Handbook of Classroom Management

The field of classroom management is not a neatly organized line of inquiry but rather consists of many disparate topics and orientations that draw from multiple disciplines. Given the complex nature of the field, this comprehensive second edition of the handbook is an invaluable resource for those interested in understanding it. It provides the field with up-to-date summaries of research on the essential topics from the first edition, as well as fresh perspectives and chapters on new topics. It is the perfect tool for both graduate students and practitioners interested in a field both fascinating and not immediately accessible without the proper guidance.

Edmund T. Emmer is Professor of Educational Psychology, Department of Educational Psychology, The University of Texas at Austin, USA.

Edward J. Sabornie is Professor of Special Education, Department of Curriculum, Instruction, and Counselor Education, North Carolina State University, USA.

Handbook of Classroom Management

Second Edition

Edited by

Edmund T. Emmer and Edward J. Sabornie

Routledge
Taylor & Francis Group

NEW YORK AND LONDON

Second edition published 2015
by Routledge
711 Third Avenue, New York, NY 10017

and by Routledge
2 Park Square, Milton Park, Abingdon, Oxon, OX14 4RN

Routledge is an imprint of the Taylor & Francis Group, an informa business

© 2015 Taylor & Francis

First edition published by Routledge, 2006

Library of Congress Cataloging-in-Publication Data
Handbook of classroom management / edited by Edmund Emmer, Edward
    Sabornie. — Second edition.
        pages cm
    Includes bibliographical references and index.
  1. Classroom management—Handbooks, manuals, etc.   I. Emmer, Edmund T.
II. Sabornie, Edward James.
    LB3013.H336 2014
    371.102'4–dc23
    2014009537

ISBN: 978-0-415-66005-1 (hbk)
ISBN: 978-0-415-66033-4 (pbk)
ISBN: 978-0-203-07411-4 (ebk)

Typeset in Minion Pro
by Apex CoVantage, LLC

Printed and bound in the United States of America by Publishers Graphics,
LLC on sustainably sourced paper.

CONTENTS

PREFACE

This new edition of the *Handbook of Classroom Management* follows the original by almost a decade. During that period, a large amount of research has been published with implications for classroom management. The goal of this volume is to bring that research to the attention of researchers, teacher educators, administrators, teachers, and students. Because the field of classroom management research draws on a wide array of disciplines and topics, a handbook is necessary to pull together into one source a comprehensive picture of the field.

The field has evolved in the last decade, producing increasing emphasis on some topics while moving away from others. The shifts are gradual and seen mainly in the ebb and flow of articles addressing particular topics over time. These shifts in researcher attention reflect changing conceptualizations about the importance of topics for understanding classroom management as well as changing school practice. Thus, readers will see increased coverage in this edition of content related to School-Wide Positive Behavior Supports, social-emotional learning, and teacher–student relationships, and Tier 2/Tier 3 interventions. Not all shifts necessarily reflect desired trends, of course, since reduced funding for some topics has limited research and publication in important areas. For example, if there were significantly greater financial support for classroom-based research on prevention and intervention strategies, there surely would be other chapters that address more facets of these topics. Readers familiar with a particular chapter from the first edition should not assume, however, that its absence in this edition necessarily means that the field has passed it by. Instead the topic may be combined with another topic in a new chapter.

This book could not have been created without the willingness of chapter reviewers whose critiques were invaluable in pointing a way toward chapter revisions. We are grateful for their willingness to share their scholarly expertise. The following individuals were reviewers: Catherine Bradshaw, Kevin Brady, Darla Castelli, Doug Cullinan, Heather Davis, Laurie deBettencourt, Robert A. Duke, Chan Evans, Andrea Flower, Hunter Gelbach, Kristine Jolivette, John Maag, Patricia Marshall, Dorothy McCoach, Christopher McCarthy, Linda Mechling, Erin O'Connor, Nancy Perry, Paul Schutz, Cheryl Torrez, Hill Walker, Herschel C. Waxman, Noreen Webb, Carol Weinstein, Stacy Weiss, and Jessica Wery.

We also extend our gratitude and appreciation to Carolyn Evertson and Carol Weinstein, the coeditors of the first *Handbook of Classroom Management*. Their pioneering work in defining and organizing the field was the foundation on which this volume was constructed, and it will continue to influence the conceptualization of the field for years to come. We are also extremely grateful to the publisher, Taylor and Francis, and its production team, including Lane Akers, Rebecca Novack, and Trevor Gori, who from the beginning have skillfully guided us along the way to completion of the project. Without their confidence, patience, and expert assistance, we could not have finished the task.

I

Introduction

1

INTRODUCTION TO THE SECOND EDITION

EDMUND T. EMMER
UNIVERSITY OF TEXAS AT AUSTIN

EDWARD J. SABORNIE
NORTH CAROLINA STATE UNIVERSITY

The first edition of the *Handbook of Classroom Management* (Evertson & Weinstein, 2006) organized the field by identifying its core areas and subfields. At the core of the field are the management strategies used by teachers to maintain order, promote student engagement, and respond to problems. Different teaching contexts and instructional formats (e.g., elementary grade settings, specific content areas, group formats) give rise to variation in teacher and student behavior, creating subfields that add depth and complexity to our understanding of classroom management (CM). Management programs respond to this variation and are influenced by values, goals, and social factors, creating more subareas that contribute to our overall picture of the field. The first edition also identified many of the methodologies for studying classrooms. These methodologies reflect different paradigms that have shaped our understanding of classroom management. How teachers acquire managerial skills and knowledge is another subfield that relies on findings from the primary field; the field, in turn, is informed by work in policy studies and equity. The first edition addressed these core areas and subfields in 42 chapters and over 1200 pages. Such a large handbook was needed for several reasons. One was to adequately review a large body of research and theory that had accumulated over a long period; another was the pluralistic and complex nature of the field. Finally, it was important to represent broadly the persons and topics that had helped shape the discipline.

The task for the second edition is different. Now the goal is to identify the lines of inquiry that have attracted the greatest amount of new research so that readers can see how these lines have been extended during the decade since the publication of the first edition. Chapters in the second edition that address the same topics as in the first edition emphasize recent research. Instead of repeating the content of their parent chapters, the contributors were asked to incorporate short summaries so that readers would have a sense of prior work, but the main focus is on research since the first edition. It was also important to add new topics representing ideas and research that expand or fill out the conceptualization of the field of classroom management. The chapters that address new topics are of necessity more comprehensive because they typically have a longer history to report.

The second edition addresses the continuing lines of inquiry and the new topics in 28 chapters and approximately half the page length of the first edition. The slimmer version results from concentrating on the past decade of developments in the field and from limiting the number of new topics introduced in the volume. Therefore, readers seeking more extensive coverage of important historical ideas and research in the field will find chapters in the first edition good companions for chapters in the second.

RESEARCH TRADITIONS IN CLASSROOM MANAGEMENT

Readers unfamiliar with the history of research in CM may wonder how the field developed and what are the major contributing traditions. We will provide a very brief overview of important developments in the field's history; more comprehensive discussions can be found in Doyle (1986) and Brophy (2006).

One of the more important influences comes from observational research on teaching and learning in classrooms. Drawing from the methodology of systematic classroom observation initiated by Flanders, Medley, and others in the 1950s and 1960s, and continued by Brophy, Good, Evertson, and others in the 1970s and 1980s, researchers in the process–product tradition sought to identify predictors of teacher effectiveness. One of the more consistent of these predictors was a set of behaviors and characteristics connected to the teacher's ability to organize and manage time use, classroom activities, and student engagement (Wang, Haertel, & Walberg, 1993). Subsequent researchers building on this base used both systematic observation and a broader array of methodologies influenced by the qualitative research paradigm. This body of research led to greater understanding of the complex set of teacher strategies needed to establish and maintain a productive classroom. In particular, the teacher's role at the beginning of the year was emphasized, along with a multidimensional perspective on management tasks. For more on this line of inquiry, see Doyle (1986), Brophy (1999), and Emmer & Gerwels (2006).

Important conceptual and methodological contributions were also made by Kounin (1970), Gump (1982), and others working in the ecological psychology tradition. Using videotape and observational methods, these researchers highlighted the importance of group management and of organizing and maintaining the classroom environment. From this perspective came the key idea of the importance of activity management, including how the teacher engages students and minimizes disruptive behavior by keeping activities on track, preventing intrusions, and maintaining activity flow.

An influential research tradition whose applications to classroom management began in the 1960s and 1970s is applied behavior analysis (Landrum & Kauffman,

2006). This tradition emphasizes management of antecedents and consequences by careful programming of reinforcement, extinction, response cost, and other forms of punishment to encourage desirable behaviors and to reduce undesirable behaviors. Early educational research in this tradition often occurred in special education settings and usually focused on managing the behaviors of individuals; more recent research has broadened the scope of its application to groups, to classrooms, and to schools.

Another tradition considers classroom management broadly as part of a system within a school. Behavior management is considered to be a school-wide concern; classroom management is a central component that needs to be coordinated across administrators, teachers, and other staff. Several different approaches that have a school-wide perspective on classroom management can be identified. One important branch of this tradition became known as school-wide positive behavior support (SWPBS) during the 1990s. Drawing substantially from applied behavior analysis, but also including components of systems theory and the research on teaching tradition, this branch emphasizes prevention at the classroom level as the foundation of effective management. Considerable attention is also given to intervention strategies for those students for whom prevention is insufficient. Another branch of the school-wide tradition emphasizes children's social and emotional development as a necessary component of the overall management system. Children learn communication skills, how to deal with emotions, and how to solve problems as part of their school's classroom management program. Social-emotional learning curricula, bullying prevention programs, and conflict resolution/peer mediation programs are examples of this branch of the school-wide systems tradition. Teacher and student thought, motivation, and relationships have become more influential concerns in recent decades. It is apparent that internal states mediate how antecedent conditions, teacher behaviors, and other environmental factors influence student behaviors and other outcomes. Thus, extensive programs of contemporary research study the influence on classroom management of teacher–student relationships, the use of intrinsic and extrinsic reinforcement, and teacher stress and anxiety.

Another tradition, whose origins are in counseling and clinical psychology, emphasizes interpersonal and communication skills along with teacher–student relationships. It is obvious that these concepts are central to any classroom management approach; programs must be implemented by the teacher, and student cooperation is essential. Moreover, teachers have to be able to work and communicate effectively with all sorts of individuals, including distressed parents, students who are experiencing a variety of developmentally appropriate and inappropriate problems, and administrators with other concerns. Early work in this tradition, in the 1960s and 1970s, emphasized models developed by Glasser, Gordon, Rogers, and Dreikurs, among others. These theorists' models emphasized communication and interpersonal skills with direct application to classroom practice. Although these models were popular, the research on their impact was limited. In recent decades, the emphasis in the field shifted away from direct application via program development and toward a more nuanced examination of the nature of teacher–student relationships (Pianta, 2006). Thus, the research base in this tradition is growing and has resulted in better knowledge about the causes, contexts, and consequences of interpersonal relationships in the classroom.

This description of the major traditions for research in classroom management is necessarily a limited one and emphasizes the unique features of each tradition. Contemporary research in an area of classroom management, although relying mainly on one tradition, may borrow from multiple sources for its identification of research questions, methodology, and interpretive framework. Similarly, educators who engage in program development might do well to be eclectic in their search for interventions with the greatest chance for addressing the complex social setting of classrooms and schools.

DEFINING CLASSROOM MANAGEMENT

As the reader may surmise from the presence of several traditions of research on the topic, classroom management's definition includes some widely agreed-upon components but also is not static. A frequently cited definition originates with Evertson & Weinstein (2006) in the first edition of this *Handbook of Classroom Management*: "[T]he actions teachers take to create an environment that supports and facilitates both academic and social–emotional learning . . . [I]t not only seeks to establish and sustain an orderly environment so students can engage in meaningful academic learning, it also aims to enhance students' social and moral growth" (p. 4). Thus, order is not the primary goal, but it serves the ultimate goals of pupil learning and social and moral growth. A similar definition is offered by Henley (2010), who identifies classroom management parsimoniously as the "essential teaching skill" (p. 4) and characterizes effective teachers as those who reduce disruptions and create learning environments that allow for students' intellectual and emotional growth. According to Henley, by proactively providing activities that lead to student self-control, a teacher is likely to spend less time dealing with misbehavior in the classroom and more time on meaningful academic instruction and related tasks. In other words, effective classroom management over time leads to greater student growth in areas that are used to judge teacher effectiveness—an important index in today's era of "value-added" teacher effects.

Another influential definition of classroom management is from Walter Doyle's seminal chapter (1986). Doyle noted that classroom management is often equated with classroom discipline, which emphasizes the treatment of misbehavior, but that the concept is much broader and includes the variety of activities teachers engage in to gain student cooperation and to establish order such as planning, establishing routines, organizing activities, monitoring students, and so on. "Classroom management refers to the actions and strategies teachers use to solve the problem of order in classrooms," wrote Doyle (p. 397). The process is complex because "order is jointly accomplished by teachers and students" in an environment characterized by multi-dimensionality, simultaneity, fast-moving events, and unpredictability, among other complicating factors.

New directions in the definition of classroom management are found in Martin and colleagues (2013), who emphasize *antecedents* of teacher action that guide classroom activity. For example, one often ignored antecedent that has an effect on how a classroom is managed is teacher self-management. Teachers who are in control of their own emotions and behavior will have a better chance of success dealing with many situations that require prompt and sensitive response and will be good models of self-control and appropriate emotional expression for students. Another direction might be to define classroom management through an antecedent, temperament-based prism. "Temperament-based classroom management is establishing and maintaining a classroom that focuses the emotional and academic development of individual students and of the classroom community" (p. 9). With this definition, teachers are expected to learn and recognize student temperaments and subsequently adapt their expectations for appropriate classroom interactions. Research applications of this definitional model (see O'Connor et al., 2012) have shown positive results related to greater teacher efficacy in classroom management and decreased levels of disruptive behavior of students at school. Other possible extensions of the definition of classroom management include developmental and cultural responsiveness.

Another definition of classroom management that flows from an antecedent perspective is related to teachers' preconceived notions about students' development and teachers' own cultural responsiveness in the classroom. A focus on developmentally and culturally responsive classroom management is related to the separation between behavior management (BM) and instructional management (IM). "Preplanned efforts to prevent misbehavior" (Martin et al., 2013, p. 12), along with how a teacher responds to misconduct, are related to BM, whereas IM includes the plans, goals, and tactics teachers use to deliver instruction in a classroom. Both constructs are related, and they interact in classrooms at all levels, but understanding the exact characteristics of the bond between the two factors awaits future research (Martin et al., 2013). Teachers' preconceived notions of a student's development and cultural influences are likely to affect his or her actions in the classroom and are interrelated with the type of classroom management that follows.

Authors of chapters in this *Handbook* exhibit similar variation in their views about the essential features of classroom management. For example, Wubbels and colleagues (Chapter 19 of this volume) extend the classroom management definition of Evertson and Weinstein (2006) in this way: "the actions teachers take to create an environment that supports and facilitates both academic and social-emotional learning." Wubbels and associates thus give prominence to the social-emotional-relational perspective of teacher actions and of teacher–student contacts. In accordance with this definition, effective classroom management is a derivative of healthy interactions between the students and teachers who populate instructional environments and is also dependent on teacher attitudes and thoughts. Another author, Bear (Chapter 2 of this volume) suggests an integration of ecological, behavioral, and social-emotional learning approaches similar to Baumrind's (1996) authoritative parenting concept. In Bear's view, such an approach offers the best way toward establishing "order, engagement, compliance, and developing self-discipline."

From this sampling of views on the definition of classroom management and its major research traditions, it is apparent that it would be difficult to encapsulate the diversity of classroom management components within a single succinct definition. Classroom management is clearly about establishing and maintaining order in a group-based educational system whose goals include student learning as well as social and emotional growth. It also includes actions and strategies that prevent, correct, and redirect inappropriate student behavior. But in addition to these core attributes, many components contribute depth, emphasis, and direction to the overall view of the concept. This diversity gives the field its vitality and has led to an expanding body of research. In the chapters of this *Handbook*, readers will find both consideration of the core features of classroom management and diversity in the perspectives adopted by their authors.

ORGANIZATION AND CONTENT OF THE SECOND EDITION

This volume has 28 chapters organized into six parts. Part I consists of this first chapter, an introduction to this edition of the *Handbook.* Part II, "Programs and Strategies," consists of six chapters that cover a wide range of approaches to prevention and intervention. George Bear (Chapter 2) describes approaches to the prevention of inappropriate behavior and concludes that teachers at all levels need to integrate the various behavioral, ecological, and social-emotional learning approaches in order to prevent inappropriate behaviors and to be successful in classroom management. Lewis, Mitchell, Trussell, and Newcomer (Chapter 3) present SWPBS as an alternative to intensive (e.g., zero tolerance) and punitive school-based consequences for inappropriate behavior. The authors recommend reconsidering disciplinary practices for students who do not enter school with a strong foundation in social skills and self-control. They conclude with a discussion of the limitations of SWPBS and recommendations for its use in schools. Sugai and Simonsen (Chapter 4) discuss techniques that are used when students do not respond to general classroom management procedures used in a school-wide and classroom-based tiered program for the reduction and elimination of inappropriate behavior. Tiered behavior practices related to small group behavior intervention (Tier 2) and individual student behavior support (Tier 3) are reviewed, and classroom examples are provided. The authors give suggestions for establishing, sustaining, and implementing a multitiered system of school and classroom management procedures. In Chapter 5, "Emerging Issues in Bullying Research and Prevention," Dorothy Espelage summarizes what is known about the causes and outcomes of bullying. She also reviews research on school bullying prevention and intervention programs, describes what is known about their effectiveness, and points to factors that must be addressed in order to move the field of bullying research forward. Schwab and Elias (Chapter 6) discuss the latest research on social-emotional learning (SEL) in the classroom. They outline the premises of SEL enacted via four teacher actions: (1) teach SEL skills, (2) build caring relationships, (3) set firm and fair behavior boundaries in the classroom, and (4) share responsibilities with students. By following these actions, teachers foster student growth in social skills and emotional health—as well as academic learning. This section concludes with Chapter 7, by Skiba and Rausch, in which they review research showing that exclusionary classroom and school management disciplinary procedures (e.g., expulsions and out-of-school suspensions) do not serve the purpose of improving student behavior or academic achievement. Such consequences are inequitable and set the stage for juvenile justice involvement and dropping out of school. Skiba and Rausch recommend alternative strategies for changing school discipline and classroom management, such as school-wide positive behavior intervention and support and enhanced social-emotional learning.

Part III, "Contexts for Classroom Management," consists of seven chapters that address environments and settings. In Chapter 8, "Early Childhood Classroom Management," Gettinger and Fischer focus on preschool classrooms and strategies that support social-emotional growth and prevent inappropriate behavior. Three classroom management aspects that foster early learning are emphasized: (1) relationships between the child and teacher, (2) consistent environmental control interventions, and (3) treatments that attempt to eliminate difficult behaviors. In Chapter 9, Richard Milner notes the need for culturally relevant management strategies to accommodate the diversity of urban settings. He also argues for better classroom management training and for consideration of teachers' emotions and the affective dimensions of teaching experiences. He concludes with a review of teaching practices and programs relevant for classroom management in urban contexts. Sabornie and Pennington (Chapter 10) review research since 2005 that examines various classroom and behavior management techniques found in noninclusive special education settings (e.g., self-contained classrooms, special schools for students with disabilities). The authors note that extreme inappropriate behavior is often problematic in such restrictive educational settings, and they highlight the importance of teaching group contingency and self-management skills. Lane and Menzies (Chapter 11) consider interventions that benefit students with disabilities in full-inclusion programs. Advantages are cited for "low-intensity" behavior supports, such as (1) incorporating student choice in the inclusive classroom, (2) increasing opportunities for students to respond, and (3) delivering appropriate reinforcement. Lane and Menzies also discuss the benefits of multitiered systems of behavioral assistance. The central role of classroom management in music settings is highlighted in Chapter 12, "Classroom Management in Music Education," by Byo and Sims. They provide a historical review of research, with commentary on commonly used methodologies. The special challenges of music instruction in urban settings are also addressed. Cothran and Kulinna (Chapter 13) describe management skills used by physical education teachers, such as identifying and implementing routines and using active supervision. They describe the effects of student (mis)behavior, as well as teachers' responses to it, and they review research on ways to promote positive behavior. In Chapter 14, Robyn Gillies reviews research on small group instruction and elaborates on the essential management task of teaching students about learning goals and how to interact with peers in groups. Strategies for improving the quality of student interaction are described and discussed.

Part IV, "Social and Psychological Perspectives," includes seven chapters that utilize social and psychological perspectives to explore classroom management issues and practices. These chapters identify the interactive, emotional, and perceptual features of both students and teachers. After providing an extensive review of the literature on teacher thinking about classroom management, Bullough and Richardson (Chapter 15) identify the topics of knowledge, values, and ethics as needing more emphasis. They also recommend using biographical and life history methods in order to better represent the complexity of teacher thought about classroom management. In Chapter 16, "Teacher Stress, Emotion, and Classroom Management," McCarthy, Lineback, and Reiser note, "When teachers perceive that professional demands exceed their capacities for coping, they can become stressed and vulnerable to job dissatisfaction, emotional exhaustion, and burnout." The critical role of appraisals and resources is described, along with the mediating role of classroom management skills and other factors involved in effective coping. How teachers can support student self-regulation of learning, motivation, and emotion is the focus of Chapter 17 by McCaslin, Sotardi, and Vega. The authors compare different perspectives on self-regulation, examine the influence of stress and coping, and describe shared regulation in small group formats. They conclude with a discussion of strategies and contexts for promoting the development of student self-regulatory skills. Montuoro and Lewis (Chapter 18) review the literature on student perceptions, especially of misbehavior. Using the standpoint of Raven's theory of social power, they examine what students consider misbehavior and their reasons for engaging in it. The chapter also looks at research on student perceptions of teachers' responses to misbehavior and provides recommendations for teaching practice. Wubbels and colleagues (Chapter 19) examine how teacher–student associations can be reconceptualized into a relational approach to classroom management. The authors provide a relational-based, seminal definition of classroom management that emphasizes creating a positive social and emotional climate. They emphasize the importance of student interpretation of teacher actions and advocate additional research that examines teacher–student reciprocal influences. Raczynski and Horne (Chapter 20) identify crucial interpersonal skills for teaching. School-wide, classroom, and individual behavior management plans depend on teachers for implementation, so the ability of a teacher to communicate is of consummate importance. This chapter provides a review of essential elements such as listening and problem solving.

Part V, "Influential Forces and Factors," contains five chapters. Culturally responsive classroom management and instruction are the focus of Chapter 21 by Cartledge, Lo, Vincent, and Robinson-Ervin. The authors advocate the use of culturally responsive interventions to address concerns about the disproportional use of punishment. Culturally responsive classroom management leads schools to concentrate on behavioral prevention and on providing positive learning experiences for students who, in turn, learn how to respect and value others. In Chapter 22, Yell, Rozsalski, and Miller are concerned with the influence of law on administrative policy and actions, as well as with its influence on how teachers use behavior management strategies. They discuss important legal issues involved in daily educational practice, emphasizing that teachers and school administrators must not only ensure that classroom and school management techniques are efficacious, but also follow accepted constitutional, federal, and case law. Teacher preparation in classroom management is reviewed by Stough and Montague in Chapter 23. They note extensive variation in the extent of preservice teachers' classroom management preparation, and they also identify promising models for in-service teacher preparation. In Chapter 24, Walker and Hoover-Dempsey stress that when parents are actively involved with their child's education, classroom management and instruction can be made more effective. They explain how the teacher–parent interface can improve student–teacher interaction, and they describe strategies for effective parent–teacher collaboration. Mason Bolick and Bartels (Chapter 25) examine how technology has assisted teachers, and caution that 21st-century technologies have the potential to both assist and disrupt the lives of educators. Noting that the literature on technology and management has been mainly descriptive and exploratory, the authors provide information on technology management in low- and high-use environments, as well as for instructional and noninstructional applications. In Chapter 26, Reeve discusses the controversial role of rewards in the classroom management procedures of teachers. His contention is that rewards for behavior in the classroom have more negative consequences than positive and that teachers should use such behavioral control techniques in moderation. Reeve advocates a structured classroom that is "highly autonomy supportive" for students, citing recent research in support of such an emphasis.

Finally, Part VI, "Research Methodology," consists of two chapters. Readers familiar with the first edition will remember that this topic was addressed extensively in a number of chapters. Instead of revisiting those earlier topics, for which not much additional literature on methodological advances was evident, we include a chapter on modeling techniques, which was not addressed in the first edition, and a chapter on single-case methodology, which expands on the previous edition's coverage. Researchers with large data sets or those interested in mining databases that have information related to classroom management topics often use multilevel modeling or structural equation modeling for data analysis. Beretvas, Whittaker, and Stafford (Chapter 27) provide readers with the tools needed for comprehending this growing literature. Kratochwill, Altschaefl, Bice-Urbach, and Kawa (Chapter 28) discuss the use of single-case research methods. They focus on the use of this approach to study well-known classroom management treatments, such as self-management techniques and token economy systems, and they consider single case design standards and criteria.

CONCLUDING COMMENTS

Classroom management as a field of research is pluralistic with contributions from diverse traditions and perspectives. At its core is a direct connection with classroom practice and the teacher's instructional role. Because those practices are so varied and the instructional role is so vital, not to mention the added complexity of engaging large groups of students, researchers can look forward to a growing array of topics and problems to address. Doing classroom management research is difficult work, gaining access to sites is fraught with political and ethical issues, and researchers in the field are chronically underfunded. We therefore celebrate the perseverance and commitment of the researchers whose work is represented in this volume, as well as the teachers and students who ultimately may be the beneficiaries of their efforts.

REFERENCES

Baumrind, D. (1966). Effects of authoritative parental control on child behavior. *Child Development, 37,* 887–907.

Brophy, J. (1999). Perspectives of classroom management: Yesterday, today, and tomorrow. In H. J. Freiberg (Ed.), *Beyond behaviorism: Changing the classroom management paradigm* (pp. 43–56). Boston: Allyn & Bacon.

Brophy, J. (2006). History of research on classroom management. In C. Evertson & C. Weinstein (Eds.), *Handbook of classroom management: Research, practice, and contemporary issues* (pp. 17–43). Mahwah, NJ: Erlbaum.

Doyle, W. (1986). Classroom organization and management. In M. C. Wittrock (Ed.), *Handbook of research on teaching* (3rd ed.) (pp. 392–431). New York: Macmillan.

Emmer, E. T., & Gerwels, M. C. (2006). Classroom management in middle and high school classrooms. In C. Evertson & C. Weinstein (Eds.), *Handbook of classroom management: Research, practice, and contemporary issues* (pp. 407–437). Mahwah, NJ: Erlbaum.

Evertson, C. M., & Weinstein, C. S. (Eds.). (2006). *Handbook of classroom management: Research, practice, and contemporary issues.* Mahwah, NJ: Erlbaum.

Gump, P. (1982). School settings and their keeping. In D. Duke (Ed.), *Helping teachers manage classrooms* (pp. 98–114). Alexandria, VA: Association for Supervision and Curriculum Development.

Henley, M. (2010). *Classroom management: A proactive approach* (2nd ed.). Boston: Pearson.

Kounin, J. (1970). *Discipline and group management in classrooms.* New York: Holt, Rinehart & Winston.

Landrum, T. L., & Kauffman, J. M. (2006). Behavioral approaches to classroom management. In C. M. Evertson & C. S. Weinstein (Eds.), *Handbook of classroom management: Research, practice, and contemporary issues* (pp. 47–71). Mahwah, NJ: Erlbaum.

Martin, N. K., Schafer, N. J., McClowry, S., Emmer, E. T., Brekelmans, M., Mainhard, T., & Wubbels, T. (2013). Expanding the definition of classroom management: Recurring themes and new conceptualizations. Manuscript submitted for publication.

O'Connor, E. E., Rodriquez, E. T., Capella, E., Morris, J. G., Collins, A., & McClowry, S. G. (2012). Child disruptive behavior and parenting sense of competence: A comparison of the effects of two models of INSIGHTS. *Journal of Community Psychology, 40,* 555–572. doi: 10.1002/jcop.21482

Pianta, R. C. (2006). Classroom management and relationships between children and teachers: Implications for research and practice. In C. M. Evertson & C. S. Weinstein (Eds.), *Handbook of classroom management: Research, practice, and contemporary issues* (pp. 685–709). Mahwah, NJ: Erlbaum.

Wang, M. C., Haertl, G. D., & Walberg, H. J. (1993). Toward a knowledge base for school learning. *Review of Educational Research, 63,* 249–294.

II

Programs and Strategies

2

PREVENTIVE AND CLASSROOM-BASED STRATEGIES

GEORGE G. BEAR
UNIVERSITY OF DELAWARE

Over one hundred years ago, in his book entitled *Classroom Management*, William Bagley (1908) posited that two opposing theories of classroom management were dominant at that time: the rigid "machinelike" theory and the "self-government" theory (p. 30). Whereas the former emphasized rules and punitive consequences to manage student behavior, the latter emphasized developing self-discipline. Both claimed to best prevent behavior problems in the classroom. Bagley's century-old conceptualization of classroom management is largely consistent with the dual meanings of the term "discipline," as well as the two traditional and primary aims of school discipline in American education (Bear, 2005). The first meaning and aim refer to creating and maintaining an orderly learning environment conducive to learning. Correcting behavior problems, most often with punitive consequences (e.g., the *use* of discipline) has been a major part of this meaning, but so too has the use of more positive and antecedent-based techniques for preventing problem behavior, particularly since the early 20th century. The second meaning of discipline and of the primary aim of education refers to *teaching*, or developing, *self-discipline* within students, also often referred to as "self-regulation," "responsibility," and "autonomy." *Self-discipline* refers to students' inhibiting inappropriate behavior and exhibiting prosocial behavior under their own volition, or willingly, which involves an integration of social, emotional, and behavioral competencies.

Consistent with Bagley's (1908) conceptualization of classroom management and of many researchers since him (as will be seen), in this chapter classroom management is viewed as having the dual aims of (1) maintaining order, engagement, and cooperation, and (2) developing self-discipline. Evidence-based classroom strategies and techniques for achieving both aims are reviewed. This is done while drawing from the three most popular evidence-based approaches to school discipline and classroom management (Osher, Bear, Sprague, & Doyle, 2010): the ecological approach, the behavioral approach, and the social-emotional learning (SEL) approach. Particular attention is given to *preventive* techniques of classroom management. Given that the focus of this chapter is preventive strategies, and due to space limitations, techniques for the correction and treatment of behavior problems are not covered. Prior to reviewing the ecological, behavioral, and SEL approaches, the dual meanings of classroom management and school discipline are discussed briefly in historical context. Whereas emphasis on adults either managing student behavior or developing self-discipline for purposes of preventing problem behavior has shifted back and forth since the early 19th century, both aims are of utmost importance. It is argued that achieving both aims calls for the integration of multiple strategies and techniques found across the ecological, behavioral, and SEL approaches.

SHIFTING VIEWS OF CLASSROOM MANAGEMENT AND PREVENTION

Bagley (1908) noted that at the turn of the 20th century, "most of the advanced and progressive educators" supported the self-government theory of classroom management (p. 31). This was in contrast to educators in previous centuries who embraced the machine-like and "military organization" (p. 30) style of classroom management. Indeed, throughout the first half of the 20th century, developing self-discipline was viewed as part of classroom management and a primary aim, as seen in the popularity of John Dewey's progressive education. Using a combination of teacher-centered and student-centered techniques, with greater emphasis on the latter, all teachers were expected to teach character education, with the understanding that character traits, including self-discipline, prevented behavior problems. How educators conceptualized classroom management changed markedly in the second half of the 20th century. In response to increasing behavior problems, including school violence (Reese, 1995), the focus of classroom management and prevention shifted away from developing self-discipline to establishing order and managing student behavior (McClellan, 1999). Increased behavior problems were reflected in nearly every Gallup poll conducted in the 1970s and 1980s on the public's views about public schools' finding that discipline was the greatest problem.

Classroom management became equated with classroom order and with the behavior management, or control, of student behavior, using teacher-centered techniques of prevention and correction. In both practice and research, the focus was on preventing and correcting misbehavior. Two major lines of research and three general approaches to classroom management dominated the field (Brophy, 2006). The first line of research was seen in the ecological and process–product approaches to studying classroom management (Anderson, Evertson, & Emmer, 1979; Brophy, 1979; Emmer, Evertson, & Anderson, 1980; Kounin, 1970). These two approaches shared the primary goal of identifying qualities, practices, or processes of teachers and the characteristics of classroom settings that were associated with important student outcomes (or products). There were more similarities than differences in these two approaches, with the same studies frequently cited in reviews of both approaches (see Doyle, 2006; Gettinger & Kohler, 2006). For this reason, as well as for the sake of brevity, throughout this chapter both approaches will be referred to as the "ecological approach." In general, however, ecological researchers focused on classroom order, as observed in student attention, engagement, cooperation, as well as the lack of student misbehavior, whereas process–outcome researchers studied a broader range of academic, behavioral, and social-emotional outcomes and the classroom processes that accounted for them. Both approaches found that effective teachers devoted more effort to prevention than to correction: They prevented most behavior problems by running their classrooms smoothly, establishing clear routines and procedures, engaging students in learning, and so forth.

The second dominant line of research on classroom management was the behavioral approach, or more specifically at that time, the behavior modification approach to managing student behavior. It too recognized the importance of prevention, but its strategy of choice for preventing misbehavior was the strategic use of positive reinforcement. Relative to the ecological and process–product approaches, the behavioral approach also directed much greater attention to techniques for *correcting* behavior problems, especially extinction and nonphysical forms of punishment (e.g., verbal warnings and reprimands, response cost, time-out). Numerous books on classroom management (e.g., O'Leary & O'Leary, 1977) guided teachers in the use of various types of positive reinforcement (e.g., primary, secondary, social, tangible, differentiated reinforcement of other behavior) and schedules thereof (e.g., continuous, fixed, variable) and in the use of additional techniques, such as extinction, punishment, token economies (O'Leary & Drabman, 1971), group contingencies (e.g., including the Good Behavior Game, Barrish, Saunders, & Wolf, 1969), direct social skills training (Cartledge & Milburn, 1978;), and school–home communication (including daily report cards, Dougherty & Dougherty, 1977). Each of those techniques continues to be emphasized in the behavioral approach today. Although self-management techniques also received attention among behavioral researchers (e.g., Rosenbaum & Drabman, 1979), they were greatly overshadowed in use by the previously mentioned more teacher-centered techniques for obtaining compliance.

Thus, from the 1960s and into the 1990s, classroom management had taken on a new meaning that was in stark contrast to the one that guided educators and researchers in the first half of the century. As noted by Emmer and Stough (2001), most definitions now referred to classroom management as "actions taken by the teacher to establish order, engage students, or elicit their cooperation" (p. 103). The ecological and behavioral approaches were consistent with this definition. In general, classroom management, which included the management of student behavior, was viewed to be related to the development of self-discipline. However, classroom management and the development of self-discipline (or socialization) were now generally conceptualized as separate functions of teachers (e.g., Brophy, 1996). To be sure, there were models for developing self-discipline, or processes believed to be related to it, that were popular during the 1970s, 1980s, and 1990s, but none claimed to be approaches to classroom management or behavior management. Few remained popular for long, and none was shown empirically to be effective in managing student behavior or developing self-discipline. These included values clarification (Raths,

Harmin, & Simon, 1966), the self-esteem approach (California Task Force to Promote Self-Esteem and Personal and Social Responsibility, 1990), the moral development approach (Power, Higgins, & Kohlberg, 1989), and various models grounded in psychotherapy that focused on both mental health and "positive," or nonpunitive, ways to correct behavior problems, such as logical consequences (Dreikurs & Grey, 1968), teacher effectiveness training (Gordon, 1974, 2003), and reality therapy (Glasser, 1965).

Recently, the inclusion of developing self-discipline as part of classroom management, and particularly in prevention, has reemerged, with theorists and researchers conceptualizing classroom management and school discipline more broadly than that of order and compliance (Bear, 2005, 2010; Emmer & Stough, 2001; Evertson & Weinstein, 2006). For example, in summarizing recurrent themes across the 47 chapters in the previous volume of this handbook, Evertson and Weinstein (2006) concluded that "[a]uthors consistently call for an approach to classroom management that fosters the development of self-regulation and emotional competence" (p. 12). That call was voiced most strongly by authors who would best be characterized today by the social and emotional learning (SEL) approach to preventing behavior problems and promoting social, emotional, and behavioral competencies. Note that when *prevention* is viewed in this manner, it includes the *promotion*, or development, of social, emotional, and behavioral competencies that underlie self-discipline. This is consistent with how most researchers now view mental health prevention (National Research Council and Institute of Medicine, 2009). That is, promoting social, emotional, and behavioral competencies is viewed as helping to prevent emotional and behavioral disorders, as well as behavior problems in general. However, it is important to note that many of those competencies also are important in their own right (National Research Council and Institute of Medicine, 2009).

Consistent with how classroom management was conceptualized by Bagley (2008) and progressive educators in the first half of the 20th century, Evertson and Weinstein (2006) further noted that "classroom management has two distinct purposes: It not only seeks to establish and sustain an orderly environment so students can engage in meaningful academic learning, it also aims to enhance students' social and moral growth. From this perspective, *how* a teacher achieves order is as important as *whether* a teacher achieves order" (p. 4). Evertson and Weinstein's (2006) distinction between *how* and *whether* an orderly environment is achieved is an important one because it is the *how* an orderly environment is created and behavior problems are prevented that most greatly distinguishes among the various models and approaches to classroom management today and in the past. That is, a teacher might prevent behavior problems in a classroom in various ways, such as by captivating student attention and motivation in a lesson, developing within students the social and emotional competencies that underlie self-discipline, building strong teacher–student and student–student relationships and norms that support an orderly and positive classroom climate, using praise and rewards, or using punitive techniques and threats of it. Models and approaches to classroom management differ in their emphases on the use of those techniques. But what also greatly distinguishes different models and approaches from one another is their primary aim—whether it is achieving order, engagement, and compliance; developing self-discipline; or both. The distinctions between the aims of classroom management and *how*, or the means, to achieve them are lost when classroom management is defined only in terms of order, engagement, and compliance.

THREE APPROACHES TO PREVENTION IN CLASSROOM MANAGEMENT

The distinctions between the dual aims of classroom management and how to achieve them should be kept in mind when reviewing the three most popular general approaches to classroom management and school discipline. They are the ecological, behavioral, and SEL approaches.

Ecological Approach

Much of the advice given to future and current teachers in today's textbooks on how best to organize and structure their classrooms in order to facilitate teaching and prevent misbehavior is based on the early research of those who adhered to the ecological approach (Brophy, 2006; Doyle, 2006). That research peaked in the 1980s, with much of it being part of the "school effectiveness" research, particularly that concerning classroom management (Doyle, 2006; Gettinger, 1988). Using primarily descriptive and correlational methodologies, Gump and Kounin (Gump, 1982; Kounin, 1970) showed that what best differentiated effective from ineffective classroom managers was not how teachers *corrected* misbehavior but how they *prevented* it from occurring in the first place and from escalating and spreading. The importance of prevention was a not a new idea (e.g., Bagley, 1908), but Gump and Kounin were among the first educational psychologists to describe characteristics of the most effective classroom managers based on actual research.

Although different terms are often used to describe the characteristics or skills identified by Gump and Kounin, the following ones have continued to be supported by researchers (Brophy, 2006; Doyle, 2006): (1) *withitness*—closely monitoring students' behavior and intervening early when misbehavior is first observed (or anticipated) and before the misbehavior interferes with learning and instruction and becomes contagious; (2) *overlapping*—dealing with multiple events or demands at the same time; (3) *momentum*—starting and presenting lessons at a brisk pace, while allowing for only brief and efficient transitions; (4) *smoothness*—presenting lessons at an even flow, free from interruptions; and (5) *group alerting*—establishing and maintaining the attention of all students.

Following the classic studies of Gump and Kounin (Gump, 1982; Kounin, 1970), other researchers working within the ecological framework have identified additional and more specific characteristics that best differentiate the least and most effective classroom managers (see Brophy, 1983; Cotton, 1995; Doyle, 2006; Emmer & Evertson, 2012; Evertson & Emmer, 2012; Gettinger & Kohler, 2006). Those characteristics are now described briefly.

High Expectations, or Standards, That Are Clear, Reasonable, and Communicated in Procedures, Routines, Rules, and Consequences

The most effective classroom managers set high expectations, or standards, during the first few days of the school year and maintain them thereafter. Behaviors consistent with their expectations are communicated often and in a number of ways: They are taught directly, modeled, discussed, retaught as needed, practiced, reinforced, and linked to supports and consequences when they are not met. High expectations are applied to *all* students, and the expectations are responsive to developmental and individual (including cultural) differences. Researchers often highlight two practices that teachers widely use to communicate their high expectations and to facilitate order in the classroom: (1) predictable and efficient procedures and routines and (2) clear and fair rules and consequences (e.g., Weinstein & Novodvorsky, 2010; Weinstein, Romano, & Mignano, 2010). Each is now described briefly.

1. *Predictable and Efficient Procedures and Routines.* Procedures and routines help provide structure and predictability and provide for quick and efficient transitions, or what Kounin referred to as "smoothness." They reduce time away from learning and from unstructured activities that often foster misbehavior. They commonly apply to the use of the room; individual work and teacher-led activities; small-group instruction; cooperative learning group activities; transitions into and out of the classroom and other areas of the school; and general tasks such as students going to the bathroom, getting a drink, and using their lockers or teachers taking attendance or making morning announcements.

2. *Fair Rules and Consequences.* Students who perceive rules to be clear and fair, including the fairness of consequences imposed for rule violations, tend to exhibit less misbehavior and to view their teachers and schools more favorably (Arum, 2003; Gottfredson, Gottfredson, Payne, & Gottfredson, 2005). Although the clarity of behavioral expectations and rules has received the greatest attention by behaviorists today (e.g., Sugai et al., 2010), research also shows that students' perceptions of fairness may be equally or more important than clarity in determining their behavior. For example, in a national study of over 30,000 students, Arum (2003) found students' perceptions of fairness to be associated with multiple positive outcomes. A curvilinear relationship between fairness and strictness was demonstrated. That is, students' perceptions of fairness tended to be correlated positively and significantly with their willingness to obey the rules, but rules were perceived to be most fair when they were neither too lenient nor overly harsh. When rules were perceived as fair, students were not only more likely to obey them but also more likely to receive higher grades. When rules were perceived as strict and unfair, there was a 35% chance that students expressed a willingness to *disobey* rules.

Arum (2003) emphasized that moderately strict rules are particularly effective when students perceive them as being imposed by adults with *legitimate* moral authority, which refers to adults whom students respect and view as fair, supportive, and not overly controlling. This finding is supported by research in social psychology on procedural justice (Tyler, 2006), which shows that adults are more likely to comply with police and judges whom they trust and believe to be fair (Gregory et al., 2010). Research in moral development, particularly social domain theory (Turiel, 2006), also supports the importance of students' perceptions of fairness. Such research shows that children and adolescents perceive rules to be fairer, justifying harsher punishment for violations of the rules, when they concern behaviors in the moral domain (prescriptive judgments and universal principles pertaining to human welfare, rights, and justice) and to a lesser extent to the social conventional domain (alterable rules and regulations that govern behavior and social interactions in a given social context). It is when rules concern behaviors perceived to be in the personal domain (e.g., clothing, hairstyle, foods to eat) that they are most likely to be viewed as unfair and thus not followed.

Frequent Monitoring of Student Behavior and Quick Response to Early Signs of Misbehavior

As seen in *withitness* and *overlapping* (Gump, 1982; Kounin, 1970), effective teachers closely monitor student behavior and respond immediately to early signs of misbehavior. They frequently scan and move about the classroom and respond quickly to the earliest signs of potential or actual behavior problems. In doing so, they use eye contact, physical proximity, verbal prompts, reminders, praise, and warnings, and they do so in a seamless fashion such that the use of these techniques rarely interferes with teaching.

Academic Instruction and Activities That Engage and Motivate Learning

This includes Kounin's concepts of *momentum and smoothness* (Gump, 1982; Kounin, 1970). It encompasses a wide variety of instructional methods and activities found in research to motivate student engagement in learning. These would include matching or adapting content/materials with the individual interests, skill levels, and needs of students; providing students with reasonable choices; ensuring high rates of success, especially when new concepts are first introduced (i.e., behavioral momentum); providing constructive and positive feedback; reteaching, as needed, to ensure mastery; progress monitoring and making changes in instruction based on such monitoring; cooperative learning; peer-assisted learning; and computer-assisted learning. It also includes providing students with opportunities to participate in instructional decisions, where appropriate and reasonable, and communicating that both teachers and students are accountable for academic success in the classroom.

Physical Environment That Is Conducive to Teaching and Learning

In general, aggression and violence are more likely to occur in environments that are crowded, unattractive, and uncomfortable (e.g., poor cooling, heating, seating) (Berkowitz, 1989). Crowding, or close physical proximity to peers, is a common problem in schools, especially when adult supervision is lacking, and behavior problems are more likely to occur under those circumstances (Astor, Benbenishty, Marachi, & Meyer, 2006). Although teachers often are limited in the extent to which they can alter their physical environment (e.g., increasing the size of the room or playground, improving room temperature), effective teachers do their best in adapting the physical environment to prevent behavior problems. This includes their arrangement of furniture, supplies, and materials; where they locate themselves; the control of the flow of student traffic via scheduling and supervision; and making the classroom generally more attractive, yet nondistracting (Hunley, 2008).

Behavioral Approach

Application of the behavioral approach is perhaps most widely seen today in the School-Wide Positive Behavioral Supports and Interventions (SWPBIS) approach (Sugai et al., 2010; Sugai & Horner, 2009). This is particularly true in the recommended application of techniques of applied behavior analysis for preventing problem behavior at the school-wide, classroom, and individual levels. In light of its popularity, the SWPBIS approach of Sugai and Horner is referred to when the behavioral approach is discussed in this chapter. It is recognized, however, that other behavioral models of SWPBIS, as well as of classroom and behavior management, exist and that there are behavioral approaches other than that of applied behavior analysis (e.g., cognitive and social cognitive).

In general, the primary focus of the behavioral approach has been on observable antecedents to behavior problems, especially demonstrating how teachers can manipulate antecedents to improve observable behaviors. In recent reviews of the literature on antecedent-based classroom-wide behavioral techniques, the following were identified as being the most common (Kern & Clemens, 2007; Sugai & Horner, 2008; Wehby & Lane, 2009):

- Clear rules and expectations
- Routines and other practices that increase predictability (e.g., schedules, visual displays)
- Praise and rewards
- Task difficulty (i.e., matching the curriculum to students' instructional levels)
- Opportunities to respond
- Seating arrangements
- Effective instruction and commands
- Sequencing of instructional activities (including high probability requests)
- Pacing of instruction
- Student choice
- Preferred activities
- Proximity control

Although often called different names, nearly all of these techniques are the same as those identified earlier in the ecological approach. What the behavioral approach has added to the research literature on classroom management has been demonstrating causal relations between antecedents and behavior—that these techniques not only characterize effective teachers but are modifiable actions, arrangements, or events that actually determine teachers' effectiveness in establishing order, engagement, and compliance. Another major contribution to the literature has been identifying specific features of each technique and steps for implementing it. A good example is seen in Jenson, Clark, and Burrow-Sanchez's (2009) review of precision requests, an antecedent-based technique for controlling behavior in which verbal requests are given that are clear, precise, and most likely to elicit compliance. Citing research in support of each feature or step, Jenson and colleagues documented that effective precisions requests are (1) presented as statements, not as questions (e.g., "I need you to get started"), (2) are made close to the student (a distance of about 3 feet), especially when noncompliance is observed or anticipated, (3) are made in a firm and quiet voice, (4) are accompanied with eye contact, (5) are followed by a 5-to10-second uninterrupted time period that allows for a response, (6) specify exactly what is requested, and (7) are followed by verbal reinforcement upon compliance.

A similar direct behavioral approach to teaching is seen in how students are taught social skills, which is one of the defining features of the SWPBIS approach (Sugai & Horner, 2010). Applying principles of applied behavioral analysis, social skills are taught directly. In their review of the research literature on behaviorally oriented social skills training programs, Elliott and Gresham (2007) identified six common components or phases of effective social skills programs: (1) *tell* (which includes discussing the skills' importance and steps for the behavior), (2) *show* (the instructor modeling and students role-playing the skill), (3) *do* (students state the steps and model them, as peers provide feedback), (4) *practice* (students apply the social skill in the classroom and are reinforced by the instructor), (5) *monitor progress* (students reflect upon and self-evaluate skill performance), and (6) *generalize* (students are asked to apply the skill in multiple contexts via homework and other opportunities). In the SWPBIS approach, teachers are to follow similar phases, with social skills taught being identified in a behavior matrix that includes where students are to exhibit the specific social skill. In a recent national survey of social skills taught in SWPBIS schools (Lynass, Tsai, Richman, & Cheney, 2012), the most common social skills found in matrices are those that "emphasize student compliance" (p. 159) and that fall under three general categories of behavioral expectations: responsibility, respect, and safety. Thus, in learning responsibility, students are repeatedly directed (and reinforced) to "keep hands and feet to self" in hallways, to "raise your hand for assistance" in the cafeteria, and to "accept consequence of your behavior" in the classroom. Likewise, in learning respect they are directed to "work quietly" in the classroom, use "voice Level 2" in the cafeteria, and to "allow others to pass" in hallways (p. 155). This is consistent with SWPBIS schools' aim of "systematically teaching rule-following behaviors within each school routine and setting" (Simonsen & Sugai, 2009, p. 136).

Although not specific to social skills training in the SWPBIS approach, in general reviews of the research literature on social skills training in school settings have yielded mixed results. Effect sizes tend to be small to moderate, either when behavioral and cognitive-behavioral approaches to social skills training are examined separately (Lösel & Beelmann, 2003; Wilson & Lipsey, 2007) or when they are combined (Elliott, Frey, & DiPerna, 2012; Cook et al., 2008). A common shortcoming of the behavioral approach to social skills training is the lack of maintenance and generalization of skills taught (Bullis, Walker, & Sprague, 2001; DuPaul & Eckert, 1994; Maag, 2006). This is less of a problem with cognitive-behavioral programs, as shown in effect sizes being twice as large for cognitive behavioral programs compared to behavior programs in follow-up studies of the effectiveness of social skills training (Lösel & Beelmann, 2003). Another shortcoming of the behavioral approach to social skills training is that the bulk of the research supporting its application comes from studies in which social skills training is applied to individual or small groups of students with disabilities or who are at risk of exhibiting social skill deficits. There is a lack of research demonstrating that a systematic, direct behavioral approach to social skills training, as just described and recommended in the SWPBIS approach, is necessary for most students, especially beyond the early grades, in teaching skills such as responsibility and respect (especially beyond simple compliance) or that such an approach is equally or more effective than other approaches.

Social and Emotional Learning (SEL) Approach

The SEL approach is a general approach to the promotion of mental health and well-being that is not specific to classroom management and school discipline. It is much broader, encompassing programs often referred to as positive youth development, resilience, character education, positive psychology, emotional development, and moral education, as well as more specifically targeted programs for preventing a number of mental health problems and risk behaviors, such as teen pregnancy, alcohol and drug abuse, bullying, school violence, and suicide (Durlak, Weissberg, Dymnicki, Taylor, & Schellinger, 2011). With respect to classroom management, however, the SEL approach is perhaps best seen in the Responsive Classroom (Brock, Nishida, Chiong, Grimm, & Rimm-Kaufman, 2008) and the Caring Schools Community (formerly the Child Development Project; Watson & Battistich, 2006).

The SEL approach shares systems and process–product perspectives with the ecological approach but focuses much more on how children think, feel, and act. Actions and processes of teachers are certainly viewed as important, but as only one of multiple factors, including individual student, peer, cultural, developmental, home, school, and community factors, that operate in a transactive, dynamic fashion in determining student behavior (Dodge, Coie, & Lynam, 2006; National Research Council and Institute of Medicine, 2009). Those external risk and protective factors influence student behavior indirectly, with their effects determined largely by social cognitive and emotional processes. A central position of the SEL approach is that, whereas teachers can prevent behavior problems using techniques highlighted previously in the ecological and behavioral approaches, they also can prevent them by developing within students the social and emotional competencies associated with self-discipline and by establishing close and supportive relationships. In doing so, they prevent behavior problems and promote mental health not only in childhood and adolescence but also in adulthood.

In a recent meta-analysis of 213 studies of universal-level SEL programs, which included 270,034 students, Durlak and colleagues (2011) found that when compared to students in control programs, students in SEL programs had significantly more favorable outcomes in all six areas they examined. Those areas were social and emotional skills (e.g., emotion regulation, perspective taking, and social problem solving), attitudes toward self and others (e.g., including self-esteem, perceptions of relations with teachers, liking of school, and beliefs about aggression,), positive social behavior, conduct problems (e.g., classroom disruption, noncompliance, aggression, and bullying), emotional distress, and academic performance. Effect sizes ranged from 0.22 to 0.57 for the total sample. Similar favorable results have been reported in other reviews of the literature on school-based programs for promoting mental health and preventing conduct problems and aggression that are consistent with the SEL approach (Lösel & Beelman, 2003; Wilson, Gottfredson, & Najaka, 2001; Wilson & Lipsey, 2007), as well as programs for classroom management (Freiberg & Lapointe, 2006).

To one degree or another, each of the teacher-centered preventive techniques presented previously under the ecological and behavioral approaches can be found in classroom management programs consistent with the SEL approach. However, in general, the SEL approach is more similar to that of the ecological approach than the behavioral approach in that the application of those techniques is not as prescribed, refined, directive, and systematic as in the behavioral approach (e.g., in teaching social skills and use of tokens and rewards). Perhaps the greatest distinction between the SEL approach and the other two approaches, however, is its greater emphasis on two preventive strategies and techniques therein: (a) lessons and activities for developing SEL skills and (b) relationship building.

Lessons and Activities for Developing SEL Skills

As in the behavioral approach, the SEL approach targets social skills, but instead of focusing on observable behaviors of compliance, it targets a broad range of prosocial and antisocial behaviors and the social cognitive and emotional processes underlying them. The two approaches also differ in the techniques used to teach social skills and develop self-discipline. Whereas the behavioral approach relies primarily on direct instruction and techniques of applied behavior analysis, the SEL approach employs additional techniques found in cognitive behavioral and emotional theories. Common among the social cognitive and emotional processes that are targeted in SEL programs and that have been shown to underlie antisocial and prosocial behavior are anger and its regulation (Lochman, Powell, Clanton, & McElroy, 2006, for a review); feelings of responsibility, as seen in the emotions of guilt and shame (Frick & White, 2008; Tangney, Stuewig, & Mashek, 2007); moral reasoning and motivation (Manning & Bear, 2011; Stams et al., 2006); awareness of and sensitivity to emotions of others and to social and moral problems (Eisenberg, Fabes, & Spinrad, 2006); recognition of the intention of others/hostile attributional bias (de Castro, Veerman, Koops, Bosch, & Monshouwer, 2002); generating alternative solutions and evaluating their consequences (see Dodge, Coie, & Lynam, 2006); mechanisms of moral disengagement (also referred to as "cognitive distortions") (Bandura, Caprara, Barbaranelli, Pastorelli, & Regalia, 2001; Weiner, 2006); perceptions of self-efficacy (Bandura, 1997); and happiness, sense of self-worth, and life satisfaction (Gilman, Huebner, & Furlong, 2009).

These social cognitive and emotional processes can be found in five core social and emotional competencies highlighted in SEL programs: self-awareness, self-management of emotions and behavior, social awareness, relationship skills, and responsible decision making (Collaborative for Academic, Social, and Emotional Learning [CASEL], 2013; Durlak, Weissberg, Dymnicki, Taylor, & Schellinge, 2011). A number of packaged curriculum programs, such as the empirically supported Second Step (Fitzgerald & Edstrom, 2011) and Promoting Alternative Thinking Strategies (PATHS; Greenberg & Kusche, 2006) programs, have been shown to be effective in teaching those competencies (see CASEL, 2013). Research shows that lessons are most effective in achieving a range of positive social, emotional, and academic outcomes when they are developmentally appropriate, evidence-based, and consistent with the acronym SAFE (Durlak, Weissberg, Dymnicki, Taylor, & Schellinge, 2011). That is, they are sequenced (step-by-step lessons are taught within and across school years), active (students play an active, rather than passive, role in learning), focused (sufficient time is devoted to skill development), and explicit (goals are clearly articulated). Integrating, or infusing, lessons throughout the general curriculum, such as in literacy and social studies, also is often recommended (Bear, 2005; Jones & Bouffard, 2012) and is likely done by many teachers, either deliberately or part of the "hidden" curriculum. However, research is lacking on the effectiveness of this method compared to the use of packaged curriculum programs.

Whether in a curriculum package or infused throughout the curriculum, lessons are taught both directly and indirectly using a combination of instructional techniques, but especially techniques in which students are actively involved. This would include applying social problem-solving steps to real-life problems in the classroom, moral reasoning discussions, social perspective taking, relaxation training, anger management training, and communication training. To enhance maintenance and generalization of social and emotional skills learned in curriculum lessons, students are provided with ample opportunities to practice the SEL skills taught (and to learn new ones), such as class meetings, peer mediation, conflict resolution and extracurricular activities (including student government and sports), cooperative learning, and service learning activities, (Bear, 2010; Elias et al., 1997).

Relationship Building and Prevention of Behavior Problems

Within the framework of the SEL approach, developing and maintaining warm, close, and supportive relationships is instrumental to both maintaining order and developing self-discipline (as well as in correcting misbehavior). The importance of relationships in classroom management also is recognized in the ecological and behavioral approaches, but it receives much less attention in those two approaches and is viewed more as a product of classroom management techniques, especially positive reinforcement, rather than as a preventive technique per se. Teacher–student relationships receive the greatest attention in the SEL approach, but student–student relationships, and to a lesser extent teacher-parent relationships, also are typically targeted.

Teacher–Student Relationships

A number of leading researchers in developmental and educational psychology argue that teachers' building positive relationships with students should be a primary focus of preventive efforts (e.g., Hughes, 2012; Sabol & Pianta, 2012). This view is supported by studies demonstrating that positive teacher–student relationships are related to a number of social, emotional, and learning outcomes for students. For example, students who perceive positive teacher–student relationships experience greater on-task behavior (Battistich & Hom, 1997) and academic engagement (Danielsen, Wiium, Wilhelmsen, & Wold, 2010; Hughes, Luo, Kwok, & Loyd, 2008) and academic achievement (Hamre & Pianta, 2001; Hughes, Wu, Kwok, Villarreal, & Johnson, 2012) and are motivated to act responsibly and prosocially (Wentzel, 1996). They engage in less oppositional and antisocial behaviors (Bru, Stephens, & Torsheim, 2002; Hamre, Pianta, Downer, & Mashburn, 2008), including bullying (Gregory et al., 2010). That students misbehave less when relationships with their teachers are positive holds true for all students, irrespective of the degree of problem behavior (Hamre & Pianta, 2001; Hamre, Pianta, Downer, & Mashburn, 2008). The preventive value of teacher–student relationships is especially important for students who lack support from other sources, such as from parents, peers, and close friends (Pianta, 1999; Sabol & Pianta, 2012). Teacher-student relationships also are important in prevention (and developing self-discipline) in that students are likely to internalize their teachers' values when they perceive their teachers as caring, warm, fair, respectful, and supportive (Hughes, 2012; Wentzel, 2006).

In sum, ample research shows that warm and supportive teacher–student relationships serve as a protective asset for students and decelerate the negative effects of multiple risk factors for children with externalizing and internalizing problems (Sabol & Pianta, 2012). As discussed further in Chapter 19, intervention programs and techniques, such as Banking Time (Driscoll & Pianta, 2010), that focus on building close relationships between students and teachers (or other adults in school) have been found to be effective in reducing behavior problems, especially with students at risk (Anderson, Christenson, Sinclair, & Lehr, 2004; Tsai & Cheney, 2012).

Student–Student Relationships

Positive student–student relationships, as seen in friendships and peer acceptance, are associated with a number of positive academic and social-emotional outcomes (Buhs, Ladd, & Herald, 2006; Danielsen, Wiium, Wilhelmsen, & Wold, 2010; French & Conrad, 2001). As is true with teacher–student relationships, supportive student-student relationships help buffer the negative impact of stressors, such as peer victimization, on students' behavior and emotional adjustment (Davidson & Demaray,

2007). Students and the relations among them also influence classroom management through classroom norms. Students are more likely to misbehave in classrooms in which disruptive and aggressive behavior is socially accepted or normalized (Kellam, Ling, Merisca, Brown, & Ialongo, 1998; Henry et al., 2000; Thomas, Bierman, & The Conduct Problems Prevention Research Group, 2006). This is true irrespective of the students' knowledge or repertoire of social skills; it is well established that knowledge and skills are not sufficient for prosocial behavior (Eisenberg, Fabes, & Spinrad, 2006). Thus, it makes sense that many behavior problems might be prevented by building student–student relationships that do not support or value antisocial and aggressive behavior, by teachers being attuned to peer group affiliations, and by targeting for intervention antisocial beliefs, values, and norms in the classroom where they exist. Such interventions have been shown to be effective (Hamm, Farmer, Dadisman, Gravelle, & Murray, 2011; Henry et al., 2000) and now are the primary component of many bullying prevention programs (Swearer, Collins, Fluke, & Strawhun, 2012).

Teacher–Parent Relationships

Although less so than with teacher–student and student–student relationships, teacher–parent relationships also are often targeted for improvement in programs that are consistent with the SEL approach (e.g., Comer, Haynes, Joyner, & Ben-Avie, 1996; Elias et al., 1997). This is in recognition of research showing the strong influence of parents on the academic, social, and emotional development of their children (Parke & Buriel, 2006). In general, however, and with respect to classroom management and student behavior, most empirical research in this area has centered on communication and collaboration in the correction of behavior problems rather than in their prevention. For example, in their review of evidence-based interventions using home–school collaboration, none of the studies were on the prevention of misbehavior but were on correction. With respect to correction, techniques that entailed home–school communication were found to be effective, such as in the use of daily report cards (Vannest, Davis, Davis, Mason, & Burke, 2010). Although it is certainly logical that close teacher–parent relations, especially communication and collaboration, are likely to prevent misbehavior, research has not consistently demonstrated its added value to other classroom management techniques in preventing misbehavior in the schools (Durlak, Weissberg, Dymnicki, Taylor, & Schellinge, 2011). Further research is needed in this area.

TOWARD INTEGRATION: AUTHORITATIVE DISCIPLINE

As just seen, the ecological, behavioral, and SEL approaches share many of the same techniques for preventing misbehavior, especially teacher-centered techniques for maintaining order and managing student behavior (e.g., close monitoring of behavior, pacing of instruction, praise, clear rules and expectations, sanctions). It is in the use of student-centered techniques for developing self-discipline (while also preventing misbehavior) that they differ the greatest. The SEL approach places much greater emphasis than the other two approaches on the techniques for developing self-discipline. If one views classroom management as consisting of the dual aims of managing students and developing self-discipline, it makes sense to integrate techniques across all three approaches (Bear, 2010; Bear, Whitcomb, Elias, & Blank, in press; Osher, Bear, Sprague, & Doyle, 2010). The SEL approach is the most integrative of the three. Few, if any, preventive techniques are found in the ecological and behavioral approaches that are not found in the SEL approach; it is largely the manner in which those techniques are applied that differentiates the behavioral and SEL approaches.

An integrated approach to classroom management would be similar to the authoritative approach to parenting, or child rearing (Baumrind, 1966, 2013). Over the past 40 years, a number of cross-sectional and longitudinal studies have demonstrated that an authoritative style to parenting, especially when compared to *authoritarian* (similar to the zero tolerance approach), *permissive, and neglectful* styles, is associated with greater positive outcomes for children, including higher self-esteem, moral maturity, social competence, and academic achievement, as well as fewer behavior problems (Lamborn, Mounts, Steinberg & Dornbusch, 1991; Steinberg, Elmen, & Mounts, 1989).

The observation that effective teachers and effective parents have many characteristics and techniques in common is not new (e.g., Bear, 1998; Hughes, 2002; Wentzel, 2002), but in recent years it has gained increased recognition and empirical support. An authoritative approach has been found to characterize the most effective teachers and schools (Bear, Gaskins, Blank, & Chen, 2011; Brophy, 1996; Gregory et al., 2010; Pellerin, 2005). Like authoritative parents, authoritative teachers prevent misbehavior and elicit compliance in the short term but also develop self-discipline in the long term. They do so by balancing of basic dimensions with child rearing and classroom management: *responsiveness* and *demandingness*, also referred to in the classroom management literature as *structure* and *support* (Gregory et al., 2010). The ecological, behavioral, and SEL approaches all recognize the importance of demandingness and responsiveness. However, relative to the SEL approach, the ecological and behavioral approaches place greater emphasis on demandingness, or structure, as seen in close monitoring and supervision, clear and high behavioral expectations, fair rules, and behavior replacement and reductive techniques. In contrast, relative to the other two approaches, the SEL approach places much greater emphasis on responsiveness to children's social, emotional, physical, and cognitive needs, as seen in supportive relationships and developing social and emotional assets.

As noted, a combination of demandingness and responsiveness characterizes the most effective classrooms and schools. However, there is a lack of empirical research demonstrating that such a combination is best achieved by integrating the ecological, behavioral, and SEL approaches per se, and how to best do so, or that such a combination is more effective than any one of the three approaches alone. It is likely that most teachers and schools already integrate techniques across approaches, although not in a planned, deliberate, and systematic fashion. In a recent study of the effectiveness of seven social and character development programs, which included PATHS (Greenberg & Kusche, 2006), Second Step (Fitzgerald & Edstrom, 2011, and a program very similar to the SWPBIS approach (Academic and Behavioral

Competencies), teachers in the control group reported using many of the same social and character development strategies, often to the same extent, as teachers implementing the seven social and character development programs investigated. For example, 95% of teachers in the control group reported using cooperative learning, 85% reported using peer group discussions, 69% reported integrating social and character education activities into the academic curriculum, and 92% reported using rewards for positive behavior on a daily or weekly basis. Moreover, principals in the control schools reported that 86% of the teachers and staff had participated in social and character development training within the past year. These findings are quite consistent with earlier research on the characteristics of the most effective classroom managers, which found that they combine techniques commonly found across various approaches to classroom management, including the techniques presented previously (Brophy & McCaslin, 1992).

That many, if not most, teachers already integrate techniques found in the ecological, behavioral, and SEL approaches also is evident in studies of the SWPBIS approach. For example, Maryland and Illinois, where a large number of studies on the SWPBIS approach have been conducted (e.g., Bradshaw, Mitchell, & Leaf, 2010; Simonsen, Eber, Sugai, Lewandowski, Sims, & Myers, 2012) require a character education or SEL program in each school. Many other states require the same, and many also require bullying prevention programs (many of which follow the SEL approach). Bradshaw, Mitchell, and Leaf (2010) reported that an average of 5.1 programs for preventing behavior and social-emotional problems were being implemented in the SWPBIS schools in their randomized controlled group study, while often focusing on "character education and /or development, social-emotional or social skills, bullying prevention, drug prevention (e.g., D.A.R.E.), and conflict resolution and/or peer mediation" (p. 146). Thus, it is very likely that to one degree or another, all teachers integrate the ecological, behavioral, and SEL techniques listed in this chapter.

The evidence-based Good Behavior Game (GBG), an interdependent group contingency program, is a good example of how combining features of all three approaches can be and has been done (Bear, 2010). The GBG was developed to improve the classroom management of teachers in classrooms in which order was greatly lacking, but it also serves to "socialize children into the role of student and to teach them to regulate their own and their classmates' behavior" (Kellam et al., 2008, p. S7). In several longitudinal and randomized control group studies on the GBG, researchers (Kellam et al., 2008; Petras et al., 2008; van Lier, Vuijk, & Crijnen, 2005) found that the game prevented behavior problems in both the short term and long term, although its long-term effects were not consistently found across cohorts or for students not at greatest risk for aggressive and delinquent behavior. Those researchers attributed the effectiveness of the GBG to a combination of mechanisms that operate during its implementation. Those mechanisms, which are found in the ecological, behavioral, and SEL approaches, are (1) the contingent use of rewards, together with clear expectations, rules, and consequences; (2) positive peer pressure; (3) early learning of social skills and students' increased self-efficacy in those skills; (4) reduced off-task behavior and greater engagement in learning; (5) increased time devoted to teaching and learning; (6) less negative peer influence, especially models of aggressive and antisocial behavior (and supporting cognitions and values); (7) increased prosocial interaction with peers; and (8) the fun and motivational game-like atmosphere in which the GBG is played.

MIGHT REWARDS BE DETRIMENTAL?

Perhaps the greatest obstacle to the integration of the behavioral approach with the ecological approach and especially the SEL approach concerns the systematic and frequent use of tangible rewards, and to a lesser extent praise, in classroom management (Bear et al., in press). The frequent and systematic use of praise and rewards is strongly endorsed by behaviorists and special educators, but it is often discouraged in general teacher education training programs (Brownell, Ross, Colón, & McCallum, 2005; Landrum & Kauffman, 2006). Over the past 40 years, perhaps no other issue has generated as much debate as the frequent use of rewards and praise. But, as is true with the use of other preventive techniques listed previously, even here researchers agree more than they differ (which is often overlooked in articles on the debate). That is, regardless of their theoretical framework, few researchers believe that rewards and particularly praise *should not* be used in classrooms or would argue against the commonly recommended four-to-one ratio of praise to corrective statement (e.g., Epstein, Atkins, Cullinan, Kutash, & Weaver, 2008). Most recognize that rewards and praise often serve as positive reinforcers (although not always), and are often needed when student motivation is lacking. They recognize that rewards are valuable in many ways other than positive reinforcement, such as providing positive feedback and guidance and helping establish positive teacher–student relationships (Brophy, 1981). These have not been points of debate and contention. Instead, at issue have been (1) the practicality of the frequent and systematic use of rewards and praise, as recommended by behaviorists, and whether such use is necessary and worth the time and (2) the potential harm to intrinsic motivation when not used wisely and strategically.

It is common for behaviorists to posit that teachers need to use praise and rewards much more frequently and systematically (Epstein, Atkins, Cullinan, Kutash, & Weaver, 2008; Kern & Clemens, 2007; Maag, 2001; Sugai & Horner, 2009). This is in contrast to Brophy's (1981) conclusion in his classic comprehensive review of the literature of praise, in which he stated the effectiveness of praise "has been seriously oversold" (p. 21). Likewise, Emmer (1987) reached a similar conclusion in his review of the literature on praise, noting that although praise is effective under certain conditions, "[r]esearch does *not* indicate that its effects are uniformly positive. . . ." (p. 38). Another interesting observation by Brophy was that the frequent use of praise and rewards might simply reflect that "the teacher is not doing enough of the more fundamental and positive things that tend to sustain student engagement" (p. 21). This observation is supported by research showing that the most effective tutors use praise sparingly (Lepper & Woolverton, 2002).

While not recommending against the wise and strategic use of rewards and praise, Brophy (1981) and others (e.g., Bear, 2010; Emmer, 1987; Hattie & Timperley, 2007) cite additional limitations inherent in their use that would lead to Brophy's conclusion that they are seriously oversold. Among them are (1) within and across age groups, individuals differ in their preferences and responses to praise and rewards with many students, especially adolescents, preferring not to be praised or rewarded publically; (2) teachers and schools often do not have access to, or control over, the rewards that are the most powerful reinforcers of behavior; (3) praise, especially rewards, can be satiating; (4) to maximize their usefulness in teaching new behaviors, praise and rewards must be given immediately and contingently, which often is difficult for teachers to do; and (5) the effects of praise and rewards often do not generalize outside of the setting in which they are systematically applied.

The second major point of debate among researchers has been the potential harm that praise and rewards—especially rewards—might have on intrinsic motivation and moral reasoning. It is beyond the scope of this chapter to review the many nuances in this debate (see Chapter 26). Although often fused into one argument, there are two distinct, yet interrelated, issues here. The first pertains to a reliance on the systematic use of praise and rewards (and also punishment) as the primary, if not exclusive, means of managing children's behavior, whether at home or school. It is argued that such a practice fosters immature, self-centered, hedonistic moral reasoning—the very low-level moral reasoning that is common among young children but also among older children who exhibit the most frequent and serious behavior problems (Manning & Bear, 2011; Stams et al., 2006). When given a restricted diet of rewards, praise, and punishment for targeted observable behaviors, especially when SEL techniques are lacking, students are likely to learn there is little reason *not* to misbehave in the absence of rewards and punishment (or adult supervision).

The second issue pertaining to the potential harmful effects is more specific to the impact of rewards on intrinsic motivation, irrespective of one's level of moral reasoning. It is argued that rewards may undermine intrinsic motivation—that students often act in a self-determined prosocial manner (i.e., for intrinsic reasons)—but that after being rewarded for such behavior, they are less likely to continue to act prosocially, especially in the absence of the promise of rewards. In general, those who voice this argument support it with research they interpret as showing that rewards harm intrinsic motivation *if* used in certain ways, particularly in a controlling (versus informative) manner, and when social comparisons are highlighted (Deci, Koestner, & Ryan, 1999, 2001). In contrast, when reviewing research studies on the effectiveness of reward, behaviorists tend to conclude that there is little empirical research supporting that rewards, especially as commonly used in most classrooms, harm "intrinsic motivation" (note that behaviorists also question whether intrinsic motivation exists or should be the subject of empirical research) (Akin-Little & Little, 2009; Cameron, 2001).

Both of these arguments have merit. That is, if one's aim is the short-term management of student behavior (versus the development of self-discipline), especially with students with behavior problems, research supports the effectiveness of rewards (despite their limitations). But if one's aim extends beyond managing student behavior and encompasses the development of social and emotional competencies, including moral reasoning and other social cognitive and emotional skills underlying self-discipline, warnings about reliance on the frequent and systematic use of praise and rewards to manage behavior and obtain compliance should be heeded. As noted previously, however, any potential negative effects of rewards and praise are likely to be avoided by combining ecological, behavioral, and SEL techniques and by using praise and rewards wisely and strategically, which includes not solely for the purpose of managing or controlling student behavior (i.e., following rules, compliance, and obedience) but also to help develop social and emotional competencies of self-discipline.

CONCLUSION

What preventive techniques "work" in classroom management depends on how one defines classroom management, which in turn determines the aim of classroom management and the most effective techniques to achieve it. In the first half of the 20th century, classroom management was conceptualized as consisting of the dual aims of (1) order, engagement and compliance and (2) developing self-discipline. For most of the second half of the 20th century, however, developing self-discipline no longer was viewed as part of classroom management. Ecological and behavioral researchers focused on observable teacher practices and on specific techniques that were effective in managing student behavior in the classroom. More recently, researchers, including those with an ecological orientation (e.g., Doyle, 2006), but particularly those with a SEL orientation, have returned to conceptualizing classroom management as having the dual aims of (1) order, engagement, and compliance and (2) self-discipline. In contrast, the behavioral approach continues to view classroom management more narrowly, with its primary aim being teachers' management of student behavior and with a particular emphasis on teacher-centered techniques that bring about compliance. To be sure, compliance *is* important, and behavioral and cognitive-behavioral techniques can be used not only to achieve it but also to help develop social and emotional competencies, including those of self-discipline. However, such a use of behavioral and especially cognitive-behavioral techniques is rarely seen in today's popular behavioral approaches to classroom management and school discipline (e.g., Canter, 2010; Knoff, 2012; Sugai & Horner, 2009; Sugai et al., 2010). With the support of research on authoritative parenting and teaching, it makes sense that teachers and schools strive to achieve the dual aims of classroom management, while integrating techniques across the ecological, behavioral, and SEL approaches.

REFERENCES

Akin-Little, A., & Little, S.G. (2009). The true effects of extrinsic reinforcement on "intrinsic" motivation. In A. Akin-Little, S.G. Little, M.A. Bray, & T. J Kehle (Eds), *Behavioral intervention in schools: Evidence-based positive strategies* (pp. 73–91). Washington, DC: American Psychological Association.

Anderson, A. R., Christenson, S. L., Sinclair, M. F., & Lehr, C. A. (2004). Check and connect: The importance of relationships for promoting engagement with school. *Journal of School Psychology, 42*, 95–113. doi: 10.1016/j.jsp.2004.01.002

Anderson, L. M., Evertson, C. M., & Emmer, E. T. (1980). Dimensions in classroom management derived from recent research. *Journal of Curriculum Studies, 12*, 343–356. doi: 10.1080/0022027800120407

Arum, R. (2003). *Judging school discipline: The crisis of moral authority*. Cambridge, MA: Cambridge University Press. doi: 10.1086/498999

Astor, R. A., Benbenishty, R., Marachi, R., & Meyer, H. A. (2006). In S. R. Jimerson & M. J. Furlong (Eds.), *Handbook of school violence and school safety: From research to practice* (pp. 221–233). Mahwah, NJ: Erlbaum.

Bagley, W. (1908). *Classroom management*. New York: Macmillan.

Bandura, A. (1997). *Self-efficacy: The exercise of control*. New York: Freeman.

Bandura, A., Caprara, G. V., Barbaranelli, C., Pastorelli, C., & Regalia, C. (2001). Sociocognitive self-regulatory mechanisms governing transgressive behavior. *Journal of Personality and Social Psychology, 80*, 125–135. doi: 10.1037/0022-3514.80.1.125 Retrieved from http://psycnet.apa.org/doi/10.1037/0022-3514.80.1.125

Battistich, V., & Hom, A. (1997). The relationship between students' sense of their school as a community and their involvement in problem behaviors. *American Journal of Public Health, 87*, 1997–2001. doi: 10.2105/AJPH.87.12.1997

Barrish, H. H., Saunders, M., & Wolf, M. M. (1969). Good behavior game: Effects of individual contingencies for group consequences on disruptive behavior in a classroom. *Journal of Applied Behavior Analysis, 2*, 119–124.

Baumrind, D. (1966). Effects of authoritative parental control on child behavior. *Child Development, 37*, 887–907. doi: 10.2307/1126611

Baumrind, D. (2013). Authoritative parenting revisited: History and current status. *Authoritative parenting: Synthesizing nurturance and discipline for optimal child development* (pp. 11–34). Washington, DC: American Psychological Association. doi: 10.1037/13948-002

Bear, G. G. (1998). School discipline in America: Strategies for prevention, correction, and long term development. *School Psychology Review, 27*(1), 14–32.

Bear, G. G. (with A. Cavalier & M. Manning). (2005). *Developing self-discipline and preventing and correcting misbehavior*. Boston: Allyn & Bacon.

Bear, G. G. (2010). *School discipline and self-discipline: A practical guide to promoting prosocial student behavior*. New York: Guilford.

Bear, G. G. (2012). Self-discipline as a protective asset. In S. Brock, P. Lazarus, & S. Jimerson (Eds), *Best practices in crisis prevention and intervention in the schools* (2nd ed.) (pp. 27–54). Bethesda, MD: National Association of School Psychologists.

Bear, G. G. (2013). Teacher resistance to frequent rewards and praise: Lack of skill or a wise decision? *Journal of Educational and Psychological Consultation, 23*, 4, 318–340. doi: 10.1080/10474412.2013.845495

Bear, G. G., Gaskins, C., Blank, J., & Chen, F.F. (2011). Delaware School Climate Survey—Student: Its factor structure, concurrent validity, and reliability. *Journal of School Psychology, 49*, 157–174. doi: 0.1016/j.jsp.2011.01.001

Bear, G. G., Whitcomb, S., Elias, M., & Blank, J. (in press). SEL and Schoolwide Positive Behavioral Interventions and Supports. In J. Durlak, T. Gullotta, C. Domitrovich, P. Goren, & R. Weissberg (Eds.), *Handbook of social and emotional learning*. New York: Guilford Press.

Berkowitz, L. (1989). Situational influences on aggression. In J. Groebel & R. A. Hinde (Eds.), *Aggression and war: Their biological and social bases* (pp. 91–100). Thousand Oaks, CA: Sage.

Bradshaw, C. P., Mitchell, M. M., & Leaf, P. J. (2010). Examining the effects of schoolwide positive behavioral interventions and supports on student outcomes. *Journal of Positive Behavior Interventions, 12*, 133–148. doi: 10.1177/1098300709334798

Brock, L. L., Nishida, T. K., Chiong, C., Grimm, K., & Rimm-Kaufman, S. E. (2008). Children's perceptions of the classroom environment and social and academic performance: A longitudinal analysis of the contribution of the Responsive Classroom approach. *Journal of School Psychology, 46*, 129–149. doi: 10.1016/j.jsp.2007.02.004

Brophy, J. (1979). Teacher behavior and its effects. *Journal of Educational Psychology, 71*, 733–750. doi: 10.1037/0022-0663.71.6.733

Brophy, J. E. (1981). On praising effectively. *The Elementary School Journal, 81*(5), 269–278.

Brophy, J. E. (1983). Classroom organization and management. *The Elementary School Journal, 83*, 265–285. doi: 10.1086/461318

Brophy, J. E. (1996). *Teaching problem students*. New York: Guilford.

Brophy, J. (2006). History of research on classroom management. In C. M. Evertson & C. S. Weinstein (Eds.), *Handbook of classroom management: Research, practice, and contemporary issues* (pp. 17–43). Mahwah, NJ: Erlbaum.

Brophy, J., & McCaslin, M. (1992). Teachers' reports of how they perceive and cope with problem students. *Elementary School Journal, 93*, 3–68. doi: org/10.1086/461712

Brownell, M. T., Ross, D. D., Colón, E. P., & McCallum, C. L. (2005). Critical features of special education teacher preparation: A comparison with general teacher education. *The Journal of Special Education, 38*, 242–252. doi: 10.1177/00224669050380040601

Bru, E., Stephens, P., & Torsheim, T. (2002). Students' perceptions of class management and reports of their own misbehavior. *Journal of School Psychology, 40*, 287–307. doi: 10.1016/S0022-4405(02)00104-8

Buhs, E. S., Ladd, G. W., & Herald, S. L. (2006). Peer exclusion and victimization: Processes that mediate the relation between peer group rejection and children's classroom engagement and achievement. *Journal of Educational Psychology, 98*, 1–13. doi: 10.1037/0022-0663.98.1.1

Bullis, M., Walker, H., & Sprague, J. R. (2001). A promise unfulfilled: Social skills training with at-risk and antisocial children and youth. *Exceptionality, 9*, 67–90. doi: 10.1207/S15327035EX091&2_6

California Task Force to Promote Self-Esteem and Personal and Social Responsibility. (1990). *Toward a state of esteem: The final report of the California Task Force to Promote Self-Esteem and Personal and Social Responsibility*. Sacramento, CA: Author.

Cameron, J. (2001). Negative effects of reward on intrinsic motivation—a limited phenomenon: Comment on Deci, Loestner, and Ryan. *Review of Educational Research, 71*, 29–42. doi: 10.3102/00346543071001029

Canter, L. (201). *Assertive discipline: Positive Behavior Management for Today's Classroom*. Bloomington, IN: Solution Tree Press.

Cartledge, G., & Milburn, J. F. (1978). The case for teaching social skills in the classroom: A review. *Review of Educational Research, 48*, 133–156. doi: 10.2307/1169912

Collaborative for Academic, Social, and Emotional Learning. (2013). *2013 CASEL guide: Effective social and emotional learning programs—Preschool and elementary school edition*. Chicago: Author.

Comer, J. P., Haynes, N. M., Joyner, E. T., & Ben-Avie, M. (Eds.). (1996). *Rallying the whole village: The Comer process for reforming education*. New York: Teachers College Press.

Cook, C. R., Gresham, F. M., Kern, L., Barreras, R. B., Thornton, S., & Crews, S. D. (2008). Social skills training with secondary students with emotional and/or or behavioral disorders: A review and analysis of the meta-analytic literature. *Journal of Emotional and Behavioral Disorders, 16*, 131–141. doi: 10.1177/1063426608314541

Danielsen, A. G., Wiium, N., Wilhelmsen, B. U., & Wold, B. (2010). Perceived support provided by teachers and classmates and students' self-reported academic initiative. *Journal of School Psychology, 48*, 247–267. doi: 10.1016/j.jsp.2010.02.002

Davidson, L. M., & Demaray, M. K. (2007). Social support as a moderator between victimization and internalizing–externalizing distress from bullying. *School Psychology Review, 36*(3), 383–405.

de Castro, B. O., Veerman, J. W., Koops, W., Bosch, J., & Monshouwer, J. J. (2002). Hostile attribution of intent and aggressive behavior: A meta-analysis. *Child Development, 73*, 916–934. doi: 10.1111/1467-8624.00447

Deci, E. L., Koestner, R., & Ryan, R. M. (1999). A meta-analytic review of experiments examining the effects of extrinsic rewards on intrinsic motivation. *Psychological Bulletin, 125*, 627–668. doi: 10.1037/0033-2909.125.6.627

Deci, E. L., Koestner, R., & Ryan, R. M. (2001). Extrinsic rewards and intrinsic motivation in education: Reconsidered once again. *Review of Educational Research, 71*, 1–27. doi: 10.3102/00346543071001043

Dodge, K. A., Coie, J. D., & Lynam, D. (2006). Aggression and antisocial behavior in youth. In W. Damon & R. M. Learner (Series Eds.) & N. Eisenberg (Vol. Ed.), *Handbook of child psychology*: Vol. 3. *Social, emotional, and personality development* (6th ed.) (pp. 719–788). New York: Wiley. doi: 10.1002/9780470147658

Dougherty, E. H., & Dougherty, A. (1977). The daily report card: A simplified and flexible package for classroom behavior management. *Psychology in the Schools, 14*, 191–195. doi: 10.1002/1520-6807(197704)14:2

Doyle, W. (2006). Ecological approaches to classroom management. In C. M. Evertson & C. S. Weinstein (Eds.), *Handbook of classroom management: Research, practice, and contemporary issues* (pp. 97–125). Mahwah, NJ: Erlbaum.

Dreikurs, R., & Grey, L. (1968*). Logical consequences: A handbook of discipline*. New York: Meredith Press.

Driscoll, K. C., & Pianta, R. C. (2010). Banking time in Head Start: Early efficacy of an intervention designed to promote supportive teacher–child relationships. *Early Education and Development, 21*, 38–64. doi: 10.1080/10409280802657449

DuPaul, G. J., & Eckert, T. L. (1994). The effects of social skills curricula: Now you see them, now you don't. *School Psychology Quarterly, 9*, 113–132. doi: 10.1037/h0088847

Durlak, J. A., Weissberg, R. P., Dymnicki, A. B., Taylor, R. D., & Schellinger, K. B. (2011). The impact of enhancing students' social and emotional learning: A meta-analysis of school-based universal interventions. *Child Development, 82*, 405–432. doi: 10.1111/j.1467-8624.2010.01564.x

Eisenberg, N., Fabes, R. A., & Spinrad, T. L. (2006). Prosocial behavior. In W. Damon & R. M. Learner (Series Eds.) & N. Eisenberg (Vol. Ed.), *Handbook of child psychology*: Vol. 3, *Social, emotional, and personality development* (6th ed.) (pp. 646–718). New York: Wiley.

Elias, M. J., Zins, J. E., Weissberg, R. P., Frey, K. S., Greenberg, M. T., Haynes, N. M., et al. (1997). *Promoting social and emotional learning: Guidelines for educators*. Alexandria, VA: Association for Supervision and Curriculum Development.

Elliott, S. N., Frey, J. R., & DiPerna, J. C. (2012). Promoting social skills: Enabling academic and interpersonal successes. In S. Brock, P. Lazarus, & S. Jimerson (Eds.), *Best practices in crisis prevention and intervention in the schools* (2nd ed.) (pp. 55–77). Bethesda, MD: National Association of School Psychologists.

Elliott, S. N., & Gresham, F. M. (2007). *Social Skills Improvement System Classwide Intervention Program.* San Antonio, TX: Pearson Assessments.

Emmer, E. T. (1987). Praise and the instructional process. *Journal of Classroom Interaction, 23*(2), 32–39.

Emmer, E. T., & Evertson, C. M. (2012). *Classroom management for middle and high school teachers* (9th ed.). New York: Pearson.

Emmer, E. T., Evertson, C. M., & Anderson, L. M. (1980). Effective classroom management at the beginning of the school year. *Elementary School Journal, 80,* 219–231. doi: 10.1037/0022-0663.74.4.485

Emmer, E. T., & Stough, L. M. (2001). Classroom management: A critical part of educational psychology, with implications for teacher education. *Educational Psychologist, 36,* 103–112. doi: 10.1207/S15326985EP3602_5

Epstein, M., Atkins, M., Cullinan, D., Kutash, K., & Weaver, R. (2008). *Reducing behavior problems in the elementary school classroom: A practice guide* (NCEE #2008–012). Washington, DC: National Center for Education Evaluation and Regional Assistance, Institute of Education Sciences, U.S. Department of Education. Retrieved from http://ies.ed.gov/ncee/wwc/publications/practiceguides.

Evertson, C. M., & Emmer, E. T., (2012). *Classroom management for elementary teachers* (9th ed.). New York: Pearson.

Evertson, C. M., & Weinstein, C. S. (Eds.). (2006). *Handbook of classroom management: Research, practice, and contemporary issues.* Mahwah, NJ: Erlbaum.

Fitzgerald, P. D., & Edstrom, L. V. S. (2011). *Social and emotional skills training with second step: A violence prevention curriculum.* New York: Routledge/Taylor & Francis.

Freiberg, H. J., & Lapointe, J. M. (2006). In research-based programs for preventing and solving discipline problems. In C. M. Evertson & C. S. Weinstein (Eds.), *Handbook of classroom management: Research, practice, and contemporary issues* (pp. 735–786). Mahwah, NJ: Erlbaum.

French, D. C., & Conrad, J. (2001). School dropout as predicted by peer rejection and antisocial behavior. *Journal of Research on Adolescence, 11,* 225–244. doi: 10.1111/1532-7795.00011

Frick, P. J., & White, S. F. (2008). Research review: The importance of callous–unemotional traits for developmental models of aggressive and antisocial behavior. *Journal of Child Psychology and Psychiatry, 49,* 359–375. doi: 10.1111/j.1469-7610.2007.01862.x

Gettinger, M. (1988). Methods of proactive classroom management. *School Psychology Review, 17*(2), 227–242.

Gettinger, M., & Kohler, K. M. (2006). In C. M. Evertson & C. S. Weinstein (Eds.), *Handbook of classroom management: Research, practice, and contemporary issues* (pp. 73–95). Mahwah, NJ: Erlbaum.

Gilman, R., Huebner, E. S., & Furlong, M. (Eds.). (2009). *Handbook of positive psychology.* New York: Routledge.

Glasser, W. (1965). *Reality therapy.* New York: Harper & Row.

Gordon, T. (1974, 2003). *TET: Teacher effectiveness training.* New York: Three Rivers Press.

Gottfredson, G. D., Gottfredson, D. C., Payne, A. A., & Gottfredson, N. C. (2005). School climate predictors of school disorder: Results from a national study of delinquency prevention in schools. *Journal of Research in Crime and Delinquency, 42,* 412–444. doi: 10.1177/0022427804271931

Greenberg, M. T., & Kusche, C. A. (2006). Building social and emotional competence: The PATHS curriculum. In S. R. Jimerson & M. J. Furlong (Eds.), *Handbook of school violence and school safety: From research to practice* (pp. 395–412). Mahwah, NJ: Erlbaum.

Gregory, A., Cornell, D., Fan, X., Sheras, P., Shih, T., & Huang, F. (2010). High school practices associated with lower student bullying and victimization. *Journal of Educational Psychology, 102,* 483–496. doi: 10.1037/a0018562

Gresham, F. M. (2004). Current status and future directions of school-based behavioral interventions. *School Psychology Review, 3*(3), 326–343.

Gresham, F. M., McIntyre, L. L., Olson-Tinker, H., Dolstra, L., McLaughlin, V., & Van, M. (2004). Relevance of functional behavioral assessment research for school-based intervention and positive behavior support. *Research in Developmental Disabilities, 25,* 19–37. doi: 10.1016/j.ridd.2003.04.003

Gump, P. V. (1982). School settings and their keeping. In D. L. Duke (Ed.), *Helping teachers manage classrooms* (pp. 98–114). Alexandria, VA: Association for Supervision and Curriculum Development.

Hahn, R., Fuqua-Whitley, D., Wethington, H., Lowy, J., Crosby, A., Fullilove, M., et al. (2007). Effectiveness of universal school-based programs to prevent violent and aggressive behavior: A systematic review. *American Journal of Preventive Medicine, 33* (Suppl. 2S), 114–129. doi: 10.1016/j.amepre.2007.04.012

Hamm, J. V., Farmer, T.W., Dadisman, K., Gravelle, M., & Murray, A.R. (2011). Teachers' attunement to students' peer group affiliations as a source of improved student experiences of the school social–affective context following the middle school transition. *Journal of Applied Developmental Psychology, 32,* 267–277. doi: 10.1016/j.appdev.2010.06.003

Hamre, B., & Pianta, R. (2001). Early teacher–child relationships and the trajectory of children's school outcomes through eighth grade. *Child Development, 72,* 625–638. doi: 10.1111/1467-8624.00301

Hamre, B.K., Pianta, R.C., Downer, J.T., & Mashburn, A.J. (2008). Teachers' perceptions of conflict with young students: Looking beyond problem behaviors. *Social Development, 17,* 115–136. doi: 10.1111/j.1467-9507.2007.00418.x

Hattie, J., & Timperley, H. (2007). The power of feedback. *Review of Educational Research, 77,* 81–112. doi: 10.3102/003465430298487

Henry, D., Guerra, N., Huesmann, R., Tolan, P., VanAcker, R., & Eron, L. (2000). Normative influences on aggression in urban elementary school classrooms. *American Journal of Community Psychology, 28,* 59–81. doi: 10.1023/A:1005142429725

Hughes, J. N. (2002). Authoritative teaching: Tipping the balance in favor of school versus peer effects. *Journal of School Psychology, 40,* 485–492. doi: 10.1016/S0022-4405(02)00125-5

Hughes, J. N. (2012). Teachers as managers of students' peer context. In A. M. Ryan & G. W. Ladd (Eds.), *Peer relationships and adjustment at school* (pp. 189–218). Charlotte, NC: Information Age.

Hughes, J.N., Luo, W., Kwok, O., & Loyd, L.K. (2008). Teacher–student support, effortful engagement, and achievement: A 3-year longitudinal study. *Journal of Educational Psychology, 100,* 1–14. doi: 10.1037/0022-0663.100.1.1

Hughes, J.N., Wu, J., Kwok, O., Villarreal, V., & Johnson, A. Y. (2012). Indirect effects of child reports of teacher–student relationship on achievement. *Journal of Educational Psychology, 104,* 350–365. doi: 10.1037/a0026339

Hunley, S. (2008). Best practices for preparing learning space to increase engagement. In A. Thomas & J. Grimes (Eds.), *Best practices in school psychology V* (pp. 813–826). Bethesda, MD: National Association of School Psychologists.

Jenson, W.R., Clark, E., & Burrow-Sanchez, J. (2009). Practical strategies in working with difficult students. *Behavioral interventions in schools: Evidence-based positive strategies* (pp. 247–263). Washington, DC: American Psychological Association. doi: 10.1037/11886-016

Jones, S. M., & Bouffard, S. M. (2012). Social and emotional learning in schools: From program to strategies. *Social Policy Report, 26*(4), 3–22.

Kellam, S. G., Brown, C. H., Poduska, J., Ialongo, N., Wang, W., Toyinbo, P., et al. (2008). Effects of a universal classroom behavior management program in first and second grades on young adult behavioral, psychiatric, and social outcomes. *Drug and Alcohol Dependence, 95,* S5–S28. doi: 10.1016/j.drugalcdep.2008.01.006

Kellam, S. G., Ling, X., Merisca, R., Brown, C. H., & Ialongo, N. (1998). The effect of the level of aggression in the first grade classroom on the course and malleability of aggressive behavior into middle school. *Development and Psychopathology, 10,* 165–185. doi: 10.1017/S0954579498001564

Kern, L., & Clemens, N.H. (2007). Antecedent strategies to promote appropriate classroom behavior. *Psychology in the Schools, 44,* 65–75. doi: 10.1002/pits.20206

Kounin, J. (1970). *Discipline and group management in classrooms.* New York: Holt, Rinehart & Winston.

Knoff, H.M. (2012). *School discipline, classroom management, and student self-management: A PBS implementation guide.* Thousand Oaks, CA: Corwin.

Lamborn, S. D., Mounts, N. S., Steinberg, L., & Dornbusch, S. M. (1991). Patterns of competence and adjustment among adolescents from authoritative, authoritarian, indulgent, and neglectful families. Child Development, 62, 1049–1065. doi: 10.2307/1131151

Landrum, T. J., & Kauffman, J. M. (2006). Behavioral approaches to classroom management. In C. M. Evertson & C. S. Weinstein (Eds.), *Handbook of classroom management: Research, practice, and contemporary issues* (pp. 47–71). Mahwah, NJ: Erlbaum.

Lassman, K. A., Jolivette, K., & Wehby, J. H. (1999). "My teacher said I did good work today!" Using collaborative behavioral contracting. *Teaching Exceptional Children, 31*(4), 12–18.

Lepper, M. R., & Woolverton, M. (2002). The wisdom of practice: Lessons learned from the study of highly effective tutors. In J. Aronson (Ed.), *Improving academic achievement: Contributions of social psychology* (pp. 135–158). Orlando, FL: Academic Press.

Lochman, J. E., Powell, N. R., Clanton, N., & McElroy, H. K. (2006). Anger and aggression. In G. G. Bear & K. M. Minke (Eds.), *Children's needs III: Development, prevention, and intervention* (pp. 115–133). Bethesda, MD: National Association of School Psychologists.

Lösel, F., & Beelmann, A. (2003). Effects of child skills training in preventing antisocial behavior: A systematic review of randomized evaluations. *Annals of the American Academy of Political and Social Science, 587*, 84–109. doi: 10.1177/0002716202250793

Lynass, L. L., Tsai, S-F., Richman, T. D., & Cheney, D. (2012). Social expectations and behavioral indicators in school-wide positive behavior supports: A national study of behavior matrices. *Journal of Positive Behavior Interventions, 14*, 153–161. doi: 10.1177/1098300711412076

Maag, J. W. (2001). Rewarded by punishment: Reflections on the disuse of positive reinforcement in schools. *Exceptional Children, 67*(2), 173–186.

Maag, J. W. (2006). Social skills training for students with emotional and behavioral disorders: A review of reviews. *Behavioral Disorders, 32*(1), 5–17.

Manning, M. A., & Bear, G. G. (2011). Moral reasoning and aggressive behavior: Concurrent and longitudinal relations. *Journal of School Violence, 10*, 258–280. doi: 10.1080/15388220.2011.579235

McClellan, B. E. (1999). *Moral education in America: Schools and the shaping of character from colonial times to the present*. New York: Teachers College Press.

National Research Council (NRC) and Institute of Medicine (IOM). (2009). *Preventing mental, emotional, and behavioral disorders among young people*. Washington, DC: National Academies Press.

O'Leary, K. D., & Drabman, R. S. (1971). Token reinforcement programs in the classroom: A review. *Psychological Bulletin, 75*, 379–398. doi: 10.1037/h0031311

O'Leary, K. D., & O'Leary. S. G. (Eds.). (1977). *Classroom management: The successful use of behavior modification* (2nd ed.). New York: Pergamon.

Osher, D., Bear, G. G., Sprague, J. R., & Doyle, W. (2010). How can we improve school discipline? *Educational Researcher, 39*, 48–58. doi: 10.3102/0013189X09357618

Parke, R. D., & Buriel, R. (2006). Socialization in the family: Ethnic and ecological perspectives. In W. Damon & R. M. Learner (Series Ed.) & N. Eisenberg (Vol. Ed.), *Handbook of child psychology*: Vol. 3, *Social, emotional, and personality development* (6th ed.) (pp. 429–504). New York: Wiley.

Pellerin, L. A. (2005). Applying Baumrind's parenting typology to high schools: Toward a middle-range theory of authoritative socialization. *Social Science Research, 34*, 283–303. doi: 10.1016/j.ssresearch.2004.02.003

Petras, H., Kellam, S. G., Brown, C. H., Muthén, B. O., Ialongo, N. S., & Poduska, J. M. (2008). Developmental epidemiological courses leading to ASPD and violent and criminal behavior: Effects by young adulthood of a universal preventive intervention in first- and second-grade classrooms. *Drug and Alcohol Dependence, 95*, S45–S59. doi: 10.1016/j.drugalcdep.2007.10.015

Pianta, R. C. (1999). *Enhancing relationships between children and teachers*. Washington, DC: American Psychological Association.

Power, F. C., Higgins, A., & Kohlberg, L. (1989). *Lawrence Kohlberg's approach to moral education*. New York: Columbia University Press.

Raths, L., Harmin, M., & Simon, S. (1966). *Values and teaching*. Columbus, OH: Merrill.

Reese, W. J. (1995). Reefer madness and a Clockwork Orange. In D. Ravitch and M. A. Vinovskis (Eds.), *Learning from the past* (pp. 355–381). Baltimore, MD: Johns Hopkins University Press.

Rosenbaum, M. S., & Drabman, R. S. (1979). Self-control training in the classroom: A review and critique. *Journal of Applied Behavior Analysis, 12*(3), 467–485.

Sabol, T. J., & Pianta, R. C. (2012). Recent trends in research on teacher–child relationships. *Attachment and Human Development, 14*, 213–231. doi: 10.1080/14616734.2012.672262

Simonsen, B., Eber, L., Black, A. C., Sugai, G., Lewandowski, H., Sims, B., & Myers, D. (2012). Illinois state-wide positive behavioral interventions and supports: Evolution and impact on student outcomes across years. *Journal of Positive Behavior Intervention, 14*, 5–16. doi: 10.1177/1098300711412601

Simonsen, B., & Sugai, G. (2009). School-wide positive behavior support: A systems-level application of behavioral principles. In A. Akin-Little, S. G. Little, M. A. Bray, & T. J. Kehle (Eds.), *Behavioral interventions in schools: Evidence-based positive strategies* (pp. 125–140). Washington, DC: American Psychological Association.

Stams, G. J., Brugman, D., Dekovic, M., van Rosmalen, L., van der Laan, P., & Gibbs, J. C. (2006). The moral judgment of juvenile delinquents: A meta-analysis. *Journal of Abnormal Child Psychology, 34*, 697–713. doi: 10.1007/s10802-006-9056-5

Steinberg, L., Elmen, J. D., & Mounts, N. S. (1989). Authoritative parenting, psychosocial maturity, and academic success among adolescents. *Child Development, 60,* 1424–1436. doi: 10.2307/1130932

Sugai, G., & Horner, R. H. (2009). Defining and describing schoolwide positive behavior support. In W. Sailor, G. Dunlap, G. Sugai, & R. Horner (Eds.), *Handbook of positive behavior support* (pp. 307–326). New York: Springer.

Sugai, G., Horner, R. H., Algozzine, R., Barrett, S., Lewis, T., Anderson, C., et al. (2010). *School-wide positive behavior support: Implementers' blueprint and self-assessment.* Eugene: University of Oregon. Retrieved from www.pbis.org.

Swearer, S. M., Collins, A., Fluke, S., & Strawhun, J. (2012). Preventing bullying behaviors in schools. In S. Brock, P. Lazarus, & S. Jimerson (Eds), *Best practices in crisis prevention and intervention in the schools* (2nd ed.) (pp. 177–202). Bethesda, MD: National Association of School Psychologists.

Tangney, J. P., Stuewig, J., & Mashek, D. J. (2007). Moral emotions and moral behavior. *Annual Review of Psychology, 58,* 345–372. doi: 10.1146/annurev.psych.56.091103.070145

Thomas, D. E., Bierman, K. L., & The Conduct Problems Prevention Research Group. (2006). The impact of classroom aggression on the development of aggressive behavior problems in children. *Development and Psychopathology, 18,* 471–487. doi: 10.1017/S0954579406060251

Tsai, S-F., & Cheney, D. (2012). The impact of the adult–child relationship on school adjustment for children at risk of serious behavior problems. *Journal of Emotional and Behavioral Disorders, 20,* 105–114. doi: 10.1177/1063426611418974

Turiel, E. (2006). The development of morality. In W. Damon (Series Ed.) & N. Eisenberg (Vol. Ed.), *Handbook of children psychology:* Vol. 3, *Social, emotional and personality development* (6th ed.) (pp. 789–857). New York: Wiley.

Tyler, T. (2006). Psychological perspectives on legitimacy and legitimation. *Annual Review of Psychology, 57,* 375–400. doi: 10.1146/annurev.psych.57.102904.190038

van Lier, P. A. C., Vuijk, P., & Crijnen, A. M. (2005). Understanding mechanisms of change in the development of antisocial behavior: The impact of a universal intervention. *Journal of Abnormal Child Psychology, 33,* 521–535. doi: 10.1007/s10802-005-6735-7

Vannest, K. J., Davis, J. L., Davis, C. R., Mason, B. A., & Burke, M. D. (2010). Effective intervention for behavior with a daily behavior report card: A meta-analysis. *School Psychology Review, 39*(4), 654–672.

Watson, M., & Battistich, V. (2006). Building and sustaining caring communities. In C. M. Evertson & C. S. Weinstein (Eds.), *Handbook of classroom management: Research, practice, and contemporary issues* (pp. 253–279). Mahwah, NJ: Erlbaum.

Wehby, J. H., & Lane, L. (2009). Proactive instructional strategies for classroom management. In A. Akin-Little, S. G. Little, M. A. Bray, & T. J. Kehle (Eds.), *Behavioral intervention in schools: Evidence-based positive strategies* (pp. 141–156). Washington, DC: American Psychological Association.

Weiner, B. (2006). *Social motivation, justice, and the moral emotions: An attributional approach.* Mahwah, NJ: Erlbaum.

Weinstein, C. S., & Novodvorsky, I. (2010). *Middle and secondary classroom management and practice* (4th ed.). New York: McGraw Hill.

Weinstein, C. S., Romano, M. E., & Mignano, J. R. (2010). *Elementary classroom management: Lessons from research and practice* (5th ed.). New York: McGraw Hill.

Wentzel, K. R. (1996). Social and academic motivation in middle school: Concurrent and long-term relations to academic effort. *Journal of Early Adolescence, 16,* 390–406. doi: 10.1177/0272431696016004002

Wentzel, K. R. (2002). Are effective teachers like good parents? Teaching styles and student adjustment in early adolescence. *Child development, 73,* 287–301. doi: 10.1111/1467-8624.00406

Wentzel, K. R. (2006). A social motivation perspective for classroom management. In C. M. Evertson & C. S. Weinstein (Eds.), *Handbook of classroom management: Research, practice, and contemporary issues* (pp. 619–643). Mahwah, NJ: Erlbaum.

Wilson, D. B., Gottfredson, D. C., & Najaka, S. S. (2001). School-based prevention of problem behaviors: A meta-analysis. *Journal of Quantitative Criminology, 17,* 247–272. doi: 10.1037/0022-006X.71.1.136

Wilson, S. J., & Lipsey, M. W. (2007). School-based interventions for aggressive and disruptive behavior: Update of a meta-analysis. *American Journal of Preventive Medicine, 33* (Suppl. 2S), 130–143. doi: 10.1016/j.amepre.2007.04.011

3

SCHOOL-WIDE POSITIVE BEHAVIOR SUPPORT

Building Systems to Prevent Problem Behavior and Develop and Maintain Appropriate Social Behavior

TIMOTHY J. LEWIS[1] AND BARBARA S. MITCHELL
UNIVERSITY OF MISSOURI

ROBERT TRUSSELL
UNIVERSITY OF TEXAS–EL PASO

LORI NEWCOMER
UNIVERSITY OF MISSOURI

INTRODUCTION

School discipline continues to be reported as one of the top concerns of educators and the American public (Elam, Rose, & Gallup, 1996; Rose & Gallup, 2006; U.S. Department of Education, 1998). For example, Myers and Holland (2000) indicated that general education teachers reported on average that one in five of their students exhibited disruptive/off-task behavior and one in 20 exhibited aggressive behaviors to the point that intervention was necessary. Data suggest that students in middle and high schools are even more at risk for encountering serious violence (Heaviside, Rowand, Williams, & Farris, 1998), with an estimated 16% of all high school students in this country involved in one or more physical fights on school property in the course of a year (Lockwood, 1997). Although the majority of students will not experience exceedingly violent or aggressive behavior, the frequency and intensity of these behaviors still disrupt and can overwhelm the process of schooling for all students (Walker, Ramsey, & Gresham, 2004). Teachers and administrators indicate that addressing school discipline issues is one of the single greatest demands on their time, citing that problem behaviors interfere with the their ability to educate and are the most common reason for the removal of students from classroom and school settings (Miller-Richter, Lewis, & Hagar, 2012).

Further compounding the challenge that schools face is the relationship between low-level nonviolent behavioral offenses (noncompliance, disrespect, insubordination) and later emergence of more serious or violent offenses (Heaviside, Rowand, Williams, & Farris, 1998; Powell, Fixsen, Dunlap, Smith, & Fox, 2007). In one study, 52% of the teachers and administrators who were surveyed reported an increase in violence at the middle and high school levels; however, they perceived that minor offenses such as verbal intimidation, threats, shoving, and harassment were escalating at a far greater rate than more serious violations (Peterson, Beekley, Speaker, & Pietrzak, 1996). Suspensions and expulsions have increased due in large part to such minor infractions as noncompliance, tardiness, and truancy (Brooks, Schiraldi, & Ziedenberg, 1999; Ingersoll, & LeBoeuf, 1997; Skiba, Peterson & Williams, 1997). Mayer and Leone (1999) point out that school personnel spend more time and resources on punitive and reactive measures (e.g., security guards, metal detectors, video surveillance systems) aimed at inhibiting aggression and violence than on positive, preventive measures. These findings are significant in that they suggest that schools should spend equal energy on addressing the overall school climate and focusing efforts to reduce minor disruptions. The magnitude of concern regarding the discipline and the mental health needs of children and youth prompted the Surgeon General more than a decade ago to call for a national agenda that fosters social and emotional health in children as a national priority (U.S. Department of Health and Human Services, 2000). To more fully respond to the issue of creating improved school environments to curb disruptive, aggressive, and violent behavior in schools, informed policy and interventions are urgently needed.

Factors That Contribute to the Problem

The Institute on Violence and Destructive Behavior has identified several risk factors that lead to the development of problem behavior patterns among children (Walker, Ramsey, & Gresham, 2004). The list includes (1) poverty, neglect, and abuse, (2) harsh and inconsistent parenting, (3) drug and alcohol use by the caregiver, (4) modeling of aggressive behavior, (5) media violence, (6) a negative attitude in the home toward schooling, (7) family transitions such as death or divorce, and (8) parent criminality. Sadly, contextual factors found in schools also contribute to the development and occurrence of persistent problem behaviors. Mayer (1995, 2001) identified within-school factors that exacerbate antisocial behavior, including: (1) an overreliance on punitive methods of control, (2) unclear rules for student behavior, (3) lack of administrative support for staff and lack of staff agreement with policies, (4) misuse of behavior management procedures, (5) failure to respond to individual student differences, and (6) academic failure. The significance of school-related contextual factors is emphasized in a U.S Department of Education publication (2000a, p. 10) that states: "Studies indicate that approximately four of every five disruptive students can be traced to some dysfunction in the way schools are organized, staff members are trained, or schools are run."

At the school and district level, discipline codes and policies are likely to include "get tough" responses (e.g., containment, punishment, suspension, or zero tolerance) designed to send a strong message that certain types of problem behaviors are unacceptable and will result in stringent consequences. Although these responses may lead to temporary reductions in problem behavior, they have little effect on increasing school safety or on the long-term reduction of problem behavior (DeVoe et al., 2003; Skiba, 2002; Skiba, Reynolds, Graham, Sheras, Conoley, & Garcia-Vazquez, 2006). Exclusionary responses increase the probability of future grade retention, subsequent suspensions, expulsion, and dropping out, factors associated with increased academic risk and juvenile crime (Sulzer-Azaroff & Mayer, 1994). Nor do such policies meet the challenge of creating a positive school climate or prevent the development and occurrence of problem behavior (Mayer, 1995; Patterson, Reid, & Dishion, 1992).

A Promising Solution

Altering contextual factors (e.g., clear routines, high rates of positive vs. negative feedback, clear adult presence) has also been associated with the creation of more positive school environments that are conducive to learning and result in increases in student time on task, teacher use of praise, and improved perceptions of school safety (Mayer, Mitchell, Clementi, Clement-Robertson, Myatt, & Vullara, 1993; Metzler, Biglan, Rusby, & Sprague, 2001; Walker, Ramsey, & Gresham, 2004). Consistent with this body of research, the Center on Crime, Communities, and Culture (1997) summarized findings indicating that a quality education may be the most important protective factor available to counter the risk factors that lead to problem behavior. To this end, there is a growing expectation that schools deliver effective and efficient interventions to ensure safe, productive school environments where norm-violating behavior is minimized and prosocial behavior is promoted (U.S. Department of Education, 2000a). A promising solution is the use of proactive school-wide behavior management strategies to address the contextual factors within schools that lead to problem behavior (Horner & Sugai, 2005; Lewis, Jones, Horner, & Sugai, 2010; Sugai et al., 2000). School-Wide Positive Behavior Support (SW-PBS) is one way to effectively (1) reduce chronic challenging behavior, (2) promote cultures of social competence that foster prosocial behavior and academic achievement, and (3) meet the needs of children with significant behavioral challenges (Lewis & Sugai, 1999; Sugai et al., 2000).

What Is Positive Behavior Support?

"Positive behavior support" is a general term that refers to the culturally appropriate application of positive behavioral interventions and systems to achieve socially important behavior change (U.S. Department of Education, 2000b). School-wide PBS focuses on three key elements: (1) adoption of evidence-based practices, (2) data to identify current status and effectiveness of intervention, and (3) systems that enable staff to implement and sustain practices with accuracy.

SW-PBS establishes behavioral expectations and supports for all staff and students across multiple settings and applies a three-tiered approach to prevention (Horner & Sugai, 2005; Lewis, Jones, Horner, & Sugai, 2010; Lewis & Sugai, 1999; Walker et al., 1996). *Universal, or Tier I, supports* focus on preventing the development and occurrence of problem behaviors. *Small group/targeted, or Tier II,* focuses on providing efficient and rapid response to reduce the number of existing cases. *Intensive/individualized, or Tier III*, focuses on reducing the intensity and complexity of existing cases that are not responsive to universal, or Tier II, supports. A functional perspective in which factors that reinforce appropriate behaviors and maintain problem behaviors (i.e., positive and negative reinforcement) guides the development of effective, efficient, and relevant interventions and is applied across the full continuum of supports. Finally, SW-PBS promotes an instructional emphasis in which behavioral expectations are clearly defined and taught to all students. For students who are at risk of social failure, social skills are taught in the same way as academic skills, and behavioral deficits are addressed by teaching functional replacement behaviors (Sugai et al., 2010). The remainder of this chapter provides an overview of the essential features of school-wide systems of PBS and is organized around (1) the essential features of school-wide systems of PBS, (2) current research, and (3) implications for research and practice.

SCHOOL-WIDE POSITIVE BEHAVIOR SUPPORT

Problem behavior occurs on a continuum from occasional mild misbehavior to behavior that is severe, chronic, and disruptive to the learning environment. SW-PBS emphasizes a continuum of support in which the intensity of intervention increases to match the intensity and complexity of the presenting problem.

Universal Supports

Universal systems of support focus on prevention and the creation of a safe, predictable environment with a common set of expectations and consistent supports applied across three interrelated systems: school-wide, nonclassroom, and classroom.

School-Wide Systems

A leadership team is established to guide all processes of SW-PBS. The team is comprised of a building administrator, classroom teachers, specialists, and support staff representatives. The leadership team takes responsibility for assessment of current discipline procedures and staff perceptions of what is in place, as well as what is working and not working. The information is used by the team to develop and implement SW-PBS policy and procedures. Components of proactive systems of school-wide PBS include (1) a statement of purpose, (2) a clear definition of expected behaviors, (3) procedures for teaching expected behaviors, (4) procedures for discouraging problem behaviors, and (5) procedures for record keeping and decision making (Sugai et al., 2010).

A statement of purpose is used to capture the proactive objectives of the discipline plan. The statement reflects an approach that is agreed upon by the administration and staff, focuses on all members of the school community and emphasizes behavioral as well as instructional outcomes. A key component of SW-PBS is a clear understanding of expected student behavior. To guide the identification of universal expectations, the team focuses not on the problem behaviors but on prosocial "replacement behaviors." In other words, they emphasize the behaviors that they would like children to demonstrate. The expectations, or school rules, should be five or fewer and positively stated. For example, the staff at Elysium Elementary School wanted their students to be "safe," "respectful" "learners." With input from faculty and staff, the leadership team completed a matrix that operationally defined what each of those expectations would look like across all settings in their school. The examples of appropriate behavior were then used as a foundation for social skill instruction.

Behavior is a skill, just as reading and mathematical computations are skills. As such, behavioral skills are taught paralleling the same process as academic instruction; educators introduce and teach a concept (e.g., quadratic equations in algebra), provide practice opportunities (e.g., homework, in-class work), and give feedback on performance (e.g., grades). Only after the student demonstrates mastery does the instructor move on to new concepts. If a student does not master the skill, reteaching, additional support, and practice are provided. Behavioral skills are taught and learned in the same way.

The leadership team also develops procedures to acknowledge appropriate behaviors on a regular basis. This serves three purposes. First, principles of reinforcement teach us that the provision of positive consequences following a desired behavior results in an increase in the future probability of that behavior occurring. Second, procedures to acknowledge appropriate behavior serve to increase the ratio of positive interactions between teachers and students, creating a positive school environment. Third, acknowledgment and reinforcement encourage students to self-manage their own behavior. Schools use a range of reinforcement strategies, from token systems to positive social acknowledgment. The form of the reinforcer is less critical than the related frequency and consistency of acknowledgment of appropriate behavior by teachers and staff.

Even with the school-wide positive procedures in place, there is still a need to develop procedures to discourage problem behaviors. A continuum of consequence responses should be available to respond to problem behavior. Consistency can be increased by providing clear definitions of problem behaviors and by differentiating between the behaviors that should be managed by teachers and supervisory staff and the behaviors that warrant a referral for administrative involvement. A full range of response procedures allows for more effective interventions across the continuum of mild misbehavior to serious and chronic behavior challenges. Students who repeatedly fail to meet behavioral expectations require a different level of response than students who only occasionally misbehave. For these students, systems that focus on teaching and supporting appropriate replacement behaviors come into play.

The use of data to assess current conditions, to guide implementation, and to evaluate the effectiveness of procedures is a critical feature of SW-PBS. An efficient system of data collection and reporting is used to summarize data in a usable format (e.g., graphs that allow visual analysis) for the purpose of evaluation and informed decision making. The data should be flexible enough to provide a summary of key indicators of problem behavior such as (1) number of office referrals per day for any given month, (2) number of office referrals per behavior (e.g., disrespect, fighting, inappropriate language), (3) number of office referrals per location (e.g., cafeteria, classroom, playground), (4) number of office referrals by consequences (e.g., detention, suspension) and (5) cumulative number of office referrals per individual students. The leadership team analyzes the data regularly to discern patterns of problem behavior and to guide the decision-making process. Data decision rules are also established to determine when individual students may need more intensive supports.

Nonclassroom Systems

Nonclassroom settings include areas of the school that are characterized by large numbers of students, strong social interaction among students, minimal adult supervision, and low structure (e.g., cafeteria, hallway transitions, bathrooms, assemblies) and that present a different set of management challenges than the classroom does. The school-wide expectations are extended to address specific behaviors unique to these settings through direct instruction and opportunities to practice. In addition, the physical characteristics and routines of these settings are assessed to determine whether modifications are necessary to promote safety and effective supervision. Modifications may include physical adjustments, such as removing unsafe objects, eliminating objects or areas with obstructed views, altering traffic patterns or adjusting schedules to reduce the number of students in a particular setting. Setting routines are designed to address both student and adult behavior in order to promote efficiency in the execution of activities and to reduce the likelihood of problem behaviors occurring.

Two strategies, precorrection and active supervision, are important features of nonclassroom setting supports. *Precorrection* procedures are used to make adjustments before a student has a chance to behave inappropriately and are used when a teacher anticipates the occurrence of problem behavior. For example, a teacher may anticipate students having difficulty with an assignment. Based on the predictable errors, she will preteach difficult vocabulary words before students are asked to read a passage (Kame'enui & Simmons, 1990). The same strategy is applied to behavioral errors. The teacher provides a precorrect, based on predictable problem behavior, to remind students of the routines and expectations before they transition to a nonclassroom setting. Precorrects consist of identifying the context and the likely problem behavior, identifying the expected behavior, conducting behavioral rehearsals, and providing reinforcement for expected behaviors. Effective use of precorrects can prevent the need to respond reactively to inappropriate student behavior after the fact (Colvin, Sugai, & Patching, 1993).

A second strategy for nonclassroom settings is *active supervision.* Elements of active supervision include (1) movement around the setting in close proximity to students, (2) visual scanning, and (3) high rates of interaction with students comprised of prompts, feedback, praise, correction, and encouragement (Newcomer, Colvin, & Lewis, 2009). After students are instructed in the expectations, rules, and routines, active supervision can promote generalized responding to other settings in the school environment.

Classroom Systems

Paralleling universal school-wide systems, classroom systems also emphasize teaching clearly defined behavioral expectations to prevent the occurrence of problem behavior. Key components of universal classroom systems include (1) identification and instruction in rules and routines, (2) effective instructional strategies, and (3) a strong emphasis on positive teacher–student interactions.

Classroom rules and expectations should reflect the unique characteristics of an individual classroom but link back to and reflect the greater school-wide expectations. Linking the rules to the school-wide expectations extends the language into the classroom and supports the generalization of behavioral performance across settings. For example, if the school-wide expectations are "Be Respectful, Be Responsible, Be Cooperative," each classroom teacher should align his or her classroom rules with these three expectations. By linking back to the language of the school-wide expectations, the students learn the specific behaviors that are important in the classroom and become able to relate how those expectations fit into the school context as a whole.

Because instruction that is too difficult or to easy creates conditions that foster problem behavior (Cooper et al., 1992), teaching and management strategies that focus on instructional, curricular, and organizational adjustments are linked to improved behavior (Conroy, Sutherland, Snyder, & Marsh, 2006; Simonson, Fairbanks, Briesch, Myers, & Sugai, 2008; Simonson, Myers, & DeLuca, 2010). Students learn best when there are frequent opportunities to respond to and actively engage in the instruction and to be positively reinforced. Frequent opportunities to respond and high rates of correct response are associated with increased on-task behavior (Burns & Boice, 2009; Haydon et al., 2010) and a decrease in disruptive behavior (Christle & Schuster, 2003; Gunter & Reed, 1997). High rates of student response results in increased opportunity for a teacher to praise and correct student responses and allows assessment of student understanding. Effective, well designed instruction incorporates student supportive strategies to minimize errors, support skill acquisition, and encourage active participation by creating opportunities for successful learning.

The quality of teacher–student interactions is another component of SW-PBS in classrooms. Research has demonstrated that in most classrooms, the rate of reprimands exceeds the rate of positive feedback and praise (Sutherland, Lewis-Palmer, Stichter, & Morgan, 2008; Sutherland & Wehby, 2001; Sutherland, Wehby, & Copeland, 2000). Altering interaction patterns to increase teacher praise and positive attention in the classroom can result in an increase in appropriate behaviors and a decrease in disruptive behaviors. An effective classroom teacher strives for a ratio of four positive praise statements to every reprimand or correction.

Tier II Supports

Approximately 10–15% of students will require support beyond the universal level (Sugai et al., 2010). While these students exhibit problem behaviors at degrees and frequencies that place them at risk for establishing chronic problem behavioral patterns, developing individualized interventions is beyond the time and resources of most schools. As part of the three-tiered approach to prevention outlined earlier in this chapter, Tier II systems of prevention and intervention present an efficient and effective intermediate level of intervention to target students who are clearly linked to universal supports. Students who require this level of intervention typically have a profile of ongoing, low-level problem behaviors (e.g., talking out, minor disruptions, work completion), frequent (three to five) office referrals, and they exhibit problem behavior across multiple settings within the school (Sugai et al., 2010).

Tier II supports focus on a range of intervention procedures and are developed and driven by data indicators. Tier II interventions have included (1) self-management, (2) social skill instruction, (3) informal, brief functional assessments and behavior support plans, and (4) academic support (Mitchell, Stormont, & Gage, 2011). Key features of Tier II supports include continuous availability, rapid access to the intervention, and low effort by teachers for referral and implementation. In addition, they are implemented by all staff across multiple settings and are continuously monitored for effectiveness and decision making. Because Tier II strategies are implemented within the universal school-wide system, they are designed to support the existing classroom expectations and create a common focus and expected outcomes that are consistent throughout the setting (Mitchell, Stormont, & Gage, 2011).

As with universal supports, data-based decision making guides the Tier II process. Students are identified at the first signs of risk, based on data or teacher referral. A multiple gating approach efficiently identifies students who need additional academic and social supports (Lane et al., 2012). First, teachers identify students who may be at risk and make referrals based on their assessments. Second, review of archival data such as attendance, academic performance, and office referrals are used to identify patterns or problems that require support. Third, a team reviews the information to determine which Tier II is appropriate for the student. Daily performance data are used to monitor student progress.

Tier III Supports

With universal and Tier II systems firmly in place, schools should experience a decrease in the number of students who need intensive individual supports (Lewis, Jones, Horner, & Sugai, 2010). With the number of referrals for individual interventions reduced, the system can respond more efficiently and effectively to those students who do require a more intense level of support (Bradshaw, Koth, Thornton, & Leaf, 2009). However, even with effective implementation of SW-PBS at the universal and Tier II levels, approximately 5–10% of students in a school will require intense, individualized interventions (Sugai et al., 2010). These students typically display serious, chronic behavior patterns and higher rates of behavior infractions (e.g., six or more major behavioral infractions or displaying high rates of risk) and require specially designed individualized supports that are comprehensive, function based, and person centered. Efficient and effective systems of individual support are based on technical competence in functional behavioral assessment and intervention design from an applied behavior analysis perspective. Within the three-tiered approach to SW-PBS, the Tier III level provides systems to build the capacity for schools to understand and assess the function of behavior and to design, implement, evaluate, and modify effective behavior support plans for individuals with serious behavior problems.

A team-based approach is the foundation of a sustainable system of individual behavior support (Benazzi, Horner, & Good, 2006). Team members should possess the technical expertise to conduct functional behavioral assessments (FBA) and to design behavior support plans that are based on assessment outcomes. At least one member of the team should have expertise in applied behavior analysis, behavioral theory, FBA, and intervention. Other logical team members would include school psychologists, special and general educators, and a building administrator. The team must also have predictable and efficient procedures to "(a) manage teacher requests for assistance, (b) ensure that teachers and students receive support in a timely and meaningful manner, (c) provide a general forum for discussions and possible solutions for individual student behavioral concerns, and (d) organize a collaborative effort to support the teacher" (Todd, Horner, Sugai, & Colvin, 1997, p. 74). The organizational features of the team promote the efficient use of time, efficient documentation, a system of accountability for task, and implementation responsibilities and clearly defined systems for making data-based decisions (Benazzi, Horner, & Good, 2006).

Summary

SW-PBS builds a continuum of research-based strategies with a central focus on increasing appropriate behavior. School-wide systems provide the processes, structures, and routines to prevent problem behavior; they promote early intervention at the first signs of problem behavior; and they utilize comprehensive individual support plans. An instructional approach built on a central theme of teaching appropriate behavior, building multiple opportunities for practice, and altering environments to promote success is emphasized through a continuum of three levels of support: universal, targeted, and individual.

RESEARCH TO DATE ON THE EFFICACY OF SCHOOL-WIDE POSITIVE BEHAVIOR SUPPORT

An emerging body of research has shown that implementing a continuum of tiered supports—(1) universals, (2) targeted/small group/Tier II, and (3) individual/Tier III student support—will impact overall rates of problem behavior in school. In addition, preliminary research has demonstrated improvements in behavior, academic gains, and increases in instructional time following implementation of interventions as part of a fully integrated approach across a continuum of supports. Research to date on the efficacy of each of the three levels is provided in this section.

Universal Supports

Over the past decade, a growing body of research has demonstrated a multi-impact on student social and academic behavior. Quasi experimental studies have demonstrated impact on overall rates of problem behavior from preschool to high school, including alternative settings (Barrett, Bradshaw, & Lewis-Palmer, 2008; Bohanon et al., 2006; Chapman & Hofweber, 2000; Curtis, Van Horne, Robertson, & Karvonen, 2010; Duda, Dunlap, Fox, Lentini, & Clarke, 2004; Farkas, Simonson, Migdole, Donovan, Clemens, Cicchese, 2012; Lohrmann-O'Rourke, Knoster, Sabatine, Smith, Horvath, & Llewellyn, 2000; Nelson, Martella, & Galand, 1998; Putnam, Luiselli, & Sunderland, 2002; Simonson, Britton, & Young, 2010); the interactive impact on behavior and academics (Algozzine, Wang, & Violette, 2011; Luiselli, Putnam, Handler, & Feinberg, 2005; McIntosh, Chard, Boland, & Horner, 2006; McIntosh, Horner, Chard, Dickey, & Braun, 2008; McIntosh, Flannery, Sugai, Braun, & Cochrane, 2008; McIntosh, Sadler, & Brown, 2012); as well as impact on interventions targeted in the classroom and nonclassroom settings within the continuum of SW-PBS (De Pry & Sugai, 2002; Hirsch, Lewis-Palmer, Sugai, & Schnacker, 2004; Lewis, Colvin, & Sugai, 2000; Lewis, Powers, Kelk, & Newcomer, 2002; Putnam, Handler, Ramirez-Platt, & Luiselli, 2003; Stichter, Lewis, Richter, & Johnson, 2006). Recently, several randomized control trial studies have confirmed similar outcomes including proactive and sustained changes in disciplinary practices that have resulted in decreases in problem behavior and increases in appropriate behavior (Bradshaw, Mitchell, & Leaf, 2010; Bradshaw, Reinke, Brown, Bevans, & Leaf, 2008; Horner, Sugai, Smolkowski, Eber, Nakasato, Todd, & Esperanza, 2009), as well as the impact on overall school climate (Bradshaw, Koth, Bevans, Ialongo, & Leaf, 2008; Bradshaw, Koth, Thorton, & Leaf, 2009) and the reduction of specific behavioral challenges including bullying behavior (Bradshaw, Waasdorp, & Leaf, in press; Waasdorp, Bradshaw, & Leaf, 2012).

Tier II Supports

For an estimated 10–15% of students who require more intensive supports in addition to the universal school-wide PBS system, several different "manualized" interventions are commonly implemented. Example Tier II interventions include check-in/check-out, social skills groups, and Check & Connect (Horner, Sugai, & Anderson, 2010). Each of these interventions has a body of evidence indicating positive effects on socially important behavior change such as reductions in problem behavior, improved social skills, increases in attendance, reduced incidence of dropout, or higher rates of student engagement. A brief description of current research for each intervention follows.

Check-in/Check-out

Check-in/check-out (CICO) is a proactive, positive, research-supported self-management intervention that combines a number of individually effective components to be used with students identified at risk for behavioral concerns (Crone, Hawken, & Horner, 2010). Numerous investigations show that the use of the CICO intervention is associated with reductions in problem behavior and/or increases in prosocial behavior (Filter et al., 2007; Hawken, 2006; Hawken & Horner, 2003; Hawken, MacLeod, & Rawlings, 2007; McCurdy, Kunsch, & Reibstein, 2007; Mong, Johnson, & Mong, 2011; Simonsen, Myers, & Briere, 2011; Todd, Campbell, Meyer, & Horner, 2008). In addition, several studies also demonstrate that CICO can be delivered with fidelity in school settings using typical personnel (Campbell & Anderson, 2011; Campbell & Anderson, 2008; Ennis, Jolivette, Swoszowski, & Johnson, 2012; Fairbanks, Sugai, Guardino, & Lathrop, 2007; Filter et al., 2007; Hawken, MacLeod, & Rawlings, 2007; Hawken, MacLeod, & O'Neill, 2011; McIntosh, Campbell, Carter, & Dickey, 2009; Mong, Johnson, & Mong, 2011; Simonsen, Myers, & Briere, 2011; Todd, Campbell, Meyer, & Horner, 2008). Finally, student, family, and teacher participants give positive ratings for the CICO intervention when surveyed about impact on problem behavior, improvement in academic outcomes, being worth the time and effort to implement, and recommending it as a treatment for other children with similar challenges (Filter et al., 2007; Hawken & Horner, 2003; Hawken, MacLeod, & Rawlings, 2007; Hawken, MacLeod, & O'Neill, 2011; Lane et al., 2012; Mong, Johnson, & Mong, 2011; Simonsen, Myers, & Briere, 2011; Todd, Campbell, Meyer, & Horner, 2008).

Social Skills Instructional Groups

Two relatively recent studies provide examples of social skills instruction as a Tier II intervention. First, Gresham, Bao Van, and Cook (2006) provided 60 hours of social skills instruction for a group of elementary-level students using a commercially published curriculum. In addition to small-group instruction led by a trained facilitator, classroom teachers implemented differential reinforcement of other behaviors as a strategy for promoting the generalization of skills across settings. Direct observation data indicated reductions in problem behavior for each of the participants. In addition, teacher ratings of problem behavior and social skill use also improved (Gresham, Bao Van, & Cook, 2006).

In a second example, students participated in a social skills group designed to increase effective communication and appropriate play. Social skills lessons were supported by the use of a self-management strategy, peer- and adult-mediated attention, and positive reinforcement for meeting behavioral goals (Marchant et al., 2007). In addition, a unique aspect of the study was the purposeful selection of students identified with internalizing characteristics. Results showed improvements for all participants.

Check & Connect

Check & Connect is an engagement model that incorporates the use of a mentor who conducts regularly scheduled checks of alterable risk indicators (e.g., attendance, work completion, grades, disciplinary events, credit accrual, etc.) with a structured process for connecting with students and families (Christenson, Stout, & Pohl, 2012). Mentors provide specific feedback about student data, teach problem-solving skills, and maintain ongoing positive relationships among students, families, and school personnel. Early investigations conducted with high school–level participants identified with learning disabilities and/or emotional/behavioral disorders showed that students who received the Check & Connect treatment were more likely to stay enrolled in school, to persist through ninth grade, and to complete their course assignments than were students in a control group who did not participate in the program (Sinclair, Christenson, Evelo, & Hurley, 1998). In addition, students in Check & Connect earned more credits during their first year of high school, were more likely to be on track for graduation, and received better teacher ratings for behavior and academic competence than did control students (Sinclair, Christenson, Evelo, & Hurley, 1998). Subsequent studies of Check & Connect have expanded by including students without disabilities and have examined effects across grade levels spanning kindergarten through twelfth grade (Anderson, Christenson, Sinclair, & Lehr, 2004; Kaibel, Sinclair, & Vanden Berk, 2008; Lehr, Sinclair, & Christenson, 2004; Sinclair & Kaibel, 2002).

Although each of these interventions, as well as others described in previous sections of the chapter, indicate positive outcomes when implemented in isolation, the added value of providing small-group/targeted interventions within the framework of a school-wide PBS system is less known, but evidence is beginning to emerge. In one recent study, Nelson and colleagues (2009) used a quasi experimental longitudinal cohort design to examine the extent to which use of a three-tier model of behavioral interventions was associated with prevention of problem behavior and sustained behavioral improvements over time. Teacher ratings of problem behavior and social skills were assessed pre- and postintervention (i.e., fall and spring during the year of treatment) and then again at one- and two-year follow-up points (i.e., spring of the next two consecutive years). Students in the Tier II group showed immediate decreases in problem behavior, along with improved social skills when the Tier II intervention was provided in the context of a universal prevention framework (Nelson et al., 2009).

Tier III Supports

The application of universal and targeted interventions will greatly reduce but not eliminate the number of students who require intense individualized support. What is emerging from the field is that SW-PBS may increase the capacity of schools to deliver more systematic and intensive targeted small-group and individual interventions (Crone, Hawken, & Bergstrom, 2007; Crone & Horner, 2003; Crone, Horner, & Hawken, 2004). Preliminary data from pilot studies are showing that functional-based interventions are outperforming traditional behavioral interventions (Ingram, 2002; Ingram, Lewis-Palmer, & Sugai, 2005; Newcomer & Lewis, 2004) and that plans are of higher quality if linked to school-wide PBS systems (McIntosh et al., 2008; Newcomer & Lewis, 2004). More research is needed to show what additional benefit school-wide systems of PBS value-add to small-group and individual student support plans (Farmer, Lane, Lee, Hamm, & Lamber, 2012; Bradshaw, Koth, Thornton, & Leaf, 2009).

Limitations of the Research Base

The study of SW-PBS represents a move from studies that evaluate the behavioral mechanism of single and small groups of students to large-scale randomized control trials. To an extent, many of the application studies have been conducted within the framework of scientific methodology, testing observable events with objective, reliable, and quantifiable data and using replicable procedures. However, the processes of SW-PBS represent a multicomponent package that is quite complex and bridges the gap between basic and applied science. Although data to date have shown encouraging results at the universal level, the value-add of the system approach in addressing small-group/targeted and individual supports is best described as emerging (Bradshaw, Koth, Thornton, & Leaf, 2009). The challenge remains to identify under what conditions the model yields significant outcomes and the active components that contribute to those outcomes. The following section briefly describes some of the issues associated with measuring large-scale system efforts to date.

Measures

The science that underlies PBS, applied behavior analysis, provides a methodology for understanding and predicting target behaviors in a given context. As investigation and application move from controlled situations such as laboratories and clinics to the less structured school environment, greater flexibility is needed in using correlation analysis, data sources, and case studies (Carr et al., 2002). Because SW-PBS interventions are always multicomponent in nature, validity concerns arise due to the multiple interacting variables that come into play. Such interaction makes it difficult to measure the impact of individual variables. Analysis must take into consideration multiple-component interventions. Such analysis, however, does not meet the standards of the single-variable experimentation necessary to ascribe causality. Applied research practices must be flexible enough to study the pragmatic effectiveness of multicomponent interventions as well as the causal mechanisms of intervention package components to explain why a model worked and to specify the active components of the model.

Connections to Individual Supports

In 1968, Baer, Wolf, and Risley established the importance of functional analysis to identify the environmental variables associated with the occurrence of target behaviors. In so doing, they laid the foundation for the application of applied behavior analysis to the study of human behavior and the functional relations between academic and social changes in adult and child behaviors. In the ensuing years, compelling evidence has accumulated to document the effectiveness of functional behavioral assessment and of positive behavior interventions and supports as having direct relevance for addressing disruptive and chronic problem behavior in schools (Blair, Umbreit & Bos, 1999; Grow, Carr, & LeBlanc, 2009; Ingram, Lewis-Palmer, & Sugai, 2005; Lewis & Sugai, 1996a, 1996b). Although the technology exists to respond to the challenges of problem behavior, it has not "fit" the unique problem context schools present (Lewis & Sugai, 1999; Sugai & Horner, 1999; Sugai et al., 2010). Research has yet to identify a well-defined procedure that delivers precise, usable, valid information with the limited time and resources available to school professionals (Farmer, Lane, Lee, Hamm, & Lamber, 2012). Zins and Ponti (1990) suggest that establishing a "host environment" that can support and maintain evidence-based practices is essential to achieve specialized and individualized behavior supports for students with chronic problem behaviors and at-risk backgrounds. The systems perspective of SW-PBS provides the requisite structure to support the adoption and sustained use of effective practices (Sugai, Horner, & Sprague, 1999); however, to date, the systemic examination of function-based individualized interventions within the context of a complete SW-PBS continuum has not been undertaken (Farmer, Lane, Lee, Hamm, & Lamber, 2012).

As demonstrated in the research previously reviewed, a school-wide systems approach to PBS effectively reduces chronic challenging behavior, promotes cultures of social competence, and meets the needs of children with significant behavioral challenges, creating a host environment that emphasizes the development of a positive school climate, practical policies, well-defined physical spaces, and monitoring systems to improve academic and social outcomes for all students, but especially those who are considered at risk for behavior problems. With school-wide systems of PBS in place, schools increase their capacity to support students who present challenges by shifting away from traditional responses of solving behavior problems through suspension and exclusion to an approach that emphasizes the development of specially designed and individualized interventions based on functional behavioral assessments to generate an understanding of how the social and instructional context influence an individual student's behavior. In doing so, these schools have redefined the roles and responsibilities of educators and all school personnel for promoting positive behavioral interventions, strategies, and support for students with chronically challenging behavior. Individual systems of PBS focus on integrated, team-based planning and problem solving to design individual support plans to prevent, reduce, and replace problem behaviors and to develop, maintain, and strengthen socially desirable behaviors. From research and application, we have learned the importance of a school-wide foundation of integrated systems, collaboration, and the development of proactive, practical interventions. When school personnel routinely reinforce positive behaviors and dedicate themselves to teaching social skills, then they increase the likelihood that individual support plans will be implemented with a high degree of integrity.

CONCLUSION

School-wide PBS is defined as consisting of systemic and individualized strategies implemented through a continuum of supports based on data-based decision making. The literature on behavioral problems is clear in that early intervention and prevention are our best hopes at making schools safe and productive learning environments (Ziglar, Taussig, & Black, 1992). Unfortunately, many educators have been slow to implement best practice until problems become chronic and entrenched (Kauffman, 1999), even though recent research has shown a clear link between "minor" discipline problems and later significant problems (Skiba & Peterson, 2000). Given that the school-wide PBS in essence is a process rather than a curriculum or packaged program, we are not suggesting that it is "the answer." Yet work to date has demonstrated that schools can implement best practices at the prevention and early intervention levels. Essential components that characterize each level of the continuum include empirically validated practices such as clearly defined student expectations, strategies to teach expectations, and providing feedback during practice opportunities. The intensity of application of these basic components are then matched to the intensity of problem behavior, and connections are made to other resources necessary to support students and their families. The selection, application, and evaluation of practices are simultaneously supported through data-based decision making, using a team process that supports faculty and staff.

NOTE

1. The preparation of this manuscript was supported in part by the Technical Assistance Center on Positive Behavioral Interventions and Supports and by a grant from the Office of Special Education Programs, U.S. Department of Education (H326S980003). Opinions expressed herein do not necessarily reflect the position of the U.S. Department of Education, and such endorsements should not be inferred. For information about the Center, go to www.pbis.org, or for information related to this manuscript, contact Tim Lewis at lewistj@missouri.edu.

REFERENCES

Algozzine, B., Wang, C., & Violette, A. S. (2011). Reexamining the relationship between academic achievement and social behavior. *Journal of Positive Behavioral Interventions, 13*, 3–16.

Anderson, A. R., Christenson, S. L., Sinclair, M. F., & Lehr, C. A. (2004). Check & Connect: The importance of relationships for promoting engagement with school. *Journal of School Psychology, 42*(2), 95–113.

Baer, D. M., Wolf, M. M., & Risley, T. R. (1968). Some current dimension of applied behavior analysis. *Journal of Applied Behavior Analysis, 1*(1), 91–99.

Barrett, S., Bradshaw, C., & Lewis-Palmer, T. (2008). Maryland state-wide PBIS initiative. *Journal of Positive Behavior Interventions, 10*, 105–114.

Benazzi, L., Horner, R. H., & Good, R. H. (2006). Effects of behavior support team composition on the technical adequacy and contextual fit of behavior support plans. *Journal of Special Education, 40*(3), 160–170.

Blair, K., Umbreit, J., & Bos, C. (1999). Using functional assessment and children's preferences to improve the behavior of young children with behavioral disorders. *Behavioral Disorders, 24*(2), 151–166.

Bohanon, H., Fenning, P., Carney, K. L., Minnis-Kim, M. J., Anderson-Harriss, S., Moroz, K. B., Hicks, K. J., Kasper, B. B., Culos, C., Sailor, W., & Pigott, T. D. (2006). Schoolwide application of positive behavior support in an urban high school: A case study. *Journal of Positive Behavior Interventions, 8*, 131–145.

Bradshaw, C. P., Koth, C. W., Bevans, K. B., Ialongo, N., & Leaf, P. J. (2008). The impact of school-wide Positive Behavioral Interventions and Supports (PBIS) on the organizational health of elementary schools. *School Psychology Quarterly, 23*(4), 462–473.

Bradshaw, C. P., Koth, C. W., Thornton, L. A., & Leaf, P. J. (2009). Altering school climate through school-wide Positive Behavioral Interventions and Supports: Findings from a group-randomized effectiveness trial. *Prevention Science, 10*(2), 100–115.

Bradshaw, C. P., Mitchell, M. M., & Leaf, P. J. (2010). Examining the effects of School-Wide Positive Behavioral Interventions and Supports on student outcomes: Results from a randomized controlled effectiveness trial in elementary schools. *Journal of Positive Behavior Interventions, 12*, 133–148.

Bradshaw, C. P., Reinke, W. M., Brown, L. D., Bevans, K. B., & Leaf, P. J. (2008). Implementation of school-wide Positive Behavioral Interventions and Supports (PBIS) in elementary schools: Observations from a randomized trial. *Education & Treatment of Children, 31*, 1–26.

Bradshaw, C. P., Waasdorp, T. E., & Leaf, P. J. (2012). Effects of school-wide positive behavioral interventions and supports on child behavior problems. *Pediatrics.* Online October 15, 2012.

Brooks, K., V. Schiraldi, V., & Ziedenberg, J. (1999). *School house hype: Two years later.* San Franciso: Center on Juvenile and Criminal Justice.

Burns, M. K., & Boice, C. H. (2009). Comparison of the relationship between words retained and intelligence for three instructional strategies among students with below-average IQ. *School Psychology Review, 38*(2), 284–292.

Campbell, A., & Anderson, C. (2008). Enhancing effects of targeted interventions with function-based support. *Behavioral Disorders, 33*(4), 233–245.

Campbell, A., & Anderson, C. M. (2011). Check-in/check-out: A systematic evaluation and component analysis. *Journal of Applied Behavior Analysis, 44*, 315–326.

Carr, E. G., Dunlap, G., Horner, R. H., Koegel, R. L., Turnbull, A. P., Sailor, W., Anderson, J. L., Ablbin, R. W., Koegel, L. K., & Fox, L. (2002). Positive behavior support: Evolution of an applied science. *Journal of Positive Behavior Intervention, 4*, 4–16.

Center on Crime, Communities, and Culture (1997). *Education as crime prevention.* Occasional Paper Series No. 2: New York: Author.

Chapman, D., & Hofweber, C. (2000). Effective behavior support in British Columbia. *Journal of Positive Behavior Interventions, 2* (4), 235–237.

Christenson, S. L., Stout, K., & Pohl, A. (2012). *Check & Connect: A comprehensive student engagement intervention: Implementing with fidelity.* Minneapolis: University of Minnesota, Institute on Community Integration.

Christle, C. A., & Schuster, J. W. (2003). The effects of using response cards on student participation, academic achievement, and on-task behavior during whole-class, math instruction. *Journal of Behavioral Education, 12*(3), 147–165.

Colvin, G., Sugai, G., & Patching, W. (1993). Pre-correction: An instructional approach for managing problem behavior. *Intervention in School and Clinic, 28*, 143–150.

Conroy, M. A., Sutherland, K. S., Snyder, A. L., & Marsh, S. (2006). Classwide intervention: Effective instruction makes a difference. *Teaching Exceptional Children, 40*(6), 24–30.

Cooper, L. J., Wacker, D. P., Thursby, D., Plagmann, L. A., Harding, J., Millard, T., & Derby, M. (1992). Analysis of the effects of task preferences, task demands, and adult attention on child behavior in outpatient and classroom settings. *Journal of Applied Behavior Analysis, 25*(4), 823–840.

Crone, D., Hawken, L., & Bergstrom, M., (2007). A demonstration of training, implementing and using functional behavioral assessment in 10 elementary and middle school settings. *Journal of Positive Behavior Interventions, 9*(1), 15–29.

Crone, D., Hawken, L. S., & Horner, R. H. (2010). *Responding to problem behavior in schools?: The behavior education program* (2nd ed.). New York: Guilford.

Crone, D. A. & Horner, R. H. (2003). *Building positive behavior support systems in schools: Functional behavioral assessment.* New York: Guilford Press.

Crone, D. A., Horner, R. H., & Hawken, L. S. (2004). *Responding to problem behavior in schools: The behavior education program.* New York: Guilford.

Curtis, R., Van Horne, J., Robertson, P., & Karvonen, M. (2010). Outcomes of a school-wide positive behavior support program. *Professional School Counseling, 13*(3), 159–164.

De Pry, R. L., & Sugai, G. (2002). The effect of active supervision and precorrection on minor behavioral incidents in a sixth grade general education classroom. *Journal of Behavioral Education, 11*, 255–267.

DeVoe, J., Peter, K., Ruddy, S., Miller, A., Planty, M., Snyder, T., & Rand, M. (2003). *Indicators of school crime and safety (NCES 2004004).* Washington, DC: U.S. Department of Education, National Center for Education Statistics.

Duda, M. A., Dunlap, G., Fox, L., Lentini, R., & Clarke, S. (2004). An experimental evaluation of positive behavior support in a community preschool program. *Topics in Early Childhood Special Education, 24*(3), 143–155.

Elam, S. J., Rose, L. C., & Gallup, A. M. (1996). 28th annual Phi Delta Kappa/Gallup poll of the public's attitudes toward the public schools. *Kappan, 78*(1), 41–59.

Ennis, R. P., Jolivette, K., Swoszowski, N. C., & Johnson, M. L. (2012). Secondary prevention efforts at a residential facility for students with emotional and behavioral disorders: Function-based check-in, check-out. Residential Treatment for Children and Youth, 29(2), 79–102.

Fairbanks, S., Sugai, G., Guardino, D., & Lathrop, M. (2007). Response to intervention: Examining classroom behavior support in second grade. *Exceptional Children*, 73(3), 288–310.

Farkas, M., Simonson, B., Migdole, S., Donovan, M., Clemens, K., & Cicchese, V. (2012). Schoolwide positive behavior support in an alternative school setting: An evaluation of fidelity, outcomes and social validity of Tier I implementation. *Journal of Emotional and Behavioral Disorders*, 2 (4), 275–288.

Farmer, T. W., Lane, K. L., Lee, D. L., Hamm, J. V., & Lamber, K. (2012). The social functions of antisocial behavior: Considerations for school violence prevention strategies for students with disabilities. *Behavioral Disorders*, 37, 149–162.

Filter, K. J., McKenna, M. K., Benedict, E. A., Horner, R. H., Todd, A. W., & Watson, J. (2007). Check in/check out: A post-hoc evaluation of an efficient, secondary-level targeted intervention for reducing problem behaviors in schools. *Education and Treatment of Children*, 30(1), 69–84.

Gresham, F., Bao Van, M., & Cook, C. R. (2006). Social skills training for teaching replacement behaviors: Remediating acquisition deficits in at-risk students. *Behavioral Disorders*, 31(4), 363–377.

Grow, L. L., Carr, J., & LeBlanc, L. (2009). Treatments for attention-maintained problem behavior: Empirical support and clinical recommendations. *Journal of Evidence-Based Practices for Schools*, 10, 70–92.

Gunter, P. & Reed, T. M. (1997). Academic instruction of children with emotional and behavioral disorders using scripted lessons. *Preventing School Failure*, 42, 33–37.

Hawken, L. S. (2006). School psychologists as leaders in the implementation of a targeted intervention: The behavior education program. *School Psychology Quarterly*, 21, 1, 91–111.

Hawken, L. S., & Horner, R. H. (2003). Evaluation of a targeted intervention within a schoolwide system of behavior support. *Journal of Behavioral Education*, 12(3), 225–240.

Hawken, L., & MacLeod, S., & O'Neill, R. (2011). Effects of function of problem behavior on the responsiveness to the Behavior Education Program. *Education and Treatment of Children*, 34, 551–574.

Hawken, L. S., MacLeod, K. S., & Rawlings, L. (2007). Effects of the behavior education program (BEP) on office discipline referrals of elementary school students. *Journal of Positive Behavior Interventions*, 9(2), 94–101.

Haydon, T., Conroy, M. A., Scott, T. M., Sindelar, P. T., Barber, B. R., & Orlando, A. (2010). A comparison of three types of opportunities to respond on student academic and social behaviors. *Journal of Emotional and Behavioral Disorders*, 18, 1, 27–40.

Heaviside, S., Rowand, C., Williams, C., & Farris, E. (1998). *Violence and discipline problems in U.S. Public Schools: 1996–97 (NCES 98–030)*. Washington, DC: U.S. Department of Education, National Center for Education Statistics.

Hirsch, E. J., Lewis-Palmer, T., Sugai, G., & Schnacker, L. (2004). Using school bus discipline referral data in decision making: Two case studies. *Preventing School Failure*, 48, 4, 4–9.

Horner, R. H., & Sugai, G., (2005). School-wide positive behavior support: An alternative approach to discipline in schools. (pp. 359–390). In L. Bambara & L. Kern (Eds.), Positive Behavior Support. New York: Guilford Press.

Horner, R. H., Sugai, G., & Anderson, C. A. (2010). Examining the evidence base for school-wide positive behavior support. *Focus on Exceptional Children*, 42(8), 1–16.

Horner, R., Sugai, G., Smolkowski, K., Eber, L., Nakasato, J., Todd, A., & Esperanza, J. (2009). A randomized, wait-list controlled effectiveness trial assessing school-wide positive behavior support in elementary schools. *Journal of Positive Behavior Interventions*, 11, 133–145.

Ingersoll, S., & LeBoeuf, K. (1997, February). Reaching out to youth out of the education mainstream. *Juvenile Justice Bulletin*, U.S. Department of Justice, Office of Juvenile Justice and Delinquency Prevention, 1–11.

Ingram, K. (2002). Comparing effectiveness of intervention strategies that are based on functional behavioral assessment information and those that are contra-indicated by the assessment. Unpublished doctoral dissertation, Eugene, University of Oregon.

Ingram, K., Lewis-Palmer, T., & Sugai, G. (2005). Function-based intervention planning: Comparing the effectiveness of FBA indicated and contra-indicated intervention plans. *Journal of Positive Behavior Interventions*, 7, 224–236.

Kaibel, C., Sinclair, M. F., & VandenBerk, E. (2008). *Check & Connect/AchieveMpls Bush Foundation interim report*. Minneapolis, MN: Minneapolis Public Schools.

Kame'enui, E. J., & Simmons, D. C. (1990). *Designing instructional strategies: The prevention of academic learning problems*. Columbus, OH: Merrill.

Kauffman, J. M. (1999). How we prevent the prevention of emotional and behavioral disorders. *Exceptional Children*, 65, 448–468.

Lane, K. L., Menzies, H. M., Oakes, W. P., Lambert, W., Cox, M., & Hankins, K. (2012). A validation of the student risk screening scale for internalizing and externalizing behaviors: Patterns in rural and urban elementary schools. *Behavioral Disorders, 37*, 244–270.

Lehr, C. A., Sinclair, M. F., & Christenson, S. L. (2004). Addressing student engagement and truancy prevention during the elementary years: A replication study of the Check & Connect model. *Journal of Education for Students Placed At Risk, 9*(3), 279–301.

Lewis, T. J., Colvin, G., & Sugai, G. (2000). The effects of precorrection and active supervision on the recess behavior of elementary school students. *Education and Treatment of Children, 23*, 109–121.

Lewis, T. J., Jones, S. E. L., Horner, R. H., & Sugai, G. (2010). School-wide positive behavior support and students with emotional/behavioral disorders: Implications for prevention, identification and intervention. *Exceptionality 18*(2), 82–93.

Lewis, T. J., & Sugai, G. (1996a). Functional assessment of problem behavior: A pilot investigation of the comparative and interactive effects of teacher and peer social attention on students in general education settings. *School Psychology Quarterly, 11*(1), 1–19.

Lewis, T. J., & Sugai, G. (1996b). Descriptive and experimental analysis of teacher and peer attention and the use of assessment-based Intervention to improve pro-social behavior. *Journal of Behavioral Education, 6*(1), 7–24.

Lewis, T. J., & Sugai, G. (1999). Effective behavior support: A systems approach to proactive schoolwide management. *Focus on Exceptional Children, 31*(6), 1–24.

Lewis, T. J., Powers, L. J., Kelk, M. J., & Newcomer, L. (2002). Reducing problem behaviors on the playground: An investigation of the application of school-wide positive behavior supports. *Psychology in the Schools, 39*, 181–190.

Lockwood, D. (1997). *Violence among middle school and high school students: Analysis and implications for prevention.* Washington, DC: National Institute of Justice, U.S. Department of Justice.

Lohrmann-O'Rourke, S., Knoster, T., Sabatine, K., Smith, D., Horvath, G., & Llewellyn, G. (2000). School-wide application of PBS in the Bangor Area School District. *Journal of Positive Behavior Interventions, 2*(4), 238–240.

Luiselli, J. K., Putnam, R. F., Handler, M. W., & Feinberg, A. B. (2005). Whole-school positive behaviour support: Effects on student discipline problems and academic performance. *Educational Psychology, 25*(2–3), 183–198.

Marchant, M. R., Solano, B. R., Fisher, A. K., Caldarella, P., Young, K. R., & Renshaw, T. L. (2007). Modifying socially withdrawn behavior: A playground intervention for students with internalizing behaviors. *Psychology in the Schools, 44*(8), 779–794.

Mayer, G. R. (1995). Preventing antisocial behavior in the schools. *Journal of Applied Behavior Analysis, 28*(4), 467–478.

Mayer, G. R. (2001). Antisocial behavior: It causes and prevention within our schools. *Education & Treatment of Children, 24*, 414–429.

Mayer, G. R., & Leone, P. (1999). A structural analysis of school violence and disruption: Implications for creating safer schools. *Education & Treatment of Children, 22*(3), 333–356.

Mayer, G. R., Mitchell, L., Clementi, T., Clement-Robertson, E., Myatt, R., & Vullara, D. T., (1993). A dropout prevention program for at-risk high school students: Emphasizing consulting to promote positive classroom environments. *Education and Treatment of Children, 16*, 135–146.

McCurdy, B. L., Kunsch, C., & Reibstein, S. (2007). Secondary prevention in the urban schools: Implementing the behavior education program. *Preventing School Failure, 51*(3), 2–19.

McIntosh, K., Campbell, A. L., Carter, D. R., & Dickey, C. R. (2009). Differential effects of a tier two behavior intervention based on function of problem behavior. *Journal of Positive Behavior Interventions, 11*(2), 82–93.

McIntosh, K., Chard, D. J., Boland, J. B., & Horner, R. H. (2006). Demonstration of combined efforts in school-wide academic and behavioral systems and incidence of reading and behavior challenges in early elementary grades. *Journal of Positive Behavioral Interventions, 8*, 146–154.

McIntosh, K., Flannery, K. B., Sugai, G., Braun, D., & Cochrane, K. L. (2008). Relationships between academics and problem behavior in the transition from middle school to high school. *Journal of Positive Behavior Interventions, 10*(4), 243–255.

McIntosh, K., Horner, R. H., Chard, D. J., Dickey, C. R., and Braun, D. H. (2008). Reading skills and function of problem behavior in typical school settings. *Journal of Special Education, 42*, 131–147.

McIntosh, K., Sadler, C., & Brown, J. A. (2012). Kindergarten reading skill level and change as risk factors for chronic problem behavior. *Journal of Positive Behavior Interventions, 14*(1) 17–28.

Metzler, C. W., Biglan, A., Rusby, J. C., & Sprague, J. (2001). Evaluation of a comprehensive behavior management program to improve school-wide positive behavior support. *Education & Treatment of Children, 24*, 448–479.

Mitchell, B. S., Stormont, M. A., & Gage, N. A. (2011). Tier 2 interventions within the context of school-wide positive behavior support. *Behavioral Disorders, 36*(4).

Miller-Richter, M., Lewis, T. J., & Hagar, J. (2012). The relationship between principal leadership skills and school-wide positive behavior support: An exploratory study. *Journal of Positive Behavior Interventions, 14*, 69–77.

Mong, M., Johnson, K., & Mong, K., (2011). Effects of check in/check out on behavioral indices and mathematics generalization. Behavioral Disorders, 36(4), 225–240.

Myers, C. L., & Holland, K. L. (2000). Classroom behavioral interventions: Do teachers consider the function of the behavior? *Psychology in the Schools, 37*(3), 271–280.

Nelson, J. R., Duppong Hurley, K., Synhorst, L., Epstein, M. H., Stage, S., & Buckley, J. (2009). The child outcomes of a behavior model. *Exceptional Children, 76*(1), 7–30.

Nelson, J. R., Martella, R., & Galand, B. (1998). The effects of teaching school expectations and establishing a consistent consequence on formal office disciplinary actions. *Journal of Emotional and Behavioral Disorders, 6*, 153–161.

Newcomer, L., Colvin, G., & Lewis, T. J. (2009). Behavior supports in nonclassroom settings. In W. Sailor, G. Dunlap, G. Sugai, & R. Horner (Eds.), *Handbook of positive behavior support* (pp. 497–520). New York: Springer.

Newcomer, L., & Lewis, T. (2004). Functional behavioral assessment: An investigation of assessment reliability and effectiveness of function-based interventions. *Journal of Emotional and Behavioral Disorders, 12*(3), 168–181.

Peterson, G. J., Beekley, C. Z., Speaker, K. M., & Pietrzak, D. (1996). An examination of violence in three rural school districts. *Rural Educator, 19*(3), 25–32.

Patterson, G. R., Reid, J. B., & Dishion, T. J. (1992). *Antisocial boys.* Eugene, OR: Castalia Press.

Powell, D., Fixsen, D., Dunlap, G., Smith, B., & Fox, L. (2007). A synthesis of knowledge relevant to pathways of service delivery for young children with or at risk of challenging behavior. *Journal of Early Intervention, 29*, 81–106.

Putnam, R. F., Handler, M. W., Ramirez-Platt, C. M., & Luiselli, J. K. (2003). Improving student bus-riding behavior through a whole-school intervention. *Journal of Applied Behavior Analysis, 36*, 583–589.

Putnam, R. F., Luiselli, J. K., & Sunderland, M. (2002). Longitudinal evaluation of behavior support intervention in a public middle school. *Journal of Positive Behavior Interventions, 4*, 182–188.

Rose, L. C., Gallup, A. (2006). The 38th annual Phi Delta Kappa/Gallup poll of the public's attitudes toward the public schools. *Phi Delta Kappan, 88*, 1, 41–56.

Skiba, R. (2002). Special education and school discipline: A precarious balance. *Behavioral Disorders, 27*, 81–97.

Simonson, B., Britton, L., & Young, D. (2010). School-wide positive behavior support in an alternative school setting: A case study. *Journal of Positive Behavior Interventions, 12*, 180–191.

Simonson, B., Fairbanks, S., Briesch, A., Myers, D., & Sugai, G. (2008). Evidence-based practices in classroom management: Considerations for research to practice. *Education and Treatment of Children, 31*(3), 351–380.

Simonsen, B., Myers, D., & Briere, D. E. (2011). Comparing a behavioral check-in/check-out (CICO) intervention to standard practice in an urban middle school setting using an experimental group design. *Journal of Positive Behavior Interventions, 13*(1), 31–48.

Simonsen, B., Myers, D., & DeLuca, C. (2010). Providing teachers with training and performance feedback to increase use of three classroom management skills: Prompts, opportunities to respond, and reinforcement. *Teacher Education in Special Education, 33*, 300–318.

Sinclair, M. F., Christenson, S. L., Evelo, D. L., & Hurley, C. M. (1998). Dropout prevention for youth with disabilities: Efficacy of a sustained school engagement procedure. *Exceptional Children, 65*, 1, 7–21.

Sinclair, M. F., & Kaibel, C. (2002). *Dakota County: Secondary Check & Connect programs: School Success Check & Connect program evaluation final summary report.* Minneapolis: University of Minnesota, Institute on Community Integration.

Skiba, R. J., & Peterson, R. L. (2000). School discipline at a crossroads: From zero tolerance to early response. *Exceptional Children, 66*, 335–356.

Skiba, R. J., Peterson, R. L., & Williams, T. (1997). Office referrals and suspensions: Disciplinary intervention in middle schools. *Education & Treatment of Children, 20*, 295–315.

Skiba, R., Reynolds, C. R., Graham, S., Sheras, P., Conoley, J. C., & Garcia-Vazquez, E. (2006). Are zero toler-ance policies effective in the schools? An evidentiary review and recommendations. *American Psycho-logical Association Zero Tolerance Task Force* (August), 40–51.

Stichter, J. P., Lewis, T. L. Richter, M., & Johnson, N. (2006). Assessing antecedent variables: The effects of instructional variables on student outcomes through in-service and peer coaching professional develop-ment models. *Education and Treatment of Children, 29*, 665–692.

Sugai, G., & Horner, R. H. (1999). Discipline and behavioral support: Preferred processes and practices. *Effec-tive School Practices, 17*(4), 10–22.

Sugai, G., Horner, R. H., Algozzine, R., Barrett, S., Lewis, T., Anderson, C., Bradley, R., Choi, J. H., Dunlap, G., Eber, L., George, H., Kincaid, D., McCart, A., Nelson, M., Newcomer, L., Putnam, R., Riffel, L., Rovins, M., Sailor, W., & Simonsen, B. (2010). *School-wide positive behavior support: Implementers' blueprint and self-assessment.* Eugene: University of Oregon.

Sugai, G., Horner, R. H., Dunlap, G., Hieneman, M., Lewis, T. J., Nelson, C. M., Scott, T., Liaupsin, C., Sailor, W., Turnbull, A. P., Turnbull, W., Wickham, D., Ruef, M., & Wilcox, B. (2000). *Applying positive behav-ioral support and functional behavioral assessment in schools.* Washington, DC: OSEP Center of Positive Behavioral Interventions and Supports.

Sugai, G., Horner, R., & Sprague, J. (1999). Functional-assessment-based behavior support planning: Research to practice to research. *Behavioral Disorders, 24*(3), 253–257.

Sulzer-Azaroff, B., & Mayer, G. R. (1994). *Achieving educational excellence: Behavior analysis for achieving classroom and schoolwide behavior change.* San Marcos, CA: Western Image.

Sutherland, K. S., Lewis-Palmer, T., Stichter, J., & Morgan, P. L. (2008). Examining the influence of teacher behavior and classroom context on the behavioral and academic outcomes for students with emotional or behavioral disorders. *The Journal of Special Education, 41*(4), 223–233.

Sutherland, K. S., & Wehby, J. H. (2001). Exploring the relationship between increased opportunities to respond to academic requests and the academic and behavioral outcomes of students with EBD. *Reme-dial and Special Education, 22*(2), 113–121.

Sutherland, K. S., Wehby, J. H., & Copeland, S. (2000). Effects of varying rates of behavior-specific praise on the on-task behavior of students with EBD. *Journal of Emotional and Behavioral Disorders, 8*(2), 2–8.

Todd, A. W., Campbell, A. L., Meyer, G. G., & Horner, R. H. (2008). The effects of a targeted intervention to reduce problem behaviors: Elementary school implementation of check-in check-out. *Journal of Positive Behavior Interventions, 10*(1), 46–55.

Todd, A. W., Horner, R., Sugai, G., & Colvin, G. (1997). Individualizing school-wide discipline for students with chronic problem behaviors: A team approach. *Effective School Practices, 17*, 72–82.

U.S. Department of Education (1998). *Violence and discipline problems in U.S. public schools: 1996–97.* Wash-ington, DC: U.S. Department of Education, National Center for Educational Statistics.

U.S. Department of Education (2000a). *Effective alternative strategies: Grant competition to reduce student sus-pensions and expulsions and ensure educational progress of suspended and expelled students.* Washington, DC: Safe and Drug Free School Programs, OMB#1810–0551.

U.S. Department of Education. (2000b). *Twenty-second annual report to Congress on the implementation of the Individuals with Disabilities Education Act.* Washington, DC: Author.

U.S. Department of Health and Human Services (2000). *Report of the Surgeon General's conference on chil-dren's mental health: A national action agenda.* Washington, DC: Author.

Waasdorp, T. E., Bradshaw, C. P., & Leaf, P. J. (2012). The impact of School-Wide Positive Behavioral Interven-tions and Supports (SWPBIS) on bullying and peer rejection: A randomized controlled effectiveness trial. *Archives of Pediatrics and Adolescent Medicine, 116*(2), 149–156.

Walker, H. M., Horner, R., Sugai, G., Bullis, M., Sprague, J., Bricker, D., & Kaufman, J. (1996). Integrated approaches to preventing antisocial behavior patterns among school-age children and youth. *Journal of Emotional and Behavioral Disorders, 4*, 193–256.

Walker, H. M., Ramsey, E., & Gresham, R. M. (2004). *Antisocial behavior in school: Evidence-based practices* (2nd ed.). Belmont, CA: Wadsworth.

Ziglar, E., Taussig, C., & Black, K. (1992). Early childhood intervention: A promising preventative for juvenile delinquency. *American Psychologist, 47*, 997–1006.

Zins, J. E., & Ponti, C. R. (1990). Best practices in school-based consultation. In A. Thomas & J. Grimes (Eds.), *Best practices in school psychology—II* (pp. 673–694). Washington, DC: National Association of School Psychologists.

4

SUPPORTING GENERAL CLASSROOM MANAGEMENT

Tier 2/3 Practices and Systems[1]

GEORGE SUGAI AND BRANDI SIMONSEN
UNIVERSITY OF CONNECTICUT

With the most appropriate highly engaging and effective instruction, teachers can maximize academic learning for most students; however, teachers also know that some students require more intensive and specified instruction to be successful. A response-to-intervention approach is used to guide this process by emphasizing (1) regular universal screening; (2) continuous progress monitoring; (3) team-driven, data-based decision making; and (4) high-fidelity implementation of evidence-based instructional practices (Griffiths, Parson, Burns, VanDerHeyden, & Tilly, 2007; Sugai & Horner, 2009). These practices are organized along a multitiered prevention continuum such that all students experience an effective core or foundation curriculum, some students receive additional academic supports in small groups, and a few students receive highly individualized interventions (Griffiths, Parson, Burns, VanDerHeyden, & Tilly, 2007).

This same multitiered support logic is applied to teach and promote the positive social behavior of students and to prevent the development and occurrence of problem behavior (e.g., Simonsen et al., 2014; Sugai & Horner, 2002, 2009; Sugai et al., 2000; Walker et al., 1996). As in the academic context, most students benefit from a classroom-wide behavior management plan, and some students require more intensive and specified behavior supports to be successful. The purpose of this chapter is to describe classroom practices and systems for supporting those students whose behaviors are unresponsive to general classroom management practices. To achieve this purpose, four main questions are addressed. First, how does school-wide relate to classroom-wide behavior support? Second, what are the practices and systems of classroom-wide positive behavior support (Tier 1)? Third, what are the classroom practices and systems of small-group behavior support (Tier 2)? Finally, what are the classroom practices and systems of individual student behavior support (Tier 3)?

As this purpose and these questions are addressed, an application example is provided to illustrate how an actual implementation might appear. Sonkei School is presented as a fictitious generic illustration of the core features of classroom management Tier 2 and 3 practices and systems. Users of these materials must adapt implementation to the unique cultural, contextual, and learning features of their students, faculty, schools, families, and neighborhoods (Fallon, O'Keeffe, & Sugai, 2012; Sugai, O'Keeffe, & Fallon, 2012). We conclude with a description of how a classroom multitiered system of behavior support is established, sustained, and monitored.

HOW DOES SCHOOL-WIDE RELATE TO CLASSROOM-WIDE BEHAVIOR SUPPORT?

Effective classroom behavior support is integrated into the formal practices and systems of school-wide behavior support. The characteristics of effective school-wide discipline and classroom management have been widely described and documented (e.g., Colvin, Kame'enui, & Sugai, 1993; Evertson & Weinstein, 2006; Horner, Sugai, & Anderson, 2010; Marzano & Pickering, 2003; Simonsen, Fairbanks, Briesch, Myers, & Sugai, 2008; Simonsen et al., 2014) and generally consist of the seven key elements: (1) school-based leadership team that is charged with leading implementation of school-wide discipline; (2) a formal and brief purpose statement that gives priority and visibility to effective behavior support; (3) three to five positively stated behavior expectations (e.g., *Respect Self, Others, and Environment; Safety, Respect, and Responsibility*) that serve as the foundation for behavior communications and practices; (4) formal lesson plans, schedules, and procedures for teaching these behavior expectations across typical and important school-wide settings (e.g., hallways, buses, assemblies, sporting events, playgrounds, common areas) and with contextually and culturally relevant positive examples that are specific to these settings; (5) continuum of practices and strategies for recognizing and acknowledging displays of these expectations across all school settings; (6) continuum of practices, strategies, and procedures for preventing and responding to norm- or rule-violating behaviors; and (7) a data system for monitoring the impact of behavior support on student behavior and fidelity of practice implementation.

Assisted by effective academic instruction and engaging teaching practices, these same school-wide discipline elements are represented within the classroom to support student social behavior success. However, a few classroom differences exist. First, grade-level or department teams might be extensions of the school-wide leadership team. Second, the purpose statement might highlight the academic instructional emphasis of the classroom. Third, behavior expectation lesson plans emphasize classroom settings and routines (e.g., transitions, teacher-directed instruction, small-group activities, independent study) and specific related behaviors. Fourth, strategies and practices for acknowledging and recognizing student behavior might be tailored to individual teachers and instructional contexts. Fifth, minor and major classroom norm- and rule-violating behavior might be emphasized in relation to academic instructional activities and classroom activities. Finally, data systems might be adapted to the instructional and content routines of the teacher and classroom.

Highlighting the relationship between school-wide and classroom-based behavior and discipline practices and systems is important for (1) emphasizing a common behavior support approach; (2) enabling a common language for

Table 4.1 Description of school-wide multitiered system of behavior support at Sonkei School.

Students and staff and family members at Sonkei School have established a school-wide multitiered system of behavior support. A school climate committee comprised of one student from each grade level, school administrator, content and grad-level teachers, school counselor, two parents, and special educator meet weekly. During weekly meetings, the team developed a behavior purpose statement (*"Sonkei School is a community of learners where respect for self, others, environment and learning are practiced daily by everyone across the whole school."*).

The team also developed four school-wide value statements (*"We respect ourselves, we respect each other, we respect our environment, and we respect learning."*) and a matrix that defines those statements in the context of typical school settings (see Figure 4.1). They also developed lesson plans and teaching procedures delivering explicit social skills instruction, based on the matrix, throughout the school year (i.e., initial instruction plus periodic review opportunities). All staff agreed to teach and use these value statements in their daily communications and to acknowledge with verbal praise and daily Respect Cards anytime students displayed these valued behaviors (Figure 4.2).

Because their system for handling rule violations was fairly complete, the team's major tasks were to (1) clarify definitions for minor (classroom-managed) versus major (office-referred) problem behaviors, (2) develop a procedural flowchart for handling noncompliance and repeated problem behavior occurrences, and (3) establish a reteaching procedure after consequences for rule violations have been completed.

The team used their existing data system to develop a weekly routine of reviewing the number of office discipline referrals (ODR) by type, location, student, and time of day. Information from these reviews was used to decide action plan activities (e.g., reteach expected behavior, increase supervision, enhance positive acknowledgments).

To implement these Tier 1 elements, the team developed a schedule for team meetings, data review, staff professional development, and teaching expectations to students. In addition, the school counselor facilitated weekly reviews of teacher enrollment lists to determine whether any students required additional behavior supports (i.e., Tiers 2/3).

After one year of implementation, the school climate team reported that 513 of their 790 (65%) students had 0 or 1 ODRs for major rule violations. Upon further inspection, the team noticed that classroom teachers wrote a majority of the ODRs for "disrupting teaching," which triggered a discussion about curriculum, design of instruction, and general classroom management. When they examined how many and where Respect Cards were being distributed, classroom settings had the lowest weekly averages. They realized they needed to increase their focus on classroom-wide positive behavior support.

student-to-student, student-to-adult, and adult-to-adult communications; and (3) developing truly school-wide experiences and routines for all students and staff members. Academic and social behavior success for *most* students is more likely if school- and classroom-wide Tier 1 practices and systems are implemented in a manner that is contextually and culturally responsive, highly accurate and fluent, and available to all students across all settings by all staff. In addition, effective, efficient, and relevant implementation of Tier 1 serves as the basis for screening for students who may require additional behavior supports to be successful, especially in the classroom. A description of Sonkei School's multitiered system of behavior support is provided in Table 4.1, and samples of their school-wide expectation teaching matrix and Respect Card are illustrated in Figures 4.1 and 4.2, respectively.

Four SW Expectations	Four Priority Skill Teaching Settings			
	Hallways	*Cafeteria*	*Bus Loading Zone*	*School Assemblies & Events*
Respect Yourself	• Have a plan • Bring needed materials	• Make healthy choices for food and beverages • Eat only until full	• Be prepared before your stop • Use safety equipment	• Arrive early • Make note of important content
Respect Others	• Walk to the right • Keep hands, feet, and objects to self	• Use a conversational volume • Stay seated while eating	• Use a conversational volume • Share seats when needed	• Save side conversations until event is over • Use active listening
Respect Environment	• Put litter in trash cans • Report damage	• Recycle plastic and paper • Leave your area neat	• Keep backpacks on your lap • Save your drinks and snacks for off the bus	• Return chairs • Put any litter in trash cans as you leave
Respect Learning	• Use quiet voice when transitioning	• Use quiet voice when entering/ exiting cafeteria	• Have something to read for long rides	• Maintain a distraction-free environment (technology off)

Figure 4.1 Sonkei school-wide expectation teaching matrix.

SONKEI SCHOOL RESPECT CARD	Student Name _____ Date _____ Teacher Name _____		
☐ *Respect Yourself*	☐ *Respect Others*	☐ *Respect Environment*	☐ *Respect Learning*
☐ *Classroom* ☐ *Hallways* ☐ *Cafeteria* ☐ *Bus Loading* ☐ *Events*			

Figure 4.2 Front of Sonkei School Respect Card.

WHAT ARE THE PRACTICES AND SYSTEMS OF CLASSROOM-WIDE POSITIVE BEHAVIOR SUPPORT (TIER 1)?

The practices and systems highlighted in the previous section are enhanced and supported by what teachers do on a daily and lesson basis. Simonsen and her colleagues (Simonsen, Fairbanks, Briesch, Myers, & Sugai, 2008; Simonsen et al., 2012) described a specific set of evidence-based classroom management practices that should be considered in all classrooms for all students. First, structure and predictability across all classroom settings, personnel, and activities are maximized by explicitly (1) teaching, prompting, modeling, and acknowledging typical behavior routines and (2) arranging the classroom environment to minimize crowding and distractions. Second, a small number (usually the same three to five used for school-wide) of positively stated expectations are explicitly and actively taught, reviewed, monitored, prompted, precorrected (reminded), supervised, and reinforced in and across all classroom routines and settings. Third, all students are actively engaged by providing high rates of opportunities to respond during instruction, highly engaging teacher-directed materials and activities, and ensuring high-fidelity implementation of evidence-based instructional curricula and methods. Fourth, a continuum of classroom-based strategies (e.g., praise, tokens, social positives, behavior contracts) that are effective, efficient, and relevant (i.e., appropriate developmentally, culturally, linguistically, etc.) is established for contingently acknowledging student displays of appropriate academic and social behavior. Finally, a continuum of classroom-based strategies that are effective, efficient, and relevant is specified for contingently responding to student displays of norm- or rule-violating social behavior. A description of classroom multitiered systems of behavior support at Sonkei School is provided in Table 4.2, and a sample of a classroom expectation teaching matrix is illustrated in Figure 4.3.

Table 4.2 Description of classroom multitiered system of behavior support at Sonkei School.

Every classroom teacher at Sonkei School was responsible for developing and implementing his or her individual classroom and behavior management systems. However, after seeing the ODR data, which indicated that most of the problem behaviors were occurring in the classroom, and learning from the students that inconsistencies across classroom teachers were creating difficulties for many students and teachers, they agreed to use the four school-wide expectations as the basis for their classroom management system so that a common language, a set of behavioral expectations, and a preventive approach would be established and aligned with the school-wide practices and expectations. Because of variations in content (e.g., music vs. literature, science vs. Spanish), teaching format (e.g., lecture vs. small group), or learning phase (e.g., new vs. practice knowledge), the settings or contexts for the matrices varied by teacher and classroom. See Figure 4.3 for an example.

(Continued)

Table 4.2 (Continued)

During homeroom, all teachers used the classroom-teaching matrix to teach and practice what good examples of each school-wide expectation would look like in the classroom. They emphasized that each setting might require different behavior variations, but collectively they would still represent one of the four school-wide expectations. Then, throughout the day over the following weeks, opportunities for reminders, practice, and reteaching were integrated into classroom instruction. Initially, Respect Cards were used to acknowledge individual students who displayed respectful behavior; however, eventually teachers provided the feedback and recognition to whole classrooms.

When classroom management was discussed in grade-level team meetings, teachers concluded that they couldn't determine which practices were evidence based. As a result, the team did a thorough search for experimentally documented behavior management practices and started training that was (1) embedded in their usual faculty and staff activities and (2) focused on increasing appropriate behavior while preventing classroom disruptions. Each teacher selected a colleague to be a peer-mentor, and observations and conversations focused on the accurate and fluent use of recommended classroom management practices (e.g., active supervision, opportunities to respond, positive recognition).

After three months of implementing, the ODR data by location indicated a relatively equal distribution of ODRs and Respect Cards, and 690 (87%) out of 790 students had received 0 or 1 ODRs.

Four SW Expectations	Four Priority Skill Teaching in Classroom Settings			
	Independent Study Time	*Lesson Transitions*	*Teacher Directed Activity*	*Collaborative Learning Activity*
Respect Yourself	• Have a plan • Use your time efficiently	• Gather personal belongings	• Sit in a ready to learn position • Minimize distractions	• Know your role and responsibilities • Be ready to collaborate
Respect Others	• Use "Hello" card to obtain teacher attentiont • Maintain a quiet learning environment	• Use inside voice • Keep hands, feet, and objects to self	• Keep belongings under desk • Use active listening skills	• Listen before speaking • Use calm and constructive language
Respect Environment	• Keep feet on the floor • Stay in your seat	• Push chair under desk • Put any litter in the trash can	• Keep area clean for next group	• Return area to original arrangement • Leave area neat
Respect Learning	• Have your materials ready • Try all activities and ask for help if needed	• Gather supplies for next activity • Maintain a quiet environment for other classes	• Take notes for main ideas • Write down assigned tasks	• Remind of purpose activity • Actively participate in group activity

Figure 4.3 Classroom expectation teaching matrix for Sonkei School.

WHAT ARE THE PRACTICES AND SYSTEMS OF SMALL-GROUP BEHAVIOR SUPPORT (TIER 2)?

These classroom-wide behavior support practices and systems are integrated into the school-wide discipline system to establish a unifying common language for communication and a consistent set of expectations and routines across all school settings (also known as Tier 1). If implemented with high fidelity (accurately and fluently) and adapted to represent the developmental, linguistic, and cultural characteristics of all students, family, and staff, most students are likely to be responsive and successful to these classroom and school-wide supports (Bradshaw, Mitchell, & Leaf, 2010; Horner et al., 2009). However, some students may be identified as needing supports that are more specified and intensive (i.e., Tier 2/3) because their behaviors are not sufficiently responsive to Tier 1 supports.

Tier 2 practices and systems are described generally as being more targeted and are supplemental to what is provided at the general classroom and school-wide levels (Crone, Hawken, & Horner, 2010). Although individual classroom teachers may independently develop and implement Tier 2 supports, a team (i.e., grade level, department, school-wide) is usually responsible because students interact with multiple teachers across multiple settings. For example, at the elementary level, students may have a homeroom teacher, music and art specialists, physical education teacher, and playground monitor; at the secondary level, students may have multiple academic content teachers, elective course teachers, and hallway and cafeteria supervisors.

This team usually comprises an administrator, individuals who have behavioral expertise (e.g., counselor, social worker, special educator, school psychologist), and one or more teachers. Their collective responsibilities include (1) screening for entering and exiting students, (2) monitoring of implementation fidelity, (3) monitoring of student progress, (4) enhancements and adaptations based on student responsiveness, (5) orienting students and teachers to the Tier 2 practices, and (6) communications with parents, students, administrators, and teachers. The team leader or coordinator is responsible for scheduling and facilitating weekly meetings, summarizing data for discussions and decision making, and communicating implementation and outcome information to others, especially to the school-wide behavior support team.

Although the specifics may vary based on size of school enrollment, developmental level, grade range, contextual and cultural demographics, Tier 2 behavior supports generally have the following features (Crone, Hawken, & Horner, 2010). First, direct and explicit social skills instruction is provided on self-management skills (e.g., goal setting, self-assessment, self-reinforcement), classroom routines, and school-wide expectations. Second, frequent and regular reminders about what these behaviors and skills would look like are scheduled and provided in different classroom contexts. Third, frequent and regular opportunities are arranged for self- and teacher monitoring of behavior. Fourth, frequent and regular opportunities for feedback are delivered contingently for displays of expected behavior. Fifth, self-evaluation and/or adult-facilitated reviews are conducted on current and cumulative student progress and implementation fidelity. Finally, daily and/or weekly progress reports are communicated to family members and teachers.

These features may be present in a range of empirically supported Tier 2 interventions, including check-in/check-out (Crone, Hawken, & Horner, 2010; Fairbanks,

Sugai, Guardino, & Lathrop, 2007); check, connect, and expect (Cheney et al., 2009); and small-group social skills instruction (Lane et al., 2003). Students who are involved in Tier 2 supports continue to participate in and experience Tier 1 practices and systems. The goal is to maintain a truly inclusive and positive school-wide social culture for all students. An example of Tier 2 check-in/check-out at Sonkei School is described in Table 4.3, and samples of the Sonkei School HONOR Respect Card and check-in/check-out student card are provided in Figures 4.4 and 4.5, respectively.

Table 4.3 Description of Tier 2 Check-in/Check-out system at Sonkei School.

Although most students were experiencing success with the implementation of school- and classroom-wide systems, 13% of the students continued to experience behavior difficulty (two or more ODRs); so the school climate team formed a subcommittee to extend their supports to these students. The core of this subcommittee comprised the school administrator, school counselor, and special education staff. Teachers were ad hoc members depending on whether they were involved with these students.

The team developed a peer group-based intervention (i.e., check-in/check-out, CICO) in which individual students would pick up a general or common behavior-monitoring card (see Figure 4.4) each morning at the counselor's office and return completed cards at the end of the day. During these pickup (check-in) and drop-off (check-out) opportunities, the counselor would remind students of the expectations, make sure they had their needed materials, and provide positive attention. Classroom settings and teacher involvement were emphasized in the orientation training and actual implementation, and the classroom teaching matrix was copied on the back of the Respect Card. On the hour, teachers would evaluate student progress in the classroom on the school-wide expectations. If a student met his or her goal, an Honors Respect Card (similar to Respect Card but of a different color and size; see Figure 4.5) was given to students to make a selection from the school supply store and to take home to share with their family. If more than 80% of all the students who were participating in the CICO system met their daily goal, they were given the privilege of selecting the items for the lunch menu on Friday or some other classroom- or school-wide activity privilege.

At end of each week, the school counselor would meet with each student and review his or her weekly progress, reteach for any problem areas, and adjust the goals as needed. Teachers and family members also received a report of their child/student's progress.

SONKEI SCHOOL **HONOR** RESPECT CARD	Student Name _____ Date _____ Homeroom Teacher _____		
Respect Yourself	*Respect Others*	*Respect Environment*	*Respect Learning*
Bearer of this card has earned a free selection at the school store.			

Figure 4.4 Sonkei School HONOR Respect Card.

Name											Date		
	2 = Great			1 = OK			0 = Try Again						
Time & Activity/Class	Respect Yourself			Respect Others			Respect Environment			Respect Learning			Teacher Initials
8 a.m. (_____)	2	1	0	2	1	0	2	1	0	2	1	0	
9 a.m. (_____)	2	1	0	2	1	0	2	1	0	2	1	0	
10 a.m. (_____)	2	1	0	2	1	0	2	1	0	2	1	0	
11 a.m. (_____)	2	1	0	2	1	0	2	1	0	2	1	0	
12 p.m. (_____)	2	1	0	2	1	0	2	1	0	2	1	0	
1 p.m. (_____)	2	1	0	2	1	0	2	1	0	2	1	0	
2 p.m. (_____)	2	1	0	2	1	0	2	1	0	2	1	0	
3 p.m. (_____)	2	1	0	2	1	0	2	1	0	2	1	0	
Today's Goal						Today's Total Points _____/64							
Signatures & Comments													
CICO Coordinator						Parent(s)/Guardian(s)							

Figure 4.5 Sample of check-in/check-out student card.

WHAT ARE THE PRACTICES AND SYSTEMS OF INDIVIDUAL STUDENT BEHAVIOR SUPPORT (TIER 3)?

If Tier 1 or 2 practices and systems are in place and being implemented with high fidelity, we still expect a few students to have behaviors that require even more intensive and individualized behavior supports (Tier 3). These behaviors are of such intensity, frequency, and/or duration that the student is at high risk of failure, including behaviors that range from high rates of verbal and physical aggression to low rates of verbal social engagement, from long-duration episodes of crying and negative self-statements to short but repeated incidences of self-injurious behaviors. In many instances, needed supports are based upon previous efforts (i.e., Tier 1/2), except that intervention decisions are linked more specifically and directly to individualized or personalized assessment information.

Although a team-based approach is continued, a Tier 3 team is individualized and includes active participation by family members, the student, a behavioral expert, and the student's teachers. When appropriate, students are actively involved in the assessment and intervention development process to become more student or person centered. From a social validation perspective, students, for example, are given opportunities to interpret information about their behavior, set and comment on behavior goals, individualize behavior intervention features, monitor the quality of progress toward behavior goals, and participate in overall program evaluations.

In addition, based on the nature of the problem behaviors, specialists from other disciplines (e.g., physicians, speech-language specialists, mental health providers, social workers) participate in the development of comprehensive treatment plans through a wraparound process that systematically considers the unique needs and circumstances of the student and his or her family (Eber, Sugai, Smith, & Scott, 2002; Scott & Eber, 2003).

In school settings, a function-based approach is particularly important for designing and implementing effective individualized behavior intervention plans in the classroom. Specifically, the objective is to specify the conditions under which problem behavior is more or less likely to be observed within a given situation or routine. This process is called a functional behavioral assessment (FBA) (Crone & Horner, 2003; Ingram, Lewis-Palmer, & Sugai, 2005; O'Neill, Horner, Albin, Storey, & Sprague, 1997; Sugai & Horner, 1999–2000; Sugai & Lewis-Palmer, 2004), and its purposes are to (1) establish hypothesis statements that describe the antecedent and consequence events or conditions most likely to be associated with the occurrence of the problem behavior in a particular setting or routine (i.e., the function) and (2) guide the development of a behavior intervention plan (BIP). If a series of systematic (experimental) manipulations are conducted to test and increase our confidence in the accuracy of hypothesis statements or gain more insight into a particularly challenging problem behavior, the process is called a functional analysis (Cooper, Heron, & Heward, 2007).

In classroom settings, teachers directly and actively implement and monitor Tier 3 interventions during times and places when problem behavior is most likely to occur. Intervention manipulations for the BIP are based on information obtained from the functional assessment and address three primary areas (see Figure 4.6): (1) before (antecedent manipulations), (2) during (behavior teaching), and (3) after (consequence manipulations). A description of the Tier 3 function-based approach at Sonkei School is provided in Table 4.4, and an abbreviate example of the FBA and BIP for a student named Hisao is provided in Figure 4.7.

In addition, assessments and evaluations may be broadened to include other types of data (e.g., physiology, neurology, endocrinology, behavioral, psychology) that might

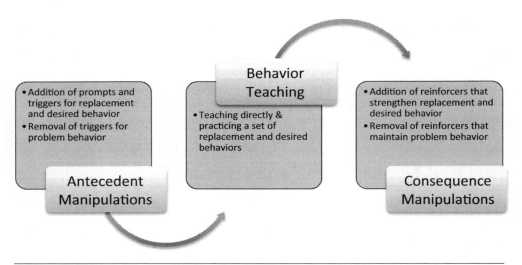

Figure 4.6 Behavior intervention manipulations.

Table 4.4 Description of Tier 3 function-based support system at Sonkei School.

> After 2 weeks of CICO implementation, Hisao failed to meet his daily goal on 6 of 10 school days (unexcused absence on one day), despite three adjustments during that time by the CICO team. The school psychologist and his homeroom teacher (T) conducted a formal FBA and reviewed the results during a support team meeting that included Hisao, his father, and the music teacher. They determined that his verbal noncompliance and name-calling behaviors were related to access to peer attention in nonclassroom settings (e.g., hallways, lunchroom), access to teacher attention during teacher lecturing in history and science, and escaping difficult academic work during independent study in history and math. They also determined that Hisao was more likely to display these behaviors on Mondays and Friday when he would spend the weekend with his stepmother.
>
> This FBA information was used to develop a comprehensive BIP that had three variations, one for each function-based condition (access to peer attention, access to adult attention, and escape from difficult independent work). The school psychologist (SP) would meet with Hisao each Wednesday to practice specific social behavior skills related to the four school-wide expectations and to the three function-based conditions. Hisao continued to use his CICO card, except that he received extra bonus points for success in math, history, and science class. To support this school plan, Hisao and his father (F) received support from the local community mental health (CMH) worker, who developed a plan to ease the shared-custody transition to Hisao's stepmother's (M's) house.

be influencing a student's academic and social behavior functioning in the classroom. Within the many physical and social settings and contexts of the classroom, assessments include careful academic achievement and performance measures, as well as sensory and physiological screenings.

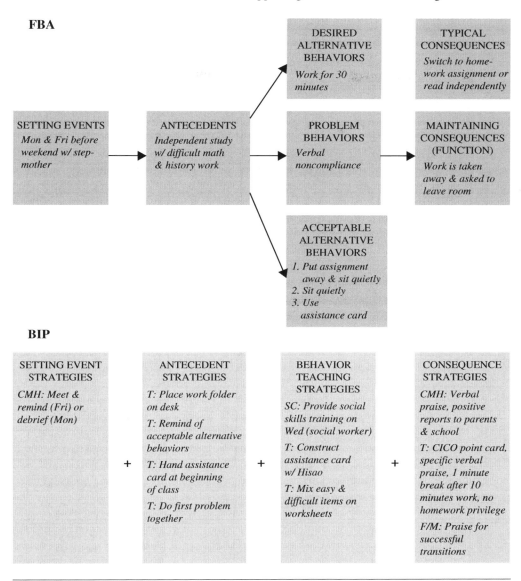

FBA

SETTING EVENTS	ANTECEDENTS		

DESIRED ALTERNATIVE BEHAVIORS
Work for 30 minutes

TYPICAL CONSEQUENCES
Switch to home-work assignment or read independently

SETTING EVENTS
Mon & Fri before weekend w/ step-mother

ANTECEDENTS
Independent study w/ difficult math & history work

PROBLEM BEHAVIORS
Verbal noncompliance

MAINTAINING CONSEQUENCES (FUNCTION)
Work is taken away & asked to leave room

ACCEPTABLE ALTERNATIVE BEHAVIORS
1. Put assignment away & sit quietly
2. Sit quietly
3. Use assistance card

BIP

SETTING EVENT STRATEGIES
CMH: Meet & remind (Fri) or debrief (Mon)

ANTECEDENT STRATEGIES
T: Place work folder on desk
T: Remind of acceptable alternative behaviors
T: Hand assistance card at beginning of class
T: Do first problem together

BEHAVIOR TEACHING STRATEGIES
SC: Provide social skills training on Wed (social worker)
T: Construct assistance card w/ Hisao
T: Mix easy & difficult items on worksheets

CONSEQUENCE STRATEGIES
CMH: Verbal praise, positive reports to parents & school
T: CICO point card, specific verbal praise, 1 minute break after 10 minutes work, no homework privilege
F/M: Praise for successful transitions

Figure 4.7 Abbreviated sample of FBA and BIP for Hisao.

ESTABLISHING, SUSTAINING, AND MONITORING A CLASSROOM-WIDE MULTITIERED SYSTEM OF BEHAVIOR SUPPORT

Establishing a full continuum of behavior support in the classroom requires the careful alignment of evidence-based practices into a system in which all students experience positive and preventive behavior management (Tier 1) and in which students whose behaviors are not sufficiently responsive have access to more intensive and specified interventions (Tiers 2/3). The establishment and sustainability of such a multitiered system requires careful attention to a number of implementation guidelines: (1) working as teams so that key stakeholders are actively participating; (2) using classroom and school-wide data to guide decisions; (3) establishing a multitiered school-wide system to support and integrate classroom practices and systems; (4) adapting implementation to the values, learning histories, and routines of the local culture (family, school, neighborhood); (5) establishing regular (e.g., weekly, monthly) and formal meetings to review, evaluate, and adjust implementation; (6) integrating behavior and academic behavior support in a comprehensive multitiered system; (7) investing in the selection of the fewest number of evidence-based practices and interventions that have the largest and most durable benefits for all students; (8) integrating initiatives and programs that have similar expected behavior outcomes and eliminating those that are ineffective, inefficient, and/or irrelevant; and (9) guiding decision making with school- and classroom-wide data that are collected through universal screening and continuous progress monitoring. A description of strategies for linking school-wide and classroom behavior supports in a sustainable manner is provided in Table 4.5, and an example of one teacher's continuum of classroom behavior supports is illustrated in Figure 4.8.

Table 4.5 Description of strategies to link school-wide and classroom behavior supports sustainably.

Every classroom at Sonkei has a classroom and behavior management plan that is linked to the agreed-upon school-wide behavior support structure. On the first day and week of each semester, the school-wide behavior expectations are taught and practiced, and each teacher uses the school-wide expectations to support her or his classroom routines and schedules. All staff have agreed to use HONOR Respect Cards to acknowledge expectation-following behaviors in nonclassroom settings. Each teacher blends the use of HONOR Respect Cards with her or his individual classroom acknowledgment systems. In addition, each teacher develops a full continuum of classroom supports that parallels and includes school-wide behavior supports.

Classroom Continuum of Behavior Support at Sonkei School

Teacher: *Ms. Kane-Helihy*   **Room:** *17A*

Tier	Classroom Supports
All	• *Teach, review, & practice 4 school-wide Respect expectations (Yourself, Others, Environment, & Learning) for typical school settings and classroom routines at the beginning of every week* • *At least 10 times each day acknowledge displays of respect in classroom and nonclassroom settings using "HONOR Respect Cards," verbal praise, homeroom teacher positive reports, positive office referrals*

Figure 4.8 Classroom continuum of behavior support strategies at Sonkei School.

Tier	Classroom Supports
	• *Teach & follow procedures for handling rule violations (discipline handbook)* • *Maximize student engagement & opportunities to respond during all academic lessons* • *Actively supervise across all school environments & classroom routines* • *Review academic progress & discipline data weekly for classroom student lists & screen for students who have one or more major office discipline referral*
Some	• *Conduct morning/afternoon & hourly student Check In/Out* • *Meet weekly with School Counselor to monitor goal achievement on weekly Check In/Out summary* • *Review academic progress & discipline data weekly for classroom student lists & screen for students whose behaviors are unresponsive to Check In/Out supports* • *Provide morning expected behavior reminders during high problem behavior hours* • *Collaborate with school counselor in weekly social skills booster sessions*
Individual	• *Participate in FBA/BIP teaming process* • *Participate in school-community-family mental health wraparound meetings* • *Implement & monitor individual student BIPs* • *Review weekly progress of individual student BIPs*

Figure 4.8 (Continued)

CONCLUDING COMMENTS

The purpose of this chapter is to describe classroom practices and systems for supporting those students whose behaviors are unresponsive to general classroom management practices within a school-wide and classroom multitiered behavior support logic and framework. This approach extends one-dimensional classroom management systems that lack a formal continuum of decision rules, practices, and implementation systems so that differentiated support is provided for students with behavior difficulties.

General classroom management practices have been discussed and recommended for decades to support the academic mission. In this chapter, an integrated link between school-wide and classroom tiered systems of support is also described. Having a consistent language and routine regarding behavior expectations can improve communication consistency and promote a more positive school climate. These expectations are supported by structured social skills lesson plans or matrices that are applied at the classroom and school-wide levels, that highlight the context in which specific behavior examples are expected, and that provide consistent feedback and acknowledgment strategies that inform students about their appropriate and inappropriate behaviors.

School-wide or classroom practices and systems (Tier 1) may be sufficient for most students, but more specialized options will be necessary to support students whose behaviors are not responsive. For some students, additional and smaller group-based structures that provide more frequent, regular, and overt social skills instruction and practice and performance feedback are required (Tier 2). For a few students, additional and more individualized or function-based behavior supports are necessary (Tier 3). This multitiered approach is implemented at both the school-wide and classroom levels with a common language, routine, and expectations to ensure efficiency, effectiveness, and relevance across all students, staff and family members, and administrators.

Finally, in this chapter, samples from Sonkei School are provided as generic illustrations of important aspects of multitiered school-wide and classroom behavior support systems. Users should focus on the main features of these samples rather than modeling them directly because every classroom and school has unique cultural, contextual, and experiential features that should be considered to enhance instructional access and impact.

NOTE

1. The development of this chapter was supported in part by a grant from the Office of Special Education Programs, U.S. Department of Education (H029D40055). Opinions expressed herein are the author's and do not necessarily reflect the position of the U.S. Department of Education, and such endorsements should not be inferred. Contact: George Sugai (george.sugai@uconn.edu), OSEP Center on Positive Behavioral Interventions and Supports (www.pbis.org), Center for Behavioral Education and Research (www.cber.org), Neag School of Education, University of Connecticut, Storrs.

REFERENCES

Bradshaw, C. P., Mitchell, M. M., & Leaf, P. J. (2010). Examining the effects of School-Wide Positive Behavioral Interventions and Supports on student outcomes: Results from a randomized controlled effectiveness trial in elementary schools. *Journal of Positive Behavior Interventions, 12,* 133–148.

Cheney, D. A., Stage, S. A., Hawken, L. S., Lynass, L., Mielenz, C., & Waugh, M. (2009). A 2-year outcome study of the check, connect, and expect intervention for students at risk for severe behavior problems. *Journal of Emotional and Behavioral Disorders, 17,* 226–243.

Colvin, G., Kame'enui, E. J., & Sugai, G. (1993). School-wide and classroom management: Reconceptualizing the integration and management of students with behavior problems in general education. *Education and Treatment of Children, 16,* 361–381.

Cooper, J. O., Heron, T. E., & Heward, W. L. (2007). *Applied behavior analysis* (2nd ed.). Upper Saddle River, NJ: Pearson.

Crone, D. A., Hawken, L. S., & Horner, R. H. (2010). *Responding to problem behavior in schools; The behavior education program* (2nd ed.). New York: Guilford.

Crone, D. A., & Horner, R. H. (2003). *Building positive behavior support systems in schools: Functional behavioral assessment.* New York: Guilford.

Eber, L., Sugai, G., Smith, C. R., & Scott, T. M. (2002). Wraparound and positive behavioral interventions and supports in the schools. *Journal of Emotional and Behavioral Disorders, 10,* 171–181.

Evertson, C. M., & Weinstein, C. S. (Eds.) (2006). *Handbook of classroom management: Research practice, and contemporary issues.* New York: Routledge.

Fairbanks, S., Sugai, G., Guardino, D., & Lathrop, M. (2007). Response to intervention: Examining classroom behavior support in second grade. *Exceptional Children, 73,* 288–310.

Fallon, L. M., O'Keeffe, B. V., & Sugai, G. (2012). Consideration of culture and context in School-wide Positive Behavior Support: A review of current literature. *Journal of Positive Behavior Interventions, 14*, 209–219. doi: 10.1177/1098300712442242

Griffiths, A. J., Parson, L. B., Burns, M. K., VanDerHeyden, A., & Tilly, W. D. (2007). *Response to intervention: Research for Practice.* Alexandria, VA: National Association of State Directors of Special Education. Retrieved from www.nasdse.org/Portals/0/Documents/RtI_Bibliography2.pdf.

Horner, R. H., Sugai, G., & Anderson, C.M. (2010). Examining the evidence base for school-wide positive behavior support. *Focus on Exceptional Children, 42*, 1–14.

Horner, R. H., Sugai, G., Smolkowski, K., Eber, L., Nakasato, J., & Todd, A., et al. (2009). A randomized, wait-list controlled effectiveness trial assessing school-wide positive behavior support in elementary schools. *Journal of Positive Behavior Interventions, 11*, 133–144.

Ingram, K., Lewis-Palmer, T., & Sugai, G. (2005). Function-based intervention planning: Comparing the effectiveness of FBA indicated and contra-indicated intervention plans. *Journal of Positive Behavior Interventions, 7*, 224–236.

Lane, K. L., Wehby, J., Menzies, H. M., Doukas, G. L., Munton, S. M., & Gregg, R. M. (2003). Social skills instruction for students at risk for antisocial behavior: The effects of small-group instruction. *Behavioral Disorders, 28*, 229–248.

Marzano, J. S., & Pickering, D. (2003). *Classroom management that works: Research-based strategies for every teacher.* Alexandria, VA: Association for Supervision and Curriculum Development.

O'Neill, R. E., Horner, R. H., Albin, R. W., Storey, K., & Sprague, J. R. (1997). *Functional analysis of problem behavior: A practical assessment guide* (2nd ed.). Pacific Grove, CA: Brookes/Cole.

Scott, T. M., & Eber, L. (2003). Functional assessment and wraparound as systemic school processes: Primary, secondary, and tertiary systems examples. *Journal of Positive Behavior Interventions, 5*, 131–143.

Simonsen, B., Fairbanks, S., Briesch, A., Myers, D., & Sugai, G. (2008). A review of evidence-based practices in classroom management: Considerations for research to practice. *Education and Treatment of Children, 31*, 351–380.

Simonsen, B., MacSuga-Gage, A. S., Briere, D. E., Freeman, J., Myers, D., Scott, T., Sugai, G. (2014). Multi-tiered support framework for teachers' classroom management practices: Overview and case study of building the triangle for teachers. *Journal of Positive Behavior Interventions, 16*, 179–190. doi: 10.1177/1098300713484062

Simonsen, B., Myers, D., Everett, S., Sugai, G. Spencer, R., & LaBreck, C. (2012). Explicitly teaching social skills school-wide: Using a matrix to guide instruction. *Intervention in School and Clinic, 47*, 259–266. doi: 10.1177/1053451211430121

Sugai, G., & Horner, R. H. (1999–2000). Including the functional behavioral assessment technology in schools (invited special issue). *Exceptionality, 8*, 145–148.

Sugai, G., & Horner, R. H. (2002). The evolution of discipline practices: School-wide positive behavior supports. *Child and Family Behavior Therapy, 24*, 23–50.

Sugai, G., & Horner, R. H. (2009). Responsiveness-to-intervention and school-wide positive behavior supports: Integration of multi-tiered approaches. *Exceptionality, 17*, 223–237.

Sugai, G., Horner, R. H., Dunlap, G., Hieneman, M., Lewis, T. J., Nelson, C. M., et al. (2000). Applying positive behavior support and functional behavioral assessment in schools. *Journal of Positive Behavior Interventions, 2*, 131–143.

Sugai, G., & Lewis-Palmer, T. (Eds.) (2004). Invited special issue: Function-based assessment. *Assessment for Effective Instruction, 30*.

Sugai, G., O'Keeffe, B. V., & Fallon, L. M. (2012). A contextual consideration of culture and school-wide positive behavior support. *Journal of Positive Behavior Interventions, 14*, 197–208. doi: 10.1177/1098300711426334

Walker, H. M., Horner, R. H., Sugai, G., Bullis, M., Sprague, J. R., Bricker, D., & Kaufman, M. J. (1996). Integrated approaches to preventing antisocial behavior patterns among school-age children and youth. *Journal of Emotional and Behavioral Disorders, 4*, 194–209.

5

EMERGING ISSUES IN SCHOOL BULLYING RESEARCH AND PREVENTION

DOROTHY L. ESPELAGE, PHD
UNIVERSITY OF ILLINOIS, URBANA-CHAMPAIGN

Bullying and peer victimization among school-age children are associated with serious academic and psychosocial problems that can harm students' school performance in the form of school avoidance, lowered levels of academic achievement, heightened conflictual relations with teachers and students, and poorer school adjustment (Cook, Williams, Guerra, Kim, & Sadek, 2010; Espelage, Hong, Rao, & Low, 2013; Glew, Fan, Katon, & Rivara, 2008; Juvonen, Nishina, & Graham, 2000; Nansel, Haynie, & Simons-Morton, 2003). In addition to negative school consequences, victims, bullies, and bully-victims often report adverse psychological effects, which have the potential to lead to subsequent victimization or perpetration (Espelage, Basile, & Hamburger, 2012; Espelage, Low, & De La Rue, 2012; Juvoven, Nishina, & Graham, 2000) and long-term effects into later adolescence and adulthood (Copeland, Wolke, Angold, & Costello, 2013; Espelage, Low, Rao, Hong, & Little, 2013). As a result, many schools and communities are struggling to understand how to prevent bullying and peer victimization to offset these adverse outcomes. This chapter includes a review of the most up-to-date research findings to help practitioners and researchers understand the etiology of bullying and how best to effectively reduce these behaviors.

DEFINITION OF BULLYING AND PEER VICTIMIZATION

Almost four decades of research have been conducted on bullying and peer victimization, ranging through prevalence studies, etiological investigations, and systematic reviews and evaluations of prevention and intervention programs (see Espelage & Holt, 2012, for review). However, a rigorous debate has recently emerged about how best to define bullying and how to distinguish it from other forms of aggression and/or peer victimization (American Educational Research Association, 2013; Rodkin, Espelage, & Hanish, under review). One of the first predominant definitions of bullying that continues to be used in the literature and in the legal arena is, "A student is being bullied or victimized when he or she is exposed, repeatedly and over time, to negative actions on the part of one or more students" (Olweus, 2010, p. 11). Other definitions have been more explicit. For example, as Smith and Sharp write, "A student is being bullied or picked on when another student says nasty or unpleasant things to him or her. It is also bullying when a student is hit, kicked, threatened, locked inside a room, sent nasty notes, and when no one ever talks to him" (Sharp & Smith, 1991, p. 1). More recent definitions of bullying emphasize observable or nonobservable aggressive behaviors, the repetitive nature of these behaviors, and the imbalance of power between the individual/group perpetrator and victim (Espelage & Swearer, 2011; Ybarra, Espelage, & Mitchell, in press). An imbalance of power exists when the perpetrator or group of perpetrators has more physical, social, or intellectual power than the victim. In a recent examination of a nationally representative study, early and late adolescents who perceived that their perpetrator had more power than they did reported greater adverse outcomes (e.g., depression, suicidal ideation) than victims who did not perceive a power differential (Ybarra, Espelage, & Mitchell, in press). Finally, repetition should be evaluated carefully given that youth who are victims of bullying often change their behaviors in order to minimize the probability of it happening again (Batanova, Espelage, & Rao, in press; Kingsbury & Espelage, 2007). For example, they might stop riding the bus or attending lunch and avoid school and other places where the victimization is occurring.

Since 2010, leading violence and victimization scholars have convened in several meetings hosted by the Department of Education and the Centers for Disease Control to develop a uniform *research* definition. This group defined bullying "as any unwanted aggressive behavior(s) by another youth or group of youths who are not siblings or current dating partners that involves an observed or perceived power imbalance and is repeated multiple times or is highly likely to be repeated. Bullying may inflict harm or distress on the targeted youth including physical, psychological, social, or educational harm" (Gladden, Vivolo-Kantor, Hamburger, & Lumpkin, 2014, p. 7). These behaviors include verbal and physical aggression that ranges in severity from making threats, spreading rumors, and exclusion to physical attacks causing injury, and they can occur face to face and/or through technology (e.g., cell phones, computers). Finally, some bullying behaviors may overlap with aggression that meets the legal definition of harassment, but not all incidents of harassment constitute bullying. Given that bullying co-occurs with other forms of aggression and school violence (Espelage, Low, & De La Rue, 2012; Rodkin, Espelage, & Hanish, in press), educators and scholars should not limit themselves to the traditional definition but rather assess all forms of aggression and victimization. Finally, victimization should not be limited to peer-on-peer experiences only but should be examined as occurring among all school community members, including youth, teachers, school staff, parents, and others (Espelage et al., 2013).

PREVALENCE OF BULLYING AND PEER VICTIMIZATION

Worldwide incidence rates for bullying among school-age youth range from 10% to 30%, and there is a notable increase during the middle school years (see Cook, Williams, Guerra, Kim, & Sadek, 2010, for review). Research findings consistently demonstrate that specific populations are at increased risk of being victimized and/ or bullied by their peers, including students with disabilities (Rose & Espelage, 2012), sexual minority youth (Espelage, Aragon, Birkett, & Koenig, 2008), and African American youth (Low & Espelage, 2013). Two of these groups will be reviewed here. This is in no way an exhaustive review of those youth that are particularly at risk for victimization or those who are overrepresented as bully perpetrators.

Bullying among Students with Disabilities

Early research on bullying and peer victimization emerged from the field of special education (Hoover & Hazler, 1994; Hoover, Oliver, & Thomson, 1993), but a dearth of research addressed bullying experiences among this population until a few years ago. This research indicates that students with disabilities are twice as likely to be identified as perpetrators and victims than students without disabilities (Rose, Espelage, Aragon, & Elliott, 2011; Rose & Espelage, 2012). Students with disabilities that are characterized or have diagnostic criteria associated with low social skills and low communication skills have a higher likelihood for involvement in bullying incidents (Rose, Monda-Amaya, & Espelage, 2011). Indeed, a meta-analysis of 152 studies found that 8 of 10 children with a learning disability (LD) were peer-rated as rejected; 8 of 10 were rated as deficient in social competence and social problem solving; LD students were less often selected as friends by their peers (Baumeister, Storch, & Geffken, 2008).

Recent empirical investigations have suggested that victimization may be predicted by the severity of the disability (Rose, 2010). For example, students with autism may be victimized more (Bejerot & Mörtberg, 2009) and students with learning disabilities may be victimized less than other subgroups of students with disabilities (Wallace, Anderson, Bartholomay, & Hupp, 2002; White & Loeber, 2008). To address subgroup differences among students with disabilities, Rose and Espelage (2012) examined rates of bullying involvement and the intersection of individual attributes among middle school students identified with specific disabilities and their peers without disabilities. Students with emotional and behavioral disorders (EBD) engaged in significantly higher levels of bullying and fighting than other subgroups of students. Additionally, higher levels of anger predicted higher levels of bully perpetration for students with EBD, where higher levels of victimization predicted higher levels of bully perpetration for students with disabilities other than EBD. These findings demonstrate the importance of recognizing the influence of the characteristic differences between subgroups of students with disabilities, as well as the unique influence these characteristics may have on student involvement within the bullying dynamic.

Bullying and the Lesbian, Gay, Bisexual (LGB) Community

A large percentage of bullying among students involves the use of homophobic teasing and slurs, called homophobic teasing or victimization (Espelage, Basile, & Hamburger, 2012; Poteat & Espelage, 2005; Poteat & Rivers, 2010). Bullying and homophobic victimization occur more frequently among LGB youth in American schools than among students who identify as heterosexual (Espelage, Aragon, Birkett, & Koenig, 2008; Robinson & Espelage, 2011, 2012). Some LGB youth report greater depression, anxiety, suicidal behaviors, and truancy than their straight-identified peers (Espelage, Aragon, Birkett, & Koenig, 2008; Robinson & Espelage, 2011). However, peer victimization does not appear to explain all of mental health disparities between LGB and heterosexual youth (Robinson & Espelage, 2012).

Russell, Kosciw, Horn, and Saewyc (2010) highlight four practices that have been shown to promote safety and well-being for LGB youth in schools. First, administrators and staff need to ensure that school nondiscrimination and antibullying policies specifically include statements about actual or perceived sexual orientation or gender identity or expression. Second, it is imperative that teachers receive training and ongoing professional development on how to intervene when homophobic teasing or name-calling occurs. Third, school-based support groups or clubs (e.g., gay–straight alliances; Poteat, Sinclair, DiGiovanni, Koenig, & Russell, 2013) should be created and supported, provided their presence is associated with less victimization related to gender nonconformity and/or sexual orientation. Finally, it is important to include LGB role models or issues in school curricula, including bullying-prevention programming, and access to information and resources through the library, school-based health centers, and other avenues.

BULLYING, PEER VICTIMIZATION, ACADEMIC ACHIEVEMENT, AND ENGAGEMENT

Several national and international research studies relying on cross-sectional data have documented that experiences of being victimized or of bullying other students are associated with decreased academic achievement. Findings from a sample of seventh-, ninth-, and eleventh-graders in an urban public school district also revealed that for each 1-point increase in grade point average, the odds of being a victim versus a bystander decreased by 10% (Glew, Fan, Katon, & Rivara, 2008). These associations are also found when students are followed over time in longitudinal studies (e.g., Juvonen, Wang, & Espinoza, 2011; Schwartz, Gorman, Nakamoto, & Toblin, 2005). Juvonen and colleagues (2011) documented that peer victimization can account for an average of a 1.5 letter grade decrease in one academic subject (e.g., math) across three years of middle school. Moreover, the researchers found that greater self-reported victimization was associated with lower grades and lower teacher-rated academic engagement.

However, a meta-analytic review of 33 studies conducted by Nakamoto and Schwartz (2010) reported that empirical research on this association has produced an incongruent pattern of findings and modest correlations. In fact, the authors reported a small but significant negative correlation between peer victimization and academic achievement under both a random effects model ($r = -.12, p < .001$) and the fixed-effects model ($r = -.10, p < .001$). To complicate the picture, a small number of researchers have also concluded that peer victimization and academic performance are unrelated phenomena (Woods & Wolke, 2004). This research suggests that peer victimization or engaging in bullying results in academic challenges from some students but not all in the same way. Thus, there are likely third variables that explain this association, and these variables are called mediators or moderators. For example, poor academic performance might be a result of victimization at school through mediating influences of internalizing behaviors (DeRosier & Mercer, 2009; Graham, Bellmore, & Mize, 2006; Nishina, Juvonen, & Witkow, 2005). Studies have documented that victims often experience depression, social anxiety, and low self-esteem, which then could contribute to academic challenges; bullies and bully-victims report similar problems (see Cook, Williams, Guerra, Kim, & Sadek, 2010, for meta-analysis).

In addition, some victimized children blame themselves for their victimization, which leads to negative self-perceptions (Batanova, Espelage, & Rao, in press; Graham, Bellmore, & Mize, 2006) and difficulty concentrating on their schoolwork. Consequently, they are likely to receive lower grades (Graham, Bellmore, & Mize, 2006; Lopez & DuBois, 2005; Nakamoto & Schwartz, 2010). Other mediators have also been identified. For example, Beran (2009) reported that peer victimized adolescents are at risk for poor academic achievement if they exhibit disruptive behaviors. Friendship quality and peer social support appear to have a complex moderating role in the association between peer victimization and academic performance (Schwartz, Gorman, Dodge, Pettit, & Bates, 2008).

ETIOLOGY OF BULLYING AND PEER VICTIMIZATION: SOCIAL-ECOLOGY PERSPECTIVE

The onset of bullying, aggression, and peer victimization is best understood from a social-ecological perspective in which individual characteristics of children interact with environmental factors to promote victimization and perpetration (Basile, Espelage, Rivers, McMahon, & Simon, 2009; Espelage, 2004, 2012; Hong & Espelage, 2012). A social ecological framework has been used to explore the risk and protective factors of bullying and peer victimization whereby child and adolescent behavior is shaped by a range of nested contextual systems, including family, peers, and school environments (Bronfenbrenner, 1979; Hong & Espelage, 2012; Espelage & Swearer, 2011). The ecological perspective provides a conceptual framework for investigating the independent and combined impacts of these social contexts and their dynamic, transactional influences on behavioral development. The microsystem includes structures with which children and adolescents have direct contact, such as families, peers, and schools. The mesosystem, another component of the ecological framework, comprises the interrelations among microsystems. This ecological framework has been applied to the conceptualization of bullying perpetration and victimization and highlights reciprocal influences on bullying behaviors among individual, family, school, peer group, community, and society (Espelage, Holt, & Henkel, 2003; Espelage, 2012; Hong & Espelage, 2012).

INDIVIDUAL CHARACTERISTICS

Certain individual characteristics have been implicated in increasing the risk of being a victim of bullying. Boys are victimized more often than girls (Cook, Williams, Guerra, Kim, & Sadek, 2010; Espelage & Holt, 2001), although this depends somewhat on the form of victimization. Boys are more likely to experience physical bullying victimization (e.g., being hit), whereas girls are more likely to be targets of indirect victimization (e.g., social exclusion) (Jeffrey, Miller, & Linn, 2001). One of the few studies that addressed influences of race on bullying found that African American students reported less victimization than white or Hispanic youth (Nansel, Haynie, & Simons-Morton, 2001). Other factors increase the likelihood of bullying others. Boys are more likely to bully peers than girls (Espelage, Holt, & Henkel, 2003; Espelage, Green, & Polanin, 2011), and individuals with behavioral, emotional, or learning problems are more likely to perpetrate bullying than their peers (Rose & Espelage, 2012). Bullies, particularly male bullies, tend to be physically stronger than their peers. Juvonen, Graham, and Schuster (2003) found that black middle school youth were more likely to be categorized as bullies and bully-victims than white students. Another study found that the reported incidences of bullying perpetration were slightly higher for Hispanic students than for their black and white peers (Nansel, Haynie, & Simons-Morton, 2001).

FAMILY CHARACTERISTICS

Parental monitoring and supervision play an important role in youth's experiences with bullying and victimization. Bullies tend to have parents who do not provide adequate supervision or who are not actively involved in the lives of their children (Espelage, Bosworth, & Simon, 2000; Georgiou & Fanti, 2010; Low & Espelage, 2013). Adolescents are likely to engage in bullying behaviors when their daily activities are not monitored by adults, when they are not held accountable for their actions, or when the family unit is not able to intervene and correct the bullying behaviors. In other instances, parents may encourage the use of aggressive and retaliatory behaviors. Children who learn to be aggressive from their parents or who learn that bullying is an acceptable means of retaliation are more likely to bully others in school (Espelage, Low, Polanin, & Brown, 2013; Georgiou & Fanti, 2010). The family environment can also influence whether children become victims of bullying. Children who are victims of bullying more often come from families with histories of abuse or inconsistent parenting (Espelage, Low, & De La Rue, 2012; Georgiou & Fanti, 2010), potentially because they may not be prepared to counteract the bullying they encounter at school.

Supportive familial relations can also buffer the impact of involvement with bully experiences. When victims of bullying have warm relationships with their families, they have more positive outcomes, both emotionally and behaviorally (Bowes, Maughan, Caspi, Moffitt, & Arseneault, 2010; Holt & Espelage, 2007). These positive parent–child interactions provide children with the opportunity to talk about their bullying experiences or can provide guidance on how to cope with these events. Bowes and colleagues (2010) also found that supportive relationships with siblings could serve to aid in bully-victims' resilience.

SCHOOL CHARACTERISTICS

Teachers and Staff Attitudes/Behaviors

It has been noted that there are discrepancies between how teachers and staff perceive bullying and how their students perceive it. Many teachers are unaware of how serious and extensive the bullying is within their schools and are often ineffective in being able to identify bullying incidents (Bradshaw, Sawyer, & O'Brennan, 2007; Kochenderfer-Ladd & Pelletier, 2008). Divergences between staff and student estimates of the rates of bullying are seen in elementary, middle, and high school, with staff consistently underestimating the frequency of these events (Bradshaw, Sawyer, & O'Brennan, 2007). In a study conducted by Bradshaw and colleagues (2007), these differences were most pronounced in elementary school, where less than 1% of elementary school staff reported bullying rates similar to that reported by students.

Very few teachers reported that they would ignore or do nothing if a student reported an incident of bullying; instead, many teachers reported that they would intervene with the bully and the victim (Bradshaw, Sawyer, & O'Brennan, 2007). Despite the good intentions of school officials, many students feel that teachers and staff are not doing enough to prevent bullying (Bradshaw, Sawyer, & O'Brennan, 2007). This belief of students that teachers will not be able to help them or that if they "tattle," the situation may become worse is the reason many students hesitate to report incidents to teachers, which may also explain why teachers perceive a lower prevalence of bullying (Craig, Henderson, & Murphy, 2000).

Broader School Climate

Studies consistently report that negative school environmental factors (e.g., policies, staff reaction to bullying) can lead to an increase in the frequency of bullying, aggression, and victimization and reduce the likelihood of students feeling safe in their school (Espelage, Bosworth, & Simon, 2000; Goldweber, Waasdorp, & Bradshaw, 2013). In contrast, youth with positive perceptions of their school environment are less likely to exhibit externalizing behaviors (e.g., aggression) (Espelage, Bosworth, & Simon, 2000; Goldweber, Waasdorp, & Bradshaw, 2013; Totura et al., 2009). In a recent multi-informant study, Espelage and colleagues (in press) surveyed 3616 sixth-grade students across 36 middle schools in the Midwest and nearly 1500 teachers/staff to examine school-level predictors of aggression and willingness to intervene. In schools where teachers/staff perceived that their school was committed to bully prevention had fewer student reports of aggression and victimization and a greater willingness to intervene. The authors concluded that schools need to have an ongoing plan to prevent and intervene when bullying occurs.

Classroom-Level Predictors

Studies that employ social network analysis to examine classroom structure and its impact on aggression find that when classrooms have rigid hierarchical social structures, victimization becomes more stable because there are few opportunities to maneuver into different roles or social positions (Schäfer, Korn, Brodbeck, Wolke, & Schulz, 2005). On the other hand, when classrooms are more democratic and the social power is more evenly distributed, a less hostile environment for students is created (Ahn, Garandeau, & Rodkin, 2010). These studies, taken together, suggest that prevention should intervene at all levels of the school's ecology.

PEERS' CHARACTERISTICS

Peers can be a source of enormous support for students, but the lack of this peer connection can make incidents of bullying more severe. Additionally, the way classmates respond to bullying has significant effects on whether the bullying continues. Bullying rarely takes place in an isolated dyadic interaction but instead often occurs in the presence of other students (Espelage, Holt, & Henkel, 2003). Students may serve to perpetuate bullying by actively joining in or passively accepting the bullying behaviors, while on the other hand students can intervene to stop bullying or defend the victim (Espelage, Green, & Polanin, 2011; Flaspohler, Elfstrom, Vanderzee, Sink, & Birchmeier, 2009; Salmivalli, 2010). Inaction on behalf of other students seems to be more prevalent; most students reinforce bullies by passively watching the bullying occur (Flaspohler, Elfstrom, Vanderzee, Sink, & Birchmeier, 2009).

Although decades of research point to the role of empathy in promoting prosocial behavior and inhibiting antisocial behavior, only recently have studies specifically examined how empathy relates to willingness to intervene in bullying scenarios or defender behavior (Caravita, DiBlasio, & Salmivalli, 2009; Gini, Albiero, Benelli, & Altoe, 2007; Gini, Pozzoli, & Hauser, 2011; Gini, Pozzoli, Borghi, & Franzoni, 2008; Nickerson, Mele, & Princiotta, 2008; Pöyhönen, Juvonen, & Salmivalli, 2010; Stavrinides, Georgiou, & Theofanous, 2010). Taken together, these studies find that among early adolescent samples, defending behavior is associated with greater empathy (Gini, Albiero, Benelli, & Altoe, 2007; Gini, Pozzoli, Borghi, & Franzoni, 2008; Nickerson, Mele, & Princiotta, 2008; Stavrinides, Georgiou, & Theofanous, 2010), and bullies appear to be morally competent but lacking in morally compassionate behavior in comparison to victims or defenders (Gini, Pozzoli, & Hauser, 2011). However, peer influence appears to interact with individual behavior. Consistent with Rigby and Johnson's study, Pozzoli and Gini (2010) found that perceived positive peer pressure to defend a victim interacted with personal responsibility to predict defending. That is, students who held moderate or high levels of personal responsibility were more likely to defend a victim if they perceived their peers to hold a positive view toward defender behavior. Finally, only one recent empirical study found that greater bullying perpetration within one's peer group was highly predictive of less individual willingness to intervene, suggesting that any prevention efforts to address bystander or defender intervention must first reduce the level of bullying within peer groups (Espelage, Green, & Polanin, 2011).

Increasingly, school-based bullying prevention programs are focusing their attention on encouraging bystanders to intervene (e.g., students and teachers who are watching bullying situations or know about the bullying). A recent meta-analysis synthesized bullying prevention programs' effectiveness in altering bystander behavior to intervene in bullying situations (Polanin, Espelage, & Pigott, 2012). Evidence from 12 school-based interventions, involving a total of 12,874 students, revealed that overall the programs were successful (Hedges' $g = 0.20$, C.I.: 0.11, 0.29, $p < .001$), with larger effects for high school samples compared to K–8 student samples (HS ES = 0.43, K–8 ES = 0.14; $p < .05$). This meta-analysis indicated that programs were effective at changing bystander intervening behavior, both on a practical and on a statistically significant level.

Bystander approaches need to consider the developmental trends in victim and bully status. The association between peers and bullying can also look different depending on the age of students. For younger students in primary (or elementary) school, there tends to be a lack of stability for the victim role, whereas students who engage in bullying tend to remain in this role for a longer, more stable period of time (Schäfer, Korn, Brodbeck, Wolke, & Schulz, 2005). At this age, bullying perpetration seems to be directed at multiple targets, resulting in multiple victims and lower stability. The environment of primary schools is such that social hierarchies are not as pronounced; therefore, students will more often confront a bully or retaliate when bullied. By the time students are in secondary school (or middle school), the bully and victim roles are relatively stable (Schäfer, Korn, Brodbeck, Wolke, & Schulz, 2005). Those students who are in the victim role are less likely to be able to maneuver away from this. In addition, students who occupy the bullying role appear to continue to target the same individuals (Schäfer, Korn, Brodbeck, Wolke, & Schulz, 2005). The social structure of students in secondary schools is more visible, which makes maneuvering to different roles more challenging.

WHAT WORKS IN BULLYING PREVENTION?

Despite the personal and societal costs of youth aggression and bullying involvement and associated correlates, the efficacy of school violence and bullying prevention programs has varied across countries and contexts (Espelage, 2012; Ttofi & Farrington, 2011). More recently, there has been an increase in bullying prevention/intervention programs; however, their efficacy varies tremendously across contexts, and program effects are often modest (Ttofi & Farrington, 2011) or have produced mixed results (Pearce, Cross, Monks, Waters, & Falconer, 2011). Specific program elements that were associated with decreases in bully perpetration included (Ttofi & Farrington, 2011) parent training and meetings, improved playground supervision, disciplinary methods, classroom management, teacher training, classroom rules, whole-school antibullying policy, school conferences, information for parents, and cooperative group work among teachers and staff. Decreases in victimization were associated with cooperative group work among teachers and staff, which interestingly, was defined as teachers working together to learn how to implement cooperative learning and role-playing activities with their students around bullying. Thus, an important first step in preventing bullying and promoting student bystander intervention is to develop a comprehensive prevention approach. This approach should focus on developing and implementing a bully policy, training and supervising teachers and staff, and creating an active stakeholder group to monitor efforts.

The Olweus Bullying Prevention Program (OBPP, Olweus & Limber, 2010) is used in many U.S. school districts and is supported by a number of state departments of education. However, the efficacy of this program in the United States is questionable (Espelage, 2012). Studies conducted by the OBPP in the U.S. schools have been methodologically limited and only marginally positive. For example, a

1998 evaluation of the OBPP in six South Carolina districts did not include random assignment and did not include a long-term follow-up. Although the original design called for a two-year evaluation, pre-post data were collected only in the first year because implementation was inadequate during year two (Olweus & Limber, 2010). Moreover, the pre-post data have yet to appear in a peer-reviewed publication. Since then, only one U.S.-based randomized controlled trial (RCT) study of the OBPP has been published, and that included an RCT of 10 schools, where reductions of bullying were reported only for white students (Bauer, Lozano, & Rivara, 2007). Given the dearth of support for this program, the OBPP is no longer on the Substance and Mental Health Services Health Administration (SAMSHA) National Registry of Evidence-Based Programs (www.nrepp.samhsa.gov). However, it is considered a promising program by the Blueprints for healthy youth development (www .blueprintsprograms.com). Research on the efficacy of the OBPP in U.S. schools is ongoing, and it will be important for the developers to demonstrate under what conditions this program yields reductions in bullying and victimization.

Social-Emotional Learning (SEL) Approaches

In contrast, school-based violence prevention programs that facilitate social and emotional learning skills, address interpersonal conflict, and teach emotion management have been very successful in reducing youth violence and disruptive behaviors in classrooms (Wilson & Lipsey, 2007). Many of these social-emotional and social-cognitive intervention programs target risk and promotive factors that have consistently been associated with aggression, bullying, and violence in cross-sectional and longitudinal studies (Basile, Espelage, Rivers, McMahon, & Simon, 2009; Espelage, Basile, & Hamberger, 2012; Espelage, Holt, & Henkel, 2003), including anger, empathy, perspective taking, respect for diversity, attitudes supportive of aggression, coping, intentions to intervene to help others, and communication and problem-solving skills.

Overall, social emotional learning (SEL) involves "the systematic development of a core set of social and emotional skills that help children more effectively handle life challenges and thrive in both their learning and their social environments" (Ragozzino & Utne O'Brien, 2009). SEL programs can provide schools, after-school programs, and youth community centers with a research-based approach to building skills and promoting positive individual and peer attitudes that can contribute to the prevention of bullying. Although this chapter focuses on SEL programs situated in schools, these programs or frameworks are also being developed and implemented in settings outside of schools (see www.casel.org for a review).

Social emotional learning as a framework emerged from influences across different movements that focused on resiliency and on teaching social and emotional competencies to children and adolescents (Elias et al., 1997). SEL programs use social skill instruction to address behavior, discipline, safety, and academics to help youth become self-aware, manage their emotions, build social skills (empathy, perspective taking, respect for diversity), friendship skill building, and making positive decisions (Zins, Weissberg, Wang, & Walberg, 2004). A study of more than 213 SEL-based programs found that by implementing a quality SEL curriculum, a school can expect better student behavior and an 11 percentile increase in academic test scores (Durlak, Weissberg, Dymnicki, Taylor, & Schellinger, 2011). Schools elect to implement these programs because of the gains that they see in achievement and prosocial behavior. Students exposed to SEL activities feel safer and more connected to school and academics, and SEL programs build work habits in addition to social skills, and kids and teachers build strong relationships (Zins, Weissberg, Wang, & Walberg, 2004).

In summary, social-emotional learning approaches to prevention are showing promise in reducing aggression and promoting prosocial behavior (Brown, Low, Smith, & Haggerty, 2011; Espelage, Low, Polanin, Brown, 2013; Frey et al., 2005). This success is largely due to the fact that SEL school-based programs parallel the hallmarks of the prevention science framework. First, these programs draw from the scientific literature on the etiological underpinnings of aggression, bullying, school violence, and other problematic behaviors among children and adolescents (Merrell, 2010). Second, risk (e.g., anger, impulse control) and promotive (e.g., empathy, communication skills) factors are identified from the etiological literature and targeted through direct instruction of skills and opportunities to use skills in different contexts. Third, in relation to bystander intervention, these programs include discussions and content about the barriers or challenges (e.g., fear of being targeted, losing friends) that youth face when they attempt to intervene on behalf of a victim of aggression. Several randomized controlled trials (RCTs) have attended to the rigorous evaluation of the intervention effects (Brown, Low, Smith, & Haggerty, 2011; Espelage, Low, Polanin, & Brown, 2013), which is an additional hallmark of prevention science. RCTs of SEL programs have identified implementation as a critical component of producing reductions in aggression and increases in prosocial behavior, but as the field moves forward, a more deliberate focus on implementation, dissemination, and sustainability is needed in order to fully capture the prevention science impact of SEL programs. As schools are increasingly pressed to find time in the day to address psychosocial issues, SEL programs that prevent aggression, victimization and its correlates (e.g., social rejection) and that also simultaneously improve academic engagement should be rigorously evaluated to make convincing arguments to teachers and school administrators that the use of these resources will produce noticeable benefits. The Collaborative for Academic, Social, and Emotional Learning (2003, www.casel.org) has reviewed many SEL approaches and is a great resource for teachers who want to improve the social-emotional aspects of their classrooms and schools.

Positive Behavior Support Framework

Positive behavior support framework (PBIS) is a dominant paradigm in schools internationally and emerged as a result of the 1997 reauthorization of the Individuals with Disabilities Education Act (IDEA), resulting in the formation of the National Center on Positive Behavioral Interventions and Supports at the University of Oregon. Also referred to as school-wide positive behavior support (SWPBS), this model is based on principles of applied behavior analysis and the prevention approach of positive behavior support (Lewis & Sugai, 1999; Sugai et al., 2000; Sugai & Horner, 2002). RCTs of school-wide PBIS in elementary schools have shown that high-quality implementation of the model is associated with significant reductions in office discipline referrals and suspensions (Bradshaw, Mitchell, & Leaf, 2010; Horner et al., 2009) and in teacher ratings of classroom behavior problems and aggression, emotion regulation problems, bullying perpetration, and peer rejection (Bradshaw, Waasdorp, & Leaf, 2012; Waasdorp, Bradshaw, & Leaf, 2012), yet the effect size data for reductions in peer victimization were low.

School Climate Improvement Process

Research suggests that both effective risk prevention (e.g., bullying and other forms of school violence) and health promotion (e.g., safe, supportive, engaging schools) efforts are, in essence, school climate reform efforts (Battistich, 2008; Berkowitz, 2000; Cohen, 2006, 2013). "School climate," or culture, refers to the quality and character of school life. School climate is based on patterns of people's experience of school life and reflects norms, goals, values, interpersonal relationships, teaching, learning, leadership practices, and organizational structures (National School Climate Council, 2007). The school climate improvement process reflects a series of overlapping systemic or school-wide processes that promote safe, supportive, engaging and flourishing schools (for review, see Cohen, Espelage et al., in press): (1) transparent, democratically informed *leadership* (Berkowitz, 2011) (2) *engaging* the students, parents, and ideally community members, as well as school personnel, to be colearners and coleaders in the improvement efforts (school–home–community partnerships) (Morton & Montgomery, 2011); (3) *measurement practices* that recognize the social, emotional, and civic dimensions of learning and school life (Cohen, McCabe, Michelli, & Pickeral, 2009); (4) *improvement goals that are tailored* to the unique needs of the students and school community (Espelage & Poteat, 2012); (5) *adult learning* and professional learning communities that support capacity building (Davis, Darling-Hammond, LaPointe, & Meyerson, 2005); and (6) prosocial education (Durlak, Weissberg, Dymnicki, Taylor, & Schellinger, 2011; Espelage, Low, Polanin, & Brown, 2013).

BULLYING PREVENTION AND INTERVENTION: SUMMARY OF THE FIELD

Much is understood about the correlates of bullying and about the short- and long-term outcomes for all youth involved. However, the reality is that school-based anti-bullying programs and efforts are yielding modest effects in reducing bullying and peer victimization (Espelage, 2012). I have argued for many years that the efforts in place are flawed in several ways. First, most antibullying programs that were included in previous meta-analyses did not stem from educational and developmental theory. Thus, the movement back to character education, problem solving, social-emotional learning, and school climate reform as ways to promote positive relationships within schools offers some promise. Second, many bully prevention efforts in our schools are often short term and fail to bring about sustainable change because they do not engage all members of the school family, including adults and parents (Espelage, 2012). Third, the majority of the programs fail to direct interventions at the proximal peer social ecology that promotes and sustains bullying perpetration (Espelage, 2012; Espelage & Holt, 2012). Fourth, many evaluations of these programs do not address the changing demographics of communities and fail to incorporate components addressing key potential moderators of effects such as race, fidelity, and socioeconomic status (Espelage & Poteat, 2012). Fifth, many do not target shared underlying risk factors (e.g., anger, impulsivity, lack of empathy) associated with persistent aggression. Sixth, many school-based bully prevention programs (e.g., Olweus, SEL) often require resources (e.g., funding, teacher time, instructional time) that schools are reluctant to allocate given the demands on testing (Cohen, 2006). Finally, schools have unique ecologies with varying issues, administrative support, professional development opportunities, resources, and parental involvement that may need to be considered as programs are adapted (Espelage & Poteat, 2012).

REFERENCES

Ahn, H., Garandeau, C. F., & Rodkin, P. C. (2010). Effects of classroom embeddedness and density on the social status of aggressive and victimized children. *Journal of Early Adolescence, 30,* 76–101. doi: 10.1177/0272431609350922

American Educational Research Association. (2013). *Prevention of bullying in schools, colleges, and universities: Research report and recommendations.* Washington, DC: American Educational Research Association.

Basile, K. C., Espelage, D. L., Rivers, I., McMahon, P. M., & Simon, T. R. (2009). The theoretical and empirical links between bullying behavior and male sexual violence perpetration. *Aggression and Violent Behavior, 14*(5), 336–347. doi: 10.1016/j.avb.2009.06.001

Batanova, M., Espelage, D.L., & Rao, M. (in press). Early adolescents' willingness to intervene: what roles do attributions, affect, coping, and self-reported victimization play? *Journal of School Psychology.*

Battistich, V.A. (2008). Character education, prevention, and positive youth development. *Journal of Research in Character Education, 6,* 81–90.

Bauer, N. S., Lozano, P., & Rivara, F. P. (2007). The effectiveness of the Olweus Bullying Prevention Program in public middle schools: A controlled trial. *Journal of Adolescent Health, 40,* 266–274. http://dx.doi .org/10.1016/j.jadohealth.2006.10.005.

Baumeister, A. L., Storch, E. A., & Geffken, G. R. (2008). Peer victimization in children with learning disabilities. *Child and Adolescent Social Work Journal, 25,* 11–23. doi: 10.1007/s10560-007-0109-6

Bejerot, S., & Mörtberg, E. (2009). Do autistic traits play a role in the bullying of obsessive-compulsive disorder and social phobia sufferers? *Psychopathology, 42,* 170–176. doi: 10.1159/000207459

Beran, T. (2009). Correlates of peer victimization and achievement: An exploratory model. *Psychology in the Schools, 46,* 348–361. doi: 10.1002/pits.20380

Berkowitz, M. W. (2000). Character education as prevention. In W. B. Hansen, S. M. Giles, & M. D. Fearnow-Kenney (Eds.), *Improving prevention effectiveness* (pp. 37–45). Greensboro, NC: Tanglewood Research.

Berkowitz, M. W. (2011). Leading schools of character. In A. M. Blankstein & P. D. Houston (Eds.), *The soul of educational leadership series:* Vol. 9. *Leadership for social justice and democracy in our schools* (pp. 93–121). Thousand Oaks, CA: Corwin.

Bowes, L., Maughan, B., Caspi, A., Moffitt, T. E., & Arseneault, L. (2010). Families promote emotional and behavioural resilience to bullying: Evidence of an environmental effect. *Journal of Child Psychology and Psychiatry, 51*(7), 809–817. doi: 10.1111/j.1469-7610.2010.02216.x

Bradshaw, C. P., Mitchell, M. M., & Leaf, P. J. (2010). Examining the effects of School-Wide Positive Behavioral Interventions and Supports on student outcomes: Results from a randomized controlled effectiveness trial in elementary schools. *Journal of Positive Behavior Interventions, 12,* 133–148. doi: 10.1177/1098300709334798

Bradshaw, C. P., Sawyer, A. L., & O'Brennan, L. M. (2007). Bullying and peer victimization at school: Perceptual differences between students and school staff. *School Psychology Review, 36,* 361–382.

Bradshaw, C. P., Waasdorp, T. E., & Leaf, P. J. (2012). Effects of school-wide positive behavioral interventions and supports on child behavior problems. *Pediatrics, 130*(5), e1136–e1145. doi: 10.1542/peds.2012-0243

Bronfenbrenner, U. (1979). *The ecology of human development: Experiments by nature and design.* Cambridge, MA: Harvard University Press.

Brown, E. C., Low, S., Smith, B. H., & Haggerty, K. P. (2011). Outcomes from a school-randomized controlled trial of STEPS to RESPECT: A Bullying Prevention Program. *School Psychology Review, 40*, 423–443.

Caravita, S., DiBlasio, P., & Salmivalli, C. (2009). Unique and interactive effects of empathy and social status on involvement in bullying. *Social Development, 18*, 140–163. doi: 10.1111/j.1467-9507.2008.00465.x

Cohen, J. (2006). Social, emotional, ethical and academic education: Creating a climate for learning, participation in democracy and well-being. *Harvard Educational Review, 76*(2) (Summer), 201–237. www .hepg.org/her/abstract/8

Cohen, J. (2013). Effective bully prevention efforts and school climate reform. In M. Masiello & D. Schroeder (Eds.), *A public health approach to bullying prevention.* Washington, DC: American Public Health Association.

Cohen, J., McCabe, E. M, Michelli, N. M., & Pickeral, T. (2009). School climate: Research, policy, teacher education and practice. *Teachers College Record, 111*(1), 180–213. www.tcrecord.org/Content .asp?ContentId=15220

Collaborative for Academic, Social, and Emotional Learning (CASEL). (2003). *Safe and sound: An educational leader's guide to evidence based social and emotional learning (SEL) programs.* Chicago: Author.

Cook, C. R., Williams, K. R., Guerra, N. G., Kim, T. E., & Sadek, S. (2010). Predictors of bullying and victimization in childhood and adolescence: A meta-analytic investigation. *School Psychology Quarterly, 25*, 65–83. doi: 10.1037/a0020149

Copeland, W. E., Wolke, D., Angold, A., & Costello, E. J. (2013). Adult psychiatric outcomes of bullying and being bullies by peers in childhood and adolescence. *JAMA Psychiatry.* doi: 10.1001/ jamapsychiatry.2013.504

Craig, W. M., Henderson, K., & Murphy, J. G. (2000). Perspective teachers' attitudes toward bullying and victimization. *School Psychology International, 21*, 5–21. doi: 0.1177/0143034300211001

Davis, S., Darling-Hammond, L., LaPointe, M., & Meyerson, D. (2005). *School leadership study: Developing successful principals.* Stanford, CA: Stanford University, Stanford Educational Leadership Institute.

DeRosier, M. E., & Mercer, S. H. (2009). Perceived behavioral atypicality as a predictor of social rejection and peer victimization: Implications for emotional adjustment and academic achievement. *Psychology in the Schools, 46*, 375–387. doi: 10.1002/pits.20382

Durlak, J. A., Weissberg, R. P., Dymnicki, A. B., Taylor, R. D., & Schellinger, K. B. (2011). The Impact of enhancing students' social and emotional learning: A meta-analysis of school-based universal interventions. *Child Development, 82*, 405–432. doi: 10.1111/j.1467-8624.2010.01564.x

Elias, M. J., Zins, J. E., Weissberg, K. S., Greenberg, M. T., Haynes, M., Kessler, R., et al. (1997). *Promoting social and emotional learning: Guidelines for educators.* Alexandria, VA: Association for Supervision and Curriculum Development.

Espelage, D. L. (2004). An ecological perspective to school-based bullying prevention. *The Prevention Researcher, 11*, 3–6.

Espelage, D. L. (2012). Bullying prevention: A research dialogue with Dorothy Espelage. *Prevention Researcher, 19*, 3, 17–19.

Espelage, D. L., Anderman, E., Brown, V., Jones, A., Lane, K., McMahon, S. D., Reddy, L. A., & Reynolds, C. R. (2013). Understanding and preventing violence directed against teachers: Recommendations for a national research, practice, and policy agenda. *American Psychologist* (February–March), 75–87. doi: 10.1037/a0031307

Espelage, D. L., Aragon, S. R., Birkett, M., & Koenig, B. W. (2008). Homophobic teasing, psychological outcomes, and sexual orientation among high school students: What influences do parents and schools have? *School Psychology Review, 37*, 202–216.

Espelage, D. L., Basile, K. C., & Hamburger, M. E. (2012). Bullying experiences and co-occurring sexual violence perpetration among middle school students: Shared and unique risk factors. *Journal of Adolescent Health, 50*, 60–65. doi: 10.1016/j.jadohealth.2011.07.015

Espelage, D. L., Bosworth, K., & Simon, T. R. (2000). Examining the social context of bullying behaviors in early adolescence. *Journal of Counseling and Development, 78*, 326–333. doi: 10.1002/j.1556-6676.2000. tb01914.x

Espelage, D. L., Green, H., & Polanin, J. (2011). Willingness to intervene in bullying episodes among middle school students: Individual and peer-group influences. *The Journal of Early Adolescence*, 1–26.

Espelage, D. L., & Holt, M. L. (2001). Bullying and victimization during early adolescence: Peer influences and psychosocial correlates. *Journal of Emotional Abuse, 2*(3), 123–142. doi: 10.1300/j135v02n02.08

Espelage, D. L., & Holt, M. K. (2012). Understanding and preventing bullying and sexual harassment in school. In K. R. Harris, S. Graham, T. Urdan, S. Graham, J. M. Royer, & M. Zeidner, *APA educational psychology handbook*: Vol. 2. *Individual differences and cultural and contextual factors* (pp. 391–416). Washington, DC: American Psychological Association.

Espelage, D. L., Holt, M. K., & Henkel, R. R. (2003). Examination of peer-group contextual effects on aggression during early adolescence. *Child Development, 74*,(1), 205–220. doi: 10.1111/1467-8624.00531

Espelage, D. L., Hong, J. S., Rao, M. A., & Low, S. (2013). Relationship between relational and verbal/physical victimization and academic performance in middle school students. *Theory into Practice, 52*(4), 233–240. doi: 10.1080/00405841.2013.829724

Espelage, D. L., Low, S., & De La Rue, L. (2012). Relations between peer victimization subtypes, family violence, and psychological outcomes during adolescence. *Psychology of Violence, 2*, 313–324. doi: 10.1037/a0027386

Espelage, D. L., Low, S., Polanin, J., & Brown, E. (2013). The impact of a middle-school program to reduce aggression, victimization, and sexual violence. *Journal of Adolescent Health, 53*(2), 180–186. doi: 10.1016/j.jadohealth.2013.02.021

Espelage, D. L., Low, S., Rao, M. A., Hong, J. S., & Little, T. (2013). Family violence, bullying, fighting, and substance use among adolescents: A longitudinal transactional model. *Journal of Research on Adolescence*. Online first.

Espelage, D. L., Polanin, J., & Low, S. (in press). Teacher & staff perceptions of school environment as predictors of student aggression, victimization, and willingness to intervene in bullying situations. *School Psychology Quarterly*.

Espelage, D. L., & Poteat, V. P. (2012). School-based prevention of peer relationship problems. In B. Altmaier & J-I Hansen (Eds.), *The Oxford handbook of counseling psychology* (pp. 703–722). New York: Oxford University Press.

Espelage, D. L., & Swearer, S. M. (Eds.). (2011). *Bullying in North American schools* (2nd ed.). New York: Routledge.

Flaspohler, P. D., Elfstrom, J. L., Vanderzee, K. L., Sink, H. E., & Birchmeier, Z. (2009). Stand by me: The effects of peer and teacher support in mitigating the impact of bullying on quality of life. *Psychology in the Schools, 46*(7), 636–649. doi: 10.1002/pits.20404

Frey, K. S., Hirschstein, M. K., Snell, J. L., Edstrom, L. V., MacKenzie, E. P., & Broderick, C. J. (2005). Reducing playground bullying and supporting beliefs: An experimental trial of the Steps to Respect program. *Developmental Psychology, 41*, 479–491. doi: 10.1037/0012-1649.41.3.479

Georgiou, S. N., & Fanti, K. A. (2010). A transactional model of bullying and victimization. *Social Psychology of Education, 13*(3), 295–311. doi: 10.1007/s11218-010-9116-0

Gini, G., Albiero, P., Benelli, B., & Altoè, G. (2007). Does empathy predict adolescents' bullying and defending behavior? *Aggressive Behavior, 33*, 467–476. doi: 10.1002/ab.20204

Gini, G., Pozzoli, T., Borghi, F., & Franzoni, L. (2008). The role of bystanders in students' perception of bullying and sense of safety. *Journal of School Psychology, 46*, 617–638. doi: 10.1016/j.jsp.2008.02.001

Gini, G., Pozzoli, T., & Hauser, M. (2011). Bullies have enhanced moral competence to judge relative to victims, but lack moral compassion. *Personality & Individual Differences, 50*, 603–608. doi: 10.1016/j.paid.2010.12.002

Gladden, R. M., Vivolo-Kantor, A. M., Hamburger, M. E., & Lumpkin, C. D. (2014). *Bullying surveillance among youths: Uniform definitions for public health and recommended data elements*, version 1.0. Atlanta, GA; National Center for Injury Prevention and Control, Centers for Disease Control and Prevention and U.S. Department of Education.

Glew, G. M., Fan, M., Katon, W., & Rivara, F. P. (2008). Bullying and school safety. *The Journal of Pediatrics, 152*, 123–128. doi: 10.1016/j.jpeds.2007.05.045

Goldweber, A., Waasdorp, T. E., & Bradshaw, C. P. (2013). Examining the link between bullying behaviors and perceptions of safety and belonging among secondary school students. *Journal of School Psychology, 51*, 469–485.

Graham, S., Bellmore, A. D., & Mize, J. (2006). Peer victimization, aggression, and their co-occurrence in middle schools: Pathways to adjustment problems. *Journal of Abnormal Child Psychology, 34*(3), 363–378. doi: 10.1007/s10802-006-9030-2

Holt, M. K., & Espelage, D. L. (2007). Perceived social support among bullies, victims, and bully-victims. *Journal of Youth and Adolescence, 36*(6), 984–994. doi: 10.1007/s10964-006-9153-3

Hong, J. S., & Espelage, D. L. (2012). A review of research on bullying and peer victimization in school: An ecological systems analysis. *Aggression and Violent Behavior, 17*, 311–312. doi: 10.1016/j.avb.2012.03.003

Hoover, J. H., & Hazler, R. J. (1994). Bullies and victims. *Elementary School Guidance and Counseling, 25*, 212–220.

Hoover, J. H., Oliver, R., & Thomson, K. (1993). Perceived victimization by school bullies: New research and future direction. *Journal of Humanistic Education and Development, 32*, 76–84. doi: 10.1002/j.2164-4683.1993.tb00133.x

Jeffrey, L. R., Miller, D., & Linn, M. (2001). Middle school bullying as a context for the development of passive observers to the victimization of others. *Journal of Emotional Abuse, 2*(2–3), 143–156. doi: 10.1300/J135v02n02 09

Juvonen, J., Graham, S., & Schuster, M. A. (2003). Bullying among young adolescents: The strong, the weak, and the troubled. *Pediatrics, 112*, 1231–1237. doi: 10.10.1542/Peds.112.6.12.1231

Juvonen, J., Nishina, A., & Graham, S. (2000). Peer harassment, psychological adjustment, and school functioning in early adolescence. *Journal of Educational Psychology, 92*, 349–359. doi: 10.1037/0022-0663.92.2.349

Juvonen, J., Wang, Y., & Espinoza, G. (2011). Bullying experiences and compromised academic performance across middle school grades. *Journal of Early Adolescence, 31*, 152–173. doi: 10.1177/0272431610379415

Kingsbury, W. L. & Espelage, D. (2007). Attribution style and coping along the bully-victim continuum. *Scientia Paedagogica Experimentalis, 64*, 71–102.

Kochenderfer-Ladd, B., & Pelletier, M. E. (2008). Teachers' views and beliefs about bullying: Influences on classroom management strategies and students' coping with peer victimization. *Journal of School Psychology, 46*, 431–453. doi: 10.1016/j.jsp.2007.07.005

Lewis, T. J., & Sugai, G. (1999). Effective behavior support: A systems approach to proactive school-wide management. *Focus on Exceptional Children, 31*(6), 1–24.

Lopez, C., & DuBois, D. D. (2005). Peer victimization and rejection: Investigation of an integrative model of effects on emotional, behavioral, and academic adjustment in early adolescence. *Journal of Clinical Child and Adolescent Psychology, 34*, 25–36. doi: 10.1207/s15374424jccp3401

Low, S., & Espelage, D. L. (2013). Differentiating cyber bullying perpetration from other forms of peer aggression: Commonalities across race, individual, and family predictors. *Psychology of Violence, 3*, 39–52. doi: 10.1037/a0030308

Merrell, K. W. (2010). Linking prevention science and social and emotional learning: The Oregon Resiliency project. *Psychology in the Schools, 47*(1), 55–70.

Morton, M., & Montgomery, P. (2011). Youth empowerment programs for improving self-efficacy and self-esteem of adolescents. *Campbell Systematic Reviews, 5*. doi: 10.4073/csr.2011.5

Nakamoto, J., & Schwartz, D. (2010). Is peer victimization associated with academic achievement? A meta-analytic review. *Social Development, 19*, 221–242. doi: 10.1111/j.1467-9507.2009.00539.x

Nansel, T. R., Haynie, D. L., & Simons-Morton, B. G. (2003). The association of bullying and victimization with middle school adjustment. *Journal of Applied School Psychology, 19*, 45–61. doi: 10.1300/J008v19n02_04

National School Climate Council. (2007). *The school climate challenge: Narrowing the gap between school climate research and school climate policy, practice guidelines and teacher education policy*. New York: Author. Retrieved January 29, 2012, from www.schoolclimate.org/climate/documents/policy/school-climate-challenge-web.pdf.

Nickerson, A. B., Mele, D., & Princiotta, D. (2008). Attachment and empathy as predictors of roles as defenders or outsiders in bullying interactions. *Journal of School Psychology, 46*, 687–703. doi: 10.1016/j.jsp.2008.06.002

Nishina, A., Juvonen, J., & Witkow, M. R. (2005). Sticks and stones may break my bones, but names will make me feel sick: The psychosocial, somatic, and scholastic consequences of peer harassment. *Journal of Clinical Child and Adolescent Psychology, 34*, 37–48. doi: 10.1207/s15374424jccp3401_4

Olweus, D. (2010). Understanding and researching bullying: Some critical issues. In S. R. Jimerson, S. M. Swearer, & D. L. Espelage (Eds.), *Handbook of bullying in schools: An international perspective* (pp. 9–34). New York: Routledge.

Olweus, D. & Limber, S. P. (2010). Bullying in school: Evaluation and dissemination of the Olweus Bullying Prevention Program. *American Journal of Orthopsychiatry, 80*, 124–134.

Pearce, N., Cross, D., Monks, H., Waters, S., & Falconer, S. (2011). Current evidence of best practice in whole-school bullying intervention and its potential to inform cyberbullying interventions. *Australian Journal of Guidance Counselling, 21*, 1–21. doi: 10.1375/ajgc.21.1.1

Polanin, J., Espelage, D. L., & Pigott, T. D. (2012). A meta-analysis of school-based bullying prevention programs' effects on bystander intervention behavior and empathy attitude. *School Psychology Review, 41*(1), 47–65.

Poteat, V. P., & Espelage, D. L. (2005). Exploring the relation between bullying and homophobic verbal content: The Homophobic Content Agent Target (HCAT) Scale. *Violence and Victims, 20*, 513–528. doi: 10891/vivi.2005.20.5.513

Poteat, V. P., & Rivers, I. (2010). The use of homophobic language across bullying roles during adolescence. *Journal of Applied Developmental Psychology, 31*(2), 166–172. doi: 10.1016/j.aadev.2009.11.005

Poteat, V. P., Sinclair, K. O., DiGiovanni, C. D., Koenig, B. W., & Russell, S. T. (2013). Gay–straight alliances are associated with student health: A multischool comparison of LGBTQ and heterosexual youth. *Journal of Research on Adolescence, 23*(2), 319–330. doi: 10.1111/j.1532-7795.2012.00832.x

Pöyhönen, V., Juvonen, J., & Salmivalli, C. (2010). What does it take to stand up for the victim of bullying? The interplay between personal and social factors. *Merrill-Palmer Quarterly, 56*, 2.

Pozzoli, T., & Gini, G. (2010). Active defending and passive bystanding behavior in bullying: The role of personal characteristics and perceived pressure. *Journal of Abnormal Child Psychology, 38*(6), 815–827. doi: 10.1007/s10802-010-9399-9

Ragozzino, K., & Utne O'Brien, M. (2009). Social and emotional learning and bullying prevention [issue brief]. Retrieved from http://casel.org/downloads/2009_bullyingbrief.pdf.

Robinson, J. P., & Espelage, D. L. (2011). Inequities in educational and psychological outcomes between LGBTQ and straight students in middle and high school. *Educational Researcher, 40*, 315–330. doi: 10.3102/0013189X11422112

Robinson, J. P., & Espelage, D. L. (2012). Bullying explains only part of LGBTQ-heterosexual risk disparities: Implications for policy and practice. *Educational Researcher, 41*(8), 309–319. doi: 10.3102/0013189X12457023

Rodkin, P. C., Espelage, D. L., & Hanish, L .D. (under review). A relational perspective on the social ecology of bullying. *American Psychologist*.

Rose, C. A. (2010). Bullying among students with disabilities: Impact and implications. In D. L. Espelage & S. M. Swearer (Eds.), *Bullying in North American schools: A socio-ecological perspective on prevention and intervention* (2nd ed.) (pp 34–44). Mahwah, NJ: Erlbaum.

Rose, C. A., & Espelage, D. L. (2012). Risk and protective factors associated with the bullying involvement of students with emotional and behavioral disorders. *Behavioral Disorders, 37*, 133–148.

Rose, C. A., Espelage, D. L., Aragon, S. R., & Elliott, J. (2011). Bullying and victimization among students in special education and general education curricula. *Exceptionality Education International, 21*(2).

Rose, C. A., Monda-Amaya, L. E., & Espelage, D. L. (2011). Bullying perpetration and victimization in special education: A review of the literature. *Remedial and Special Education, 32*, 114–130. doi: 10.1177/0741932510361247

Russell, S. T., Kosciw, J. G., Horn, S. S., & Saewyc, E. (2010). Safe schools policy for LGBTQ students. *Social Policy Report, 24*(4) (Washington, DC: Society for Research in Child Development).

Salmivalli, C. (2010). Bullying and the peer group: A review. *Aggression & Violent Behavior, 15*, 112–120. doi: 10.1016/j.avb.2009.08.007

Schäfer, M., Korn, S., Brodbeck, F. C., Wolke, D., & Schulz, H. (2005). Bullying roles in changing contexts: The stability of victim and bully roles from primary to secondary school. *International Journal of Behavioral Development, 29*, 323–335. doi: 10.1177/01650250544000107

Schwartz, D., Gorman, A. H., Dodge, K. A., Pettit, G. S., & Bates, J. E. (2008). Friendships with peers who are low or high in aggression as moderators of the link between peer victimization and declines in academic functioning. *Journal of Abnormal Child Psychology, 36*, 719–730. doi: 10.1007/s10802-007-9200-x

Schwartz, D., Gorman, A. H., Nakamoto, J., & Toblin, R. (2005). Victimization in the peer group and children's academic functioning. *Journal of Educational Psychology, 97*, 425–435.

Sharp, S., & Smith, P. K. (1991). Bullying in UK schools: The DES Sheffield bullying project. *Early Child Development and Care, 77*, 47–55. doi: 10.1080/0300443910770104

Stavrinides, P., Georgiou, St., & Theofanous, V. (2010). Bullying and empathy: A short-term longitudinal investigation. *Educational Psychology, 30*(7), 793–802. doi: 10.1080/01443410.2010.506004

Sugai, G., & Horner, R. H. (2002). The evolution of discipline practices: School-wide positive behavior supports. *Child and Family Behavior Therapy, 24*, 23–50. doi: 10.1300/J019v24n01_03

Sugai, G., Horner, R. H., Dunlap, G. Hieneman, M., Lewis, T. J., Nelson, C. M., Scott, T., Liaupsin, C., Sailor, W., Turnbull, A. P., Turnbull, H. R., III, Wickham, D. Reuf, M., & Wilcox, B. (2000). Applying positive behavioral support and functional behavioral assessment in schools. *Journal of Positive Behavioral Interventions, 2*, 131–143. doi: 10.1177/109830070000200302

Totura, C. M. Wienke., MacKinnon-Lewis, C., Gesten, Ellis L., Gadd, R., Divine, K. P., Dunham, S., & Larson, A. V. N. (2009). Bullying and victimization among boys and girls in middle school: The influence of perceived family and schools contexts. *Journal of Early Adolescence, 29*, 571–609.

Ttofi, M. M., & Farrington, D. P. (2011). Effectiveness of school based programs to reduce bullying: A systematic and meta-analytic review. *Journal of Experimental Criminology, 7*, 27–56. doi: 10.1007/s11292-010-9109-1

Waasdorp, T. E., Bradshaw, C. P., & Leaf, P. J. (2012). The impact of School-wide Positive Behavioral Interventions and Supports (SWPBIS) on bullying and peer rejection: A randomized controlled effectiveness trial. *Archives of Pediatrics and Adolescent Medicine, 116*(2), 149–156. doi: 10.1001/archpediatrics.2011.755

Wallace, T., Anderson, A. R., Bartholomay, T., & Hupp, S. (2002). An ecobehavioral examination of high school classrooms that include students with disabilities. *Exceptional Children, 68*, 345–359.

White, N. A., & Loeber, R. (2008). Bullying and special education as predictors of serious delinquency. *Journal of Research in Crime and Delinquency, 45*, 380–397. doi: 10.1177/0022427808322612

Wilson, S. J., & Lipsey, M. W. (2007). School-based interventions for aggressive and disruptive behavior: Update of a meta-analysis. *American Journal of Preventive Medicine, 33*, S130–S143. doi: 10.1016/j.amepre.2007.04.011

Woods, S., Wolke, D. (2004). Direct and relational bullying among primary school children and academic achievement. *Journal of School Psychology, 42*, 135–155. doi: 10.1016/j.jsp.2003.12.0022

Ybarra, M., Espelage, D. L., & Mitchell, K. J. (in press). Differentiating youth who are bullied from other victims of peer-aggression: The importance of differential power and repetition. *Journal of Adolescent Health.*

Zins, J. E., Weissberg, R. P., Wang, M. C., & Walberg, H. J. (Eds.). (2004). *Building school success through social and emotional learning.* New York: Teachers College Press.

6

FROM COMPLIANCE TO RESPONSIBILITY

Social-Emotional Learning and Classroom Management

YONI SCHWAB
THE SHEFA SCHOOL AND YESHIVA UNIVERSITY

MAURICE J. ELIAS
RUTGERS UNIVERSITY

Marzano and Marzano's (2003) meta-analytic study suggests that classroom management is the single variable with the largest impact on student achievement. Why is that? Shouldn't the quality of math or language arts instruction make the biggest difference in terms of achievement? The most obvious reason for this influence is that effective classroom management sets the stage for learning. Without it, classrooms are disorganized and chaotic, and very little academic learning can happen. Less obvious is that a teacher's classroom management practices are socializing influences on students. They communicate—subtly and not so subtly—messages about social norms and emotional behavior. Whether or not teachers are aware of it, students are constantly developing social and emotional skills (both good and bad) through modeling, experimentation, and reinforcement. Teachers' activities in the broad category called "classroom management" can help students to develop healthy habits. This chapter presents guidelines for integrating proactive social-emotional learning into classroom management so that both are effective because ultimately they are mutually dependent and inseparable.

A STUDENT-CENTERED GOAL FOR CLASSROOM MANAGEMENT

Classroom management refers to all of the teacher's practices related to establishing the physical and social environment of the classroom, regulating routines and daily activities, and preventing and correcting problems. Nearly everything a teacher does, aside from communicating the content of the academic curriculum, is part of classroom management. Indeed, even the mode of instruction (e.g., frontal lecturing, worksheets, creative group work projects) is a component of classroom management.

The traditional goal of classroom management has been for the teacher to maintain and enforce discipline so that academic instruction can proceed without distractions. The control goal of classroom management is an important, probably necessary, condition for a classroom to function effectively. However, this goal does not take into account that some discipline strategies may maintain control but may *not* foster learning. We define learning broadly here. Schools are increasingly focused on social and emotional learning, as well as academic learning. Therefore, we propose a more holistic and student-centered goal for classroom management: to create a classroom environment that fosters students' learning of academic, social, and emotional skills and the ability to put them to positive use in the world around them. Although order is necessary for this goal, it is not sufficient. Classroom management strategies must both maintain order and foster learning.

Furthermore, managing for compliance, as opposed to fostering internalized motivation, is shortsighted and often ineffective for the independent tasks required in most classrooms (McCaslin & Good, 1992, 1998). Behaviors that are reinforced through control tactics alone do not generalize well (Deci, Koestner, & Ryan, 1999), so they can be difficult to maintain in large classrooms where teachers cannot invest the time needed to constantly monitor all students, often while they work independently. And if control alone makes it difficult to maintain positive behavior within the classroom, it is even more unlikely to generalize that behavior outside the classroom and into the future. If schools are truly concerned with students becoming good citizens, successful workers, and lifelong learners, then their behavior management practices need to be consistent with and carefully calibrated to support a student-centered, skill-building instructional approach.

The converging goals of fostering academic, social, and emotional learning simultaneously have become the focus of the emerging area of social-emotional learning (SEL). SEL is aligned with research showing the inextricable interconnection between cognitive-academic, emotional, and social competencies. Therefore, SEL makes monitoring emotions the first step in solving problems and achieving self-control (see Elias & Bruene, 2005). This is one example of an insight that SEL can bring to the field of classroom management.

SOCIAL-EMOTIONAL LEARNING

Social-emotional learning is the process of gaining competencies and intrinsic motivation for emotional self-awareness and self-regulation, for safe and responsible behavior and for assertive, empathic, and skillful social interaction. SEL skills include identifying feelings in oneself and others, managing one's emotions, being responsible for one's actions and commitments, showing empathy and respect, communicating effectively, and many other challenging but necessary skills for functioning adaptively in a free society (Elias, 2003; Elias et al., 1997). (The Collaborative for Academic, Social, and

Table 6.1 CASEL's five essential SEL skills and competencies.

Self-awareness: The ability to accurately recognize one's emotions and thoughts and their influence on behavior. This includes accurately assessing one's strengths and limitations and possessing a well-grounded sense of confidence and optimism.

Self-management: The ability to regulate one's emotions, thoughts, and behaviors effectively in different situations. This includes managing stress, controlling impulses, motivating oneself, and setting and working toward achieving personal and academic goals.

Social awareness: The ability to take the perspective of and empathize with others from diverse backgrounds and cultures, to understand social and ethical norms for behavior, and to recognize family, school, and community resources and supports.

Relationship skills: The ability to establish and maintain healthy and rewarding relationships with diverse individuals and groups. This includes communicating clearly, listening actively, cooperating, resisting inappropriate social pressure, negotiating conflict constructively, and seeking and offering help when needed.

Responsible decision making: The ability to make constructive and respectful choices about personal behavior and social interactions based on consideration of ethical standards, safety concerns, social norms, the realistic evaluation of consequences of various actions, and the well-being of self and others.

Emotional Learning [CASEL] has identified five interrelated sets of cognitive, affective and behavioral competencies [CASEL, n.d.]; see Table 6.1.)

It was once thought that social and emotional skills were learned strictly by experience and that they had no place in the curriculum. Math can also be learned by experience, but it is doubtful that students would "naturally" learn math with the same level of sophistication as they do with years of instruction and practice. The same is true of social and emotional skills.

Durlak, Weissberg, Dymnicki, Taylor, and Schellinger (2011) conducted a meta-analysis of 213 studies of school-based, universal SEL programs. They found that teaching social and emotional skills in school has significant impacts across all of the domains they tested. Participation in SEL programs leads to improved SEL skill performance, more positive attitudes toward oneself and others, more positive daily social behavior, and better grades and achievement test scores. The magnitude of academic achievement gains was equivalent to an increase of 11 percentile points. SEL programs also led to fewer conduct problems and reduced emotional distress and internalizing problems (e.g., depression and anxiety). Better outcomes were achieved by programs that empowered classroom teachers to deliver the SEL instruction as compared with programs in which skills were taught by nonschool personnel (e.g., research assistants). Thirty-three of the studies in the meta-analysis collected follow-up data at least six months after the program ended. Positive effects across all six domains remained significant.

Durlak and colleagues (2011) recommend that programs provide *sequenced*, step-by-step training in specific skills and use *active* forms of learning. They must *focus* sufficient time in order to target *explicit* skills rather than positive development in general. Though many SEL programs have been marketed, many do not follow these criteria, and only a handful of them have been empirically tested and supported. For a more complete review of programs and their research support, see Collaborative for Academic, Social, and Emotional Learning (2012) and Greenberg, Domitrovich, and Bumbarger (2001).

INTEGRATING SOCIAL AND EMOTIONAL LEARNING AND CLASSROOM MANAGEMENT

Even though not every classroom can incorporate a systematic, multiyear, evidence-based SEL program, the research on SEL reinforces the need for classroom management practices that support the development of students' academic, social, and emotional skills. SEL pedagogy and classroom management are overlapping tasks, and classroom management practices can have a significant impact (positive or negative) on students' social and emotional development.

Self-Control, Self-Discipline, and Emotional Competence

Schools have traditionally relied on external control because of its expediency. However, numerous classroom management theorists and researchers have attempted to differentiate between management models that stress external control or obedience, on the one hand, and self-control, self-discipline, and responsibility, on the other (e.g., Bear, 1998, 2010; Brophy, 1999; Curwin & Mendler, 1988; Dreikurs, 1968; Elias & Trusheim, 2013; Freiberg, 1999; Glasser, 1992; Gordon, 1974, 2003; Kohn, 1996; Weinstein, 1999).

SEL theory makes an important contribution to the goal of promoting self-control and self-discipline by stressing the primacy of emotional competence for social and academic learning. "Emotional competence is the demonstration of self-efficacy in emotion-eliciting social transactions. *Self-efficacy* is used here to mean that the individual believes that he or she has the capacity and skills to achieve a desired outcome" (Saarni, 2000, p. 68, emphasis in the original). Saarni's (2000) model can be illustrated through an example.

Imagine someone tells a sixth-grade girl that her friends have been spreading rumors about her. Her ability to exert self-control relies on her emotional competence. If she does not attend to her emotional reaction or the emotions of her friends, then she may react in an unacceptable way (e.g., spreading counterrumors, physically attacking) before finding out more information. If she does attend to her emotions and label them accurately (e.g., anger, hurt, puzzlement), she may be able to regulate them until she finds out more information and decides on a plan. That gives her an opportunity to evaluate the source of the disclosure and/or to speak to her friends in a calm way to see whether they have a benign explanation. Based on her conclusions to such inquiries, she can identify her emotions and use them to choose a course of action that fits her sense of morality. For example, instead of starting a fight with her friends and getting into trouble, she may choose to suspend or end the friendships and channel her emotional energy toward strengthening her other relationships. It is clear how many times during the school day this kind of process is replicated with each and every student.

The Pedagogy of SEL and Classroom Management

This section describes four areas of action that characterize a converging pedagogy for SEL, classroom management, and academic learning:

Action 1: Teach SEL skills.
Action 2: Build caring relationships.

Action 3: Set firm and fair boundaries.
Action 4: Share responsibility with students.

Though presented sequentially, these actions overlap and are mutually reinforcing, so they are carried out simultaneously and with consistent language. SEL pedagogy is convergent with many state-of-the-art instructional practices that teachers apply to academic teaching. The most widely used framework for teacher professional development and evaluation, the Danielson Framework, devotes the second of its four domains to creating the classroom conditions for critical thinking, inquiry, problem solving, and group work (Danielson, 2008). SEL pedagogy is also highly consistent with Gardner's multiple intelligences theory (1985, 1993), Levine's "A Mind at a Time" approach (2002), McCarthy's 4MAT instructional method (1987), and principles of differentiated instruction (Tomlinson, 1999).

ACTION 1: TEACH SEL SKILLS

The first step in bringing SEL to the classroom is to plan how one will incorporate explicit SEL skill building into the curriculum and classroom management agenda. Based on the SEL approach chosen, a matching full-scale classroom management plan can then be designed. For example, if an SEL program teaches a problem-solving technique, the teacher should use the same one to address day-to-day problems that arise in the classroom.

Skills necessary for optimal functioning in the classroom can and must be taught, modeled, and practiced proactively and explicitly. When they are not, skill development is spotty (Cartledge & Milburn, 1995) and eroded by students' pervasive exposure to an array of media messages that urge them to act in ways that support neither academic excellence nor self-control (Comer, 2003).

Before, during, and after teaching individual social skills, teachers must also work to "change values and basic assumptions, particularly about the value of prosocial rather than aggressive and antisocial behaviors in problem situations" (Cartledge & Milburn, 1995, p. xi). In other words, social skills instruction is a two-component process. First, teachers help students to develop specific skills and competencies to enable students to act in prosocial ways. Second, teachers must work over the long term to foster motivation for responsible behavior and ethical growth, which bridge the gap between students' learning social-emotional skills and choosing to apply them. At first, students will not use their newly acquired skills spontaneously. Repetition, cuing, and coaching are necessary to transform discrete skills into socially competent and responsible behavior across many different situations (Elias et al., 1997). The goal is for students to be able to act responsibly and ethically without cuing or any kind of external reinforcement. These are the kinds of citizens that any democracy hopes for.

The Three Phases of Social-Emotional Skill Instruction

Cartledge and Milburn (1995) break down the process of teaching social and emotional skills into three phases: (1) instruction, (2) skill performance and feedback, and (3) practice and generalization. The evaluation of students' competence with the specific behaviors should occur frequently in order to measure the effectiveness of instruction. (CASEL [2012] contains guidelines for evaluation and links to evaluation tools used by various SEL programs.)

The instruction phase begins with providing a rationale for learning and performing the SEL skill being taught. This is best done by challenging the students to analyze the value of the skill or even to identify the behavior themselves by figuring out the best response to a hypothetical scenario. Once the value of the skill has been addressed, it is important to break down the skill into its component behaviors (Elias & Bruene, 2005). Finally, the students are presented with a model of the skill, which could be a character in literature, an actor on a videotape, a peer who role-plays the skill, and so on (Cartledge & Milburn, 1995).

The second phase of teaching SEL skills is skill performance and feedback. Like seatwork during a lesson, guided rehearsal gives the students an opportunity to perform the focal skill individually for the first time in a secure environment. Rehearsal can be covert (i.e., cognitive or imaginal), verbal, or physical. Of course, physical performance of the skill, if possible, is superior to either thinking or talking about it. Feedback is provided in order to correct mistakes, address problems, and recognize when the skill is being done properly. Feedback can be verbal, reinforcement-based, or self-evaluative (Cartledge & Milburn, 1995). Table 6.2 is a sample lesson plan that gives a classroom-based example of phases 1 and 2.

The third phase is practice. As with any other skill taught in a classroom, practice—even overlearning—is necessary to maintain the behavior. In addition to practice for maintenance, generalization to various real-world situations is a critical part of teaching social-emotional skills. Cartledge and Milburn (1995) identify key strategies for generalization based on behavioral and cognitive research: (1) Training should occur in a variety of settings, particularly settings that match "target" situations for the behavior. (2) Practice should be done in real-life conditions or under conditions that approximate real life as much as possible. (3) Training should occur with different people to show consistency across social situations, and cuing and reminding must be done frequently over time (Shure & Glaser, 2001). For the best outcomes, all school personnel should model, cue, and reinforce social skills consistently and use the same language to refer to them. This requires that school-wide policies concerning rules and behavior be established. To generalize beyond school, parents and community members should be taught to use the same social skill language, and peers can also be empowered to cue and reinforce school- or community-wide SEL skills. (4) Contingencies of reinforcement for SEL behaviors should remain consistent across different settings, both in school and, if possible, out of school. External reinforcement, however, should be tapered in order to encourage generalization to settings where reinforcement is unavailable. (5) Students should be encouraged to develop self-management for their social behaviors. Ultimately, the goal of social-emotional skill building is to make the transition from external control and reinforcement to internal motivation, responsibility, and self-control. This is perhaps the most valuable principle that the field of classroom management can learn from SEL.

Almost no students remember when and how to apply new skills until they have had many opportunities to practice them in the real world. Cuing can take many

Table 6.2 Sample lesson plan for third-grade language arts: An example of integrating academics and social-emotional skill building (based on Cartledge & Milburn, 1995).

Objectives

- Students will read and analyze literature through the lens of social and emotional skills.
- Students will become familiar with the concept of body language and its importance in social interactions.
- Students will recognize specific examples of emotional body language.
- Students will practice demonstrating emotions through body language.

Materials

- *Buffalo Before Breakfast* by Mary Pope Osborne (1999). (This lesson can be adapted for any piece of children's literature that has an example of reading body language.)

Motivation

As part of a regular reading/language arts lesson, the teacher begins by reading a passage from *Buffalo Before Breakfast* by Mary Pope Osborne (1999) in which the protagonists, Jack and Annie, first meet the Lakota people. In the passage, Jack and Annie report that even though the Lakota people are not saying anything, they do not appear to be angry.

Procedure

1. Providing a rationale:
   a. Using this passage as a jumping-off point, the teacher poses the following questions:
      "How do the characters know the Lakota people are not angry?"
      "Can you show me what the Lakota people might have looked like if they were angry?"
      "What do you look like when you are angry?"
      (Students respond by saying that there are various signs of anger in the face, arms, and shoulders of the person.)
   b. The teacher introduces the term "body language" and encourages students to make text-to-self connections:
      "Why is reading body language helpful?"
      "When Jack and Annie read body language, how does that help them?"
      "Can you give me examples of times when reading body language has helped you?"
2. Breaking down the skill into its components
   The teacher asks students to suggest different parts of the body that display anger and writes the ideas on the board: "Which parts of your face or body change when you are angry?" (e.g., clenched teeth, a furrowed brow, raised shoulders)
3. Modeling
   As they suggest angry body signs, students model the actions for their peers. The teacher also asks students to model other emotions so that their peers can guess what they are "feeling." With each example of a new emotion, the teacher uses the student model to help the class break down the body language into its components.
4. Skill performance and feedback: Guess My Emotion Game
   a. The teacher divides the students into groups and asks them to write down components of body language for fear and happy. They share these lists with their groups and then practice acting out these emotions for the other members of their group.
   b. Each group is assigned an emotion to present to the class. The class practices reading body language by guessing the other groups' emotions.

Feedback and Assessment

- The teacher circulates during group work to monitor progress and understanding.
- With each group presentation, the teacher gives specific feedback on the display of the emotion and on the class's interpretation, in addition to encouraging students to give appropriate and constructive feedback to one other.

Follow-up

- The teacher assigns students to practice reading their siblings' and friends' body language after school and report back the next day.
- The teacher will reinforce the skill of reading social and emotional cues in another two reading lessons as soon as is feasible, as well as in future lessons involving literature and other media.
- The teacher will remind students about this skill when it comes up in real-world social interactions in the classroom and throughout the school.

For a skill as complex as recognizing others' emotions through body language to be fully integrated into the students' social skill repertoire, multiple lessons along these lines would be necessary, as well as cuing and practice in real-world situations.

forms, verbal and nonverbal, all of which should be positive, brief, private, and designed to encourage rather than criticize the child. It can be helpful to have a code word or acronym for a particular skill.

Let's take an example of an SEL skill from the Social Decision Making/Social Problem Solving (SDM/SPS) curriculum that applies to classroom management directly (Elias & Bruene, 2005). If a student is not paying attention to a peer who is speaking, a teacher might be tempted to shout from across the room: "Kim, stop fiddling around with the papers in your desk. Sit up straight, turn and look at Michael, and listen to what he's trying to say." This might stop her from fiddling with the papers, but it would likely make Kim feel embarrassed and discouraged, and, because of those feelings, she would probably not hear what Michael has to say. The SDM/SPS program calls that set of listening skills "Listening Position." Saying "Use good Listening Position" in a positive tone of voice helps everyone to self-monitor and self-correct. A need for further reminders suggests that perhaps the child does not know the skill and/or has a learning or attentional impairment that should be watched more closely. Educators routinely underestimate the time needed before cues are faded. One should think in terms of months, not weeks.

Social Problem-Solving Strategies

The three building blocks of SEL competency and responsible behavior are basic/readiness skills, problem-solving strategies, and internal motivation and self-discipline. Readiness skills include turn taking, following directions, keeping calm, communicating effectively, and reading social cues. Social problem solving relies on readiness skills related to choosing and organizing actions in almost any situation. Consequently, it is at the heart of all of the empirically supported SEL programs previously discussed. Internal motivation, the third building block, drives the choice to use one's problem-solving competencies and exert self-control in a situation.

There are numerous social problem-solving strategies. Many use mnemonics to help children remember the steps. Problem-solving in SDM/SPS is called "*FIG TESPN*" (Elias & Bruene, 2005). Each letter stands for a step in the problem-solving process:

> *Feelings*—How do I feel in this situation?
> *Identify problem*—What's the problem?
> *Goal*—What is my ultimate goal? What do I want to have happen?
> *Think*—Brainstorm at least three possible solutions to this problem.
> *Envision*—What are the likely consequences of each of my possible solutions?
> *Solution*—Choose the best solution I thought of.
> *Plan*—Plan how to carry out my solution.
> *Notice results*—After I carry out my plan, evaluate it.

Other programs' problem-solving systems are substantially similar; the main differences are the names and memory devices.

Integrating SEL and Academics

SEL instruction is particularly effective when integrated with academics rather than when treated as a separate "subject" (Elias, 2004). As explained, SEL skills are vital to academic learning. Integrating the two types of learning creates synergies for both. For example, when SEL skill-building is integrated into a literature lesson, the SEL skills are raised to the level of importance of core academics rather than being viewed as a special or add-on subject. SEL is also dramatized in meaningful and complex ways in literature, which improves the learning of both SEL and the literature being studied through text-to-self connections. Table 6.2 shows how SEL gains relevance through a literature lesson and how the literature lesson is enhanced by using SEL as a paradigm for analyzing a particular passage in a read-aloud book. Problem solving can be applied to the dilemmas faced by characters at exciting junctures in stories, bringing students into the authoring process.

History and current events can be presented as a series of problems that various individuals and groups have attempted to solve. Students can try to figure out, based on their readings and other sources of information, what various individuals and groups were feeling and what their goals were. They learn the powerful impact of deficiencies in effective problem solving, empathy, and perspective taking. As students apply their social problem-solving strategies in academic areas, they are broadening and deepening the application of their skills (Elias, 2004).

ACTION 2: BUILD CARING RELATIONSHIPS

Building caring relationships is a tenet of SEL and a necessary factor in fostering students' social and emotional growth. The actions are associated with developing a caring relationships model of competent social skill behavior. Because children are learning all the time, whether we intend to teach them or not, building caring relationships in classrooms may have at least as much influence on their development of social skills as explicit teaching. (Students should be encouraged to do as we say *and* as we do.) Furthermore, a caring atmosphere (which, sadly, many students lack outside the classroom) supports students emotionally and models such emotional skills as emotion identification and regulation. Building caring relationships sets the tone for SEL skill building and provides the first vehicle for practice and improvement. It makes the classroom a living SEL laboratory.

In terms of classroom management, building an atmosphere of caring relationships can make all the difference between a functional and dysfunctional classroom. The persistent demands of academic performance, complying with rules, and interacting positively with peers and teachers can be challenging for students. Developing a supportive community in the classroom helps to impart a sense of each student's belonging, to alleviate students' social anxieties and frustration, and to motivate students to comply with teacher requests and act prosocially with peers. Consequently, as the level of respect for teachers and peers increases, negative or aggressive social behaviors are reduced, and students are more likely to comply with the rules (Elias et al., 1997). As a result, building caring relationships is the first step in the promotion of responsible behavior and prevention of misbehavior. Setting a supportive tone for the class should be the teacher's first task when students enter the classroom on the first day of school. It is worth noting that any early childhood educator reading this will recognize it as an essential tenet of their teaching. However, what SEL theory has brought into clearer focus is that the link of caring relationships to learning does not cease to become relevant after early childhood. Indeed, its importance continues through the adolescent years and persists into adult education contexts (Salovey & Sluyter, 1997).

Teacher–Student Relationships

Building caring relationships between teachers and students is necessary for many reasons. First, when students sense that a teacher cares about them, they see the teacher as more credible and as an ally rather than a foe. This increases motivation to follow directions, to adhere to rules, and to put effort into classroom activities and academics. Just as adults who feel respected and supported in the workplace are more productive, children have those same needs and respond best in school environments that they perceive as caring and respectful. Weinstein and Mignano (2003) detail nine ways in which successful classroom managers express concern for students. Effective teachers are welcoming, are sensitive to students' concerns, treat students fairly, act like real people (not just as teachers), share responsibility, minimize the use of external controls, include everyone, search for students' strengths, and communicate effectively. To this list, we would add that teachers should also show an interest in their students' lives and pursuits. Many of these ten practices not only express concern for students but are important for other action steps, a fact that highlights the integrated nature of SEL and classroom management. Multiple large meta-analyses have established that building such supportive teacher–student relationships is a reliable and strong predictor of social, emotional, and academic outcomes (Cornelius-White, 2007; Hattie, 2009; Roorda, Koomen, Spilt, & Oort, 2011).

Student-Student Relationships and the Classroom Community

Peer-to-peer relationships and the classroom community are just as important as teacher–student relations in maintaining a functional classroom and promoting social and emotional growth. This may seem like an obvious statement on the surface, but Noddings (2003) points out why the classroom community is essential for shaping success in school and life. She observes that a moral life is completely relational and that character and the habits of learning are acquired through strong, nurturant, positive relationships. The classroom as a community must teach caring as the bedrock on which other values, essential for intellectual accomplishment and ethical living, can be built: honesty, courage, responsibility.

Even though peer relationships do not always directly involve the teacher, the teacher is a vital force in establishing the conditions for social interaction and would benefit greatly from proactively intervening to help caring relationships develop positively. SEL social skill-building practices suggest a number of ways to do this. First, the teacher can begin the year by helping students feel comfortable with one another in the classroom through group-building activities, creative opportunities to share personal experiences and interests, and establishing an ethic of teamwork and helping one another with everyday tasks and problems. Second, teachers should involve students in deciding what rules should govern social interaction in the classroom and facilitate conversations on specific ways to show respect and caring. In the mode of SEL pedagogy, prosocial interactions should be role-played and modeled so that students learn what abstract values such as caring, inclusion, and respect look like in practice. Third, teachers should discuss, teach, and model a problem-solving approach to understanding and resolving personal dilemmas and mistakes (using personal examples in an appropriate way) to set a personal, supportive tone to the class. The SEL literature provides numerous models to accomplish these tasks (Charney, 2002; Elias et al., 1997).

The capacity for empathy is the keystone to intrinsically motivated prosocial behavior. Empathy and perspective taking are vital—and often absent—in our society. One SDM/SPS skill used to teach empathy is Footsteps. The goal of Footsteps is to enable students to recognize another's feelings and goals when in a conflict. The two participants in the exercise place cutouts in the shape of footsteps on the floor across from each other. They stand in their own "feet" and begin by stating their feelings and concerns using I-statements. Then they switch places, and each acknowledges the other's feelings and concerns and checks for accuracy with an active listening statement (e.g., "I heard you . . ."). They then return to their original places and talk about how it felt to be in the other's "feet." Once they understand their partner's emotions and position, they problem-solve together until a mutually agreeable solution is reached. This is a complex skill that requires adult modeling, specific feedback, and generous amounts of practice. Creative lessons that integrate this skill with academics (particularly literature and social studies) are especially beneficial. In keeping with the SEL skill-building pedagogy previously mentioned, once students have learned and practiced the Footsteps technique, its use should be prompted. This takes place by adults carrying around cutouts and dropping the "feet" when they come upon students having conflicts in hallways, assemblies, lunchrooms, or the playground. Students know that once the feet are dropped, they should "assume the position" required and begin the orderly process of conflict resolution under the adult's (or trained peer mediator's) watchful eye.

Communication

Developing effective communication is a challenging but vital step in building caring, functional relationships throughout the classroom. Effective teacher-to-student communication includes, but is not limited to, clarity and checking for understanding; active listening; facilitative and open-ended questioning; and saying far more positive, complimentary, and encouraging words to all students (even the challenging ones) than negative words.

Numerous SEL skills relate to communication, and a number of SEL skill-building methods have particular utility in classroom functioning. I-messages and active (reflective) listening are tried-and-true techniques. The SDM/SPS listening skill of Listening Position was already mentioned. But how does a student know when it's time to speak instead of listen? SDM/SPS uses a system called "Speaker Power," which involves passing an object from person to person in order to signify whose turn it is to speak. When Speaker Power is active, no one is allowed to speak without holding the object—including the teacher. The teacher gives the instructions while holding Speaker Power and then passes it to a student who is demonstrating a good Listening Position and has raised his or her hand. After the speaker is finished, the teacher takes the object back and gives it to another student. Once the class masters this procedure, the speaker becomes responsible for choosing who gets Speaker Power next. This not only reduces outbursts and quick responses but also forces students to pause before they speak and process what the previous person said. These are all important skills in the domains of listening and respecting others.

Classrooms dedicated to integrating SEL and effective classroom management should have frequent class meetings, or Share Circles (the SDM/SPS version of a class meeting), to discuss problems and continually build the classroom community. Share Circles are designated times to focus entirely on the social and emotional life of the classroom through discussions, group-building activities, SEL skill development, and group problem solving. They encourage supportive relationships throughout the classroom, set a positive tone for the classroom, help children to process any emotions that they bring to school, and give students an opportunity for input into the daily running of the classroom (Charney, 2002). Providing structured opportunities to share feelings, experiences, and interests makes the classroom the personal and supportive environment that underlies caring relationships. Some programs, notably Responsive Classroom, consider this to be a central *daily* feature of effective classroom management (Charney, 2002), and recent research supports this contention (www.responsiveclassroom.org).

ACTION 3: SET FIRM AND FAIR BOUNDARIES

Discipline is probably the first thing that comes to mind when someone mentions classroom management. Unfortunately, many teachers equate discipline with classroom management, neglecting the numerous other components of effective management (many of which have been stressed in this chapter), inevitably leading to disappointing results. For many, discipline implies a reaction to misbehavior. Throughout this chapter, we have emphasized that teachers generate management through specific actions directed toward creating a functional learning environment and preventing misbehavior. Behavior problems are minimized when students are engaged in learning, when they have developed social and emotional skills that enable them to pursue their needs and goals in prosocial ways, when the relationships in the classroom are supportive and caring, and when they feel a sense of autonomy and ownership of the class because they share responsibility for it. That being said, the presence of these conditions does not obviate the need for a clear boundary-setting structure. Students will occasionally make mistakes in their behaviors, just as they do when learning academic skills. In an SEL-infused classroom, these mistakes in judgment highlight social skill deficits. Just like mistakes in solving math problems, they are opportunities for learning and growing—in other words, social-emotional skill building for the next time.

Rules

Rules are necessary for any society or organization to function. Boundaries educate children about what is acceptable and what is not. Learning to act with self-control and respect for others is predicated on having clear rules that define responsible behavior in a particular environment. Therefore, clear rules are necessary for an SEL-oriented classroom.

Everyone agrees that class rules should be established early in the year, and most advocate that it be done on the first day of school. Brady, Forton, Porter, and Wood (2003) recommend that teachers wait a few days before initiating a collaborative rule-making process, until a sense of order, predictability, and trust in the classroom has been established. They contend that the basic elements of a caring community must be established before students can contribute meaningfully to rule making. Many experts, though not all, encourage teachers to create class rules "democratically" (e.g., Brady et al., 2003; Schaps & Solomon, 1990; Weinstein & Mignano, 2003). If the rules are truly a product of the whole class's effort, the students are far more likely to respect and show a commitment to them. The teacher must manage this process to ensure that all students feel they have contributed and that the final set of rules is reasonable, age appropriate, and fair to the students and the teacher. Establishing democratic rules is a necessity for an SEL-infused classroom because is promotes learning how to self-govern, cooperate, and choose responsible actions in a democratic environment.

Establishing and enforcing rules are necessary but not sufficient. To ensure that students understand them and are able to follow them, rules, like SEL skills, must be discussed, taught, modeled, and practiced. "Respecting oneself and others" or some variation on the theme is found in most classrooms. Respect is an abstract concept, especially to young children. What does respect look like? What types of behaviors does respect imply? Discussing, teaching, modeling, and practicing respectful behavior enable students to learn how to follow the rule. Rules are rarely learned after one lesson or discussion. The more difficult rules require practice and repetition throughout the year or across years.

Responses and Feedback

Though classroom management is primarily a proactive and preventive process, there will always be a need to respond and give feedback about student behavior—both positive and negative. Even though it is inherently a reactive task, the system of responses to problem behavior is an integral component of classroom management and should be planned out in advance.

Marshall and Weisner (2004) elegantly present a theory of discipline that enhances rather than impedes SEL development. They begin by stating a goal for classroom management that is similar to that proposed by this chapter: to promote responsible behavior guided by internal motivation. They propose a hierarchy of social development modeled on Maslow's (1970) hierarchy of needs and

Kohlberg's (1984) stages of moral development. From lowest to highest, the levels of their hierarchy are:

A—Anarchy.
B—Bossing/bullying.
C—Cooperation/conformity.
D—Democracy.

Levels A and B lead to socially destructive behaviors that are never acceptable. Level C is acceptable but has some drawbacks. Most teachers and administrators are satisfied when students' actions reflect compliance. In fact, it is often impossible to discern, from a prosocial behavior itself, whether the motivation is cooperation with authority or self-directed responsibility. For example, students may clean up the room at the end of an art lesson because it is the responsible thing to do in order to maintain a healthy, orderly environment or because the teacher will punish them if they don't. In both cases, the behavior is good, but the SEL implications are quite different.

McCaslin and Good (1998) point out the drawbacks of managing for compliance. Compliance depends on constant monitoring; there is little maintenance over time. When compliance is the only means of management, then prosocial behavior is unlikely to generalize to different settings. Further, complex instructional modalities, such as cooperative learning, are very difficult to manage through compliance alone. Students need to self-regulate in order to make cooperative learning work. Raising students' motivation to level D is necessary for the constructivist, problem-solving curriculum. "We believe that the intended modern school curriculum, which is designed to produce self-motivated active learners, is seriously undermined by classroom management policies that encourage, if not demand, simple obedience" (McCaslin & Good, 1992, p. 4). Management systems should go beyond demanding compliance and strive to foster the skills necessary for democratic values and personal responsibility.

Bear (1998, 2010) agrees that in the short term, the goal is managing the class and controlling problems. The long-term goal is developing students' self-discipline. This, he says, is the essence of the authoritative parenting style (Baumrind, 1966), which is widely regarded as the most effective and is the most compatible with SEL. Like Marshall and Weisner (2004), Bear defines self-discipline as the internalization of democratic ideals. Because it is internally motivated, it is evident only when external regulators are not present. That is why one must move beyond operant strategies to foster self-discipline.

If straightforward operant approaches to reinforcing desirable behavior and punishing undesirable behavior are not the most effective ways to build SEL skills and promote the internalization and generalization of prosocial behavior, what is more effective? Taken together, the actions described in this chapter—teaching SEL skills, building caring relationships, setting firm and fair boundaries, and sharing responsibility with students—serve that goal. This section is devoted to alternatives to traditional operant reinforcement that foster SEL skills, internalization, and generalization.

Positive Recognition and Feedback

Qualitative and meaningful feedback is absolutely necessary to developing academic, social, and emotional skills, but the way that feedback is delivered can have
profound effects on long-term social-emotional growth. Deci, Koestner, and Ryan's
(1999) meta-analysis of 128 studies of the effects of extrinsic rewards on intrinsic
motivation strongly supported their theory that, although positive feedback often
provides useful information to a child about his or her competence, it can also be
delivered in a controlling way, which undermines internal motivation. They found
that tangible rewards are more likely to undermine internal motivation than verbal praise and that verbal praise can either increase or decrease internal motivation, depending on how and in what context it was delivered. Their meta-analysis
demonstrated that the most effective praise is unexpected rather than expected and
performance-contingent rather than for just completing a task. In other words, it
needs to be given meaningfully—for real effort and good work—rather than for every
little task accomplished in the classroom. Different levels of performance should not
be praised equally. Substantial praise should be used sparingly, reserved for when it
is truly deserved. Too often, students begin to expect praise for the completion of
tasks irrespective of quality or effort, which can lead to reductions in intrinsic motivation, self-regulation, and learning (Deci et al., 1999). Such praise may even imply
that the student in *not* capable. Why else would the teacher make such a big deal
about something so pedestrian (Dweck, 1999; Willingham, 2005)?

One reliable way to avoid communicating too much control is for feedback to take
the form of self-evaluation, whenever possible. This can be done by nonjudgmen-
tally pointing out specific aspects of the student's work and teaching the student to
self-assess in a productive, realistic way. Furthermore, descriptive specificity conveys
genuine recognition of the student's work and directs the positive feedback for the
student—which provides the information that the child is seeking—while generally
avoiding undue control.

Dweck and her colleagues' extensive research on the effects of praise on achievement motivation has provided another crucial guideline. Their work suggests that
praise should be effort rather than trait oriented. "You did well on this test—you're
so smart" (an example of trait praise) can lead to a child's feeling less smart and less
motivated after a subsequent failure. Such praise suggests that each task is a refer-
endum on one's innate, static intelligence. If a student does poorly, the only conclusion is that she is not smart. And even if a student succeeds after working very hard,
he might reach a similar conclusion. The child's theory on intelligence is that it is
inversely related to effort. Someone who has to work hard is not as smart as someone who does not. Therefore, it is safest not to try. That way, if the student succeeds,
she can conclude that she is exceedingly bright. If she does not, she can use the lack
of effort as an excuse. On the other hand, praising effort (e.g., "You worked really
hard on this") can help to increase persistence and resilience when failure inevitably
occurs. When teachers give feedback about process rather than ability, they are communicating that success is within the child's control. If he did well, he can conclude
that he tried hard or used good strategies. If he did poorly, he did not put in enough

effort or did not learn the right strategies—conditions that seems much easier to change than one's intelligence (Dweck, 1999; Mueller & Dweck, 1998).

Jere Brophy (2004) points out that teachers frequently give feedback that communicates low expectations to low achievers. For example, when compared with their interactions with high achievers, teachers tend to give less time to low achievers to respond to a question before providing the answer or calling on another student, they reinforce low achievers for incorrect responses more frequently, they criticize low achievers more often and praise them less, they give low achievers less interesting and rigorous curricula, and they interact with low achievers less often and in less positive ways. Inasmuch as students' achievement and behavior are deeply influenced by their teachers' expectations, it is crucial for teachers to give feedback to students that communicates high (and reasonable) expectations.

Punishment and Natural and Logical Consequences

No matter how efficient the teacher's prevention efforts, students will test the limits of the rules, and responses will be needed to correct the behavior, control the situation, and teach positive and responsible alternatives. The following guidelines help link a "disciplinary" action constructively with SEL: (1) The response should separate the deed from the doer. The teacher should make clear that the problem is the behavior, not the child. (2) Teachers should teach children they have the power to choose their actions and that they can learn to avoid losing control. (3) Responses should encourage reflection, self-evaluation, and problem solving. Lectures and teacher-centered explaining have the same limited effectiveness for SEL skill building as they do for academic skill development. Students are more likely to own the problem if they are asked rather than told what the problem is and given an opportunity to figure out how to fix it. (4) Responses to a mistaken behavior should involve the child learning the rationale for and practicing prosocial alternatives that can be reasonably used in similar future situations. This basic SEL technique fosters feelings of responsibility for correcting and preventing the problem.

Natural and logical consequences are intended to teach children to understand, anticipate, and make decisions based on the consequences of their actions in the real world (Brady et al., 2003; Dreikurs & Loren, 1968; Nelsen, Lynn, & Glenn, 2000). For example, if a child plays too roughly with a toy and it breaks, then the consequence is that the child's toy is now ruined. There is no need for an external, punitive intervention; the child begins to learn from the direct consequences of his or her mistakes, which is the goal of this system. Logical consequences are needed when the misbehavior substantially affects others or when the potential natural consequence is too severe.

Logical consequences have three basic features that are meant to maximize their informational value while minimizing the control aspect, thereby supporting the child's need for autonomy: they must be related, reasonable, and respectful. Being related means that they must be logically related to the misbehavior. For example, if a student writes on his or her desk, a related consequence would be for the student to clean the desk, not for the student to go to detention. Reasonable means that the severity of the consequence must be mild. If a kindergartener knocks down another student's block tower, it is unreasonable to have the student sit quietly in his or her chair for 45 minutes while the rest of the class is playing. Instead, the student might help rebuild the tower. Finally, consequences must be delivered respectfully. No matter how much a teacher may want to display his or her anger, consequences are most effective when delivered calmly and matter-of-factly (Brady et al., 2003; Dreikurs & Loren, 1968; Nelsen, Lynn, & Glenn, 2000).

Natural and logical consequences are solidly aligned with SEL theory. SEL focuses a great deal on students' decision-making, problem-solving, and conflict-resolution processes. A critical reflection point of this process is the anticipation of outcomes. Early research in SDM/SPS showed that problem behaviors were most likely to occur when children anticipated positive consequences from negative actions (Leonard & Elias, 1993). The simplest example: "He was bothering me, so I hit him to make him stop." Indeed, the stoppage is a natural consequence, but it is not the only one, and students need guidance to help them understand how the world around them works so that their view of consequences is realistic and takes into account long- and short-term outcomes both for themselves and for others.

From an SEL point of view, the potential for consequences to foster empathy and perspective taking better than other forms of punishment is critical. Natural and logical consequences must increase compliance in the short term (like punishments), as well as promote long-term maintenance and generalization to situations in which the child is not being monitored. For these techniques to have their desired positive effect, they must be rooted in a caring relationship between teachers and students.

One type of logical consequence that helps to build the SEL skills of caring and perspective taking is what Brady et al. (2003) call "apology of action." An apology of action is an active way to fix a problem the child has caused interpersonally. It includes but goes beyond a verbal apology. The child is expected at least to repair the damage done (or its equivalent), which is the type of consequence that adults face all the time at work and at home. Optimally, the child suggests a way to fix the problem, which makes a far greater impression than a grudging apology and takes the teacher out of the position of being the enforcer.

SEL-Derived Skills for Preventing and Correcting Misbehavior

Problem-Solving Strategies

Problem-solving strategies, such as *FIG TESPN* (previously described), can be enormously useful in responding to behavior mistakes. They can be used to work collaboratively with a child to fix problems, come up with alternative strategies for challenging situations, and devise appropriate logical consequences. *FIG TESPN* teaches the child that he or she has the power to choose different actions and encourages the child to take ownership for the mistake and its outcomes. With copious problem-solving practice, students may begin to envision the likely consequences of their actions before they take them and feel responsible for acting constructively in new situations. Ultimately, when a child gets into "trouble" or has a conflict with a peer, a constructive, preventively oriented problem-solving strategy should be used. SDM/SPS has examples of worksheets to guide this process (Elias & Bruene, 2005).

Self-Regulation

A component skill of self-control and self-discipline is self-regulation. Emotional self-regulation involves two steps: self-monitoring and emotion management. Self-monitoring emotions requires that students are able to identify the names of the emotions they are feeling based on their bodily sensations and cognitions. Emotion words can be taught using a number of games, and the student's unique bodily sensations should be discussed in order to help the student identify feelings as they are beginning to take hold. Once students are able to identify and self-monitor their emotions, they need practical strategies to be able to manage them and use them constructively.

Feelings Fingerprints

One specific example of how these techniques are operationalized within SEL is the SDM/SPS program's Feelings Fingerprints procedure. What follows is how we present the technique to teachers who, in turn, present to their students. For children to self-monitor, they need to understand that their bodies send them signals when they are about to lose control. SDM/SPS calls these signals of anger or stress "Feelings Fingerprints." (At the secondary level, we use the term "Stress Signature" and make the appropriate adjustments in the analogy.) Why? Like fingerprints, everyone has a unique set. Some people get a headache, a nervous stomach, a stiff neck, or sweaty palms. Others get a dry mouth, a quick heartbeat, clenched fists, a flushed face, or itchy skin. Most have more than one such signal. When teachers find themselves in a stressful or difficult choice situation, they can verbalize how they are feeling and what their Feelings Fingerprints are. This bridges naturally into asking students, "You just heard how my body sends me a headache behind my left eye and a red face when I am upset and under stress. How do *your* bodies let *you* know when you are upset?"

When learning Feelings Fingerprints, students take turns generating examples of situations during which they felt upset and what their Feelings Fingerprints were. Those situations are labeled "trigger situations." They learn that being aware of their Feelings Fingerprints and anticipating trigger situations serve as warning systems that they are facing a tough situation and need to use self-control to keep calm. Teachers may use this opportunity to discuss with students what it means to use self-control. They ask students to share different times and situations in which they have to use self-control. Then teachers ask for strategies for maintaining self-control, such as Keep Calm (see the next subsection), and help students make proactive plans to disengage from problem situations.

Keep Calm

SDM/SPS relies on Keep Calm, which was derived from Lamaze childbirth preparation procedures, to reduce students' anxiety, anger, and frustration. Keep Calm is simple and short, and it helps students to maintain self-control by reducing physi-ological arousal. Keep Calm begins with a student identifying the first physical signs of anger and then saying to him or herself, "Stop. Keep calm." Then the student takes a number of slow breaths, counting to five while breathing in, two while holding one's breath, and five while breathing out. This so-called 5-2-5 technique is simple to remember, prompt, and apply, and it reduces arousal so that students can respond in productive ways. Self-monitoring worksheets with teacher feedback and guidance can be especially valuable for students who have trouble responding initially to these and other skill-building activities.

ACTION 4: SHARE RESPONSIBILITY WITH STUDENTS

The final recommended action for bringing together SEL and effective classroom management is sharing responsibility with students. If we want children to learn responsibility, we have to give them many opportunities to experiment with it and grow comfortable, confident, and skilled at taking it. Sharing responsibility with students increases their commitment to the classroom, increases their prosocial motivation and behavior, and reduces behavior mistakes that result from frustration and feeling powerless. Empowering students is the best way to encourage them to take responsibility and contribute—rather than detracting and destroying (Freiberg, Huzinec, & Borders, 2008). Furthermore, it has been directly linked to academic motivation and performance (see McCombs, 2014).

This chapter has already mentioned a number of ways in which responsibility can be shared with students, beginning with developing democratic classroom rules. Students can contribute to the physical environment of the classroom with their art-work and through representations of their individuality. Students also benefit from input in day-to-day classroom decision making. The decisions students participate in can vary from choosing a signal for quiet to requesting a friend to sit with when the class's seating arrangement changes. Even giving students' input into small choices, such as the order of the day's schedule, can increase motivation. Teachers should not and need not give over all classroom governance to the students. However, giv-ing students choices—even between two acceptable options—makes the class more manageable and productive and increases students' social-emotional competencies (Elias et al., 1997; Weinstein & Mignano, 2003).

CONCLUSION

The field of SEL provides a pedagogy that aligns classroom management, social-emotional skill building, and academic learning. We reviewed four sets of teacher actions that can be taken with the goal of creating a seamless classroom management system that promotes academic, social, and emotional learning: teaching social-emotional skills, building caring relationships, setting firm and fair boundaries, and sharing responsibility with students.

The challenges of attaining this goal cannot fall on any one teacher. Only by coor-dinated and continuous application of the principles outlined herein can the desired impact on students occur. Yet nearly two millennia ago, a Jewish educator recognized that each teacher must do his or her part, with no alibis or excuses: "You are not responsible for completing the work, nor are you free to give up on it" (Pirke Avot 2:21). No teacher can be fully responsible for the growth—academic or otherwise—of his or her students. Students are influenced by so many other factors and spend only a few months in each classroom before moving on. Nevertheless, it is each teacher's responsibility to provide students with as many useful tools as possible to enable them to build their own futures. And it is the responsibility of all educators to see that all students pass through organized, caring, and skill-enhancing classrooms and school environments so that they can become academically, socially, and emotionally competent as adults.

REFERENCES

Baumrind, D. (1966). Effects of authoritative parental control on child behavior. *Child Development, 37,* 887–907.

Bear, G. G. (1998). School discipline in the United States: Preventing, correcting, and long-term social development. *School Psychology Review, 27*(1), 14–32.

Bear, G. G. (2010). *School discipline and self-discipline: A practical guide to promoting prosocial student behavior.* New York: Guilford.

Brady, K., Forton, M. B., Porter, D., & Wood, C. (2003). *Rules in school.* Greenfield, MA: Northeast Foundation for Children.

Brophy, J. (1999). Perspectives of classroom management: Yesterday, today, and tomorrow. In H. J. Freiberg (Ed.), *Beyond behaviorism: Changing the classroom management paradigm* (pp. 43–56). Boston: Allyn & Bacon.

Brophy, J. (2004). *Motivating students to learn.* Mahwah, NJ: Erlbaum.

Cartledge, G., & Milburn, J. F. (1995). *Teaching social skills to children and youth: Innovative approaches* (3rd ed.). Boston: Allyn & Bacon.

Charney, R. (2002). *Teaching children to care: Classroom management for ethical and academic growth, K–8.* Greenfield, MA: Northeast Foundation for Children.

Collaborative for Academic, Social, and Emotional Learning. (2012). *2013 CASEL Guide: Effective social and emotional learning programs: Preschool and elementary school edition.* Chicago: Collaborative for Academic, Social, and Emotional Learning (CASEL).

Collaborative for Academic, Social, and Emotional Learning (CASEL). (n.d.). *Social and emotional learning core competencies.* Retrieved from www.casel.org/social-and-emotional-learning/core-competencies.

Cornelius-White, J. (2007). Learner-centered teacher–student relationships are effective: A meta-analysis. *Review of Educational Research, 77*(1), 113–143.

Comer, J. P. (2003). Transforming the lives of children. In M. J. Elias, H. Arnold, & C. S. Hussey (Eds.), *EQ + IQ = Best leadership practices for caring and successful schools* (pp. 11–22). Thousand Oaks, CA: Corwin Press.

Curwin, R., & Mendler, A. (1988). Packaged discipline programs: Let the buyer beware. *Educational Leadership, 46,* 2, 68–71.

Danielson, C. (2008). *The handbook for enhancing professional practice: Using the Framework for Teaching in your school.* Alexandria, VA: Association for Supervision and Curriculum Development.

Deci, E. L., Koestner, R., & Ryan, R. M. (1999). A meta-analytic review of experiments examining the effects of extrinsic rewards on intrinsic motivation. *Psychological Bulletin, 125,* 627–668.

Dreikurs, R. (1968). *Psychology in the classroom: A manual for teachers.* New York: Harper & Row.

Dreikurs, R., & Loren, G. (1968). *Logical consequences.* New York: Meredith Press.

Durlak, J. A., Weissberg, R. P., Dymnicki, A. B., Taylor, R. D., & Schellinger, K. B. (2011). The impact of enhancing students' social and emotional learning: A meta-analysis of school-based universal interventions. *Child Development, 82,* 405–32. doi: 10.1111/j.1467-8624.2010.01564.x

Dweck, C. S. (1999). Caution—Praise can be dangerous. *American Educator, 23*(1), 4–9.

Elias, M. J. (2003). *Academic and social-emotional learning.* Brussels: International Academy of Education, UNESCO.

Elias, M. J. (2004). Strategies to infuse social and emotional learning into academics. In J. E. Zins, R. P. Weissberg, M. C. Wang, & H. J. Walberg (Eds.), *Building academic success on social and emotional learning: What does the research say?* (pp. 113–134). New York: Teachers College, Columbia University.

Elias, M. J., & Bruene, L. (2005). *Social decision making/social problem solving: A curriculum for academic, social, and emotional learning, Grades 2–3, 4–5, and 6–8.* Champaign, IL: Research Press.

Elias, M. J., & Trusheim, W. (2013, July). Beyond compliance: Rethinking discipline and codes of conduct. *Education Week, 32,* 37. Retrieved from www.edweek.org/ew/articles/2013/07/25/37elias.h32.html.

Elias, M. J., Zins, J. E., Weissberg, R. P., Frey, K. S., Greenberg, M. T., Haynes, N. M., et al. (1997). *Promoting social and emotional learning: Guidelines for educators.* Alexandria, VA: Association for Supervision and Curriculum Development.

Freiberg, H. J. (1999). Beyond behaviorism. In H. J. Freiberg (Ed.), *Beyond behaviorism: Changing the classroom management paradigm* (pp. 3–20). Boston: Allyn & Bacon.

Freiberg, H. J., Huzinec, C. A., & Borders, K. (2008). The effects of classroom management on student achievement: A study of three inner-city middle schools and their comparison schools. Paper presented at the American Education Research Association Annual Meeting, New York, March 24–28.

Gardner, H. (1985). *Frames of mind.* New York: Basic Books.

Gardner, H. (1993). *Multiple intelligences: The theory in practice.* New York: Basic Books.

Glasser, W. (1992). *The quality school: Managing students without coercion* (2nd ed., expanded). New York: HarperCollins.

Gordon, T. (with Burch, N.). (1974). *TET: Teacher effectiveness training.* New York: P. H. Wyden.

Gordon, T. (with Burch, N.). (2003). *TET: Teacher effectiveness training* (1st rev. ed.). New York: Three Rivers Press.

Greenberg, M. T., Domitrovich, C., & Bumbarger, B. (2001). The prevention of mental disorders in school-aged children: Current state of the field. *Prevention & Treatment, 4,* article 1 (March 30). Retrieved from http://journals.apa.org/prevention/volume4/pre0040001a.html

Hattie, J. (2009?). *Visible learning: A synthesis of over 800 meta-analyses relating to achievement.* London: Routledge.

Kohlberg, L. (1984). *The psychology of moral development.* San Francisco: Harper & Row.

Kohn, A. (1996). *Beyond discipline: From compliance to community.* Alexandria, VA: Association for Supervision and Curriculum Development.

Leonard, C., & Elias, M. J. (1993). Entry into middle school: Student factors predicting adaptation to an ecological transition. *Prevention in Human Services, 10,* 39–57.

Levine, M. (2002). *A mind at a time.* New York: Simon & Schuster.

Marshall, M., & Weisner, K. (2004, March). Using a discipline system to promote learning. *Phi Delta Kappan, 85,* 498–507.

Marzano, R. J., & Marzano, J. S. (2003). The key to classroom management. *Educational Leadership, 61,* 1 (September), 6–13.

Maslow, A. H. (1970). *Motivation and personality* (2nd ed.). New York: Harper & Row.

McCarthy, B. (1987). *The 4MAT system: Teaching to learning styles with right/left mode techniques.* Barrington, IL: Excel.

McCaslin, M., & Good, T. (1992). Compliant cognition: The misalliance of management and instructional goals in current school reform. *Educational Researcher, 21,* 4–17.

McCaslin, M., & Good, T. (1998). Moving beyond management as sheer compliance: Helping students to develop goal coordination strategies. *Educational Horizons, 76,* 169–176.

McCombs, B. (2014). Developing responsible and autonomous learners: A key to motivating students. Retrieved from www.apa.org/education/k12/learners.aspx?item=1

Mueller, C. M., & Dweck, C. S. (1998). Intelligence praise can undermine motivation and performance. *Journal of Personality and Social Psychology, 75,* 33–52.

Nelsen, J., Lynn, L., & Glenn, H. S. (2000). *Positive discipline in the classroom: Developing mutual respect, cooperation, and responsibility in your classroom* (rev. 3rd ed.). Roseville, CA: Prima Publishing.

Noddings, N. (2003). *Happiness and education.* Cambridge: Cambridge University Press.

Osborne, M. P. (1999). *Buffalo before breakfast.* New York: Random House.

Roorda, D. L., Koomen, H. M. Y., Spilt, J. L., & Oort, F. J. (2011). The influence of affective teacher–student relationships on students' school engagement and achievement: A meta-analytic approach. *Review of Educational Research, 81*(4), 493–529.

Saarni, C. (2000). Emotional competence: A developmental perspective. In R. Bar-On & J. D. A. Parker (Eds.), *The handbook of emotional intelligence: Theory, development, assessment, and application at home, school, and in the workplace* (pp. 68–91). San Francisco: Jossey-Bass.

Salovey, P., & Sluyter, D. (Eds.). (1997). *Emotional development and emotional intelligence: Educational implications.* New York: Basic Books.

Schaps, E., & Solomon, D. (1990). Schools and classrooms as caring communities. *Educational Leadership, 48*(3) (November), 38–42.

Shure, M. B., & Glaser, A. (2001). I Can Problem Solve (ICPS): A cognitive approach to the prevention of early high-risk behaviors. In J. Cohen (Ed.), *Caring classrooms/intelligent schools: The social emotional education of young children* (pp. 122–139). New York: Teachers College, Columbia University.

Tomlinson, C. A. (1999). *The differentiated classroom: Responding to the needs of all learners.* Alexandria, VA: Association of Supervision and Curriculum Development.

Weinstein, C. S. (1999). Reflections on best practices and promising programs: Beyond assertive classroom discipline. In H. J. Freiberg (Ed.), *Beyond behaviorism: Changing the classroom management paradigm* (pp. 147–163). Boston: Allyn & Bacon.

Weinstein, C. S., & Mignano, Jr., A. J. (2003). *Elementary classroom management: Lessons from research and practice* (3rd ed.). Boston: McGraw-Hill.

Willingham, D. T. (2005). How praise can motivate—or stifle. *American Educator, 29*(4), 23–27, 48.

7

RECONSIDERING EXCLUSIONARY DISCIPLINE

The Efficacy and Equity of Out-of-School Suspension and Expulsion

RUSSELL J. SKIBA & M. KAREGA RAUSCH
INDIANA UNIVERSITY

Effective school disciplinary systems—the philosophies, policies, and practices used to create safe schools that are maximally conducive to learning for all students—are necessary to ensure that schools maximize student opportunity to learn. In the first edition of this handbook, Skiba & Rausch (2006) identified four core goals of any school disciplinary system. First, discipline is intended to ensure the safety of students and teachers, preventing incidents that could threaten the safety of students or staff. Second, effective discipline creates a climate conducive to instruction and should improve academic outcomes by increasing the amount and quality of time teachers can spend teaching, rather than responding to behavioral disruptions (Brophy, 1988; Wang, Haertel, & Walberg, 1997). Third, from a purely behavioral perspective, a discipline system can be called effective only if it actually creates a change in student behavior over time, reducing rates of negative behavior and hopefully increasing prosocial behavior toward peers and adults (Alberto & Troutman, 2013). Finally, systems of discipline teach students the skills they need to succeed in schools and society.

Although these types of goals are accepted almost universally, *how* schools go about achieving them is a matter of considerable debate. Among the most common and controversial of procedures is removing the student from the learning environment entirely through the use of out-of-school suspension and expulsion. Recent reports from advocates (Losen & Martinez, 2013), policy think tanks (Council of State Governments, 2011), and professional associations (American Academy of Pediatrics, 2013; American Bar Association, 2001; American Psychological Association, 2008) have presented data on the negative outcomes associated with suspension and expulsion and have recommended a reduction or a moratorium on their use (Dignity in Schools Campaign, 2012). Yet the removal from school for some period of time for disciplinary incidents has been and remains among the most commonly used of disciplinary techniques (Lewis, Butler, Bonner, & Joubert, 2010; Skiba, Peterson, & Williams, 1997). Losen and Martinez (2013), examining the most recent Civil Rights Data Collection of the United States Office for Civil Rights that included all middle and high schools in the country, reported that in 7000 secondary schools in that data set, 25% or more of students in at least one student group (racial group, gender, disability status) were suspended one or more times during the 2009–2010 school year. Indeed, reliance on out-of-school suspension has continued to increase from the 1970s until the present (Losen & Skiba, 2010; Wallace, Goodkind, Wallace, & Bachman, 2008).

Removal from school, however, poses an inherent risk by reducing one of the strongest predictors of student academic and social success: student opportunity to learn (see Wang, Haertel, & Walberg, 1997). Although educational decision makers at schools with higher rates of out-of-school suspension tend to believe that such approaches are necessary to preserve school order and safety (Advancement Project/ Civil Rights Project, 2000; Mukuria, 2002; Skiba & Edl, 2004), the frequent use of suspension and expulsion practices, particularly for incidents that are not threats to safety, has been found to be associated with a number of risks to studen learning, including reducing learning time (Lassen, Steele, & Sailor, 2006), damaging the student–school bond (Bracy, 2011; McNeely, Nonemaker, & Blum, 2002), and diminishing student engagement in the educational process (Greenwood, Horton, & Utley, 2002). In terms of long-term outcomes, data have begun to suggest relationships between out-of-school suspension/expulsion and school dropout (Suh & Suh, 2007) and increased risk of juvenile justice involvement (Council of State Governments, 2011; Nicholson-Crotty, Birchmeier, & Valentine, 2009).

Is frequent use of out-of-school suspension and expulsion a required element of school disciplinary systems? The purpose of this chapter is to examine school disciplinary systems, particularly what we know about the use of suspension and expulsion practices, the effectiveness of student removal in achieving critical educational and community outcomes, the extent of and reasons for its inequitable use, and the effectiveness and equitable outcomes associated with alternative disciplinary system practices.

USE OF DISCIPLINARY REMOVAL

Although often understood to be a linear event, moving directly from student misbehavior to office referral to administrative decision, student removal from school through out-of-school suspension[1] and expulsion is actually the end result of a number of converging factors, including the quality of the student–teacher relationship, student perception of school and behavior, teacher philosophy and practices, school and classroom characteristics, principal philosophies and practices, and the policy context at the local, state, and national levels (Morrison, Anthony, Storino, Cheng, Furlong, & Morrison, 2001). Thus, the extent and disproportionality of use described in this section should be understood to be the culmination of this complex process, rather than solely a response to individual student misbehavior (Skiba, Horner, Chung, Rausch, May, & Tobin, 2011).

Common and Increasing Use

Out-of-school suspension is a commonly used disciplinary technique (Council of State Governments, 2011; KewalRamani, Gilbertson, Fox, & Provasnik, 2007; Mansfield & Farris, 1992), among the most frequently used responses to disciplinary referrals (Lewis, Butler, Bonner, & Joubert, 2010; Skiba, Peterson, & Williams, 1997). In a longitudinal investigation of school disciplinary incidents for individual student cohorts as they progressed through secondary schools, the Council of State Governments (2011) found that almost one-third of all students (31%) in Texas public schools experienced at least one out-of-school suspension between seventh and twelfth grade. Skiba and colleagues, studying disciplinary referrals across all middle schools in one large urban school district, reported that one-third of all referrals to the office resulted in a one- to five-day out-of-school suspension.

The use of suspension and expulsion in America's public schools continues to increase (Krezmien, Leone, & Achilles, 2006; Losen & Martinez, 2013; Losen & Skiba, 2010). In an examination of suspension use as reported to the U.S. Department of Education's Office for Civil Rights from 1973 to 2006, Losen and Skiba reported that, nationally, out-of school suspension rates have nearly doubled, increasing from approximately 3.7% in 1973 to 6.9% in 2006. National, state, and local district reports also suggest increases in disciplinary removal rates, particularly for African American students (Losen & Martinez, 2013; Losen & Skiba, 2010; Krezmien, Leone, & Achilles, 2006; Rausch & Skiba, 2005; Richart, Brooks, & Soler, 2003; Tuzzolo & Hewitt, 2007; Wallace, Goodkind, Wallace, & Bachman, 2008).

Context of Use

Studies of school discipline find that student removal appears to be related to the locale and level of the school. Out-of-school suspension and expulsion rates tend to be highest in urban schools compared to usage at suburban, town, or rural locales (Massachusetts Advocacy Center, 1986; Noltemeyer & Mcloughlin, 2010; Rausch & Skiba, 2005; Wu, Pink, Crain & Moles, 1982). Suspensions and expulsions appear to be lowest in elementary school, increase sharply and peak in middle school, and either remain high or drop slightly in high school (Arcia, 2007; Petras, Masyn, Buckley, Ialongo, & Kellam, 2011; Raffaele Mendez & Knoff, 2003; Rausch & Skiba, 2005; Theriot & Dupper, 2010).

Variability in suspension and expulsion appears to be attributable also to individual student behavior but, to an even greater degree, school factors. Student behavior does contribute to a student's likelihood of being disciplined (Horner, Fireman & Wang, 2010; Petras et al., 2011; Tobin, Sugai, & Colvin, 1996). Yet, because school discipline is a complex process that is a combination of student behavior, teacher competence and skill, and administrative practice and policy (Morrison, Anthony,

Storino, Cheng, Furlong, & Morrison, 2001; Skiba et al., 2011; Vavrus & Cole, 2002), research has also found substantial contributions of schools and school personnel to school discipline (Gregory & Weinstein, 2008; Horner et al., 2010; Irvin, Tobin, Sprague, Sugai, & Vincent, 2004; Rocque, 2010; Skiba et al., 2011; Wu, Pink, Crain, & Moles, 1982). Studies that have compared the relative contributions of students to school factors have found classroom or school factors to be stronger predictors of student removal (Bradshaw, Mitchell, O'Brennan & Leaf, 2010; Christle, Nelson & Jolivette, 2004; Horner et al., 2010; Rocque, 2010; Skiba, Chung, Trachok, Baker, Sheya, & Hughes, in press; Wu, Pink, Crain, & Moles, 1982).

EFFICACY AND EQUITY CHALLENGES

Both federal educational legislation (United States Department of Education, 2013) and contemporary educational leadership scholarship (Slavin, Cheung, Holmes, Madden, & Chamberlain, 2013) increasingly assume a requirement that educational practices be grounded in strong or promising empirical evidence documenting their effectiveness in achieving intended outcomes. Moreover, the rapidly growing racial/ethnic diversity in schools and communities (Sandefur, Martin, Eggerling-Boeck, Mannon, & Meier, 2001) and the right of students not to be discriminated against on the basis of race, color, or national origin (Browne, Losen, & Wald, 2002) create a context by which educational practice must also be focused on creating equitable outcomes. Thus, out-of-school suspension and expulsion can be judged to be effective to the degree that they yield school contexts that maximize the ability of all students to learn and do so equitably (American Psychological Association, 2008; Skiba & Rausch, 2006). The following two sections review the evidence on the effectiveness of student removal and the degree to which student removal is equitably practiced.

Effects and Effectiveness of Out-of-School Suspension and Expulsion

How well does disciplinary removal work? In the following sections, we examine the extent to which disciplinary removal is associated with the instructional and organizational outcomes identified by Skiba and Rausch (2006) as elements of an effective disciplinary system: (1) ensuring school safety, (2) contributing to an improved climate for teaching and learning, (3) improving student behavior, and (4) promoting successful outcomes in school and society.

Contribution to Safe Schools

In its comprehensive review of zero tolerance, the American Psychological Association's Zero Tolerance Task Force (2008) concluded that there is no evidence that the use of out-of-school suspension and expulsion associated with zero tolerance has made a contribution to improved safety in schools. Indeed, some analyses have suggested a negative relationship between the use of punitive and exclusionary discipline approaches and perceptions of school safety. In a mixed method study, Steinberg, Allensworth, and Johnson (in press) found that high suspension rates resulted in lower student ratings of safety and diminished school climate, while strong student-teacher and parent-teacher relationships were associated with lower suspension rates and an increased sense of safety. Similarly, McNeely, Nonemaker, & Blum (2002), using data from the ADD Health national survey of seventh through twelfth graders, found that students reported feeling less safe in schools that use harsh punishments due to policy regulations than students in schools that use more moderate forms of punishments.

Improved Climate for Learning

One assumption of disciplinary exclusion is that the removal of disruptive students will improve school climate by reducing disruption and improving the learning environment for those who remain (Ewing, 2000). Reviews of available research (e.g., American Psychological Association, 2008), however, have yielded no evidence to support this assumption, instead finding that the increased use of suspension and expulsion is associated with student and teacher perceptions of a *less* effective and inviting school climate. Schools with higher rates of suspension have higher student/teacher ratios and a lower level of academic quality (Hellman & Beaton, 1986), spend more time on discipline-related matters (Davis & Jordan, 1994), and pay significantly less attention to issues of school climate (Bickel & Qualls, 1980).

Such relationships may be especially salient for students of color (Gregory, Cornell, & Fan, 2011; Kuperminc, Leadbeater, Emmons, & Blatt, 1997; Mattison & Aber, 2007). Mattison and Aber (2007) compared self-reported rates of detention and suspension with ratings of racial school climate and found that African American students reported more experiences of racism and lower ratings of racial fairness at school and that both of these ratings were associated with higher rates of detention and suspension. Similarly, Gregory and colleagues (2011) found that schools having the lowest levels of some indicators of school climate also had the highest rates of suspension, as well as the largest suspension gap between black and white students.

Improved Student Behavior

Given a technical definition of punishment as an event or procedure that reduces the future probability of occurrence of a behavior (Alberto & Troutman, 2013; Driscoll, 2000; Skinner, 1953), student disciplinary interventions that are effective punishers should lead to reduced rates of inappropriate or disruptive behavior. Longitudinal and descriptive studies find that, rather than reducing the likelihood of being suspended, suspension predicts higher future rates of suspension. Descriptive studies of suspension find high rates of repeat offending in out-of-school suspension, ranging from 35% (Bowditch, 1993) to 42% (Costenbader & Markson, 1998). In a longitudinal investigation, Raffaele Mendez (2003) found that the number of out-of-school suspensions a student received in fourth or fifth grade was the strongest predictor of the number of suspensions later in middle school, even after statistically controlling for student's socioeconomic status, race, special education status, teacher ratings of student behavior, and academic achievement. The lack of long-term effectiveness of disciplinary exclusion in affecting behavioral trajectory has led some authors to conclude that in many cases, "suspension functions as a reinforcer (variable interval schedule) rather than as a punisher" (Tobin, Sugai, & Colvin, 1996, p. 91).

Promoting Successful Engagement in School and Society

Certainly one of the prime purposes of any disciplinary system is to preserve an instructional climate that can support student learning. Similarly, large majorities of teachers (93%) and parents (88%) agree that one fundamental element of a school's mission is to ensure that children are able to fully and effectively participate in society (Public Agenda, 2004). Yet available evidence suggests that punitive approaches to discipline are associated with negative academic outcomes (Arcia, 2006; Davis & Jordan, 1994), school dropout (Arcia, 2007; Balfanz, Byrnes, & Fox, 2013; Council of State Governments, 2011; Ekstrom, Goertz, Pollack, & Rock, 1986; Raffaele Mendez & Knoff, 2003; Shollenberger, in press; Suh & Suh, 2007; Wehlage & Rutter, 1986), and involvement in the juvenile justice system (Council of State Governments, 2011; Nicholson-Crotty, Birchmeier, & Valentine, 2009).

Support for student achievement. One of the most consistent and widely replicated findings of educational psychology in the past 30 years has been a strong and consistent relationship between opportunity for student learning and student gains in academic achievement (Brophy, 1988; Greenwood, Horton, & Utley, 2002; Wang, Haertel, & Walberg, 1997). Time lost to suspension and expulsion may have a negative impact on school connectedness, on student engagement, and ultimately on student achievement. In a study of school discipline in New Hampshire, Muscott, Mann, and LeBrun (2008) reported that an average office disciplinary referral (ODR) resulted in 45 minutes of lost classroom instruction for students, 10 to 15 minutes of lost teaching time for teachers, and 15 to 45 minutes of lost time for school administrators. In one urban school district, 3587 African American males enrolled missed a collective 3714 school days from being suspended out-of-school in one academic year (Lewis, Butler, Bonner, & Joubert, 2010).

It is not surprising, then, that emerging evidence suggests a negative relationship between school discipline and multiple measures of student academic achievement, including state accountability examinations (Davis & Jordan, 1994; Rausch & Skiba, 2005), reading achievement (Arcia, 2006), school grades (Rocque, 2010), and writing achievement (Raffaele Mendez, Knoff, & Ferron, 2002). In a three-year longitudinal investigation of a matched sample of suspended and nonsuspended middle school students in one large and diverse school district in the Southeast, Arcia (2006) found a significant negative relationship between reading achievement growth over the three-year period and the number of days suspended over that same three-year period.

Relationship to school dropout. In a five-year longitudinal study of all students in the state of Texas, the Council of State Governments (2011) found that suspended/expelled students were five times as likely to drop out compared to students with no disciplinary action. Similarly, Suh and Suh (2007) found that being suspended at least once increased the likelihood of dropping out of school by 77.5% and that suspensions are a stronger predictor of dropout than either grade point average or socioeconomic status. Using a matched-sample longitudinal examination of suspension and dropout, Arcia (2006) found that the number of days students were suspended in the ninth grade is positively associated with their likelihood of dropping out before twelfth grade. Ethnographic field studies of school discipline suggest that the relationship between school suspension and school dropout may not be entirely accidental and that suspension may be used as a "pushout" tool to encourage low-achieving students and those viewed as "troublemakers" to leave school before graduation (Bowditch, 1993; Ferguson, 2001).

Relationship to juvenile justice system. Research connecting the overuse of punitive school disciplinary systems and contact with the juvenile justice system has been described under the construct of the so-called school-to-prison pipeline (Kim, Losen, & Hewitt, 2010; Wald & Losen, 2003). Recent studies (Council of State Governments, 2011; Nicholson-Crotty, Birchmeier, & Valentine, 2009) have provided some documentation of this connection. The Council of State Governments (2011) followed every seventh-grader in the state of Texas through the high school years. Even after controlling for more than 80 individual and school-level demographic and programmatic variables, multivariate analysis indicated that suspended or expelled students had a greater likelihood of contact with the juvenile justice system in future years; this relationship was even stronger for African American students.

Summary: Effectiveness of Exclusionary Discipline

In response to these and other data over the past decade, both the American Psychological Association and the American Academy of Pediatrics have released strong statements on the effectiveness of disciplinary removal. The American Psychological Association's Zero Tolerance Task Force (2008) concluded that "[z]ero tolerance has not been shown to improve school climate or school safety. Its application in suspension and expulsion has not proven an effective means of improving student behavior. It has not resolved, and indeed may have exacerbated, minority over-representation in school punishments" (p. 860). Similarly, the American Academy of Pediatrics (2013) concluded that "out-of-school suspension and expulsion are counterproductive to the intended goals, rarely if ever are necessary, and should not be considered as appropriate discipline in any but the most extreme and dangerous circumstances, as determined on an individual basis rather than as a blanket policy" (p. 1005).

Equity Challenges of Student Removal

Consistency of disproportionality across time and groups

The Children's Defense Fund (1975) report *Suspensions: Are They Helping Children?* first brought the issue of racial disparities in discipline to national attention. Since then, African American disparities in discipline have been consistently documented across location and type of punishment. African American students have been found to be overrepresented in a range of school disciplinary outcomes, including referrals to the office (Bradshaw, Mitchell, O'Brennan, & Leaf, 2010; Rocque, 2010; Skiba et al., 2011), out-of-school suspension and expulsion (Eitle & Eitle, 2004; Gregory & Weinstein, 2008; Hinojosa, 2008), school-based arrests (Theriot, 2009), and corporal punishment (Gregory, 1995; Owen, 2005; Shaw & Braden, 1990). In addition, African American students have been found to receive fewer mild disciplinary sanctions when referred for an infraction (McFadden, Marsh, Price, & Hwang, 1992; Payne & Welch, 2010). A number of studies have found black disproportionality in out-of-school suspension and expulsion to be increasing over time (Losen & Skiba, 2010; Wallace, Goodkind, Wallace, & Bachman, 2008).

Although there has been extensive study of disciplinary disproportionality for African American students, school discipline disparities for other student groups have been studied far less and with less consistent results. Whereas Peguero and Shekarkhar (2011) reported that both first-generation and third-generation Latino students received school punishments at a higher than expected level given their rate of misbehavior, others have found that Latino rates of out-of-school suspension do not differ significantly from the rates of white students (Horner et al., 2010; McFadden, Marsh, Price, & Hwang, 1992; Skiba et al., 1997). Studying elementary and middle schools across 17 states, Skiba and colleagues (2011) found Latino students to be overrepresented in office disciplinary referrals at the middle school level but underrepresented at the elementary school level. In a national investigation of disparate discipline across a number of racial/ethnic groups, Wallace and colleagues (2008) reported overrepresentation among American Indian students and underrepresentation among Asian students in school discipline and out-of-school suspension in particular.

Although as yet underresearched, emerging findings suggest that disciplinary disparities may also exist for students who identify as LGBTQ (lesbian, gay, bisexual, transgender, questioning). Using a nationally representative sample of adolescents in grades seven through twelve and controlling for self-reported rates of misbehavior, age, gender, race, and socioeconomic status, Himmelstein and Bruckner (2011) found that adolescents who reported same-sex attraction had significantly higher odds of being expelled from school. National surveys (e.g. Kosciw, Greytak, & Diaz, 2009), state analyses (Massachusetts Department of Elementary and Secondary Education, 2006), and comprehensive reviews of the literature (Russell, Kosciw, Horn, & Saewyc, 2010) find that LGBTQ students tend to rate school climates as hostile, punitive, unsafe, and unsupportive.

Counterintuitive Nature of Disproportionality Data

Although discussions on disproportionality are often framed as a problem found primarily in urban, high-poverty schools and districts, particularly for African American males, actual patterns of findings for disciplinary disproportionality often run counter to these expectations. Wallace and colleagues (2008) reported that, although boys of all races and ethnicities were more likely than girls to be disciplined, disparities between black and white rates of discipline were actually greater among female students. Similarly, although rates of out-of-school suspension and expulsion have consistently been found to be higher in poor urban districts than in suburban or rural settings (Losen & Skiba, 2010; Nicholson-Crotty et al., 2009; Noltemeyer & Mcloughlin, 2010), black–white disparities in suspension appear to be as great or even greater in higher-resourced suburban districts than in poor urban districts (Eitle & Eitle, 2004; Rausch & Skiba, 2004; Wallace, Goodkind, Wallace, & Bachman, 2008). Together, these findings argue that patterns of disproportionality in disciplinary consequences cannot be predicted from absolute rates of those same consequences. While males and under-resourced urban schools experience higher rates of suspension and expulsion, disproportionality in those consequences is as high or higher for females and in suburban settings.

Causes and Contributions to Disproportionality

Relationship between Socioeconomic Status and Disproportionality

Low-income students have consistently been found to be overrepresented in the use of out-of-school suspension (Brantlinger, 1991; Noltemeyer & Mcloughlin, 2010; Skiba et al., 1997; Wu et al., 1982). Hinojosa (2008) reported that a variety of variables typically associated with poverty are significantly associated with the likelihood of suspension, including the presence of a mother or father in the home, number of siblings, and quality of home resources.

Multivariate analyses have consistently found, however, that socioeconomic status is insufficient to account for racial and ethnic disproportionality in suspension and expulsion. Wallace and colleagues (2008), drawing on a national sample documenting disproportionality in major and minor offenses across a number of racial/ethnic groups over time, reported that consistent difference in rates of office referrals and suspensions for black, Latino, and American Indian tenth-graders remained significant even after controlling for family structure and parental education. Finding that urban schools consistently suspended a higher proportion of students out of school even after controlling for poverty, Noltemeyer and Mcloughlin (2010) concluded that "there is something above and beyond poverty that explains disciplinary differences between school types" (p. 33).

Differential Behavior

A related hypothesis might suggest that differential rates of discipline for African American students are due to differences in student behavior. Direct comparative classroom observation would provide the most compelling test of this hypothesis (Rocque, 2010), but such a study has yet to be conducted. Other more indirect methods—measurement of differences in severity, statistical controls for misbehavior, and controls for teacher and student ratings—have been conducted, however, to test the hypothesis that differential punishment is due to differential misbehavior.

Statistical Control for Type of Misbehavior

One line of inquiry to exploring the contribution of differential behavior to disciplinary disproportionality has examined racial/ethnic contributions to rates of suspension and expulsion using multivariate procedures (e.g., logistic regression) to control for type of misbehavior. If racial disparities in discipline are due to differential rates of disruption, the contribution of race to disciplinary outcomes should become nonsignificant when the type or severity of behavior enters the model. That hypothesis has not been supported in multivariate tests. Whether the predictor variables are a range of minor and major office disciplinary referrals at the school level (Skiba et al., 2011), major offenses (e.g., incidents of violence, weapons possession, substance use and possession) taken from a statewide suspension database (Eitle & Eitle, 2004), or self-reported data from the National Education Longitudinal Study (Peguero & Shekarkhar, 2011), controls for the extent or type of misbehavior have, at best, led to slight and nonsignificant decreases in the size of disproportionality. The continuing significance of race after controlling for a range of student behaviors strongly suggests that, in general, factors related to student behavior are insufficient to account for racial/ethnic disparities in discipline.

Differences in Behavioral Severity

Inasmuch as any referral to the office is a product of student behavior and teacher judgment (Morrison et al., 2001), simple differences in rate of office referrals or suspension/expulsion are insufficient to assess whether cross-group differences represent a function of student behavior or teacher/school response. One indicator of behavioral difference, however, might be severity of infraction.

A number of studies have examined whether black students are referred to the office for behaviors that might be considered more severe. Racial and ethnic differences that have emerged in comparative studies of school discipline tend to be minimal (McCarthy & Hoge, 1987; Wallace et al., 2008) or occur in more interactive or subjective categories of infraction (Gregory & Weinstein, 2008; Skiba, Michael, Nardo, & Peterson, 2002). Wallace and associates found few racial differences in offenses likely to lead to zero tolerance policy violations (e.g., drugs, alcohol, weapons) but in higher rates of out-of-school suspensions for black, Latino, and Native American students. Analyzing middle school disciplinary referrals, Skiba and colleagues (2002) found that white students were referred to the office significantly more frequently for offenses that appear more observable (e.g., smoking, vandalism), whereas black students were referred more often for behaviors that appear to require more subjective judgment (e.g., disrespect, excessive noise). Reviewing the suspension database of an urban, midsized high school, Gregory and Weinstein (2008) reported that *defiance* was the single most common reason for referral to the office—fully 67% of all referrals to the office were for defiance—and that black students were significantly more likely than white students to be referred for that reason.

Controlling for Teacher or Student Ratings of Behavior

As noted, any office disciplinary referral is a joint product of student behavior and teacher perception of the threat to classroom order posed by that behavior. Thus, one strategy for disentangling behavior from perceptions of student behavior involves controlling for external ratings of the severity of behavior. Even after controlling for peer ratings as aggressive or prosocial, Horner and colleagues (2010) found that African American students were significantly more likely to receive a serious disciplinary action. Hinojosa (2008) controlled for teacher perception of student behavior with a four-point teacher rating of fighting and found that black students in an urban school district were still more likely to be suspended. Two separate studies (Bradshaw, Mitchell, O'Brennan, & Leaf, 2010; Rocque, 2010) have reported that even when controlling for the classroom teacher's own ratings of externalizing or disruptive behavior, black students were significantly more likely to be referred to the office by those same teachers.

In summary, data from a number of sources appear to converge in failing to support the hypothesis that differences in school discipline are due to racial/ethnic differences in behavior. Multivariate analyses have consistently found race/ethnicity to be a robust predictor of school punishment even after controlling statistically for student misbehavior. Studies that have specifically investigated the severity of behavioral infractions have found no evidence that African American or other students are engaging in more severe behavior that would warrant higher rates of suspension or expulsion. Finally, in what is probably the strongest evidence in this area, racial/ethnic disparities in disciplinary consequences remain even when holding teachers' own ratings of the severity of student behavior constant.

What Does Predict Disciplinary Disproportionality?

Even though neither poverty nor differential rates of misbehavior appears to explain racial and ethnic disparities in discipline, recent research has identified a number of variables that have demonstrated some degree of relationship to rates of racial disparity in school discipline.

Relationship to Achievement

Gregory, Skiba, and Noguera (2010) reviewed literature on the achievement and discipline gap and found sufficient evidence to suggest a relationship between the two. The relationship between students' externalizing behavior and academic skill deficits has been well documented (Cairns & Cairns, 2000; Lopes, 2005). Students living in poverty situations also face a lower quality of resources and facilities (Kozol, 2005), higher teacher turnover and a lower proportion of highly qualified teachers (Darling-Hammond, 2004), and a general inequality of educational opportunity (Ladson-Billings, 2006). It appears that the extent to which the relationship between the achievement gap and the discipline gap is due to achievement/behavior correlations or that a systemic influence on both gaps cannot yet be determined.

Representativeness of Faculty and Students

The hypothesis that differential disciplinary outcomes are associated with the representation of faculty or students of color has begun to be explored in two separate lines of work. *Representative bureaucracy* asserts that if administrators and the groups they serve share similar characteristics, they will also be more likely to share the same norms and values and be more likely to pursue courses of action more favorable to those groups (Meier & Stewart, 1992). Applications of this construct to school discipline have found that schools with a more diverse and representative teaching force tend to exhibit lower rates of racial disparity in school discipline (Mcloughlin & Noltemeyer, 2010; Rocha & Hawes, 2009), although the race of the school administrator has not been found to be a significant contributor to disproportionality (Roch, Pitts, & Navarro, 2010). Rates of minority student enrollment have also been found to influence rates of school punishment. Regardless of levels of misbehavior and delinquency, schools with higher black enrollment have been found to be more likely to use higher rates of exclusionary discipline, court action, and zero tolerance policies and to use fewer mild disciplinary practices (Payne & Welch, 2010; Welch & Payne, 2010).

Contribution of Classroom and Office Processes

There is evidence that racial disparities in school discipline begin with classroom referral and classroom management. Skiba and colleagues (2011) reported that black students are twice as likely to receive ODRs at the elementary level and up to four times as likely in middle school. The situational nature of behavior leading to office disciplinary referral also argues for a contribution at the classroom level: Gregory and Weinstein (2008) reported that black student referrals for defiance occurred consistently across classrooms for only a small proportion (14%) of the sample they studied. Initial disparities in office referral also appear to be augmented by differential processing at the office level. Nicholson-Crotty and colleagues (2009) reported that approximately 95% of black students who committed a weapons offense received an out-of-school suspension, as opposed to 85% of white students. Skiba and colleagues (2011) found black and Latino students to be significantly more likely than white students to receive the consequences of suspension and expulsion for minor infractions, even when controlling for the previous step of teacher referral.

School Climate

Positive school climate has been found to be associated with lower rates of student misconduct and discipline (Bickel & Qualls, 1980; Welsh, 2003). At the same time, comparisons of student ratings of climate have reported that African American students' perceptions of school climate are more negative than their white peers (Kupchik & Ellis, 2008; Mattison & Aber, 2007; Ruck & Wortley, 2002; Shirley & Cornell, 2011; Watkins & Aber, 2009). It is not surprising, then, that there is evidence of a link between rates of disproportionality and student ratings of racial school climate (Mattison & Aber, 2007), as well as with more general measures of school climate (Gregory, Cornell, & Fan, 2011; Kuperminc, Leadbeater, Emmons, & Blatt, 1997; Shirley & Cornell, 2011).

Summary: Ineffectiveness and Inequity of Disciplinary Removal

Keeping children safe and learning at school requires that school disciplinary systems create a context conducive to learning, using proven evidence-based approaches to achieve those ends. Available evidence suggests that instead of creating such environments, disciplinary removal is associated with less adequate school climate (Gregory, Cornell, & Fan, 2011), lower levels of achievement (Arcia, 2006), a higher probability of future student misbehavior (Tobin, Sugai, & Colvin, 1996), and higher levels of school dropout and engagement in the juvenile justice system (Council of State Governments, 2011). Moreover, students of color—African American students in particular—appear to be placed at higher risk of experiencing these negative outcomes. While African American students continue to experience disciplinary removal at rates disproportionately higher than their peers (Losen & Skiba, 2010), there is no evidence that such removal is due to higher rates of misbehavior or higher rates of poverty among African American students (American Psychological Association, 2008). Available evidence does suggest that disproportionality in discipline may be due to a lack of diversity among faculty and the student body (Mcloughlin & Nolte-meyer, 2010), school practices and procedures (Skiba et al., 2011), and differential perceptions of school climate (Mattison & Aber, 2007).

Are there alternative elements of school disciplinary systems that are able to achieve different results for students? The next section will explore the evidence on alternative disciplinary strategies, with a particular emphasis on the degree to which these strategies are creating more positive climates and outcomes for all students.

ALTERNATIVE STRATEGIES FOR RESTRUCTURING SCHOOL DISCIPLINE

A number of universal, school-wide interventions have been shown to be effective in improving school discipline or school climate and have been suggested as having potential for reducing disproportionality (Osher, Bear, Sprague, & Doyle, 2010). These include school-wide positive behavior supports (SWPBS) (Bradshaw, Koth, Thornton & Leaf, 2009; Horner et al., 2009), social-emotional learning (SEL) (Durlak, Weissberg, & Pachan, 2010; Ialongo, Poduska, Werthamer, & Kellam, 2001; Payton et al., 2008), and restorative justice or restorative practices (International Institute for Restorative Practices, 2009; Jennings, Gover & Hitchcock, 2008; Stinchcomb, Bazemore, & Riestenberg, 2006; Strang & Braithwaite, 2001).

School-Wide Positive Behavioral Interventions and Supports (SWPBIS)

The framework of SWPBIS is intended to restructure school disciplinary practices through a comprehensive and proactive approach to school discipline. The primary goals of SWPBIS are to prevent the development and intensification of behavior problems while maximizing academic achievement (Sugai, Horner, & McIntosh, 2008). To do so, the SWPBIS framework emphasizes four elements: (1) identifying measurable behavior and academic outcomes, (2) collecting data to guide decision making, (3) using evidence-based practices that support these outcomes, and (4) leveraging systems that support effective implementation (Sugai & Horner, 2009). The SWPBIS framework is intended to be flexible enough to be responsive to the local needs of schools.

The implementation of SWPBIS with fidelity has been linked to improved behavioral outcomes. Randomized control trial comparisons have showed significant decreases in major and minor ODRs (Bradshaw, Mitchell, & Leaf, 2010), improvement in measures of school climate and organizational health (Bradshaw, Koth, Bevans, Ialongo, and Leaf, 2008), and significantly lower behavioral risk factors and improved staff reports of school safety (Horner et al., 2009). Although case studies have reported promising results when cultural adaptations are made in PBIS implementation (Jones, Caravaca, Cisek, Horner, & Vincent, 2006; Wang, McCart, & Turnbull, 2007), there are as yet no broad-scale or experimental studies exploring the effect of PBIS implementation on racial and ethnic disparities in discipline. Emerging data have tended to find that PBIS in and of itself is insufficient for reducing disproportionality in discipline (Skiba et al., 2011; Vincent, Pavel, Sprague, & Tobin, in press; Vincent & Tobin, 2011).

Social Emotional Learning (SEL)

By teaching and reinforcing life skills, SEL programs seek to facilitate the healthy development of children who are self-aware, caring and connected to others, and responsible in their decision making (Collaborative for Academic, Social, and Emotional Learning [CASEL], 2003; Greenberg et al., 2003; Ialongo, Poduska, Werthamer, & Kellam, 2001). SEL programs vary greatly but are generally regarded as a curriculum aimed at building students' skills to: (1) recognize and manage their emotions, (2) appreciate the perspectives of others, (3) establish positive goals, (4) make responsible decisions, and (5) handle interpersonal situations effectively (CASEL, 2003; Payton et al., 2008).

Several studies have linked the completion of SEL programs to an increase in prosocial behaviors and a decrease in misbehaviors (CASEL, 2003; Zins, 2001). In a meta-analysis of after-school programs aimed at enhancing the personal and social skills of students age 5 to 18, Durlak, Weissberg, and Pachan (2010) found that students who participated in SEL programs demonstrated significant increases in their self-perceptions and bonding to school, positive social behaviors, levels of academic achievement, and significant reductions in problem behaviors. Again, no studies have yet been reported in the literature designed to specifically test the utility of SEL approaches for addressing issues of racial/ethnic disparities in school discipline.

Restorative Practices

Restorative practices or *restorative justice* has been implemented in schools as a theoretical framework for responding to student misbehavior (Braithwaite, 2002; Stinchcomb, Bazemore, & Riestenberg, 2006). Based on the assumption that wrongdoing damages relationships, restorative practices aim to restore relationships and repair harm. School discipline practices built on principles of restorative justice employ the use of formal and informal conferencing, classroom conference circles, and/or other frameworks of school disciplinary practice based on relationship and community building (Karp & Breslin, 2001; Stinchcomb, Bazemore, & Riestenberg,, 2006).

Research surrounding the effects of restorative justice implementation in U.S. public schools is in its early stages, and results have been somewhat mixed (Jennings, Gover, & Hitchcock, 2008; Umbreit, Vos, Coates, & Lightfoot, 2006), showing decreases in suspensions and behavioral referrals in some but not all schools. As with PBIS and SEL, applications of restorative justice related to reduction in disproportionate discipline are currently limited to case studies (Wearmouth, McKinney, & Glynn, 2007). In sum, although the results of pilot studies reflect possibilities that these approaches can reduce problem behaviors and the need for disciplinary actions in schools, more data are needed on the overall effects of sustained restorative justice programs.

Culturally Responsive Classroom Management (CRCM)

Numerous researchers have begun to examine the components that would increase the cultural responsiveness of classroom management. Qualitative observation and interview studies have identified a number of promising conventions of these components that describe and inform culturally responsive classroom management best practices (Bondy, Ross, Gallingame, & Hambacher, 2007; Brown, 2004; Monroe & Obidah, 2004; Weinstein, Tomlinson-Clarke, & Curran 2004). Managing student behavior based on culturally appropriate strategies means teachers are considering that students from many backgrounds and experiences may exhibit different communication styles, behavioral norms, and methods of expressing parental engagement. Bondy and colleagues (2007) suggest that CRCM "makes it explicit that classroom management is grounded in teachers' judgments about appropriate behavior and that these judgments are informed by cultural assumptions" (p. 328). In a theoretical review of CRCM, Weinstein and associates (2004) identified five components that characterize CRCM: (1) recognition of one's own ethnocentrism; (2) knowledge of students' cultural backgrounds; (3) understanding of the broader social, economic, and political context; (4) ability and willingness to use culturally appropriate management strategies; and (5) a commitment to building caring classrooms. Although a conceptual basis for an explicitly culturally responsive approach to classroom management and discipline has begun to emerge in the literature (e.g., Utley, Kozleski, Smith, & Draper, 2002; Weinstein, et al., 2004), research to date on CRCM has relied on teacher interview (Brown, 2003) or ethnographic field study and observation (Bondy, Ross, Gallingame, & Hambacher, 2007; Brown, 2002; Monroe & Obidah, 2004) to identify themes of cultural responsiveness.

Policy Intervention: School and District Codes of Conduct

Available evidence suggests that written disciplinary policies, frequently called "codes of conduct," are currently misaligned with evidence-based systems. In a content analysis of 120 high school disciplinary codes of conduct in six states, Fenning and colleagues (2012) reported that schools' written responses to a range of behaviors—including minor behaviors—routinely emphasized suspension and expulsion and were very unlikely to offer alternative or prevention-oriented responses such as teaching expected behaviors. A heavy reliance on punishment and exclusion in codes of conduct appears to be prevalent even in schools implementing SWPBIS, resulting in an incoherent disciplinary system (Fenning et al., in press). In recent years, some school districts, including some of the nation's largest, have begun to restructure their district code of conduct. The Los Angeles Unified School District has revamped its discipline code for the stated purpose of reducing out-of-school suspensions, increasing the use of proactive approaches such as SWPBIS and establishing clear expectations for school conduct (Barnhart, Franklin, & Alleman, 2008). In 2012, the Chicago Public Schools significantly reorganized the district's discipline code, restricting the use of 10-day suspensions for only the most disruptive and illegal infractions, expanding antibullying policies, and refocusing on instructive and restorative approaches (Chicago Public Schools, 2012). There is virtually no research at this time on the effect of policy change on disciplinary outcomes; further research is necessary in order to examine the extent to which shifts in written disciplinary policy are sufficient to create actual change in disciplinary outcomes at the school or district level.

CONCLUSION

In an era of heightened national attention on school safety and accountability for student achievement, effective school disciplinary systems are critical in order to ensure that schools are safe to learn. The research on exclusionary discipline presents a profound quandary for the field. Disciplinary strategies that remove students from school for a set period of time—out-of-school suspension and expulsion—are among the most frequently used disciplinary responses in schools today, and their usage appears to be steadily increasing (Lewis et al., 2010; Wallace et al., 2008). Yet it is unclear how school removal contributes in any way to meeting the goals one might expect of a disciplinary system. Studies of suspension and expulsion have consistently demonstrated a negative relationship between exclusionary discipline and improved student behavior (Raffaele Mendez, 2003), positive school climate (Steinberg, Allensworth, & Johnson, in press), and improved achievement outcomes (Arcia, 2006). Perhaps more importantly, it has become increasingly clear that exclusion from educational opportunity through suspension or expulsion is in itself a risk factor for further negative outcomes (American Academy of Pediatrics, 2013), including school dropout (Suh & Suh, 2007) and increased probability for contact with the juvenile justice system (Council of State Governments, 2011). These risks continue to fall disproportionately on certain racial and ethnic groups, in particular African American students (Gregory, Skiba, & Noguera, 2010). Racial and ethnic disparities are increasing over time, and the evidence suggests that such disparities are due more to processes of classroom management, administrative decision making, and school climate than to poverty or differences in student behavior.

Alternative elements of school disciplinary systems—such as SWPBIS, SEL, restorative practices, CRCM, and changes to disciplinary policies—hold considerable promise for disciplinary reform. The evidence is relatively strong that at least some of these strategies (e.g., SWPBIS) can make a significant difference in school disciplinary outcomes (Horner et al., 2009); for other interventions, such as restorative practices, the evidence is promising but very much emerging (Wearmouth, McKinney, & Glynn, 2007). Data on the negative outcomes associated with exclusionary discipline may be the driving force behind significant changes to disciplinary codes occurring in a number of school districts; research is needed on the effects of such policy changes on student outcomes. The challenge for future research and practice is the development, testing, and implementation of disciplinary system reforms that contribute to school safety and improved student behavior without threatening students' opportunity to learn and while effectively addressing the persistent and pervasive racial/ethnic inequities in school disciplinary systems.

NOTE

1. Although school suspension can include either in-school or out-of-school suspension, this chapter focuses on out-of-school suspension for two reasons. First, given high variability in how in-school suspension is used in schools and inconsistent definitions in what constitutes an in-school suspension, there is little consistency in research findings regarding in-school suspension. Second, given the strong relationships found between time spent in learning and positive academic outcomes, it must be presumed that an intervention that removes a student totally from the opportunity to learn in a school setting is a stronger risk factor for student outcomes than one that at least potentially keeps students engaged in academic endeavors. Thus, unless otherwise stated, the term "suspension" refers to out-of-school suspension, and the terms "disciplinary removal" and "exclusionary discipline" are used in this chapter to refer to out-of-school suspension or expulsion, not in-school suspension.

REFERENCES

Advancement Project/Civil Rights Project. (2000). *Opportunities suspended: The devastating consequences of zero tolerance and school discipline.* Cambridge, MA: Author.
Alberto, P. A., & Troutman, A. C. (2013). *Applied behavior analysis for teachers* (9th ed.). Upper Saddle River, NJ: Merrill/Prentice Hall.
American Academy of Pediatrics. (2013). Policy statement on out-of-school suspension and expulsion. *Pediatrics*, 131, 1000–1007. doi: 10.1542/peds.2012-3932
American Bar Association. (2001). Resolution on "school discipline" zero tolerance policies. Retrieved from www.americanbar.org/groups/child_law/tools_to_use/attorneys/school_disciplinezerotolerancepolicies.html.
American Psychological Association. (2008). Are zero tolerance policies effective in the schools? An evidentiary review and recommendations. *American Psychologist*, 63(9), 852–862. doi: 10.1037/0003-066X.63.9.852
Arcia, E. (2006). Achievement and enrollment status of suspended students: Outcomes in a large, multicultural school district. *Education and Urban Society*, 38(3), 359–369.
Arcia, E. (2007). A comparison of elementary/K-8 and middle schools' suspension rates. *Urban Education*, 42(5), 456–469. doi: 10.1177/0042085907304879
Balfanz, R., Byrnes, V., & Fox, J. (in press). Sent home and put off-track: The antecedents, disproportionalities, and consequences of being suspended in the ninth grade. In D. J. Losen (Ed.), *Closing the school discipline gap: Research for policymakers.* New York: Teachers College Press.
Barnhart, M. K., Franklin, N. J., & Alleman, J. R. (2008). Lessons learned and strategies used in reducing the frequency of out-of-school suspensions. *Journal of Special Education Leadership*, 21(2), 75–83.
Bickel, F., & Qualls, R. (1980). The impact of school climate on suspension rates in the Jefferson County Public Schools. *The Urban Review*, 12(2), 79–86. doi: 10.1007/BF02009317

Bondy, E., Ross, D. D., Gallingane, C., & Hambacher, E. (2007). Creating environments of success and resilience: Culturally responsive classroom management and more. *Urban Education, 42*(4), 326. doi: 10.1177/0042085907303406

Bowditch, C. (1993). Getting rid of troublemakers: High school disciplinary procedures and the production of dropouts. *Social Problems, 40*(4), 493–507. doi: 10.1525/sp.1993.40.4.03x0094p

Bracy, N. L. (2011). Student perceptions of high-security school environments. *Youth and Society, 43*(1), 365–395. doi: 10.1177/0044118X10365082

Bradshaw, C. P., Koth, C. W., Bevans, K. B., Ialongo, N., & Leaf, P. J. (2008). The impact of school-wide positive behavioral interventions and supports (PBIS) on the organizational health of elementary schools. *School Psychology Quarterly, 23*(4), 462–473. doi: 10.1037/a0012883

Bradshaw, C. P., Koth, C. W., Thornton, L. A., & Leaf, P. J. (2009). Altering school climate through school-wide positive behavioral interventions and supports: Findings from a group-randomized effectiveness trial. *Prevention Science, 10*(2), 100–115. doi: 10.1007/s11121-008-0114-9

Bradshaw, C. P., Mitchell, M. M., & Leaf, P. J. (2010). Examining the effects of schoolwide Positive Behavioral Interventions and Supports on student outcomes: Results from a randomized controlled effectiveness trial in elementary schools. *Journal of Positive Behavior Interventions, 12*, 133–148. doi: 10.1177/1098300709334798

Bradshaw, C. P., Mitchell, M. M., O'Brennan, L. M., & Leaf, P. J. (2010). Multilevel exploration of factors contributing to the overrepresentation of black students in office disciplinary referrals. *Journal of Educational Psychology, 102*(2), 508–520. doi: 10.1037/a0018450

Braithwaite, J. (2002). *Restorative justice and responsive regulation.* New York: Oxford University Press.

Brantlinger, E. (1991). Social class distinctions in adolescents' reports of problems and punishment in school. *Behavioral Disorders, 17*(1), 36–46.

Brophy, J. E. (1988). Research linking teacher behavior to student achievement: Potential implications for instruction of Chapter 1 students. *Educational Psychologist, 23*(3), 235–286. doi: 10.1207/s15326985ep2303_3

Brown, D. F. (2003). Urban teachers' use of culturally responsive classroom management strategies. *Theory into Practice, 42*(4), 277–282. doi: 10.1353/tip.2003.0041

Brown, D. F. (2004). Urban teachers' professed classroom management strategies: Reflections on culturally responsive teaching. *Urban Education, 39*(3), 266–289. doi: 10.1177/0042085904263258

Brown, E. L. (2002). Mrs. Boyd's fifth grade inclusive classroom: A study of multicultural teaching strategies. *Urban Education, 37*(1), 126–141. doi: 10.1177/0042085902371008

Browne, J. A., Losen, D. J., & Wald, J. (2002). Zero tolerance: Unfair, with little recourse. In R. J. Skiba & G. G. Noam (Eds.), *New directions for youth development (no. 92: Zero tolerance: Can suspension and expulsion keep schools safe?)* (pp. 73–99). San Francisco: Jossey-Bass.

Cairns, R. B., & Cairns, B. D. (2000). The natural history and developmental functions of aggression. In A. J. Sameroff, M. Lewis, & S. M. Miller (Eds.), *Handbook of developmental psychopathology* (2nd ed.) (pp. 403–429). New York: Kluwer Academic/Plenum Publishers.

Chicago Public Schools. (2012). Board of Education approves student code of conduct to foster positive, safer learning environments and limit removal of students from school [press release, June 27]. Retrieved from www.cps.edu/News/Press_releases/Pages/06_27_2012_PR3.aspx.

Children's Defense Fund. (1975). *School suspensions: Are they helping children?* Cambridge, MA: Washington Research Project.

Christle, C., Nelson, C. M., & Jolivette, K. (2004). School characteristics related to the use of suspension. *Education and Treatment of Children, 27*(4), 509–526.

Collaborative for Academic, Social, and Emotional Learning (CASEL) (2003). *Safe and sound: An educational leader's guide to evidence-based social and emotional learning programs.* Chicago: Author.

Costenbader, V., & Markson, S. (1998). School suspension: A study with secondary school students. *Journal of School Psychology, 36*(1), 59–82. doi: 10.1016/S0022-4405(97)00050-2

Council of State Governments. (2011). *Breaking schools' rules: A statewide study of how school discipline relates to student's success and juvenile justice involvement.* New York: Council of State Governments Justice Center.

Darling-Hammond, L. (2004). Inequality and the right to learn: Access to qualified teachers in California's public schools. *Teachers College Record, 106*(10), 1936–1966. doi: 10.1111/j.1467-9620.2004.00422.x

Davis, J. E., & Jordan, W. J. (1994). The effects of school context, structure, and experiences on African American males in middle and high schools. *Journal of Negro Education, 63*, 570–587.

Dignity in Schools Campaign. (2012). *Loud and clear: Dignity in schools campaign and partners call for solutions not suspensions.* Washington, DC: Author. Retrieved from www.dignityinschools.org/blog/loud-and-clear-dsc-and-partners-call-solutions-not-suspensions.

Driscoll, M. P. (2000). *Psychology of learning for instruction* (2nd ed.). Boston: Allyn & Bacon.

Durlak, J. A., Weissberg, R. P., & Pachan, M. (2010). A meta-analysis of after-school programs that seek to promote personal and social skills in children and adolescents. *American Journal of Community Psychology, 45*(3–4), 294–309. doi: 10.1007/s10464-010-9300-6

Eitle, T. M. N., & Eitle, D. J. (2004). Inequality, segregation, and the overrepresentation of African Americans in school suspensions. *Sociological Perspectives, 47*(3), 269–287. doi: 10.1525/sop.2004.47.3.269

Ekstrom, R. B., Goertz, M. E., Pollack, J. M., & Rock, D. A. (1986). Who drops out of high school and why? Findings from a national study. *Teachers College Record, 87*(3), 357–73.

Ewing, C. P. (2000). Sensible zero tolerance protects students. *Harvard Education Letter,* 16.1 (January/February), 8, 7. Retrieved from www.edlettr.org/past/issues/2000-jf/zero.shtml.

Fenning, P., Pigott, T., Engler, E., Bradshaw, K., Gamboney, E. Grunewald, S., & Haque, T. (in press). A mixed methods approach examining disproportionality in school discipline. In D. J. Losen (Ed.), *Closing the school discipline gap: Research for policymakers.* New York: Teachers College Press.

Fenning, P., Pulaski, S., Gomez, M., Morello, M., Maciel, L., Maroney, E., et al. (2012). Call to action: A critical need for designing alternatives to suspension and expulsion. *Journal of School Violence, 11*(2), 105–117. doi: 10.1080/15388220.2011.646633

Ferguson, A. A. (2001). *Bad boys: Public schools and the making of Black masculinity.* Ann Arbor: University of Michigan Press.

Greenberg, M. T., Weissberg, R. P., O'Brien, M. U., Zins, J. E., Fredericks, L., Resnik, H., & Elias, M. J. (2003). Enhancing school-based prevention and youth development through coordinated social, emotional, and academic learning. *American Psychologist, 58,* 6–7, 466–474. doi: 10.1037/0003-066X.58.6-7.466

Greenwood, C. R., Horton, B. T., & Utley, C. A. (2002). Academic engagement: Current perspectives on research and practice. *School Psychology Review, 31*(3), 328–349.

Gregory, J. F. (1995). The crime of punishment: Racial and gender disparities in the use of corporal punishment in U.S. public schools. *The Journal of Negro Education, 64*(4), 454–462. doi: 10.2307/2967267

Gregory, A., Cornell, D., & Fan, X. (2011). The relationship of school structure and support to suspension rates for black and white high school students. *American Educational Research Journal, 48*(4), 904–934. doi: 10.3102/0002831211398531

Gregory, A., Skiba, R. J., & Noguera, P. A. (2010). The achievement gap and the discipline gap: Two sides of the same coin? *Education Researcher, 39*(1), 59–68. doi: 10.3102/0013189X09357621

Gregory, A., & Weinstein, R. S. (2008). The discipline gap and African Americans: Defiance or cooperation in the high school classroom. *Journal of School Psychology, 46*(4), 455–475. doi: 10.1016/j.jsp.2007.09.001

Hellman, D. A., & Beaton, S. (1986). The pattern of violence in urban public schools: The influence of school and community. *Journal of Research in Crime & Delinquency, 23,* 102–127. doi: 10.1177/0022427886023002002

Himmelstein, K. E. W., & Bruckner, H. (2011). Criminal-justice and school sanctions against nonheterosexual youth: A national longitudinal study. *Pediatrics, 127*(1), 49–57. doi: 10.1542/peds.2009-2306

Hinojosa, M. S. (2008). Black-white differences in school suspension: Effect of student beliefs about teachers. *Sociological Spectrum, 28*(2), 175–193. doi: 10.1080/02732170701796429

Horner, R. H., Sugai, G., Smolkowski, K., Eber, L., Nakasato, J., Todd, A. W., & Esperanza, J. (2009). A randomized, wait-list controlled effectiveness trial assessing school-wide positive behavior support in elementary schools. *Journal of Positive Behavior Supports and Interventions, 11*(3), 133–144. doi: 10.1177/1098300709332067

Horner, S. B., Fireman, G. D., & Wang, E. W. (2010). The relation of student behavior, peer status, race, and gender to decisions about school discipline using CHAID decision trees and regression modeling. *Journal of School Psychology, 48*(2), 135–161. doi: 10.1016/j.jsp.2009.12.001

Ialongo, N., Poduska, J., Werthamer, L., & Kellam, S. (2001). The distal impact of two first-grade preventive interventions on conduct problems and disorder in early adolescence. *Journal of Emotional and Behavioral Disorders, 9,* 146–160. doi: 10.1177/106342660100900301

International Institute for Restorative Practices. (2009). *Findings from schools implementing restorative practices.* Restorative Practices eforum. Retrieved September 29, 2010, from www.iirp.org/pdf/IIRP-Improving-School-Climate.pdf.

Irvin, L. K., Tobin, T. J., Sprague, J. R., Sugai, G., & Vincent, C. G. (2004). Validity of office discipline referral measures as indices of school-wide behavioral status and effects of school-wide behavioral interventions. *Journal of Positive Behavior Interventions, 6,* 131–147. doi: 10.1177/10983007040060030201

Jennings, W. G., Gover, A. R., & Hitchcock, D. M. (2008). Localizing restorative justice: An in-depth look at a Denver public school program. In H. V. Miller (Ed.), *Sociology of crime, law, and deviance,* Vol. 11 (pp. 167–187). Bingley, UK: JAI Press.

Jones, C., Caravaca, L., Cizek, S., Horner, R. H., & Vincent, C. G. (2006). Culturally responsive Schoolwide Positive Behavior Support: A case study in one school with a high proportion of Native American students. *Multiple Voices for Ethnically Diverse Exceptional Learners*, 9(1), 108–119.

Karp, D. R., & Breslin, B. (2001). Restorative justice in school communities. *Youth & Society*, 33, 249–272. doi: 10.1177/0044118X01033002006

KewalRamani, A., Gilbertson, L., Fox, M. A., & Provasnik, S. (2007). *Status and trends in the education of racial and ethnic minorities.* Washington, DC: National Center for Education Statistics, Institute of Education Sciences, U.S. Department of Education.

Kim, C. Y., Losen, D. J., & Hewitt, D. T. (2010). *The school-to-prison pipeline: Structuring legal reform.* New York: New York University Press.

Kosciw, J. G., Greytak, E. A., & Diaz, E. M. (2009). Who, what, where, when, & why: Demographic and ecological factors contributing to hostile school climates for lesbian, gay, bisexual, and transgender youth. *Journal of Youth & Adolescence*, 38(7), 976–988. doi: 10.1007/s10964-009-9412-1

Kozol, J. (2005). *The shame of the nation: The restoration of apartheid schooling in America.* New York: Crown Publishers.

Krezmien, M. P., Leone, P. E., & Achilles, G. M. (2006). Suspension, race, and disability: Analysis of statewide practices and reporting. *Journal of Emotional and Behavioral Disorders*, 14(4), 217–226. doi: 10.1177/10634266060140040501

Kupchik, A., & Ellis, N. (2008). School discipline and security: Fair for all students? *Youth & Society*, 39(4), 549–574. doi: 10.1177/0044118X07301956

Kuperminc, G. P., Leadbeater, B. J., Emmons, C., & Blatt, S. J. (1997). Perceived school climate and difficulties in the social adjustment of middle school students. *Applied Developmental Science*, 1(2), 76–88. doi: 10.1207/s1532480xads0102_2

Ladson-Billings, G. (2006). From the achievement gap to the education debt: Understanding achievement in U.S. schools. *Educational Researcher*, 35(7), 3–12. doi: 10.3102/0013189X035007003

Lassen, S. R., Steele, M. M., & Sailor, W. (2006). The relationship of school-wide Positive Behavior Support to academic achievement in an urban middle school. *Psychology in the Schools*, 43(6), 701–712. doi: 10.1002/pits.20177

Lewis, C. W., Butler, B. R., Bonner III, F. A., & Joubert, M. (2010). African American male discipline patterns and school district responses resulting impact on academic achievement: Implications for urban educators and policy makers. *Journal of African American Males in Education*, 1(1). 8–25.

Lopes, J. (2005). Intervention with students with learning, emotional and behavior disorders: Why do we take so long to do it? *Education and Treatment of Children*, 28(4), 345–360.

Losen, D. J., & Martinez, T. E. (2013). *Out of school & off track: The overuse of suspensions in American middle and high schools.* Los Angeles, CA: The Center for Civil Rights Remedies. Retrieved from http://civilrightsproject.ucla.edu/resources/projects/center-for-civil-rights-remedies/school-to-prison-folder/federal-reports/out-of-school-and-off-track-the-overuse-of-suspensions-in-american-middle-and-high-schools/Exec_Sum_OutofSchool_OffTrack_UCLA.pdf.

Losen, D. J., & Skiba, R. J. (2010). *Suspended education: Urban middle schools in crisis.* Montgomery, AL: Southern Poverty Law Center. Retrieved from www.splcenter.org/get-informed/publications/suspended-education.

Mansfield, W., & Farris, E. (1992). *Office for Civil Rights survey redesign: A feasibility study.* Rockville, MD: Westat.

Massachusetts Advocacy Center. (1986). *The way out: Student exclusion practices in Boston middle schools.* Boston: Author.

Massachusetts Department of Elementary and Secondary Education. (2006). *2005 Massachusetts youth risk behavior survey results.* Malden, MA: Author.

Mattison, E., & Aber, M. S. (2007). Closing the achievement gap: The association of racial climate with achievement and behavioral outcomes. *American Journal of Community Psychology*, 40(1), 1–12. doi: 10.1007/s10464-007-9128-x

McCarthy, J. D., & Hoge, D. R. (1987). The social construction of school punishment: Racial disadvantage out of universalistic process. *Social Forces*, 65(4), 1101–1120. doi: 10.1093/sf/65.4.1101

McFadden, A. C., Marsh, G. E., Price, B. J., & Hwang, Y. (1992). A study of race and gender bias in the punishment of handicapped school children. *Urban Review*, 24(4), 239–251. doi: 10.1007/BF01108358

Mcloughlin, C. S., & Noltemeyer, A. (2010). Research into factors contributing to discipline use and disproportionality in major urban schools. *Current Issues in Education*, 13(2), 1–20.

McNeely, C. A., Nonemaker, J. M., & Blum, R. W. (2002). Promoting student connectedness to school: From the national longitudinal study of adolescent health. *Journal of School Health*, 72(4), 138–147. doi: 10.1111/j.1746-1561.2002.tb06533

Meier, K. J., & Stewart, J. S. (1992). The impact of representative bureaucracies: Educational systems and public policies. *American Review of Public Administration, 22*(3), 157–171. doi: 10.1177/027507409202200301

Monroe, C. R., & Obidah, J. E. (2004). The influence of cultural synchronization on a teacher's perceptions of disruption: A case study of an African American middle-school classroom. *Journal of Teacher Education, 55*(3), 256–268. doi: 10.1177/0022487104263977

Morrison, G. M., Anthony, S., Storino, M., Cheng, J., Furlong, M. F., & Morrison, R. L. (2001). School expulsion as a process and an event: Before and after effects on children at-risk for school discipline. *New Directions for Youth Development: Theory, Practice, Research, 92,* 45–72.

Mukuria, G. (2002). Disciplinary challenges: How do principals address this dilemma? *Urban Education, 37*(3), 432–452. doi: 10.1177/00485902037003007

Muscott, H. S., Mann, E. L., & LeBrun, M. L. (2008). Positive behavioral interventions and supports in New Hampshire: Effects of large-scale implementation of school-wide positive behavior support on student discipline and academic achievement. *Journal of Positive Behavior Interventions, 10*(3), 190–205. doi: 10.1177/1098300708316258

Nicholson-Crotty, S., Birchmeier, Z., & Valentine, D. (2009). Exploring the impact of school discipline on racial disproportion in the juvenile justice system. *Social Science Quarterly, 90*(4), 1003–1018. doi: 10.1111/j.1540-6237.2009.00674.x

Noltemeyer, A., & Mcloughlin, C. S. (2010). Patterns of exclusionary discipline by school typology, ethnicity, and their interactions. *Perspectives on Urban Education,* 27–39. Retrieved from www.urbanedjournal.org/sites/urbanedjournal.org/files/pdf_archive/PUE-Summer2010-V7I1-pp27-40.pdf.

Osher, D., Bear, G. G., Sprague, J. R., & Doyle, W. (2010). How can we improve school discipline? *Educational Researcher, 39*(1), 48–58. doi: 10.3102/0013189X09357618

Owen, S. S. (2005). The relationship between social capital and corporal punishment in schools: A theoretical inquiry. *Youth & Society, 37*(1), 85–112. doi: 10.1177/0044118X04271027

Payne, A. A., & Welch, K. (2010). Modeling the effects of racial threat on punitive and restorative school discipline practices. *Criminology, 48*(4), 1019–1062. doi: 10.1111/j.1745-9125.2010.00211.x

Payton, J., Weissberg, R. P., Durlak, J. A., Dymnicki, A. B., Taylor, R. D., Schellinger, K. B., & Pachan, M. (2008). *The positive impact of social and emotional learning for kindergarten to eighth-grade students: Findings from three scientific reviews.* Chicago: Collaborative for Academic, Social, and Emotional Learning.

Peguero, A. A., & Shekarkhar, Z. (2011). Latino/a student misbehavior and school punishment. *Hispanic Journal of Behavioral Sciences, 33*(1), 54–70. doi: 10.1177/0739986310388021

Petras, H., Masyn, K. E., Buckley, J. A., Ialongo, N. S., & Kellam, S. (2011). Who is most at risk for school removal? A multilevel discrete-time survival analysis of individual- and context-level influences. *Journal of Educational Psychology, 103*(1), 223–237. doi: 10.1037/a0021245

Public Agenda. (2004). *Teaching interrupted: Do discipline policies in today's public schools foster the common good?* New York: Author. Retrieved from www.publicagenda.org/files/teaching_interrupted.pdf.

Raffaele Mendez, L. M. (2003). Predictors of suspension and negative school outcomes: A longitudinal investigation. In J. Wald & D. J. Losen (Eds.), *New directions for youth development (no. 99; Deconstructing the school-to-prison pipeline)* (pp. 17–34). San Francisco: Jossey-Bass.

Raffaele Mendez, L. M., & Knoff, H. M. (2003). Who gets suspended from school and why: A demographic analysis of schools and disciplinary infractions in a large school district. *Education and Treatment of Children, 26,* 30–51.

Raffaele Mendez, L. M., Knoff, H. M., & Ferron, J. M. (2002). School demographic variables and out-of-school suspension rates: A quantitative and qualitative analysis of a large, ethnically diverse school district. *Psychology in the Schools, 39*(3), 259–277.

Rausch, M. K., & Skiba, R. J. (2004). *Unplanned outcomes: Suspensions and expulsions in Indiana.* Bloomington, IN: Center for Evaluation & Education Policy.

Rausch, M. K., & Skiba, R. J. (2005). The academic cost of discipline: The contribution of school discipline to achievement. Paper presented at the Annual Meeting of the American Educational Research Association, Montreal, Canada, April.

Richart, D., Brooks, K., & Soler, M. (2003). Unintended consequences: The impact of "zero tolerance" and other exclusionary policies on Kentucky students. Retrieved from www.cclp.org/documents/BBY/kentucky.pdf.

Roch, C. H., Pitts, D. W., & Navarro, I. (2010). Representative bureaucracy and policy tools: Ethnicity, student discipline, and representation in public schools. *Administration & Society, 42*(1), 38–65. doi: 10.1177/0095399709349695

Rocha, R., & Hawes, D. (2009). Racial diversity, representative bureaucracy, and equity in multicultural districts. *Social Science Quarterly, 90*(2), 326–344. doi: 10.1111/j.1540-6237.2009.00620.x

Rocque, M. (2010). Office discipline and student behaviors: Does race matter? *American Journal of Education*, *116*(4), 557–581. doi: 10.1086/653629

Ruck, M. D., & Wortley, S. (2002). Racial and ethnic minority high school students' perceptions of school disciplinary practices: A look at some Canadian findings. *Journal of Youth and Adolescence*, *31*(3), 185–195. doi: 10.1023/A:1015081102189

Russell, S., Kosciw, S., Horn, S., & Saewyc, E. (2010). Safe schools policy for LGBTQ students. *Social Policy Report*, *24*(4), 1–24.

Sandefur, G. D., Martin, M., Eggerling-Boeck, J., Mannon, S. E., & Meier, A.M. (2001). An overview of racial and ethnic demographic trends. In N. J. Smelser, W. J. Wilson, & F. Mitchel (Eds.), *American becoming: Racial trends and their consequences*, Vol. 1 (pp. 40–102). Washington, DC: National Academies Press.

Shaw, S. R., & Braden, J. B. (1990). Race and gender bias in the administration of corporal punishment. *School Psychology Review*, *19*(3), 378–383.

Shirley, E. L. M., & Cornell, D. G. (2011). The contribution of student perceptions of school climate to understanding the disproportionate punishment of African American students in a middle school. *School Psychology International*, *33*(2), 115–134. doi: 10.1177/0143034311406815

Shollenberger, T. L. (in press). Racial disparities in school suspension and subsequent outcomes: Evidence from the National Longitudinal Survey of Youth 1997. In D. J. Losen (Ed.), *Closing the school discipline gap: Research for policymakers*. New York: Teachers College Press.

Skiba, R. J., Chung, C. G., Trachok, M., Baker, T., Sheya, A., & Hughes, R. (in press). Where should we intervene? Contributions of behavior, student, and school characteristics to suspension and expulsion. In D. J. Losen (Ed.). *Closing the school discipline gap: Research for policymakers*. New York: Teachers College Press.

Skiba, R. J., & Edl, H. (2004). *The disciplinary practices survey: How do Indiana's principals feel about discipline?* Bloomington, IN: Center for Evaluation and Education Policy.

Skiba, R. J., Horner, R. H., Chung, C. G., Rausch, M. K., May, S. L., & Tobin, T. (2011). Race is not neutral: A national investigation of African American and Latino disproportionality in school discipline. *School Psychology Review*, *40*(1), 85–107.

Skiba, R. J., Michael, R. S., Nardo, A. C., & Peterson, R. (2002). The color of discipline: Sources of racial and gender disproportionality in school punishment. *Urban Review*, *34*(4), 317. doi: 10.1023/A:1021320817372

Skiba, R. J., Peterson, R. L., & Williams, T. (1997). Office referrals and suspension: Disciplinary intervention in middle schools. *Education and Treatment of Children*, *20*(3), 295–316.

Skiba, R. J., & Rausch, M. K. (2006). Zero tolerance, suspension, and expulsion: Questions of equity and effectiveness. In C. M. Evertson & C. S. Weinstein (Eds.), *Handbook of classroom management: Research, practice, and contemporary issues* (pp. 1063–1089). Mahwah, NJ: Erlbaum.

Skinner, B. F. (1953). *Science and human behavior*. New York: Free Press.

Slavin, R. E., Cheung, A., Holmes, G., Madden, N. A., & Chamberlain, A. (2013). Effects of a data-driven district reform model on state assessment outcomes. *American Educational Research Journal*, *50*(2), 371–396. doi: 10.3102/0002831212466909

Steinberg, M. P., Allensworth, E., & Johnson, D. W. (in press). What conditions jeopardize and support safety in urban schools? The influence of community characteristics, school composition and school organizational practices on student and teacher reports of safety in Chicago. In D. J. Losen (Ed.), *Closing the school discipline gap: Research for policymakers*. New York: Teachers College Press.

Stinchcomb, J. B., Bazemore, G., & Riestenberg, N. (2006). Beyond zero tolerance: Restoring justice in secondary schools. *Youth Violence and Juvenile Justice*, *4*, 123–147. doi: 10.1177/1541204006286287

Strang, H., & Braithwaite, J. (2001). *Restorative justice and civil society*. Cambridge, Melbourne: Cambridge University Press.

Sugai, G., & Horner, R. (2009). Defining and describing school-wide positive behavior support. In W. Sailor, G. Dunlap, G. Sugai, & R. Horner (Eds.), *Handbook of positive behavior support* (pp.307–326). New York: Spring Science and Business Media.

Sugai, G., Horner, R., & McIntosh, K. (2008). Best practices in developing a broad-scale system of school-wide positive behavior support. In A. Thomas & J. Grimes (Eds.), *Best practices in school psychology-V*, Vol. 3 (pp. 765–780). Bethesda, MD: The National Association of School Psychologists.

Suh, S., & Suh, J. (2007). Risk factors and levels of risk for high school dropouts. *Professional School Counseling*, *10*(3), 297–306.

Theriot, M. T. (2009). School resource officers and the criminalization of student behavior. *Journal of Criminal Justice*, *37*(3), 280–287. doi: 10.1016/j.jcrimjus.2009.04.008

Theriot, M. T., & Dupper, D. R. (2010). Student discipline problems and the transition from elementary to middle school. *Education and Urban Society, 42*(2), 205–222. doi: 10.1177/0013124509349583

Tobin, T., Sugai, G., & Colvin, T. (1996). Patterns in middle school discipline records. *Journal of Emotional and Behavioral Disorders, 4*(2), 82–94. doi: 10.1177/106342669600400203

Tuzzolo, E., & Hewitt, D. T. (2007). Re-building inequity: The re-emergence of the school-to-prison pipeline in New Orleans. *The High School Journal, 90*(2), 59–68.

Umbreit, M. S., Vos, B., Coates, R. B., & Lightfoot, E. (2006). Restorative justice in the 21st century: A social movement full of opportunities and pitfalls. *Marquette Law Review, 89,* 253–304.

United States Department of Education. (2013). Investing in innovation fund, development grants. Retrieved from www.gpo.gov/fdsys/pkg/FR-2013-03-27/pdf/2013-07003.pdf.

Utley, C. A., Kozleski, E., Smith, A., & Draper, I. L. (2002). Positive behavior support: A proactive strategy for minimizing behavioral problems in urban multicultural youth. *Journal of Positive Behavior Interventions, 4*(4), 196–207. doi: 10.1177/10983007020040040301

Vavrus, F., & Cole, K. (2002). "I didn't do nothin": The discursive construction of school suspension. *The Urban Review, 34,* 87–111.

Vincent, C. G., Pavel, M., Sprague, J. R., & Tobin, T. J. (in press). Towards identifying school-level factors reducing disciplinary exclusions of American Indian/Alaska Native students. In D. J. Losen (Ed.), *Closing the school discipline gap: Research for policymakers.* New York: Teachers College Press.

Vincent, C. G., & Tobin, T. J. (2011). The relationship between implementation of school-wide positive behavior support (SWPBS) and disciplinary exclusion of students from various ethnic backgrounds with and without disabilities. *Journal of Emotional and Behavioral Disorders, 19*(4), 217–234. doi: 10.1177/1063426610377329

Wald, J., & Losen, D. J. (2003). Defining and redirecting a school-to-prison pipeline. In J. Wald & D. J. Losen (Eds.), *New directions for youth development,* Vol. 99. *Deconstructing the school-to-prison pipeline* (pp. 9–15). San Francisco: Jossey-Bass.

Wallace, J. M., Goodkind, S., Wallace, C. M., & Bachman, J. G. (2008). Racial, ethnic, and gender differences in school discipline among U.S. high school students: 1991–2005. *The Negro Educational Review, 59*(1–2), 47–62.

Wang, M. C., Haertel, G. D., & Walberg, H. J. (1997). Learning influences. In H. J. Walberg & G. D. Haertel (Eds.), *Psychology and educational practice* (pp. 199–211). Berkeley, CA: McCutchan.

Wang, M., McCart, A., & Turnbull, A. P. (2007). Implementing positive behavior support with Chinese American families: Enhancing cultural competence. *Journal of Positive Behavior Interventions, 9,* 38–51. doi: 10.1177/10983007070090010501

Watkins, N. D., & Aber, M. S. (2009). Exploring the relationships among race, class, gender, and middle school students' perceptions of school racial climate. *Equity & Excellence in Education, 42*(4), 395–411. doi: 10.1080/10665680903260218

Wearmouth, J., McKinney, R., & Glynn, T. (2007). Restorative justice: Two examples from New Zealand schools. *British Journal of Special Education, 34*(4), 196–203. doi: 10.1111/j.1467-8578.2007.00479.x

Wehlage, G. G., & Rutter, R. A. (1986). Dropping out: How much do schools contribute to the problem? *Teachers College Record, 87,* 374–393.

Weinstein, C. S., Tomlinson-Clarke, S., & Curran, M. (2004). Toward a conception of culturally responsive classroom management. *Journal of Teacher Education, 55,* 25–38. doi: 10.1177/0022487103259812

Welch, K., & Payne, A. A. (2010). Racial threat and punitive school discipline. *Social Problems, 57*(1), 25–48. doi: 10.1525/sp.2010.57.1.25

Welsh, W. N. (2003). Individual and institutional predictors of school disorder. *Youth Violence and Juvenile Justice, 1*(4), 346–368. doi: 10.1177/1541204003255843

Wu, S. C., Pink, W. T., Crain, R. L., & Moles, O. (1982). Student suspension: A critical reappraisal. *The Urban Review, 14,* 245–303. doi: 10.1007/BF02171974

Zins, J. E. (2001). Examining opportunities and challenges for school-based prevention and promotion: Social and emotional learning as an exemplar. *The Journal of Primary Prevention, 21,* 441–446. doi: 10.1023/A:1007154727167

III

Contexts for Classroom Management

8

EARLY CHILDHOOD EDUCATION CLASSROOM MANAGEMENT

MARIBETH GETTINGER & COLLETTE FISCHER
UNIVERSITY OF WISCONSIN–MADISON

INTRODUCTION

Educators, researchers, and policy makers increasingly recognize that high-quality early childhood education prepares young children for long-term social-emotional and academic success. A critical aspect of early childhood education is classroom management. Teachers' effective management of behavior is an important mechanism for promoting young children's school readiness. When teachers are able to create nurturing classroom environments that promote positive behavior, children demonstrate a high level of task engagement, self-regulation, and social competence (Thompson, 2002). Moreover, by preventing misbehavior and effectively dealing with challenging behavior when it does occur, teachers' classroom management skills contribute to children's early literacy and language learning (Espinosa, 2002). Recent research on the negative trajectories of early problem behavior also underscores the need for educators to address the behavioral needs of young children. Thus, from the vantage of strengthening young children's school readiness and literacy skills, as well as preventing the occurrence or escalation of problem behavior, a focus on early childhood education classroom management is warranted.

The purpose of this chapter is to review classroom management approaches for fostering young children's social-emotional growth, enhancing literacy and language development, and minimizing the occurrence of challenging behaviors. Effective classroom management practices are conceptualized within a hierarchical framework that encompasses multiple tiers of early childhood classroom management practices (Stewart, Benner, Martella, & Marchand-Martella, 2007). Within a multitiered framework, the first tier involves the implementation of basic classroom management strategies for all children, including establishing warm, nurturing teacher–child relationships and creating well-structured classroom environments that support positive behavior. Whereas Tier 1 reflects universal, preventative approaches for all children, the upper tiers include empirically validated interventions for classrooms, small groups, or individual children who exhibit disruptive and challenging classroom behaviors that require more intensive behavioral support. In recent years, a number of interventions targeting persistent problem behavior in young children have been developed and evaluated, and several are designed to be implemented by classroom teachers in naturalistic early childhood settings (Bryant, Vizzard, Willoughby, & Kupersmidt, 2000). Thus, the chapter also describes and reviews the evidence supporting comprehensive intervention programs aimed specifically at addressing young children's problem behaviors.

RATIONALE FOR FOCUS ON CLASSROOM MANAGEMENT IN EARLY CHILDHOOD SETTINGS

The role of social-emotional and behavioral competence in promoting children's long-term adjustment and academic success underscores the importance of early education and effective classroom management. As will be summarized, the significance of early childhood classroom management stems from three broad areas of research addressing (1) the prevalence of challenging behaviors in preschool-age children, (2) the negative outcomes associated with problem behaviors in early childhood, and (3) the influence of early childhood education in preventing challenging behavior and promoting social-emotional well-being.

In recent years, there has been a renewed focus on the early childhood years as laying the groundwork for school readiness. Children who enter kindergarten with well developed social and behavioral competencies are most likely to succeed in school (Raver & Knitzer, 2002). Unfortunately, kindergarten teachers typically report that many children enter school without being able to pay attention, sit still, follow directions, or remain engaged in social and learning activities (Pianta, Cox, & Snow, 2007). Indeed, deficits in children's readiness for school are evident even before they begin kindergarten. In one study, for example, early childhood teachers reported that 40% of their students engaged in at least one challenging behavior every day (Willoughby, Kupersmidt, & Bryant, 2001). Another study found that 60% of young children from low-SES backgrounds demonstrated significant delays in self-regulation and social competence (National Center for Children in Poverty, 2006). Finally, national survey data suggest that the prevalence of significant problem behaviors in children that require early intervention services is close to 10% and may be as high as 25% for children living in poverty (Qi & Kaiser, 2003; Webster-Stratton & Hammond, 2000; West, Denton, & Germino-Hausken, 2000). Although young children from low-income backgrounds may be at high risk for behavioral issues, preschoolers from middle- and upper-income families exhibit challenging behaviors in the classroom as well (Campbell, 2002).

The frequent occurrence of misbehavior in young children is particularly troublesome given the well established link between challenging behavior in early childhood and later negative developmental and social outcomes (Campbell, Spieker, Burchinal, Poe, 2006). Children who exhibit challenging behaviors in early education settings are at significant risk for violence, substance abuse, depression, and anxiety as adults (Moffitt, 1994). Behavior problems during a child's preschool years, such as aggression, inattention, impulsivity, and noncompliance, jeopardize healthy social-emotional development and are highly predictive of delinquency in adolescence and gang membership (Gilliam, 2005).

The negative effects of problem behaviors extend to classroom peers and teachers as well. For example, peers exposed to a classmate who exhibits challenging behavior often miss out on valuable learning and social opportunities themselves as a result of disruptions (Warner & Lynch, 2004). For teachers, the occurrence of disruptive behavior interferes with their delivery of engaging lessons and activities and lowers the frequency of positive, supportive interactions with all children (Hemmeter, Santos, & Ostrosky, 2008). Furthermore, teachers in classrooms with a high number of children who exhibit problem behavior are more likely to experience stress, become dissatisfied with their job, and transfer or leave the profession (Carlson, Tiret, Bender, & Benson, 2011). Early childhood teachers report that disruptive behavior is one of the greatest challenges they face, and they identify knowledge and skills for addressing disruptive behavior as their most significant training need (Griffin, 2010).

Beyond the long-term negative impact, preschool children with challenging behaviors, particularly aggressive behavior, face more immediate consequences. They are often rejected by peers, receive less positive teacher attention, are less successful in kindergarten, and are at risk for developing negative attitudes toward school (Tremblay, 2000). Moreover, children who lack social and behavioral competence (i.e., difficulty with sharing, making friends, or engaging in social problem solving) tend to exhibit extreme forms of challenging behaviors, such as prolonged tantrums and physical aggression (Zill & West, 2001).

Given the large number of children in the United States who currently attend center-based early education programs, strengthening classroom management in early childhood settings can be an effective mechanism to reduce problem behavior and promote social competence. Results from longitudinal studies demonstrate that high-quality, early childhood programs, which include effective classroom management approaches, minimize children's risk of developing challenging behaviors (McCabe & Frede, 2007). In one large-scale, randomized control study, for example, African American children from low-income families attended an early childhood program taught by qualified teachers who had received extensive training in classroom management strategies. Children who participated in this experimental program had lower adolescent and adult crime rates nearly 40 years later compared to children who attended a control preschool program (Nores, Belfield, Barnett, & Schweinhart, 2005).

EFFECTIVE CLASSROOM MANAGEMENT PRACTICES IN EARLY EDUCATION

An effective classroom management approach is one that promotes social competence (i.e., the social skills and behaviors children need to be successful in early childhood settings), provides support for children's appropriate behavior, and prevents the occurrence of challenging behavior (Jolivette & Steed, 2010). A number of models for early childhood classroom management that achieve these goals have been described in the literature (e.g., Brown, Odom, & Conroy, 2001). In this chapter, we have adopted a model of classroom management that focuses on supporting children's positive behavior through a multitiered approach. Hemmeter, Ostrosky, and Fox (2006) describe an application of a tiered framework, called the Teaching Pyramid Model, as a continuum of scientifically validated practices designed to build social competence and prevent challenging behavior in young children. Hemmeter and associates' model conceptualizes early childhood classroom management within a multitiered framework. Specifically, in their Pyramid Model, early educators incorporate universal strategies into their everyday practices to promote the development of appropriate behaviors for all children (e.g., using classroom rules and clear behavioral expectations), and they implement more focused prevention programs and specialized curricula for children who are not responsive to high-quality, well managed classrooms. These second-tier strategies are often delivered through individualized or small-group formats, although many may be applied to whole classrooms as well (Fox, Dunlap, Hemmeter, Joseph, & Strain, 2003).

Inherent in a multitiered approach to classroom management are several key principles about children's behavior and classroom management. First, effective classroom management is about prevention. It involves designing classrooms such that problem behaviors are less likely to occur, setting positive goals and strengthening positive behavior, and teaching and promoting the development of social competence and appropriate behaviors for all children. Research consistently demonstrates that problem behaviors in young children can be minimized by creating environments that teach, encourage, and support desired behaviors (Kaiser & Rasminsky, 2011). Second, classroom management strategies that involve responding to problem behaviors by attempting to eliminate them through negative or punitive procedures (such as giving reprimands) are neither preventive nor remedial and have not been shown to improve children's behavior (Hester, Baltodano, Hendrickson, Tonelson, Conroy, & Gable, 2004). Finally, effective approaches for addressing the behavioral needs of children are grounded in two critical assumptions about their behavior (Crone & Horner, 2005). First, young children's behavior is purposeful in nature and occurs for a reason. That is, appropriate as well as inappropriate behavior persists because it serves a critical function for the child, for example, to gain attention from the teacher or peers. Second, children's behavior is related to the context in which it occurs. Specifically, children's behaviors (appropriate as well as inappropriate) are typically predictable responses or reactions to a situation or specific set of events.

Despite the importance and validity of these key principles of effective classroom management, there remains a disparity between what is known about promoting behavioral competence in young children and the typical classroom practices and services they receive (Dunlap et al., 2006). In one study, for example, although early education teachers reportedly embraced the principles of positive behavior support, classroom observations revealed that many teachers failed to implement certain practices related to effective management (e.g., teaching and clarifying behavior expectations or providing children with choices [Branson & Demchek, 2011]). The researchers also noted that many teachers did not consistently teach appropriate classroom behavior or effective social skills in an intentional and systematic manner. Although teachers in this study recognized the importance of talking about emotions and helping children negotiate social situations, they did not consistently provide explicit instruction to teach these skills. Moreover, there continues to be an overemphasis on the use of negative or reductive procedures to eliminate problem behaviors, rather than positive approaches to support the development of appropriate behavior (Maag, 2001). Many strategies for dealing with misbehavior in early childhood classrooms involve the use of various forms of punishment such as removal from the classroom, loss free time, or even suspension and expulsion (Gilliam, 2005). These punitive management approaches have little effect on encouraging young children to develop and exhibit appropriate behavior patterns.

The early years provide teachers with many opportunities to promote the development of positive behavior and to intervene early and effectively with young children who display challenging behaviors. Moreover, numerous researchers have identified effective classroom management strategies aimed at both prevention and intervention for challenging behaviors (Conroy, Dunlap, Clark, & Alter, 2005; Dunlap et al., 2006). In general, the evidence suggests that an effective approach to behavior management in preschools relies on the adoption of a multitiered approach, such as the Teaching Pyramid Model, to promote development of social and behavior competence, provide support for children's appropriate behavior, and prevent challenging behavior.

EARLY CHILDHOOD CLASSROOM ENVIRONMENTS

The importance of high-quality classroom environments and supportive adult–child relationships for supporting the development of positive behaviors is well established in early education (Lloyd & Bangser, 2009). Within a multitiered framework, enhancing early childhood environments constitutes a first-tier approach to classroom management. The Tier 1, or universal, basic management strategies are designed to provide all children with effective practices that prevent problem behaviors from emerging and reduce the need for more intensive interventions. Two specific aspects of early childhood environments—teacher–child relationships and the physical classroom arrangement—have garnered substantial research support as contributing to effective behavior management (McCabe & Frede, 2007).

Positive Relationships between Teachers and Students

Researchers agree that a critical aspect of well managed classrooms is the quality of the relationship between teachers and students (Davis, 2003; Griggs, Gagnon, Huelsman, Kidder-Ashley, & Ballard, 2009; Hamre & Pianta, 2001; Hughes, Cavell, & Willson, 2001; Pianta & Stuhlman, 2004). Young children in particular need trusting, warm, and nurturing relationships with teachers and caregivers to promote development of social and behavioral competence. Most behavior management strategies will not be effective unless there is a positive relationship between the teacher and children.

Several studies have investigated the manner in which teacher–child relationships influence young children's classroom behavior. Whereas many factors may have an impact on children's adjustment and behavior during their early childhood years, the student–teacher relationship has consistently emerged as an important predictor of children's concurrent and long-term social competence (Birch & Ladd, 1997). According to Birch and Ladd, as adults build nurturing relationships with students, their direct influence on children's behavior grows significantly. Young children are more readily guided by teachers with whom they are emotionally invested. They pay particular attention to what a teacher says and does, and they seek ways to ensure even more positive attention from teachers with whom they have a caring relationship (Edwards & Raikes, 2002). Moreover, children are more likely to develop a positive self-concept, confidence, and a sense of security in the context of supportive relationships. Studies demonstrate that children who have secure relationships with their teachers exhibit lower levels of challenging behavior in early childhood classrooms compared to children with insecure or conflictual relationships (Joseph & Strain, 2004).

The interactions that occur between children and teachers are also critical in providing opportunities for children to observe and develop social competence. For instance, when teachers demonstrate kindness and respect toward others through the use of affectionate words or appropriate physical contact, young children engage in similar behaviors toward peers and other adults in the classroom (Hamre & Pianta, 2006; Powell, Dunlap, & Fox, 2006). Finally, positive teacher–child relationships are particularly important for children with a history of disruptive or challenging behavior. Huffman, Mehlinger, and Kerivan (2000) found that close relationships with early childhood teachers served as a protective factor for young children at risk for behavior problems due to family characteristics and early aggression. Other researchers have suggested a similar moderating role for positive teacher–child relationships in the link between early risk factors and later behavior problems (Burchinal, Peisner-Feinberg, Pianta, & Howes, 2002; Hughes, Cavell, & Willson, 2001; Ladd & Burgess, 2001; Meehan, Hughes, & Cavell, 2003).

In early education settings, many practices promote the formation of secure attachments and positive teacher–child relationships. Descriptive and correlational research has identified teacher characteristics that are essential to developing positive relationships and, in turn, creating well managed classrooms (LaCourse et al., 2002). For example, teachers who are successful in establishing well managed classrooms are attuned to children's developmental needs. Specifically, they demonstrate an understanding of children's physical, attentional, and emotional needs through responsive interactions; they also listen to children before responding, make eye contact, and engage children in frequent one-on-one conversations (Grining, Raver, Champion, Sardin, Metzger, & Jones, 2010). Moreover, effective teachers plan for and provide children with a variety of choices in the classroom to accommodate individual differences (Hojnoski & Missall, 2010). Early childhood teachers in well managed classrooms also model prosocial behavior and appropriate interactions toward others. Children who observe and receive more frequent, positive interactions with adults have been shown to be more competent in their own interactions with peers and adults (Powell, Dunlap, & Fox, 2006). Teachers who are warm and attentive are also more successful in motivating and engaging children in academic learning activities (Edwards & Raikes, 2002).

Unfortunately, when children display disruptive behaviors, teachers often have a difficult time establishing positive relationships with them. Children with challenging behaviors are more likely to have interactions with teachers and caregivers that are directive in nature or focused on their problem behavior, rather than interactions that provide positive feedback for appropriate behavior and support for learning new skills (Arnold, McWilliams, & Arnold, 1999; Newman, Caspi, Moffitt, & Silva, 1997; Tremblay, 2000). An important goal for all early childhood teachers is to engage in positive, supportive interactions with every child in their classroom each day.

Adult attention and positive feedback are important for managing young children's behavior as well. This may take the form of guiding a child through a difficult social problem, providing positive feedback about something the child has done well, modeling appropriate ways to communicate emotions or interact with peers, or engaging in a conversation about something that interests the child (Warner & Lynch, 2004). Effective early educators understand the importance of monitoring their interactions with children to ensure that they are spending a greater proportion of time acknowledging and teaching appropriate behaviors and less time responding to or punishing challenging behavior. When teachers attend to children's appropriate behavior and provide assistance as needed, children are less likely to exhibit problem behaviors (Hemmeter, Fox, Jack, Broyles, & Doubet, 2007).

Overall, the importance of teacher–child interactions and relationships in early childhood settings as the foundation for effective classroom management cannot be overstated. Developing a supportive relationship with each child begins with the use of positive attention and feedback for appropriate behavior. Teachers can use their interactions with children in ways that promote positive behavior and prevent challenging behavior. Positive attention, encouragement, and praise for appropriate behavior are powerful tools for managing and shaping behavior. In addition, nurturing teacher–child relationships contribute to active engagement among preschoolers and support the development of behavioral competence by reducing levels of challenging behavior and increasing opportunities for learning (National Research Council, 2001).

Arrangement and Structure of Early Childhood Environments

The National Research Council (2001) report, *Eager to Learn*, confirms that the way in which early childhood classroom environments are arranged has a direct influence on young children's participation, peer interactions, learning, and behavior. Thus, effective Tier 1 classroom management practices include strategies to structure early childhood environments to promote the development of positive behaviors and prevent the occurrence of challenging behaviors.

A key component of effective behavior management is creating a predictable and organized classroom setting. When early education environments are structured such that children feel safe and supported, and when they know what to do, when to do it, and what is expected of them, children are less likely to engage in challenging behavior (Lawrey, Danko, & Strain, 1999). Three broad types of environmental strategies have been identified by researchers as being effective in minimizing challenging behavior. These strategies focus on (1) the physical arrangement of the classroom environment, (2) rules and behavioral expectations, and (3) classroom schedules and routines.

Physical Arrangement, Activity Selection, and Active Monitoring

The physical environment of a classroom includes the layout and boundaries of activity areas, selection and display of materials and equipment, and opportunities for monitoring behavior. Whereas strategic arrangement of classroom space may seem like a simple management strategy, studies consistently demonstrate that it has a significant impact on children's behavior (Simonsen, Fairbanks, Briesch, Myers, & Sugai, 2008).

Multiple features of environmental arrangements in early childhood classrooms have been linked to effective behavior management (Ratcliff, 2001). First, activity areas can be arranged to promote engagement and social interaction. Engagement is the key to preventing challenging behavior. When children are actively involved in doing something they enjoy, they are less likely to engage in challenging behavior (Sugai & Horner, 2002). Several strategies for arranging the physical environment to promote engagement have been documented in the literature. Examples include (1) incorporating children's development levels and natural interests into activities to sustain their motivation, (2) setting up areas to be free from other distractions to allow children to become deeply engaged in their work, (3) arranging adjoining areas to encourage "spillover" of play or to increase social interaction (e.g., putting the writing center next to dramatic play area), (4) limiting the number of children in each center to ensure adequate space and to avoid overcrowding, and (5) arranging the classroom to ensure visual monitoring of all children by teachers and aides (Warner & Lynch, 2004).

Recently, a zone defense schedule (ZDS) system in early childhood settings has been researched as a method for organizing both the adults in a classroom and the physical environment (Casey & McWilliam, 2005). Within this system, teachers or other adults are assigned specific roles and tasks during designated times of the day, and the children move between and among teachers rather than having teachers follow children around the classroom. The primary goal of the ZDS is to decrease the rate of child nonengagement by having at least one adult directly observing and interacting with children at all times. Organizing adults using the ZDS system has been shown to facilitate transitions between activities, increase opportunities for instruction, and decrease behavior challenges (Casey & McWilliam, 2011).

Similar considerations of physical arrangement should be given to the materials available in a classroom as well. Not surprisingly, children are more likely to use materials if they are made available. For example, when books are easily accessible in the classroom, children are likely to read them. Young children are also more likely to be engaged and interested in materials that are systematically rotated over time to provide novelty (Dobbs-Oates, Kaderavek, Guo, & Justice, 2011). Furthermore, materials should be selected to support specific skill development. For example, the use of social materials, such as puppets and dramatic play props, has been shown to increase cooperative peer interactions (Ostrosky & Meadan, 2010). Materials can also be distributed intentionally to encourage interaction between peers. For example, if two children are painting, one child may be given two colors and the other child two different colors to share. Finally, allowing children to pick out materials on their own and requiring them to return materials to the appropriate place foster independence and responsibility (McCormick, Jolivette, & Ridgely, 2003).

Consistent Rules and Clear Expectations

A second component of the environment that decreases the likelihood of challenging behaviors is the establishment and communication of classroom rules and behavior expectations (Ratcliff, 2001). When implementing rules, there are several research-based guidelines to consider. First, rules should be simply worded, few in number, and provide preschoolers with sufficient clarity to teach them to discriminate between behaviors that are appropriate versus not appropriate in the classroom setting (McGinnis, Frederick, & Edwards, 1999). Second, young children require explicit instruction and guided practice to understand and comply with rules and expectations. Specifically, children need to be taught rules and expectations using an instructional model that incorporates step-by-step teaching, positive and specific feedback, and repeated practice over time until all children understand and are able to engage in appropriate behaviors (Dunlap et al., 2006). Finally, clarity and consistency in expectations help young children learn self-regulation and minimize the occurrence of problem behavior (Powell, Dunlap, & Fox, 2006). The use of pictures that illustrate the behavioral expectations (e.g., Walking Feet) provides a comprehensible visual cue for teaching expectations for classroom behavior to young children. Moreover, visual supports serve as reminders to children to follow classroom expectations as well as to teachers to reinforce children who demonstrate behavior expectations.

Predictable Schedules and Routines

Researchers have also demonstrated that schedules and routines influence children's classroom behaviors. Predictable and consistent schedules in early childhood classrooms help children feel secure and comfortable, thus reducing the frequency of behavior problems. Activity schedules that provide children with choices and balanced activities (e.g., small- and large-group activities, quiet and active time periods, teacher-directed and child-directed tasks, etc.) result in a high rate of child engagement and minimal disruptive behavior (Jolivette, McCormick, Jung, & Lingo, 2004).

Lawrey and colleagues (1999) delineated three components of a well planned schedule. The first component is consistency in the schedule. When a schedule changes from day to day, it is difficult for children to learn and remember the routine. Children feel comfortable and confident if they are able to anticipate what will come next during the school day. The second component of an effective schedule is the occurrence of few, if any, transition periods during which children spend time waiting without anything to do. When transitions in a schedule are necessary and unavoidable, it is important that all children are not required to move at exactly the same time in the same way (e.g., stagger transitions to and from snack time and other standard activities; Hemmeter, Ostrosky, Artman, & Kinder, 2008). Transition times can also be structured so that children have a consistent activity or routine to follow while they wait for other children, such as listening to a story, singing a song, or playing a game. The final component of effective schedules identified by Lawrey and associates is the use of explicit instruction and practice to teach classroom routines. Whereas some children will learn routines simply by participating in them, most will need to be taught routines in more systematic ways through the use of picture schedules, visual prompts, and teacher-assisted rehearsal with feedback (Dunlap et al., 2006).

In sum, within a multitiered approach to classroom management, the deliberate use of effective environmental strategies creates classroom settings that minimize the occurrence of problems and promote positive behavior among all children. When early educators combine warm, nurturing relationships with consistent routines, clear expectations regarding classroom behavior, physical arrangements that promote engagement and peer interactions, and positive attention for appropriate behavior, the likelihood of challenging behavior is significantly reduced (Dunlap et al., 2006; Lloyd & Bangser, 2009; McCabe & Frede, 2007; Powell, Dunlap, & Fox, 2006).

EARLY CHILDHOOD BEHAVIOR INTERVENTION PROGRAMS AND CURRICULA

Even when early educators are responsive to young children and structure their classrooms to promote the development of social and behavioral competence, some children continue to be at risk for problem behavior. These are children whose behavior deviates from what is developmentally normative, who often disrupt the learning of other children in the classroom, and who are unresponsive to the efforts of teachers to meet their needs. Within a multitiered framework, these children require more intensive and focused behavior management strategies than what is provided at the universal level.

In recognition of the need to intervene early to put children back on healthy developmental trajectories necessary for school success, a number of programs have been developed and demonstrated to ameliorate behavior challenges in young children (Dunlap et al., 2006; Joseph & Strain, 2003). The social-emotional and behavior programs described in this section represent approaches that early childhood educators can use to teach prosocial skills and to intervene with incipient behavior problems with the goal of remediating behaviors before they escalate to more severe and intractable levels. Although programs are most often delivered through small-group formats, they can be implemented by teachers with whole classrooms or with individual children in early childhood settings. Moreover, whereas the interventions described in this section can be used as preventive universal approaches for all children, many have been developed specifically for children who are at risk for, or already exhibit, challenging behaviors (Powell, Dunlap, & Fox, 2006). As such, these tier two, or supplemental, behavioral programs are designed for narrower purposes than are Tier 1 strategies, such as teaching explicit behavior or social skills to a subgroup of children. In a multitiered framework, these interventions are intended to supplement the universal, first-tier behavioral supports (i.e., responsive teacher–child relationships and well structured classroom environments) that are provided to all students.

Incredible Years

First developed in the early 1980s for children with early onset conduct problems who were referred to clinical settings, the Incredible Years (IY) series was later adapted for dissemination and implementation in school settings, including early childhood programs (Webster-Stratton & Reid, 2009). Today, the series includes three training programs specifically developed for (1) preschool and elementary school-aged children with challenging behaviors, (2) parents, and (3) classroom teachers.

The IY series is embedded in a broad theoretical framework that includes cognitive social learning, modeling, developmental, self-efficacy, and relationship theories specifically as they pertain to the development of antisocial behaviors (Webster-Stratton, Reinke, Herman, & Newcomer, 2011). Extensively researched over the last three decades, the IY series has received considerable empirical support (Center for the Study and Prevention of Violence, 2001; Greenberg, Domitrovich, & Bumbarger, 2000).

Whole-Child Approach

Although the focus of this chapter is on classroom-based interventions, a discussion of the IY series would not be complete without addressing the synergy of the parent, child, and teacher training components. Indeed, the authors of the program have long emphasized the importance of a whole-child approach to treating early onset conduct problems (Webster-Stratton & Reid, 2009). Extensive research on the IY series supports this claim, with data suggesting that optimal improvements in internalizing and externalizing symptoms are achieved when children are treated with a combination of training programs (Beauchaine, Webster-Stratton, & Reid, 2005; Herman, Borden, Reinke, & Webster-Stratton, 2011).

1. *Parent training.* The IY parent training component involves a series of 12 weekly workshops, during which parents learn about and discuss various topics related to their children's social, emotional, and behavioral development. Topics include modeling positive thoughts and attitudes, praising and rewarding positive behaviors, setting limits, supporting social and emotional competencies, and collaborating with schools and community organizations.
2. *Child training.* In the early childhood and elementary school classroom settings, the manualized IY child training program, entitled *Dinosaur Social Skills and Problem Solving Curriculum*, can be used as a universal classroom

prevention curriculum for all children or as a small-group treatment program specifically for children who have persistent problem behaviors. The year-long child training program consists of seven units, which include topics such as school readiness, social and emotional competence, empathy, problem solving, and anger management. In a randomized control trial conducted by Webster-Stratton, Reid, and Hammond (2004), children (4–8 years) who participated in the IY child-training-only condition showed significant improvements on measures of social skills.

3. *Teacher training.* The teacher training program complements the child training program. It consists of six, full-day workshops throughout the year in which teachers learn about topics such as nurturing student–teacher interactions, using effective individualized and classroom-wide behavior management strategies, promoting social competency, reinforcing positive behaviors, and collaborating with families. Findings from the Webster-Stratton and associates (2004) study showed that children whose teachers had participated in the teacher training program had significantly lower reports of behavior problems posttreatment compared to children in the child-training-only condition.

Maintenance and Generalization

The IY's broad-based treatment approach has been shown to promote maintenance and generalization of positive behavior change. A two-year follow-up study conducted by Reid, Webster-Stratton, and Hammond (2003), for example, found that when teacher training supplemented parent- or child-training-only conditions, the long-term outcomes for children with persistent behavior problems were significantly improved. The multicomponent aspect of IY also affords flexibility in accommodating the individual needs of children. That is, the specific combination of parent, child, and teacher training programs may differ on a case-by-case basis. If a child exhibits persistent challenging behaviors across home and school settings, then an emphasis on combined parent and teacher training and communication is warranted (Reid, Webster-Stratton, & Hammond, 2003).

Chicago School Readiness Project

The Chicago School Readiness Project (CRSP) was developed in response to a perceived shortage of structured, classroom-based behavioral intervention programs for preschool-age children from low-SES backgrounds (Raver & Knitzer, 2002). Specifically, the developers sought to implement a comprehensive consultation program to address the unique demographics of urban early childhood settings (e.g., Head Start–funded programs), where teachers typically have limited access to training and resources to support students' academic, social, and emotional development (Raver, Jones, Li-Grining, Zhai, Metzger, & Solomon, 2009).

Because the preschool years are widely considered to be a vulnerable and critical period of development that sets the stage for later self-regulation and school readiness, the CSRP aims to introduce a focused framework for intervention, one that gives teachers the means to better understand students' internalizing and externalizing behavior problems and subsequently intervene with effective classroom management strategies. According to Raver and colleagues (2011), the CSRP is rooted in the fields of developmental psychology and prevention science, both of which provide a rationale for the program's three primary intervention components: (1) collaborative mental health consultation, (2) teacher training, and (3) teacher coaching.

Consultation

A significant body of research suggests that mental health consultants working in early childhood classrooms can serve as change agents for improved classroom environments and subsequent improved child behavioral outcomes (Benedict, Horner, & Squires, 2007; Perry, Dunne, McFadden, & Campbell, 2008). For this reason, the CSRP employs a mental health consultant (MHC), typically a master's-level social worker, who works with the classroom teacher on a weekly basis. The goal of the MHC is to provide classroom teachers with multiple levels of support and resources. Specifically, efforts to improve the overall classroom environment involve many of the same elements of behavior management approaches previously discussed in this chapter (Tier 1), including nurturing student–teacher relationships, physical classroom arrangements, and effective classroom management techniques. In addition to providing consultation for behavior management techniques, the MHCs also consult with teachers concerning three to five individual children in their classrooms, using a child-focused consultation model for addressing persistent challenging behaviors.

Teacher Training and Coaching

A major premise behind the CSRP is that early childhood classroom teachers often lack adequate training in classroom environment and behavior management techniques. The CSRP addresses this training gap by providing 30 hours of professional development through workshops for groups of classroom teachers. The training materials used at the workshops are adapted from the Webster-Stratton and colleagues' (2004) Incredible Years Teacher Training Program. Following the workshops, MHCs continue to coach early childhood teachers in implementing the learned techniques in the classroom. MHCs also provide supplemental workshops that address personal issues related to teacher burnout, helping teachers to identify factors that contribute to stress and how to address them.

Evidence Base

In a randomized controlled trial involving CSRP implementation in 35 Chicago Head Start classrooms, findings showed that teachers who received the CSRP training, coaching, and consultation services were rated by independent observers as having significantly higher-quality classroom environments, particularly in terms of classroom management, compared to control teachers (Raver et al., 2009). These same teachers also self-reported higher ratings of perceived job-related control and resources (Zhai, Raver, & Li-Grining, 2011). Furthermore, a significant decrease in children's challenging behaviors was observed (Raver et al., 2009). In the same study, teacher-report measures of children's internalizing and externalizing behaviors were also significantly more positive.

School Readiness

Data from a randomized controlled trial revealed significant gains in self-regulation skills among children who were in CSRP classrooms compared to control classrooms (Raver et al., 2011). Moreover, significant improvements were noted in the children's early literacy and math skills. Such findings suggest that the benefits of the CSRP model may have a far-reaching impact on children's school readiness beyond effective classroom management.

A compelling follow-up study found that, in the year following their participation in the CSRP, children who transitioned to high-performing schools for kindergarten had maintained their academic and behavioral gains, whereas children who transitioned to lower-performing schools did not (Zhai, Raver, & Jones, 2012). These findings suggest that, although a structured approach such as the CSRP holds great promise in preparing young children from low-SES backgrounds for school entry, continued supportive environments are necessary to sustain the behavioral and academic gains.

Positive Behavior Intervention and Support

The Positive Behavior Intervention and Support (PBIS) model is a team-based, comprehensive approach for assessing, conceptualizing, and intervening in accordance with a multitiered framework for classroom management. Currently, the PBIS model is being implemented in many school systems across the nation, and during the last decade, there has been much discussion in the literature regarding its relevance for the early childhood education settings (Benedict, Horner, & Squires, 2007; Stormont, Lewis, & Beckner, 2005; Stormont, Smith, & Lewis, 2007).

Unlike the other empirically validated programs and curricula (e.g., IY), PBIS is not a specific, manualized approach to prevention and intervention for challenging behaviors. Rather, PBIS reflects an overall paradigm shift toward behavior management, one that promotes the systematic use of effective, positive, and proactive management strategies (Fox, Dunlap, & Powell, 2002).

The PBIS paradigm is rooted in behavioral theory and well aligned with the multitiered framework of this chapter. The ultimate goal of PBIS implementation is to decrease incidents of problem behaviors and subsequently to increase students' social and emotional competence and academic performance (Simonsen, Sugai, & Negron, 2008). In an early childhood setting, this is achieved by developing responsive and nurturing school environments that are supportive of all students' needs, with additional and more intensive supports provided for children whose challenging behaviors persist. Across the multiple tiers, PBIS implementation involves defining behavioral expectations, teaching appropriate behaviors, and positively reinforcing appropriate behaviors (Stormont, Lewis, & Beckner, 2005).

Team-Based

The PBIS model hinges on collaborative team-based leadership that drives system-wide consensus building and implementation. According to Stormont and colleagues (2005), the most effective PBIS teams in early childhood settings include members who represent the multiple systems that have an impact on young children's lives (e.g., administrators, behavioral consultants, classroom teachers, paraprofessionals, support staff, and primary caregivers). These stakeholders work in collaboration to establish goals, use data-based decision making, select evidence-based assessments and interventions, and monitor individual student, classroom, and program-wide progress.

In the case of early childhood education settings, the literature stresses the importance of a PBIS model that is culturally relevant and family centered. Fox and colleagues (2002) assert that, in order to provide effective prevention and intervention practices, the PBIS team is responsible for considering the diverse life experiences of young children with challenging behaviors, whose situations are often compounded by complex family, social, and economic dynamics. Thus, it is crucial that families are viewed as key members of PBIS teams and are directly involved in the goal-setting and decision-making processes.

Challenging Behaviors

When challenging behaviors are a major concern, the PBIS model calls for additional assessment and the provision of individualized behavioral support. As Crone and Horner (2003) assert, effective PBIS interventions are best informed utilizing a functional behavioral assessment (FBA) approach. FBA involves the systematic collection of data (e.g., observations, interviews, ratings) to identify the function of a problem behavior (e.g., to escape a difficult task, to gain attention from the teacher), as well as contextual variables (e.g., lack of structure or clarify in expectations) that reliably predict or trigger the occurrence of the problem behavior (Nielsen & McEvoy, 2004). Once teams have completed an FBA, they are able to move forward and select appropriate function-based interventions to reduce the occurrence of problem behaviors and to reinforce or strengthen positive alternative, or replacement, behaviors.

In an experimental control study by Gettinger and Stoiber (2006), findings revealed better behavioral outcomes in prekindergarten through first-grade classrooms that utilized FBAs in conjunction with a collaborative, team-based PBIS model. Based on their descriptive review, Stormont and associates (2005) concluded that because system-wide PBIS implementation brings consistency to a district or school system, the model shows promise in promoting the maintenance and generalization of positive behavior outcomes.

PBIS is a broad multitiered approach that incorporates both Tier 1, universal, appropriate classroom management strategies, as well as Tier 2, supplemental, programs. For example, in their discussion of classroom management procedures within an early childhood PBIS model, Benedict and colleagues (2007) reference both the IY (described earlier) and First Step to Success (Walker, Stiller, & Golly, 1998) programs as second-tier interventions that may be implemented within the PBIS approach.

Promoting Alternative THinking Strategies

First developed in the early 1980s for use with children who are deaf and hard-of-hearing, the Promoting Alternative THinking Strategies (PATHS) curriculum was adapted for use in regular and special education elementary classrooms (for children ages 5–12); it was later revised for early childhood education classrooms (for children ages 3–5). The PATHS curriculum is a comprehensive, year-long behavior management program that aims to improve children's social and emotional competencies and subsequently to decrease the risk of internalizing and externalizing problem behaviors (Greenberg & Kusche, 1993).

Materials for the PATHS curriculum are designed to be integrated, multiyear modules; schools and districts that adopt the program are encouraged to incorporate the curriculum across multiple grade levels, including early childhood education classrooms. In the early childhood modules, classroom teachers are trained to implement turtle-themed activities within their standard circle time periods (e.g., using modeling through stories, role-plays, and puppet characters). Such activities directly teach students skills related to emotional and behavioral self-regulation, effective communication, positive peer relationships, and problem solving. These acquired skills are then incorporated into the general curriculum, with additional games and activities that reinforce the use of the skills throughout the school day.

The PATHS curriculum aligns with the ABCD (Affective-Behavioral-Cognitive-Dynamic) developmental model, which emphasizes the interrelated nature of children's affect, behaviors, cognitions, and social-cognitive awareness by developing skills for emotional and behavioral self-regulation (Greenberg & Kusché, 1993). In addition, the PATHS program views children's emotional and behavioral challenges as both a function of and a contributor to their complex environmental systems. As such, the PATHS program emphasizes the importance of generalizing outcomes to the academic curriculum and overall classroom environment (Domitrovich, Cortes, & Greenberg, 2007).

Prevention Focus

Compared to other comprehensive, modularized prevention and intervention programs (e.g., IY and First Step to Success), the PATHS curriculum does not place as much emphasis on home–school collaboration. Rather, the PATHS curriculum focuses primarily on the classroom setting, with only a few supplemental worksheets and activities that can be sent home. Domitrovich and colleagues (2007), however, recommended the development of a more intensive PATHS model for early childhood settings that incorporates caregiver modules for improved home–school communication and parent training.

The PATHS curriculum has been disseminated to hundreds of schools and districts across the world, and multiple studies have found it to be an effective program for the prevention of problem behaviors in children (Greenberg, Kusche, Cook, & Quamma, 1995; Mihalic, Irwin, Elliott, Fagan, & Hansen, 2001). In separate studies, Domitrovich and associates (2007) and Bierman and colleagues (2008) researched the implementation of the preschool-level PATHS curriculum in Head Start classrooms. In a randomized trial involving 20 Head Start programs, Domitrovich and fellow researchers (2007) found significantly improved treatment effects on direct measures of children's emotional competencies, as well as parent and teacher reports of social competencies.

School Readiness

In their randomized control study, Bierman and colleagues (2008) studied the efficacy of the PATHS curriculum when implemented as part of a Head Start multifaceted school readiness program incorporating both academic and social-emotional components. In this study, when the PATHS curriculum was supplemented with additional interventions (i.e., professional development, structured academic curriculum, and early language and emergent literacy skill programs), the findings showed significant improvements across multiple domains of academic and social-emotional school readiness, compared to children in a control condition.

Maintenance and Generalization

Findings from the Kam, Greenburg, and Wall (2003) study of first-graders in inner-city schools revealed that, in order for the PATHS curriculum to result in improved outcomes (i.e., an increase in emotional competence and a decrease in aggression), two conditions must be met: (1) support from school principals and (2) high levels of classroom implementation. Thus, coordinated school-wide efforts allow for long-term maintenance. Indeed, with consistent classroom and system-level support as well as implementation beginning during the early childhood years, the multiyear PATHS program can continue to reinforce students' social and emotional competencies as they transition from their early childhood education to elementary school classrooms.

First Step to Success

Developed in the early 1990s, the First Step to Success (FSTS) program incorporates a manualized treatment approach to early intervention and classroom management for young children who are at risk for developing significant problem behaviors. The FSTS program specifically targets those children who "show the soft signs of an antisocial pattern of behavior" (Walker, Severson, Feil, Stiller, & Golly, 1998, p. 263). The program relies on a consultant-based module system that includes three components: (1) universal screening, (2) interventions designed for the school setting (targeting the children who are identified as being most at risk based on screening measures), and (3) training for primary caregivers.

The FSTS program is similar to the IY series in that it aims to mediate at-risk, problem behaviors in a comprehensive manner. The program emphasizes the importance of training those in close proximity to the child (primary caregivers, teachers, and peers). In their description of FSTS, Walker, Kavanagh, Stiller, Golly, Severson, and Feil (1998) reference Moffit's (1994) research, which differentiates between anti-social behaviors that are adolescence-limited versus life-course-persistent. The former are behaviors that result from exposure to peers' problem behaviors, whereas the latter are behaviors that tend to be influenced by the family system and have more severe, long-term consequences. For this reason, the FSTS program includes targeted interventions for peers and primary caregivers, in addition to supporting teachers.

Consultation

Integral to the FSTS program is the role of the consultant or coach, a trained individual (typically a school support staff member) who, first, works individually with targeted children, explicitly teaching and rewarding appropriate behaviors in conjunction with a red/green card game (Walker, Severson, Feil, Stiller, & Golly, 1998). Next, under the continued direction of the consultant, the behavior system is gradually generalized to the classroom environment, with the teacher taking over implementation and the classroom peers of target children participating as well. In this way, the FSTS program supports teachers by giving them behavioral management strategies that target social and behavioral competencies at the universal classroom level. The role of the consultant also extends to the family system. Specifically, the third FSTS component involves coaching primary caregivers of the targeted children in behavior management skills, such as setting limits, rewarding positive behaviors, and supporting school readiness. Furthermore, the consultant facilitates and coordinates communication between the home and school systems.

Evidence Base

Multiple studies of the FSTS program have found it to be effective at improving academic, social, and behavioral competence for those children most at risk for anti-social and challenging behaviors (What Works Clearinghouse, 2012). As reviewers (e.g., Maag & Katsiyannis, 2010; Rodriguez, Loman, & Horner, 2009) point out, however, the majority of FSTS studies have relied on single-case design methodology; only two randomized control trials (Walker, Severson, Feil, Stiller, & Golly, 1998; Walker et al., 2009) meet rigorous standards for having an evidence-based intervention.

In the initial randomized control trial by Walker and colleagues (1998), findings suggested a causal relationship between the intervention and improved behavioral outcomes in kindergarten students. The study also included first-grade and second-grade follow-up phases and demonstrated that gains were maintained across all phases and measures of teacher ratings and observations. In a later study (Walker et al., 2009), findings of improved outcomes were replicated in a diverse urban school district. Although children, on average, made significant gains, about one-third of individual children did not demonstrate improved outcomes postimplementation. To examine more closely variables that contribute to children's progress, several researchers have conducted multiple baseline single-case studies investigating the role of teacher fidelity of implementation and the effect of adding individualized functional behavioral assessment and function-based support plans to the FSTS protocol; these studies reveal that implementation fidelity and added supports allow a greater number of children to benefit from FSTS (e.g., Carter & Horner, 2009; Rodriguez, Loman, & Horner, 2009).

Kindergarten Screening

In the context of early childhood interventions, one notable limitation of the FSTS program is that the manualized approach has been targeted and tested only for students in kindergarten through third grade, at which point the opportunity to intervene to promote early school readiness skills has already past. Initially, the developers explained that a benchmark of kindergarten entry is the best time for proactive, universal screening efforts (Walker, Stiller, & Golly, 1998). It should be noted, however, that at this time the program developers are in the final phases of a grant funded by the National Institute of Child Health and Human Development (NICHD), adapting the FSTS program for use in the early childhood setting. Considering that the literature is now supporting earlier prevention and intervention efforts for children at risk for challenging behaviors, the results of this project will make important contributions to the research on early childhood classroom management.

Summary of Early Childhood Behavioral Intervention Programs

In the face of mounting evidence that early behavior problems are linked to later negative developmental and social outcomes, educators, researchers, and policy makers are charged with developing ways to identify and intervene when the initial signs that children may be on such a trajectory occur. By viewing this inherently complex issue from the conceptual framework of a multitiered approach to classroom behavior management, a structured response begins to take shape.

The establishment of effective classroom management begins with a focus on universal management techniques within Tier 1 (e.g., nurturing teacher–child relationships and creating well structured classroom environments) and expands to include the supplemental, Tier 2 behavior management programs described in this section that offer more intensive and focused intervention strategies and behavioral support. Separately, these five programs—i.e., IY, CSRP, PBIS, PATHS, and FSTS—are exemplary models for evidence-based, structured approaches to addressing persistent challenging behaviors. Each program is conceptualized to provide a unique and effective approach to the early identification, prevention, and intervention of problem behaviors.

Although it is important to look at the programs separately and contrast their distinct frameworks, it is also advantageous to consider them as a whole. Together, these programs provide a clear rationale and strong evidence base for a myriad of components that are involved in the effective prevention and intervention for persistent challenging behaviors in early childhood. First, for schools and districts, multiple intervention components are necessary, including system-level program implementation; supplemental support and resources for teachers to prevent burn-out; advanced teacher training and coaching in classroom management strategies; consultation; team-based leadership; establishing goals; data-based decision making; considerations for long-term maintenance and generalization; and monitoring individual student, classroom, and program-wide progress. Collaboration with families is also critical for effective classroom management; this collaborative component typically requires culturally relevant and family-centered practices, parent training, and home–school communication. Collectively, this continuum of system-wide, family, and classroom components comprise the key features for developing and sustaining an effective, multitiered framework for early childhood classroom management.

CONCLUSIONS AND FUTURE DIRECTIONS

The occurrence of challenging behaviors in young children presents serious implications for all aspects of their development. Preschool-age children who display challenging behaviors are likely to experience immediate and long-term negative social-emotional and academic outcomes. As awareness of these issues grows, it will be increasingly important for teachers in early childhood education settings to adopt and implement a systematic approach to classroom management. In this chapter, we have framed effective behavior management within a multitiered model that includes universal as well as supplemental, comprehensive approaches to addressing challenging behavior and promoting social and behavioral competence among all children.

Despite this call for effective and efficient classroom management in early childhood classrooms, research continues to demonstrate that early childhood teachers often lack the knowledge and skills to implement effective classroom management strategies with fidelity. Implementation fidelity refers to the extent to which strategies and interventions are implemented accurately and as intended (Noell, Gresham, & Gansle, 2002). There is growing evidence that fidelity of implementation of classroom management strategies is related to behavioral outcomes (Fiske, 2008). Recent research has been directed to toward development of measures to evaluate the extent to which effective classroom management procedures are used in early childhood classrooms. For example, the Preschool-Wide Evaluation Tool (PreSET; Steed & Webb, 2013) was designed specifically for use in early childhood education settings to assess the level of implementation of universal management strategies described in this chapter (e.g., supportive relationships, consistent routines, etc.). Another measure, the Teaching Pyramid Observation Tool (TPOT) for Preschool Classrooms (Hemmeter, Fox, Snyder, 2013), is directly aligned with the multitiered approach addressed in this chapter and examines teachers' use of strategies related to both universal and supplemental intervention.

There is general agreement regarding the benefits of incorporating a focus on effective behavioral interventions and classroom management strategies into both preservice and in-service teacher training initiatives; however, there is less consensus about how to support and sustain teachers' implementation of research-supported strategies in the "real-world" contexts of their classrooms (Kratochwill & Shernoff, 2004). Evidence from several small-scale studies indicates that providing technical support and on-site coaching as teachers "try out" classroom management strategies may be one mechanism for enhancing skill development and implementation (Strain & Joseph, 2004). For example, when early childhood teachers received individualized coaching, feedback, and technical assistance to implement strategies for increasing positive social interactions, the rates of positive teacher–child and child–child interactions increased significantly compared to teachers who did not receive on-site coaching (Kohler, Anthony, Steighner, & Hoyson, 2001). Similarly, research has documented greater changes in young children's positive classroom behavior in classrooms where teachers received direct consultation and ongoing feedback and support for implementing evidence-based management strategies (Hemmeter, Fox, Jack, Broyles, & Doubet, 2007). Although limited, this research underscores the need for future work aimed at developing and evaluating effective professional development approaches to facilitate teachers' implementation of early childhood classroom management strategies.

REFERENCES

Arnold, D. H., McWilliams, L., & Arnold, E. H. (1999). Teacher discipline and child misbehavior in day care: Untangling causality with correlational date. *Developmental Psychology, 34*, 276–287.

Beauchaine, T. P., Webster-Stratton, C., & Reid, M. J. (2005). Mediators, moderators, and predictors of 1-year outcomes among children treated for early-onset conduct problems: A latent growth curve analysis. *Journal of Consulting and Clinical Psychology, 73*, 371–388.

Benedict, E. A., Horner, R. H., & Squires, J. K. (2007). Assessment and implementation of positive behavior support in preschools. *Topics in Early Childhood Special Education, 27*, 174–192.

Bierman, K. L., Domitrovich, C. E., Nix, R. L., Gest, S. D., Welsh, J. A., Greenberg, M. T., et al. (2008). Promoting academic and social-emotional school readiness: The Head Start REDI program. *Child Development, 79*, 1802–1817.

Birch, S. H., & Ladd, G. W. (1997). The teacher–child relationship and children's early school adjustment. *Journal of School Psychology, 35*, 61–79.

Branson, D., & Demchek, M. (2011). Toddler teachers' use of Teaching Pyramid practices. *Topics in Early Childhood Special Education, 30*, 196–208.

Brown, W. H., Odom, S. L., & Conroy, M. A. (2001). An intervention hierarchy for promoting preschool children's peer interactions in natural environments. *Topics in Early Childhood Special Education, 21*, 162–175.

Bryant, D., Vizzard, L. H., Willoughby, M., & Kupersmidt, J. (2000). A review of interventions for preschoolers with aggressive and disruptive behavior. *Early Education and Development, 10*, 47–68.

Burchinal, M. R., Peisner-Feinberg, E., Pianta, R., & Howes, C. (2002). Development of academic skill from preschool through second grade: Family and classroom predictors of developmental trajectories. *Journal of School Psychology, 40*, 415–436.

Campbell, S. (2002). *Behavior problems in preschool children: Clinical and developmental issues* (2nd ed.). New York: Guilford.

Campbell, S., Spieker, S., Burchinal, M., Poe, M., & National Institute of Child Health and Human Development Early Child Care Research Network. (2006). Trajectories of aggression from toddlerhood to age 9 predict academic and social functioning through ages 12. *Journal of Child Psychology and Psychiatry, 47*, 791–800.

Carlson, J. S., Tiret, H. B., Bender, S. L., & Benson, L. (2011). The influence of group training in the Incredible Years teacher classroom management program on preschool teachers' classroom management strategies. *Journal of Applied School Psychology, 27*, 134–154.

Carter, D. R., & Horner, R. H. (2009). Adding functional behavioral assessment to First Step to Success: A case study. *Journal of Positive Behavior Interventions, 9*, 229–238.

Casey, A. M., & McWilliam, R. A. (2005). Where is everybody? Organizing adults to promote child engagement. *Young Exceptional Children, 8*(2), 2–10.

Casey, A. M., & McWilliam, R. A. (2011). The impact of checklist-based training on teachers' use of the zone defense schedule. *Journal of Applied Behavior Analysis, 44*, 397–401.

Center for the Study and Prevention of Violence. (2001). *Blueprints for violence prevention.* Boulder, CO: Author.

Conroy, M. A., Dunlap, G., Clarke, S., & Alter, P. (2005). A descriptive analysis of positive behavioral intervention research with young children with challenging behavior. *Topics in Early Childhood Special Education, 25*, 157–166.

Crone, D. A., & Horner, R. H. (2003). *Building positive behavior support systems in schools: Functional behavioral assessment.* New York: Guilford.

Crone, D. A., & Horner, R. H. (2005). Changing the way we think about assessment and intervention for problem behavior. In L. M. Bambara & L. Kern (Eds.), *Individualized support for students with problem behaviors* (pp. 11–24). New York: Guilford.

Davis, H. A. (2003). Conceptualizing the role and influence of student–teacher relationships on children's social and cognitive development. *Educational Psychologist, 38*, 207–234.

Dobbs-Oates, J., Kaderavek, J. N., Guo, Y., & Justice, L. M. (2011). Effective behavior management in preschool classrooms and children's task orientation: Enhancing emergent literacy and language development. *Early Childhood Research Quarterly, 26*, 420–429.

Domitrovich, C. E., Cortes, R., & Greenberg, M. T. (2007). Improving young children's social and emotional competence: A randomized trial of the preschool PATHS curriculum. *Journal of Primary Prevention, 28*, 67–91.

Dunlap, G., Strain, P., Fox, L., Carta, J., Conroy, M., Smith, B., et al. (2006). Prevention and intervention with young children's challenging behavior: Perspectives regarding current knowledge. *Behavioral Disorders, 32*, 29–45.

Edwards, C. P., & Raikes, H. (2002). Extending the dance: Relationship-based approaches to infant/toddler care and education. *Young Children, 57*(4), 10–17.

Espinosa, L. (2002). The connection between social-emotional development and early literacy. *The Kauffman Early Education Exchange, 1*, 30–44.

Fiske, K. E. (2008). Treatment integrity of school-based behavior analytic interventions: A review of the research. *Behavior Analysis in Practice, 1*(2), 19–25.

Fox, L., Dunlap, G., Hemmeter, M., Joseph, G., & Strain, P. (2003). The Teaching Pyramid: A model for supporting social competence and preventing challenging behavior in young children. *Young Children, 58*(4), 48–52.

Fox, L., Dunlap, G., & Powell, D. (2002). Young children with challenging behavior: Issues and considerations for behavior support. *Journal of Positive Behavior Interventions, 4*, 208–217.

Gettinger, M., & Stoiber, K. C. (2006). Functional assessment, collaboration, and evidence-based treatment: Analysis of a team approach for addressing challenging behaviors in young children. *Journal of School Psychology, 44*, 231–252.

Gilliam, W. S. (2005). *Pre-kindergarteners left behind: Expulsion rates in state pre-kindergarten programs (FCD Policy Brief Series No. 3).* New York: Foundation for Child Development.

Greenberg, M. T., Domitrovich, C., & Bumbarger, B. (2000). *Preventing mental disorders in school-age children: A review of the effectiveness of prevention programs.* State College: Prevention Research Center for the Promotion of Human Development, Pennsylvania State University.

Greenberg, M. T., & Kusche, C. A. (1993). *Promoting social and emotional development in deaf children: The PATHS project.* Seattle: University of Washington Press.

Greenberg, M. T., Kusche, C. A., Cook, E. T., & Quamma, J. P. (1995). Promoting emotional competence in school-aged children: The effects of the PATHS curriculum. *Development and Psychopathology, 7*, 117–117.

Griffin, J. A. (2010). Research on the implementation of preschool intervention programs: Learning by doing. *Early Childhood Research Quarterly, 25*, 267–269.

Griggs, M. S., Gagnon, S. G., Huelsman, T. J., Kidder-Ashley, P., & Ballard, M. (2009). Student–teacher relationships matter: Moderating influences between temperament and preschool social competence. *Psychology in the Schools, 46*, 553–567.

Grining, C. L., Raver, C. C., Champion, K., Sardin, L., Metzger, M., & Jones, S. M. (2010). Understanding and improving classroom emotional climate and behavior management in the "real world." *Early Education and Development, 21*, 65–94.

Hamre, B. K., & Pianta, R. C. (2001). Early teacher–child relationships and the trajectory of children's school outcomes through eighth grade. *Child Development, 72*, 625–638.

Hamre, B. K., & Pianta, R. C. (2006). Student–teacher relationships. In G. G. Bear & K. M. Minke (Eds.), *Children's needs III: Development, prevention, and intervention* (pp. 59–72). Bethesda, MD: National Association of School Psychologists.

Hemmeter, M. L., Fox, L., Jack, S., Broyles, L., & Doubet, S. (2007). A program-wide model of positive behavior support in early childhood settings. *Journal of Early Intervention, 29*, 337–355.

Hemmeter, M. L., Fox, L., & Snyder, P. (2013). *Teaching Pyramid Observation Tool for Preschool Classrooms (TPOT) manual*. Baltimore, MD: Brookes.

Hemmeter, M. L., Ostrosky, M., Artman, K., & Kinder, K. (2008). Moving right along: Planning transitions to prevent challenging behavior. *Young Children, 63*(3), 18–22.

Hemmeter, M. L., Ostrosky, M., & Fox, L. (2006). Social emotional foundations for early learning: A conceptual model for intervention. *School Psychology Review, 35*, 583–601.

Hemmeter, M. L., Santos, R. M., & Ostrosky, M. (2008). Preparing early childhood educators to address young children's social-emotional development and challenging behavior: A survey of higher education programs in nine states. *Journal of Early Intervention, 30*, 321–340.

Herman, K. C., Borden, L. A., Reinke, W. M., & Webster-Stratton, C. (2011). The impact of the Incredible Years parent, child, and teacher training programs on children's co-occurring internalizing symptoms. *School Psychology Quarterly, 26*, 189–201.

Hester, P. P., Baltodano, H. M., Hendrickson, J. M., Tonelson, S. W., Conroy, M. A., & Gable, R. A. (2004). Lessons learned from research on early intervention: What teachers can do to prevent children's behavior problems. *Preventing School Failure, 49*, 5–11.

Hojnoski, R. L., & Missall, K. N. (2010). Social development in preschool classrooms: Promoting engagement, competence, and school readiness. In M. R. Shinn and H. M. Walker (Eds.), *Interventions for achievement and behavior in a three-tier model including RTI* (pp. 703–728). Bethesda, MD: National Association of School Psychologists.

Huffman, L. C., Mehlinger, S. L., & Kerivan, A. S. (2000). *Risk factors for academic and behavioral problems at the beginning of school*. Bethesda, MD: National Institute of Mental Health.

Hughes, J. N., Cavell, T. A., & Willson, V. (2001). Further support for the developmental significance of the student–teacher relationship. *Journal of School Psychology, 39*, 289–301.

Jolivette, K., McCormick, K. M., Jung, L. A., & Lingo, A. S. (2004). Embedding choices into the daily routines of young children with behavior problems: Eight reasons to build social competence. *Beyond Behavior, 13*, 21–26.

Jolivette, K., & Steed, E. A. (2010). Classroom management strategies for young children with challenging behavior within early childhood settings. *NHSA Dialog, 13*, 198–213.

Joseph, G. E., & Strain, P. S. (2003). Comprehensive evidence-based social-emotional curricula for young children: An analysis of efficacious adoption potential. *Topics in Early Childhood Special Education, 23*, 65–76.

Joseph, G. E., & Strain, P. S. (2004). Building positive relationships with young children. *Young Exceptional Children, 7*(4), 21–28.

Kaiser, B., & Rasminsky, J. S. (2011). *Challenging behavior in young children: Understanding, preventing, and responding effectively* (3rd ed.). Upper Saddle River, NJ: Pearson.

Kam, C. M., Greenberg, M. T., & Walls, C. T. (2003). Examining the role of implementation quality in school-based prevention using the PATHS curriculum. *Prevention Science, 4*(1), 55–63.

Kohler, F. W., Anthony, L. J., Steighner, S. A., & Hoyson, M. (2001). Teaching social interaction skills in the integrated preschool: An examination of naturalistic tactics. *Topics in Early Childhood Special Education, 21*, 93–103.

Kratochwill, T. R., & Shernoff, E. S. (2004). Evidence-based practice: Promoting evidence-based interventions in school psychology. *School Psychology Review, 33*, 34–48.

LaCourse, E., Cote, S., Nagin, D. S., Vitaro, R., Brendgen, M., & Tremblay, R. E. (2002). A longitudinal-experimental approach to testing theories of antisocial behavior development. *Development and Psychopathology, 14*, 909–924.

Ladd, G. W., & Burgess, K. B. (2001). Do relational risks and protective factors moderate the linkages between childhood aggression and early psychological and school adjustment? *Child Development, 72,* 1579–1601.

Lawrey, J., Danko, C. D., & Strain, P. (1999). Examining the role of the classroom environment in the prevention of problem behaviors. In S. Sandall & M. Ostrosky (Eds.), *Practical ideas for addressing challenging behavior* (pp. 49–62). Longmont, CO: Sopris West.

Lloyd, C. M., & Bangser, F. (2009). *Promoting preschool quality through effective classroom management.* New York: MDRC.

Maag, J. W. (2001). Rewarded by punishment: Reflections on the disuse of positive reinforcement in schools. *Exceptional Children, 67,* 173–186.

Maag, J. W., & Katsiyannis, A. (2010). Early intervention programs for children with behavior problems and at risk for developing antisocial behaviors: Evidence- and research-based practices. *Remedial and Special Education, 31,* 465–475.

McCabe, L. A., & Frede, E. C. (2007). Challenging behaviors and the role of preschool education. New Brunswick, NJ: National Institute for Early Education Research.

McCormick, K. M., Jolivette, K., & Ridgely, R. (2003). Choice making as an intervention strategy for young children. *Young Exceptional Children, 6*(2), 3–10.

McGinnis, J. C., Frederick, B. P., & Edwards, R. (1999). Enhancing classroom management through proactive rules and procedures. *Psychology in the Schools, 32,* 220–224.

Meehan, B. T., Hughes, J. N., & Cavell, T. A. (2003). Teacher–student relationships as compensatory resources for aggressive children. *Child Development, 74,* 1145–1157.

Mihalic, S. F., Irwin, K., Elliott, D., Fagan, A., & Hansen, D. (2001). *Blueprints for violence prevention.* Washington, DC: U.S. Department of Justice, Office of Justice and Delinquency Prevention.

Moffitt, T. (1994). Adolescence-limited and life-course-persistent antisocial behavior: A developmental taxonomy. *Psychological Review, 100,* 674–701.

National Center for Children in Poverty. (2006). *Basic facts about low-income children: Birth to age 6.* New York: Author.

National Research Council. (2001). *Eager to learn: Educating our preschoolers.* Washington, DC: National Academies Press.

Newman, D. L., Caspi, A., Moffitt, T. E., & Silva, P. A. (1997). Antecedents of adult interpersonal functioning: Effects of individual differences at age 3 temperament. *Developmental Psychology, 33,* 206–217.

Nielsen, S., & McEvoy, M. (2004). Functional behavioral assessment in early education settings. *Journal of Early Intervention, 26,* 115–131.

Noell, G. H., Gresham, F. M., & Gansle, K. A. (2002). Does treatment integrity matter? A preliminary investigation of instructional implementation and mathematics performance. *Journal of Behavioral Education, 11,* 51–67.

Nores, M., Belfield, C. R., Barnett, W. S., & Schweinhart, L. (2005). Updating the economic impacts of the High/Scope Perry Preschool Program. *Educational Evaluation and Policy Analysis, 27,* 245–261.

Ostrosky, M. M., & Meadan, H. (2010). Helping children play and learn together. *Young Children, 65*(4), 104–110.

Perry, D. F., Dunne, M. C., McFadden, L., & Campbell, D. (2008). Reducing the risk for preschool expulsion: Mental health consultation for young children with challenging behaviors. *Journal of Child and Family Studies, 17,* 44–54.

Pianta, R. C., Cox, M. J., & Snow, K. L. (Eds.). (2007). *School readiness and the transition to kindergarten in the era of accountability.* Baltimore, MD: Paul Brookes.

Pianta, R. C., & Stuhlman, M. W. (2004). Teacher–child relationships and children's success in the first years of school. *School Psychology Review, 33,* 444–458.

Powell, D., Dunlap, G., & Fox, L. (2006). Prevention and intervention for the challenging behaviors of toddlers and preschoolers. *Infants and Young Children, 19,* 25–35.

Qi, C. H., & Kaiser, A. P. (2003). Behavior problems of preschool children from low-income families: Review of the literature. *Topics in Early Childhood Special Education, 23,* 188–216.

Ratcliff, N. (2001). Use the environment to prevent discipline problems and support learning. *Young Children, 56*(5), 84–87.

Raver, C. C., Jones, S. M., Li-Grining, C. P., Zhai, F., Bub, K., & Pressler, E. (2011). CSRP's impact on low-income preschoolers' pre-academic skills: Self-regulation as a mediating mechanism. *Child Development, 82,* 362–378.

Raver, C. C., Jones, S. M., Li-Grining, C. P., Zhai, F., Metzger, M., & Solomon, B. (2009). Targeting children's behavior problems in preschool classrooms: A cluster-randomized controlled trial. *Journal of Consulting and Clinical Psychology, 77,* 302–316.

Raver, C. C., & Knitzer, J. (2002). *Ready to enter: What research tells policymakers about strategies to promote social and emotional school readiness among three- and four-year-old children.* New York: National Center for Children in Poverty.

Reid, M. J., Webster-Stratton, C., & Hammond, M. (2003). Follow-up of children who received the Incredible Years intervention for oppositional-defiant disorder: Maintenance and prediction of 2-year outcome. *Behavior Therapy, 34,* 471–491.

Rodriguez, B. J., Loman, S. L., & Horner, R. H. (2009). A preliminary analysis of the effects of coaching feedback on teacher implementation fidelity of First Step to Success. *Behavior Analysis in Practice, 2*(2), 11–21.

Simonsen, B., Fairbanks, S., Briesch, A., Myers, D., & Sugai, G. (2008). Evidence-based practices in classroom management: Considerations for research to practice. *Education and Treatment of Children, 31,* 351–380.

Simonsen, B., Sugai, G., & Negron, M. (2008). School-wide positive behavior supports: Primary systems and practices. *Teaching Exceptional Children, 40*(6), 32–40.

Steed, E. A., & Webb, M. L. (2013). The psychometric properties of the Preschool-Wide Evaluation Tool (Pre-SET). *Journal of Positive Behavior Interventions, 15,* 231–241

Stewart, R. M., Benner, G. J., Martella, R. C., & Marchand-Martella, N. E. (2007). Three-tier models of reading and behavior: A research review. *Journal of Positive Behavior Interventions, 9,* 239–253

Stormont, M., Lewis, T. J., & Beckner, R. (2005). Positive behavior support systems: Applying key features in preschool settings. *Teaching Exceptional Children, 37*(6), 42–49.

Stormont, M. A., Smith, S. C., & Lewis, T. J. (2007). Teacher implementation of pre-correction and praise statements in Head Start classrooms as a component of a program-wide system of positive behavior support. *Journal of Behavioral Education, 16,* 280–290.

Strain, P. S., & Joseph, G. E. (2004). Engaged supervision to support evidence-based practices for young children with challenging behavior. *Topics in Early Childhood Special Education, 24,* 39–50.

Sugai, G., & Horner, R. (2002). The evolution of discipline practices: School-wide positive behavior supports. *Child and Family Behavior Therapy, 24,* 23–50.

Thompson, R. (2002). The roots of school readiness in social and emotional development. *The Kauffman Early Education Exchange, 1,* 8–29.

Tremblay, R. (2000). The development of aggressive behavior during childhood: What have we learned in the past century? *International Journal of Behavioral Development, 24,* 129–141.

Walker, H. M., Kavanagh, K., Stiller, B., Golly, A., Severson, H. H., & Feil, E. G. (1998). First Step to Success: An early intervention approach for preventing school antisocial behavior. *Journal of Emotional and Behavioral Disorders, 6,* 66–80.

Walker, H. M., Seeley, J. R., Small, J., Severson, H. H., Graham, B. A., Feil, E. G., et al. (2009). A randomized controlled trial of the First Step to Success early intervention demonstration of program efficacy outcomes in a diverse, urban school district. *Journal of Emotional and Behavioral Disorders, 17,* 197–212.

Walker, H. M., Severson, H. H., Feil, E. G., Stiller, B., & Golly, A. (1998). First Step to Success: Intervention at the point of school entry to prevent antisocial behavior patterns. *Psychology in the Schools, 35,* 259–269.

Walker, H. M., Stiller, B., & Golly, A. (1998). First Step to Success. *Young Exceptional Children, 1*(2), 2–6.

Warner, L., & Lynch, S. A. (2004). *Preschool classroom management.* Beltsville, MD: Gryphon House.

Webster-Stratton, C., & Hammond, M. (2000). Conduct problems and level of social competence in Head Start children: Prevalence, pervasiveness, and associated risk factors. *Clinical Child and Family Psychology Review, 1,* 101–123.

Webster-Stratton, C., & Reid, M. J. (2009). The Incredible Years program for children from infancy to preadolescence: Prevention and treatment of behavior problems. In R. Murrihy, A. Kidman, & T. Ollendick (Eds.), *Clinician's handbook for the assessment and treatment of conduct problems in youth* (pp. 117–138). New York: Springer.

Webster-Stratton, C., Reid, M. J., & Hammond, M. (2004). Treating children with early-onset conduct problems: Intervention outcomes for parent, child, and teacher training. *Journal of Clinical Child and Adolescent Psychology, 33,* 105–124.

Webster-Stratton, C., Reinke, W. M., Herman, K. C., & Newcomer, L. L. (2011). The Incredible Years teacher classroom management training: The methods and principles that support fidelity of training delivery. *School Psychology Review, 40,* 509–529.

West, J., Denton, K., & Germino-Hausken, E. (2000). *America's kindergartener: Findings from the Early Childhood Longitudinal study, kindergarten class of 1990–99.* Washington, DC: National Center for Educational Statistics.

What Works Clearinghouse. (2012). *Children classified as having an emotional disturbance: First Step to Success.* Washington, DC: U.S. Department of Education, Institute of Education Sciences.

Willoughby, M., Kupersmidt, J. B., & Bryant, D. (2001). Overt and covert dimensions of antisocial behavior in early childhood. *Journal of Abnormal Child Psychology, 29,* 177–187.

Zhai, F., Raver, C. C., & Jones, S. M. (2012). Academic performance of subsequent schools and impacts of early interventions: Evidence from a randomized controlled trial in Head Start settings. *Children and Youth Services Review, 34,* 946–954.

Zhai, F., Raver, C. C., & Li-Grining, C. (2011). Classroom-based interventions and teachers' perceived job stressors and confidence: Evidence from a randomized trial in Head Start settings. *Early Childhood Research Quarterly, 26,* 442–452.

Zill, N., & West, J. (2001). *Entering kindergarten: A portrait of American children when they begin school.* Washington, DC: U.S. Department of Education.

9

RESEARCH ON CLASSROOM MANAGEMENT IN URBAN SCHOOLS

H. RICHARD MILNER IV
UNIVERSITY OF PITTSBURGH

Since the publication of the inaugural *Handbook on Classroom Management* (2006), approximately 26 new scholarly articles have been published on the topic of classroom management in urban education as identified in searches using Education Full Text (H.W. Wilson), ProQuest ERIC, and Google Scholar. Keywords searched in some combination included *urban*, *classroom*, and *management*. In this chapter, I focus mostly on this new scholarship, drawing particular attention to themes that emerged and aspects of the scholarship that need to be addressed in order to move the field of classroom management forward and especially to contribute to *urban* classroom management.

In the next section, I conceptualize what I mean by "urban" and also discuss what makes urban environments particularly critical sites for research and practice related to classroom management. The discussion then shifts to a brief explanation of what I mean by "urban classroom management." I stress in that section how urban classroom management needs to consider more than specific, predetermined strategies that might well be effective in suburban or even rural environments, mainly because of the range of student diversity in urban classrooms. I briefly tackle the diversity and classroom management nexus. The discussion then moves to themes that emerged from my review of the most current scholarship available and published in scholarly journals since 2006. Based on my review, four broad themes emerged from the literature and will be covered in this chapter: I conceptualized these themes as I read, analyzed and organized the extant literature. It is important to note that I suggest these themes as possible sites for further inquiry and development in order to capture and organize a more effective and structured knowledge base for research and theory on urban classroom management because, with some exceptions (Freiberg & Lamb, 2009, for instance), collectively the studies are a bit sporadic and disparate in the literature. The sporadic nature of these studies is not necessarily a function of what researchers have examined but of a lack of common, agreed-upon, synergistic organization among the various areas of focus. In other words, similar to how other disciplines have organized the focus of their work, perhaps around teaching and learning subject matter/content, I propose a similar focus on organization for urban classroom management. In the final sections of the chapter, I provide thematic critiques of this scholarship and make recommendations to advance the field, followed by a section with conclusions and implications. First, however, what do I mean by "urban"?

DEFINING URBAN

There is no generally agreed-upon definition of the term "urban" in the educational literature or a definition that is focused specifically on classroom management. In an attempt to address this void, I offer a typological framework to help clarify the term "urban." Based on what I have come to understand about urban environments, three types of urban districts exist. The first is *urban intensive*, which refers to large cities in which schools are located. The size and density of a particular community make these environments unique and particularly intensive. Metropolitan cities such as Chicago, Atlanta, Los Angeles, Philadelphia, and New York, with populations in excess of one million people, provide a layer of intensity in that sometimes limited resources are expected to service an immense number of students in schools and the surrounding city. What sets these cities apart from other cities is their mere size— their sheer density. In sum, "urban intensive" speaks to the scope and concentration of people in a particular locale. The broader environment, which includes outside-of-school factors such as housing, poverty, and transportation, is directly connected to what happens inside the school. There are also positive features of living in large cities, such as transportation options and business infrastructure.

A second type of urban is *urban emergent*, wherein schools and districts are in large cities but typically have populations smaller than or very close to 1 million people. Nonetheless, these cities are still faced with many of the same problems as urban intensive schools but not on the same scale. Examples of such cities are Nashville, Tennessee; Austin, Texas; Columbus, Ohio; and Charlotte, North Carolina.

A third type is *urban characteristic*, where districts are not necessarily located in or even near large cities but may be located in suburban or rural areas. Yet these communities are beginning to experience some of the shifts and realities seen in much larger districts—increasingly diverse populations, as well as increases in the number of immigrant families and students and in those from lower socioeconomic backgrounds. Table 9.1 summarizes these types of environments.

The reality of large, growing cities and districts is that there is a need to rethink the manner in which teachers are equipped to manage student learning. In many ways, all teachers, even those in urban emergent and urban characteristic contexts, are seeing some, if not many, of the characteristics that are prevalent in urban intensive schools.

Generally, in some combination, urban education and urban sociocultural contexts can be conceptualized related to (1) the *size* of the city in which schools are

Table 9.1 Conceptualization of urban districts.

Category	Definition
Urban intensive	These schools are concentrated in large, metropolitan cities across the United States, such as New York, Chicago, Los Angeles, and Atlanta.
Urban emergent	These schools are typically located in large cities but not as large as the major cities. They typically have some of the same characteristics as urban schools and districts in terms of resources, qualification of teachers, and academic development of students. Examples of such cities are Nashville, Tennessee; Austin, Texas; Columbus, Ohio; and Charlotte, North Carolina.
Urban characteristic	These schools are not located in big cities but may be beginning to experience increases in features that are sometimes associated with urban contexts, such as an increase in English language learners (ELLs) in a community. These schools may be located in what might be considered rural or even suburban areas.

located—dense, large, metropolitan areas; (2) the *students* in the schools—a wide range of student diversity, including racial, ethnic, linguistic, and socioeconomic; and (3) the *resources*—the amount and number of resources available in a school, such as technology and financial structures funded through federal programs as well as property taxes. Currently, approximately 6.9 million students are enrolled in public schools across the United States.

Next, what is meant by "urban classroom management" in this chapter?

CONCEPTUALIZING URBAN CLASSROOM MANAGEMENT

In the first handbook, established research and theory suggested that classroom management in urban classrooms should concern more than teachers' ability to get students to behave in any certain way. Indeed, classroom management in urban classrooms should highlight students' opportunities and access to learning. Student learning should not only focus on learning subject matter but also provide learning opportunities that help students think critically and analytically about issues both within and outside the school as they develop social and academic skills. Perhaps especially in urban environments, classroom management should help students develop inquisitive dispositions and perspectives about power structures and hierarchies that shape what happens in society and school. Freiberg and Lamb (2009), drawing on the research of Rogers and Freiberg (1994), who conducted extensive interviews with students, discussed the importance of teacher–student relationships. The core of these relationships related to trust and respect, caring and committed teachers (and other adults), students' feeling connected to others in the various contexts, and students' choices and perspectives in managing their own learning.

In addition, classroom management in urban classrooms should help students recognize the social and political landscape of their schools and their communities and support students in understanding and mitigating the culture of power (Delpit, 1995) in the school, in the classroom, and in society. It should empower students to participate in and critique pervasive power discourses in their classrooms. Classroom management in urban schools is about teachers' ability to manage student learning, not to control students, so that students can engage and participate meaningfully in the teaching and learning exchange—regardless of the subject matter being taught. In short, teachers should not restrict their attention to students' behavioral needs but expand it to include their cognitive, social, and humanistic needs as well (Freiberg & Lamb, 2009; Milner, 2010). They should be aware of students' cognitive, social, academic, and socioemotional needs, as well as their political needs, so that they can be responsive to the various aspects and dimensions of who students are (their identity) and who they are becoming (developing identity). Thus, classroom management in urban classrooms is curricular; it is instructional and is also about social and political justice. It is about teachers' skill and ability to transform their practices, belief systems, and thinking to meet the complex needs of the diverse learners they teach by drawing from and building on the assets of their students. Indeed, student diversity is a critical aspect of understanding classroom management in urban environments, a topic I briefly explore in the next section.

CLASSROOM MANAGEMENT AND DIVERSITY

Although both classroom management and student cultural diversity are essential in the teaching and learning exchange, "the literature on classroom management has paid scant attention to issues of cultural diversity" (Weinstein, Tomlinson-Clarke, and Curran, 2004, p. 26), and the literature on diversity and classroom practices has focused limited attention to classroom management. It seems that matters of classroom management, instruction, learning, and diversity are almost inseparable, although many past and more current studies do not seem to agree about these intersections, at least in terms of how they conceptualize the focus of their studies. Although the literature regarding the interrelated nature of diversity and classroom management is underdeveloped, three salient trends seem to be present:

1. The terms and constructs used to elucidate, study, and conceptualize classroom management and diversity vary.
2. The populations—that is, the racial and ethnic identities of the students studied in this literature—extend beyond black and white to include a range of culturally and racially diverse students.
3. The contexts—urban intensive, emergent, or characteristic—vary across studies and need clearer definition.

In addition to these three larger trends, a number of key terms and constructs have emerged in these studies as well. These key terms include the conceptualization of a "discipline gap" (Monroe, 2006, p. 164); the need for "culturally specific disciplinary techniques" (p. 165), particularly with culturally and linguistically diverse learners; "culturally relevant classroom management strategies" (Hammond, Dupoux, & Ingalls, 2004, p. 3); and "culturally responsive classroom management" (Weinstein, Curran & Tomlinson-Clarke, 2003, p. 269).

Additionally, the research has focused on a range of racial and ethnic diversity among the populations studied, including American Indian students (Hammond,

Dupoux, & Ingalls, 2004), Navajo middle school students (McCarthy & Benally, 2003), and American and Korean students (Shin & Koh, 2007). Contexts studied with a focus on classroom management include urban emergent schools (Milner & Tenore, 2010; Milner, 2008), as well as contexts outside of traditional schools such as an examination of classroom management techniques in prisons with incarcerated adult students (Shobe, 2003). With a glimpse on literature regarding classroom management and diversity established, the chapter focus shifts to recent scholarship on classroom management.

RECENT SCHOLARSHIP ON CLASSROOM MANAGEMENT

Although there are books, research reports, and book chapters that focus on classroom management in and for urban classrooms, the focus of this chapter is on published, refereed journal articles of empirical studies. In just a few cases, a conceptual or review article or chapter is included in this section in order to help elucidate a particular point that was introduced or referenced in one of the empirical studies. Indeed, the available literature since 2006 provides important insights about classroom management in urban classrooms, schools, and districts. The analysis is organized around the following topical areas: (1) teacher learning and teacher education; (2) teacher knowledge, beliefs, and emotions; (3) program and model evaluation and assessment; and (4) classroom practices.

Teacher Learning and Teacher Education

In general, literature suggests that teacher education programs are not doing an adequate job of developing appropriate attitudes, practices, and skills to meet Prekindergarten–12 students' needs related to classroom management. In some cases, there are very few (if any) courses in teacher education programs on classroom management and even fewer focused on urban classroom management. This preparation gap seems to be common in both traditional and nontraditional teacher education programs.

For instance, research has examined features of both alternative and traditional pathways into teaching (Hammerness, 2011) in an attempt to capture learning opportunities for teachers in classroom management. In examining the classroom management preparation of new teachers in New York City, one study focused on the 31 childhood teacher education programs that prepared 460 graduates and found evidence revealing that

> less than half of the traditional programs required any coursework in classroom management. Early entry candidates were more likely to have had a course in classroom management . . . [T]eachers in traditional programs may encounter more foundational knowledge in such courses, while early entry teachers may have more opportunities to learn practical, concrete strategies. (Hammerness, 2011, p. 151)

Clearly and overwhelmingly, critiques were prevalent in the literature about the preparation of teachers in both traditional and nontraditional programs, based on empirical data with teachers in urban classrooms as well as in teacher education programs themselves. For instance, investigations of the daily diaries of 252 new teachers in New York City over a two-week period revealed some important insights (Schonfeld & Feinman, 2012). Seventy percent were certified through New York City Teaching Fellows, an alternative teaching program, and the other 30% were certified through traditional programs. The study found the following regarding the two routes into teaching:

> Alternatively certified teachers were more likely to experience stressors such as violent incidents and classroom management problems. No differences were found in exposure to stressors/difficulties such as problematic adults, student learning problems, and students experiencing emotional upset . . . [T]he high absolute rates of management problems and violence in both groups of teachers were striking and need to be addressed. (p. 215)

Unlike many studies reviewed since 2006, this study provided important, detailed descriptions of the context of the study and urban environments explored. On a broader-level analysis, the authors found "the less extensively trained alternatively certified teachers, compared to their traditionally certified colleagues, experienced more classroom management difficulties. The classroom management problems included students disrupting lessons, not paying attention, refusing to work, and confronting the teacher" (p. 233). However, it is important to note that the alternatively certified teachers were observed more often by administrators than were those of traditional certification. The point, however, is that, according to the study, teachers were not well trained in either program, but traditionally educated teachers did have more foundational coursework in classroom management.

Although in general teacher education programs (both traditional and alternative) were critiqued about their preparation of teachers for classroom management in urban schools, one recent study focused on the success of a school–university partnership program. Preservice teachers' development of classroom management skills in an urban context was examined (Dobler, Kesner, Kramer, Resnik, & Devin, 2009). Through a collaborative partnership among principals, mentors, and a university supervisor, the design of the study allowed for a supportive environment for teachers to critically examine and discuss what they were learning in diverse settings. Through the partnership, experienced and effective educators played an important role in teacher learning. The researchers were mostly focused on how they could improve their own work as teacher educators, as well as the practices of preservice teachers, both in their learning to teach and also when they transitioned into their own classrooms as teachers. The major features of the partnership were preservice teacher placement in "diverse" settings, dialogue and discussion, and critical reflection. The overall message of the research was that these activities in particular helped support teacher learning and development.

Attention has been placed on preservice teachers' conflicts related to management strategies in an urban elementary school (Higgins & Moule, 2009). Important tensions were identified, especially those that shed light on how preservice teachers were trained and what was actually practiced in the classroom. In particular, the researchers pointed out dilemmas because preservice teachers were actually educated in their teacher education program to develop and implement "democratic" (p. 132) strategies, but more authoritarian strategies were actually found in their practices in elementary urban classrooms. The mixed-race research pair (one black and one white) reflected the practices and tensions they observed and were able to point out "subtle forms of racism and strong cultural norms" (132) that impacted the teachers' practices in the study.

In summary, research on teacher learning and teacher education identified several important features. A central finding was that both traditional and nontraditional teacher education programs need to do a better job of preparing teachers with classroom management knowledge, skills, and practices. Traditional teacher education programs seem to provide more foundational learning opportunities with a classroom management focus, whereas nontraditional classroom management programs seem to provide more observations and feedback for teachers while they teach. Moreover, even though several of the studies focused on classroom management with "diverse" learners, it is unclear what teacher learning in teacher education programs looks like or should emphasize for urban classrooms. Future research should continue examining the various features, successes, and challenges of both traditional and nontraditional teacher education programs in preparing teachers to teach in urban classrooms. Moreover, concentrated effort needs to examine the programmatic philosophies and consequent practices that characterize *urban* classroom management learning opportunities for teachers. Results from this research should be used to influence practices in teacher education. However, these research findings should be implemented with caution so that teachers do not reinforce stereotypes about urban communities and the people in them. Importantly, how do traditional and nontraditional teacher education programs prepare teachers to be effective classroom managers in urban environments and simultaneously reject generalized misconceptions and stereotypes about what it means to teach, learn, and manage in urban contexts?

Teacher Knowledge, Beliefs, and Emotions

While the studies in the previous section focused on teacher learning and development in particular, some literature examined the knowledge, beliefs, and emotions of teachers. A general message of these articles is that understanding the independence or intersection of these areas was essential because each contributes to teachers' practices of classroom management with their students. Teachers' knowledge—that is, what they knew and understood—about classroom management in urban environments, especially, appears to be underdeveloped. Again, I differentiate between teachers' knowledge of classroom management and their knowledge about urban classroom management.

In a study of teachers' practical knowledge in "multicultural classrooms" (p. 453), 12 teachers in Dutch classrooms were identified as effective classroom managers (Tartwijk, Brok, Veldman, & Wubbels, 2009). The research sought to determine the practical knowledge and practices of teachers who were successful in creating a positive working environment with their students. Results of the study, based on video-stimulated interviews, focused on the awareness these teachers had about establishing and communicating clear rules and building teacher–student relationships. The study also found that these teachers adjusted their instructional practices to meet student needs, "anticipating students' responses" (p. 453). As Gay (2010) explained, it is essential for teachers to modify some of their practices rather than expect students to always modify their behaviors in the classroom in order to maximize potential learning opportunities. In short, the study determined that teachers' practical knowledge was essential in addressing the needs of the Dutch students and that teachers had to modify their practices so that conflicts did not escalate (Tartwijk, Brok, Veldman & Wubbles, 2009).

Research has also examined teachers' beliefs about classroom management strategies for "American" and "Korean" students (Shin & Koh, 2007). Data were collected from self-reports of 116 American teacher surveys and 167 Korean teacher surveys on the Attitudes and Beliefs on Classroom Control Inventory. The cross-country analysis between the two sets of educators revealed no statistically significant cross-cultural differences in terms of their years of teaching experiences. A statistically significant cross-cultural difference was reported in the teachers' instruction and management styles. According to the study, American teachers tended to develop classrooms that were more teacher-directed, where they attempted to control students through a behaviorist approach, whereas Korean teachers developed classroom environments that were more student directed and driven.

In a summative article that captured several studies, the review focused on teachers working to adjust and regulate their own emotions (Sutton, Mudrey-Camino, & Knight, 2009). The research determined that teachers' ability to regulate their affect played a role in the success of their classroom management. In their words, "teachers are much more confident that they can communicate their positive emotions than reduce their negative emotions, and they use a variety of emotion regulation strategies, including preventative and reactive methods" (p. 130). Conceptually, the focus of this research examines the interrelated nature of teachers' affect (emotion), motivation and regulation, and beliefs. In the words of these researchers:

> Recent research indicates that teaching is an emotional enterprise and that teachers believe that regulating their emotions when teaching makes them more effective. These beliefs of teachers are supported by some studies indicating that students are adversely influenced by teachers' expression of negative emotions . . . Although the majority of teachers seek to down-regulate their negative emotions, teacher anger can serve to enforce accepted standards of classroom conduct and so be effective. (p. 136)

Thus, this review article provides important insights about the role of teacher emotion and beliefs in teacher decision making. Although affective and social dynamics among students have been examined and stressed as essential in classroom management (Freiberg & Lamb, 2009), this research redirects attention to such importance among teachers themselves—mainly because teachers' practices (what they do and teach) are shaped by their emotions; consequently, student learning is influenced by what teachers do and teach. Examining this area seems essential in light of the pressure and stress teachers face in their work. For instance, how do teachers identify and regulate their own emotion as they attempt to manage their classrooms and when they encounter unrealistic expectations and stress related to student test score results, especially those of value-added models?

In summary, the literature focused on teacher knowledge, beliefs, and emotions provides some important implications for enhancing what we know about classroom management in urban classrooms. Research has examined the role and salience of teachers' practical knowledge, but as a field, it seems that more studies need to focus on teachers' cultural knowledge (Gay, 2010; Milner, 2010) in understanding and responding to students in urban classrooms. For instance, how does teachers' cultural knowledge influence what they teach and how? How do teachers negotiate and draw on their cultural knowledge in responding to students in urban classrooms? Additionally, better capturing the nexus between what teachers believe and what they do can shed light on why teachers' managerial practices manifest as they do. Although understanding teacher beliefs and teacher knowledge are essential from a cross-national analysis, examinations within the United States or within a particular country can also shed light on some of the complexities surrounding tensions between teacher and student identity. Finally, as mentioned, examining teacher emotion and other affective dimensions of teachers' experiences, especially in urban environments, has the potential to help the field chart a research agenda focused on connections between and among teacher emotion (McGee, in progress), their classroom management practices, and urban classroom contexts in particular.

Program and Model Evaluation and Assessment

Much of the available empirical literature concerning classroom management in urban classrooms consists of evaluations and assessments of particular classroom management programs and models. According to the literature, "recent meta-analyses indicate that 87% to 92% of published studies on school-based interventions targeting student problem behaviors report results from demonstration projects (involving highly trained staff under ideal circumstances) rather than routine practice programs" (Burke, Oats, Ringle, Fichtner, & DelGaudio, 2011, p. 201). Collectively, the programs and projects possess particular characteristics and features that may or may not be transferable or generalizable to other contexts.

Attention has been placed on a multicomponent professional development model for teachers early in their careers as teachers (Shernoff et al., 2011). The model focused on

> linking novices with peer-nominated . . . teachers and an external coach who work together to (1) provide intensive support in evidence-based practices for classroom management and engaging learners, and (2) connect new teachers with their larger network of colleagues. (p. 465)

The research found that because teacher attrition is linked to teachers' ability to manage classrooms and engage students, models are needed to support teachers as they work to meet the needs of their students. In particular, the results revealed "varying attendance rates throughout the school year and . . . although seminars and professional learning communities were delivered as intended . . . adaptations to enhance the relevance, authenticity, level, and type of instructional support were needed" (p. 465).

Lannie and McCurdy (2007) examined a program, The Good Behavior Game, to determine its effects on student behavior. Consistent with previous findings, the results of this study with 22 first-graders in an urban elementary classroom revealed that student on-task, positive behavior increased and disruptive behavior decreased. In these researchers' words, "although the level of classroom disruption decreased with a concomitant behavior for the teacher to praise, there was not an increase in teacher praise statements. Alternatively, the teacher neutral and negative statements (largely negative) did vary with the level of disruptive behavior" (p. 94).

With a special education focus, a study examined the effectiveness of the Class-Wide Function-Related Intervention Teams (CW-FIT) program (Kamps et al., 2011). CW-FIT, according to the researchers, is a "group contingency intervention for whole classes, and for students with disruptive behaviors who are at-risk for emotional/behavioral disorders" (p. 154). The program was designed to enhance communication skills, to eliminate problem behavior, and to strengthen alternative positive behavior and self-maintenance. The researchers found "clinically important improvements" (p. 154). Because this study focused on emotional/behavioral disorders (EBD), there is little attention to structural challenges or systems of discrimination that disproportionately place many African American and Latino students in this category. Researchers, like practitioners, adopt color-blind lenses when examining the causes and consequences of enrollment patterns in special education, and very little is known about consequences (beyond individual factors) related to why a disproportionate number of African American and Latino American students are referred for special education, especially for EBD.

In another program evaluation study, the focus was on two pilot studies related to Cultivating Awareness and Resilience in Education (CARE) (Jennings, Snowberg, Coccia, & Greenberg, 2011). According to the researchers, CARE is a "professional development program designed to reduce stress and improve teachers' performance" (p. 37). According to the researchers, several tenets shaped the CARE model: emotion skills instruction, mindfulness/stress reduction practices and caring, as well as listening practices. Indeed, the purpose of the study was to examine "whether the CARE professional development program improves teachers' and student teachers' socio-emotional skills (motivation/efficacy and mindfulness) and well-being and consequently improves their ability to develop and maintain a well-managed learning environment and provide optimal emotional and instructional support to their students" (p. 45). The results of the two pilot studies suggested that CARE might be most effective in "high-poverty urban settings" in comparison to suburban or semirural settings. Although grouped with the program evaluation studies, this study examines an area that seems to have a promising focus—emotion (also see Sutton, Mudrey-Camino, & Knight 2009, reviewed previously in this chapter).

A program evaluation of the Developmental Designs classroom management approach and professional development model was conducted in its inaugural year of enactment across 22 middle schools in urban districts in the Midwest (Hough, 2011) and revealed some interesting insights. In particular, the research focused on participants' levels of competence, efficacy/confidence, and implementation. An important finding from the study was "the need for a minimum of 2 year's training and classroom use to achieve significant improvement in teachers' confidence in and implementation of new strategies for classroom management" (p. 177).

In examining the effects of a prosocial classroom and instructional management program (Consistency Management & Cooperative Discipline, CMCD) of 14 elementary schools in a large urban district, an evaluation determined that students in CMCD schools scored higher on achievement exams than those in the control group (Freiberg, Huzinec & Templeton, 2009). In the researchers' words, "in mathematics, on average, CMCD students ranked at the 67th percentile, while control students ranked at the 50th percentile" (p. 63). It is unclear what other variables may have contributed to the test score gap and gain, but the effects of the program are compelling nonetheless. The CMCD program, coupled with the established research and theoretical literature, would suggest the following interrelated features of success in urban classrooms committed to increased and sustained student outcomes: a heavy emphasis on social-emotional aspects of students, school connectedness among students, student-positive school and classroom climate, and student ability to self-discipline and direct (Freiberg & Lamb, 2009). Importantly, the Freiberg and Lamb model challenges the types of behavior-oriented disciplinary practices in many schools and argues for a more person-centered approach.

Program evaluation has also focused on the effects of preservice teachers' differential reinforcement (Auld, Belfiore, & Scheeler, 2010) of a model learned in their teacher education program. This investigation centered on the learning and implementation of the Differential Reinforcement of Alternate Behavior Strategy (DRA), an approach teachers learned when they were student teaching. Seven teachers teaching in rural, suburban, and urban schools participated in the study. Drawing from the research, the researchers maintained that:

> [r]esults showed that (a) student teachers increased their number of correct DRA responses as measured by accurate teacher feedback to students, and (b) students showed increased hand-raising and decreased talk-outs. (p. 169)

A major component of this study was the researchers' suggestion that general education students be taught special education strategies to work in different types classroom structures—in general classroom settings, not only in special education. However, the researchers explained that many teacher education programs do not provide this type of training and support for general education students.

Another evaluation project studied 56 second-, third-, and fourth-grade teachers after three years training in a classroom management program, The Well-Managed Classroom (WMC) (Burke, Oats, Ringle, Fichtner, & DelGaudio, 2011). According to the researchers, this program emerged from the Teaching-Family Model and Boys Town Family Home Program, which were "designed to help at-risk youth in residential care who are typically functioning 1 to 2 years below academic grade level" (p. 203). Through observations and teacher self-ratings, the research determined high program fidelity related to classroom behaviors and practices, such as stronger academic engagement and fewer suspensions but not better report card grades. The major program features concerned student academic engagement and reducing suspension rates.

Although not an empirical study, a prosocial classroom environment model was advanced to support teachers in developing social and emotional competence (Jennings & Greenberg, 2009). Drawing from their own research and their review of extant literature, this synthesis stressed the importance of teacher–student relationships, effective classroom management, and social and emotional learning as essential to the production of positive classroom environments. An important aspect of this review and proposed model was the authors' finding that when teachers social and emotional learning was in place, teacher burnout and stress were reduced.

In summary, most of the model evaluation research reviewed since 2006 demonstrated a range of positive outcomes, such as a decrease in student suspensions, an increase in student test scores, fewer distractions from learning, and stronger teacher–student relationships. What these findings suggest is that programs and models designed to meet the needs of learners in urban contexts have the potential to improve teaching practices and student learning. Several challenges to such models exist, however. For instance, research in this area indicated differential implementation in practice among teachers who learned particular models in teacher education programs. Further, because urban contexts are extremely complex both on a systems level as well as on an individual level (macro/micro), replicating and transferring models between and across various contexts make it very difficult and should be done with caution. Research about particular features across the range of urban environments should be conducted to help build research and theory about model and program development so that teachers can draw from these effective programs and models for practice in their particular urban context. Moreover, this line of research suggests that more longitudinal studies are needed to help build these features, over time, across different models and programs.

Classroom Practices

Although a large number of recent studies concerned program/project evaluation, another healthy number of studies were situated in classroom practices. While these studies were often small in scale and provided nuanced accounts of teachers' practices that seemed to "work" in a particular urban context, one study examined a national representative sample of 10,700 first-graders' mental health outcomes based on practices in the classroom (Milkie & Warner, 2011). This study examined how classroom learning milieus influence students' affective and behavioral problems. It was found that students experienced more emotional and behavioral challenges in classrooms with low academic standards, disruptive behavior of peers, and "low" peer skills.

Another study challenged traditional conceptions of urban classroom management where students are characterized as substandard, disrespectful, and unteachable (Ullucci, 2009). This study of respected teachers (five female and one male) in urban schools demonstrated how these teachers moved away from traditional classroom management practices to relevant, respectful, and responsive practices. Unlike many current studies on classroom management, the analyses were grounded in theory related to culture and teaching, as well as culturally responsive teaching practices. In some compelling ways, this study disrupts commonly held myths about students in urban schools and appropriate classroom management strategies in urban classrooms. Based on her study, Ullucci wrote:

> The mythology concerning discipline in urban schools is deeply rooted; the typical portrait involves unruly children and disrespectful behavior . . . Teachers believe they must create highly structured, punitive measures in which to control their students . . . Community takes a backseat to the more pressing needs of punishments and military-like routines. (p. 24)

Teachers in the study used humor to build relationships with students. Students were encouraged and allowed to talk with each other to problem-solve; teachers developed norms in the classroom that made students feel as if they belonged and mattered (also consistent with Freiberg & Lamb, 2009). In short, according to Ullucci, "teachers in this study were direct and sharp with their discipline. However, this style did not tear at the dignity and self-concept of children" (p. 25).

In my own research with Tenore (Milner & Tenore, 2010), we focused on particular practices of teachers in urban schools that were responsive and met the needs of learners. Our research found that classroom management continues to be a serious concern for teachers, especially in urban and diverse learning environments. Drawing from established theory on culturally responsive classroom management, our study showcased the culturally responsive classroom management practices of two teachers from an urban and diverse middle school in order to extend the construct of culturally responsive classroom management. The principles that emerged in this study included the importance and centrality of teachers' (1) understanding equity and equality, (2) understanding power structures among students, (3) immersion in students' life worlds, (4) understanding the self in relation to others, (5) granting students entry into their worlds, and (6) conceiving school as a community with family members. We concluded the discussion with implications for teachers and researchers, suggesting that more theory is needed to guide research in the area and that teacher education researchers need to examine successful practices in P–12 schools and to adapt their practices for preservice and in-service teachers in teacher education programs.

Another snapshot of classroom practices concerned two classroom teachers in an urban high school English classroom who successfully implemented practices grounded in culturally responsive classroom management (Adkins-Coleman, 2010). The research revealed teachers constructed a classroom context where students understood and met high behavioral expectations and were engaged in class both socially and cognitively.

Although much of the published work on classroom management is atheoretical, one study attempted to build a theory that described the interactions between teachers and students in the study of alternative learning environments (Kennedy, 2011). Through interviews and observations, the research examined and determined how essential student and teacher interactions are in responding to students who exhibit challenging behavior. This article provided additional evidence of particular classroom practices that appear to make a positive, impactful difference for students and teachers. The study addressed the interrelated nature of "student engagement, student–teacher relationship building, alternative education and early adolescence" (p. 7). The research examined the practices and interactions that students and teachers both found as essential in student development. This study provides perspectives from teachers as well as students. It also presented challenges (a negative case), as well as successful practical examples. In essence, the study found "early adolescence is a crucial time in which students face decisions about who they will become and how they will behave . . . [T[he interactions that occur in the classrooms studied do have positive impacts on students and teachers" (Kennedy, 2011, pp. 23–24). In essence, teachers were nonjudgmental in their interactions with students, both in terms of addressing academic development and social development. For instance, teachers did not ridicule or embarrass students when they did not know the answers to questions teachers posed. Teachers helped students think through the content being covered by means of the questions they posed, and students felt supported.

Another study was guided by theories of psychologically supportive classroom environments and building resilience (Bondy, Ross, Gallingane, & Hambacher, 2007). Through videotaping and interviewing, the study examined three effective novice teachers during their first two hours of the first day of an academic year. The research revealed that the teachers developed positive relationships with their students and high expectations. The teachers "insisted" that the students engage in the classroom and adapted a culturally responsive communication style with their students. In essence, this study focused on how three teachers set the stage for a successful academic year and were able to develop community; the authors explained that the teachers in the study were deliberate in their practices of "earning respect rather than demanding it" (p. 328). Several important features emerged from this study. For instance, from the onset, teachers worked to build relationships, establish expectations, and communicate in culturally responsive ways; the teachers also insisted that students were accountable and would meet the high expectations that were established. By culturally responsive, the authors meant that teachers attempted to understand the cultural backgrounds of their students and respond to those backgrounds through their curriculum and instructional practices.

In another study, the inquiry focused on how to de-escalate student misbehavior (Henninger & Coleman, 2008). The researchers explained that de-escalation is a set of "teacher behaviors that, when working in combination, help teachers limit the impact of students' misbehavior on the maintenance of order" (p. 12). The central tenets of de-escalation included "knowing students, proactive skills related to giving students respect and getting respect from students, and reactive skills focused on soft imperatives and re-direction, patience, and humor" (p. 12). Similarly, another study highlighted "mindful reflection" as a process in developing culturally responsive practices (Dray & Wisneski, 2011). A motivation for their framework was shaped by the researchers' observation that "teachers are not often aware of how diversity affects the way that they interpret students' actions and the ways that they interact with their students on a daily basis" (p. 29). Drawing from the research, several important reflection questions are provided for teachers, ranging from teacher bias to understanding the outside-of-school realities of students. The authors outlined a six-step plan for practitioners: (1) explain the attributions that teachers have about a particular student; (2) write out and reflect on feelings and thoughts when working with a particular student or students; (3) consider alternative explanations by reviewing documentation and reflections; (4) check and reflect on assumptions; (5) make a plan; and (6) continuously revisit this process to reassess attributions and progress with students.

Research has examined the narratives of 364 fourth- to sixth-graders addressing personal experiences with conflict (Harris & Walton, 2009). According to the researchers, "several features of the narrative were reliably coded, including level of violence described in the story, children's descriptions of internal states, moral evaluations, and responses to conflict" (p. 281). The data revealed that communication was a critical aspect in students' being able to resolve and work through conflict.

The researchers provided recommendations and implications for helping teachers empower students to work through conflict in the urban classroom through writing. Indeed, this research suggested that teachers need to "give voice to [student] experiences" (p. 308) and cautioned against silencing the student voices and experiences that teachers may not view as important. According to this research, providing narrative space for students can help them think, reflect, and work through tensions in the classroom.

In summary, the line of research focused on classroom practices provides important cases and illustrative examples of teacher practice, centralizing classroom management, with particular groups of students in urban classrooms. This research, similar to that on models and programs, provides important insights on a specific context. However, how do teachers transfer effective practices in one context to another? How do teachers build on these effective qualities to meet the idiosyncrasies of different environments? Although not the norm, one study focuses on a negative, difficult situation of a teacher and how the negative case can shed light on the moves the teacher makes in the classroom. In addition to continuing this line of small-scale research and providing examples for teachers on the nuances in a particular context, research should also examine and reveal examples where teachers are not successful classroom managers in these environments.

THEMATIC CRITIQUES AND RECOMMENDATIONS

Several important trends have emerged in the literature since 2006, many of which were consistent with and some inconsistent with previous work in the area. I now provide some general critiques of the scholarship and make some recommendations based on my analyses.

- In my chapter published in the first *Handbook of Classroom Management* (Milner, 2006), I pleaded for more studies with a focus on culture, race, and inequity. I reviewed literature both within and outside the field of classroom management in an attempt to cultivate and galvanize researchers to design studies that were explicitly equity focused. Much of that work addressed teacher thinking and instructional practices that were culturally centered. Since then, there appears to be some emphasis on issues of equity but certainly not a collective movement toward such a focus. Because so many more students attending urban schools are not having their needs met (Milner & Lomotey, 2014), again, researchers should design more studies that specifically focus on equity—posing research questions that attempt to get at the core of why students in these contexts are too often unsuccessful.
- Although classroom management has a heavy emphasis on students in urban environments, much of the recent literature since 2006 focused on teachers, not on students. More studies are needed that focus on students. Providing insights about students based on their test scores, suspension rates, or grades on report cards provide one level of evidence regarding students. Studies should also include student voices and the observable behavior of students, as well as providing triangulation between what students say and what researchers actually observe.
- Many studies do not define what they mean by "urban" environments or "urban" classroom management. This is a serious problem and does not adequately allow the field to build knowledge about these contexts. Who were the students in these environments? What were their racial and ethnic backgrounds? What material and capital resources were available to them? What was the size of these environments?
- Most of the quantitative studies provided only limited information about the populations under study. In many of the studies reviewed, the large-scale ones do not provide enough descriptive statistics or data to make sense of the populations under study. Studies that provide information such as "students in poverty" or "students on free and reduced lunch" provide only a basic, superficial level of information regarding students and do not provide a more complex picture of the identities of the students. We need to know more about who the students (and teachers) were, the structures in place to support teachers and students, as well as what the authors meant by their use of the term "urban."
- In many cases, researchers did not define or conceptualize what was meant by "classroom management" itself. This is a definition issue that makes it difficult to build synergy between and among studies.
- Much of the large-scale, quantitative research does not reference or build on established theory or qualitative research in the field (or beyond it) related to urban classroom management. This failure to build on previous studies leaves

holes in the knowledge base about classroom management. Similarly, qualitative studies often do not build on findings from other, related quantitative studies.

- Some researchers, especially in quantitative studies, misuse and inappropriately employ terms like "at-risk," "urban," "minority," and "low-income" when they are discussing students in studies on classroom management. This language carries with it a deficit orientation. In other words, researchers approach the research context (i.e., urban) and the people in it focused on what this community does not have or what it lacks rather than focusing on what it actually has or possesses (their assets).
- Many of the studies do not adequately review the established research literature, and many of them do not build on existing theory. In this way, many studies in the area are atheoretical and do not contribute much to theory building related to classroom management in urban contexts. More emphasis on theory building is important to contributing to the intellectual rigor of the field. Qualitative studies were more likely to incorporate theory, but even those studies tended to be thin on theory.

CONCLUSIONS AND IMPLICATIONS

In conclusion, classroom management remains a serious problem for teachers, especially those who struggle with management in urban classrooms. Research continues to forge ahead in urban classrooms, schools, and districts, but, collectively, more synergy is needed to build a comprehensive knowledge base. I suggest that the themes that have emerged in this chapter be used as sites to organize and advance what we know about classroom management in research, theory, practice, and policy: (1) teacher learning and teacher education; (2) teacher knowledge, beliefs, and emotions; (3) program and model evaluation and assessment; and (4) classroom practices. With more emphasis on students in this research, a potential fifth organizational theme could centralize the role(s) of students or student voices in the discourse on classroom management. Again, the point is not that student voices are completely absent in the literature (see, for instance, Kennedy, 2011); the point is that research on students is underdeveloped in comparison to that in other areas.

My analysis suggested a continuing need for emphasis on classroom practices, particularly urban classrooms. We still do not know enough about what actually happens inside urban classrooms that can allow the field to prepare teachers to manage classrooms successfully in urban environments. In this way, we need to design teacher education programs and practices with what we know about good practice in P–12 environments. According to Tartwijk, Brok, Veldman, and Wubbels (2009), "further research is needed to investigate the strategies that teachers use to develop positive relationships with their students from [various] cultural and ethnic backgrounds outside the context of the formal lesson, or even outside the classroom." (p. 460). Moreover, Schonfeld and Feinman (2012) wrote:

Some teachers complained that the graduate courses they anticipated would help them did not provide sufficient content in the area of classroom management, consistent with evidence that many professors in schools of education do not emphasize practical matters such as classroom discipline. (p. 237)

These are serious challenges that should be addressed. However, it is important to note that researchers continue to investigate programs, models, teacher practices, and teacher beliefs. This provides a hopeful space for what is possible in developing classroom management practices that meet the needs of all students. Still, much more work has to be done to address the structural and systemic challenges embedded in urban communities, districts, and schools and consequently in their classrooms.

ACKNOWLEDGMENTS

I am grateful to Elizabeth Self for helping me gather the documents I reviewed in this chapter and to Heather Cunningham for helpful edits on it.

REFERENCES

Adkins-Coleman, T. A. (2010). "I'm not afraid to come into your world": Case studies of teachers facilitating engagement in urban high school English classrooms. *Journal of Negro Education, 79*(1), 41–53.

Auld, R. G., Belfiore, P. J., & Scheeler, M. C. (2010). Increasing pre-service teachers' use of differential reinforcement: Effects of performance feedback on consequences for student behavior. *Journal of Behavioral Education, 19*, 169–183.

Bondy, E., Ross, D. D., Gallingane, C., & Hambacher, E. (2007). Creating environments of success and resilience: Culturally responsive classroom management and more. *Urban Education, 42*(4), 326–348.

Burke, R. V., Oats, R. G., Ringle, J. L., Fichtner, L. O. N., & DelGaudio, M. B. (2011). Implementation of a classroom management program with urban elementary schools in low-income neighborhoods: Does program fidelity affect student behavior and academic outcomes? *Journal of Education for Students Placed at Risk, 16*(3), 201–218.

Delpit, L. (1995). *Other people's children: Cultural conflict in the classroom.* New York: New Press.

Dobler, E., Kesner, C., Kramer, R., Resnik, M., & Devin, L. (2009). A collaborative model for developing classroom management skills in urban professional develop school settings. *School-University Partnerships, 3*(1), 54–68.

Dray, B. J., & Wisneski, D. B. (2011). Mindful reflection as a process for developing culturally responsive practices. *Teaching Exceptional Children, 44*(1), 28–36.

Freiberg, H. J., & Lamb, S. M. (2009). Dimensions of person-centered management. *Theory into Practice, 48*, 99–105.

Freiberg, H. J., Huzinec, C. A., & Templeton, S. M. (2009). Classroom management—A pathway to student achievement: A study of fourteen inner-city elementary schools. *The Elementary School Journal, 110*(1), 63–80.

Gay, G. (2010). *Culturally responsive teaching: Theory, research, and practice* (2nd ed.). New York: Teachers College Press.

Hammerness, K. (2011). Classroom management in the United States: A view from New York City. *Teaching Education, 22*(2), 151–167.

Hammond, H., Dupoux, E., & Ingalls, L. (2004). Culturally relevant classroom management strategies for American Indian students. *Rural Special Education Quarterly 23*(4), 3–9.

Harris, A. R., & Walton, M. D. (2009). "Thank you for making me write this." Narrative skills and the management of conflict in urban schools. *Urban Review, 41*, 287–311.

Henninger, M., & Coleman, M. (2008). De-escalation: How to take back control in your urban physical education classes. *Strategies*, 11–14.

Higgins, K. M., & Moule, J. (2009). "No more Mr. Nice Guy": Preservice teachers' conflict with classroom management in a predominantly African-American urban elementary school. *Multicultural Perspectives, 11*(3), 132–138. doi: 10.1080/15210960903116530

Hough, D. L. (2011). An evaluation of the developmental designs approach and professional development model on classroom management in 22 middle schools in a large, midwestern school district. *Middle Grades Research Journal,* 6(3), 177–192.

Jennings, P. A., & Greenberg, M. T. (2009). The prosocial classroom: Teacher social and emotional competence in relation to student and classroom outcomes. *Review of Educational Research,* 79(1), 491–525.

Jennings, P. A., Snowberg, K. E., Coccia, M. A., & Greenberg, M. T. (2011). Improving classroom learning environments by Cultivating Awareness and Resilience in Education (CARE): Results of two pilot studies. *Journal of Classroom Interaction,* 46(1), 37–48.

Kamps, D., Wills, H. P., Heitzman-Powell, L., Laylin, J., Szoke, C., Petrillo, T., et al. (2011). Class-wide function-related intervention teams: Effects of group contingency programs in urban classrooms. *Journal of Positive Behavior Interventions,* 13(3), 154–167.

Kennedy, B. L. (2011). The importance of student and teacher interactions for disaffected middle school students: A grounded theory study of community day schools. *Urban Education,* 46(1), 4–33.

Lannie, A. L., & McCurdy, B. L. (2007). Preventing disruptive behavior in the urban classroom: Effects of the good behavior game on student and teacher behavior. *Education & Treatment of Children,* 30(1), 85–98.

McCarthy, J., & Benally, J. (2003). Classroom management in a Navajo middle school. *Theory into Practice* 42(4), 296–304.

McGee, E. (in progress). Dying to succeed: The extreme price of STEM college success for Black students.

Milkie, M. A., & Warner, C. H. (2011). Classroom learning environments and the mental health of first grade children. *Journal of Health and Social Behavior,* 52(1), 4–22.

Milner, H. R. (2006). Classroom management in urban classrooms. In C. M. Evertson & C. S. Weinstein (Eds.), *The handbook of classroom management: Research, practice & contemporary issues* (pp. 491–522). Mahwah, NJ: Erlbaum.

Milner, H. R. (2008). Disrupting deficit notions of difference: Counter-narratives of teachers and community in urban education. *Teaching and Teacher Education* 24(6), 1573–1598.

Milner, H. R. (2010). *Start where you are, but don't stay there: Understanding diversity, opportunity gaps, and teaching in today's classrooms.* Cambridge, MA: Harvard Education Press.

Milner, H. R., & Lomotey, K. (Ed.), (2014). *Handbook of urban education.* New York: Routledge.

Milner, H. R., & Tenore, F. B. (2010). Classroom management in diverse classrooms. *Urban Education,* 45(5), 560–603.

Monroe, C. R. (2006). Misbehavior or misinterpretation? Closing the discipline gap through cultural synchronization. *Kappa Delta Pi Record 42(4),* 161–165.

Monroe, C. R. (2009). Teachers closing the discipline gap in an urban middle school. *Urban Education,* 44(3), 322–347.

Rogers, C., & Freiberg, H. J. (1994). Freedom to learn (3rd ed.). Columbus, OH: Merrill.

Schonfeld, I. S., & Feinman, S. J. (2012). Difficulties of alternatively certified teachers. *Education and Urban Society,* 44(3), 215–246.

Shernoff, E. S., Maríñez-Lora, A. M., Frazier, S. L., Jakobsons, L. J., & Atkins, M. S. (2011). Teachers supporting teachers in urban schools: What iterative research designs can teach us. *School Psychology Review,* 40(4), 465–485.

Shin, S., & Koh, M.-S. (2007). A cross-cultural study of teachers' beliefs and strategies on classroom behavior management in urban American and Korean school systems. *Education and Urban Society,* 39(2), 286–309.

Shobe, R. (2003). Respecting diversity: A classroom management technique: A survey of incarcerated adult students. *Journal of Correctional Education,* 54(2), 60–64.

Sutton, R. E., Mudrey-Camino, R., & Knight, C. C. (2009). Teachers' emotion regulation and classroom management. *Theory into Practice,* 48, 130–137. doi: 10.1080/00405840902776418

Ullucci, K. (2009). "This has to be family": Humanizing classroom management in urban schools. *Journal of Classroom Interaction,* 44(1), 13–28.

Tartwijk, J. van, Brok, P. den., Veldman, I., & Wubbels, T. (2009). Teachers' practical knowledge about classroom management in multicultural classrooms. *Teaching and Teacher Education,* 25, 453–460.

Weinstein, C. S., Thomlinson-Clarke, S., & Curran, M. (2003). Culturally responsive classroom management: Awareness into action. *Theory into Practice,* 42(4), 269–276.

Weinstein, C. S., Thomlinson-Clarke, S., & Curran, M. (2004). Toward a conception of culturally responsive classroom management. *Journal of Teacher Education,* 55(1), 25–38.

10

CLASSROOM AND BEHAVIOR MANAGEMENT RESEARCH IN SPECIAL EDUCATION ENVIRONMENTS

EDWARD J. SABORNIE AND MALINDA LEIGH PENNINGTON
NC STATE UNIVERSITY

Since 2005, notwithstanding the number of students with disabilities receiving instruction in a general education setting (i.e., participating with nondisabled peers for 80% or more of the school day), a significant number of students with disabilities continue to be educated in more restrictive educational settings, such as resource rooms, self-contained classrooms, and special day and residential school settings. Recent data (i.e., U.S. Department of Education, 2012) show that roughly 20% of students with disabilities are served in resource room settings (i.e., with 40–79% of the remaining school day with typical peers) and that 14% are served in separate or self-contained classrooms (i.e., with 39% or less of remaining school day with nondisabled peers). Even though both of these numbers represent a decrease from 2005 rates, it is notable that the number of students served in separate schools and residential settings (including hospital/homebound and other institutional facilities) has increased from 3.9 to 5.1%.

Many students with disabilities—particularly those with high-incidence disabilities (i.e., learning disabilities, mild intellectual disability, emotional and behavioral disability)—received all of their instruction in general education classrooms prior to eligibility for special education. In other words, failure in general education settings led to special education referral and later eligibility. Oftentimes what leads to placement in more restrictive educational environments such as self-contained special education classrooms are inappropriate student behaviors beyond the control or behavior change expertise of general education teachers. Students with disabilities who demonstrate disruptive behaviors such as noncompliance and hostility are likely to elicit feelings of rejection from their inclusion environment teachers (Cook & Cameron, 2010), and such students (particularly those with autism) are likely to receive intrusive behavioral interventions in the classroom (Mayton, Carter, Zhang, & Wheeler, 2014). Moreover, students with emotional and behavioral disabilities

(EBD) often exhibit higher levels of acting out or aggressive behavior than other students with special needs. Serious inappropriate behaviors usually require specifically designed instruction and behavioral interventions (e.g., functional behavior analysis and intervention; see Chapter 4 in this volume) that can be best delivered by trained special educators (Sabornie, Evans, & Cullinan, 2006). Additionally, students with disabilities who are placed in the most restrictive educational settings, such as separate day or residential schools, often have the trisected issues of academic, behavioral, and social difficulties (Chmelka, Trout, Mason, & Wright, 2011). Given the troublesome behavioral characteristics of many students with disabilities, it is no surprise that teachers in more restrictive educational settings spend a substantive amount of time dealing with student conduct.

If students with disabilities are to receive an appropriate education in more restrictive settings, they should benefit from individualized attention and supports. Even some special education teachers, however, are not always adequately prepared to assess and address the behavioral needs of their students (Begeny & Martens, 2006). Although specific pre- and in-service training can enhance the ability to manage classroom behaviors, some teachers hold negative perceptions toward their most disruptive students (Gao & Merger, 2011).

There are several evidence-based practices for classroom and behavior management in special education settings, such as functional behavior assessments leading to behavior intervention and replacement plans, positive reinforcement procedures, self-management techniques, behavior reduction procedures, and structured positive learning environments (Regan & Michaud, 2011). Landrum and Kauffman (2006) discussed many of these techniques used in special education settings in the first edition of *Handbook of Classroom Management*. This chapter, in contrast, reviews research (i.e., published since the first edition of the *Handbook of Classroom Management*) that examined classroom and behavior management techniques in order to evaluate the efficacy of such interventions as used in special education settings. To find the studies reviewed herein, we conducted database searches in ERIC, PsychINFO, PsychARTICLES, and Sociological Abstracts, using the terms "classroom management," "behavior management," "special education classrooms," "special education self-contained classrooms," "special education resource room classrooms," "special education special schools," "segregated educational environments," and "special education instruction." After finding the articles discussed in this chapter, we also searched the reference lists of each study in an attempt to find additional, related studies. This resulted in a total of 27 studies for discussion.

REVIEW OF SPECIAL EDUCATION CLASSROOM AND BEHAVIORAL MANAGEMENT RESEARCH

In this section, we review selected quantitative research (i.e., group and single-case design [SCD]) that has been published since 2005 and that used various methods of classroom and behavior management to affect student conduct in special education settings. Those with autism attention deficit hyperactivity disorder (ADHD), EBD, learning disabilities (LD), intellectual disabilities (ID), and other health impairments

(OHI) served as participants in these peer-reviewed investigations. Special education self-contained classrooms, resource rooms, and special education (only) schools were used as the research sites. The studies examined in this chapter relate only to the United States and are diverse in terms of samples studied and interventions. By reviewing the quantitative research on this topic, we attempt to inform the reader that behavioral management is a large component and *the* typical form of classroom management research found in special education settings in schools. The studies are grouped into those pertaining to type of special educational setting in order to show the variety of methods that have been used in the more restrictive school placements. We highlight the interventions, experimental design features, findings, and implications for each study as they apply to classroom and behavioral management. An additional section highlights studies that examined special education teacher time use related to classroom management, as well as teachers' views of the cost-benefit relationships of numerous classroom and behavior management interventions. These last studies are reviewed to show how classroom and behavioral management activities fit into the daily routine of special education settings.

It is beyond the scope of this chapter to provide a complete discussion of the technical adequacy of all the group design and SCD studies reviewed here based on the *What Works Clearinghouse* (WWC) standards. Interested readers should see Chapter 28 in this volume and the Council for Exceptional Children (2014) report for additional, related information in this domain.

Resource Room Research

Creel, Fore, Boon, and Bender (2006) examined the use of self-management skills in an attempt to improve the classroom preparedness of four students with ADHD in a sixth-grade language arts resource room. The instructional setting was used to teach seven or fewer students identified with high-incidence disabilities. The participants were taught elements of self-monitoring (i.e., self-recording and self-evaluation) and were then measured on completing various "preparedness" behaviors in the classroom, such as having work materials ready, submitting homework on time, completing assigned work during class without teacher prompting, and staying in their seats. Students were expected to display at least 80% mastery of all self-preparedness behaviors presented on a checklist. A multiple baseline across participants design was used. The participants and a science teacher (who also taught the students) completed a questionnaire in a pre-post intervention schedule to verify the study's social validity.

Results showed that the participants' classroom preparedness behaviors improved dramatically across all four participants and were maintained for at least two weeks in a maintenance phase. The science teacher saw measurable results in the students' science class preparedness, and the students were highly accurate in recording their own behaviors. No effect size calculations were included in the report. A visual inspection of the results of this study shows that disorganized students can become structured with comprehensive and consistent classroom behavior management techniques.

In a group design study that surveyed special education teachers, Evans, Weiss, and Cullinan (2012) attempted to uncover what classroom and behavioral management interventions were used regularly for various types of student behaviors, as well as whether such strategies differed across public school instructional settings. Students of interest in the survey were those with EBD; how teachers interacted with such pupils in different types of education placements (i.e., general education classes, resource or separate classes, and separate school classes) was also of interest. Twenty teachers from 36 schools in a rural district completed a two-part survey that included questions related to student characteristics and behavior management strategies. The data related to the teachers' behavior and classroom management strategies in only the special education settings are discussed here.

Evans and colleagues (2012) asked respondents to provide classroom and behavior management strategies that they used to address academic difficulties, as well as externalizing and internalizing problem behaviors. Teacher responses were classified as those that were used by teachers "frequently" or "sometimes." With regard to dealing with academic problems in special education settings, teachers frequently used explicit direct instruction, classroom rules, verbal reinforcement, and teacher proximity. When faced with externalizing behavior problems in special education classrooms teachers regularly used point-and-level systems, direct instruction, classroom rules, teacher proximity, and verbal reinforcement. Teachers in resource or separate classrooms repeatedly used verbal reinforcement to deal with students' internalizing behavior problems, but special educators in separate school classes used behavioral contracts, response cost, self-management, and token reinforcement, among the five other techniques mentioned previously, to address internalizing behavior issues. Teachers did not rank-order the frequency of usage for each classroom and behavior management strategy. It is apparent, however, that special education teachers in separate schools used a greater variety of techniques in comparison to those serving students with externalizing and internalizing behavior problems in resource or separate classrooms in typical schools. Effect size calculations were provided for some variable comparisons. The Evans and associates results show that teachers of students with EBD—regardless of the special education setting—frequently use a multitude of behavioral and classroom management strategies to address the varied and serious problems of such students.

Jones, Boon, Fore, and Bender (2008), in an SCD reversal (ABAB) study, attempted to reduce the number of verbally disrespectful behaviors of seven middle school students with LD and ADHD in a special education resource room. The independent variable included a group contingency intervention in which one of the seven participants was secretly designated as the Mystery Hero each day. The hero was required to reduce his or her number of verbally disrespectful comments in the resource room (from the count registered on the previous school day) in order for the entire class to receive the Mystery Surprise. The identity of the randomly selected hero was unknown until the end of the class period. The dependent variable, "verbally disrespectful behaviors," consisted of any spoken message from one student to another (or from student to teacher) that included name-calling, impolite comments, or disparagement during a reading instructional period. Event recording was used to count the number of occurrences of the target behavior for each of the seven participants, along with the total of all who were present.

Jones and colleagues (2008) showed that the Mystery Hero intervention program was highly successful in reducing the total number of disrespectful comments said by the seven participants as a group. A functional relationship between the dependent and independent variables was also shown for the majority of the individual participants and their singular ability to reduce disrespectful comments over baseline levels. Effect size, social validity, and treatment fidelity data were not described in the report, nor were full descriptions of the Mystery Surprise group reinforcements. In spite of these limitations, the Mystery Hero and Surprise classroom behavior management strategies appear worthy of implementation for teachers seeking to decrease the amount of disrespectful language used in classrooms.

Ness, Sohlberg, and Albin (2011), in a reversal SCD study, used an assignment management intervention package in an attempt to improve the project completion of three seventh-graders with disabilities educated in a resource room. The three study participants differed in the type of disability (i.e., autism, LD, EBD), and each was selected because he demonstrated low "assignment attack" behavior in the resource room setting. Three additional students with disabilities were also present in the resource room at the time of data collection, as well as a special education teacher and paraprofessional. The classroom assignment attack organizational system consisted of a bulletin board listing the students' assignments from all daily classes; assignment "tickets," which were a method for gathering new assignments (i.e., details, due dates, etc.) from all classes attended; posting new assignments on the bulletin board correctly; and student reinforcement for correctly gathering and posting assignments. The participants' assignment attack behavior during the resource room period was measured via direct observation using a five-point rating scale (completed by the first author and a research assistant) for (1) correctly recalling the assignment details, (2) gathering materials to complete the assignment, (3) beginning the work without incident, and (4) degree of task engagement. A total score for one session of assignment attack could range, therefore, from four to 20 (i.e., scores could range between 1 and 5 for each of the four target behaviors involved with assignment attack).

Results showed that a functional relationship was established between the dependent and independent variables for two of the three participants, and it was maintained for one month following the end of the second intervention phase. Two of the three participants showed clear changes in assignment attack trends during the intervention phases (i.e., in comparison to baselines), and variability of performance decreased during those same treatment periods. Scattered and unpredictable performance was shown for the one participant with EBD who did not demonstrate dependent variable performance improvement. Social validity was addressed through the special education teacher's report and follow-up phone interview, and treatment fidelity was shown to be 100% when checked by the research assistant and principal investigator. Effect sizes were not reported for the participants individually, nor were they stated for the entire treatment group. The assignment attack strategy, as reported by Ness and associates (2011), seems worthy of implementation for any teacher who has difficulty keeping students on task and completing obligations. When students are off task and do not complete assignments, classroom and behavioral management are likely to suffer.

Terenzi, Ervin, and Hoff (2010) implemented a class-wide self-management system in a special education resource room to improve on-task behavior and decrease disruptive behavior of three sixth-grade boys with LD and ADHD. The participants were chosen in light of their unsuccessful prior experience with an existing Positive Behavior Intervention and Support (PBIS) system in place at the K–6 elementary school they attended and to prevent the participants from exhibiting additional problem behaviors. The language arts resource room class composition ranged from 6 to 11 pupils, and it was staffed by one special educator and one paraprofessional. Active (e.g., writing answers on a sheet of paper) and passive engaged time (e.g., looking at a computer screen) were combined to indicate on-task behavior in a momentary time-sampling behavior recording system; disruptive off-task behavior included both off-task verbal (e.g., talking without raising one's hand) and off-task motor (i.e., leaving one's assigned desk) in a partial interval behavior recording scheme. An A-B-A-B-C-C'-A-C' SCD was used in the study. Phase A included baselines; B was the "gold slips" period when the students received a high level of positive reinforcement for rule following in the school-wide PBIS system; C included the class-wide self-management regimen where students recorded their own behavior, as well as their peers', in 5-minute segments; and the C' phases integrated the C phase components but extended the observation period to seven minutes. The participants were trained in the self-management recording and treatment regimen, including the teaching of rules for how to be respectful (e.g., follow directions from adults, among four other components) and for safety (e.g., both feet on the floor, among four other safety-related behaviors). Participants rated their own behavior, as well as that of the entire class, during the class-wide self-management intervention using a letter grade system where A indicated excellent conduct and F specified "could be better."

Terenzi and colleagues (2010) showed that, across the three participants, the class-wide self-management behavior system was clearly successful in increasing on-task behavior and decreasing disruptive, off-task behavior. Successful maintenance of the target behaviors occurred in the last experimental phase when the self-recording increased to longer periods. Moreover, the removal of the self-management routine within the last baseline phase led to a return to preintervention levels of on-task and disruptive behavior. The resource room teacher mentioned that the intervention package was successful in changing the behavior of the participants in the desired direction but that it was time intensive and difficult to achieve. Procedural integrity assessments were conducted throughout the project, but effect size calculations were not reported. The authors concluded that the self-management of student conduct is an effective Tier 2 (see Chapter 4 in this volume) behavioral and classroom management treatment within a response to intervention paradigm.

Williamson, Campbell-Whatley, and Lo (2009) used a dependent group contingency to affect the on-task behavior of six high school students (five boys, one girl) with high-incidence disabilities (i.e., LD, OHI with ADHD, and EBD) in a tenth-grade special education resource room. The participants were selected for intervention because they displayed frequent off-task behavior during independent seatwork in the 90-minute English period in the resource room; each had been receiving special education services for at least one year prior to study initiation. The special education teacher (first author) was also present in the classroom and collected much of the data, as well as implementing the intervention. Momentary time sampling (in five-minute intervals) was used to measure the dependent variable, on-task behavior, defined as actively involved with independent seatwork such as reading or completing a written assignment, silently working on an assigned task, and staying in the work area. An A-B-A-B (reversal) SCD structure guided the investigation. The intervention consisted of randomly selecting a student at the end of the English period and checking whether he or she met a predetermined criterion of on-task behavior. The student's name was never revealed to participants. When the on-task performance standard was met for the selected student, all class members received the reinforcement (homework pass, extra free time, etc.). If poor on-task behavior was shown by the randomly selected participant, the teacher simply encouraged all the students to do better next time.

Williamson and associates (2009) showed that the mean level of on-task behavior during the first baseline was 43% but that level jumped to 84% in the first intervention phase of the study. During the second baseline, the participants' mean level of the target behavior decreased (63%) but not to the level of the first baseline. When the group contingency condition was reinstated, the mean level of on-task behavior increased to only 67%, and only three participants showed increased levels of the target behavior. The intervention was selectively successful in that only three students made substantive on-task behavior progress over the course of the study. Procedural integrity was checked informally in a post hoc manner, but no social validity verification was provided. Effect size calculations were not conducted with the data. The Williamson and colleagues study provides additional evidence, in addition to that of Hansen and Lignugaris/Kraft (2005; discussed in the next section), that a dependent group contingency can improve students' behavior and assist in the teacher's goal of successful classroom and behavior management.

Self-Contained Classroom Research

Foxx and Garito (2007), in a four-phase, multitreatment-site SCD study, attempted to reduce the severe and dangerous behaviors of a 12-year-old boy with autism in three different settings. The participant, whom we'll call Ned, engaged in inappropriate behaviors such as self-injury (e.g., head banging), aggression (e.g., throwing objects at others), property destruction (e.g., breaking objects), inappropriate toileting (e.g., urinating anywhere other than in a toilet), and vomiting (e.g., putting his fingers down his throat to induce vomiting) in all settings included for examination in the study. Because the many inappropriate behaviors occurred in multiple settings, a multisite intervention, with the hope of generalization to his "home" classroom in a primary school, was deemed necessary. Event recording was used to record the target behaviors desired for reduction across four experimental phases. Phase one (baseline) was conducted in Ned's self-contained, public school classroom in which he was the only student; his teacher, two paraprofessionals, and a therapeutic support staff member were also present in the classroom. Phase two (in the first treatment setting) was conducted in Ned's home and later moved to a large room at the family's church; a special education teacher, paraprofessional, and support staff person implemented treatment. Phase three (the second treatment environment) continued in the large room at the church with a different special education teacher, the second author, and a support staff person present. Phase four (the third treatment site) was a self-contained classroom in a new school where Ned never attended; the same staff as in phase three were present. The intervention included an extensive "package" of differential reinforcement of appropriate behavior, a token economy system, a response cost system where earned tokens were removed when inappropriate behavior was demonstrated, contingent physical exercise, overcorrection, contingent movement, and physical restraint.

Results showed that Ned's severe inappropriate behavior increased to over 110 occurrences per day during the four-month baseline phase but decreased dramatically to at or near zero for 14 months in the self-contained classroom of phase four. Aggression levels increased in phase two, leading to changing the treatment environment from home to the large room in the church. During the final phase four, however, aggression was reduced to a level of 95% of baseline. At the end of the study, Ned was able to display more elaborate social skills and language and to enjoy activities with other students. No effect size calculations were provided in the study narrative. Foxx and Garito (2007) demonstrated the power of using multiple behavioral management techniques to improve behavior in the classroom (and in other environments) of a student in desperate need of intervention. Notwithstanding the impressive results over time, unless extensive and expert support staff beyond a single teacher is available to students in serious need, the external and social validity of this study is open to discussion.

Spriggs, Gast, and Ayres (2007), in an SCD study, used picture activity schedule books in an attempt to improve the on-schedule and on-task behaviors of four students with disabilities in a self-contained classroom. The four participants, aged 12–13, each had moderate ID and were selected for intervention because they showed great difficulty completing assigned tasks and following the schedule in the classroom. The picture activity schedule books used for intervention stimuli consisted of a photo album with four pictures showing the activity the participant should complete during the instructional period, along with a card at the end that indicated task completion. Five phases were included in the study: (1) a generalization pretest, (2) a no-picture-activity schedule book condition, (3) an instructional (intervention) phase, (4) a picture-book-only stage, and (5) a generalization posttest. The target behaviors were recorded using presence or absence of on-schedule and on-task behavior via time sampling and event recording methods.

Results showed low levels of on-schedule and on-task behavior of the four participants during baseline, but dramatic improvements occurred during the instructional phase, as well as when the students used the picture activity schedule books alone without instruction. On-schedule and on-task behavior also generalized to

other activities not used during the instructional phase. Social validity was measured by surveying the teachers and other professionals who worked directly with the
four participants and showed that the raters agreed that the students became more
independent when using the picture activity schedule books. No effect size measurements were reported in the narrative of the study; this is unfortunate because a visual
inspection of the participants' performance graphs indicates a dramatic change in
their target behaviors over baseline levels. Picture activity schedule books appear to
be a viable method to increase on-schedule and on-task behavior—and to decrease
nonscheduled behaviors—of early adolescents with ID and, in doing so, can greatly
assist a teacher in classroom and behavior management.

Gulchak (2008), in an application of 21st-century technology, used a handheld
computing device in an effort to improve the on-task behavior of a third-grade boy
with EBD. The participant, Jay, was educated in a public school self-contained classroom for students with EBD along with nine other students, had measured intelligence scores in the average range, and showed both internalizing and externalizing
behaviors that led to his classification of EBD. A handheld computer (Palm Zire 72
device; one each for the student and researcher recording the target behavior) was
used to record on-task behavior of the participant (defined as "keep hands away
from face, complete work assigned, and raise hand to ask questions," p. 571) for
30-minute periods during reading instruction. A 30-second whole interval recording method was used to record the target behavior. Whenever Jay heard a distinct
tone through his earphone connected to the Palm device, he checked a yes or no
box on the screen indicating whether he was on-task for the 30-second interval.
An ABAB reversal design was used to test the efficacy of the self-monitoring-of-
attention independent variable.

Gulchak (2008) showed that Jay could successfully use the handheld device in an
effort to self-monitor his attention to task behavior. Jay's baseline levels of on-task
behavior averaged 67% during the reading period but increased to an average of 94%
during the two intervention phases. Jay was excited to use the handheld device, and
his other classmates in the self-contained classroom also wanted to use it for their
own attention-to-task behavior. Treatment integrity was measured in the investigation, but effect size, social validity, and maintenance of the target behavior were not.
The second baseline (A_2) and second intervention (B_2) phases each lasted only two
sessions. In spite of these shortcomings, the Gulchak study deserves replication to
determine whether newer handheld devices that have become ubiquitous in schools
(e.g., smartphones, tablets, etc.) can also show the same results in increasing on-task
behavior in special education classrooms.

Miller, Lane, and Wehby (2005) used a social skills instructional program in an
attempt to improve the inappropriate behavior and academic engaged time (AET)
of seven students (five boys, two girls) with high-incidence disabilities in a self-
contained special education setting. Three of the participants were identified as
having EBD; others were identified as LD, ID, OHI, and speech and language
impairment, and they ranged in age from six to nine. The participants were assessed
using various standardized measures prior to the study (i.e., social skills, problem
behaviors, academic competence) to determine their present levels of performance

on skills important to the aim and scope of the study. A multiple baseline across two groups of students and two dependent variables (i.e., inappropriate behavior, academic engaged time) SCD was used. Intervention groups were matched on grade level and gender, and the groups received social skill instruction three or four times a week for 30 minutes each session, over a six-week period. The *Social Skills Intervention Guide: Practical Strategies for Social Skills* (Elliott & Gresham, 1991) curriculum was used to deliver social skill instruction to the participants. The Multi Option Observation System for Experimental Studies (MOOSES; Tapp, Wehby, & Ellis, 1995), a computer program used for direct observation, was used to collect and quantify the dependent variable data.

Results showed that inappropriate classroom behavior of both experimental groups decreased from baseline to intervention phases and that the lower rates were held through the postintervention phase. In terms of AET, both groups' increased their time on-task, but one of the two experimental groups, while increasing AET in the intervention phase, did not maintain the same level of AET in the follow-up phase (i.e., in comparison to the first intervention stage). Social validity measurements showed that the teacher and student teacher in the classroom found the intervention worthwhile but that the paraprofessional assisting in the class was less enthusiastic about the experimental methods and results. More than half of the students viewed the intervention positively, but one participant did not. Effect size calculations were extensive (i.e., covering both groups and individual participants), and treatment integrity was checked consistently. The Miller and colleagues (2005) study showed that comprehensive social skill instruction can affect classroom behavior in a positive manner and can ease the difficulty of teachers seeking uneventful classroom and behavior management.

Holifield, Goodman, Hazelkorn, and Heflin (2010) used self-monitoring in a multiple baseline across participants SCD study to enhance the academic performance and attention to task behavior of two boys with autism in an elementary-level, special education self-contained classroom. Tony (age 10) and Graham (age 9) were in the self-contained classroom for five months when the study began, along with four additional students, a paraprofessional, and the teacher. The two participants received all their daily instruction in the self-contained classroom except for physical education, art, and music; both had a history of difficulty in attending to task and completing assigned work. The multiple baseline across the two participants design was implemented during the students' language arts and math classes for a total of 40 minutes of observation and behavior recording for each student and session. Momentary time sampling was used to record the students' attention to task at the end of a 10-second interval, and accuracy of performance data were recorded using a permanent product methodology (i.e., the teacher-graded student work papers each day). Tony and Graham were taught the self-monitoring behavior in a staggered manner after the baseline data were collected. This consisted of the self-monitoring sheet placed on the students' desks and instructions from the teacher to circle yes or no related to attending to task when cued. Both participants were able to independently use the self-monitoring measurement system after six days of teacher instruction.

Holifield and associates (2010) were able to show that the self-monitoring procedure was effective in increasing the attention to task of both participants in language arts, but that the experimental effect related to increased accuracy during language arts was modest. In math, the intervention was responsible for immediate and convincing growth of both participants in accuracy and attention to task. A maintenance phase beyond the intervention stage was not included, nor were effect size measurements, social validity confirmation, and fidelity of implementation data. While these omissions lead to reserved conclusions regarding the technical adequacy of the Holifield and colleagues study, other research (see Ness, Sohlberg, & Albin, 2011) shows classroom and behavior management value in using the self-monitoring of behavior for students with autism.

Hansen and Lignugaris/Kraft (2005) used social skill instruction and a group contingency plan in a withdrawal SCD study to improve the verbal interactions of nine boys with EBD in a junior high school. Each of the participants had been educated in a self-contained EBD classroom for at least three years, six were on probation for a criminal offense when the study was conducted, and the majority (i.e., seven of nine) had previously exhibited delinquent behavior. The study was conducted during the students' 45-minute math class, and a special education teacher and a paraeducator were also in the classroom with the students. The classroom behavior management structure in place consisted of a point-and-level system in which the students earned reinforcement for positive classroom behavior and privileges were limited when inappropriate behavior was displayed. The dependent variables in the study, positive and negative statements spoken during the math class, were recorded using a frequency count in a one-minute partial interval system over the 15-minute observation period.

Participants were taught how to provide positive statements toward another via the Social Skills Strategies (Gawerski & Mayo, 1989) curriculum. The dependent group contingency was also used for providing positive statements in that each day two students were randomly selected and kept anonymous. For the entire class to receive the reinforcement, the two selected participants had to give at least four positive statements to another peer in the classroom during the observation session. Four phases were included in the study design: (1) baseline, (2) social skills training with role-playing, (3) the dependent group contingency, and (4) faded group contingency.

The results showed that during the initial baseline, only two participants exhibited positive statements toward a peer and that all the pupils with EBD said at least one negative statement to another student. When the social skills intervention was in place, five of the participants increased the number of positive statements made toward a peer (although at a low rate), and the number of students speaking negative statements decreased. When the group contingency was implemented, however, all students increased their number of positive statements and decreased their number of negative statements. In the fading (maintenance) contingency, all participants continued to provide positive statements toward peers and to limit their number of negative statements as well. Effect sizes were not reported, and social validity statements from the students or teachers were not mentioned in the narrative. Treatment fidelity assessments were also not provided. The results of the Hansen and Lignugaris/Kraft (2005) study show positive changes in the participants and provide additional evidence (cf. Jones, Boon, Fore, & Bender, 2008) of the benefits of a group contingency intervention to improve classroom and behavior management.

Research in Special Schools

Stahr, Cushing, Lane, and Fox (2006), in an SCD (i.e., multiple baseline across two settings in conjunction with a withdrawal procedure), used a function-based treatment to assist a nine-year-old boy with ADHD, EBD, and speech and language impairment attending a special school for students with EBD. The participant, Shawn, officially classified as OHI, demonstrated high rates of off-task behavior in two of his fourth-grade classes, math and language arts, and this interfered with the instruction of all the students present in the classroom. Shawn's classroom included a total of nine other students with EBD, a special education teacher, one paraprofessional, and an intermittent counseling therapist. The package intervention consisted of (1) a signaling system in which the student communicated his level of comfort in completing a task, (2) a self-monitoring, six-item checklist that Shawn used to measure his level of on-task behavior in the classroom, and (3) an extinction procedure in which the teacher and paraprofessional ignored Shawn's inappropriate attempts to gain attention.

Results showed that in the initial baseline phases, Shawn's percentage of time on task was consistently at low levels during both subject periods and frequently at or near zero during math class. During the two intervention phases, however, his mean on-task behavior increased dramatically, as shown by a percentage of nonoverlapping data (PND) points of 89% in language arts and 50% in math period. In the second baseline period, Shawn's on-task behavior returned to low levels in both subject periods but increased quickly in the second intervention phase. Social validity, treatment integrity, and PND data collected indicated that the intervention was valuable to the teaching staff and to Shawn, that the specifics of the intervention were delivered with fidelity, and that the effect size of the behavior change was moderate to strong. It appears that the intervention package used in the Stahr and associates (2006) study is well worth attempts at replication in less restrictive instructional settings, such as resource rooms and self-contained classrooms in typical public schools.

Foxx and Meindl (2007) implemented a comprehensive intervention package aimed at decreasing the aggressive and destructive behaviors of an early adolescent boy, Johnny, with autism. The study's baseline period began in a self-contained special education classroom for three months, but because of the participant's severe inappropriate behavior, the intervention setting was changed to a special education school for the next year. Examples of the inappropriate behavior that Johnny exhibited included head-butting anyone who came near to him in the classroom (breaking the nose of one teacher and having another lose teeth), as well as biting, hitting, pinching, and aggressing toward others with objects as weapons. In the end, physical aggression toward others and destructive behavior were selected as his target behaviors to improve at the special school; they were measured via frequency recording throughout the school day. In the special school, Johnny was the only student in the classroom, which included a teacher, a paraeducator, and an applied behavior analysis intern. The intervention consisted of a package of treatments including "a token economy system, differential reinforcement of other behaviors (DRO), response cost, overcorrection, and physical restraint" (Foxx & Meindl, pp. 88–89). Classroom rules were also implemented in the investigation.

The target behavior reduction that was shown by Johnny over the 12-month course of the intervention package was remarkable. In baseline, his target behavior frequency averaged 102 occurrences of the inappropriate behavior per day. During the first month of intervention, it was reduced to an average of five per day, and by the sixth month it averaged less than one per day. Over the course of the entire 12-month treatment phase, Johnny's aggressive behavior (destructive behavior had completely vanished) averaged 1.6 incidents per day. Physical restraint was used a total of nine times in the treatment phase, and it was used zero times in seven of the last eight months of the study. Negative verbal behaviors were also extinguished during the lengthy intervention phase. Social validity was reported via the anecdotal notes taken by Foxx and Meindl (2007) throughout the one-year intervention, but interobserver reliability measurement techniques and coefficients were not included in the report, nor were treatment integrity descriptions, effect size calculations, and an intervention maintenance phase. The simple A-B experimental design used also limits the strength of the recommendations that can be drawn from the study. Moreover, the fact that Johnny was the only student in the classroom and was supervised by three adults restricts the external and social validity of the investigation. Nevertheless, the classroom-based inappropriate behaviors that were changed in the participant were impressive and lasted for one year—a much longer period than typically noted in most SCD studies.

Special Education Teacher Time Use

Two studies (i.e., Vannest & Hagan-Burke, 2010; Vannest, Hagan-Burke, Parker, & Soares, 2011) provide a snapshot of the classroom and behavior management practices of special education teachers in different types of educational environments. In both studies, Vannest and colleagues asked special education teachers in self-contained classrooms, resource rooms, content mastery classrooms (i.e., a "pull-out" setting with a special education teacher that is used for academic instruction assistance), and coteaching environments (where special and general educators teach side by side in the same classroom) to document their daily activities. The purpose of the studies was to describe teacher time usage within the four different classroom types over a period of one year. Teacher time usage was subdivided into 10 categories, such as academic instruction, nonacademic instruction, instructional support, preventive behavior management, and responsive behavior management, among others. Teachers were asked to estimate how long they spent in each of the 10 categories during a one-hour instructional period, and the researchers closely monitored teacher time usage through many observations and reliability checks over the one-year span of data collection. Study data were entered into an electronic database for additional analysis.

Results in both studies showed that special education teachers usually spend less than 50% of their available class time involved in actual academic instruction. Behavior management and discipline issues comprised from 7 to 9% of total class time, with teachers in the most restrictive settings (i.e., self-contained classrooms) spending more time on discipline than teachers in less restrictive ones. Preventive (i.e., teaching students correct behaviors) and responsive (i.e., responding to inappropriate behavior) behavior management time occurred at nearly equal amounts across special education setting types. Effect size and interobserver reliability calculations were performed in both studies. Vannest and colleagues concluded that special education teachers in different types of instructional settings are involved in extremely diverse types of classroom and behavior management activities and that they are busy with noninstructional tasks. Based on the Vannest and colleagues research, it is likely to be difficult to measure value-added special education teacher effects that are related to student and school accountability indices.

Special Educators' Views of Behavior Management Strategies

Kaff, Zabel, and Milham (2007), in a descriptive study, surveyed special education teachers to determine their "use, intensity, and effectiveness of communication and behavior management strategies" (p. 35) in the classroom. A total of 211 special education teachers completed a questionnaire; 44% were resource room teachers, 33% taught in self-contained classrooms, and fewer than 1% taught in "other" settings. The remaining teachers (23%) taught in inclusive settings. All teacher/respondents taught only students with high-incidence disabilities. The teachers rated their communication strategies ($n = 24$; e.g., using verbal praise; verbally encouraging appropriate behavior) and behavior management interventions ($n = 33$; e.g., changing the seating of a student; sending a student to the office for discipline), using a Likert scale related to (1) how likely they would use the treatment in the classroom, (2) the labor intensity of the procedure, and (3) intervention effectiveness, among other factors.

Kaff and associates (2007) found that special education teachers were more likely to use communication-related (vs. behavior management) strategies to maintain order in the classroom. The high-use communication-related teacher behaviors included classroom rules and verbal praise. High-use behavior management practices included physical proximity to students, using prompts and gestures, and contacting parents. Behavior management strategies were found to be less labor intensive in comparison to communication interventions, and several communication-related procedures (e.g., modeling appropriate behavior) were found to be more effective than behavior management tactics (e.g., individualizing student instruction). Not one of the 57 communication-related or behavior management strategies was found to be classified as both high use and high intensity among the teachers. Although descriptive in nature and lacking any comparison group (e.g., general education teachers), the Kaff and colleagues study confirms that special education teachers across instructional settings are likely to first focus their attention on antecedent events that prevent problem behavior in the classroom (see Chapter 2 in this volume), and then explore ways to deal effectively with behavior problems after they occur.

Table 10.1 Other related studies not reviewed.

Study	Design	Setting(s)	Sample(s)	Dependent Variable(s)
Anderson (2007)	Qualitative	SCC	EBD	Self-regulation and de-escalation of behaviors
Azrin, Vinas, & Ehle (2007)	SCD	SCC	ADHD, IDMO	Attention to task; calmness
Bennett, Reichow, & Wolery (2011)	SCD	SCC	AU, DD	Engagement; task completion stereotypic behavior
Causton-Theoharis, Theoharis, Orsati, & Cosier (2011)	Qualitative	SCC	LD, AU, ID, POHI	Self-contained classroom efficacy
DeSchipper & Schuengel (2010)	Quantitative	Group care	IDMO, IDSP, AU	Attachment behavior
Hume & Odom (2007)	SCD	SCC	AU	On-task responding; task completion
Hume, Plavnick, & Odom (2012)	SCD	SCC	AU	Task completion; prompting
Lang, Davis, O'Reilly, Machalicek, Rispoli, Sigafoos, Lancioni, & Regester (2010)	SCD	RR	AU	Elopement
Lang, Shogren, Machalicek, Rispoli, O'Reilly, Baker, & Regester (2009)	SCD	SS	AU	Classroom rules
Mays & Heflin (2011)	SCD	SCC	AU	Self-care

Note. ADHD = attention deficit with hyperactivity disorder; AU = autism; DD = Developmental Disability; EBD = emotional behavioral disorder; ID = intellectual disability; IDMO = moderate intellectual disability; IDSP = severe-profound intellectual disability; LD = learning disability; POHI = physical and other health impaired; RR = resource room; SCC = self-contained classroom; SCD = single-case design; SS = special education school.

Space limitations prevent a thorough review of all the research since 2005 that examined classroom and behavior management issues in special education settings. Table 10.1 includes a summary of other studies in special education classroom and behavior management that were not discussed in detail in this chapter.

CONCLUSIONS

Among other factors, effective classroom and behavior management in any type of classroom requires the teacher to increase certain desirable student behaviors and decrease other inappropriate behaviors (Sabornie & deBettencourt, 2009). Unfortunately, countless general and special education teachers report that they struggle to deal with students' challenging behaviors in the classroom and admit to being ill prepared to successfully solve such problems (Regan & Michaud, 2011). Considering the severity of some of the inappropriate behaviors (see Foxx & Garito, 2007; Foxx & Meindl, 2007) that some special education teachers are likely to see in self-contained classrooms and special schools, it is little wonder that teachers working in those more restrictive types of educational environments (i.e., in comparison to inclusive classrooms and schools) feel inadequate in their preparation. The types of student behaviors that special education teachers will need to increase or decrease in order to achieve classroom management success in the most restrictive educational settings will certainly challenge their skills and may not be seen in the most inclusive classrooms and schools. Many times, a student is educated in the most restrictive educational setting available because his or her inappropriate behaviors are so severe that constant and robust behavior management is necessary before any functional behavior acquisition occurs. In many self-contained special education classrooms and special schools, student and staff safety is also an important part of classroom management, and it requires diligence at all times. In other words, extreme inappropriate behaviors sometimes need to be matched in intensity with potent interventions, and such treatments are not likely to be possible or successful in general education settings. Contrary to the criticism aimed at self-contained classrooms and special schools (see Causton-Theoharis, Theoharis, Orsati, & Cosier, 2011) such environments serve an important role in the continuum of available school placements for students with severe behavior problems.

The research that included self-management and monitoring techniques (four studies reviewed in this chapter) is encouraging for successful classroom management in special education. When effective, such methods allow for greater ownership of behavior on the part of students and removes the need for teachers to pay constant attention to inappropriate student behavior, which can be reinforcing to offending students. Similarly, the use of group contingency interventions (found in three studies) is also heartening, given its successful use in resource rooms and self-contained special education settings. One unique aspect of the group contingency intervention includes using an anonymous student's conduct as the standard for reinforcement delivered to all other students present. By doing so, the "unknown" student is free from group reproach when his or her behavior does not meet the criterion desired and leads to better student harmony and classroom management.

It is noteworthy that one of the old standards in special education classroom and behavior management, the token economy system, was used in only one study in our review since 2005 (i.e., Foxx & Garito, 2007). It is safe to say that over the last 40+ years, few instructional methods texts in special education neglected to discuss the token economy system as an effective tool for successful classroom management in different types of educational and therapeutic settings. Several books were written on the design and use of token economy systems in many different educational settings, with the original text by Ayllon and Azrin (1968) still cited today. Maggin, Chafouleas, Goddard, and Johnson (2011), however, in an extensive review of the research literature on token economy systems, found insufficient evidence to conclude that such systems were a robust, evidence-based practice supported by WWC standards. Maggin and associates found that student behavior can be changed via token economy systems, but methodological problems in the research led to complications in the interpretation of the findings as a whole.

The methodological problems in the classroom and behavior management research reviewed in this chapter are also recurrent. Reporting of effect sizes was a common omission, along with SCD execution issues such as omitting treatment fidelity, too few observation sessions in an experimental phase, and the lack of a maintenance or follow-up stage in some studies. These are common limitations that are mentioned in many of the studies, but such lapses do lead to tentative recommendations (at best) for replication in classrooms and do not assist in the transfer of knowledge from research to practice.

Without high-quality research on effective classroom and behavior management techniques in special education settings, and successful ways to disseminate it to practitioners, little progress will be made, and negative comments about the disconnect between research and everyday usage in the hands of educators will persist. It is imperative to train teachers in the essential ways to organize, operate, and manage their instructional settings because, among other important reasons, classroom management self-efficacy has been shown to deter teacher burnout (Aloe, Amo, & Shanahan, 2014). In this chapter, we synthesized instructional methods shown in research that are related to classroom and behavior management success in special education settings; we hope this information lands in the hands of those who can make it meaningful for many—in higher education as well as in public schools.

REFERENCES

Aloe, A.M., Amo, L.C., & Shanahan, M.E. (2014). Classroom management self-efficacy and burnout: A multivariate meta-analysis. *Educational Psychology Review, 26*, 101–126. doi: 10.1007/s10648-013-9244-0

Anderson, K.L. (2007). Who let the dog in? How to incorporate a dog into a self-contained classroom. *Teaching Exceptional Children Plus, 4*(1). Retrieved from http://search.ebscohost.com/login.aspx?direct=true&db=eric&AN=EJ967469&site=ehost-live&scope=site

Ayllon, T., & Azrin, N.H. (1968). *The token economy: A motivational system for therapy and rehabilitation.* New York: Appleton-Century-Crofts.

Azrin, N.H., Vinas, V., & Ehle, C.T. (2007). Physical activity as reinforcement for classroom calmness of ADHD children: A preliminary study. *Child & Family Behavior Therapy, 29*, 1–8.

Begeny, J.C., & Martens, B.K. (2006). Assessing pre-service teachers' training in empirically validated behavioral instruction practices. *School Psychology Quarterly, 21*, 262–285.

Bennett, K., Reichow, B., & Wolery, M. (2011). Effects of structured teaching on the behavior of young children with disabilities. *Focus on Autism and Other Developmental Disabilities, 26*, 143–152. doi: 10.1177/1088357611405040

Causton-Theoharis, J., Theoharis, G., Orsati, F., & Cosier, M. (2011). Does self-contained special education deliver on its promises? A critical inquiry into research and practice. *Journal of Special Education Leadership, 24*(2), 61–78.

Chmelka, M.B., Trout, A.L., Mason, W.A., & Wright, T. (2011). Children with and without disabilities in residential care: Risk at program entry, departure and six-month follow-up. *Emotional and Behavioural Difficulties, 16*, 383–399.

Cook, B.G., & Cameron, D.L. (2010). Inclusive teachers' concern and rejection toward their students: Investigating the validity of ratings and comparing student groups. *Remedial and Special Education, 31*, 67–76.

Council for Exceptional Children (2014). *Council for exceptional children standards for evidence-based practices in special education.* Arlington, VA: Author.

Creel, C., Fore, C., Boon, R.T., & Bender, W.N. (2006). Effects of self-monitoring on classroom preparedness skills of middle school students with Attention Deficit Hyperactivity Disorder. *Learning Disabilities: A Multidisciplinary Journal, 14*, 105–113.

De Schipper, J.C., & Schuengel, C. (2010). Attachment behaviour towards support staff in young people with intellectual disabilities: Associations with challenging behaviour. *Journal of Intellectual Disability Research, 54*, 584–596. doi: 10.1111/j.1365-2788.2010.01288.x

Elliott, S., & Gresham, F.M. (1991). *Social skills intervention guide.* Circle Pines, MN. American Guidance.

Evans, C., Weiss, S.L., & Cullinan, D. (2012). Teacher perceptions and behavioral strategies for students with emotional disturbances across educational environments. *Preventing School Failure, 56*(2), 82–90. doi: 10.1080/1045988X.2011.574170

Foxx, R.M., & Garito, J. (2007). The long term successful treatment of the very severe behaviors of a preadolescent with autism. *Behavioral Interventions, 22*, 69–82. doi: 10.1002/bin.232

Foxx, R. M., & Meindl, J. (2007). The long term successful treatment of the aggressive/destructive behaviors of a preadolescent with autism. *Behavioral Interventions*, *22*, 83–97. doi: 10.1002/bin.233

Gao, W., & Merger, G. (2011). Enhancing preservice teachers' sense of efficacy and attitudes towards school diversity through preparation: A case of one U.S. inclusive teacher education program. *International Journal of Special Education*, *26*, 92–107.

Gawerski, M., & Mayo, P. (1989). *SSS: Social skills strategies*. Eau Claire, WI: Thinking Publications.

Gulchak, D. J. (2008). Using a mobile handheld computer to teach a student with an emotional and behavioral disorder to self-monitor attention. *Education and Treatment of Children*, *31*, 567–581.

Hansen, S. D., & Lignugaris/Kraft, B. (2005). Effects of a dependent group contingency on the verbal interactions of middle school students with emotional disturbance. *Behavioral Disorders*, *30*, 170–184.

Holifield, C., Goodman, J., Hazelkorn, M., & Heflin, L. J. (2010). Using self-monitoring to increase attending to task and academic accuracy in children with autism. *Focus on Autism and Other Developmental Disabilities*, *25*, 230–238. doi: 10.1177/1088357610380137

Hume, K., & Odom, S. (2007). Effects of an individual work system on the independent functioning of students with autism. *Journal of Autism and Developmental Disorders*, *37*, 1166–1180. doi: 10.1007/s10803-006-0260-5

Hume, K., Plavnick, J., & Odom, S. L. (2012). Promoting task accuracy and independence in students with autism across educational setting through the use of individual work systems. *Journal of Autism and Developmental Disorders*, *42*, 2084–2099. doi: 10.1007/s10803-012-1457-4

Jones, M., Boon, R. T., Fore, C., & Bender, W. N. (2008). *Our Mystery Hero!* A group contingency intervention for reducing verbally disrespectful behaviors. *Learning Disabilities: A Multidisciplinary Journal*, *15*, 61–69.

Kaff, M. S., Zabel, R. H., & Milham, M. (2007). Revisiting cost-benefit relationships of behavior management strategies: What special educators say about usefulness, intensity, and effectiveness. *Preventing School Failure*, *51*(2), 35–45. doi: 10.3200/PSFL.51.2.35-45

Landrum, T. J., & Kauffman, J. M. (2006). Behavioral approaches to classroom management. In C. M. Evertson & C. S. Weinstein (Eds.), *Handbook of classroom management: Research, practice, and contemporary issues* (pp. 47–71). New York: Erlbaum/Taylor & Francis.

Lang, R., Davis, T., O'Reilly, M., Machalicek, W., Rispoli, M., Sigafoos, J., Lancioni, G., & Regester, A. (2010). Functional analysis and treatment of elopement across two school settings. *Journal of Applied Behavior Analysis*, *43*, 113–118. doi: 10.1901/jaba.2010.43-113

Lang, R., Shogren, K. A., Machalicek, W., Rispoli, M., O'Reilly, M., Baker, S., & Regester, A. (2009). Video self-modeling to teach classroom rules to two students with Asperger's. *Research in Autism Spectrum Disorders*, *3*, 483–488. doi: 10.1016/j.rasd.2008.10.001

Maggin, D. M., Chafouleas, S. M., Goddard, K. M., & Johnson, A. H. (2011). A systematic evaluation of token economies as a classroom management tool for students with challenging behavior. *Journal of School Psychology*, *49*, 529–554. doi: 10.1016/ j.jsp.2011.05.001

Mays, N. M., & Heflin, L. J. (2011). Increasing independence in self-care tasks for children with autism using self-operated auditory prompts. *Research in Autism Spectrum Disorders*, *5*, 1351–1357. doi: 10.1016/ j.rasd.2011.01.017

Mayton, M. R., Carter, S. L., Zhang, J., & Wheeler, J. J. (2014). Intrusiveness of behavioral treatments for children with Autism and developmental disabilities: An initial investigation. *Education and Training in Autism and Developmental Disabilities*, *49*, 92–101.

Miller, M. J., Lane, K. L., & Wehby, J. (2005). Social skills instruction with high-incidence disabilities: A school-based intervention to address acquisition deficits. *Preventing School Failure*, *49*(2), 27–39.

Ness, B. M., Sohlberg, M. M., & Albin, R. W. (2011). Evaluation of a second-tier classroom-based assignment completion strategy for middle school students in a resource context. *Remedial and Special Education*, *32*, 406–416. doi: 10.1177/0741932510362493

Regan, K. S., & Michaud, K. M. (2011). Best practices to support student behavior. *Beyond Behavior*, *20*(2), 40–47.

Sabornie, E. J., & deBettencourt, L. U. (2009). *Teaching students with mild and high-incidence disabilities at the secondary level* (3rd ed.). Upper Saddle River, NJ: Pearson.

Sabornie, E. J., Evans, C., & Cullinan, D. (2006). Comparing characteristics of high-incidence disability groups: A descriptive review. *Remedial and Special Education*, *27*, 95–104.

Spriggs, A. D., Gast, D. L., & Ayres, K. M. (2007). Using picture activity schedule books to increase on-schedule and on-task behaviors. *Education and Training in Developmental Disabilities*, *42*, 209–233.

Stahr, B., Cushing, D., Lane, K. & Fox, J. (2006). Efficacy of a function-based intervention in decreasing off-task behavior exhibited by a student with ADHD. *Journal of Positive Behavior Interventions, 8,* 201–211. doi: 10.1177/10983007060080040301

Tapp, J. T., Wehby, J. H., & Ellis, D. M. (1995). A multiple option observation system for experimental studies: MOOSES. *Behavior Research Methods Instruments and Computers, 27,* 25–31.

Terenzi, C. M., Ervin, R. A., & Hoff, K. E. (2010). Classwide self-management of rule following: Effect on the on-task and disruptive behaviors of three students with specific learning disabilities and attention deficit/hyperactivity disorder. *Journal of Evidence-Based Practices for Schools, 11*(2), 87–116.

U.S. Department of Education. (2012). Office of Special Education Programs, Data Analysis System (DANS), OMB #1820–0517 (2012). Part B, Individuals with Disabilities Education Act, Implementation of FAPE Requirements. Percent of all students ages 6 through 21 served under IDEA, Part B, by educational environment and state. Fall 2011. Updated July 15, 2012. Retrieved from www.ideadata.org/arc_toc13.asp#partbLRE

Vannest, K. J., & Hagan-Burke, S. (2010). Teacher time use in special education. *Remedial and Special Education, 31,* 126–142. doi: 10.1177/0741932508327459

Vannest, K. J., Hagan-Burke, S., Parker, R. I., & Soares, D. A. (2011). Special education teacher time use in four types of programs. *The Journal of Educational Research, 104,* 219–230. doi: 10.1080/00220671003709898

Williamson, B. D., Campbell-Whatley, G. D., & Lo, Y. (2009). Using a random dependent group contingency to increase on-task behaviors of high school students with high-incidence disabilities. *Psychology in the Schools, 46,* 1074–1083. doi: 10.1002/pits.20445

11

CLASSROOM MANAGEMENT FOR INCLUSIVE SETTINGS

KATHLEEN LYNNE LANE
UNIVERSITY OF KANSAS

HOLLY MARIAH MENZIES
CALIFORNIA STATE UNIVERSITY, LOS ANGELES

As discussed in other chapters in this *Handbook*, classroom management is complex and nuanced, requiring an understanding of multiple perspectives as well as of varied bodies of knowledge. This is particularly true when considering classroom management from the perspective of inclusive settings. Without a safe and orderly learning environment, it is difficult for teachers and students to attend to the business of teaching and learning. Yet, in a survey from the National Center for Educational Statistics (2008), nearly 40% of responding teachers indicated that student misbehavior interfered with their teaching.

This is highly unfortunate given that teachers are under enormous pressure to achieve academic excellence with the use of evidenced-based practices (No Child Left Behind Act, 2001; Tankersley & Cook, 2013), while supporting a wide range of students who vary tremendously in their academic, behavioral, and social competencies (Lane, Oakes, & Menzies, 2010). Although many students come to school with the requisite skills and are able to meet teachers' expectations by engaging in behaviors that optimize instruction (e.g., cooperating with peers, following teachers' instructions, and calmly making their needs known), others are less prepared. Some students lack the necessary skills to be successful in school and actually exhibit behaviors that impede the instructional process (e.g., limited self-determined behaviors, noncompliance, and splintered academic skills; Davis & McLaughlin, 2013; Walker, Ramsey, & Gresham, 2004) and reflect what some refer to as the growing problem of incivility in America (Shandwick & Tate, 2012).

Some educators might contend that students with challenging behaviors such as emotional or behavioral disorders (EBD)—which include internalizing (e.g., excessive

205

shyness, somatic complaints) or externalizing (e.g., aggressive, noncompliant) behaviors—are more appropriately served in special education. However, the reality is less than 1% of school-age students will go on to receive special education services for emotional disturbances (ED) under the Individuals with Disabilities Education Improvement Act (IDEA, 2004). Given that prevalence estimates indicate approximately 12% of school-age students have moderate to severe EBD (Forness, Freeman, Paparella, Kauffman, & Walker, 2012), the vast majority of students will be supported by the general education community. Coupling this expectation with the goal of inclusive programming for all students, including those with special needs such as emotional disturbance, it is essential to empower general education teachers with effective classroom management skills to meet students' multiple needs (Burstein, Sears, Wilcoxen, Cabello, & Spagna, 2004; Lane, Menzies, Bruhn, & Crnobori, 2011). Furthermore, teachers must be supported in recognizing the transactional relation between behavior and academic performance: How teachers instruct influences how students behave, and how students behave influences how teachers instruct (Hinshaw, 1992).

Most schools are shifting to instructive and proactive behavior management where time is taken to establish and teach expectations, as well as to provide support to students who have difficulty meeting them. A number of researchers are promoting reform efforts that focus on the entire school (Desimone, 2002; Waldron & Mcleskey, 2010), rather than singling out a specific population within the school or emphasizing a particular strategy. There are a range of multitiered systems of support to address this charge: response to intervention (RTI) models, focusing mainly on academic domains (Fuchs & Fuchs, 2006); positive behavior interventions and supports (PBIS), focusing mainly on behavioral domains (Sugai & Horner, 2006; see Chapter 22 of this volume); and comprehensive, integrated, three-tiered (CI3T) models (Lane, Oakes, & Menzies, 2010; Sugai & Horner, 2009), integrating academic, behavior, and social domains. These data-informed models include three levels of prevention: primary support (Tier 1, for all students), secondary support (Tier 2, for some students), and tertiary support (Tier 3, for a few students). Academic and behavior screening data are used to determine which students may benefit from supports beyond primary prevention efforts (see Chapter 23 of this volume).

These models hold particular benefit for inclusive classrooms because they capitalize on a coordinated, shared system focusing on collaborative efforts between general and special education teachers to support all students by (1) preventing learning and behavior problems from occurring and (2) responding effectively to existing concerns in a timely manner, with evidence-based strategies and practices at each level of prevention (Lane, Menzies, Oakes, & Kalberg, 2012). However, in comprehensive models, an essential task is to carefully examine the classroom or school context to determine whether a support should be student centered (addressed either in a small group or individually for a particular student) or the teacher can adjust an aspect of the environment instead. For example, if behavior screening data suggest 20–30% of students are exhibiting moderate behavioral challenges, it may be more efficient to fine-tune teacher strategies (instructionally and otherwise) to increase the percentage of students performing at optimal levels behaviorally and academically (Lane, Menzies, Ennis, & Bezdek, 2013). In this case, a teacher might consider shifting to higher rates of reinforcement to increase on-task behavior for everyone in the class rather than developing a self-monitoring intervention for students with high rates of off-task behavior. Similarly, classroom management routines and expectations could be revisited to be sure they are adequately addressing overall behavioral concerns. Antecedent-based strategies (those that anticipate and avoid behavior problems) will reduce the overall number of consequence-based interventions (those implemented in response to problems that do occur) that teachers will have to manage. Antecedent-based strategies facilitating engagement and instruction (Lane, Menzies, Bruhn, & Crnobori, 2011) should be well integrated into a teacher's everyday practice. Efficiently decreasing relatively low-level behavioral issues caused by boredom, peer influence, academic difficulties, and misunderstanding of expectations saves teacher time by reserving more intensive interventions for behaviors that must be managed individually (Long, 2013).

PURPOSE

In this chapter, we focus on instructional considerations and low-intensity behavioral supports to build teachers' capacity to provide high-quality inclusive experiences for all learners. In terms of instruction, we emphasize lesson planning that addresses a student's zone of proximal development (Vgotsky, 1978) as well as differentiating content, process, and product (Tomlinson, 2005) to maximize student engagement and minimize the likelihood that problem behaviors will occur. In terms of behavioral supports, we focus on three research-based strategies: incorporating choice (Kern, Mantegna, Vorndran, Bailin, & Hilt, 2001), increasing opportunities to respond (Conroy, Sutherland, Snyder, & Marsh, 2008), and proving appropriate reinforcement (Cooper, Heron, & Heward, 2007). We define each low-intensity behavioral support and provide evidence of the effectiveness of these strategies for students with or at risk for learning and behavior challenges. We conclude with a brief summary and discussion of the educational implications of antecedent-based strategies to facilitate engagement and instruction.

INSTRUCTIONAL CONSIDERATIONS

An implicit and essential part of implementing primary prevention efforts in multitiered models is strong, proactive classroom management. While a school-wide effort provides cohesion, efficiency, and standardizes effective practices across the school, teachers individually contribute to this overall effect by establishing warm classroom climates focused on learning. Teachers who are skillful instructors make academic work engaging and create a classroom community that values learning and mutual respect. Collectively, these classrooms are the foundation for multitiered systems of support. The entire system rests on the aggregate performance of accomplished teachers whose effects are then amplified when part of a school-wide system.

Many factors contribute to classroom climate, which is the overall feel or tone a teacher establishes, including physical arrangement of a classroom, the way a teacher interacts with students, how instruction is offered, and values implicitly and explicitly demonstrated by both teacher and students throughout the school day (Evertson & Weinstein, 2006). Although all are important, we focus this first section on instructional techniques that emphasize scaffolded support and differentiation. These ensure that students are working at the appropriate level of challenge while avoiding frustration.

Appropriate and Supported Instruction

While a teacher's goal is to have students meet or exceed grade-level standards, this does not mean all content in a classroom should be introduced at the same level of difficulty. It is rare a teacher has a class of students who are equally adept at every skill, and if instruction were to proceed as if they are, little learning would occur. If tasks are too difficult, many students (especially those with behavior issues) may react negatively by acting out or shutting down to escape the too-difficult task. Students who consistently view the academic work as too hard will often go to great lengths to distract their classmates (externalizing behavior patterns) or quietly withdraw from the learning experiences or say they do not feel well (internalizing behavior patterns) to keep their teacher from noticing their lack of ability. However, teachers can avoid situations like these by choosing tasks that are slightly above the learner's competence level but that can be done with the assistance of the teacher or a more skilled peer. This is called the zone of proximal development (ZPD) (Vygotsky, 1978). Working in a student's ZPD is equally important for students whose skills are advanced. If the work they encounter is always too easy, students will be bored and uninspired without the optimal level of challenge (Umbreit, Lane, & Dejud, 2004). In addition to ensuring the academic task is neither too difficult nor too easy, the teacher must think about how to scaffold the lesson so there is enough support to reduce frustration. It should be structured so the student can successfully complete the steps while learning the task. Once the steps are mastered, the student can leave the "scaffold" behind when it is no longer required.

For example, a teacher may want students to create a written summary for a section of expository text. Students can already identify the main idea and supporting details, so the task is novel but not too hard. The teacher would initially model how to create a written summary by organizing the main ideas and supporting details in a logical and brief sequence in a "think-aloud" (orally narrating how she is thinking about the steps of the task as she completes them). After modeling, students would be closely guided through the assignment. The teacher would provide a graphic organizer linked to a specific section of text that already included some of the required elements in a predetermined order. After having students read the section, the class and teacher would work together to complete the organizer and generate a written summary from it. Then students would be given another portion of text and work in pairs to complete a new organizer that required them to generate all the necessary elements themselves. When completed, the teacher would have students check their work against a teacher-created model and note the elements they had missed. Finally, each student would write a summary paragraph using their organizer. The student pairs could read their completed paragraphs to one another. This lesson (taught over several days) would not yet be over. The teacher would provide many opportunities to summarize expository text. Students would use their graphic organizers as long as they needed them, but eventually most would be able to abandon the use of this tool because they will have learned and routinized the task. In this scenario, the teacher has chosen a task of appropriate difficulty based on what students already know how to do and created a lesson that included integral scaffolding to support students until they mastered the skill. When instructional tasks are carefully planned so that they are in a student's ZPD and offer adequate support, students will have an opportunity to be more fully engaged and less likely to exhibit escape-motivated behaviors that manifest in either externalizing or internalizing facets of EBD.

Differentiation

Another technique for promoting student engagement is to differentiate instruction. Tomlinson's (2001; Tomlinson & McTighe, 2006) work on differentiation is a useful guide for thinking about how to offer instruction that specifically targets students' interests and skill level and is still manageable when working with large groups of students. Differentiation acknowledges students' varying abilities and provides the teacher with structures for addressing those differences. Tomlinson suggests thinking about the curriculum along three dimensions—content, process, and product—to provide students with multiple approaches to the information they are expected to learn. She also emphasizes the importance of providing support for challenging work, establishing a community of learners where taking risks is respected, and offering activities in a variety of formats including whole-class, small-group, and individually. Even though it is impossible to do justice to Tomlinson's work in the available pages, we offer a brief overview of differentiating along content, process, and product. Another way to think of these elements is (1) what you teach, (2) how you teach it, and (3) what students create to further learn the concepts or to demonstrate their understanding.

Teachers must make many decisions when it comes to content. Often, there is not enough time in a school year to explicitly teach all the content specified for a particular grade level. While a school's curriculum is prescribed by state or district (e.g. adoption of the Common Core Standards), it is the teacher's responsibility to decide which aspects of the curriculum, or content, to emphasize and what level of mastery a student must hold for a particular skill or area of knowledge. For example, when a fifth-grade student is given a writing assignment, many standards could be addressed, but depending on a student's skill level in mechanics, grammar, or rhetorical effectiveness, the teacher may ask the student to pay particular attention to one or two areas of the writing task. He or she may choose one skill the student should demonstrate with near perfect performance and another on which to show progress. Alternately, the student could choose a writing focus of interest, either to explore or to practice. Tomlinson (2001) also suggests techniques such as curriculum compacting, concept-based teaching, and learning contracts, among others, as strategies for content differentiation.

Process is what Tomlinson refers to as a "sense-making activity" (2001, p. 79) or an opportunity for students to work with the new material until they understand it. The differentiation occurs when the teacher offers more than one way to encounter or make meaning of the information. For example, a third-grade class might be identifying geographical features in their local region. After a whole-class lesson on the topic, the teacher offers students the choice of three projects for learning more about the local geography. One activity could be completing a graphic organizer that lists various geographic features. The student does online research using preselected websites to find out which features occur locally and provides a written description of them. Another activity covering the same information would have students examine various maps to make a list of local features. Tomlinson (2005) lists many strategies for differentiating process, including journals, learning centers, literature circles, collaborative grouping (e.g., Jigsaw), and role-playing. In addition to capitalizing on students' interest and skill, offering multiple avenues for engaging with material promotes the use of student choice, which itself is intrinsically motivating.

Teachers are familiar with using products as a way for students to reinforce concepts and as a culminating activity. Whereas sense-making activities are short and highlight only a few concepts or skills, products are more substantial endeavors that require students to engage substantively with content they have spent an extended time learning. Allowing students to prepare different types of products in response to learning is key. This is how learning is individualized for a particular student's skill or interests. It is not to say that every single student must do something different but that a variety of choices are offered—which also serves as a behavioral support (choice making), as discussed later in this chapter. Teachers will want to determine the basic requirements of what the product must demonstrate and set the criteria for quality work. Students may require a certain amount of scaffolding to plan for and create a product, so they should not simply be assigned a product and left to their own devices. Products can range from constructing simple models to giving a live performance depending on the grade, student, and knowledge to be demonstrated.

At first look, one may not consider instructional concerns such as ZPD, scaffolding, and differentiation to be behavior management techniques. However, the quality of instruction is an integral aspect of creating an environment that fosters positive student work habits. When students are engaged and feel successful, they have fewer opportunities and less desire to misbehave. This is especially true for students whose school experience has been less than successful.

LOW-INTENSITY BEHAVIOR SUPPORTS

Low-intensity behavioral supports are critical hallmarks of classrooms that take a proactive and instructive approach to classroom management rather than a punitive or reactive one. How a teacher handles each of these areas is critical to both classroom climate and, subsequently, effective classroom management. When students are actively engaged in learning, feel supported, and are reminded in respectful ways to make good behavior choices, teachers will encounter fewer behavioral issues. By focusing on antecedent-based interventions, teachers can prevent many behavioral challenges from occurring in the first place, and effective instructional and behavioral strategies are an integral part of good classroom management (Simonsen, Myers, & DeLuca, 2010). In this section, we introduce three effective, feasible, low-intensity behavior supports: incorporating choice, increasing opportunities to respond, and providing appropriate reinforcement. Studies demonstrating the effectiveness of these techniques are also briefly discussed.

Choice

As noted previously, creating opportunities for students to have choices in their instructional experiences (e.g., how they demonstrate what they have learned, Tomlinson, 2001) can be a relatively simple yet highly effective behavioral support. Interventions examining the incorporation of "choice" into instruction demonstrate an increase in students' academic engagement and a decrease in undesirable behaviors (e.g., for disruption, Dunlap, Foster-Johnson, Clarke, Kern, & Childs, 1995; Kern, Delaney, Clarke, Dunlap, & Childs, 2001; Kern & Manz, 2004).

Choice making does not mean students have the option of *not* working. Instead, it provides the opportunity to choose between two or more activities (or the order in which activities will be completed) that will produce the same (or similar) learning outcomes. Choice can be easily incorporated throughout various academic tasks. For example, choice might involve the option of starter activities (e.g., writing a three- to four-sentence paragraph about what they learned or two or three unanswered questions from yesterday's lecture); which book to read for a term paper on transcendentalism (e.g., *Moby Dick* or *Walden*); the order in which a student completes daily tasks for a given instructional block (e.g., lab, workbook problems, and daily journal); the creation of a presentation, YouTube video, or written report to demonstrate how to give instructions in a foreign language; or even whether to complete the evens or odds on a math homework assignment. Incorporating choice is intrinsically motivating to students and develops their sense of autonomy. Choice also communicates that a teacher respects students' preferences and interests (Tomlinson, 2005).

Choice making has been studied since the mid-1990s, offering ample evidence to suggest it is associated with increases in academic engagement, decreases in behavior problems, and—in some instances—improvements in students' learning. For example, Dunlap and colleagues (1995) conducted a study exploring the impact of choice with eight students with EBD. In this study, choice was introduced by allowing students to select six of eight assignments to complete. Results demonstrated a functional relation between the introduction of choices and decreases in the level of disruptive behavior. Similarly, Cosden, Gannon, and Haring (1995) conducted a study in which students were given a list of 10 potential activities, such as work problems, writing assignments, and answering science questions, and were offered the opportunity to choose which assignments they would like to complete. Results indicated student work was more accurate in the choice condition as compared to rates of accuracy in the no-choice condition. Kern and colleagues (2001) demonstrated that simply offering students the opportunity to select which assignment to complete *first* in a series of tasks was effective as evidenced by increased engagement and decreased problem behaviors. It is important to note that students did not escape any assignments—they had to complete all tasks assigned—but had control over the order in which they could complete them. Collectively, the evidence suggests choice-making strategies—many of which require very low investments in terms of teacher time and resources—can be implemented with a high degree of accuracy (with integrity) and yield the desired changes in student performance.

Opportunities to Respond

Increasing opportunities to respond (OTR) is a technique initially studied within the context of special education; yet it can be used in general education classrooms to increase the participation of all students. As is evident from the term, OTR promotes response modes enabling students multiple opportunities to answer questions and receive rapid corrective feedback (Greenwood, Delquadri, & Hall, 1984). The more opportunities students have to successfully participate in class activities, engage in discussions, and respond accurately to teacher-initiated questions, the more they will be academically engaged. When a student is answering questions and responding to instruction, such behaviors are incompatible with off-task and disruptive behavior.

Too often classrooms are characterized by very low rates of opportunities to respond. For example, teachers frequently check for understanding or conduct discussions by asking a single student to respond (e.g., "Katie, what were three contributing factors to the Civil War?"; Armendariz & Umbreit, 1999). This approach can be improved by including the students' name at the end of the question because doing so is more likely to capture all students' attention until they know for certain who will be asked to respond (e.g., "What were three contributing factors to the Civil War . . . Katie?"). While this strategy of calling on one student at a time is appropriate in some contexts, it restricts active participation for the class as a whole because only a few students can be called on during a typical instructional block. If only a few students are participating, it provides ample opportunity for other students (particularly those who struggle behaviorally and/or academically) to engage in tasks not related to the instructional objective. Increasing OTRs enhances academic and behavioral performance because it facilitates active participation, which is incompatible with either active or passive off-task behaviors.

Teachers using OTR as a behavioral support should target high rates of accurate participation: (1) 4–6 responses per minute with 80% accuracy when introducing new content and (2) 8–12 responses per minute at 90% accuracy when practicing skills acquired to build fluency (Sutherland & Wehby, 2001). This can occur in a number of ways, such as gestures (e.g., thumbs-up, -down, or sideways for yes, no, or not sure, respectively), displaying a visual cue (e.g., stacking one of three cups on top: green for "I agree" or "I understand"; yellow for "I am unsure" or "I am unclear but can continue working while I wait for clarification"; or red for "I disagree" or "I have no idea, and I need help right now"), choral responding, response cards, mini whiteboards, or digital response systems where students use "clickers" to have their responses instantly recorded and displayed on the classroom whiteboard. Specifically, OTRs involve the following steps: (1) use a repeated prompt to cue answers (e.g., verbal and/or visual as suggested previously); (2) include information that directs students to the correct response (e.g., "There were three key causes of the Civil War x, y, and z. . . . What were the three key causes of the Civil War?"); (3) incorporate modifications to support students at different levels of performance; (4) allow for sufficient wait time using the teacher-selected system (e.g., response cards); and (5) provide appropriate feedback (e.g., corrective feedback) to ensure students are accurate in their responses (Conroy, Sutherland, Snyder, & Marsh, 2008).

OTR is a quick-paced, feedback-rich instructional technique affording students an opportunity to be both highly engaged and highly accurate in their participation (Lane, Oakes, Menzies, & Germer, 2014). By experiencing high rates of success, students are less likely to be anxious about answering a question incorrectly and suffering the embarrassment of being "wrong" in front of their peers. In turn, students will have less need to escape tasks that previously felt beyond their skill sets. Too often students "act out" to "get out" of tasks that are either too difficult (and in some cases, too simple) (Umbreit, Lane, & Dejud, 2004).

During the past decade, several studies have demonstrated the effectiveness of using OTR to increase accurate responding and decrease disruptive behavior for a variety of students in a range of settings, particularly for students with EBD (Sutherland & Wehby, 2001). For example, Sutherland, Alder, and Gunter (2003) conducted a study using OTRs with eight students with EBD. Results showed an increase in the percentage of time on task from 55 to 79%. As expected, students also demonstrated an increase in the number of correct responses and a decrease in disruptive behavior. Christle and Schuster (2003) conducted a study exploring use of OTRs in a fourth-grade general education math class. When the teacher shifted from a hand-raising to a response card procedure, students demonstrated an increase in participation as well as improved performance on weekly math quizzes. The response card approach employed by Christle and Schuster (2003) was equally successful for students with highly challenging behavior problems. Haydon, Mancil, and Van Loan (2009) also demonstrated similar outcomes in a general education science class. When the teachers increased OTRs via choral responding, a female student exhibited less disruptive behavior and increased the number of questions answered correctly. Just recently, Haydon, Conroy, Scott, Sindelar, Barber, and Orlando (2010) examined the impact of three types of OTRs (individual, choral, and mixed responding) on syllable and sight word practice with six second-grade students at risk for EBD identified according to the Systematic Screening for Behavior Disorders (SSBD) (Walker & Severson, 1992). Results indicated mixed responding appeared to be a more effective strategy for five of the six students in decreasing disruptive behavior than either choral or individual responding in isolation. Also, results suggested choral responding was more effective than individual responding for five out of six students in decreasing disruption as well as off-task behavior. Findings from these studies support the utility and feasibility of using OTR procedures to support students' accurate and active participation.

Reinforcement

The last behavioral support we address is reinforcement. Over the course of any given instructional day, teachers spend a great deal of time interacting with students and giving feedback on performance (Lane, Oakes, Menzies, & Germer, 2014). In considering the nature of these interactions and feedback, it is important to recognize that all behavior is maintained by the consequences that follow it (Cooper, Heron, & Heward, 2007). From a behavioral perspective, students engage in any behavior—desired (e.g., working on an assigned task) or undesired (e.g., arguing with a teacher)—to access or avoid attention, tasks or tangibles, or sensory stimuli (Umbreit, Ferro, Liaupsin, & Lane, 2007). In essence, behavior serves a communicative purpose, meaning it is occurring for a reason—to tell the teacher something, with the function being either positive reinforcement (e.g., accessing teacher attention) or negative reinforcement (e.g., avoiding too difficult or too easy tasks) (Umbreit, Ferro, Liaupsin, & Lane, 2007). If the goal is to increase engagement, work production, and other similar academic objectives, it must be clear what maintains maladaptive behaviors, such as disruptive and coercive acts, and competes with desired behaviors.

In some instances, teachers unintentionally reinforce undesirable behavior. For example, a student who frequently complains his or her stomach hurts (which it actually does, due to anxiety) before transitioning to physical education (PE) is communicating that he or she does not want to participate in PE. If the teacher continually allows the student to go to the nurse's office and skip PE, the teacher is unintentionally reinforcing escape-motivated behavior. In essence, the teacher is using the principle of negative reinforcement in which the task demands or experience of participating in PE is avoided by becoming ill. If this pattern of behavior suggests an increase in the instances or rate of a student's becoming ill in the future (increasing the future probability of the target behavior—becoming ill), then we are certain the behavior is being maintained by negative reinforcement.

Similar instances also happen with respect to positive reinforcement when teachers unintentionally reinforce behaviors they do not want to occur in their classroom, such as talking out of turn (e.g., without hand raising). For example, consider a classroom in which a teacher has taught a routine for students to raise their hands and wait to be called upon by the teacher before responding. If the teacher acknowledges students who violate this routine by shouting out answers (e.g., "Jack, that is correct; there are five kingdoms of living things.") rather than students who follow the routine (e.g., Sally, who is raising her hand and waiting quietly, but is not called on), they are positively reinforcing shouting out by demonstrating to Jack and Sally, as well as to the other students in the class, that shouting out is the quickest way to secure the teacher's attention. If the intent is to increase desired behaviors and decrease undesired behaviors, teachers must be cognizant of (1) behavioral functions and (2) how they apply principles of positive and negative reinforcement in their classroom (intentionally and otherwise).

One very effective strategy teachers can employ to increase the likelihood of desired behaviors (e.g., working on an assignment, turning work in on time, using positive language in cooperative learning groups) is behavior-specific praise (BSP). BSP can be used to maximize feedback and capitalize on opportunities to increase the future probability of desired behaviors occurring. Instead of making general statements (e.g., "Good job!" or "Nice work!"), which do not make it clear to a student what is being reinforced. BSP involves teachers providing a praise statement directly linked to the behavior it describes, such as "Thank you for making those revisions on your essay. I appreciate your time and effort!" or "Thank you for being in class on time." When delivering BSP, make certain to praise effort (something the students can control, "Katie, I appreciate all the time you put into your clay tile art project—it really turned out nicely!") rather than ability (something students cannot control, "Katie, you are such a talented artist!"). In other words, reinforce malleable behaviors—those that can be altered.

Several studies that have been conducted over almost 30 years demonstrate the feasibility and effectiveness of using behavior-specific praise in school-based settings. Although it is beyond the scope of this chapter to discuss all applications, it has been used to increase compliance to teacher instructions, increase academic engaged time, increase work completion, and decrease disruptive behavior (Craft, Alber, & Heward, 1998; Goetz, Holmberg, & LeBlanc, 1975; Musti-Rao & Haydon, 2011; Sutherland, 2000; Sutherland, Wehby, & Copeland, 2000). Musti-Rao and Haydon (2011) recently published an article offering eight tips for increasing the use of BSP in inclusive contexts. They emphasize collecting frequency data (counting the number of BSP statements in a given period of time) to determine how often a teacher is currently using BSP. These baseline data can be used to set a goal and serve as a comparison metric. They also suggest focusing on either a specific student or identifying a certain behavior (e.g., polite comments to peers or on-time arrival to school) to help teachers remember to use BSP. Teachers might also consider a prompting device such as the MotivAider app or a timer on their cell phone that would vibrate on a fixed or variable interval (e.g., every 3 minutes) to cue the teacher to deliver BSP.

Another benefit of this brief and relatively simple strategy is that it contributes to a positive learning environment. Rather than relying on reprimands (e.g., "Stop talking and get back to work."), this strategy assists teachers in focusing on the positive and yet requires little planning or preparation to implement with integrity.

SUMMARY

In reflecting on how to support an increasingly diverse group of students in inclusive environments, we are encouraged to see many schools and districts embracing multitiered systems of support. Graduated systems of support such as RTI, PBIS, and CI3T models of prevention hold promise for all students, including those with externalizing and internalizing facets of EBD as they promote focused collaboration between general and special education communities. The success of these models is premised on teachers' strong classroom management skills and ability to use antecedent-based strategies to provide engaging and effective instruction (Lane, Menzies, Ennis, & Bezdek, 2013). Although a common practice in multitiered systems of support is to analyze academic and behavior screening data to determine which students need supports beyond primary prevention efforts, we contend it may be more efficient and effective to begin with teacher-focused supports—instructionally and behaviorally (Lane, Menzies, Ennis, & Bezdek, 2013). Specifically, we encourage teachers to offer instructional experiences within students' zone of proximal development (Vgotsky, 1978), provide instructional scaffolding, and differentiate along the dimensions of content, process, and product (Tomlinson, 2005). These techniques maximize student engagement and minimize the likelihood that problem behaviors will occur in inclusive environments. We also suggest the use of low-intensity behavioral supports, such as incorporating choice, increasing opportunities to respond, and careful reinforcement of desired behavior to build teachers' capacity and confidence in preventing behavioral challenges from occurring.

We conclude by offering the following suggestions to support implementation within the context of multitiered systems of support (Lane, Menzies, Ennis, Oakes, & Kalberg, 2012; Lane, Oakes, Menzies, & Germer, 2014). First, we encourage school sites to begin with a self-assessment for all faculty and staff who provide instruction to students to determine areas of strength as well as areas in need of improvement (e.g., see self-assessment surveys in Lane, Menzies, Bruhn, & Crnobori, 2011). It is important to determine the extent to which teachers are knowledgeable and confident in instructional and behavioral strategies and concepts. By mapping a staff's professional development needs, school site and district-level leadership teams can make data-informed decisions about how to allocate professional development resources.

Second, we also encourage leadership teams to capitalize on their teachers' strengths. For example, if a teacher indicates she is knowledgeable about OTRs but lacks the confidence to implement this strategy in her classroom, she could be paired with a teacher-partner at the school site who is knowledgeable about the strategy, confident about implementing it, and is currently using the technique. This teacher can model the technique and provide on-site coaching and support for the teacher interested in making this behavioral support part of her repertoire. Ideally, each teacher could be a "coach" for one or more strategies or concepts and a "learner" of others. When assigning the role of coach, we encourage leadership teams to choose two partner coaches for each strategy or concept. For example, two teachers might be the coaches for differentiating products, while another pair of teachers assists with BSP, and so on. In this way, we build school site capacity, recognize the talent at the school site, and protect against attrition (e.g., when teachers are out on leave or retire) (Lane, Menzies, Bruhn, & Crnobori, 2011). Yet this requires time for professional development activities. These activities should be built into the academic calendar and academic day to avoid adding to teachers' already very demanding set of responsibilities.

Third, we recognize that many other instructional and behavioral supports can be used in inclusive instruction to enhance strong classroom management and to promote academic engaged time (e.g., behavior contracts) (Downing, 2002). When considering other supports, we recommend selecting those with sufficient evidence to warrant adoption (Tankersley & Cook, 2013). Teachers' energy and instructional time are simply too valuable to invest in strategies and practices with insufficient evidence to indicate that the desired outcomes will be achieved (e.g., increased rate of academic engagement, increased academic performance, and decreased levels of disruption). Practice guides published by the U.S. Department of Education Institute of Education Sciences (IES, n.d.) are good resources when reviewing potential strategies and practices.

We respectfully offer the instructional and behavioral strategies reviewed in this chapter as research-based options for meeting students' multiple academic, behavioral, and social needs in inclusive classrooms. By beginning with these antecedent-based strategies, we may prevent the need for more resource-intensive, student-focused Tier 2 and 3 supports for students requiring assistance beyond Tier 1 efforts. We continue to be impressed by the tremendous talent in many school sites and encourage the use of these and other strategies to optimize student learning.

REFERENCES

Armendariz, F., & Umbreit, J. (1999). Using active responding to reduce disruptive behavior in a general education classroom. *Journal of Positive Behavior Interventions, 1*, 152–158.

Burstein, N. N., Sears, S. S., Wilcoxen, A. A., Cabello, B. B., & Spagna, M. M. (2004). Moving toward inclusive practices. *Remedial and Special Education, 25*(2), 104–116.

Christle, C. A., & Schuster, J. W. (2003). The effects of using response cards on student participation, academic achievement, and on-task behavior during whole-class, math instruction. *Journal of Behavioral Education, 12*, 147–165.

Conroy, M. A., Sutherland, K. S., Snyder, A. L., & Marsh, S. (2008). Classwide interventions: Effective instruction makes a difference. *Teaching Exceptional Children, 40*(6), 24–30.

Cooper, J. O., Heron, T. E., & Heward, W. L. (2007). *Applied Behavior Analysis.* Upper Saddle River, NJ: Pearson Education.

Cosden, M., Gannon, C., & Haring, T. G. (1995). Teacher-control versus student-control over choice of task and reinforcement for students with severe behavior problems. *Journal of Behavioral Education, 5*, 11–27.

Craft, M. A., Alber, S. R., & Heward, W. L. (1998). Teaching elementary students with developmental disabilities to recruit teacher attention in a general education classroom: Effects of teacher praise and academic productivity. *Journal of Applied Behavior Analysis, 31*, 399–415.

Davis, C. A., & McLaughlin, A. (2013). Strategies to improve compliance. In K. L. Lane, B. G. Cook, & M. G. Tankersley (Eds.), *Research-based strategies for improving outcomes in behavior* (pp. 46–58). New York: Pearson.

Desimone, L. (2002). How can comprehensive school reform models be successfully implemented. *Review of Educational Research, 72*(3), 433–479.

Downing, J. A. (2002). Individualized behavior contracts. *Intervention in School and Clinic, 37*, 168–172.

Dunlap, G., Foster-Johnson, L., Clarke, S., Kern, L., & Childs, K. (1995). Modifying activities to produce functional outcomes: Effects on the problem behaviors of students with disabilities. *Journal of the Association for Persons with Severe Handicaps, 20,* 248–258.

Evertson, C. M., & Weinstein, C. S. (2006). *Handbook of classroom management: Research, practice, and contemporary issues.* Mahwah, NJ: Erlbaum.

Forness, S. R., Freeman, S. F. N., Paparella, T., Kauffman, J. M., & Walker, H. M. (2012). Special education implications of point and cumulative prevalence for children with emotional or behavioral disorders. *Journal of Emotional and Behavioral Disorders, 20,* 4–18.

Fuchs, D., & Fuchs, L. (2006). Introduction to response to intervention: What, why, and how valid is it? *Reading Research Quarterly, 41,* 93–99.

Goetz, E. M., Holmberg, M. C., & LeBlanc, J. M. (1975). Differential reinforcement of other behavior and noncontingent reinforcement as control procedures during the modification of a preschooler's compliance. *Journal of Applied Behavior Analysis, 8,* 77–82.

Greenwood, C. R., Delquadri, J., & Hall, R. V. (1984). *Opportunity to respond and student academic performance*. Kansas City: University of Kansas, Juniper Gardens Children's Project.

Haydon, T., Conroy, M. A., Sindelar, P. T., Scott, T. M., Barber, B., & Orlando, A.M. (2010). A comparison of three types of opportunities to respond on student academic and social behaviors. *Journal of Emotional and Behavioral Disorders, 18*, 27–40.

Haydon, T., Mancil, G., & Van Loan, C. (2009). Using opportunities to respond in a general education classroom: A case study. *Education and Treatment of Children, 32*, 267–278.

Hinshaw, S. P. (1992). Externalizing behavior problems and academic underachievement in childhood and adolescence: Causal relationships and underlying mechanisms. *Psychological Bulletin, 111*, 127–155.

Individuals with Disabilities Education Improvement Act of 2004, 20 U.S.C. 1400 *et seq.* (2004) (reauthorization of Individuals with Disabilities Act 1990).

Kern, L., Delaney, B., Clarke, S., Dunlap, G., & Childs, K. (2001). Improving the classroom behavior of students with emotional and behavioral disorders using individualized curricular modifications. *Journal of Emotional and Behavioral Disorders, 9*, 239–247.

Kern, L., Mantegna, M. E., Vorndran, C. M., Bailin, D., & Hilt, A. (2001). Choice of task sequence to reduce problem behaviors. *Journal of Positive Interventions, 3*, 3–10.

Kern, L., & Manz, P. (2004). A look at current validity issues of school-wide behavior support. *Behavioral Disorders, 30*, 47–59.

Lane, K. L., Menzies, H., Bruhn, A., & Crnobori, M. (2011). *Managing challenging behaviors in schools: Research-based strategies that work*. New York: Guilford.

Lane, K. L., Menzies, H. M., Ennis, R. P., & Bezdek, J. (2013). School-wide systems to promote positive behaviors and facilitate instruction. *Journal of Curriculum and Instruction, 7*, 6–31.

Lane, K. L., Menzies, H. M, Oakes, W. P., & Kalberg, J. R. (2012). *Systematic screenings of behavior to support instruction: From preschool to high school*. New York: Guilford.

Lane, K. L., Oakes, W. P., & Menzies, H. M. (2010). Systematic screenings to prevent the development of learning and behavior problems: Considerations for practitioners, researchers, and policy makers. *Journal of Disabilities Policy Studies, 21*, 160–172.

Lane, K. L., Oakes, W. P., Menzies, H. M., & Germer, K. (2014). Increasing instructional efficacy: A focus on teacher variables. In S. G. Little and A. Akin-Little (Eds.) *Academic assessment and intervention*. (pp. 300–315). New York: Routledge.

Long, R. (2013). Beyond classroom "management": Understanding students with SEBD and building their executive skills. In T. Cole, H. Daniels, & J. Visser (Eds.), *The Routledge international companion to emotional and behavioural difficulties* (pp. 226–236). London: Routledge.

Musti-Rao, S. & Haydon, T. (2011). Strategies to increase behavior-specific teacher praise in an inclusive environment. *Intervention in School and Clinic, 47*, 91–97.

National Center for Education Statistics. (2008). Table 77. Teachers' perceptions about teaching and school conditions, by control and level of school: Selected years, 1993–94 through 2007–08. Retrieved from http://nces.ed.gov/programs/digest/d11/tables/dt11_077.asp.

No Child Left Behind Act, 2001, 20 U.S.C. 70 § 6301 *et seq.*

Shandwick, W. & Tate, P. (2012). *Civility in America 2012*. Washington, DC: KRC Research.

Simonsen, B., Myers, D., & DeLuca, C. (2010). Teaching teachers to use prompts, opportunities to respond, and specific praise. *Teacher Education and Special Education, 33*, 300–318.

Sugai, G., & Horner, R. H. (2006). A promising approach for expanding and sustaining school-wide positive behavior support. School Psychology Review, 35, 245–260.

Sugai, G., & Horner, R.H. (2009). Responsiveness-to-intervention and school-wide positive behavior supports: Integration of multi-tiered system approaches. *Exceptionality, 17*(4), 223–237. doi: 10.1080/09362830903235375

Sutherland, K. S. (2000). Promoting positive interactions between teachers and students with emotional/ behavioral disorders. *Preventing School Failure, 44*, 110–115.

Sutherland, K. S., Alder, N., & Gunter, P. L. (2003). The effect of varying rates of opportunities to respond to academic requests on the classroom behavior of students with EBD. *Journal of Emotional & Behavioral Disorders, 11*, 239–248.

Sutherland, K. S., & Wehby, J. H. (2001). Exploring the relationship between increased opportunities to respond to academic requests and the Academic and behavioral outcomes of students with EBD: A review. *Remedial and Special Education, 22*, 113–121.

Sutherland, K. S., Wehby, J. H., & Copeland, S. R. (2000). Effect of varying rates of behavior-specific praise on the on-task behavior of students with EBD. *Journal of Emotional and Behavior Disorders, 8,* 2–8.

Tankersley, M. & Cook, B. (Eds.). (2013). *Effective practices in special education.* Boston: Pearson.

Tomlinson, C. A. (2001). *How to differentiate instruction in mixed-ability classrooms.* Upper Saddle River, NJ: Pearson Education, Inc.

Tomlinson, C. (2005). *An educator's guide to differentiating instruction.* Boston: Houghton-Mifflin.

Tomlinson, C.A. & McTighe, J. (2006). *Integrating differentiated instruction and understanding by design.* Alexandria, VA: Association for Supervision and Curriculum Development.

Umbreit, J., Ferro, J., Liaupsin, C., & Lane, K. (2007). *Functional behavioral assessment and function-based intervention: An effective, practical approach.* Upper Saddle River, NJ: Prentice-Hall.

Umbreit, J., Lane, K. L., & Dejud, C. (2004). Improving classroom behavior by modifying task difficulty: The effects of increasing the difficulty of too-easy tasks. *Journal of Positive Behavior Interventions, 6,* 13–20.

U.S. Department of Education, Institute for Education Sciences. (n.d.). *What Works Clearinghouse practice guides.* Retrieved from http://ies.ed.gov/ncee/wwc/.

Vygotsky, L. S. (1978). *Mind in society.* Cambridge, MA: Harvard University Press.

Waldron, N. L., & McLeskey, J. (2010). Establishing a collaborative school culture through Comprehensive School Reform. *Journal of Educational & Psychological Consultation, 20*(1), 58–74.

Walker, H. M., Ramsey, E., & Gresham, F. M. (2004). *Antisocial behavior in school: Strategies and best practices* (2nd ed.). Pacific Grove, CA: Brooks/Cole.

Walker, H.M., & Severson, H. (1992). *Systematic screening for behavior disorders: Technical manual.* Longmont, CO: Sopris West.

12

CLASSROOM MANAGEMENT IN MUSIC EDUCATION

JAMES L. BYO
LOUISIANA STATE UNIVERSITY

WENDY L. SIMS
UNIVERSITY OF MISSOURI

On a list of music teaching competencies, classroom management may appear as a single item; however, unlike other items, it is not a monolith. Rather, classroom management is "a multidimensional construct—a constellation of multiple teacher behaviors and attitudes, curricular matters, and student proclivities" (Evertson & Weinstein, 2006, p. 5). Research in areas such as effective teaching and learner motivation, while not labeled "classroom management," has clear classroom management implications. As we explore related areas in this comprehensive summary of research on classroom management in music, we are cognizant of this definition:

> [T]he actions teachers take to create an environment that supports and facilitates both academic and social-emotional learning. In other words, classroom management has two distinct purposes: It not only seeks to establish and sustain an orderly environment so students can engage in meaningful academic learning, it also aims to enhance students' social and moral growth . . . From this perspective, *how* a teacher achieves order is as important as *whether* a teacher achieves order. (Evertson & Weinstein, 2006, p. 4)

In this definition, we see all of 20th-century thinking about classroom management pass before our eyes—literal management according to a one-way, teacher-centered paradigm with learners as passive receptors and post-1950s learners as empowered agents of their own thinking. Behaviorism, a guiding theory in the middle to late 20th century, is now considered at best a part of the story, at worst wrong-headed. In the currently accepted social cognitive theory, the learner, as agent, has the capacity to decide and act with intention, independent of a teacher. Learners as empty vessels and learners with agency perhaps serve as useful endpoints on a continuum that informs music teachers' approaches to classroom management.

This chapter presents an overview of research in classroom management as applied to music teaching and learning. We organize, define, and focus "a scattered array of research and scholarship" (Chapter 1 of this volume) with the intention of providing a useful resource for researchers, teacher educators, school administrators, and school music teachers. We begin by setting the context, presenting classroom management as a teacher competency priority, and defining and describing the music "classroom setting" and the nature of music teaching and learning, with a focus on aspects common to and different from teaching in other disciplines. We then summarize research specific to aspects of classroom management in music education, beginning with a historical perspective emanating from empirical/positivistic methods to more recent postpositivist perspectives regarding learner attributes, including a discussion of how these techniques have informed the discipline. We also discuss a body of research related to the significant management challenges encountered by teachers of music in urban schools. We conclude with implications for educators and researchers.

CHARACTERISTICS OF MUSIC CLASSROOMS

Music classrooms present unique challenges for teachers, compared with other school subjects, because of the specialized nature of music as a field of study. Music classes focus primarily on the production, interpretation, and analysis of sound, as well as on reading and writing using a complex symbol system. Students must simultaneously employ and integrate cognitive, psychomotor, and affective skills in increasingly sophisticated ways as they progress through the school music curriculum. Whole-group, teacher-directed classroom instruction is typical and appropriate at all levels due to the abstract and complex nature of the subject, the involvement of students in group music making, large class sizes, the potential noise level and chaotic environment that asynchronous individual or small group singing or playing in a classroom provide, and the reality that students often don't have the music literacy skills and knowledge to work productively alone or in small groups.

The responsibilities, schedules, and workloads of music teachers differ in important ways from those of most other teachers. A music teacher at the elementary school level typically teaches multiple class sections of all grade levels from kindergarten through grade five or six, often seeing 400 or even more children for two 20- to 30-minute classes per week. Secondary school music teachers most often meet students in ensemble classes, frequently with enrollments of 50 to 100 students (or even more in the case of marching band), which is two to four times as many students as are found in most other classes; sometimes there is a co-teacher, sometimes one teacher alone. As Gordon (2002) explained, "larger class sizes imply that more students will present more problems and have larger 'audiences' when infractions occur" (p. 164). Music teachers at all levels regularly take small and large groups of students to performances in the community and at the secondary level may travel with student ensembles for longer distances to festivals, competitions, and on tours.

Elementary music teachers incorporate a variety of activities into every class period in order to meet curricular goals. Children are engaged in singing, playing instruments, perceptive listening activities, creative or structured movement activities, creating and improvising, evaluating performances and compositions, and discussing music in relation to history and culture and the other arts. The elementary music teacher who has back-to-back classes of children for only a half-hour at a time has little flexibility to implement behavior management plans, as compared with the classroom teachers who are with the same children for the greater part of each day and thus have much more control of the children's schedules.

Secondary school music teachers primarily teach students in performing ensembles, implementing curricula and preparing for concerts, while maintaining budgets for instruments and uniforms, music, supplies, and travel. The pressure of preparation for public performances places time management demands on the teachers and students. Secondary students who choose and persist in music performance often are independent and motivated. At the other end of the spectrum are the middle/junior high and senior high school "general music" classes, primarily composed of students who are in exploratory class rotations or who need a fine arts credit, who are reluctant to perform, and/or who are not highly motivated by the content.

Music educators have long recognized that in order to facilitate productive learning environments with diverse and large groups of students, whether in classrooms or rehearsal halls, on concert stages or football fields, music teachers would need to be especially good at managing their teaching environments. As a result, some of the earliest research conducted in music classrooms, considered cutting-edge at its time, was related to various aspects of teacher and student behaviors that fall under the aforementioned inclusive definition of classroom management.

TEACHER COMPETENCIES

The Competency Based Education movement of the 1960s and 1970s (Mountford, 1976) was a stimulus for the study of music teacher competencies. Competencies related to classroom management continuously arise in studies that identify, describe and/or prioritize preservice and in-service teachers' skills and concerns about their teaching ability. Researchers have sought to identify competencies necessary for success in the music classroom to assist with the development of preservice teacher education curricula and coursework. Research with experienced teachers has helped to identify management-related competencies, while research with preservice teachers has sought to identify their related concerns.

Among teaching competencies that music teachers have considered important are the ability to establish excellent classroom management, elicit appropriate student behavior, and motivate students (Forsythe, Kinney, & Braun, 2007; MikVSza, Roeder, & Biggs, 2010; Rohwer & Henry, 2004; Taebel, 1980; Teachout, 1997). The results of a research survey about behaviors important to music teaching indicated that experienced teachers ranked "maintain student behavior" as the most important music teaching skill out of the 40 listed, followed by "motivating students," "being organized," "being enthusiastic," and "displaying confidence"—all related to the personal attributes of the teacher as opposed to musical or general teaching skills (Teachout, 1997). Miksza and colleagues' (2010) analysis of the responses of successful teachers to survey items regarding important characteristics of music teachers indicated the highest ranked teacher characteristic was enthusiasm/energy. They found in analyzing their open-ended questions that the most common struggle in school band directing was "motivating students/classroom management" (p. 374).

Several studies with preservice teachers have focused on the undergraduates' teaching fears and concerns. When asked to write about their three greatest fears related to the upcoming student teaching internship, senior music education majors' responses "revealed considerable fear of inadequacy in the area of discipline and classroom management" (Madsen & Kaiser, 1999, p. 29). Results of a study that collected data at several points throughout both a prestudent teaching practicum and the student teaching experience itself indicated that music education students identified management-related strategies as concerns (Miksza & Berg, 2013). Similarly, Killian, Dye, and Wayman (2013) found that self-reported concerns of preservice music teachers included in the category the researchers labeled "discipline" remained among the most frequently mentioned concerns in both pre- and poststudent teaching. Brand (1982) found not only that student teachers' classroom management beliefs remain unchanged as a result of eight weeks of student teaching but that their skills did not change significantly either. Developing classroom management skills prior to student teaching via curricular, cocurricular, extracurricular, and nonmusic teaching experiences has been recognized by music students as valuable preparation (Hourigan & Scheib, 2009).

One of the more recent concerns in music education is teacher shortages, either currently in existence or the future anticipated retirement of a large number of teachers in coming years (Kim & Barg, 2010). An inability to structure and manage school and classroom environments that support academic and social-emotional learning puts music teachers at high risk of attrition or migration (Hancock, 2008).

Classroom management has been found to be a prevalent source of stress and common source of anxiety for both in-service (Gordon, 2002) and preservice (Madsen & Kaiser, 1999) music teachers. Although there is some fairly old research at this point that investigated ways to teach "behavior management skills" to undergraduate students (Brand, 1977), it seems imperative that those currently responsible for music teacher preparation programs, as well as professional development for in-service teachers, develop effective strategies to help develop these important teacher competencies.

HISTORICAL INFLUENCES: BEHAVIORAL RESEARCH IN MUSIC CLASSROOMS

Much of the early research related to the management of music classrooms was influenced by behavioral psychology, which provided both the theoretical framework and the paradigm for data collection and analysis. Substantial bodies of such research were published in the 1970s through 1990s. Much of this descriptive and experimental research was based on classroom observations, taking advantage of, and perhaps a result of, the relatively new "portable" technologies that permitted audio and subsequently video recording to take place in the schools.

The nature of music making in groups requires that performers remain attentive, synchronizing their actions with each other and the leader/conductor of the ensemble. Thus, it is logical that some of the earliest research in music classrooms was related to student attentiveness, operationally defined as on-task/off-task behavior. Given the teacher/conductor as a focal point in the music classroom, exploring the effects of various teacher attributes on attentiveness was the goal of quite a few studies.

The results of these bodies of research were integrated into and thus have continued to influence conceptualizations of best practice for the music classroom. Even as research methodologies have advanced, much of the older literature is still cited frequently and has served as the basis for more modern iterations of research in music classrooms. For example, a 1975 study by Yarbrough, related to the effects of various teacher behaviors on student performance, attentiveness, and attitude, was listed in April 2013 by Sage Publications as the most frequently cited article published in the *Journal of Research in Music Education*, the premier research journal in the field (http://jrm.sagepub.com/reports/most-cited). The second most frequently cited study was also a classroom observation study, investigating relationships among several conductor behavior variables and rates of student off-task behavior (Yarbrough & Price, 1981). Thus, it seems important to pay homage to the seminal studies in the field by including a brief summary of the research here, although an extended review is beyond the scope of this chapter.

The primary dependent variable related to classroom management in this body of behavioral studies was student attentiveness (which may be considered a subset of "engagement," the term used in more current research). This was measured by systematic observation of on-/off-task behavior across increments of time, either directly in the classrooms or from video recordings. Customized forms were developed based on the independent variables of interest, on which observers recorded their observations of specified behaviors, typically using time-sampling procedures to observe and record the data and sometimes continuous observations. Independent observers' responses were compared to ensure interobserver reliability.

One set of observable teacher behaviors that served as independent variables in this body of literature included characteristics such as eye contact, pacing, delivery of content, and expressiveness or enthusiasm conveyed by voice, face, or gesture. Varying combinations of these characteristics were observed or experimented with, operationally defined and labeled by some of the researchers with terms such as "magnitude" (Yarbrough, 1975), "affect" (Sims, 1986) or "intensity" (Standley & Madsen, 1987). Results of these studies indicated that students of various age levels, from preschool through high school, were most attentive when teachers demonstrated higher and/or more positive and/or more varied levels of the characteristics or constructs under investigation, particularly eye contact (Brendell, 1996; Byo, 1990; Hughes, 1992; Madsen, Standley, Cassidy, 1989; Sims, 1986; Standley & Madsen, 1987; Yarbrough, 1975; Yarbrough & Price, 1981).

Another independent variable investigated by many authors was effects of teachers' use of time in the classroom on student attentiveness. Participants represented in these studies ranged from preschool-aged children through college students. In general, results indicated higher levels of student attentiveness when students were engaged in activities such as singing, playing instruments, or moving in conjunction with music listening, especially as compared with times when the teacher was talking or the class was in transition between activities (Forsythe, 1977; Hughes, 1992; Madsen & Geringer, 1983; Moore, 1981 & 1987; Sims, 1986; Spradling, 1985; Yarbrough & Price, 1981; Witt, 1986).

Relationships between teacher feedback and student attentiveness were of interest to several early researchers. Teacher feedback or lack thereof was investigated (Dunn, 1997), as were effects of teacher verbal approval/disapproval (Forsythe, 1975; Madsen & Alley, 1979; Madsen & Duke, 1985; Murray, 1975; Price, 1983; Yarbrough & Price, 1981). According to an analysis of this research by Duke (1999/2000), there was "little empirical evidence that higher proportions of positive teacher feedback lead to greater student attentiveness." (p. 15).

LEARNER ATTRIBUTES

Motivation

Student motivation as a factor in academic and social-emotional learning, orderly classroom environment, and student engagement is not only relevant but integral in the discussion of classroom management. Teachers' understanding of motivation informs their understanding of classroom management. Evertson and Weinstein (2006) understandably placed the onus for classroom management on the teacher; the teacher makes it happen. Of course, what the teacher does is predicated in part on what students bring, specifically their motivation to choose, value, put forth effort, and persist—in other words, to be engaged in the class being "managed." Motivation in the social-cognitive paradigm is viewed as a process internal to the learner. Learners behave in accord with how they think, and this is the "primary source of motivation" (Austin & Vispoel, 1992, p. 3). Perhaps because of the influence of the behavioral psychology framework through the 1990s, learner-centered theories of motivation have been underresearched in music education, save perhaps attribution theory and self-regulation.

Theories of motivation are divided according to locus of control, that is, the individual's belief that outcomes are contingent on one's actions (internal) or independent of one's actions (external). Achievement goal theory addresses why learners want to achieve. There are two general orientations. In task goal orientation, motivation is drawn from the task itself as well as the variable process involved in acquiring understanding and skill. In ego goal orientation, motivation is drawn from conditions external to the task, for example, success as determined by outsiders, competition with others, and public acknowledgment of accomplishment (Nichols, 1984). Ames (1992) applied different labels, "mastery goals" and "performance goals," similarly defined. Task goal orientation is more conducive to perseverance behavior because the learner seeks out ways to control the process. In a study of 300 secondary school instrumental musicians, participants chose mastery motivation (or task goal orientation) and cooperative motivation prompts as the most salient explanations for their success in music (Schmidt, 2005).

Dweck (2000) proposed two theories of intelligence/ability based on learners' perceptions of whether intelligence and ability are modifiable. She postulated a continuum anchored by entity, the sense that intelligence is set and not subject to change, and by incremental, the sense that intelligence can increase (see Pintrich, 2000, on learners' adoption of entity and incremental simultaneously). The common perception that innate talent is the primary determinant of success in music performance (e.g., Asmus, 1986) illustrates entity theory. Colvin (2008) pieced together empirical research to refute the talent-as-primary notion (see also Chase & Simon, 1973) and explained elite performances on the basis of a certain kind of intense effort, practiced in large doses (see Ericsson, Krampe, & Tesch-Romer, 1993, on deliberate practice and Sosniak, 1985, on developing talent among elite pianists).

The most self-enhancing and classroom management–friendly goal orientations are those in which learners demonstrate adaptive behaviors. Learning and skill development are viewed as dynamic *processes* marked by episodes of success and failure. Obstacles to achievement are inevitable. The path to success, sometimes linear, sometimes not, requires the thoughtful attention of both learner and teacher. The learner finds pleasure in working through adversity. Task goal and incremental orientations are conducive to this adaptive process. On the other end of the spectrum, the maladaptive helpless-oriented learner tends to respond to failure with negative emotion and by avoiding challenges and giving up (Dweck, 2000). Individuals' motivational, cognitive, affective, and behavioral responses, viewed through goal orientations, are sensitive to situational context. Teachers have an important role in setting contexts and thus shaping learners' goals (Schunk, Pintrich, & Meece, 2008, p. 197).

Class goal structures are classroom environments shaped by how students are evaluated, both formally and informally. Goal structure, whether competitive or individualistic,[1] can affect learner motivation. Secondary school music education in the United States tends to be competition driven, for both individual students and ensembles. A competitive structure compares one student to another (similar to ego orientation) and, in music performance, manifests in rank ordering students based primarily on quality of performance. Frequently, an audition determines whether students are placed in school bands, orchestras, and choirs and constitutes the manner in which students are "seated" (placed in order from strongest to weakest player, often resulting in playing/singing more to less challenging musical parts) within like-instrument or voice sections. Subsequent competitive "challenges" for seat placement are designed to tap into students' desire for upward mobility within the rank order. In a challenge, a lower-ranked student attempts to take the seat of a higher-ranked student via an audition that allows direct comparison of performance skill. Research indicates that students who perceive themselves as successful musicians tend to favor a challenge system and cite effort, ability, and knowledge as the reasons for their success. Students on the other end of the success spectrum tend to hold challenges in disfavor and cite factors outside their control for their failure (Chandler, Chiarella, & Auria, 1987). Some teachers' practice of rotating seating would seem to reduce the zero-sum nature of a fixed rank order arrangement. By distributing roles differentially among students, rotating seating is an option that seems to be a pedagogically sound practice.

Many school bands, orchestras, and choirs across the United States function within the context of a competitive *program* structure, a vestige of the popular band contest movement of the 1930s and a staple activity of many state music organizations (e.g., the Ohio Music Educators Association, the Florida Music Educators Association). Curricula are developed according to competitively designed endpoints, such as a marching band contest, a solo and chamber ensemble contest, a large ensemble festival. As a motivator of musicians, evidence indicates that competition is favored by high school juniors and seniors and college freshmen (Burnsed, Sochinksi, & Hinkle, 1983). In the schools' elective course environment, where students "vote with their feet" (Humphreys, 1995, p. 43), students may be attracted to competitive experiences.[2] Only a few studies in music have examined a causal relationship between competition and music achievement and attitude, and results are mixed. A competitive music performance environment produced significant gains in music achievement and self-concept among fifth- and sixth-grade musicians (Austin, 1988). In contrast, fifth- and sixth-graders' responses to competitive and noncompetitive goal structures showed no performance differences (Austin, 1991). Noncompetitors, those seeking to simply perform their best, performed as well as or better than students who competed against standards.

Students who participate in school music run the gamut from those who crave competition to those who prefer a noncompetitive experience. The pursuit of effective classroom management might warrant caution with respect to competition. A rank ordering of students by performance achievement accentuates ability and social comparisons and is ripe for strengthening the motivation of "winners" and weakening that of "losers" (Ames, 1984). Given the inevitability of competition among students in music ensembles, it is likely best for teachers to promote the simultaneous adoption of task and ego goal orientations in doses that vary according to individual students' needs.

Teachers need to understand the conditions under which music students persevere because perseverance implies continued engagement in a thing of interest, and when that thing is good and appropriate, perseverance is conducive to an effectively managed classroom. One perspective on motivation is attribution theory (Heider, 1958; Weiner, 1974), the idea that individuals are driven to action or inaction by how they explain their own and others' success and failure, in terms of either effort or ability. Effort explanations, given their internal-to-the-learner nature and modifiability, are thought to beget continued effort. In an analysis of open-ended responses of fourth- to twelfth-graders to questions about why students do or do not do well in music, Asmus (1986) identified a tendency for effort attributions to change to ability attributions as young people get older. Importantly, effort can be thought of generally, as in trying hard, or specifically, as in types (e.g., strategic efforts). There was motivational advantage when fifth- to eighth-graders attributed the cause of failure to the need for better strategy and general effort (see Austin and Vispoel, 1992, in music performance, and Vispoel and Austin, 1993, in general music). When failure can be blamed on type of effort rather than on effort in general, there is no dead-end to the process that seeks forward progression toward a goal.

Austin and Vispoel (1998) expanded the attributions list to include family influence (the degree of music involvement among family members), teacher influence, peer influence, metacognition, persistence, interest, and strategy. Seventh-graders in classroom music responded to success and failure differently, and, disturbingly, effort and strategy attributions were not salient. It is important that teachers be aware of individual students' attribution tendencies and, when not conducive to perseverance (e.g., family influence and ability attributions), educate or re-educate in the direction of effort and strategy. Ability explanations, although internal to the learner, are worrisome if ability is considered unmodifiable. Task difficulty explanations as external elements are out of the control of the learner, although importantly they are within the control of the teacher in instances where teachers assign tasks. Austin and Vispoel (1998) warned that "most achievement outcomes probably reflect the collective influence of a number of different factors rather than a single factor" (p. 41).

Self-Regulation and Self-Efficacy

If learners are active in teaching themselves, as is the case in the goal-directed processes of self-regulation that are important for music learning (McPherson & Zimmerman, 2002; Zimmerman, 1998; Zimmerman & Martinez-Pons, 1988), they are engaged in "an environment that supports and facilitates academic and social-emotional learning" (Evertson & Weinstein, 2006, p. 4). Self-regulation is therefore germane to classroom management. The self-regulatory "environment" emanates from the learner's perception of events in his external environment. Imagine a school orchestra, each member with an internal, personal classroom management operating within the managed external classroom. Learners monitor their own learning. In music performance, they listen to their performance, analyze its quality, and make adjustments in the direction of a known goal. The self-regulatory learner is an independent, self-sufficient learner. There is evidence indicating an absence or low-level of self-regulatory behavior in the music practice of young musicians generally (McPherson & Renwick, 2001; Pitts, Davidson, & McPherson, 2000; Renwick & McPherson, 2002). Young musicians, however, distinguished among themselves by showing nascent and varied signs of self-regulatory behavior (e.g., silent fingering, silent thinking)—more so in those who demonstrated strong interest in music making at the outset, maintained interest for an extended period, were supported by parents, and persevered willingly through periods of less motivation (McPherson & Renwick, 2001; Pitts, Davidson, & McPherson, 2000) and if they were motivated by personal choice rather than teacher choice of music (Renwick & McPherson, 2002). According to McPherson and Renwick (2001): "Students who are more cognitively engaged while practising not only tend to do more practice, but enjoy learning more and are also more efficient in their work" (p. 170).

The more music teachers understand self-regulation, the greater the likelihood of teaching in ways that support student self-sufficiency. As proposed by McPherson (2005), the answer regarding how best to acquire music performance skills resides more in the study of learners' mental practice strategies than in the amount of time practiced or the assessment of practiced music. Some learners walk in the door "wired" to self-regulate. McPherson wrote that "the best players possessed more sophisticated strategies for playing their instruments very early in their development" (p. 27). They believed in personal effort and were rewarded by smart, strategic effort. Other students need to be taught the processes of cognitively engaged practice. As such, self-regulation is "no longer viewed as a fixed characteristic of students but rather as context-specific processes that are selectively used to succeed in school" (Zimmerman, 1998, p. 74). The processes include goal setting, task strategies, imagery, self-instruction, time management, self-monitoring, and self-evaluation.

The self-report nature of much of the data for musicians' practice behavior has been the impetus for studying the validity and reliability of measures of self-regulation. Miksza (2012) found a four-factor model to be well-suited to middle school band students. The factors of self-regulated learning were self-efficacy, method and behavior combined, time management, and social influences.

Opportunities abound for learners to self-regulate during performance classes, ensemble rehearsals, and individual practice done independently of a teacher. There is much literature calling for music teachers to facilitate self-regulation among learners in school settings. To do so, teachers must design rehearsals and develop assessment techniques aimed at reaching individuals within the group setting (rather than address the ensemble as one undifferentiated unit), probe students about their cognitive processes, and encourage them to reflect on personal performance quality in the context of decision making in practice.

Across students and situations, self-regulation exists on a continuum of strong to weak self-efficacy (Bandura, 1986; McPherson & McCormick, 2006). When students are engaged in monitoring their own thinking about personal performance quality (listening, judging, and adjusting toward a known goal), they are likely engaged willingly in the class managed. On the surface, the listen-judge-adjust model of music performance appears simple and direct. A social-cognitive perspective (Bandura, 1986), putting student perception front and center, reveals intricacies relevant to classroom management. Social-cognitive theory resonates in the connection of agency and human development. Bandura (2002) wrote more to the point: "To be an agent is to influence intentionally one's own functioning" (p. 270). Self-efficacy is one's answer to the question to what extent am I able to make positive change in my performance toward this specific goal? Situational specificity distinguishes self-efficacy from self-concept. The young piano player's belief that she can play the F major scale with correct notes, correct fingerings, good hand position, legato articulation, and even tone at a designated tempo is an efficacy thought (whereas her belief that she is a good pianist would reflect a positive self-concept). Self-efficacy is a mediator of choices—to persist in music, to persist in practice, to behave in one way or the other. Self-efficacy may be the means by which to refine thinking about self-confidence.

Research in academic areas has shown self-efficacy to be an important precursor to achievement (e.g, Jinks & Lorsbach, 2003; Pajares & Miller, 1994). Pajares (2003) situated students' personal perceptions of writing competence as central to the processes of teaching and learning. In music, self-efficacy was found to be the primary predictor of accomplishment on juried performance (McPherson & McCormick, 2006; McCormick & McPherson, 2003). This depicts a continuum of personal judgment spanning self-enhancing and self-debilitating outcomes and as such is likely to affect one's behavior in the managed music classroom. Self-efficacy is under-researched in music education—this despite the likelihood that collective efficacy (Bandura, 2002) is a construct ripe for study in the group-oriented/collective effort setting of the music rehearsal.

Flow

Flow is a state of mind that occurs when one's skill level and the challenge of a structured activity are ideally matched and thus thrust one into optimal engagement and enjoyment (Csikszentmihalyi, 1990). Like self-regulation, flow is an internal experience that supports and facilitates academic and social-emotional learning. To the degree that music teachers structure environments that create "flow" potential among students, those teachers are likely involved with effective classroom management (O'Neill, 1998; Sinnamon, Moran, & O'Connell, 2012; Waite & Diaz, 2012). Flow has been studied in work environments, sports, and leisure activities but less so in music performance. Nine dimensions or correlates define flow in various domains; so too in music settings (Martin & Jackson, 2008; Sinnamon, Moran, & O'Connell, 2012). Custadero (2005), through behavior observation, reported a range of flow experiences in the music making of children; likewise did Sinnamon and associates (2012) through self-report of professional-track and amateur musicians. Flow as a "group" experience has been documented in the music rehearsals of college and professional musicians (Kraus, 2003; Sutton, 2004). It tends to occur during rehearsals late in the sequence of rehearsals when there is more continuous performance of music. In the group context, whether an individual experiences flow is dependent on factors ranging from one's own goals and self-imposed focus of attention to the behaviors and skill level of others. Psychometric measures show that flow can be measured reliably (Jackson, Martin, & Eklund, 2008; Sinnamon, Moran, & O'Connell, 2012).

URBAN EDUCATION

Although teacher behaviors and student attributes have been of interest to music education researchers for many years, classroom context is a more recent focus of attention. A growing body of research and pedagogical writing about urban music education has emerged over the past six to seven years because this is one of the most challenging environments for music teachers. As the book title *Teaching Music in the Urban Classroom: A Guide to Survival, Success, and Reform* (Frierson-Campbell, 2006) indicates, the urban context for music education is complex and problematic.

In Frierson-Campbell's words: "Whether because of rigid training or professional nearsightedness, the cultural disconnect between music teachers and urban students is a theme that permeates the discussion of music in urban schools" (p. xiii). Music education in urban schools was recognized and formalized as an area for concern in the late 1960s (Choate, 1968) by the primary professional organization for music educators, the National Association for Music Education (previously called the Music Educators National Conference).

Several authors have expressed the idea that music teacher education curricula should be designed to assuage prospective teachers' apprehensions about urban teaching (Fiese & DeCarbo, 1995; Kindall-Smith, 2004; Nierman, Zeichner, & Hobbel, 2002). McKoy (2013) studied the cross-cultural competence of music education students and student teachers. She concluded:

> As with general teacher preparation programs, music teacher preparation programs continue to evidence teacher candidate populations that are racially and ethnically homogeneous. Thus, the attainment of cross-cultural competence continues to be at the forefront of identified competencies for teacher candidates. (p. 389)

Urban teachers were surveyed by Baker (2012) "to determine a profile of an effective urban music educator in an effort to provide strategies for university training programs to prepare students to teach in urban schools" (p. 44). When asked in a free-response question to indicate "challenges they felt were unique to urban music educators" (p. 46), responses categorized as *discipline issues* were the most frequent. When asked about their advice for university training programs, the most frequent responses were to provide observations and field experiences in urban schools and to teach discipline/classroom management and urban culture and diversity.

Fitzpatrick's (2011) portrait of urban instrumental music education is another of the few empirical studies in music that examined urban education in ways that expose elements of classroom management. She wrote, "little is known about the experiences of urban music teachers and the ways that they think about and connect to the urban context that surrounds them" (p. 231). Many urban students come from home and community environments that do not promote managed lives, let alone managed classrooms, so teachers begin the process at a disadvantage. Several of Fitzpatrick's findings have implications for classroom management: (1) Teachers reported personal emotions ranging from extreme frustration with daily challenges to the satisfaction brought by student success; (2) the ability to cope with the frustration and work toward student success was attributed to the teachers' skill in overcoming "disconnectedness;" they learned their students' life contexts; (3) knowledge of life context was used to modify teaching; and (4) modified teaching led to the development of a "specialized set of skills, understandings, and dispositions" (p. 240) for success in the urban classroom. The teachers believed in holding students to high standards. They reported that their classroom management was better than that in the rest of the school. This statement from one of the participating teachers was typical: "They [the students] want to be respected and that's a huge inner city thing. These kids don't get respect at home—they don't get respect in real life, so if you give them that respect, they appreciate it. Even if they don't always show it, they do appreciate it" (p. 239).

This student-centered theme is echoed in Abril's (2006) study of three successful urban music teachers situated in high-poverty schools. Teachers connected with their students by "seeing issues through their lenses" (p. 93). This perspective necessitated that neither subject matter nor pedagogy be rigidly conceived, so each could be modified in the context of student needs. Abril's teacher participants, like Fitzpatrick's, were both frustrated by conditions and elated by evidence of student improvement. Recommendations for confronting the challenges of urban education included (1) assigning novice music teachers to schools where the opportunity to succeed is not remote, (2) connecting novice teachers with a committed and knowledgeable mentor, (3) providing in teacher education meaningful fieldwork in urban schools (see also Fiese & DeCarbo, 1995; Kindall-Smith, 2004; Nierman, Zeichner, & Hobbel, 2002), and (4) advancing teachers' grant-writing skills in order to acquire funding that otherwise does not find its way to urban school bands (Costa-Giomi & Chappell, 2007), orchestras (Smith, 1997), and elementary general music programs (Costa-Giomi, 2008). Urban public schools with "fewer minorities and with lower proportions of disadvantaged students had more financial resources, more adequate facilities, and more supportive parents than schools with a higher proportion of minority students or disadvantaged students" (Costa-Giomi & Chappell, 2007, p. 1). Of the approximately 21% of 2004 high school seniors who were members of school performing ensembles, group makeup was oriented toward females, whites, families of high socioeconomic status, native English speakers, students with high test scores, and students whose parents had earned advanced degrees (Elpus & Abril, 2011). Kinney (2008, 2010) found that among urban middle school students, school band appeared to be a magnet for higher academic achievers and students of two-parent/ two-guardian families. In the context of classroom management, it is helpful perhaps to consider the positive effect of participation in ensemble performance (see Shields, 2001, about at-risk students); participation in music, visual art, drama, and dance (see Center for Music Research, 1990, on at-risk students); and membership in the school subcultures of band, orchestra, or choir (Adderly, Kennedy, & Berz, 2003; Morrison, 2001). The potential for second-home status of music classrooms for performance group members may facilitate classroom management by providing an environment that promotes all learner attributes described previously.

IMPLICATIONS FOR EDUCATORS

A number of guidelines for teachers and teacher educators may be drawn from the literature reviewed. It should be noted that although many of these have been examined by some empirical research, only the early behavioral research actually has large enough bodies of research on which to base more definitive statements.

Teachers are most successful in eliciting attention from students in general music classes and ensemble rehearsals when they use high levels of eye contact and expressiveness while keeping students actively engaged and reducing time spent in transitions and talking. To ensure maximum student engagement, teachers should strive to emphasize task goal motivation (intrinsic motivation) vs. ego goal motivation (extrinsic motivation). They should set appropriate contexts for success and help students learn to attribute success as a musician to effort, hard work, and strategic practice, regardless of "talent." Emphasizing self-efficacy rather than self-concept is an advisable pedagogical approach. Teachers should view excessive competition with caution because although it may function well as motivation for students who already have been successful, it may function badly for those who have had less success. To help students become independent, music teachers should work toward developing and facilitating self-regulatory behavior, especially with respect to individual practicing. By structuring classes and rehearsals for maximum engagement, teachers can help students recognize and value flow experiences.

Teacher educators should work to prepare future teachers with the delivery skills that facilitate student attentiveness and with the strategies that will help them and their students establish appropriate perspectives on the sources of motivation and engagement. Preservice teacher preparation coursework should be responsive to the literature that explains the challenges of teaching music in urban settings or other at-risk environments, as well as to the strategies used and attitudes held by teachers who have been successful in these situations. By facilitating student placement in diverse field experiences, teacher education programs may help students achieve cross-cultural competence.

IMPLICATIONS FOR RESEARCHERS

Given the importance of successful classroom management to successful learning environments, especially for music teachers who face demanding schedules, encounter many and/or large groups of students each week, and implement performance-oriented classes and curricula, relatively little research in this area has taken place in actual music classrooms. Very little is known, as well, about best practices for preparing preservice music teachers to be proactive in setting appropriate classroom expectations and to deal with classroom management issues that may arise, especially in more challenging school settings.

The early research related to classroom management ideas primarily took place in classrooms. Far less of the more recent research seems to have done so. Future researchers could make valuable contributions by going "back to the future" and pursue observational, experimental, and qualitative research in classrooms with music students and teachers, using the areas provided in this review as starting points for conceptualizing theoretical frameworks and research designs.

CONCLUSION

One key question in the early classroom management research was under what teaching conditions are music students attentive, based on the recognition that "[t]eachers at every level of instruction are concerned with each student's ability to focus attention and stay on task" (Madsen, Geringer, & Madsen, 2009, p. 16; see also Sims, 2002)? As paradigms and theoretical frameworks have shifted over time, questions turned to issues related to more learner-centered behaviors. Answers reside among students, teachers, and environmental factors. Students bring to their experiences in music motivations, perceptions, behaviors, and attitudes to the classroom that run the gamut between self-enhancing and self-debilitating responses. Teachers bring knowledge of individual students' proclivities and with this knowledge choose an appropriate curriculum, deliver it in some form along an autocratic/democratic continuum, and provide feedback aimed at shaping students to be motivated according to incremental and task goal orientations, to attribute success to strategic effort and failure to lack of strategic effort, to regulate their own learning and skill development, and to feel self-efficacious in doing so. Environment (e.g., the home from which students come and the school facilities and equipment), when detrimental to effective management, creates challenges that must be mitigated by the teacher to the extent possible.

Under the umbrella of the social cognitive paradigm, we have included coverage of a variety of areas of study, each with formidable research streams, if not in music education per se, then in a combination of education, psychology, and music. To compress coverage of this research in the limited scope of a book chapter runs the risk of diminishing the importance of each research study. There is no desire on our part to trivialize this research; far from it, classroom management is an incredibly complex construct that warrants every bit of research into its component parts.

It is striking that, despite autonomy among research streams, there is much interrelatedness. In a big picture view, research results lead to the same place: To achieve effective classroom management, it is optimal when students, both individually and collectively, are lead by teachers who demonstrate high levels of magnitude, affect, and intensity and who are engaged in relevant and meaningful endeavors over which they exercise some control and at which they experience some success. If students believe that their engagement will make a positive difference, the likelihood that they will persist and be willing participants in music classes and ensembles increases.

NOTES

1. One type of individual goal structure compares one's current performance quality to a high-standards performance quality, a sort of norm-referenced idea. Another individual goal structure compares one's current performance quality to previous performance quality, a sort of criterion-referenced idea.
2. Humphrey's article was published initially in 1992. The reference to a substantial and stable school band population may not hold today, over 20 years later. In a recent philosophical essay, Allsup (2012) argued that band should be a model for moral education and in so doing steers our thinking away from external modes of motivation: "We must look more carefully at what intrinsically motivates children" (p. 3). See also Kratus (2007).

REFERENCES

Abril, C. R. (2006). Teaching music in urban landscapes: Three perspectives. In Carol Frierson-Campbell (Ed.), *Teaching music in the urban classroom* (pp. ix–xviii). Lanham, MD: Rowman & Littlefield.
Adderly, C., Kennedy, M., & Berz, W. (2003). "A home away from home": The world of the high school music classroom. *Journal of Research in Music Education, 51*(3), 190–205.

Allsup, R. E. (2012). The moral ends of band. *Theory into Practice, 51*(3), 179–187. Retrieved from www .tandfonline.com/doi/abs/10.1080/00405841.2012.690288 #preview.

Ames, C. (1984). Competitive, cooperative, and individualistic goal structures: A cognitive-motivational analysis. In R. Ames & C. Ames (Eds.), *Research on motivation in education,* Vol. 1 (pp. 177–207). New York: Academic Press.

Ames, C. (1992). Classrooms: Goals, structures, and student motivation. *Journal of Educational Psychology, 84,* 261–271.

Asmus, E. P. (1986). Student beliefs about the causes of success and failure in music: A study of achievement motivation. *Journal of Research in Music Education, 34,* 262–278.

Austin, J. R. (1988). The effect of contest format on self-concept, motivation, achievement, and attitude of elementary band students. *Journal of Research in Music Education, 36*(2), 95–107.

Austin, J. R. (1991). Competitive and non-competitive goal structures: An analysis of motivation and achievement among elementary band students. *Psychology of Music, 19,* 142–158.

Austin, J. R., & Vispoel, W. P. (1992). Motivation after failure in school music performance classes: The facilitative effects of strategy attributions. *Bulletin of the Council for Research in Music Education, 111,* 1–23.

Austin, J. R., & Vispoel, W. P. (1998). How American adolescents interpret success and failure in classroom music: Relationships among attributional beliefs, self-concept and achievement. *Psychology of Music, 26,* 26–45.

Baker, V. D. (2012). Profile of an effective urban music educator. Update: *Applications of Research in Music Education, 31,* 44–54.

Bandura, A. (1986). *Social foundations of thought and action: A social cognitive theory.* Englewood Cliffs: Prentice-Hall.

Bandura, A. (2002). Social cognitive theory in cultural context. *Applied Psychology: An International Review, 51*(2), 269–290.

Brand, M. (1977). Effectiveness of simulation techniques in teaching behavior management. *Journal of Research in Music Education, 25,* 131–138.

Brand, M. (1982). Effects of student teaching on the classroom management beliefs and skills of music student teachers, *Journal of Research in Music Education, 30,* 255–265.

Brendell, J. K. (1996). Time use, rehearsal activity, and student off-task behavior during the initial minutes of high school choral rehearsals. *Journal of Research in Music Education, 44,* 6–14.

Burnsed, V., Sochinski, J., & Hinkle, D. (1983). The attitude of college band students toward high school marching band competition. *Journal of Band Research, 19,* 11–17.

Byo, J. L. (1990). Recognition of intensity contrasts in the gestures of beginning conductors. *Journal of Research in Music Education, 38,* 157–163.

Center for Music Research. (1990). *The role of the fine and performing arts in high school dropout prevention.* Tallahassee, FL (ERIC 354 168).

Chandler, T., Chiarella, D., & Auria, C. (1987). Performance expectancy, success, satisfaction, and attributions as variables in band challenges. *Journal of Research in Music Education, 35,* 249–259.

Chase, W. G., & Simon, H. A. (1973). Perception in chess. *Cognitive Psychology, 4*(1), 55–81.

Choate, R. A. (Ed.). (1968). *Documentary report of the Tanglewood Symposium* (LoC 68–57958). Washington, DC: Music Educators National Conference. Retrieved from www.bu.edu/tanglewoodtwo/about/document-report.pdf.

Colvin, G. (2008). *Talent is overrated: What really separates world-class performers from everybody else.* New York: Penguin.

Costa-Giomi, E. (2008). Characteristics of elementary music programs in urban schools: What money can buy. *Bulletin of the Council for Research in Music Education, 177,* 19–28.

Costa-Giomi, E., & Chappell, E. (2007). Characteristics of band programs in a large urban school district: Diversity or inequality? *Journal of Band Research, 42*(2), 1–18.

Csikszentmihalyi, M. (1990). *Flow: The psychology of optimal experience.* New York: Harper & Row.

Custadero, L. A. (2005). Observable indicators of flow experience: A developmental perspective on musical engagement in young children from infancy to school age. *Music Education Research, 7,* 185–209. doi: 10.1080/14613800500169431

Duke, R. A. (1999/2000). Measures of instructional effectiveness in music research. *Bulletin of the Council for Research in Music Education, 143,* 1–48.

Dunn, D. E. (1997). Effect of rehearsal hierarchy and reinforcement on attention, achievement, and attitude of selected choirs. *Journal of Research in Music Education, 45,* 547–567.

Dweck, C. S. (2000). *Self-theories: Their role in motivation, personality, and development.* Philadelphia: Psychology Press.

Elpus, K., & Abril, C. R. (2011). High school music ensemble students in the United States: A demographic profile. *Journal of Research in Music Education, 59,* 128–145.

Ericsson, K. A., Krampe, R. T., & Tesch-Romer, C. (1993). The role of deliberate practice in the acquisition of expert performance. *Psychological Review, 100,* 363–406.

Evertson, C. M., & Weinstein, C. S. (2006). Classroom management as a field of inquiry. In C. M. Evertson & C. S. Weinstein (Eds.), *Handbook of classroom management: Research, practice, and contemporary issues* (pp. 3–15). New York: Routledge.

Fiese, R. K., & DeCarbo, N. J. (1995). Urban music education: The teachers' perspective. *Music Educators Journal, 82*(1), 32–35.

Fitzpatrick, K. R. (2011). A mixed methods portrait of urban instrumental music teaching. *Journal of Research in Music Education, 59,* 229–256.

Forsythe, J. L. (1975). The effect of teacher approval, disapproval, and errors on student attentiveness: Music versus classroom teachers. In C. K. Madsen, R. D. Greer, & C. H. Madsen Jr. (Eds.), *Research in music behavior* (pp. 49–55). New York: Teachers College Press.

Forsythe, J. L. (1977). Elementary student attending behavior as a function of classroom activities. *Journal of Research in Music Education, 25,* 228–239.

Forsythe, J. L., Kinney, D. W., & Braun, E. L. (2007). Opinions of music teacher educators and preservice music students on the National Association of Schools of Music standards for teacher education. *Journal of Music Teacher Education, 16,* 19–33. doi: 10.1177/10570837070160020104

Frierson-Campbell, C. (2006). Introduction: Perspectives on music in urban schools. In Carol Frierson-Campbell (Ed.), *Teaching music in the urban classroom: A guide to survival, success, and reform,* Vol. 1 (pp. ix–xviii). Lanham, MD: Rowman & Littlefield.

Gordon, D. G. (2002). Discipline in the music classroom: One component contributing to teacher stress. *Music Education Research, 4,* 157–165.

Hancock, C. B. (2008). Music teachers at risk for attrition and migration: An analysis of the 1999–2000 schools and staffing survey. *Journal of Research in Music Education, 56,* 130–144.

Heider, F. (1958). *The psychology of interpersonal relations.* New York: Wiley.

Hourigan, R. M., & Scheib, J. W. (2009). Inside and outside the undergraduate music education curriculum: Student teacher perceptions of the value of skills, abilities, and understandings. *Journal of Music Teacher Education, 18,* 48–61.

Hughes, W. O. (1992). The effect of high versus low teacher affect and active versus passive student activity during music listening on high school general music students' attention. *Research Perspectives in Music Education, 46*(2), 16–18.

Humphreys, J. T. (1995). Instrumental music in American education: In service of many masters. *Journal of Band Research, 30,* 25–51.

Jackson, S. A., Martin, A. J., & Eklund, R. C. (2008). The long and short measures of flow: The construct validity of the FSS-2 and DFS-2, and new brief counterparts. *Journal of Sport and Exercise Psychology, 30,* 561–587.

Jinks, J., & Lorsbach, A. (2003). Introduction: Motivation and self-efficacy belief. *Reading and Writing Quarterly, 19,* 113–118.

Killian, J. N., Dye, K. G., & Wayman, J. B. (2013). Music student teachers: Pre-student teaching concerns and post-student teaching perceptions over a 5-year period. *Journal of Research in Music Education, 61,* 63–79.

Kim, S. E., & Barg, D. (2010). Reducing music teacher turnover and its consequences. *Music Education Policy Briefs, 2,* 1–7.

Kindall-Smith, M. (2004). Teachers teaching teachers: Revitalization in an urban setting. *Music Educators Journal, 91*(2), 41–46.

Kinney, D. (2008). Selected demographic variables, school music participation and achievement test scores of urban middle school students. *Journal of Research in Music Education, 56,* 145–161.

Kinney, D. (2010). Selected nonmusic predictors of urban students' decisions to enroll and persist in middle school band programs. *Journal of Research in Music Education, 57,* 334–350.

Kratus, J. (2007). Music education at the tipping point. *Music Educators Journal, 94,* 42–48.

Kraus, B. N. (2003). Musicians in flow: Optimal experience in the wind ensemble rehearsal. PhD dissertation, Arizona State University, Tempe: Retrieved from Proquest Dissertations and Theses (UMI 3084646).

Madsen, C. K., & Alley, J. M. (1979). The effect of reinforcement on attentiveness: A comparison of behaviorally trained music therapists and other professionals with implications for competency-based academic preparation. *Journal of Music Therapy*, 16, 70–82.

Madsen, C. K. & Duke, R. A. (1985). Perception of approval/disapproval in music. *Bulletin of the Council for Research in Music Education*, 85, 119–130.

Madsen, C. K., & Geringer, J. M. (1983). Attending behavior as a function of in-class activity in university music classes. *Journal of Music Therapy*, 20, 30–38.

Madsen, C. K., Geringer, J. M., & Madsen, K. (2009). Adolescent musicians' perceptions of conductors within musical context. *Journal of Research in Music Education*, 57, 16–25.

Madsen, C. K., & Kaiser, K. A. (1999). Pre-internship fears of student teaching. Update: *Applications of Research in Music Education*, 17(2), 27–32.

Madsen, C. K, Standley, J. M, & Cassidy, J. W. (1989). Demonstration and recognition of high and low contrasts in teacher intensity. *Journal of Research in Music Education*, 37, 85–92.

Martin, A. J., & Jackson, S. A. (2008). Brief approaches to assessing task absorption and enhanced subjective experience: Examining "short" and "core" flow in diverse performance domains. *Motivation and Emotion*, 32, 141–157. doi 10.1007/s11031–008–9094–0

McCormick, J., & McPherson, G. E. (2003). The role of self-efficacy in a musical performance examination: An exploratory structural equation analysis. *Psychology of Music*, 31, 37–51.

McKoy, C. L. (2013). Effects of selected demographic variables on music student teachers' self-reported cross-cultural competence. *Journal of Research in Music Education*, 60, 375–394.

McPherson, G. E. (2005). From child to musician: Skill development during the beginning stages of learning an instrument. *Psychology of Music*, 33(1), 5–35.

McPherson, G. E., & McCormick, J. (2000). The contribution of motivational factors to instrumental performance in a music examination. *Research Studies in Music Education*, 15, 31–39.

McPherson, G. E., & McCormick, J. (2006). Self-efficacy and music performance. *Psychology of Music*, 34, 322–336.

McPherson, G. E., & Renwick, J. M. (2001). A longitudinal study of self-regulation in children's musical practice. *Music Education Research*, 3, 169–186.

McPherson, G. E., & Zimmerman B. J. (2002). Self-regulation of musical learning: A social-cognitive perspective. In R. Colwell & C. Richardson (Eds.), *The new handbook of research on music teaching and learning* (pp. 327–347). New York: Oxford University Press.

Miksza, P. (2012). The development of a measure of self-regulated practice behavior for beginning and intermediate instrumental music students. *Journal of Research in Music Education*, 59, 321–338.

Miksza, P., & Berg, M. H. (2013). A longitudinal study of preservice music teacher development: Application and advancement of the Fuller and Bown teacher-concerns model. *Journal of Research in Music Education*, 61, 44–62.

Miksza, P., Roeder, M., & Biggs, D. (2010). Surveying Colorado band directors' opinions of skills and characteristics important to successful music teaching. *Journal of Research in Music Education*, 57(4), 364–381.

Moore, R. S. (1981). Comparative use of teaching time by American and British elementary school specialists. *Bulletin of the Council for Research in Music Education*, 66–67, 62–68.

Morrison, S. (2001). The school ensemble: A culture of our own. *Music Educators Journal*, 88(2), 24–28.

Mountford, R. D. (1976). Competency-based teacher education: The controversy and a synthesis of related research in music from 1964–1974. *Bulletin of the Council for Research in Music Education*, 46, 1–12.

Murray, K. C. (1975). The effect of teacher approval/disapproval on musical performance, attentiveness, and attitude of high school choruses. In C. K. Madsen, R. D. Greer, & C. H. Madsen Jr. (Eds.), *Research in music behavior* (pp. 165–180). New York: Teachers College Press.

Nichols, J. (1984). Achievement motivation: Conceptions of ability, subjective experience, task choice, and performance. *Psychological Review*, 91, 328–346.

Nierman, G. E., Zeichner, K., & Hobbel, N. (2002). Changing concepts of teacher education. In R. C. Colwell & C. Richardson (Eds.), *The new handbook of research on music teaching and learning* (pp. 818–839). Oxford: Oxford University Press.

O'Neill, S. (1998). Flow theory and the development of musical performance skills. *Bulletin of the Council for Research in Music Education*, 141, 129–134.

Pajares, F. (2003). Self-efficacy belief, motivation, and achievement in writing: A review of the literature. *Reading and Writing Quarterly*, 19, 139–158.

Pajares, F., & Miller, M. D. (1994). Role of self-efficacy and self-concept beliefs in mathematical problem-solving: A path analysis. *Journal of Educational Psychology*, 86, 193–203.

Pintrich, P. R. (2000). Multiple goals, multiple pathways: The role of goal orientation in learning and achievement. *Journal of Educational Psychology, 25,* 92–104.

Pitts, S., Davidson, A., & McPherson, G. E. (2000). Models of success and failure in instrumental learning: Case studies of young players in the first 20 months of learning. *Bulletin of the Council for Research in Music Education, 146,* 51–69.

Price, H. E. (1983). The effect of conductor academic task presentation, conductor reinforcement, and ensemble practice on performers' musical achievement, attentiveness, and attitude. *Journal of Research in Music Education, 31,* 245–257.

Renwick, J. M., & McPherson, G. E. (2002). Interest and choice: Student-selected repertoire and its effect on practicing behavior. *British Journal of Music Education, 19,* 173–188.

Rohwer, D., & Henry, W. (2004). University teachers' perceptions of requisite skills and characteristics of effective music teachers. *Journal of Music Teacher Education, 13,* 18–27. doi: 10.1177/10570837040130020104

Schmidt, C. P. (2005). Relations among motivation, performance achievement, and music experience variables in secondary instrumental music students. *Journal of Research in Music Education, 53,* 134–147.

Schunk, D. H., Pintrich, P. R., & Meece, J. L. (2008). *Motivation in education: Theory, research, and applications.* Upper Saddle River, NJ: Pearson.

Shields, C. (2001). Music education and mentoring as intervention for at-risk urban adolescents: Their self-perceptions, opinions, and attitudes. *Journal of Research in Music Education, 49,* 273–286.

Sims, W. L. (1986). The effect of high versus low teacher affect and passive versus active student activity during music listening on preschool children's attention, piece preference, time spent listening, and piece recognition. *Journal of Research in Music Education, 34,* 173–191.

Sims, W. L. (2002). Individual differences in music listening responses of kindergarten children. *Journal of Research in Music Education, 50,* 292–300.

Sinnamon, S., Moran, A., & O'Connell, M. (2012). Flow among musicians: Measuring peak experiences of student performers. *Journal of Research in Music Education, 60,* 6–25.

Smith, C. (1997). Access to string instruction in American public schools. *Journal of Research in Music Education, 45,* 650–662.

Sosniak, L. A. (1985). Phases of learning. In B. Bloom (Ed.), *Developing talent in young people* (pp. 409–438). New York: Ballantine Books.

Spradling, R. L. (1985). The effect of timeout from performance on attentiveness and attitude of university band students. *Journal of Research in Music Education, 33,* 123–138.

Standley, J. M., & Madsen, C. K. (1987). Intensity as an attribute of effective client/therapist interaction. *Quodlibet* (Summer), 15–20.

Sutton, R. C. (2004). *Peak performance of groups: An examination of the phenomenon in musical groups.* Malibu: Pepperdine University.

Taebel, D. K. (1980). Public school music teachers' perception of the effect of certain competencies on pupil learning. *Journal of Research in Music Education, 28*(3), 185–195.

Teachout, D. J. (1997). Preservice and experienced teachers' opinions of skills and behaviors important to successful music teaching. *Journal of Research in Music Education, 45*(1), 41–50.

Vispoel, W. P., & Austin, J. R. (1993). Constructive response to failure in music: The role of attribution feedback and class goal structure. *British Journal of Educational Psychology, 63,* 110–129.

Waite, A. K., & Diaz, F. M. (2012). The effect of skill level on instrumentalists' perceptions of flow. *Missouri Journal of Research in Music Education, 49,* 40–51.

Weiner, B. (1974). *Achievement motivation and attribution theory.* Morristown, NJ: General Learning Press.

Witt, A. C. (1986). Use of class time and student attentiveness in secondary instrumental music rehearsals. *Journal of Research in Music Education, 34,* 34–42.

Yarbrough, C. (1975). Effect of magnitude of conductor behavior on students in selected mixed choruses. *Journal of Research in Music Education, 23,* 134–146.

Yarbrough, C., & Price, H. E. (1981). Prediction of performer attentiveness based on rehearsal activity and teacher behavior. *Journal of Research in Music Education, 29,* 209–217.

Zimmerman, B. J., (1998). Academic studying and the development of personal skill: A self-regulatory perspective. *Educational Psychologist, 33*(2/3), 73–86.

Zimmerman, B. J., & Martinez-Pons, M. (1988). Construct validation of a strategy model of student self-regulated learning. *Journal of Educational Psychology, 80,* 283–290.

13

CLASSROOM MANAGEMENT IN PHYSICAL EDUCATION

DONETTA COTHRAN
INDIANA UNIVERSITY

PAMELA KULINNA
ARIZONA STATE UNIVERSITY

It was the first day of PE for this Kindergarten class. We went over the rules. We practiced moving safely in the gym. We practiced our formation signals. We were about to line up when a child raised his hand and asked "When can I do that?" I asked, "Do what?" He said, "Stand in front of the class and tell everyone what to do."

This teacher story, submitted to a teacher resource website (pecentral.org), captures much of what this chapter is about. What do effective managers in physical education do, when do they do it, and how did they learn to do it? What happens when a teacher stands in front of the class to tell everyone what to do and some students do what was asked and others do not? Under what conditions are students most likely to do what is asked, and how can the teacher influence those conditions? Accordingly, the purpose of this chapter is to answer those questions and more about classroom management in physical education. The chapter starts with an overview of the unique conditions physical educators work in, recommended practices, and teacher knowledge and time use. The second section of the chapter focuses on the complexity of student behaviors in physical education, ways in which students can be off-task, why those behaviors might occur, and the effects of such behaviors. Discipline strategies and creating more positive student behaviors form the basis of the third section, and the chapter closes with a short discussion of some current issues and recommendations for future research.

CONTEXT, RECOMMENDED PRACTICE, TEACHER KNOWLEDGE AND TIME USE

Given that management is context specific, this section presents information about the physical education environment and recommended best practices with regard to maximizing student learning time and minimizing student off-task behavior. How teachers learn those practices and their use of class time are also discussed.

The Context

Understanding context is a key to management, and the context of physical education is unique and variable. Beyond the obvious factor of students moving in a large space, the context is influenced by variability in teaching sites, poor acoustics, a diverse student population, large class sizes, and the need to safely incorporate simultaneously moving bodies, implements, and objects. For these and other reasons, class management in physical education may be more difficult than in the classroom (Chepyator-Thomson & Liu, 2003).

Physical educators must have flexible skills that are adaptable to different teaching spaces. Note the use of the plural, "spaces," because physical education occurs in a wide variety of settings. Teachers at well resourced secondary schools might rotate their class through a classroom, weight room, pool, gymnasium, and outdoor teaching sites throughout the year. In contrast, at the elementary level, schools often have a single multiuse facility, sometimes jokingly called a "cafegymatorium," that serves many roles. The result is that the teacher often finds that the gymnasium will be used for a special event and today's lesson will need to take place on a stage or in the hallway. Each of those settings presents a unique set of challenges for management and the need to develop clear and consistent, yet flexible rules and routines for the varied settings.

Common teaching sites in physical education are likely to suffer from poor acoustics and/or high noise levels making effective teaching and management difficult. Sometimes those noise levels are a function of the educational activity as forty bouncing balls make a great deal of noise. Contributing to the high noise level is the design of the space with the typical gymnasium having a large area, hard surfaces, high ceilings, and no soundproofing. Whether indoors or outside, physical education settings often have high levels of noise that affect both student learning and teacher health (Ryan & Mendel, 2010).

In addition to environmental challenges, physical education is also unique in that teachers may be assigned a wide range of student grade levels to teach. Teacher licensure is often kindergarten through twelfth grade with some states and university programs also offering preschool certification. The result is that physical educators need flexible skills to meet the educational and management needs of students ages 3–21.

In addition to the wide range of students' ages and skill levels, physical educators must also deal with large class sizes. It is not unusual for a physical education teacher to have double or even triple classes at one time. Both teachers (O'Sullivan

& Dyson, 1994) and students (Dyson, Coviello, DiCesare, & Dyson, 2009) report problems with large class sizes. Hastie and Sanders (1991) found that in addition to curricular limitations created by large class sizes, there were significantly more students off-task in large classes (over 44 students) and that less time was devoted to academic tasks. One possible explanation for the larger class sizes in physical education is that principals and teachers disagree on acceptable class sizes in physical education, with principals believing larger classes are acceptable (Heitman, Kovaleski, Pugh, & Vicory; 2007). Bevans, Fitzpatrick, Sanchez, Riley, and Forrest (2010) also report challenges with large class sizes and the managerial demands placed on the teacher.

A final unique context challenge for physical educators is the use of equipment in a lesson. The distribution, use, and collection of equipment are challenging tasks that require significant management skills. The physically active nature of class with moving equipment and bodies also creates safety challenges that teachers must be aware of and plan for (Hastie & Martin, 2006). A lack of equipment can also be a problem in maintaining student interest and quality instruction (Misner & Arbogast, 1990), both of which can contribute to off-task behavior.

Recommended Practices to Promote Learning and Order

Doyle (1986) famously described two of the major tasks of management as promoting learning and order. The two are interrelated with a shared goal of using class time efficiently and in engaging ways to capture students' interest and cooperation, if not authentic engagement. When students are engaged in appropriate, motivating learning activities, their opportunity to learn is obviously increased, and their opportunity to be off-task is reduced. This section focuses on strategies to promote learning and order. What happens when students are off-task in ways that threaten learning and order is discussed in a later section.

Given the challenge and variability in the physical education context, recommended best practices in physical education are more a list of principles than prescriptions. Effective managers take time to develop and practice rules and routines, start class on time with an engaging task, plan equipment use as well as transitions, and carefully manage the challenge and pace of the lesson (Siedentop & Tannehill, 2000). As is true with many management practices, the devil is in the details of how a teacher accomplishes these tasks. For example, what is a good start and stop signal in an acoustically challenging space like a soccer field, and will those same signals be used when the class rotates to the weight room? Some teachers will choose to use the same signals while others will develop outdoor and indoor signals. The key is that effective teachers from both groups recognize the need for the management principle of clear stop and go signals.

Teacher education textbooks in the field (e.g., Darst, Pangrazi, Sariscsany, & Brusseau; 2012; Graham, Holt-Hale, & Parker, 2009; Pangrazi & Beighle, 2013; Rink, 2010; Siedentop & Tannehill, 2000) offer full descriptions of the steps and strategies teachers should consider for various needed components of a management plan in physical education. For example, Rink provides a list of needed routines related to various aspects of management: the locker room (e.g., what to wear, time allowed for dressing), before class (e.g. attendance, what to do when entering the gymnasium), when giving the lesson (e.g., boundaries, equipment, stop/start signals), and at end of lesson (e.g., cleanup, leaving the gym). Each of those categories has multiple considerations within it. Graham and colleagues and Pangrazi and Beighle offer specific game ideas to teach basic rules and routines to young students.

Active supervision is another trait common to best practice recommendations. This strategy involves a great deal of physical movement around the teaching space with a common strategy of keeping one's "back to the wall" (Arbogast & Chandler, 2005) to maximize viewing the most students at one time. Other commonly promoted strategies focus on short periods of teacher talk and always saying "when" before "what" (e.g., "When I say 'go,' I want you to . . .") when giving directions. Other key strategies include effective routines for moving students into groups quickly, as well as how to distribute and collect equipment efficiently.

At least some of these recommendations are based on research in the field with teachers. For example, the advice to keep moving and strive to keep most of the class in view is informed by investigations of teacher supervision patterns and its relationship to student learning time. Van der Mars, Vogler, Darst, and Cusimano (1994) analyzed supervision patterns (location, rate of movement, feedback) of elementary physical education teachers and examined their relationship with learning time. The teachers were moving constantly, and investigators found that teachers' location (primarily around the periphery) and movement correlated significantly with students' appropriate practice time. Another finding was that positive behavior feedback was correlated with student on-task behavior. Similar support for the importance of active monitoring on student on-task behavior is provided by other investigators (e.g., Hastie, Sanders, & Rowland, 1999).

Building on this basic concept of teacher use of time and student behavior, Hastie (1994) analyzed the teaching behaviors of three teachers to determine specific teacher behaviors that were linked with higher levels of appropriate practice. He found the most effective teacher was always "busy" offering encouragement, clarifying task expectations, and holding students accountable for their performance. The least effective teacher spent more time in observation, was less interactive with students, and rarely clarified tasks or held students accountable. Behets (1997) found similar results of the importance of actively observing students and reported that more effective teachers provided more activity time and less instructional time.

With regard to rules and routines, Fink and Siedentop (1989) observed seven elementary teachers at the start of the school year to learn how routines and rules were established. The most important routine taught by the teachers was the attention/quiet routine, and teachers taught it explicitly and practiced it often. In another start of the year investigation, Oslin (1996) found that middle school teachers spent a great deal of time on "housekeeping" duties like uniform distribution and locker room procedures.

The ability to manage locker rooms and uniforms for several hundred students is a significant managerial task (O'Sullivan & Dyson, 1994). The locker room is a problematic area for supervision inasmuch as teachers must simultaneously supervise male and female locker rooms, often on opposite sides of the gymnasium, while also preparing the teaching space for the next class. The crowded, small spaces and difficulty of supervision can lead to many problems including locker room bullying (Stoudt, 2006). Students who do not change clothes are a common management problem that is multifaceted. Given that wearing the school uniform is often part of the student's grade, teachers must first have an accurate recording system for such infractions. Second, many schools offer a "loaner uniform" to students willing to change clothes but who forgot their uniform, and that distribution and collection must be monitored. Finally, students who do not change clothes and therefore cannot participate create what is essentially a second class within a class that must be monitored with alternate assignments and/or locations like sitting in the bleachers while the rest of the class is actively engaged elsewhere.

Students can also supply insights into the effectiveness of teachers' management practices. Suppaporn's (2000) secondary students reported that teachers should have a clearly communicated and fair system. Students also suggested that the teacher have a learning focus and use smaller groups. Finally, they recommend that the teacher respond to student misbehavior and not just ignore it. Students in the Cothran, Kulinna, and Garrahy (2003) study recommended that their teachers set student behavior expectations early in the school year. A student described the need this way: "[T]his is kind of giving the secret way, but you've gotta lay down rules on the very first day . . . Don't let us break the rules and then try the rules later 'cause no one will pay attention" (p. 437). Students also recommended being consistent and developing relationships with students.

Increasingly, physical educators are being asked to facilitate physical activity across the curriculum (e.g., Let's Move Active Schools), and as such they may be asked to provide activity break strategies for non–physical education teachers. Given that teachers' confidence in their management skills when students are moving is a key factor in their willingness to use activity breaks, classroom teachers need management as well as lesson content strategies (Cothran, Kulinna, & Garn; 2010). Kulinna and colleagues (2013) report that modifying physical education practices to fit the classroom can help teachers. Five key management principles for the classroom are (1) the start and stop signals are different and used consistently (e.g., use a verbal command to start and a sound, perhaps a bell, to stop; (2) use "when" before "what" in directions (e.g., "When I say go, please . . ."; (3) organize students into groups efficiently; (4) deliver instructions quickly (e.g., 30 seconds or less); and (5) have equipment ready.

Employing evidenced-based strategies like these decreases student opportunity to be off-task and increases student opportunity for on-task behaviors and learning time. The next section on teacher knowledge provides some insights into the mechanisms for learning effective management principles.

Teacher Knowledge

Given that management is so critical to teacher success and satisfaction, as well as to student learning, how do teachers learn to implement these recommended practices and effectively manage such a complex environment? Garrahy, Cothran, and Kulinna (2005) found that teachers rarely credited their university programs with preparing them for successful classroom management and instead gave the most credit to trial and error, students, and colleagues. Teachers in the Hill and Brodin (2004) investigation also reported being unprepared for class management by their teacher education program. McCormack (1997) had teachers rate the factors that influenced their management practice. Previous teaching experience, personal values, their own experiences as students, and fellow teachers all scored highly. Two of the lowest rankings were given to in-service training and preservice training. Student teachers in the Fernandez-Balboa (1991) investigation largely ignored methods taught in their teacher education programs and instead relied on how their former teachers and coaches handled similar situations.

The report from Chepyator-Thomson and Liu (2003) is a bit more positive, suggesting that at least the student teaching experience is important for management knowledge growth. When university programs do receive credit for classroom management preparation, field experiences are often a key source of knowledge gain. Field experiences themselves, however, may need careful supervision and reflection skill building to increase students' management knowledge. Some research suggests that current field experiences may serve to move preservice teachers from a focus on student learning to a custodial and authoritarian approach to teaching (O'Sullivan, 2003).

Perhaps it is not surprising that little credit is given to university programs because the topic of classroom management does not often receive significant curricular focus in physical education teacher education programs. Lavay, Henderson, French, and Guthrie (2012) found that although university professors recognized the importance of teaching management, only six of the 134 surveyed institutions in the United States offered a course specific to the topic. The others taught a unit in one or more courses. In general, students received 5–23 hours specific to management in their course work, most often as part of teaching methods classes.

Teacher Use of Time

One of the goals of class management is to maximize student opportunity to learn; thus understanding how teachers use their time to create those student opportunities can provide insights into both learning and management practices. Van der Mars, Vogler, Darst, and Cusimano (1995) suggest that examining teachers' behaviors like transition time can illustrate their organizational and managerial ability. Much of what is known about teacher use of time is from systematic observations using the Academic Learning Time–Physical Education (ALT-PE) instrument (Siedentop, Tousignant, & Parker, 1982).

At one level, ALT-PE is a direct measure of teacher use of time. The instrument begins with the available class time and then subdivides that available time into managerial and organizational activities and activity time. Each of those categories has subcategories. Efficient use of time in management duties (e.g., equipment distribution, grouping students) logically leads to more available activity time. From studies using systematic observation instruments, we know that management time varies widely and is influenced by a number of factors including lesson content. For example, Kulinna, Silverman, and Keating (2000) reported that across 84 observed classes of 42 K–12 teachers, 23% of class time was spent in class management. Although the specifics vary widely for different classes, a finding of at least 20% in management time is fairly standard. This finding that management fills a large part of class time has also been confirmed using a variety of instruments across different lesson content (e.g., Hall et al., 2012; Roberts & Fairclough, 2011).

STUDENT (MIS)BEHAVIOR, ATTRIBUTIONS, AND EFFECTS

The previous section focused on teacher strategies to maximize student learning time and order. Student cooperation with teacher tasks is needed for those strategies to be effective. Students, however, are not always on-task. This section provides insights into the difficulty of observing student behavior and then examines the range of possible student responses to a task. Some of those task responses will be labeled "misbehavior," an off-task response that threatens the learning and order of the class. Although when an off-task behavior should be considered a misbehavior is a fuzzy line whose interpretation can vary from teacher to teacher, from student to student, and definitely between teacher and student. The frequency of, attributions for, and effects on others of off-task behavior comprise the final section in this chapter.

Complexity of Observing Student Behavior

One fundamental need for understanding class management is to understand what behaviors are actually occurring in the class. That seems like a relatively simple question but the complexity of the physical education environment means that an accurate description of student behaviors is a challenge. One challenge is the sheer volume of events happening in a large space at any one time. The overlapping nature of class events means it is nearly impossible for any individual, whether that is a teacher, observer, or student, to be aware of every behavior (Suppaporn, 2000). Add those overlapping events to the large and varied spaces that must be monitored, and one begins to envision the difficulty of observing accurately what is happening at any one time. A second challenge to accurately describing student behavior is that students can and do conceal their behaviors from their teachers (Hastie & Siedentop, 1999; Stork & Sanders, 2002a). A third challenge is the differing perspective of teachers and students on the same class events (e.g., Cothran & Ennis, 1997; Stork & Sanders, 2002b) makes it hard to even define what is a misbehavior when viewed by different participants. Students may not even agree on when a student action is merely a different behavior or a misbehavior, particularly when a teacher's management system has not clearly defined acceptable actions (Suppaporn, Dodds, & Griffin; 2003).

Four Ways Students Respond to Tasks

Students exhibit a wide range of behaviors in class, some that support the learning environment and some that do not. Tousignant and Siedentop (1983) reported four specific ways that students responded to teachers' stated tasks: (1) Students completed the task as described by the teacher; (2) students modified the task to make it easier or harder depending on their skill and interest level; (3) students acted as "competent bystanders" who were off-task but at first glance did not appear to be so; and (4) students participated in deviant off-task behavior.

Students Complete Tasks

Students engaging appropriately in and completing the stated task of the teacher is a primary goal of class management. Offering developmentally appropriate, challenging tasks that students value can increase their willingness to stay on-task. Similarly, holding students accountable for their learning and giving them some choice in it also creates a more positive and on-task class environment.

Students Modify Tasks

The second category of student behaviors, students who modify the task, may or may not be disruptive to the class. Sometimes the changes students make to a stated task are related to altering the task to meet their individual skill levels, but the behavior itself is still appropriate in that the student is learning engaged. For example, students might change the distance from which they are shooting a basketball or challenge another student to a shooting contest, even though competition was not part of the stated task. At other times, the student off-task behavior is clearly working against the learning environment.

Sanders and Graham (1995) describe a "zone of acceptable responses" with regard to off-task behavior. Students are granted some leeway by the teacher to task change, but at some point the teacher defines the change as off-task and redirects students to appropriate behavior. When taken to its extreme, this "zone of acceptable responses" can focus strictly on behavioral compliance with little expectation that students will engage appropriately in the learning task, a condition Lund (1992) calls "instructional pseudoaccountability." In these situations, the teacher holds students accountable only for good behavior, not learning. This focus on behavior, not learning, is a widespread phenomenon described by Placek (1983) as "busy, happy and good" programs in physical education.

Altered tasks and a range of acceptable options can be the result of task modifications to meet students' skill needs, but the same processes are also at work as students pursue their social agendas in class. Students are often motivated by noneducational goals (Cothran & Ennis, 1998), and their active pursuit of goals like fun and time with friends is an additional aspect of the class ecology (Hastie & Siedentop, 1999). Hastie and Pickwell (1996) and Carlson and Hastie (1997) offer detailed analyses of how the student social agenda contributes to decreased learning expectations from the teachers in a trade for increased appropriate behavior by the students.

Stork and Sanders (2002a) offer another perspective on off-task behavior by examining elementary students' task changes and why those occurred. Three possible reasons were offered to explain why a student might not follow the teacher's directions. First, the students' developmental level meant they sometimes had trouble recalling a sequence of instructions and were easily distracted by other class events. Second, comprehension did not necessarily reflect understanding. Because students did not always understand the point of the task, students sometimes had low levels of engagement or changed the task. Finally, they noted that students had internalized the teacher's focus on management and that their primary focus may then have been on behavioral compliance more than learning skills.

This failure to understand the purpose of the task was a significant finding in Hopple and Graham's (1995) examination of students' perceptions of and behaviors related to a mile run fitness test. Because the students did not understand the purpose and the test was not fun, many students became "test dodgers." These misunderstandings about the purposes of physical education and appropriate student behavior appear to start as early as kindergarten (Sanders & Graham, 1995). How teachers can best address such student off-task behavior will be discussed at length in later sections of this chapter.

Students Are Not Fully Engaged but Look Engaged

The "test dodgers" described by Hopple and Graham (1995) represent a third task response option. In this case, students are not fully engaged in the learning task but have developed skills in looking as though they are. The original description of "competent bystander" comes from work by Tousignant and Siedentop (1983), who described students who strategically seek less active positions in the field/court, give up turns, and engage in a wide range of behaviors to limit their actual involvement without being so off-task as to draw the teacher's attention.

Seminal research by Griffin (1984, 1985) focused on middle school physical education and how a student's skill level interacted with the curriculum and other students to create participation patterns. Some of the students were very active and on-task, while several negative participation patterns were described. These included "invisible players and wimps" for the boys who were minimally involved in the class and "cheerleaders" for the girls who were enthusiastic supporters of their team but rarely were involved in the game. Often teachers fail to notice competent avoidance, or if they do notice, they willingly acquiesce to the behavior to allow time and energy to focus on more serious threats to class management.

Deviant Off-Task

These are the behaviors that are commonly described as misbehaviors and that most observers would classify as detracting from learning and order. As one of the high school students in Suppaporn's (2000) investigation explained, "Misbehavior is when students do something wrong or something we are not told to, or they are doing something that they know they are not supposed to" (p. 126). These types of behaviors are more fully explored in the next section.

Misbehaviors and Attributions

Misbehaviors

Perhaps the largest investigation related to the frequency of physical education student misbehaviors was conducted in the United States. Over 2,300 students (Cothran

& Kulinna, 2007) and 300 teachers (Kulinna, Cothran, & Regualos, 2006) completed the Physical Education Classroom Instrument (Kulinna, Cothran, & Regualos, 2003; Krech, Kulinna, & Cothran, 2010), rating the frequency of misbehaviors in physical education settings. The misbehaviors were divided into mild, moderate, and severe categories. There were some differences between teacher and student responses, but in general the two groups reported similar findings. Both groups reported a wide range of behaviors in class with regard to the frequency and severity of behaviors. Most of the misbehaviors were mild or moderate (e.g., fails to pay attention, inappropriate language), and misbehavior happened frequently. It is important to note that mild does not equate to nonproblematic. Using an observation instrument instead of self-report, Goyette, Dore, and Dion (2000) reported that 23% of misbehaviors occurred in the mildest category, 42% in the next most serious category, and 35% in the most serious category.

Secondary students reported more misbehavior than elementary students with the largest number of misbehaviors being with students in grades 7–10 (Cothran & Kulinna, 2007). Teacher reports also indicated the most misbehaviors at the secondary level and the fewest at the elementary level. Although there are likely many reasons for the increased misbehaviors at the secondary level, one key consideration is the failure of the curriculum to meet student needs. Instead of engagement, alienation may be the norm in some settings (Carlson, 1995; Cothran & Ennis, 1999; Dyson, Coviello, DiCesare, & Dyson, 2009). Teachers in urban settings reported more misbehaviors than their suburban or rural counterparts. Female students perceived more misbehaviors in their class than did male students, a pattern also true for the teachers; female teachers reported more student misbehaviors.

Working with preservice and in-service teachers in Australia, McCormack (1997) similarly found a range of student misbehaviors with the most common misbehaviors being "talking out of turn" and "idleness and slowness." McCormack also found gender differences with these teacher reports. Fernandez-Balboa (1991) focused on preservice teachers and found they reported mostly individually deviant students (86%) with the three main types of misbehavior being off-task, nonparticipation, and aggression.

Hardy, Hardy, and Thorpe (1994) took a slightly different approach; they observed 119 secondary classes in England and examined student sex and time-of-day differences in student behavior. They found that the time of day (morning or afternoon) when the class met did not affect behavior, but there were significant relationships between student behavior and the sex of the student and teacher. Specifically, males were responsible for roughly twice as many misbehaviors as female students. Interestingly, though, students were more likely identified as misbehaving by teachers of the same sex.

Attributions: A Matter of Perspective

It is important to know what misbehaviors occur in class, but perhaps it is just as important to understand why those misbehaviors occur. Only with that understanding can effective interventions be planned and implemented.

Teacher attributions

Cothran, Kulinna, and Garrahy (2009) explored secondary physical education teachers' and students' attributions for student misbehavior. Teachers most often attributed student misbehavior to students' poor home life where parents did not care, give attention, or teach proper behavior. Blaming students' home life was also reported by Ennis (1995), who examined teachers' responses to noncompliant students, and by Fernandez-Balboa (1990, 1991), who reported on preservice teachers' attributions for student misbehavior. Teachers in the Ennis study also noted their urban students' disinterest in school in general and the lack of importance the students placed on school outcomes or grades, leaving teachers frustrated and confused. Cothran and colleagues (2009) also found that teachers were seemingly confused by student behavior and often replied "Who knows?" when asked to explain student behavior, as though, from the teacher perspective, there was no logical explanation for how some students behaved.

Student Attributions

In contrast, students almost never mentioned home life as a cause of misbehavior. Student explanations for misbehavior focused on student attempts to get attention from either peers or the teacher. Particularly for male students, misbehavior could lead to increased popularity among peers. A second attribution reported by students was that when school was boring, students would "act bad" to alleviate the boredom and to provide the fun that the lesson failed to provide. Interestingly, teachers never attributed student misbehavior to curricular choices or lesson activities, although they did describe differences in student behavior based on how popular a particular class topic was for students.

In a high school study, students suggested that student grouping and the type of activity contributed to misbehavior (Suppaporn, 2000). They suggested that the peer group and size of the group could make a student more or less likely to stay on-task. Specifically, the larger the group and the smaller the space, the more misbehavior was likely. A second behavioral influence was how much students enjoyed the activity. If students did not like the activity, they were more likely to misbehave or at least not participate.

Cothran's and Kulinna's (2007) survey also examined student reported reasons for misbehavior. The top three reasons across all age groups were that the lesson was boring, the student wanted attention, and the students did not think they could do the lesson, so they did not try. Interestingly, Cothran and Kulinna also asked students to self-rate what kind of students they were with regard to behavior, and that rating influenced why students believed misbehavior occurs. For students who self-rated themselves as often failing to comply with school rules, their rationale for misbehavior was different. For these students, their top three attributions for misbehavior were (1) lesson is boring, (2) they don't like the teacher, and (3) they are just bad kids. Not liking the teacher suggests that personal relationships are key, a finding substantiated by other investigations (e.g., Cothran, Kulinna, & Garrahy, 2003; Dyson, Coviello, DiCesare, & Dyson, 2009).

The Effects of Student Misbehavior

Regardless of the cause, the effects of misbehavior on teachers and students are significant. Cothran and associates (2009) shared stories from teachers and students in very diverse school settings about the effects of student misbehavior on the class. First, both groups recognized that student misbehavior meant lost learning time. Second, curricular offerings had been eliminated (e.g., archery, gymnastics) due to safety concerns, while other content (e.g. dance) was dropped or minimized because of perceived student apathy toward the topic. Finally, teachers and students both reported the negative effect that misbehavior had on teacher attitude and energy, as well as on the quality of teacher–student and student–student relationships.

Specific to lost learning time, it seems logical that if a teacher does not have good routines or must take time to deal with student misbehavior, then less time is available for learning. Both teachers and students also noted the time it takes to "write someone up"—the increased paperwork demands of school-wide management systems that have letters of referral, demerits, and so on (Cothran, Kulinna, & Garrahy, 2009). Fernandez-Balboa (1991) also reported that misbehavior can distract both teachers and students from a learning focus.

Changes to the offered curriculum have also been described by other investigators. Ennis (1996) found that teachers across various subject matters, including physical education, actively planned to avoid direct confrontations with their urban high school students. Teachers avoided content that was (1) not of immediate interest to students, (2) related to minimal or no student participation, and (3) a stimulus for student discussions that the teachers wanted to avoid. Rovegno (1994) shared similar reports of preservice teachers who retreated into a "curricular zone of safety" in an attempt to limit conflict with students in a secondary setting. Even when teachers did not avoid content, student behavior is a critical factor in implementing curricula. Hall and colleagues (2012) report that student misbehavior was the number one barrier (60% of all reported) to implementing the HEALTHY curriculum, a standardized curricular program across a wide range of schools.

As might be expected given their relatively short tenure at their schools, students never commented on curricular change over time, but they were cognizant of how their engagement shaped the class period (Cothran, Kulinna, & Garrahy, 2009). Students were even able to describe specific strategies they used in class to affect content choices of the teacher. As Erik, a secondary student, explained, "If we're not interested, you [the teacher] can't get it done" (Cothran & Ennis, 1997, p. 546). Specifically, the students reported using nonparticipation, powerful personality persuasion, disruption, and rewards to affect the teacher's choice of content and structure. The reward students offered their teachers was compliance. In return, teachers were expected to offer favorite content in a low-accountability environment. This negotiated compromise allowed teachers to gain the order that they and their administration valued but at the cost of student learning.

It is also clear that student misbehavior affects the individuals in the class in a number of ways. Numerous studies suggest that student misbehavior is a major cause of teacher job dissatisfaction (e.g., Cothran & Ennis, 1997; McCormack, 1997). If the management challenges and failures continue, a negative cycle of blame and feeling helpless builds, which can result in teachers leaving the profession (Fernandez-Balboa, 1990). In the short term, the daily stress affects teacher's energy (O'Sullivan & Dyson, 1994) and attitude (Cothran, Kulinna, & Garrahy, 2009; Dyson, Coviello, DiCesare, & Dyson, 2009). The Dyson and associates (2009) middle school students offered examples of "Teachers are uptight" when describing their program. Telesa, a student in an urban high school, described the cause and effect of her teacher's lack of patience: "I think that's just because they're frustrated with the kids who don't wanna learn. And the ones that wanna learn, she wanna help them, but she can't help the ones that don't wanna learn because the ones that don't wanna learn don't pay attention and be quiet so teachers sometimes be frustrated." (Cothran, Kulinna, & Garrahy, 2009, p. 163). Students who did want to learn also sometimes reported being frustrated with other students' misbehavior. The teachers in the O'Sullivan and Dyson (1994) study suggested that misbehaving students took enjoyment from the class from other students. Suomi, Collier, and Brown (2003) proposed that when teachers fail to address students' social skills, negative experiences occur for at least some students, particularly those with disabilities. Although students report that misbehavior is not always a negative factor, from the student perspective, misbehavior can sometimes lead to more fun and increased peer status (Cothran, Kulinna, & Garrahy, 2009).

CHANGING STUDENT BEHAVIOR

Given the frequency and effects of misbehaviors, teachers clearly have a responsibility for intervention. Following Doyle's (1986) lead of defining discipline as a subset of order focused more on curbing student misbehavior than on promoting engagement and order, this section examines teacher discipline strategies for student misbehavior and ways in which teachers might design their programs to teach and motivate students to exhibit more positive behaviors.

Teacher Discipline Strategies

Textbooks in the field (e.g., Lavay, French, & Henderson, 2006) offer suggested disciplinary strategies, but there are surprisingly little data on what strategies teachers actually use. An early attempt to explore this issue by Kennedy (1982) described 17 teacher techniques at the secondary level, with the most common intervention being a verbal order to stop. Henkel (1991) developed an instrument to examine elementary teachers' strategies and whether they were used before or after a misbehavior. He found that teachers' use of strategies varied and that the differences were a function of philosophy, lesson content, and equipment availability. Perron and Downey

(1997) used the same instrument to examine secondary teachers' strategies. Much like their elementary counterparts, the teachers used a range of strategies, including some not on the original instrument (e.g., detention, conferencing), but used praise and rewarding less often. Working with physical educators in Britain, Curtner-Smith, Kerr, and Hencken (1995) found that teachers frequently used positive psychosocial development strategies (e.g., encouragement, positive reinforcement) and that those strategies remained fairly constant across various curricular units.

There is some suggestion that teacher use of strategy is developmental. McCormack (1997) found differences in strategy use between preservice and experienced teachers. Preservice teachers tended to focus on rules, commands, and clear directions, while experienced teachers tended to focus on prevention with top-rated strategies of positive relationships, praise and encouragement, and being genuine. O'Sullivan and Dyson (1994) report similar findings with experienced secondary teachers who focused on respect, showing interest, and communication—a finding echoed by the elementary teachers in the Garrahy and associates (2005) investigation.

In contrast to these multiple strategy teachers, Suppaporn, Dodds, and Griffin's (2003) investigation of secondary physical education found that the primary strategy was to ignore behavior unless it seriously disrupted the class or could lead to injury. Fernandez-Balboa (1991) also noted limited action systems with his student teachers inasmuch as they rarely considered options like positive reinforcement, improved tasks and work systems, or assertive strategies. The three most common strategies were verbal interaction with the student (e.g., warning, talk about the behavior), relocate the student (e.g., move away from group or a time-out), and implement a sanction (e.g., grade point deduction, detention).

One discipline tool that is largely unique to physical education is exercise. Despite a national position paper against the practice (National Association for Sport and Physical Education, 2009), exercise continues to be used in some school settings (e.g., Dyson, Coviello, DiCesare, & Dyson, 2009; O'Sullivan & Dyson, 1994). Its persistent use is attributed to the socialization process of teachers and the complex interplay between sport and physical education experiences of teachers (Pagnano & Langley, 2001).

Promoting Positive Behavior

Ward (2006) suggests that social skills, much like motor skills, can be developed but that teachers too often assume that students have social skills, so misbehavior must be intentional. Siedentop and Tannehill (2000) go so far as to describe the belief that all students will have needed social skills as one of the major myths of class management. Rimm-Kaufman, Pianta, and Cox (2000) found that kindergarten teachers across the nation report significant and growing deficits in children's social skills needed for success. As one example, 20% of the teachers reported at least half their class had problems with social skills. Those are not problems that the children will "grow out of," and that lack of skills places the children at academic risk. Specific to physical education, a number of approaches have been proposed, including behavior management strategies, curricular models, and instructional techniques to create a positive classroom community and promote social skills.

Behavior Management

One skill promoting option for teachers to consider is behavior management (see Ward & Barrett, 2002, for a review). Vidoni and Ward (2006) used group-oriented contingencies to promote fair play behaviors in a middle school setting. The intervention produced more positive behaviors, and some of those were maintained during a follow-up check. Interestingly, Vidoni and Ward also asked the classes involved about the use of group contingencies. Over 80% of the students would like to use the strategy again. Group contingencies have also been used successfully to increase participation in running laps (Ward & Dunaway, 1995) and with reducing inappropriate behavior while increasing appropriate behavior (Patrick, Ward, & Crouch, 1998). Given the reported success of these interventions, it is difficult to understand why behavior management strategies are used so rarely by teachers.

Curricular and Instructional Models

Probably the best known and most studied of the curricular models designed to help students learn personal and social skills was proposed by Hellison (2013). The curriculum provides a developmental perspective on personal and social responsibility. The five levels in the model provide a useful framework for working with students to develop social skills. Level 1 is respecting the rights and feelings of others, and students are prompted to reflect on and exhibit participation and effort in Level 2. Self-direction becomes the focus of Level 3, and Level 4 focuses on caring. Level 5 asks students to use their skills outside the gym to become difference makers in their family and community. Hellison suggests that teachers need new strategies to promote student development. Those strategies might include awareness talks, reflection time, decision-making opportunities, group meetings, and counseling time. In a review of research on 26 programs (Hellison & Walsh, 2002) that had adopted the personal and social responsibility model, strong support was shown for the effectiveness of parts of the program. Watson and Clocksin (2013) offer a companion text to the Hellison model that provides sample teaching units, strategies, and assessments consistent with the model.

The Exemplary Physical Education Curriculum (Michigan Fitness Foundation, 2002) has also been used to increase students' social skills. Findings from more than 1,000 students in 30 schools indicated that social behaviors significantly increased (e.g., "I put the ball in the basket when the teacher tells me to") for elementary students after the teachers used the curricular model for one year (Martin, Kulinna, McCaughtry, & Barnard, 2005). Positive reports from teachers also support the curriculum model Dynamic Physical Education (Pangrazi & Beighle, 2013) as enhancing elementary class management (Kloeppel, Kulinna, Stylianou, & van der Mars, 2013). At the secondary level, Sport for Peace has shown promise in promoting positive and on-task student behavior (Ennis et al., 1999). Sport for Peace combines the Sport Education curricular model (Siedentop, 1994) with concepts of care theory and conflict negotiation skills. Teachers were initially resistant to the increased organizational duties of the model but, over time, reported positive experiences with the model and the resultant student behaviors and learning.

Other curricular models like Adventure Education and Sport Education, although not developed specifically to teach social skills as a primary goal, have reported positive impacts on students' trust and communication (Dyson, 1995) and students' cooperation, effort, and teamwork (MacPhail, Kirk, & Kinchin, 2004). Additionally, instructional models like cooperative learning also hold promise in developing student social skills. In both secondary (Dyson & Strachan, 2000) and elementary settings (Dyson, 2001, 2002), the use of cooperative learning increased student cooperation and responsibility. Although not specifically an instructional model, the motivational environment that a teacher creates also influences students' on-task behavior (e.g., Moreno-Murcia, Sicilia, Cervello, Huescar, & Dumitru, 2011; Papaioannou, 1998; Spray, 2002). For example, Solmon (1996) manipulated task- and ego-involved learning environments for a motor task and found that a task-focused environment resulted in more student learning and fewer teacher-reported problems.

In one of the few experimental studies to examine teachers' actual teaching of social skills, Sharpe, Crider, Vyhlidal, and Brown (1996) found that urban teachers who implemented specific lessons that addressed well-defined appropriate behavior, taught conflict resolution skills, and used a rotating class roster to provide leadership opportunities increased prosocial characteristics like effort, helping, and respect.

Building Community

Rethinking the traditional teacher–student hierarchy may also be a necessary step in promoting positive student behaviors. Students report they want connection with the content and with caring, respectful classmates and teachers (Cothran & Ennis, 1999, 2000). Enacting a caring curriculum (e.g., Larson & Silverman, 2005; Owens & Ennis, 2005) will also require new ways of thinking about teaching. Curricular models like Sport Education (Siedentop, 1994) offer some of the meaning that students request, but the field may also need to move beyond sport as a primary content area to connect with students.

LOOKING BACK AND FORWARD

This chapter began with a series of questions about management in physical education, and hopefully those questions have been at least partially answered. As is often the case with review chapters, however, a review of the old means new questions arise about where the field has been and where it should go.

The first question that should prompt serious thought is why is there so little research specific to class management? That is not to say that the field has ignored the topic, but given that management is central to any discussion of teacher satisfaction, retention, and effectiveness, as well as student success and arguably enjoyment, why doesn't management dominate the field's research agenda? Instead, much of what we know about management comes as a corollary to other topics like teacher socialization or curriculum implementation. Given that management is a core foundation on which all class processes rests, one might expect that the field would address the topic more directly and more often.

A second and related question is what class management strategies do physical educators actually use and how effective are those practices? There is some research to support recommended practice, particularly with regard to preventive strategies like teacher use of time, but there is almost no evidence to guide teachers seeking the most effective discipline strategies. For example, time-out is a widely used strategy in elementary schools, but does it work? At an intuitive level, time-out seems an effective strategy, and the practical knowledge of teachers should not be dismissed, but no studies document an actual change in student behavior and/or attitude from having experienced time out. Similarly we have little to no evidence examining the effectiveness of various management practices in different settings. Are the field's principles of practice equally effective in urban and rural settings? What impact does the increasing multicultural nature of schools play in management systems for today and tomorrow? Evidence-based practice is a foundational concept today in many fields, including education. If that practice were applied to physical education management, the field would have very little to recommend to teachers as data-based guidance.

This lack of data-based guidance may be related to the perennial question in teacher education, not just physical education, of why teacher education programs have so little influence on teacher practice. Clearly, socialization and the limited time that university programs actually have with students are primary influences on the washout effect of teacher education, but perhaps if we had more specific practices that we strongly believed could positively impact class management practice, then maybe university programs and preservice teachers would both be more willing to engage regularly in using and mastering those strategies. Certainly the lack of time specifically spent on class management in teacher education programs is also a point for the field to ponder and change.

Interestingly, a small but relatively robust body of work suggests that behavioral techniques like group contingency are effective in changing individual student and class behavior, yet almost no teachers report using those techniques, and textbooks in the field are often mute on the topic. Additional work is needed to explore the promise of these techniques and, just as importantly, to understand why teachers do not use them.

Two other areas that need additional attention are teacher and student attributions for behavior, as well as the link between curricular offerings and student behavior. First, with regard to attributions, it seems a necessary first step to learn more about how individuals explain behavior if the field is to design more effective management strategies. The work by Cothran and colleagues (2009) suggests that neither teachers nor students accept responsibility for the behaviors happening in class. Both play a role, and both therefore need to be involved in the solution. The Hellison (2013) responsibility curriculum model may provide a framework for reflection and developmental growth of student responsibility, but what strategies can help teachers become more accountable for their decision making and the role it plays in student behavior? For example, it is clear that teacher curricular offerings and the motivational environment they create play a large role in students' engagement or resistance, yet teachers do not directly attribute student engagement to those factors.

In contrast, two of the top three reasons for misbehavior, as explained by students (Cothran & Kulinna, 2007), were curricular in nature. Specifically, if the lesson is boring or too hard, students report they are more likely to misbehave. Teachers in physical education have a great deal of curricular freedom, so how can they use that freedom to offer challenging yet engaging learning environments instead of retreating into a curricular zone of safety (Rovegno, 1994) that results in only minimal compliance by students?

Students who self-rate themselves as likely to misbehave agree that boring lessons lead to misbehavior, but they also report not liking the teacher as a primary reason for misbehaving (Cothran & Kulinna, 2007). Several other reports also note the importance of teacher caring and respect to student on-task behavior. Effective class management cannot separate the technical (e.g., time use, quick transitions) from the personal (e.g., caring, respect). How to understand that merger and to teach merging those skills to teachers are other areas the field has yet to address directly in significant ways.

CONCLUSION

This chapter provided some initial insights into the unique context of physical education and how effective teachers have attempted and might alternately try to manage their classes to achieve the dual goals of learning and order. Those goals, however, cannot be considered separate from student goals and student–teacher relationships. Additional work is needed to fully explore these options and relationships to provide a more complete understanding of effective class management in physical education.

REFERENCES

Arbogast, G., & Chandler, J. P. (2005). Classroom management behaviors of effective Physical Educators. *Strategies, 19*, 7–11.

Behets, D. (1997). Comparison of more and less effective teaching behaviors in secondary physical education. *Teaching and Teacher Education, 13*, 215–224.

Bevans, K. B., Fitzpatrick, L. A., Sanchez, B. M., Riley, A. W., & Forrest, C. (2010). Physical education resources, class management, and student physical activity levels: A structure-process-outcome approach to evaluating physical education effectiveness. *Journal of School Health, 80*, 573–580.

Carlson, T. (1995). We hate gym: Student alienation from physical education. *Journal of Teaching in Physical Education, 14*, 467–477.

Carlson, T., & Hastie, P. (1997). The student social system within sport education. *Journal of Teaching in Physical Education, 16*, 176–195.

Chepyator-Thomson, J. R., & Liu, W. (2003). Pre-service teachers' reflections on student teaching experiences: Lessons learned and suggestions for reform in PETE programs. *Physical Educator, 60*, 2–12.

Cothran, D. J., & Ennis, C. D. (1997). Students' and teachers' perceptions of conflict and power. *Teaching and Teacher Education, 13*, 541–553.

Cothran, D. J., & Ennis, C. D. (1998). Curricula of mutual worth: Comparisons of students' and teachers' curricular goals. *Journal of Teaching in Physical Education, 17*, 307–327.

Cothran, D. J., & Ennis, C. D. (1999). Alone in a crowd: Meeting students' needs for relevance and connection in urban high school physical education. *Journal of Teaching in Physical Education, 18*, 234–247.

Cothran, D. J., & Ennis, C. D. (2000). Building bridges to engagement: Communicating respect and care for students in urban high schools. *Journal of Research and Development in Education, 33*, 106–118.

Cothran, D. J., & Kulinna, P. H. (2007). Students' reports of misbehavior in physical education. *Research Quarterly for Exercise and Sport, 78*, 216–224.

Cothran, D. J., Kulinna, P. H., & Garn, A. (2010). Classroom teachers and physical activity integration. *Teaching and Teacher Education, 26*, 1381–1388.

Cothran, D. J., Kulinna, P. H., & Garrahy, D. A. (2003). "This is kind of giving a secret away. . .": Students' perspectives on effective classroom management. *Teaching and Teacher Education, 19*, 435–444.

Cothran, D. J., Kulinna, P. H., & Garrahy, D. A. (2009). Attributions for and consequences of student misbehavior. *Physical Education and Sport Pedagogy, 14*, 155–167.

Curtner-Smith, M. D., Kerr, I .G., & Hencken, C. L. (1995). Teacher behaviors related with pupil psychosocial development in physical education: A descriptive-analytic study. *Educational Research, 37*, 267–277.

Darst, P. W., Pangrazi, R. P., Sariscsany, M. J., & Brusseau, T. A. (2012). *Dynamic physical education for secondary school students* (7th ed.). Boston: Benjamin Cummings.

Doyle, W. (1986). Classroom organization and management. In Merlin C. Wittrock (Ed.), *Handbook of Research on Teaching* (4th ed.). New York: MacMillan.

Dyson, B. (1995). Students' voices in two alternative elementary physical education programs. *Journal of Teaching Physical Education, 14*, 394–407.

Dyson, B. (2001). Cooperative learning in an elementary school physical education program. *Journal of Teaching in Physical Education, 20*, 264–281.

Dyson B. (2002). The implementation of cooperative learning in an elementary school physical education program. *Journal of Teaching in Physical Education, 22*, 69–84.

Dyson, B., Coviello, N., DiCesare, E., & Dyson, L. (2009). Students' perspectives of urban middle school physical education programs. *Middle Grades Research Journal, 4*, 31–52.

Dyson, B., & Strachan, K. (2000). Cooperative learning in a high school physical education program. *Waikato Journal of Education, 6*, 19–37.

Ennis, C. D. (1995). Teachers' responses to noncompliant students: The realities and consequences of a negotiated curriculum. *Teaching & Teacher Education, 11*, 445–460.

Ennis, C. D. (1996). When avoiding confrontation leads to avoiding content: Disruptive students' impact on curriculum. *Journal of Curriculum and Supervision, 11*, 145–162.

Ennis, C. D., Solmon, M. A., Satina, B., Loftus, S. J., Mensch, J., & McCauley, M. T. (1999). Creating a sense of family in urban schools using "Sport for Peace" curriculum. *Research Quarterly for Exercise and Sport, 70*, 273–285.

Fernanadez-Balboa, J. M. (1990). Helping novice teachers handle discipline problems. *Journal of Physical Education, Recreation, and Dance, 66*, 50–54.

Fernandez-Balboa, J. M. (1991). Beliefs, interactive thoughts, and actions of physical education student teachers regarding pupil misbehaviors. *Journal of Teaching in Physical Education, 11*, 59–78.

Fink, J., & Siedentop, D. (1989). The development of routines, rules and expectations at the start of the school year. *Journal of Teaching in Physical Education, 3*, 198–212.

Garrahy, D. A., Cothran, D. J., & Kulinna, P. H. (2005). Voices from the trenches: An exploration of teaches' management knowledge. *Journal of Educational Research, 99*, 56–63.

Goyette, R., Dore, R., & Dion, E. (2000). Pupils' misbehaviors and the reactions and causal attributions of physical education student teachers: A sequential analysis. *Journal of Teaching in Physical Education, 20*, 3–14.

Graham, G., Holt-Hale, S. A., & Parker, M. (2009). *Children moving: A reflective approach to teaching physical education* (8th ed.). Mountain View, CA: Mayfield.

Griffin, P. (1984). Girls' participation patterns in a middle school team sports unit. *Journal of Teaching in Physical Education, 4*, 30–38.

Griffin, P. (1985). Boys' participation styles in a middle school team sports unit. *Journal of Teaching in Physical Education, 4*, 100–110.

Hall, W. J., Zeveloff, A., Steckler, A., Schneider, M., Thompson, D., Pham, T., Volpe, S. L., Hindes, K., Sleigh, A., & McMurray, R. G. (2012). Process evaluation results from the HEALTHY physical education intervention. *Health Education Research, 27*, 307–318.

Hardy, C. A., Hardy, C. E., & Thorpe, R. D. (1994). Pupil misbehavior in secondary school mixed-sex physical education lessons. *British Journal of Physical Education, 15*, 7–11.

Hastie, P. A. (1994). Selected teacher behaviors and student ALT-PE in secondary school physical education. *Journal of Teaching in Physical Education, 13*, 242–259.

Hastie, P. A., & Martin, E. (2006). *Teaching elementary physical education: Strategies for the classroom teacher.* New York: Pearson.

Hastie, P.A., & Pickwell, A. (1996). A description of a student social system in a secondary school dance class. *Journal of Teaching in Physical Education, 15,* 171–187.

Hastie, P. A., & Sanders, J. E. (1991). The effects of class size and equipment availability on student lesson involvement in primary school physical education. *Journal of Experimental Education, 59,* 212–224.

Hastie, P. A., Sanders, S. W. & Rowland, R. S. (1999). Where good intentions meet harsh realities: Teaching large classes in physical education. *Journal of Teaching in Physical Education, 18,* 277–289.

Hastie, P., & Siedentop, D. (1999). An ecological perspective on physical education. *European Physical Education Review, 5,* 9–19.

Heitman, R. J., Kovaleski, J. E., Pugh, S. F., & Vicory, J. R. (2007). A comparison of principals' and physical educators' perceptions of program quality in physical education. *Research Quarterly for Exercise and Sport, 78*(1), A-70.

Hellison, D. (2013). *Teaching responsibility through physical activity* (3rd ed.). Champaign, IL: Human Kinetics.

Hellison, D., & Walsh, D. (2002). Responsibility-based youth programs evaluation: Investigating the investigations. *Quest, 54,* 292–307.

Henkel, S. A. (1991). Teachers' conceptualization of pupil control in elementary school physical education. *Research Quarterly for Exercise and Sport, 62,* 52–60.

Hill, G., & Brodin, K. L. (2004). Physical education teacher' perceptions of the adequacy of university coursework in preparation for teaching. *Physical Educator, 61,* 1–15.

Hopple, C., & Graham, G. (1995). What children think, feel, and know about physical fitness testing. *Journal of Teaching in Physical Education, 14,* 408–417.

Kennedy, E. F. (1982). Discipline in the physical education setting. *Physical Educator, 39,* 91–94.

Kloeppel, T., Kulinna, P. H., Stylianou, M., & van der Mars, H. (2013). Teacher fidelity to one physical education curricular model. *Journal of Teaching in Physical Education, 32,* 186–204.

Krech, P. R., Kulinna, P. H., & Cothran, D. (2010). Development of a short-form version of the physical education classroom instrument: Measuring secondary pupils' disruptive behaviours. *Physical Education and Sport Pedagogy, 15,* 209–225.

Kulinna, P. H., Cothran, D., & Regualos, R. (2003). Development of an instrument to measure student disruptive behaviors. *Measurement in Physical Education and Exercise Science, 7,* 25–41.

Kulinna, P. H., Cothran, D. J., & Regualos, R. (2006). Teachers' reports of students' misbehavior in physical education. *Research Quarterly for Exercise and Sport, 77,* 32–40.

Kulinna, P. H., Silverman, S., & Keating, X. D. (2000). Relationship between teachers' belief systems and actions toward teaching physical activity and fitness. *Journal of Teaching in Physical Education, 19,* 206–221.

Kulinna, P. H., Stylianou, M., Lorenz, K., Martin, J., Hodges, M., & Houston, J. (2013). Using social cognitive theories to investigate teacher behavior change in integrating physical activity breaks. Paper presented at the American Educational Research Association 2013 annual meeting, San Francisco, California, April.

Larson, A., & Silverman, S. (2005). Rationales and practices used by caring physical education teachers. *Sport, Education & Society, 10,* 175–193.

Lavay, B. W., French, R., & Henderson, H. L. (2006). *Positive behavior management in physical activity settings* (2nd ed.). Champaign, IL: Human Kinetics.

Lavay, B., Henderson, H., French, R., & Guthrie, S. (2012). Behavior management instructional practices and content of college/university physical education teacher education (PETE) programs. *Physical Education and Sport Pedagogy, 17,* 195–210.

Lund, J. (1992). Assessment and accountability in secondary physical education. *Quest, 44,* 352–360.

MacPhail, A., Kirk, D., & Kinchin, G. (2004). Sport education: Promoting team affiliation through physical education. *Journal of Teaching in Physical Education, 23,* 106–122.

Martin, J. J., Kulinna, P. H., McCaughtry, N., & Barnard, S. D. (2005). Influences of professional development on elementary students' personal and social development. *Research Quarterly for Exercise and Sport, 76* (March), A16–17.

McCormack, A. (1997). Classroom management problems, strategies and influences in physical education. *European Physical Education Review, 3,* 102–115.

Michigan Fitness Foundation. Michigan's Exemplary Physical Education Curriculum (EPEC). (2002). *EPEC lessons: Grades K, 1, 2, 3, 4, 5, and user's manual.* Lansing: Author.

Misner, J., & Arbogast, G. (1990). Strategies for improving student learning and the status of physical education. *Physical Educator, 47,* 50–54.

Moreno-Murcia, J. A., Sicilia, A., Cervello, E., Huescar, E., & Dumitru, D. C. (2011). The relationship between goal orientations, motivational climate and self-reported discipline in physical education. *Journal of Sports Science and Medicine, 10*, 119–129.

National Association for Sport and Physical Education. (2009). *Physical activity used as punishment and/or behavior management* [position statement]. Reston, VA: Author.

Oslin, J. (1996). Routines as organizing features in middle school physical education. *Journal of Teaching in Physical Education, 15*, 319–337.

O'Sullivan, M. (2003). Learning to teach physical education. In S. Silverman and C. Ennis (Eds.), *Student learning in physical education: Applying research to enhance instruction* (pp. 275–294). Champaign, IL: Human Kinetics.

O'Sullivan, M., & Dyson, B. (1994). Rules, routines, and expectations of 11 high school physical education teachers. *Journal of Teaching in Physical Education, 13*, 361–374.

Owens, L., & Ennis, C. (2005). The ethic of care in teaching: An overview of supportive literature. *Quest, 57*, 392–425.

Pagnano, K., & Langley, D. J. (2001). Teacher perspectives on the role of exercise as a management tool in physical education. *Journal of Teaching in Physical Education, 21*, 57–74.

Pangrazi, R., & Beighle, A. (2013). *Dynamic physical education for elementary school children* (17th ed.). Boston: Pearson.

Papaioannou, A. (1998). Goal perspectives, reasons for behaving appropriately and self-reported discipline in physical education lessons. *Journal of Teaching in Physical Education, 17*, 421–441.

Patrick, C. A., Ward, P., & Crouch, D. W. (1998). Effects of holding students accountable for social behaviors during volleyball games in elementary physical education. *Journal of Teaching in Physical Education, 17*, 143–156.

Perron, J., & Downey, P. J. (1997). Management techniques used by high school physical education teachers. *Journal of Teaching in Physical Education, 17*, 72–84.

Placek, J.H. (1983). Conceptions of success in teaching: Busy, happy, and good? In T. Templin and J. Olsen (Eds.). *Teaching in physical education* (pp. 45–56). Champaign, IL: Human Kinetics.

Rimm-Kaufman, S. E., Pianta, R. C., & Cox, M. J. (2000).Teacher's judgments of problems in the transition to kindergarten. *Early Childhood Research Quarterly, 15*, 147–166.

Rink, J. E. (2010). *Teaching physical education for learning* (6th ed.). Boston: McGraw-Hill.

Roberts, S., & Fairclough, S. (2011). Observational analysis of student activity modes, lesson contexts and teacher interactions during games classes in high school (11–16 years) physical education. *European Physical Education Review, 17*, 255–268.

Rovegno, I. (1994). Teaching within a curricular zone of safety, school culture and the knowledge of student teachers' pedagogical content knowledge. *Research Quarterly for Exercise and Sport, 65*, 269–279.

Ryan, S., & Mendel, L. L. (2010). Acoustics in physical education settings: The learning roadblock. *Physical Education and Sport Pedagogy, 15*, 71–83.

Sanders, S., & Graham, G. (1995). Kindergarten children's initial experiences in physical education: The relentless persistence for play clashes with the zone of acceptable responses. *Journal of Teaching in Physical Education, 14*, 372–383.

Sharpe, T., Crider, K., Vyhlidal, T. & Brown, M. (1996). Description and effects of prosocial instruction in an elementary physical education setting. *Education and Treatment of Children, 19*, 4, 435–457.

Siedentop, D. (1994). *Sport education*. Champaign, IL: Human Kinetics.

Siedentop, D., & Tannehill, D. (2000). *Developing teaching skills in physical education* (4th ed.). Mountainview, CA: Mayfield.

Siedentop, D., Tousignant, M., & Parker, M. (1982). *Academic learning time-physical education: Coding manual* (2nd ed.). Columbus: The Ohio State University.

Solmon, M. A. (1996). Impact of motivational climate on students' behaviors and perceptions in a physical education setting. *Journal of Educational Psychology, 88*, 731–738.

Spray, C. (2002). Motivational climate and perceived strategies to sustain pupils' discipline in physical education. *European Physical Education Review, 8*, 5–20.

Stork, S., & Sanders, S.W. (2002a). Why can't students just do as they're told?! An exploration of incorrect responses. *Journal of Teaching in Physical Education, 21*, 208–228.

Stork, S., & Sanders, S. W. (2002b). You say potāto, I say potáto: Problems associated with the lack of shared meaning in instruction and learning. *Quest, 52*, 60–78.

Stoudt, B. G. (2006). You're either in or you're out: School violence, peer discipline, and the (re)production of hegemonic masculinity. *Men and Masculinity, 8,* 273–287.

Suomi, J., Collier, D., & Brown, L. (2003). Factors affecting the social experiences of students in elementary physical education classes. *Journal of Teaching in Physical Education, 22,* 186–202.

Suppaporn, S. (2000). High school students' perspectives about misbehavior. *Physical Educator, 57,* 124–135.

Suppapporn, S., Dodds, P., & Griffin, L. (2003). An ecological analysis of middle school misbehavior through student and teacher perspectives. *Journal of Teaching in Physical Education, 22,* 328–349.

Tousignant, M., & Siedentop, D. (1983). A qualitative analysis of task structures in required secondary physical education classes. *Journal of Teaching in Physical Education, 3,* 47–57.

van der Mars, H., Vogler, B., Darst, P., & Cusimano, B. (1994). Active supervision patterns of physical education teachers and their relationship with student behaviors. *Journal of Teaching in Physical Education, 14,* 99–112.

van der Mars, H., Vogler, E.W., Darst, P., & Cusimano, B. (1995). Novice and expert physical education teachers: Maybe they think and decide differently . . . but do they behave differently? *Journal of Teaching in Physical Education, 14,* 340–347.

Vidoni, C., & Ward, P. (2006). Effects of a dependent group-oriented contingency on middle school physical education students' fair play behaviors. *Journal of Behavioral Education, 15,* 81–92.

Ward, P. (2006). The philosophy, science and application of behavior analysis in physical education. *The Handbook of Physical Education* (pp. 3–20) London: Sage.

Ward, P., & Barrett, T. (2002). A review of behavior analysis research in physical education. *Journal of Teaching in Physical Education, 21,* 242–266.

Ward, P., & Dunaway, S. (1995). Effects of contingent music on laps run in a high school physical education class. *Physical Educator, 52,* 2–7.

Watson, D., & Clocksin, B. (2013). *Using physical activity and sport to teach personal and social responsibility.* Champaign, IL: Human Kinetics.

14

SMALL-GROUP WORK

Developments in Research

ROBYN M. GILLIES
THE UNIVERSITY OF QUEENSLAND

INTRODUCTION

Schools are being encouraged to adopt pedagogical practices that promote students-centered learning, and foremost among many of these practices is cooperative group learning or peer-mediated learning. Interest in cooperative group learning has arisen because a large volume of research shows that it has been used successfully to promote learning achievements across a range of curricula such as enhanced understanding in science, mathematics, and technology (Lou, Abrami, & d'Apollonia, 2001; Webb & Farivar, 1999), better conceptual development and concept mapping in physics (Howe, Tolmie, Greer, & MacKenzie, 1995), enhanced computational problem solving in chemistry (Bilgin & Geban, 2006), improved literacy and reading outcomes (Slavin, 1996), and better reasoning and problem-solving skills (Gillies & Khan, 2008), to name just a few.

In the affective area, cooperative learning influences the development of positive student attitudes toward other group members (Tolmie et al., 2010; Johnson & Johnson, 2002) and motivation to learn (Johnson & Johnson, 2003), improved self-confidence and self-esteem (Roseth, Johnson, & Johnson, 2008), and more positive attitudes to school in general and to children with diverse learning and adjustment needs (Emmer & Stough, 2001). Cooperative learning has also been used as a teaching strategy to help students learn to manage conflicts and for students identified as bullies to learn appropriate interpersonal skills (Cowie & Berdondini, 2001). In effect, cooperative learning has helped to enhance the achievement of a range of cognitive and affective goals in students.

However, while the benefits of cooperative learning are widely acknowledged, many teachers still struggle with implementing this pedagogical practice in their classrooms, possibly because of the challenges it poses to their control of the learning process, the demands it places on curriculum reorganization involving the need for more open communication among teachers and students, and the personal commitment teachers need to make to sustain their efforts (Kohn, 1992). Difficulties may also arise because of teachers' lack of understanding of how to use this pedagogical practice in their classrooms and, in particular, how to structure the groups so that the benefits widely attributed to this approach to learning are maximized (Gillies, 2008). This chapter discusses how teachers can structure small-group learning in classrooms so that students understand what they are expected to learn and how they are expected to interact. Three linguistic tools that have been demonstrated to enhance student discourse during small-group learning are presented and discussed, along with other successful peer-mediated strategies such as peer tutoring and peer collaboration.

Key Components in Cooperative Group Work

Placing students in groups and expecting them to work together will not necessarily promote cooperation. In fact, groups often struggle with knowing what to do, and, in the process, discord often occurs as members grapple with the demands of the task as well as with managing the processes involved in learning, including how to deal with conflicting opinions expressed by other group members or working with students who only contribute minimally to the group's task. It is widely recognized that, to avoid these pitfalls, groups need to be established so that the five key components of successful cooperative learning are embedded in their structure. These components involve ensuring that group members understand that:

1. They are linked positively to each other so that in order for one to succeed, they must all succeed.
2. They have a responsibility to contribute to the group's goals.
3. They must interact with other group members to facilitate their learning.
4. They need to demonstrate appropriate interpersonal and small group skills.
5. They need to participate in periodic and regular group processing activities (Johnson & Johnson, 1990).

There is no doubt that when students work in well structured cooperative small groups, they learn to listen to what others have to say and understand their different perspectives, share information and ideas, communicate respectively, clarify misunderstandings, and work constructively to develop new understandings. The result is that cooperation creates a group ethos where members realize that they "sink or swim" together and that it is in their interests to coordinate their efforts to help and support the endeavors of other group members if they are to succeed. The values that Johnson and Johnson (2000) identify that underpin cooperation include the following:

- Commitment to the common good
- Recognition that mutual goals will only be attained by combining the resources of all
- Facilitation, promotion, and success of others as a natural way of life

- Satisfaction derived from helping others succeed
- Acknowledgment that other individuals are potential contributors to one's own success
- Acceptance of the worth of others

It has been argued that the academic and social benefits that accrue to students who work cooperatively together to achieve a common goal are unequivocal (Cohen, 1994; Johnson & Johnson, 2002). In fact, it is the apparent success of this approach to learning that led Slavin (1999) to propose that it is one of the greatest educational innovations of recent time, while Johnson and Johnson (1999) noted that "this is so well confirmed that it stands as one of the strongest principles of social and organizational psychology" (p. 72).

USING COOPERATIVE LEARNING IN CLASSROOMS

Despite the benefits widely attributed to cooperative learning, Baines, Blatchford, and Kutnick (2003), in a study of grouping practices in the UK, reported that elementary students rarely worked in groups although they often sat in small groups. Most children worked individually under the direction of an adult attached to their group. By secondary school, students either worked in dyads or in groups of 11 or more students with little autonomy over the task they were required to complete. In most instances, grouping practices were aimed at the teacher maintaining control of the learning process, keeping students focused and on-task, and maximizing teacher-directed learning. In reporting on cooperative learning in Dutch primary classrooms, Veenman, Kenter, and Post (2000) noted that effective learning and cooperation were not promoted because teachers devoted little time to teaching students group work skills. Similar observations were made by Gillies (2003) about grouping practices in Australian schools.

However, despite the difficulties teachers have in implementing this pedagogical practice, research indicates that when students have opportunities to work in small groups where teachers have been encouraged to focus on supporting the quality of collaborative group work, there were significant increases in both the frequency and quality of students' discourse and marked improvements in the classroom learning environment (Christie, Tolmie, Thurston, Howe, & Yopping, 2009). Baines, Rubie-Davies, and Blatchford (2009) found that when teachers trained students in relational and group working skills, students exhibited higher levels of participation, engagement, active and sustained discussion, and higher levels of inferential joint reasoning, and lower levels of group disruptive and blocking behaviors than peers who had not been taught these skills. Similar results were obtained by Galton, Hargreaves, and Pell (2009), who found secondary students (11–14 years old) who worked in groups demonstrated more sustained and higher-level cognitive interactions and obtained higher academic outcomes than their peers who worked in whole-class settings. Interestingly, the authors argued that group work could have been improved if the teachers had given more time to training students in the communication skills needed to promote successful cooperation and had devoted more time to debriefing the groups after their small group experiences.

TEACHER-MEDIATED LEARNING STRATEGIES

The key role teachers play in teaching students how to ask and answer questions is critically important if students are to learn to participate in reasoned argumentation, problem solving, and learning. However, research indicates that students rarely engage in such high-level discourse unless they are explicitly taught to do so. Generally, students do not elaborate on information, ask challenging questions, or spontaneously link prior knowledge with current information unless provided with relevant external guidance to do so (Chinn, O'Donnell, & Jinks, 2000).

In a study of teacher interaction patterns in primary classrooms from 1976 to 1996, Galton, Hargreaves, and Pell (1999) reported that "teaching in today's primary schools . . . is very much a matter of teachers talking and children listening" (p. 33) with teachers primarily making statements or asking questions designed to elicit facts or to recall the correct answer to a problem. Students are rarely asked thought-provoking or challenging questions about their learning. In fact, Galton and colleagues (1999) found that this type of one-way communication pattern where teachers talk and students listen was so entrenched that over the 20-year period under observation, teachers' tendency to talk and provide students with facts and ideas had actually increased from about 57% to over 80% of their total classroom talk.

The Importance of Asking Questions

Teaching teachers how to engage in dialogic interactions where they learn to ask thought-provoking and challenging questions is critically important if children, in turn, are to learn to be active participants in the learning process. Gillies (2004), in a study that compared the effects of training teachers in specific communication skills designed to promote thinking and scaffold learning on teachers' and students' dialogic interactions during cooperative group work, found that the trained teachers, in contrast to their untrained peers, engaged in more mediated-learning interactions or interactions designed to scaffold and challenge students' thinking. Interestingly, in turn, the children in these teachers' classrooms modeled many of the responses they gave their teachers in their interactions with each other (see Table 14.1), providing more detailed explanatory responses than children in the untrained teachers' classrooms, responses that Webb and Mastergeorge (2003) found are associated with positive learning outcomes.

Research shows clearly that teachers can be taught to use specific communication strategies designed to facilitate student–teacher interactions and to promote students' thinking and learning during cooperative group work. Rojas-Drummond and Mercer (2003) found that when teachers were taught to use Exploratory Talk as an approach to inducting students into the communicative and intellectual activities of the classroom, they, in turn, use questions that encourage students to make explicit their thoughts, reasons, and knowledge and share them with the class. They also model useful ways of using language that children can appropriate during their discussions, and they provide opportunities for students to express their understandings or articulate their difficulties. Similarly, Gillies and Khan (2008) found that when teachers had participated in professional development activities where

Table 14.1 Types and examples of teacher communication skills.

Types of Communication Skills	Examples of Specific Communication Skills
Probing and clarifying	• Can you explain that a little more? • Perhaps you can tell me a little more about what you're trying to say?
Acknowledging and validating	• You've worked really hard to demonstrate the link between these two variables in your experiment.
Confronting discrepancies and clarifying options	• I'm not sure what you mean. On the one hand you're saying . . . , and yet on the other you're saying . . . . How do you account for this discrepancy? • I wonder how you can include . . . when you've already mentioned . . . ?
Tentatively offering suggestions	• Have you thought about doing it this way? • Perhaps you could have a go at this and see if it is suitable?

they had learned how to use such specific linguistic tools such as Exploratory Talk (i.e., asking questions and providing reasons, Mercer, 1996), Ask to Think–Tel Why (i.e., asking cognitively challenging questions; King, 1997), and Cognitive Tools and Intellectual Roles (i.e., giving students specific tasks and roles to perform in their groups; Palincsar & Herrenkohl, 2002), they not only demonstrated more challenging and scaffolding behaviors in their interactions with their students, but the students, in turn, provided more elaborative assistance to one another than their peers in the untrained teachers' classes. It appears when teachers are explicit in the types of thinking they want students to use, it triggers in students the recognition that they need to provide more help and explanations to others in their group.

Rojas-Drummond and Zapata (2004) also observed that when teachers explicitly teach children how to engage in exploratory talk where they are expected to provide reasons for their decisions, they produce significantly more and better arguments than their comparison peers. Similarly, Mercer, Dawes, Wegerif, and Sams (2004), in a study that aimed to develop children's abilities to use language as a tool for thinking both collectively and individually in science, found that children who had been explicitly taught how to engage in providing reasons for their answers recorded better-quality language and higher reasoning skills and obtained significantly higher scores in science than students in classes who had not been taught these skills. Likewise, Mercer and Sams (2006), in a study that taught children how to use language as a tool for thinking in mathematics, also found that that those children who had been explicitly taught how to make their reasoning visible used talk more effectively, which helped in the development of their mathematical reasoning, understanding, and problem-solving skills.

Teachers' Instructional Practices

Teachers' instructional practices have the potential to influence students' learning. McNeill and Krajcik (2008) found that instructional practices such as defining and modeling scientific explanations, making the rationale for scientific explanations explicit, and connecting these explanations to everyday explanations positively influenced students' learning during inquiry science. Similarly, Chin (2007) found that students were more successful at constructing scientific knowledge when their teachers asked questions that challenged them to generate ideas, apply concepts, formulate hypotheses, draw inferences, and evaluate information—practices that encouraged them to think more deeply about issues under discussion.

Michaels, O'Connor, and Resnick (2008) argue that teachers need to establish classroom practices that can lead to reasoned participation by all students. These practices emphasize the importance of ensuring that all students have the right to speak and the obligation to explicate their reasoning, providing evidence for their claims so that others can understand and critique their arguments in an environment that is respectful of their opinions. In this type of environment, teachers act to facilitate discussion by using conversation openers or extenders, commonly called "open-ended questions"; they give voice to students' comments by acknowledging their ideas and contributions, and they engage in explicit modeling of teacher-guided discussion to enhance students' problem solving and reasoning. In such classrooms, the authors argue, teachers successfully build a discourse culture that involves risk taking and the explicit modeling and practice of particular talk moves so that over time new forms and norms of discourse are developed that involve students learning to listen to each other, build on each other's ideas, and participate productively in complex deliberative practices.

In a study that investigated teachers' questioning and interaction patterns during inquiry science, Erdogan and Campbell (2008) found that teachers who acted as facilitators in classrooms where students were actively involved in learning with their peers asked significantly more questions designed to facilitate knowledge construction than teachers who facilitated in classrooms where students had minimal opportunities to interact with their peers. In these latter classrooms, teacher instruction appeared to be the dominant form of interaction with questions focusing on knowledge reproduction rather than knowledge construction.

There is no doubt that teachers' instructional practices affect students' thinking about learning and their learning experiences. In a study of student participation in collaborative student-led conversations, teacher practices, and student achievement in three elementary classrooms, Webb and colleagues (2008) found that giving correct and complete explanations were positively related to achievement scores while giving only an answer and giving neither an answer nor an explanation were negatively related to achievement. Even though all three teachers in the Webb and associates study encouraged students to explain their thinking, students' success at explaining was dependent on the extent to which their teachers encouraged further explanation of students' thinking beyond the initial explanation, whether they asked for further elaboration for both correct and incorrect strategies, and whether they pushed students to give correct and complete explanations. It was these specific practices that showed a strong correspondence with the nature and frequency of students' explaining in different classroom contexts and that also corresponded to classroom differences in achievement (see Table 14.2).

Given that teachers' instructional practices affect students' interactions and thinking during small-group learning, the following section presents three specific

Table 14.2 Specific teachers' verbal behaviors used to promote student thinking and learning.

Behaviors Used to Promote Student Thinking and Learning

• Requests information on how student solved a problem
• Responds to student's explanation by drawing attention to the explanation, asking further questions about the explanation, repeating or rephrasing it, adding details to it, or inviting students to respond to it
• Modeling how to solve the problem
• Exploring students' conceptions or misconceptions. For example, "Can you tell me why you think that?"
• Encouraging students to be active participants in their learning

linguistic tools that have been demonstrated to promote student discourse during their small group discussions. Although the first two tools, Ask to Think–Tel Why (King, 1997) and Philosophy for Children (Lipman, 1988) have been shown to promote students' higher-level thinking, the third tool, Collaborative Strategic Reading (Vaughn, Klingner, & Bryant, 2001) can be used to help low-achieving students learn the skills successful readers use to comprehend text.

LINGUISTIC TOOLS TO PROMOTE STUDENT DISCOURSE

Ask to Think–Tel Why

Ask to Think–Tel Why is an inquiry-based model of peer tutoring developed by Alison King (1997) in which children are taught to ask a sequence of questions designed to scaffold each other's thinking and learning to progressively higher levels. The advantage of this type of sequence is not only that it encourages children to focus on summarizing and elaborating information, but it also helps them to ask cognitively challenging questions that encourage them to draw on previous understandings and knowledge that connect with current information. King (2008) has identified a list of question stems that can be used to challenge students' thinking and elicit high-level thinking responses:

• Explain why . . .
• How would you use . . . to . . . ?
• What is the significance of . . . ?
• What is the difference between . . . and . . . ?
• What do you think would happen if . . . ?
• Compare . . . with . . .
• What do you think causes . . . . Why?
• What are the strengths and weaknesses of . . . ?
• What evidence is there to support your answer? (King, 2008, p. 80).

In generating these types of questions King (2008) maintains that the questioner needs to think about how ideas in the task relate to each other, and respondents must be able to generate an answer that connects the ideas or provides a rationale or explanations to justify their responses. Because respondents have been taught to provide elaborated responses such as explanations, justifications, and rationales to the questions they are asked, they realize the importance of explaining, justifying, and rationalizing how they have connected ideas and information to support their responses. In so doing, students often develop new ways of explaining and arguing their points of view as new knowledge is often generated and the quality of the discourse is enhanced.

To guide students' responses in the Ask to Think–Tel Why model of peer tutoring, students are taught a procedure for explaining, elaborating, and inferencing so that their responses to the cognitively challenging questions their peers pose are likely to be equally thoughtful. This procedure includes reminders such as:

- Telling what they know about a topic.
- Explaining why and how they know this.
- Linking the information being presented to something their partner already knows so they will understand.
- Telling why and how they know this.

The Ask to Think–Tel Why procedure is an acronym designed to keep students' attention focused on the characteristics of effective explanations, elaborations, and inferences by prompting them to explain their thinking and link it to previous experiences that they and their partner share.

The five types of questions that King (1997) identified as part of this sequence of questions designed to promote higher-level thinking include the following:

1. Review questions ("Tell me what you know about . . .")
2. Probing questions ("Tell me more about . . . .")
3. Hint questions ("I wonder have you thought about . . . ?")
4. Intelligent-thinking questions ("What is the difference between . . . and . . . ?")
5. Self-monitoring questions ("Have I covered all the points I need to?")

As partners engage in the question-asking-answering process that is typical of the interactions in the Ask to Think–Tel Why strategy, they learn that each question posed is often highly dependent on previous responses and that these, in turn, help to shape subsequent questions. In this sense, partners are highly dependent on each other in these reciprocal dialogues for scaffolding and guiding each other's learning. King maintains that this reciprocity of questioning and answering creates a transactive process where the partners are equal participants in providing mutual assistance and mutual learning, together promoting higher-level thinking and complex learning. The following vignette is an example of this transactive process.

In the following vignette, Michael and Susan are discussing the effects of tsunamis from their unit of work on Natural Disasters in their sixth-grade science class. In this vignette, Michael is the tutor, and Susan is the respondent.

Michael: Tell me what you know about the tsunami that hit Fukushima, Japan. (review question)

Susan: The tsunami was a large series of waves that were caused by the earthquake off the east coast of Japan, and even though they had large sea walls to protect the people, the tsunami was too big, and it flowed over the walls and raced inland and caused a lot of damage. (statement showing comprehension)

Michael: Is there anything else that you can say about the causes of the tsunami and its effects? (probing question)

Susan: The earthquake was caused by two tectonic plates colliding . . . the Pacific Plate subducted under the North American Plate and caused the 8.9 earthquake. The earthquake forced the seabed up and pushed the water forward. It raced toward the coast and hit land, causing the damage. (statement showing the integration of cause and effect)

Michael: Can you tell me more about the tsunami? You said it was a series of waves that caused the damage. How big was it? (probing question)

Susan: It was a powerful series of waves that were up to 30 meters high that just flowed over the sea walls, and it moved very fast. People couldn't run away from it because it moved too quickly. Cars and houses were swallowed up. (statement showing the integration of the concepts of speed, using the example of people trying to run away from it, and its power, being able to swallow cars and houses)

Michael: You mentioned the Boxing Day tsunami that hit the island of Sumatra in Indonesia in 2004. How were they the same and how were they different? (thinking question)

Susan: This tsunami was caused again by subducting. The Indian Plate slipped under the Sumatra plate (?). I mean the Eurasian Plate. Hundreds of thousands of people were killed, whereas in Japan only a few thousand were killed. There was lots of mud and trees and stuff in it. It was moving very fast, and people couldn't get away from it, but I did see people riding on the debris. They were different because one was near Japan and one was near Indonesia, but they were mostly the same. (statement showing the integration of concepts by linking different aspects)

In this vignette, Michael acts as the tutor posing questions designed to encourage Susan to think about the information on tsunamis that they have been learning in their science class. Michael's role as the tutor is only to ask questions. He is not expected to provide answers to any of the questions, whereas Susan's role is to explain and not ask questions. King (2008) maintains that by encouraging the tutor to ask thinking questions only, the tutee is more likely to respond with explanations or other elaborated information that is known in order to promote learning in both the tutor and tutee.

In this interaction, Michael begins by asking Susan to state what she knows about the tsunami that hit Fukushima, and she responds with a detailed account of the information she has been reading (see turn 2). Michael follows this up with a probing question to see whether there is anything else about the causes of the tsunami and its effects. His question provides a hint that he'd like her to discuss the effects of the tsunami in more detail (see turn 3). Susan responds with more detailed information on the causes of the tsunami along with an explanation of how it forced the seabed up and pushed the water forward, causing the damage as it hit land (see turn 4). Michael continues to scaffold Susan's responses as he probes for information on the size of the tsunami (see turn 5). This helps Susan to respond in more detail as she integrates different concepts of speed and power that illustrate how quickly it moved and the force of its power (see turn 6).

Michael follows this response with a thinking question that asks Susan to identify the similarities and differences between the Boxing Day tsunami and the Fukushima one. In effect, Michael is asking a thinking question that involves a compare-and-contrast assessment (see turn 7). Susan responds by demonstrating that she is able to integrate concepts by linking different aspects of the two tsunamis (see turn 8).

An examination of the questions that were asked and the responses provided in the vignette indicates that the discourse became more detailed and elaborate as Michael moved beyond asking review questions to ones that probed Susan's thinking and challenged her to link information and integrate concepts. In effect, Susan was asked to think more deeply about the topic, leading to her generating more detailed explanations and cognitively sophisticated responses.

Evidence Supporting Ask to Think–Tel Why

Gillies and Khan (2008) found that students who had been taught to use the Ask to Think–Tel Why strategy provided significantly more elaborative and help-giving behaviors to group members than peers who had not been taught this linguistic strategy, and they obtained higher scores on follow-up reasoning and problem-solving activities. Similarly, Gillies and colleagues (2012) found that students who had been taught to use the Ask to Think–Tel Why strategy were more verbally interactive than peers who had not been taught to use this questioning strategy, and they also obtained higher scores on their reasoning and problem-solving tasks. In short, both studies demonstrate that when students are explicitly taught to ask questions that promote higher-level thinking, these thinking and reasoning skills transfer to written reasoning and problem-solving tasks.

Philosophy for Children

In the Philosophy for Children (P4C) approach, developed by Matthew Lipman (1988), children are taught how to work together using philosophical thinking centered on dialogue and collaborative activity where they engage in critical and creative thought. The lessons often begin with students identifying a topic they want to discuss. However, before they begin, their teacher will encourage them to take some time to think about the questions they would like to ask and from the list of questions they develop the children choose a question that is of interest to them and, with the teacher's help, discuss it together. The discussion often involves the children questioning assumptions, developing opinions with supporting reasons, analyzing significant concepts and generally applying the best reasoning and judgment they are capable of to the question they are discussing. In the longer term, the teacher aims to build the children's skills and concepts through appropriate follow-up activities, such as thinking games, and by developing connections among philosophical discussions, life, and the rest of the school curriculum. P4C aims to teach children to be more thoughtful and reflective during their discussions and to go beyond information to seek understanding.

The process of conducting a good inquiry begins by having students identify a question that they wish to explore in more depth. While there are no set questions that students learn to ask, they are, however, guided to ask a range of questions such as the following:

- Probe alternative perspectives (e.g., "What are the alternatives?")
- Explore causal connections and relationships (e.g., "How are they similar, and how are they different?")
- Pose hypothetical problems (e.g., "I wonder what would happen if . . . ?")
- Provide reasons (e.g., "What evidence is there for believing that?")
- Give examples (e.g., "Can someone think of an example of this? Can someone think of an alternative example?")
- Draw distinctions (e.g., "Can we make a distinction here?")
- Make connections (e.g., "Is anyone able to build on that idea? Can you link that with another idea?")
- Indicate intentions (e.g., "Is that what is really meant? Is that what they're really saying?")
- Identify criteria (e.g., "What are the things that really count here?")
- Demonstrate consistency (e.g., "Does that conclusion follow? Are these principles consistent?")

Other questions challenge students to be more self-reflective and self-monitoring (e.g., "What would the consequences be if one of those alternatives were chosen?"). It is through the dialogic exchanges that children learn to engage in reasoned argumentation that helps them to clarify their understandings and facilitate their thinking (Reznitsakaya et al., 2007).

Evidence Supporting P4C

In order to evaluate the effectiveness of the Philosophy for Children (P4C) program on children's thinking, Trickey and Topping (2004) undertook a systematic review of 10 experimental studies conducted in primary and secondary schools that measured outcomes by norm-referenced tests of reading, reasoning, cognitive ability, listening skills, mathematical skills, expressive language, self-esteem, and emotional intelligence and found that there were significant improvements across all studies with low variance, indicating a consistently moderate positive effect for P4C on a range of outcome measures.

A follow-up study by Trickey and Topping (2006) that investigated the socio-emotional effects of Collaborative Philosophical Enquiry, an adaptation of Lipman's P4C (1988) approach, on children's self-esteem and social behavior found that there were significant gains in self-esteem in the way students in the experimental classes perceived themselves in contrast to their peers who did not participate in the Collaborative

Philosophical Enquiry program (control classes). There were also significant differences in teachers' perceptions of the way students managed failure, with students in the experimental classes managing failure more resiliently than their peers in the control classes. A further study by Topping and Trickey (2007a) investigated the effects of Collaborative Philosophical Enquiry on students' verbal cognitive ability and their nonverbal reasoning ability and found that students who had participated in this program showed significant standardized gains in verbal cognitive ability and that these gains also generalized to nonverbal and quantitative reasoning ability as well. This was in contrast to their peers who did not participate in the program and who showed no gains in either the verbal or nonverbal reasoning ability tests.

Importantly, Topping and Trickey (2007b) found that when the children in the Topping and Trickey (2007a) study were followed up two years later, after they had transferred from primary school to secondary school, the pre- to posttest cognitive ability gains that were evident in the students who had participated in the P4C program were maintained, whereas the control group of children showed an insignificant but persistent deterioration in scores from pre- to posttest follow-up. The study demonstrated that not only are the cognitive gains maintained even though the students had not had any further experience with P4C but that they transferred across contexts. In short, Trickey and Topping (2004, 2006) and Topping and Trickey (2007a, 2007b) demonstrated that training in P4C for an hour a week leads to cognitive gains and enhanced affective outcomes.

Collaborative Strategic Reading

Collaborative strategic reading (CSR) (Vaughn, Klingner, & Bryant, 2001) is an adaption of reciprocal teaching where students are taught how to dialogue together to construct meaning and understanding by using strategies that successful readers use to assist in their comprehension of written text. During CSR, students work in small, cooperating groups with each member having the opportunity of leading the group and employing a number of specific strategies to assist their discussion of the text. These strategies include:

1. Preview strategy (making predictions about the passage prior to reading it).
2. Click and clunk strategy (identifying passages that "click" because they recognize material they know and those that "clunk" because they are more difficult to understand).
3. Get the gist strategy (identifying the main idea in a passage).
4. Wrap-up strategy (summarizing the main idea).

These four strategies (preview, click and clunk, get the gist, and wrap-up) are introduced one at a time and modeled by the teacher before students practice them in their small groups. For example, the preview strategy is designed to help students activate background knowledge so that they can make informed predictions about the text. Students are taught to scan the text and search for clues such as pictures, key words and phrases, and headings to try and predict what the passage is about. When they have mastered the preview strategy, the click and clunk strategy is introduced, modeled, and again practiced in small groups. This strategy involves students' monitoring their own reading so they "click" when they recognize material they know and "clunk" material, words, or concepts they need to find out more about. This process continues until the students have learned all four strategies.

4.3.1 Evidence Supporting CSR

There is considerable support in the literature for the efficacy of Collaborative Strategic Reading, possibly because it makes instruction visible and explicit; it involves implementing procedural strategies to facilitate learning; it uses interactive groups or partners; and it provides opportunities for students to dialogue together and with their teachers. Bryant, Vaughn, Linan-Thompson, Ugel, Hamff, and Hougen (2000) used CSR as part of a multicomponent reading intervention strategy with students with reading disabilities, low-achieving students, and average-achieving students in the middle years and found that all students' reading outcomes (i.e., word identification, fluency, and comprehension) increased significantly as a result of the intervention, although a small group of very poor readers made little progress. Interestingly, teachers reported that the percentage of their students who passed high-stakes tests increased from the previous year as a result of their participation in the intervention. Similarly, Klinger, Vaughn, Arguelles, Hughes, and Leftwich (2004) examined teachers' yearlong implementation of CSR in five elementary classrooms and found that students in the CSR classrooms improved significantly in reading comprehension when compared with students in the control classrooms. Furthermore, when students were compared by achievement level (i.e., high/average, low, or learning disabled), all students, irrespective of achievement level, outperformed their peers in the control condition.

In short, Bryant and colleagues (2000) and Klinger and associates (2004) demonstrate that CSR has the potential to benefit all students, irrespective of achievement level. Moreover, these benefits are likely to be additive when teachers ensure that students are explicitly taught the four CSR strategies and are given the opportunity of practicing them in small cooperating groups.

PEER-MEDIATED LEARNING STRATEGIES

Numerous studies over the years have documented how peers can be used to help each other learn. These include studies in peer tutoring where less able students are tutored by more able students, such as occurs in cross-age tutoring or collaborative tutoring where students of similar ability work together on a task that neither can solve independently and cooperative learning where students, often of mixed ability, work together (Fuchs, Fuchs, Hamlett, & Karns, 1998; Topping, 2005). In all instances, groups are generally structured so students understand what they are expected to learn and how they are to interact (Greenwood, Delquadri, & Hall, 1989; Fuchs, Fuchs, Bentz, Phillips, & Hamlett, 1994). In effect, the students are interdependently linked to achieve a common goal. When these conditions exist, Lou,

Abrami, and Spence (2000) found that small group cooperative instruction had a positive effect (effect size = 1) for elementary students of all ability levels. That is, average students at the 50th percentile performed at the 84th percentile or well above average compared to students in classrooms without these grouping arrangements. The authors hypothesized that the positive peer interaction that occurred when students worked together, listened to one another's perspectives on issues, elaborated on ideas, and both gave and received help may have provided more opportunities to engage in knowledge construction and learning than their peers who worked in unstructured groups where group members were not interdependently linked to achieve a common goal.

Peer Tutoring

From a very early age, children learn from their peers, and teachers have used this approach to learning as a way of providing additional help to children experiencing difficulties in class. Peer tutoring usually involves a more able child (tutor) helping a less able child (tutee) master specific information or skills. Greenwood and colleagues (1989) reported on a Classwide Peer Tutoring (CPT) approach that had been implemented across a four-year period in low-SES schools and found that the students in these schools attained significantly higher academic gains than their comparison low-SES peers. The authors attributed these gains to the processes involved in implementing CPT, particularly the training teachers and students received, the requirement that students had opportunities to participate in CPT on a daily basis across core subject areas, and the careful monitoring of students' progress.

Tutor Training

Training in how to interact and provide assistance to peers during peer tutoring appears to be critical to its success. Fuchs, Fuchs, Bentz, Phillips, and Hamlett (1994) examined the effects of training versus no training on students' interactions during peer tutoring and found that tutors who had been trained provided more explanations that incorporated sounder instructional principles than untrained tutors. In a follow-up study that investigated how students helping behaviors could be enhanced during peer tutoring in mathematical tasks, Fuchs and associates (1997) examined the differences in achievement for students who were taught how to provide elaborated and detailed conceptual help to one another in contrast to students who provided elaborated help only or to those who did not participate in this training. The results showed that the students who had been taught to provide elaborated and conceptual help asked more participatory, procedural questions and provided more explanations than students who had been trained to provide elaborated help only, which, in turn, surpassed that of the control group. Moreover, the achievement of the students who were taught to provide elaborated and conceptual help was higher than the achievement of students in the elaborated group only, and they, in turn, outperformed students in the control group.

The training that Fuchs and colleagues (1997) found worked most effectively included the following two processes. First, the students in the peer-mediated learning groups employed the following steps to help each other master the procedure:

1. The tutor models and scaffolds the procedure about the directions to complete the task.
2. The tutor provides step-by-step feedback to affirm correct responses and explains and models strategic behavior when answers are incorrect.
3. Both tutors and tutees engage in verbal and written interaction.
4. Both tutor and tutee reverse roles during each session.

Once the students had mastered these steps, the second part of the training was undertaken. This included teaching students how to seek elaborated help with conceptual understanding. Elaborated help included such behaviors as asking for detailed help and continuing to do so until it is received and providing elaborated help to one's partner when it is needed. Conceptual understanding was achieved when students have the opportunity to:

1. Relate material under discussion to real life examples.
2. Use visual representations such as pictures.
3. Use manipulatives that represent numbers.
4. Discuss the problem and how to solve it.
5. Ask questions that begin with "what," "where," "when," "how," and "why."

Follow-up studies indicate students in kindergarten can be taught how to provide help and assistance to their partner during peer tutoring in mathematics classes (Fuchs, Fuchs, & Karns, 2001) and during reading lessons (Fuchs & Fuchs, 2005). Peer-assisted learning strategies have been used effectively to help English language learners with learning disabilities with their comprehension of text (Saenz, Fuchs, & Fuchs, 2005) and to assist students with mathematics disabilities improve on their number combination fluency and problem-solving skills (Fuchs et al., 2008).

Additionally, cross-age peer tutoring has been used effectively to promote thinking and learning. Topping and Bryce (2004) demonstrated that 11-year-old students can be trained to tutor 7-year-old students in a peer-tutoring reading intervention involving the use of specific verbal instructions, demonstration, practice, coaching, and feedback and that this had a positive effect on the tutees' thinking skills as measured by their ability to be able to make explanatory inferences about the text under discussion. Similarly, Topping, Peters, Stephen, and Whale (2004) found that 8- to 9-year-old students can be used effectively to tutor 7- to 8-year-olds in science with significant gains in scientific concepts and key words in comparison to control peers, who made no gains.

Evidence Supporting Peer-Mediated Learning Strategies

Peer-mediated learning strategies have been used across different age groups, ability levels, and curriculum areas to assist students to learn. Although the research is generally positive in that many studies have supported this approach to learning, large-scale randomized studies or meta-analyses of studies are often needed to ensure that the results obtained or the trends that are evident are strong and not likely to be contested. One such study involved a best-evidence synthesis of 87 studies that focused on improving elementary students' achievements in mathematics through the implementation of the mathematics curricula, computer-assisted instruction, and instructional processes (e.g., cooperative learning, peer tutoring) (Slavin & Lake, 2008). The results indicated that there was limited evidence for the different effects of various mathematics curricula and only moderate effects for computer-assisted instruction. The strongest effects were for the instructional processes, such as cooperative learning, classroom management and motivational programs, and peer-tutoring programs. The authors concluded that programs that focus on changing daily teaching practices appear to be more promising than those that focus on curriculum or technology interventions alone.

Topping, Thurston, McGavock, and Conlin (2012) conducted a large randomized controlled study across 87 primary schools in Scotland that investigated the effects of a two-year peer-tutoring program in reading on students' reading achievements. It also investigated the effectiveness of cross-age versus same-age peer tutoring, light versus intensive peer tutoring interventions, and reading versus reading and mathematics peer tutoring. The results showed that there were significant gains for reading attainment for cross-age tutoring across the two years, that tutoring involving reading and mathematics together was more effective than tutoring in reading alone, and that light versus intensive peer tutoring were equally effective.

In short, Slavin and Lake (2008) and Topping, Thurston, McGavock, and Conlin (2012) demonstrate that peer-mediated learning strategies such as cooperative learning and peer tutoring can be used effectively to promote student learning. Students obtain clear benefits when they have opportunities to interact with others in reciprocal dialogues where they coach, prompt, model, and provide feedback to assist understanding and learning. Moreover, both tutees and tutors benefit from the resulting interaction. Tutees benefit because of the additional assistance they receive, and tutors benefit because they have to explain the task clearly, forcing them to cognitively restructure the information to be taught and, in so doing, often gain a better understanding of this information than they had previously.

IMPLICATIONS FOR TEACHERS

Research indicates that there is much to be gained by implementing peer-mediated learning strategies such as small-group learning in classrooms. These benefits include enhanced understanding and learning, the development of positive student attitudes toward self and others, and improved self-confidence and motivation to learn. Moreover, these benefits apply across different grade levels from kindergarten to college and across different subjects such as science, mathematics, language learning, and enhanced reading and problem-solving skills.

However, despite the documented benefits of peer-mediated learning, teachers are often reluctant to implement these practices in their classrooms, possibly because of the time it takes to organize and establish the tasks and teach the students the skills they need to work successfully in groups. Structuring the group task so that students know what they are expected to do and teaching them how to interact with others is critically important if students are to demonstrate the appropriate interpersonal behaviors that will help them engage in dialogic interactions where they learn to how to seek help while responding to the requests for help from their peers.

Three linguistic tools that have been demonstrated to promote student discourse during small group work include: *Ask to Think-Tel Why*, an inquiry-based model of peer tutoring; *Philosophy for Children*, a dialogic approach to teaching children how to engage in critical and creating thinking; and *Collaborative Strategic Reading*, an approach to teaching students how to use strategies that successful readers use to assist in their understanding of written text. The first two linguistic tools have been shown to promote students' higher-level thinking, and Collaborative Strategic Reading can be used to promote students' comprehension of text. All three tools use a structured dialogic process to help students learn how to dialogue, ask questions, predict and hypothesize, connect ideas, and evaluate outcomes. Other strategies that have been used to help students dialogue include modeling by the tutor with step-by-step feedback to the tutee to affirm conceptions and correct misconceptions, relating the material to authentic real-life examples that resonate with students, using visual representations to illustrate information and ideas, and asking questions that enable students to clarify their understandings. Research indicates that these strategies have been used effectively in same-age and cross-age peer tutoring and with students with similar and different abilities.

REFERENCES

Baines, E., Blatchford, P., & Kutnick, P. (2003). Changes in grouping practices over primary and secondary school. *International Journal of Educational Research, 39*, 9–34.

Baines, E., Rubie-Davies, C., & Blatchford, P. (2009). Improving pupil group work interaction and dialogue in primary classrooms: Results from a year-long intervention. *Cambridge Journal of Education, 39*, 95–117.

Bilgin, I. & Geban, O. (2006). The Effect of Cooperative Learning Approach Based on Conceptual Change Condition on Students' Understanding of Chemical Equilibrium Concepts. *Journal of Science Education and Technology, 15*, 31–46.

Bryant, D., Vaughn, S., Linan-Thompson, S., Ugel, N., Hamff, A., & Hougen, M. (2000). *Learning Disability Quarterly, 23*, 4, 238–252.

Chin, C. (2007). Teacher questioning in science classrooms: Approaches that stimulate productive thinking. *Journal of Research in Science Teaching, 44*, 815–843.

Chinn, C., O'Donnell, A., & Jinks, T. (2000). The structure of discourse in collaborative learning. *The Journal of Experimental Education, 69*, 77–89.

Christie, D., Tolmie, A., Thurston, A., Howe, C., & Yopping, K. (2009). Supporting group work in Scottish primary classrooms: Improving the quality of collaborative dialogue. *Cambridge Journal of Education, 39*, 141–156.

Cohen, E. (1994). Restructuring the classroom: Conditions for productive small groups. *Review of Educational Research, 64*, 1–35.

Cowie, H., & Berdondini, L. (2001). Children's reactions to cooperative group work: A strategy for enhancing peer relationships among bullies, victims, and bystanders. *Learning and Instruction, 11*, 517–530.

Emmer, E., & Stough, L. (2001). Classroom management: A critical part of educational psychology with implications for teacher development. *Educational Psychologist, 36*, 103–112.

Erdogan, I., & Campbell, T. (2008). Teacher questioning and interaction patterns in classrooms facilitated with different levels of constructivist teaching practices. *International Journal of Science Education, 30*, 1891–1914.

Fuchs, D. & Fuchs, L. (2005). Peer-assisted learning strategies: Promoting word recognition, fluency, and reading comprehension in young children. *The Journal of Special Education, 39*, 34–44.

Fuchs, L., Fuchs, D., Bentz, J., Phillips, N., & Hamlett, C. (1994). The nature of student interactions during peer tutoring with and without prior training and experience. *American Educational Research Journal, 31*, 75–101.

Fuchs, L., Fuchs, D., Hamlett, C., & Karns, K. (1998). High-achieving students' interactions and performance on complex mathematical tasks as a function of homogeneous and heterogeneous pairings. *American Educational Research Journal, 35*, 227–267.

Fuchs, L., Fuchs, D., Hamlett, C., Phillips, N., Karns, K., & Dutka, S. (1997). Enhancing students' helping behavior with conceptual mathematical explanations. *The Elementary School Journal, 97*, 223–249.

Fuchs, L., Fuchs, D., & Karns, K. (2001). Enhancing kindergartners' mathematical development: Effects of Peer-Assisted learning strategies. *The Elementary School Journal, 101*, 495–510.

Fuchs, L., Fuchs, D., Powell, S., Seethaler, P., Cirino, P., & Fletcher, J. (2008). Intensive intervention for students with mathematics disabilities: Seven principles of effective practice. *Learning Disabilities Quarterly, 31*, 79–92.

Galton, M., Hargreves, L., Comber, C., Wall, D., & Pell, T. (1999). Changes in patterns of teacher interaction in primary classrooms: 1976–1996. *British Educational Research Journal, 25*, 23–37.

Galton, M., Hargreaves, L. & Pell, T. (2009). Group work and whole-class teaching with 11–14-year-olds compared. *Cambridge Journal of Education, 39*, 119–140.

Gillies, R. (2003). Structuring cooperative group work in classrooms. *International Journal of Educational Research, 39*, 35–49.

Gillies, R. (2004). The effects of communication training on teachers' and students' verbal behaviours during cooperative learning. *International Journal of Educational Research, 41*, 257–279.

Gillies, R. (2008). The effects of cooperative learning on junior high school students' behaviours, discourse, and learning during a science-based learning activity. *School Psychology International, 29*, 328–347.

Gillies, R., & Khan, A. (2008). The effects of teacher discourse on students' discourse, problem-solving and reasoning during cooperative learning. *International Journal of Educational Research, 47*, 323–340.

Gillies, R., Nichols, K., Burgh, G., & Haynes, M. (2012). The effects of two meta-cognitive questioning approaches on children's explanatory behaviour, problem-solving, and learning during cooperative, inquiry-based science. *International Journal of Educational Research, 53*, 93–106.

Greenwood, C., Delquadri, J., & Hall, R. (1989). Longitudinal effects of classwide peer tutoring. *Journal of Educational Psychology, 81*, 371–383.

Howe, C., Tolmie, A., Greer, K., & MacKenzie, M. (1995). Peer collaboration and conceptual growth in physics: Task influences on children's understanding of heating and cooling. *Cognition and Instruction, 13*, 483–503.

Johnson, D., & Johnson, R. (1990). Cooperative learning and achievement. In S. Sharan (Ed.), *Cooperative learning: Theory and research* (pp. 23–37). New York: Praeger.

Johnson, D., & Johnson, R. (2000). Cooperative learning, values, and culturally plural classrooms. In M. Leicester, C. Modgil, & S. Modgil (Eds.), *Classroom issues: Practice, pedagogy, and curriculum* (pp. 15–28). London: Falmer Press.

Johnson, D., & Johnson, R. (2002). Learning together and alone: Overview and meta-analysis. *Asia Pacific Journal of Education, 22*, 95–105.

Johnson, D., & Johnson, R. (2003). Student motivation in cooperative groups: Social interdependence theory. In R. Gillies & A. Ashman (Eds.), *Cooperative learning: The social and intellectual outcomes of learning in groups* (pp. 136–176). London: Routledge Falmer.

King, A. (1997). Ask to Think–Tel Why: A model of transactive peer tutoring for scaffolding higher level complex learning. *Educational Psychologist, 32*, 221–235.

King, A. (2008). Structuring peer interaction to promote higher-order thinking and complex learning in cooperating groups. In R. Gillies, A. Ashman, & J. Terwel (Eds.), *The teacher's role in implementing cooperative learning in the classroom* (pp.73–91). New York: Springer.

Klinger, J., Vaughn, S., Arguelles, M., Hughes, M., & Leftwich, S. (2004). Collaborative strategic reading: Real-world lessons from classroom teachers. *Remedial and Special Education, 25*(5), 291–302.

Kohn, A. (1992). Resistance to cooperative learning: making sense of its deletion and dilution. *Journal of Education, 174*, 38–55.

Lipman, M. (1988). *Philosophy goes to school*. Philadelphia: Temple University Press.

Lou, Y., Abrami, P., & d'Apollonia, S. (2001). Small group and individual learning with technology: A meta-analysis. *Review of Educational Research, 71*, 449–521.

Lou, Y., Abrami, P., & Spence, J. (2000). Effects of within-class grouping on student achievement: An exploratory model. *The Journal of Educational Research, 94*, 101–112.

McNeill, K., & Krajcik, J. (2008). Scientific explanations: Characterizing and evaluating the effects of teachers' instructional practices on student learning. *Journal of Research in Science Teaching, 45*, 53–78.

Mercer, N. (1996). The quality of talk in children's collaborative activity in the classroom. *Learning and Instruction, 6*, 359–377.

Mercer, N., Dawes, L., Wegerif, R., & Sams, C. (2004). Reasoning as a scientist: Ways of helping children to use language to learn science. *British Educational Research Journal, 30*, 359–377.

Mercer, N., & Sams, C. (2006). Teaching children how to use language to solve math problems. *Language and Education, 20*, 507–528.

Michaels, S., O'Connor, C., & Resnick, L. (2008). Deliberative discourse idealized and realized: Accountable talk in the classroom and civic life. *Studies in Philosophy of Education, 27*, 283–297.

Palincsar, A., & Herrenkohl, L. (2002). Designing collaborative contexts. *Theory into Practice, 41*, 26–35.

Reznitskaya, A., Anderson, R., Kuo, L. (2007). Teaching and learning argumentation. *Elementary School Journal, 107*, 449–472.

Rojas-Drummond, S., & Mercer, N. (2003). Scaffolding the development of effective collaboration and learning. *International Journal of Educational Research, 39*, 99–111.

Rojas-Drummond, S., & Zapata, M. (2004). Exploratory talk, argumentation and reasoning in Mexican primary school children. *Language and Education, 18*, 539–557.

Roseth, C., Johnson, D., & Johnson, R. (2008). Promoting early adolescents' achievement and peer relationships: The effects of cooperative, competitive, and individualistic goal structures. *Psychological Bulletin, 134*, 223–246.

Saenz, L., Fuchs, L., & Fuchs, D. (2005). Peer-assisted learning strategies. *Exceptional Children, 71*, 231–247.

Slavin, R. (1996). Research on cooperative learning and achievement: What we know, what we need to know. *Contemporary Educational Psychology, 21*, 43–69.

Slavin, R. (1999). Comprehensive approaches to cooperative learning. *Theory into Practice, 38*, 74–79.

Slavin, R., & Lake, C. (2008). Effective programs in elementary mathematics: A best-evidence synthesis. *Review of Educational Research, 78*, 427–515.

Tolmie, A., Topping, K., Christie, D., Donaldson, C., Howe, C., Jessiman, E., Livingston, K., & Thurston, A. (2010). Social effects of collaborative learning in primary schools. *Learning and Instruction, 20*, 177–191.

Topping, K. (2005). Trends in peer learning. *Educational Psychology, 25*, 631–645.

Topping, K. & Bryce, A. (2004). Cross-age peer tutoring of reading and thinking: Influence on thinking skills. *Educational Psychology, 24*, 595–621.

Topping, K., Peters, C., Stephen, P., & Whale, M. (2004). Cross-age peer tutoring of science in primary school: Influence on scientific language and thinking. *Educational Psychology, 24*, 57–75.

Topping, K., Thurston, A., McGavock, K., & Conlin, N. (2009). Outcomes and process in reading tutoring. *Educational Research, 54*, 239–258.

Topping, K., & Trickey, S. (2007a). Collaborative philosophical enquiry for school children: Cognitive effects at 10–12 years. *British Journal of Educational Psychology, 77*, 271–288.

Topping, K., & Trickey, S. (2007b). Collaborative philosophical enquiry for school children: Cognitive gains at 2-year follow-up. *British Journal of Educational Psychology, 77*, 787–796.

Trickey, S., & Topping, K. (2004). Philosophy for Children: A systematic review. *Research Papers in Education, 19*, 365–380.

Trickey, S. & Topping, K. (2006). Collaborative Philosophical Enquiry for school children: Social-emotional effects at 11 and 12 years. *School Psychology International, 27*, 599–614.

Vaughn, S., Klingner, J., & Bryant, D. (2001). Collaborative strategic reading as a means to enhance peer-mediated instruction for reading comprehension and content-area learning. *Remedial and Special Education, 22*, 66–74.

Veenman, S., Kenter, B., & Post, K. (2000). Cooperative learning in Dutch primary classrooms. *Educational Studies, 26*, 281–302.

Webb, N., & Farivar, S. (1999). Developing productive group interaction in middle school mathematics. In A. O'Donnell & A. King (Eds.), *Cognitive perspectives on peer learning* (pp. 117–150). Mahwah, NJ: Erlbaum.

Webb, N., Franke, M., Ing, M., Chan, A., De, T., Freund, D., & Battey, D. (2008). The role of teacher instructional practices in student collaboration. *Contemporary Educational Psychology, 33*, 360–381.

Webb, N., & Mastergeorge, A. (2003). Promoting effective helping in peer-directed groups. *International Journal of Educational Research, 39*, 73–97.

IV

Social and Psychological Perspectives

15

TEACHER PERSPECTIVES ON CLASSROOM MANAGEMENT

Rules, Ethics, and "Crime Control"

ROBERT V. BULLOUGH JR. AND MICHAEL RICHARDSON
BRIGHAM YOUNG UNIVERSITY

INTRODUCTION

The focus of this chapter is teachers' perspectives on classroom management. We begin with a brief overview of a previous chapter from the first *Handbook on Classroom Management*, which combined both student and teacher perspectives (Woolfolk Hoy & Weinstein, 2006). Woolfolk Hoy and Weinstein begin their chapter with an exploration of the meaning of the terms knowledge, beliefs, and perspectives, stating:

> In spite of some conceptual differences . . . , the majority of respondents perceived knowledge and beliefs as overlapping constructs; many ideas fall in the realm of what is both known *and* believed. Given that teachers often seem to define knowledge and beliefs as overlapping constructs, and a precedent set by other researchers of teacher cognition, within this review we discuss them as overlapping and somewhat interchangeable constructs. (p. 182)

This review begins at the same point of departure. Following their introduction, Woolfolk Hoy and Weinstein include two sections on student perceptions, one of the good teacher and another of disciplinary interventions. Their discussion of teachers' knowledge and beliefs about classroom management focuses on teacher "Orientations to Management" and includes descriptions of and conclusions drawn from use of the Pupil Control Ideology (PCI) form, the Beliefs about Discipline Inventory (BADI), and the Attitudes and Beliefs on Classroom Control (ABCC) framework. Additional descriptions follow of social and political perspectives of classroom management, including studies using the Problems in School (PS) questionnaire to assess teachers' "beliefs about control and autonomy support" (p. 199), of classroom management and student choice, and of teachers' views of the value of various management strategies. A section then follows on teacher beliefs about the reasons for student misbehavior, including attributions and problem ownership. A final section focuses on teacher beliefs about self, most especially emphasizing studies of teacher efficacy.

The lines of research described by Woolfolk Hoy and Weinstein in their review continue, and, most notably, the number of studies of teacher efficacy and collective efficacy (Sorlie & Torsheim, 2011) has grown in the intervening years. Given this conclusion, only a portion of this chapter is directly concerned with updating the lines of research discussed in the first *Handbook* chapter, which holds up well and is foundational to this chapter. We approached this review by conducting multiple searches using several different descriptors of published research studies from 2004 to the present. Descriptors combined classroom management, management, and discipline with teacher values, perspectives, beliefs, knowledge, attitudes, concerns, dispositions, and understanding, and cross-references to teaching and learning in primary and secondary schools and teacher education. Several dozen articles were identified in this manner, each of which was reviewed to determine those that were data-driven—either qualitative or quantitative—and on topic with explicit reference to teacher perspectives on classroom management. Through multiple readings and ongoing discussion, eventually 74 articles were identified and then outlined. The outlines were then read, reread, and discussed to identify patterns and themes, which were compared to those used by Woolfolk Hoy and Weinstein to organize their review. There are differences in emphasis including what appears to be an increase in international and cross-cultural studies, in a dominating view of classroom management as primarily being a matter of behavioral management, and in attention to students with disabilities of various kinds.

This review is organized into five sections. The first section focuses on the methods used in studies of teacher perspectives on management. The second is concerned with culture and cultural differences, a topic of importance inasmuch as more than 20 nations are represented in the studies reviewed from Australia and Botswana to Slovenia and the United States. The third section considers influences on teacher perspectives, and the fourth explores teacher concerns and attributions. Representing an underdeveloped area, the fifth section explores ethics and management. A conclusion briefly considers implications and future directions for research.

METHODS USED IN THE STUDIES

The great majority of articles reviewed employed surveys (80%). More commonly used instruments included versions of the Attitudes and Beliefs on Classroom Control Inventory (ABCC) (Martin, Yin, & Baldwin, 1998), the Pupil Control Ideology survey (PCI) (Willower, Eidell, & Hoy, 1967), and the Teacher Self-Efficacy Scales (TSES, including language adaptations; see, e.g., Abu-Teneh, Khasawneh & Khlaileh, 2011; Shin & Koh, 2007). The ABCC is a 26-item Likert-type scale intended to measure management and control. Use of the PCI typically involved a 10-item (Capa, 2005) Likert-type scale intended to measure beliefs about management ranging from custodial to humanistic. The TSES (Tschannen-Moran & Woolfolk Hoy, 2001) includes 12 Likert-type items intended to measure efficacy for instructional strategies, classroom management, and student engagement.

Studies also drew on data from the Teacher Belief Survey (TBS), in particular a seven-item Likert-type subscale of constructivist or student-centered teaching (see e.g. Ngidi, 2012); the Teacher Job Satisfaction Survey, which includes 12 Likert-type questions about job satisfaction and an open response section asking teachers to list the most prevalent and challenging student behaviors faced (see, e.g., Landers, Alter, & Servilio, 2008); the Behavior Attributions Survey (BAS), which describes behaviors and then asks teachers to indicate whether they are related to student, teacher, school, or out-of-school influences (see e.g. Kulinna, 2007–2008); a modified version of the Teacher Expectations for School Success (TESS) questionnaire (see e.g. Lane, Pierson, Stang & Carter, 2010); and the Coping Scale for Adults (CSA), which is also a Likert-type measure describing types of coping responses (see e.g. Lewis, Roache, & Romi, 2011).

Two studies explored the relationships among different measures, such as self-efficacy, pupil control, and self-reported management behavior in order to examine the construct of academic optimism (e.g., Ngidi, 2012; Woolfolk Hoy, Hoy, & Kurz, 2008). Other studies reported the development (Caldarella et al., 2009; Gotzens, Badia, Genovard & Dezcallar, 2010) or validation (Martin & Sass, 2010) of new measures, including studies in which teachers responded to vignettes describing student behavior (Alvarez, 2007; Poulou, 2005). While most of the survey research relied on Likert-type scales, Rimm-Kaufman, Storm, Sawyer, Pianta, and LaParo (2006) used a potentially promising alternative, the Teacher Belief Q-Sort (TBQ). Rather than offering a list of beliefs for teachers to rate, the TBQ has teachers sort beliefs according to how characteristic they are of their own perspectives about management. The authors argue that this method, compared to other measures, allows for a more person-oriented rather than a variable-oriented analysis.

A fourth of the studies, some of which also included use of surveys, employed structured interviews (see e.g. Chakrabortie-Ghosh, 2008; Hong, 2012; Oplatka, 2006, 2009; Watson, Charner-Laird, Kirkpatrick, Szczesiul, & Gordon, 2006). Based on her interviews of teachers in India and the United States, Chakraborty-Ghosh (2008) concluded that the conceptions of behavior by these two groups of teachers might be very different, suggesting that terms and concepts commonly used in studies of teacher perspectives of management might not be universally understood. In addition to initial surveys, Jackson (2010) conducted in-depth interviews of teachers to explore "laddishness," problematic behavior primarily attributed to boys. Her interviews revealed that some teachers, particularly male, implicated themselves in a type of laddish behavior through which they hoped to better engage laddish students but that, Jackson argues, might both encourage laddishness and alienate non-laddish students. The idea that some teachers might be in collusion with problematic student behavior represents the sort of provocative line of research unlikely to emerge from surveys of teachers' views of student behavior.

In addition to surveys and interviews, a very few studies employed case study methods (Newberry, 2010; Popp, Grant & Stronge, 2011) and teachers' written responses in journals (Chakrabortie-Ghosh, 2008; Stoughton, 2007). Missing are studies drawing on action research traditions, which, as Mitchell, Reilly and Logue (2009) suggest, hold potential for "increasing teachers' levels of self-efficacy and feelings of empower-ment . . . supporting professional development . . . [and] preventing teacher burnout" (p. 345). Also missing are self-studies, which would seem particularly promising for gaining insight into how perspectives of management develop and evolve over time and in context. A study by Snoeyink (2010) suggests some of the potential value of research designed to help teachers think through their perspectives. Snoeyink used guided self-analysis of videos, along with interviews, a rating scale designed to calcu-late "dissonance scores" and focus-group discussion to help novice teachers explore their perceptions of their teaching, including of classroom management, in the light of their actual classroom behavior. A range of changes in perception were noted, includ-ing a "heightened awareness of student behaviors" (p. 105).

All research methods have limits. Survey research allows for tapping into general perspectives on relatively narrowly defined categories of interest but may prevent recognition of deeper issues, eliminate from consideration important variables and distort potentially significant relationships. Greater emphasis on other methods is needed, including interviews, case studies, journaling, self-study, video self-analysis, and, most especially, classroom observations. We suspect that the dominance of survey methods in studies of teacher perception encourages researchers to view classroom management as being mostly a matter of student discipline and of dis-cipline primarily as a function of teacher orientations (more or less humanistic, interactionist, giving students greater say and involvement in rule development and implementation, or interventionist, i.e., more teacher directed) toward rule setting and enforcement. Rule setting is taken to be the essential component of preven-tion, and remarkably little attention is given to classroom routines or to curricular issues related to management, such as lesson organization and design and content interest and value. For this reason, Reupert and Woodcock (2010) argue that when teaching—and we would add researching—classroom management, greater atten-tion needs to be given to how "the processes involved in preventing classroom man-agement problems require an understanding of the function of behaviour within an ecological framework" (p. 1267). To better understand such frameworks, there is need for "local studies" (Bullough, 2012), studies that contextualize perspectives in persons, relationships, communities, cultures, and places.

CULTURE AND CULTURAL DIFFERENCES

As noted, a wide variety of nationalities are present in the studies reviewed. Given such diversity, it was somewhat surprising to find that with but few exceptions, rela-tively little was said about culture even when making cross-cultural comparisons. The exceptions include Gibbs and Gardiner (2008) who compared English and Irish teachers, concluding that Irish teachers are somewhat more likely than English teach-ers to locate the sources of student misbehavior in students rather than in teacher strategies. They link their conclusions to historical and contextual differences, the English system being more centralized, with the Irish offering more latitude for rec-ognizing local priorities. A very high survey return rate among Irish teachers and a very low return rate among English teachers, which necessitated a much broader sampling, may cast doubt on these conclusions. Khoury-Kassabri and Ben-Harush (2012) offer another exception. These authors compared Arab and Jewish teachers' perspectives on the use of nonpunitive and punitive methods of discipline. They found that both groups of teachers were more supportive of nonpunitive methods, but overall Arabic teachers were more supportive of punitive measures than Jewish teachers, particularly when aggression was directed toward teachers. These authors suggest that both cultural and socioeconomic differences, including differences in resources, class sizes, and training, might account for the findings.

Other studies involved comparisons across more distant and diverse cultural contexts, raising questions about study purposes. Using the ABCC Inventory, Shin and Koh (2007) reported a greater emphasis on teacher control among the 112 Americans surveyed (teaching in an urban, largely African American, school district) compared to 166 Korean teachers (working in Seoul, schools driven by college admission test scores). The authors note that Korean teachers move from class to class and the students remain, whereas in the United States students change classrooms, a factor that might influence teacher perspectives on management. Reasons for conducting this particular cross-cultural study are unclear even as the comparison made, despite the small sample size, is presented as being between American and Korean teachers writ large and, as the authors note, using an instrument that may have failed to accurately capture Korean teachers' thinking. The authors state that Korean teachers are perhaps more likely than American teachers to "choose more moderate and safe options" when marking the Inventory (p. 303). Problems arose in a qualitative study of 10 teachers, comparing attitudes toward behavioral disorders among five teachers from India and five from the United States. Highlighting difficulties of transferring concepts from one cultural context to another, Chakraborti-Ghosh (2008) concluded that teachers in India describe misbehavior more in terms of contextual contributors than as located within the student, as is more often the case among American teachers. Similar difficulties arose in a study of teacher self-efficacy and of behavior problems and labels comparing teachers from Canada and from Singapore (Klassen et al., 2008).

Perhaps most striking about the cross-cultural studies is not what is present but what is absent. Similar or identical instruments are often used with little consideration of potential difficulties not only with translation but also with the relevance of constructs and issues across cultures. The question of whether similar scores on an instrument mean the same thing in different cultural contexts remains largely unaddressed. If measures and responses are commensurate across cultures, a globalization of Western educational models may be indicated. Presently, globalization is assumed. The emphasis on classroom management as discipline, which was mentioned in the previous section and will be discussed in the sections that follow, remains largely intact regardless of cultural context—perhaps partially due to the borrowing or adaption of surveys and survey methodology—suggesting an assumed similarity prior to the search for differences.

One purpose for cross-cultural studies involves the validation of concepts across cultures. Many other purposes are ignored including questions regarding the influence of various individual and group characteristics on teacher perspectives about classroom management—such as class location, ethnicity, religion, and child-rearing patterns, among others. Questions also arise regarding differences in institutional structures and organizational practices, such as the sort mentioned when Korean teachers rather than students move from classroom to classroom. In addition, large regions of the world are not represented in the literature reviewed, notably South America, Eastern Europe, and Russia. Although no doubt there are similarities across cultures in how classroom management is understood born of the challenges associated with managing large groups of young people, there are also significant differences, and these differences likely represent potentially rich sources of understanding.

INFLUENCES ON TEACHER PERSPECTIVES

Despite giving rather little attention to broad cultural influences, the literature has identified a range of factors that affect teacher perspectives about classroom management including biographical influences, student characteristics and behavior, teacher personal characteristics, and the influence of teacher education.

Biographical Influences

A very few studies reviewed note biographical influences in how teachers define classroom management (Chakraborti-Ghosh, 2008). Included in these influences is past schooling, which affects how teachers view the students they teach. For example, Watson, Charner-Laird, Kirkpatrick, Szczesiul, & Gordon, (2006) interviewed 17 teachers, 15 of whom were white, enrolled in an urban teacher education program, and followed them into their first months of teaching. The authors conclude that for all but one of the teachers, Robert, a Latino, there were differences between perspectives on effective teaching and effective urban teaching. Teachers thought of their own experience as suburban students as normal and used "stereotypical constructions of race and class to determine who their students were and to plan their teaching accordingly" (p. 403). The authors offer the example of Molly, who, they argue, based on her experience as a student, demonstrated a stereotype of urban students as having behavior problems,

> [Molly] described the ease of teaching in a suburban classroom, "or a classroom where for whatever reason the climate of the school was such that people behaved better in class—classroom management was not such an issue" . . . Molly planned her lessons accordingly, focusing predominantly on classroom management in her teaching. In so doing, Molly's teaching responded to her *stereotype* of urban students as hard to manage, as opposed to the individual backgrounds and identities of each of her students. (p. 403)

In contrast, Robert "actually stated a plan . . . that placed the responsibility for effective urban teaching on teachers, as opposed to citing student deficits as the source of difference between effective urban teaching and teaching in other contexts" (p. 404). Watson and colleagues attribute this difference in perspective in part to Robert's "experience as a student in both urban and suburban schools" (p. 406).

Student Characteristics and Behavior

Student characteristics and behavior also influence teacher perspectives. Some studies suggest that teachers "want to be pupil-centered and constructivist to support mutual interaction with pupils and to use versatile teaching methods and learning environments" (Atjonen, Korkeakoski, & Mehtalainen, 2011, p. 285), aims widely thought central to teacher education, but conclude, because of student misbehavior, established work conditions requiring teachers to manage large numbers of students, and lack of administrative support, they cannot teach in this way. Misbehavior consistently has been identified as a major contributor to undermining teacher psychological well-being and commitment, including as a source of teacher exhaustion (Skaalvik & Skaalvik, 2007) and attrition, particularly when there is comparatively little administrative support (Tickle, Chang, & Kim, 2011). In a study involving 806 French Canadian teachers in public elementary and secondary schools, for example, Fernet, Guay, Senecal, and Austin (2012) concluded that "changes in burnout are predicted by changes in teachers' perceptions of school environment and motivational factors . . . Although we examined a limited set of variables, our findings suggest that teachers' perceptions of interpersonal factors (students' behavior and the principal's leadership behaviors) are particularly influential in the burnout process" (p. 522).

Teachers are also taught and generally believe that different types of students require different approaches to teaching and classroom management. For both good and ill, the assumptions teachers hold about students shape the judgments they make about management. For example, in a comparative study of secondary teachers in Canada and Singapore, Klassen and colleagues (2008) noted that the Canadian teachers were "more likely to discuss students in terms of their funding labels or categories" (p. 1929) rather than attending to the individual child. Students with special needs, in particular, were seen as qualitatively different from other students and more demanding. Once set, labels and supporting perceptions tend to endure, as Batzle, Weyandt, Janusis, & DeVietti (2010) conclude from their study of teacher expectations of ADHD students.

One study found that older children were thought less challenging to manage than younger children because of increasing maturity (Lane, Pierson, Stang, & Carter, 2010). Other studies report that boys are perceived as much more challenging than girls (Arbuckle & Little, 2004; Batzle, Weyandt, Janusis, & DeVietti, 2010; Jackson, 2010; Jones, 2005).

Teacher Personal Characteristics

Despite the challenges of teaching, on the whole, teachers tend to be optimistic and hopeful people (Bullough & Hall-Kenyon, 2011). Two studies of teacher academic optimism (Ngidi, 2012; Woolfolk Hoy, Hoy, & Kurz, 2008)—a construct composed of sense of efficacy, trust in parents and teachers, and academic emphasis—speak to teachers' perspectives about classroom management. Academic optimism positively correlated with humanistic management style, student-centered teaching, individual citizenship, and dispositional optimism (Woolfolk Hoy, Hoy, & Kurz, 2008). Ngidi studied academic optimism in four regions of KwaZulu-Natal, South Africa, and found that virtually all the 280 teachers surveyed reported high (63%) to moderate levels of optimism (37%); none reported low levels. "This means that the majority of teachers believe that, with the trust they have in parents and students, they are capable of teaching successfully" (p. 148), which includes effectively managing classrooms.

Differences emerge, however, between teachers who remain in teaching and those who leave. In a study comparing self-efficacy, teacher beliefs, and emotions of seven "leavers" and seven "stayers," Hong (2012) found that while there was agreement about the challenges of teaching, including the difficulties of classroom management, stayers were able to maintain higher levels of self-efficacy and positive emotions, such as joy and satisfaction, and higher levels of optimism. Leavers tended to attribute their "difficulty to their own personality or characteristics and experienced emotional burnout" (p. 431). With the assistance of administrators, stayers reported being able to "strategically set emotional lines or boundaries between themselves and students, so that they would not take negative events personally" (p. 431). Perhaps relatedly, over time, as teachers age it appears their attitudes toward classroom management become "more controlling" (Unal & Unal, 2012, p. 47) favoring an "interventionist" management style.

In a case study of six award-winning teachers working at schools with high at-risk populations, Popp, Grant, and Stronge (2011) underscore the centrality of high teacher investment in student academic success and the belief that there is a "close link between academic and affective [student] needs" (p. 284). "Planning, assessment, instruction, and classroom management were not separate activities [but] often occurred in unison" (p. 287). Teacher knowledge of students and strong relationships with them were reported as critical to positive student behavior and academic success. Similarly, Oplatka (2006, 2009) studied teachers identified as "those who do more than is needed formally in school, not to impress others but for the sake of the whole" (2006, p. 395), exhibiting what is described as organizational citizenship behavior (OCB). OCB involves seven elements: helping behavior, sportsmanship, organizational loyalty, organizational compliance, individual initiative, civic virtue, and self-development. Such teachers have a "sense of calling" (p. 407) and a high degree of self-fulfillment, satisfaction, and enthusiasm for the work of teaching (Oplatka, 2009). The author concludes from a second study—which involved interviewing 50 Israeli teachers, 25 elementary and 25 secondary with eight or more years teaching—that "[n]otably, OCB in teaching was related to fewer discipline problems in school and class. Teachers' attentiveness and care for students, even at the expense of their leisure and non-contract time, is subjectively linked to lower levels of disruptive behaviors in class" (p. 384). These and other studies (Newberry, 2010) underscore the significance of teachers being willing and able to build quality personal relationships with students and of their belief in the value of positive teacher emotions (Sutton, Mudrey-Camino, & Knight, 2009) to student learning and development of prosocial behavior.

Gender differences also emerged as salient. In a survey study of 514 Canadian preservice teachers of their perspectives on bullying, Beran (2005) concluded that "female teachers were more concerned and felt more responsible than male teachers [but] also reported feeling less confident" (p. 45). Rideout and Morton (2007) explored connections between 746 preservice teachers' philosophical orientations—their understanding of select key educational concepts—and pupil control ideologies (PCI). The authors found that "females tended to be more humanistic than males" (p. 599). In addition, the researchers noted connections between academic majors and PCI measures that may also relate to gender: "Participants with an undergraduate major in the natural sciences tended to have a more custodial PCI, while those with undergraduate majors in psychological studies, sociological studies, and the creative arts tended to have a more humanistic PCI" (ibid).

Teacher Education

Evidence is mixed on the influence of teacher education on teacher perspectives about classroom management. A U.S. study of the impact of teacher education on "teachers' proposed attributions, affective reactions, and interventions for aggressive classroom behaviour" (Alvarez, 2007, p. 1116), concluded that "trained" teachers "endorsed significantly less negative affect in response to the hypothetical vignettes as compared to those with no training" (p. 1118). Moreover, untrained teachers were more likely to report "feelings of anger, stress, helplessness, irritation, and hurt/offence" than those with training (p. 1121). And "[t]eacher training was also positively related to the likelihood that teachers would propose positive, active interventions in response to classroom aggression" (p. 1121). Conclusions from a journal study conducted by Stoughton (2007) of preservice teachers enrolled in an urban practicum are pertinent here. The cooperating teachers involved in this study emphasized clearly defined rules consistently reinforced, positive recognition of rule following, and public consequences for rule infractions of escalating severity. Only three of 48 teacher education students concluded they would organize their own classrooms in similar ways to their cooperating teachers', and eight reported being "extremely uncomfortable" with the practices used in the classrooms to which they were assigned. Thirty-seven students were uncertain about the practices, indicating difficulty balancing what they witnessed with what was being taught in their teacher education programs. Several expressed concern about "the ultimate purposes of behavioral management programmes," that the "object of many interventions was to stop misbehaviour as quickly and efficiently as possible without considering how to help children learn more effective ways to handle similar situations in the future" (p. 1033). Obedience seemed to trump student learning.

In contrast, in a roughly similar study of teacher education students, but in this instance, master's-level students, Kaufman and Moss (2010) found, to their disappointment, that "when asked what steps they would take to manage their classroom well, all mention of organization disappeared, replaced with the exclusive focus on establishing rules, expectations, rewards, and consequence for behavior" (p. 131). Not surprisingly, practica are found to be especially influential. For example, in a

Turkish study, Yilmaz and Cavas (2008) concluded that the "most important factor which affects or changes pre-service teachers' [beliefs] is the teaching practice experience" (p. 51). Using the ABCC Inventory and the Science Teaching Efficacy Belief Instrument (STEBI-B), the researchers found that the instructional management beliefs of preservice teachers in this study became somewhat more interactionist and less interventionist, but their people management beliefs became more interventionist through the teaching experience" (p. 52). Generally, there appears to be a disjunction between what is taught in preservice teacher education and what is experienced in the field, although there is some evidence of positive effects of teacher education on teacher beliefs.

TEACHER CONCERNS, ATTRIBUTIONS, AND PERCEPTUAL CHANGE

Several studies underscore that teachers generally define classroom management simply in terms of rules (Gotzens, Badia, Genovard, & Dezcallar, 2010; Kaufman & Moss, 2010); *classroom* management is thought to be synonymous with *behavior* management. Underpinning this view appears to be a belief that the development of student self-control and cooperative skills is critical for school success (Lane, Wehby, & Cooley, 2006; Lane, Pierson, Stang, & Carter, 2010). Mostly, the behavior problems that concern teachers are "not major infringements or violent behaviour, but rather they are minor infractions and repeated disruptions" (Arbuckle & Little, 2004, p. 60), including talking out of turn (TOOT). This said, there is a continuum of concern and some evidence of what may be a growing interest in school violence, including the effects of teacher fear of violence on job satisfaction (Ricketts, 2007).

Using questionnaires, a behavioral checklist, and interviews of children, parents, and teachers, Lyons and O'Connor (2006) explore a range of questions related to "misbehaviour" in an Irish primary school. The questionnaires sought to get at the "incidence, severity, and range" of misbehaviour, reasons for misbehaving, frequency, "strategies and effectiveness," "beliefs about challenging behaviour," impact and "school improvement, working conditions and job satisfaction" (p. 218). A continuum emerged. The "most serious challenging behaviours involved physical and verbal aggression and refusal to co-operate with teachers' direction" (p. 222), a view supported by Gotzens and associates (2010). As Lyons and O'Connor (2006) note, aggressive behavior was comparatively rare and involved few children. Inattentiveness and withdrawal are at the other extreme of the continuum, behaviors generally not seen as problems except by a minority of teachers. The authors conclude that this finding—that student withdrawal is generally not thought a problem—underscores the "importance of control and 'doing what you are told' in teacher perceptions of what is challenging [behaviour]" (p. 222). Interestingly, and likely signaling significant contextual and cultural differences, in a survey of 244 Chinese teachers Ding, Li, Li, and Kulm (2008) found daydreaming to be the most troublesome student behavior.

There is some minor variation in teacher attributions of student misbehavior. Generally, teachers tend to locate the source of student misbehavior in factors external or internal to the student and outside of the classroom and school. The teachers in Lyon and O'Connor's (2006) study, for example, located reasons for student misbehavior in a disjunction between school and home values, even though interviewed parents reportedly shared teachers' values. Student home lives and other "out of school factors" are similarly faulted in Kulinna's (2007–2008) study of 199 physical education teachers, a finding echoed in a survey study of 869 Greek high school teachers (Koutrouba, 2011). In a study of Botswana school teachers, Garegae (2008) found high levels of teacher frustration arising from a perceived disjunction between cultural patterns of discipline and school policies that prohibited teachers from meting out corporal punishment and instead placed primary responsibility for correction on school heads. The result of such policies, the teachers asserted, was a dramatic rise in misbehavior. Culture and class are also identified as significant contributors to student misbehavior in two studies (Jackson, 2010; Watson, et al., 2006), and internal factors were mentioned, notably in studies of teachers of children with special needs (Batzle, Weyandt, Janusis, & DeVietti, 2010). Additionally, Abu-Teneh, Khasawneh, and Khalaileh (2011) conclude from a survey of 566 randomly selected Jordanian public school teachers that teachers were aggressively involved in managing students because "they assume, children are unable to adequately monitor and control themselves" (p. 179).

The findings of Gibbs and Gardiner (2008) offer a rare contrasting conclusion. The teachers in this study "appeared to recognise that their own behaviour (in terms of responding to children's work and behaviour) was a major influence on children's behaviour" (p. 74). The authors conclude that "behavioural problems do not emanate from the individual child but are a product of social interaction" (p. 74). Noting that definitions of misbehavior, including attributions, are crucially important to intervention, Lyons and O'Conner (2006) argue for what they describe as an "interactive" model:

> Examining our expectations and their validity leads us to address contextual issues that are contributing to the expression of an individual child's needs in a way that we find challenging. Equally, the child's perspectives, responses and behavioural choices need to be explored so that their influence on their context can be clarified and possibly changed. (p. 230)

It is worth noting that Lyons and O'Connor (2006) found that in contrast to the ease of defining misbehavior, teachers and students in their study had difficulty defining just what is *good behavior*, concluding: "There appears to be a general assumption that we all know what it is to be well behaved or 'good' and that this needs little explication" (p. 222). This finding, the way in which systemic values are taken for granted and generally unquestioned, underpins issues addressed in the next section: ethics and classroom management.

Once established, teacher perceptions of classroom management are difficult to change. In an Australian study, Davies, Edwards, Gannon, & Laws (2007) attempted to alter the "neo-liberal subjectivities" of teachers by problematizing the "discursive strategies" they used to constitute students as troubled and troubling (p. 32). Based on previous research, the authors argue that two discourses dominate teacher think-ing about student behaviour: The first locates 'bad' behaviour . . . as arising when students *do not understand* the consequences of their actions and so do not make *good* choices. Students are thus read as deficient in the skills required to 'get it right' at school. Getting it right at school, in this discourse, is seen as compliance with school rules and authority/ies" (p. 27). The second discourse "sees such students as *wilfully 'bad'* rather than skills deficient" (ibid). In both discourses, the individual student is thought of as deficient and in need of correction, views consistent with the assumptions of crime control, to be discussed in the next section. The aim of the study, intended to be collaborative, was to encourage a rethinking of the "positioning of students seen to be engaging in inappropriate behaviour, with the aim of map-ping new philosophical principles from which new policies and practices might be developed" (p. 28), perhaps along the order of Lyons and O'Connor's (2006) interac-tive model. On every level, the authors report that the project failed, resulting in a withdrawal from participation of all but the research team and educators in manage-ment positions attached to the participating school districts. Noting a range of prob-lems with how the study was conceptualized and organized, the authors conclude that their failure reveals just how deeply embedded in the culture and practices of schooling are the two discourses, such that "[e]ach individual develops passionate attachments to the person/subject that they take themselves to be, to competencies that they have accomplished . . . The introduction of a new discourse can destabilise individual subjectivities, and can appear as a potential threat to the sites in which the school-based participants competently carried out their daily work" (pp. 37–38). In effect, asking the teachers to rethink their views of the sources of misbehavior meant asking them to rethink their senses of themselves as teachers, and this they did not or could not do.

ETHICS AND CLASSROOM MANAGEMENT

On the whole in the literature reviewed, there is remarkably little discussion of ethi-cal issues or of values other than those associated with maintaining classroom con-trol, although the focus of academic optimism on trust appears to be an important exception. The Kaufman and Moss (2010) study of students enrolled in the teacher education program at the University of Connecticut is in many respects representa-tive. For these intending teachers, the central almost exclusive concern was estab-lishing classroom rules. Moreover, these preservice teachers believed that classroom management was the sole responsibility of teachers; not one of the 42 respondents reportedly mentioned "co-creating rules with students" (p. 130). In a Swedish quali-tative study of 13 elementary school teachers in two schools, Thornberg (2008) extends and deepens the point, that teachers are overwhelmingly concerned about gaining student compliance. "For the teachers . . . values education is about fostering students into good manners, characters, and behaviour, to maintain rules in school and in classroom, to manage conflicts between students, and to help students develop social skills" (p. 1793). Thornberg concludes that the teaching of values was part of an "informal curriculum" and mostly about teachers "intervening when things happen . . . reactive and unplanned[;] embedded in everyday school life with a focus on students' everyday behaviour [and] partly or mostly unconsciously performed by the teachers" (pp. 1794, 1795).

In this study, Thornberg found that little, if any, attention was being given to the values teachers taught. Values were "personal rather than professional" (p. 1794). Reviewing the data, Thornberg was troubled: The concern with rules and rule enforcement appears to be sharply focused on "students' short-term behaviour in school" while giving very little attention to the "far-reaching influence of morality" (p. 1795). An "over-emphasis on rules and obeying rules can . . . undermine the goal of fostering self-discipline, critical thinking, and democratic skills in children" (p. 1797). Indirectly, a report on developments in Wales underscores the importance of Thornberg's issue. Between 2006 and 2008, a review was conducted in Welsh schools of student behavior and attendance. Noting concern about comparatively lower school attendance rates and issues with student behavior, in 2009 the Welsh Assembly published a report offering a range of suggestions for improving the situation, most of which center on increasing teacher training in "behavioural management and the promotion of positive behaviour and attendance management at the school, [local authority], inter-agency, parent and pupil level" and "refresher training" (Reid, 2011, pp. 36, 37). Only a nod is given to ethical considerations, and this appears primarily to be a matter of keeping educator actions within established legal boundaries: The report urged that school staff be given "training modules" to make certain they understand children and young people's rights as they manage their classrooms and schools.

Thornberg has a broader concern. He recognizes that managing classrooms involves teaching values and creating forms of life, ways of living (Bullough, 2014). Even as he notes a lack of language useful for thinking and talking about ethics in schools and classrooms, Thornberg argues for an explicit emphasis on ethical theory and values education as central to quality teaching and to how teachers should think about management. Sharing Thornberg's general concern, Lewis and Burman (2008) argue in two studies of Australian teachers' views of classroom management that it is "critical that teachers are aware of both the managerial and *educational* [emphasis added] functions of discipline, where the former focuses solely on efficiency, in contrast to the latter, which is concerned with what values are learnt from the experience" (p. 152). These authors are interested in how students are involved in decisions related to classroom management, what teachers think about student involvement and how they would like them to be involved, if at all. One conclusion is that the teachers would "prefer to involve students less in classroom management decision-making in their current school . . . than they would do in an ideal setting" (p. 160). The authors argue that a reason for this result is that the teachers are constrained by a number of impediments in their current positions, including, as the teachers reported, too many students, lack of administrative support for wider student involvement, classroom size and layout, too many teaching demands, and too little knowledge of how to engage students meaningfully in decision making. Under these conditions, efficiency goals easily vacate wider student learning goals.

There is surprisingly little mention in the management literature of the wider cultural and economic impediments that shape schooling and inform teachers' perceptions of their work and responsibilities. Here, we reach outside the classroom management literature. In his discussion of what he describes as the "new Taylorism," referring to the influence of Frederick Winslow Taylor's "scientific management," Au (2011), among many others (Hursh, 2007), notes the influence globally on teaching of high-stakes testing, new forms of accountability, greater standardization of the curriculum, and growing technical control of teachers' work. Narrow conceptions of efficiency dominate, altering teacher and student relations in fundamental ways and often forcing teachers to teach in ways contrary to their deepest values, including what they teach, how they teach, and how they manage their classrooms (Valli & Buese, 2007). A very few studies have called attention to the growing criminalization of student behavior, a trend that dramatically affects teachers' perceptions of classroom management and the treatment of deviance and that grows out of the same social forces that underpin the "new Taylorism" that Au discusses.

Noting an explosion in the size and influence of the criminal justice system following major economic and cultural changes, most notably in the United States, Hirschfield (2008) locates this trend in a "shift toward a crime control paradigm in the definition and management of the problem of student deviance" (p. 80). Traditionally, classroom management and student discipline have been the purview of teachers and school administrators, an assumption held by the teacher education students, previously noted, studying at the University of Connecticut and generally thought of in relationship to wider educational, school, and personal aims. But things are changing, as Hirschfield observes:

> Most legislative responses to school deviance do not codify new crimes or escalate penalties. Rather, legal reforms mandate that certain behaviors—already illegal—such as drug and weapons possession are referred to the policy when they occur on school property. Other policies stipulate that students are treated like actual or suspected criminals, for instance by subjecting them to in-school suspension or scrutiny by armed police, dogs, or metal detectors. (p. 80)

Despite evidence to the contrary (Ricketts, 2007), such policies suggest that all schools are dangerous places and everyone is potentially a victim. Presumably only preventative measures, such policies and practices strengthen and deepen the conceptual and organizational assumptions linking classroom management, rule setting, enforcement, and dispassionate student punishment.

Hirshfield (2008) illustrates how teachers' views of classroom management are changing by identifying "three dimensions of school criminalization": (1) use of "uniform procedural and disciplinary guidelines evolving around the nature of the offense rather than the discretion of teachers" (pp. 81–82), a reflection of legislated zero-tolerance policies; (2) "increased reliance on suspensions and expulsions; and (3) "increased use of criminal justice technology, methodology, and personnel for disciplinary and security purposes" (p. 82), including police, bag searches, video cameras, and metal detectors. Moreover, these changes are wide-ranging and thought good for all schools (particularly secondary schools) regardless of the actual risk of crime, as Kupchik (2009) argues from his extensive study of four very different urban and suburban schools located in two very different regions of the United States.

Kupchik concludes that the "mission of detecting and punishing misbehavior is [now] prioritized over therapeutic, mentoring and even pedagogical goals . . . harsh reactive punishments now take priority over more effective proactive strategies such as counseling or conflict resolution" (p. 305). In these schools, each operating under a "crime control" regime, the school staff, *even when they wish to respond differently* by "treating disciplinary interactions as a teaching opportunity in which students are involved and from which they learn . . . tend to treat these interactions as the occasions where punishment is applied without reflection or discussion" (p. 308). Fairness inevitably trumps justice (see Woodruff, 2011). Kupchik argues that "in all four schools, punishments often appear to have the goal of asserting the school's authority rather than correcting behavioral problems" (p. 308). Punishment is dispensed "by the book" so that teachers "can defend their actions if challenged" (p. 301). In turn, Kupchik notes that the students felt "powerless to shape the rules they face" (p. 311) and, like Thornberg (2008), wonders what the results will be if the values taught are carried over "into the realm of civic governance once these students reach the age of majority" (Kupchik, 2009, p. 312). As Hirschfield (2008) warns: "The management of student deviance, divested of its broader social aims, is prone to redefinition and reappropriation for other ends" (p. 80).

CONCLUSION

As noted, the bulk of the studies reviewed in this chapter continue along lines described by Woolfolk Hoy and Weinstein (2006), primarily centering on teacher perspectives about varying levels of and approaches to behavior control and rule enforcement. The articles reviewed in this chapter portray teachers as generally holding rather narrow conceptions of classroom management, and, as we have suggested, "crime control" may encourage a further narrowing. However, studies by Newberry (2010), Oplatka (2006, 2009), Popp, Grant, & Stronge (2011), Snoeyink (2010), Stoughton (2007), and Watson, Charner-Laird, Kirkpatrick, Szczesiul, and Gordon (2006), as well as the studies of academic optimism, suggest that the sameness of the portrayal of teacher perspectives on classroom management where management and student discipline are taken as interchangeable concepts masks a much more complex reality. As we have argued, there is a need for a broadening of researcher concern as well as of research methods. Looking toward the future, we hope this review will encourage a new generation of studies that portray more richly the complexity of teachers' thinking about classroom management, situating teacher perspectives—development, knowledge, values, beliefs—in biography and history. Most especially, like Thornberg (2008), we seek to encourage researchers to explore the ethical implications of teacher decision making about classroom management so that studies of teacher perspectives might better support the efforts of teacher educators and teachers themselves as they seek to further the educational and moral aims of schooling.

REFERENCES

Abu-Tineh, A. M., Khasawneh, S. A., & Khalaileh, H. A. (2011). Teacher self-efficacy and classroom management styles in Jordanian schools. *Management in Education, 25*(4), 175–181.

Alvarez, H. K. (2007). The impact of teacher preparation on responses to student aggression in the classroom. *Teaching and Teacher Education, 23*, 1113–1126.

Arbuckle, C., & Little, E. (2004). Teachers' perceptions and management of disruptive classroom behaviour during the middle years (years five to nine). *Australian Journal of Educational & Developmental Psychology, 4*, 59–70.

Atjonen, P., Korkeakoski, E., & Mehtalainen, J. (2011). Key pedagogical principles and their major obstacles as perceived by comprehensive school teachers. *Teachers and Teaching: Theory and Practice, 17*, 273–288.

Au, W. (2011). Teaching under the new Taylorism: High stakes testing and the standardization of the 21st century curriculum. *Journal of Curriculum Studies, 43*(1), 25–45.

Batzle, C. S., Weyandt, L. L., Janusis, G. M., & DeVietti, T. L. (2010). Potential impact of ADHD with stimulant medication label on teacher expectations. *Journal of Attention Disorders, 14*(2), 157–166.

Beran, T. (2005). A new perspective on managing school bullying: Pre-service teachers' attitudes. *Journal of Social Sciences, 8*, 43–49.

Bullough, R. V., Jr. (2012). Against best practice: uncertainty, outliers and local studies in educational research. *Journal of Education for Teaching, 38*(3), 343–357.

Bullough, R. V., Jr. (2014). The way of openness: Education, ethics, and Moral Sphere Theory. *Teachers and Teaching: Theory and Practice, 20*(3), 251–263.

Bullough, R. V., Jr. & Hall-Kenyon, K. M. (2011). The call to teach and teacher hopefulness. *Teacher Development, 15*(2), 127–140.

Caldarella, P., Shatzer, R. H., Richardson, M. J., Shen, J. Zhang, N., & Zhang, C. (2009). The impact of gender on Chinese elementary school teachers' perceptions of student behavior problems. *New Horizons in Education, 57*(2), 17–31.

Capa, Y. (2005). Factors affecting first year teachers' sense of efficacy. Doctoral dissertation, Ohio State University.

Chakraborti-Ghosh, S. (2008). Understanding behavior disorders: Their perception, acceptance and treatment—A cross cultural comparison between Indian and the United States. *International Journal of Special Education, 23*(1), 136–146.

Davies, B., Edwards, J., Gannon, S., & Laws, C. (2007). Neo-liberal subjectivities and the limits of social change in university-community partnerships. *Asia-Pacific Journal of Teacher Education, 35*(1), 27–40.

Ding, M., Li, Y., Li, X., & Kulm, G. (2008). Chinese teachers' perceptions of students' classroom misbehaviour. *Educational Psychology, 28*, 305–324.

Fernet, C., Guay, F., Senecal, C., & Austin, S. (2012). Predicting intraindividual changes in teacher burnout: The role of perceived school environment and motivational factors. *Teaching and Teacher Education, 28*, 514–525.

Garegae, K. G. (2008). The crisis of student discipline in Botswana schools: An impact of culturally conflicting disciplinary strategies. *Educational Research and Review, 3*, 48–55.

Gibbs, S., & Gardiner, M. (2008). The structure of primary and secondary teachers' attributions for pupils' misbehaviour: A preliminary cross-phase and cross-cultural investigation. *Journal of Research in Special Educational Needs, 8*(2), 68–77.

Gotzens, C., Badia, M., Genovard, C., & Dezcallar, T. (2010). A comparative study of the seriousness attributed to disruptive classroom behaviors. *Electronic Journal of Research in Educational Psychology, 8*(1), 33–58.

Hirschfield, P. J. (2008). Preparing for prison? The criminalization of school discipline in the USA. *Theoretical Criminology, 12*(1), 79–101.

Hong, J. Y. (2012). Why do some beginning teachers leave the school, and others stay? Understanding teacher resilience through psychological lenses. *Teachers and Teaching: Theory and Practice, 18*(4), 417–440.

Hursh, D. (2007). Assess No Child Left Behind and the rise of neoliberal education policies. *American Educational Research Journal, 44*(3), 493–518.

Jackson, C. (2010). "I've been sort of laddish with them . . . one of the gang": Teachers' perceptions of "laddish" boys and how to deal with them. *Gender and Education, 22*(5), 505–519.

Jones, S. (2005). The invisibility of the underachieving girl. *International Journal of Inclusive Education, 9*(3), 269–286.

Kaufman, D., & Moss, D. M. (2010). A new look at preservice teachers' conceptions of classroom management and organization: Uncovering complexity and dissonance. *The Teacher Educator, 45,* 118–136.

Khoury-Kassabri, M., & Ben-Harush, A. (2012). Discipline methods within the Israeli education system: Arab and Jewish teachers' attitudes. *The International Journal of Children's Rights, 20*(2), 265–278.

Klassen, R. M., Chon, W. H., Huan, V. S., Wong, I., Kates, A., & Hannok, W. (2008). Motivation beliefs of secondary school teachers in Canada and Singapore: A mixed methods study. *Teaching and Teacher Education, 24*(7), 1919–1934.

Koutrouba, K. (2011). Student misbehaviour in secondary education: Greek teachers' views and attitudes. *Educational Review.* doi: 10.1080/00131911.2011.628122

Kulinna, P. H. (2007–2008). Teachers' attributions and strategies for student misbehavior. *Journal of Classroom Interaction, 42*(2), 21–30.

Kupchik, A. (2009). Things are tough all over: Race, ethnicity, class and school discipline. *Punish & Society, 11*(3), 291–317.

Landers, E., Alter, P., & Servilio, K. (2008). Students' challenging behavior and teachers' job satisfaction. *Beyond Behavior, 18*(1), 26–33.

Lane, K. L., Pierson, M. R., Stang, K. K., & Carter, E. W. (2010). Teacher expectations of students' classroom behavior. *Remedial and Special Education, 31*(3), 163–174.

Lane, K. L., Wehby, J. H., & Cooley, C. (2006). Teacher expectations of students' classroom behavior across the grade span: Which social skills are necessary for success? *Exceptional Children, 72,* 153–167.

Lewis, R., & Burman, E. (2008). Providing for student voice in classroom management: Teachers' view. *International Journal of Inclusive Education, 12*(2), 151–167.

Lewis, R., Roache, J., & Romi, S. (2011). Coping styles as mediators of teachers' classroom management techniques. *Research in Education, 85*(1), 53–68.

Lyons, C. W., & O'Connor, F. (2006). Constructing an integrated model of the nature of challenging behaviour: A starting point for intervention. *Educational and Behavioural Difficulties, 11*(3), 217–232.

Martin, N. K., & Sass, D. A. (2010). Construct validation of the Behavior and Instructional Management Scale. *Teaching and Teacher Education, 26*(5), 1124–1135.

Martin, N. K., Yin, Z., & Baldwin, B. (1998). Construct validation of the Attitudes and Beliefs on Classroom Control Inventory. *Journal of Classroom Interaction, 33*(2), 6–15.

Mitchell, S. N., Reilly, R. C., & Logue, M. E. (2009). Benefits of collaborative action research for the beginning teacher. *Teaching and Teacher Education, 25*(2), 344–349.

Newberry, M. (2010). Identified phases in the building and maintaining of positive teacher–student relationships. *Teaching and Teacher Education, 26*(8), 1695–1703.

Ngidi, D. P. (2012). Academic optimism: An individual teacher belief. *Educational Studies, 38*(2), 139–150.

Oplatka, I. (2006). Going beyond role expectations: Toward an understanding of the determinants and components of teacher organizational citizenship behavior. *Educational Administration Quarterly, 42*(3), 385–423.

Oplatka, I. (2009). Organizational citizenship behavior in teaching: The consequences for teachers, pupils, and the school. *International Journal of Educational Management, 23,* 375–389.

Popp, P. A., Grant, L. W., & Stronge, J. H. (2011). Effective teachers for at-risk or highly mobile students: What are the dispositions and behaviors of award-winning teaches? *Journal of Education for Students Placed at Risk, 16*(4), 275–291.

Poulou, M. (2005). Perceptions of students with emotional and behavioural difficulties. *Emotional and Behavioural Difficulties, 10*(2), 137–160.

Reid, K. (2011). Tackling behaviour and attendance issues in school in Wales: Implications for training and professional development. *Educational Studies, 37*(1), 31–48.

Reupert, A., & Woodcock, S. (2010). Success and near misses: Pre-service teachers' use, confidence and success in various classroom management strategies. *Teaching and Teacher Education, 26*(6), 1261–1268.

Ricketts, M. L. (2007). K–12 teachers' perceptions of school policy and fear of school violence. *Journal of School Violence, 6*(3), 45–67.

Rideout, G. W., & Morton, L. L. (2007). Preservice teachers' beliefs and other predictors of pupil control ideologies. *Journal of Educational Administration, 45*(5), 587–604.

Rimm-Kaufman, S. E., Storm, M. D., Sawyer, B. E., Pianta, R. C., & LaParo, K. M. (2006). The Teacher Belief Q-Sort: A measure of teachers' priorities in relation to disciplinary practices, teaching practices, and beliefs about children. *Journal of School Psychology, 44*(2), 141–165.

Shin, S., & Koh, M. S. (2007). A cross-cultural study of teachers' beliefs and strategies on classroom behavior management in urban American and Korean school systems. *Education and Urban Society, 39*(2), 286–309.

Skaalvik, E. M., and Skaalvik, S. (2007). Dimensions of teacher self-efficacy and relations with strain factors, perceived collective teacher efficacy, and teacher burnout. *Journal of Educational Psychology, 99*(3), 611–625.

Snoeyink, R. (2010). Using video self-analysis to improve the "withitness" of student teachers. *Journal of Digital Learning in Teacher Education, 26*(3), 101–110.

Sorlie, M-A., and Torsheim, T. (2011). Multilevel analysis of the relationship between teacher collective efficacy and problem behaviour in school. *School Effectiveness and School Improvement, 22*(2), 175–191.

Stoughton, E. H. (2007). "How will I get them to behave?": Pre service teachers reflect on classroom management. *Teaching and Teacher Education, 23*(7), 1024–1037.

Sutton, R. E., Mudrey-Camino, R., & Knight, C. C. (2009). Teachers' emotion regulation and classroom management. *Theory into Practice, 48*, 130–137.

Thornberg, R. (2008). The lack of professional knowledge in values education. *Teaching & Teacher Education, 24*, 1791–1798.

Tickle, B. R., Chang, M., & Kim, S. (2011). Administrative support and its mediating effect on US public school teachers. *Teaching and Teacher Education, 27*, 342–349.

Tschannen-Moran, M., & Woolfolk Hoy, A. (2001). Teacher efficacy: Capturing an elusive construct. *Teaching and Teacher Education, 17*(7), 783–805.

Unal, Z. & Unal, A. (2012). The impact of years of teaching experience on the classroom management approaches of elementary school teachers. *International Journal of Instruction, 5*(2), 41–59.

Valli, L., & Buese, D. (2007). The changing roles of teachers in an era of high-stakes accountability. *American Educational Research Journal, 44*(3), 519–558.

Watson, D., Charner-Laird, M., Kirkpatrick, C. L., Szczesiul S. A., & Gordon, P. J. (2006). Effective teaching/effective urban teaching: Grappling with definitions, grappling with difference. *Journal of Teacher Education, 57*(4), 395–409.

Willower, D. J., Eidell, T. L., & Hoy, W. K. (1967). *The school and pupil control ideology* (Monograph no. 24). University Park: Penn State Press.

Woodruff, P. (2011) *The Ajax dilemma: Justice, fairness and rewards.* New York: Oxford University Press.

Woolfolk Hoy, A., Hoy, W. K., & Kurz, N. M. (2008). Teacher's academic optimism: The development and test of a new construct. *Teaching and Teacher Education, 24*(4), 821–835.

Woolfolk, Hoy, A., & Weinstein, C. S. (2006). Student and teacher perspectives on classroom management. In C. M. Evertson & C. S. Weinstein (Eds.), *Handbook of classroom management: Research, perspectives and contemporary issues* (pp. 181–220). New York and London: Routledge.

Yilmaz, H., & Cavas, P. H. (2008). The effect of the teaching practice on pre-service elementary teachers' science teaching efficacy and classroom management beliefs. *Eurasia Journal of Mathematics, Science & Technology Education, 4*, 45–54.

16

TEACHER STRESS, EMOTION, AND CLASSROOM MANAGEMENT

CHRISTOPHER J. McCARTHY, SALLY LINEBACK, AND JENSON REISER
UNIVERSITY OF TEXAS AT AUSTIN

> A courage which looks easy and yet is rare; the courage of a teacher repeating day after day the same lessons—the least rewarded of all forms of courage.—Honore de Balzac (1799–1850)

Teaching can be both a rewarding and a demanding job (Johnson, Cooper, Cartwright, Donald, Taylor, & Millet, 2005; Kiziltepe, 2006). When teachers perceive that professional demands exceed their capacities for coping, they can become stressed and vulnerable to job dissatisfaction, emotional exhaustion, and burnout (Klassen & Chiu, 2011). Recent research suggests that the effects of stress are linked to teachers' emotional and professional well-being, with sustained negative feelings and dissatisfaction leading to burnout and an eventual decision to leave the profession (López, Castro, Santiago, & Villardefrancos, 2010; McCarthy, Lambert, Crowe, & McCarthy, 2010). Such consequences can occur early in a teacher's career: Ingersoll (2001) noted that 40–50% of teachers leave the profession in their first five years and that the cost of replacing these teachers is significant (Reese, 2004).

In the first edition of *The Handbook of Classroom Management*, Friedman (2006) provided a thorough review of the construct of teacher burnout, a phenomenon theorized to result from chronic stress endemic among human service workers, including teachers. Freudenberger (1974) first identified burnout as a construct consisting of reduced idealism and enthusiasm, and more recently, Maslach, Schaufeli, and Leiter (2001) refined the meaning and measurement of burnout and identified three essential components: (1) emotional exhaustion, the central construct of burnout, referring to feeling overwhelmed by emotional contact with others at work; (2) depersonalization, which describes the development of a cynical attitude and emotional distancing; and (3) reduced personal accomplishment, which involves reduced feelings of competence and personal achievement. Schaufeli and Enzmann (1998) noted that teachers are one of the most frequently studied occupational groups in burnout research and comprise 22% of all samples used. In addition to a range of psychological and emotional consequences, teacher burnout has also been associated with physiological symptoms such as high blood pressure (Moya-Albiol, Serrano, & Salvador, 2010) and systemic inflammation known to contribute to atherosclerosis (von Känel, Bellingrath, & Kudielka, 2008).

Teacher burnout symptoms have been related to numerous aspects of their work, including the school environment (Gavish & Friedman, 2010; Kaufhold, Alvarez, & Arnold, 2006) and aspects of teachers' professional identity such as the lack of existential fulfillment owing to unmet expectations and needs (Friedman, 2006; Loonstra, Brouwers, & Tomic, 2009; Pines, 2002). However, one of the most frequently cited factors contributing to teacher stress is student misbehavior (Eskridge & Coker, 1985; Lopez et al., 2008; Sutton, Mudrey-Camino, & Knight, 2009). As an example, Tsouloupas, Carson, Matthews, Grawitch, and Barber (2010) found that the act of disciplining students is associated with emotional exhaustion. Ingersoll and Smith (2003) noted that student discipline problems are the second leading cause of beginning teachers leaving the profession due to dissatisfaction. Classroom management is therefore essential to teacher welfare and student achievement.

Even as student misbehavior is clearly a challenge for teachers, recent research on teacher stress suggests that classroom demands such as student misbehavior are but one component in a complex process that can lead to teachers' feeling stressed (Lopez et al., 2008). Increasingly, researchers are finding that teacher appraisals of the classroom environment are an important determinant of whether they will experience stress and burnout (Chang, 2009; Steinhardt, Jaggars, Faulk, & Gloria, 2011). Appraisals refer to cognitive evaluations that teachers make about situations that have the potential to cause them stress and that have been found in the stress literature to be teacher-specific (McCarthy, Lambert, O'Donnell, & Melendres, 2009). In other words, stress is at least partly perceptual, and teachers can vary widely in how they interpret and react to similar types of classroom demands.

Even though burnout has received most of the attention in the teacher stress literature, research shows that burnout is not the only important consequence of teacher stress. Even the early symptoms of burnout have negative consequences for teachers, and full-fledged burnout does not need to be present for teachers to suffer (McCarthy, Lambert, O'Donnell, & Melendres, 2009). Further, teachers with high demand levels can experience a range of negative emotions (Chang & Davis, 2009) and conflicts between work and personal life (Cinamon, Rich, & Westman, 2007), whether or not they fit the classic definition of burnout. It is therefore essential that stress and the full range of its consequences in the area of classroom management be understood and applied to the work of teachers.

The purpose of this chapter is threefold. First, we will present an integrative theoretical framework drawn from recent research on teacher stress that can be useful in understanding the interrelationship of teacher stress, emotion, and classroom management. Given this foundation, we will then review recent research on what types of classroom management issues are implicated in teacher stress. We will then conclude with a review of promising trends in the area of classroom management that have the potential of lowering teachers' stress levels and improving their effectiveness in the classroom.

THEORETICAL PERSPECTIVES ON TEACHER STRESS, COPING, AND EMOTION

Lazarus and Folkman's (1984) transactional model is the theoretical foundation for this chapter. It is unquestionably the dominant model in the stress and coping literature (Hobfoll, Schwarzer, & Chon, 1998), has important implications for understanding teachers' welfare, and is receiving renewed attention in the educational research literature (McCarthy, Lambert, & Ullrich, 2012). The transactions described in the model refer to how people interpret their environment vis-à-vis their capacities for coping. Specifically, when a potentially demanding life event is encountered, one must first decide whether it is relevant and congruent with existing goals and commitments. This is labeled a primary appraisal and is thought to occur more or less automatically. If the primary appraisal results in an evaluation that an event is significant and potentially negative, the individual must decide whether she or he has the resources for coping with it, which is labeled a secondary appraisal.

If resources are appraised to be roughly commensurate with demands, the individual will likely not experience stress or negative emotion and in fact may be energized by the prospect of taking on a challenge. However, if resources are appraised as insufficient for the nature of the demand, negative emotions and stress are likely to ensue. The section titled "Toward a More Unified Understanding of Teacher Stress" gives a more detailed description of the transactional model of stress.

It is interesting to note that transactional models are similar to Kyriacou and Sutcliffe's (1977) early definition of teacher stress as "a response by a teacher of negative affect . . . as a result of the demands made upon the teacher in his role as a teacher" and consists of a number of factors, including "the degree to which the teacher perceives that he is unable to meet the demands made upon him" (p. 299). The authors also note that the stress response includes an emotional component. As Lazarus (2000) stated about the transactional model of stress, "a fundamental theme of my approach is that stress and emotion can no longer be divided into two separate research and theoretical literatures" (p. 195). Linking the definition of teacher stress to the constructs used in the stress literature is also essential inasmuch as imprecision in the use of terms has plagued the stress literature for decades (Matheny, Aycock, Pugh, Curlette, & Cannella, 1986). The following section overviews the link between stress and emotion, followed by a description of the role of appraisals and coping resources in transactional models of teacher stress.

Stress and Emotion

Emotions are considered to be processes involving multiple components derived from experiential, behavioral, and physiological systems. Emotional exhaustion, the hallmark characteristic of teacher burnout, is theorized to be a precursor to the other symptoms of burnout (reduced personal accomplishment and depersonalization; Maslach, Schaufeli, & Leiter, 2001) and may result from chronically elicited emotions such as anxiety and anger. Chang (2009) suggests that classroom management issues play an important role in eliciting these particular stress-producing emotions.

Chang (2009) also identified the central role that teacher perceptions, or appraisals, play in generating these emotions. Schutz, Hong, Cross, and Osbon (2006) further specify that teacher emotions tend to emerge with appraisals related to the pursuit of a goal in a particular activity or setting and generally tend to occur without awareness. For example, a teacher identifies that her second-graders need a review lesson on adding two-digit numbers, but a particular student's frequent outbursts during the lesson continuously disrupt the lesson and distract other students, resulting in the teacher experiencing frustration and anger. According to Schutz's research, this teacher's emotions (frustration and anger) emerged from her appraisal (with or without being aware of it) that this particular student stands in the way of her goal (her students' mastery of adding two-digit numbers). Both Chang's research and Schutz's research suggest that these stress-producing emotions (frustration and anger) are a result of this teacher's perception of her classroom situation and that perhaps a change in this appraisal may hold the key to experiencing a different emotional response.

Teacher Appraisals

As was noted previously, Kyriacou and Sutcliffe's (1977) inclusion of perceptions of demands teachers face in their early definition of stress is consistent with current transactional models of stress because both definitions emphasize that much of what is stressful in daily life has to do with either perceptions or appraisals of life demands rather than with the demands themselves. Lambert, McCarthy, O'Donnell, and Wang (2009) identified a gap in the literature that exists mainly due to the difficulty associated with measuring appraisals: How can teachers' perceptions of the sufficiency of resources for coping vis-à-vis perceived demands be assessed accurately and meaningfully? To address this gap, Lambert and colleagues reported on the development of a measure to assess teachers' perceptions of classroom demands and resources, the Classroom Appraisal of Resources and Demands (CARD). This measure assesses teachers' appraisals of both the demands and resources in their classrooms and may be used to classify teachers into three groups: those viewing classroom demands as (1) exceeding, (2) equal to, or (3) less than their resources. Because teachers' appraisals of resources are theorized to be as important as demands in determining a stress response, we next review resources most relevant for teachers.

Teacher Resources

The various resources that teachers have for coping with job demands are hypothesized to be an important element of the stress process, both in the general population (Hobfoll, Schwarzer, & Chon, 1998) and in the teaching profession (Friedman,

2006). In the stress and coping literature, coping resources refer to various assets in one's personal repertoire for dealing with life demands (Matheny, Curlette, Aycock, & Junker, 1993) and can range from personal skills and personality characteristics to financial resources and strategies for living, such as time management and having a positive attitude (Matheny, Aycock, Pugh, Curlette, & Silva Cannella, 1986).

Personal coping resources and specific classroom resources, such as instructional materials and teacher aides, can help teachers in coping with stress (Kaufhold, Alvarez, & Arnold, 2006). Recent research strongly emphasizes teacher efficacy as an essential resource for coping with classroom demands (Betoret, 2009; Pas, Bradshaw, & Hershfeldt, 2012; Schwarzer & Hallum, 2008; Schwerdtfeger, Konermann, & Schönhofen, 2008). Bandura (1982) was a pioneer in the study of self-efficacy and described it as expectations of competence and control in carrying out life tasks. In the context of teaching, self-efficacy refers to teachers' expectations that they can master demands of the classroom, and the lack of self-efficacy makes teachers likely to suffer stress as a result (Schwerdtfeger, Konermann, & Schönhofen, 2008).

Although earlier research refers to teacher self-efficacy as a single construct that encompasses a wide range of teaching skills (Gibson & Dembo, 1984), later research has defined teacher self-efficacy as including three different dimensions: instructional efficacy, engagement efficacy, and classroom management efficacy (Emmer & Hickman, 1991; Tschannen-Moran & Woolfolk Hoy, 2001). For the purposes of this chapter, we will refer to teacher self-efficacy in the particular way researchers refer to the construct in specific studies, with some defining it just as teacher efficacy and others further breaking the construct down to classroom management self-efficacy and other components specifically. Inasmuch as classroom management is the focus of this chapter, it is important to define self-efficacy as it relates specifically to classroom management. Emmer and Hickman (1991) developed a scale of classroom management self-efficacy that includes the perceived ability to establish "classroom order and cooperation" and to effectively respond to student misbehavior (p. 764).

Toward a More Unified Understanding of Teacher Stress

Our review of teacher stress so far has suggested that the stress process includes a number of different hypothesized constructs and processes relevant to teachers and classroom management stress. Figure 16.1 depicts the hypothesized relationship among these constructs, which is drawn from transactional theories of stress.

At the top of the figure, the teacher's classroom circumstances are represented, contextualizing a teacher's experience (e.g., the teachers' school, particular group of students, classroom realities, etc.). Events emerging from this context as potentially significant for the teacher, such as student misbehavior or other student management issues, are hypothesized to trigger a reflexive, cognitive balancing act in which the teacher weighs the nature of the event (i.e., How serious is it? What implications does it have for my students and me?), along with the teachers' perceived capabilities for handling it (i.e., Is this something I can handle?) (McCarthy, Lambert, O'Donnell, & Melendres, 2009). Appraisals of events are labeled "primary appraisals" because they are hypothesized to

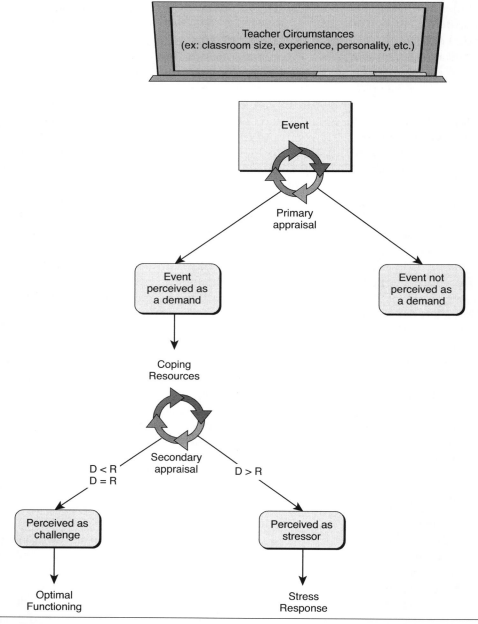

Figure 16.1 Hypothesized model of appraisals and stress.

occur automatically and immediately, and if an event is evaluated as both significant and potentially negative, it is conceptualized as a "demand" (Lazarus, 2000; see Figure 16.1). Demands therefore refer to classroom situations and requirements either self-imposed by the teacher or imposed by others, such as students, administrators, and parents, that have been appraised as both significant and potentially troublesome for the teacher.

As shown in Figure 16.1, secondary appraisals of demands follow and involve an evaluation of the sufficiency of one's resources for coping vis-à-vis the demand. Secondary appraisals are hypothesized to converge with primary appraisals, resulting in an overall evaluation of whether the demand constitutes a stressor or simply a challenge that can be met (Lazarus, 2000).

Noted previously, Lambert and colleagues (2009) developed the CARD to assess teachers' perceptions of classroom demands and resources in attempt to validate this theory. Research using the CARD supports transactional models and has shown that teachers who perceive themselves as having higher classroom demands compared to resources are different from other teachers: they report more burnout symptoms (McCarthy, Lambert, O'Donnell, & Melendres, 2009), more students with behavior problems (Lambert, Kusherman, O'Donnell, & McCarthy 2006), and more students with learning disabilities (Lambert, McCarthy, O'Donnell, & Melendres, 2007). Further, McCarthy and colleagues (2010) found that teachers reporting an intention to leave their current job for professional reasons, as opposed to personal ones, also report higher demands in the classroom, fewer resources provided by schools, and higher levels of occupational stress.

As an example of this process, if a student is off-task after the teacher asks her to follow directions, the teacher might evaluate the situation by thinking, "I need her to follow directions because her behavior is incongruent with my goals for the class [primary appraisal], so I need to think about what resources I have to address this off-task behavior [secondary appraisal]. Since I have learned a variety of techniques, I am going to choose one of them to deal with this behavior." Appraisals such as these would likely result in the evaluation that they have the resources to handle the situation ($R = D$ or $R > D$), and the teacher would view the event as a challenge, not as a stressor. On the other hand, when faced with the same off-task student, the teacher could appraise the behavior in this way: "I need her to follow directions because her behavior is incongruent with my class goals [primary appraisal]. I am pretty sure, however, that I have previously tried everything with this student, and nothing has worked [secondary appraisal], so I am not going to address this student's behavior." These appraisals would likely result in the evaluation that the teacher does not have the resources to handle the situation ($R < D$), and the teacher would view this event as a stressor.

As this example illustrates, an understanding of teachers' perceptions of the event, along with their perceptions of available resources, is important in explaining their differential reactions to a student's misbehavior. It is therefore essential to better understand what types of classroom management situations and teacher appraisals result in stress. It is to this topic we now turn.

CLASSROOM MANAGEMENT AS A SOURCE OF TEACHER STRESS

Research consistently identifies classroom management issues, particularly student misbehavior, as both a source and a consequence of teacher stress and burnout (Chang, 2009; Eskridge & Coker, 1985; Lewis, Roache, & Romi, 2011; Sutton, Mudrey-Camino, & Knight, 2009). In other words, student misbehavior can both add to teacher stress levels and also reflect the fact that a teacher's stress level is interfering with managing the class effectively. Although past research has linked student misbehavior to teacher stress (Friedman, 2006; Kuzsman & Schnall, 1987; Lambert, Kusherman, O'Donnell, & McCarthy, 2006), more recent research examines which teachers are most vulnerable to stress. As Chang stated, "If the classroom disruptive behavior is identified as the prominent source of teacher burnout, how does one teacher manage to survive while another is depleted by it?" (Chang, 2009, p. 202).

As is shown in Figure 16.1, current thinking on teacher stress points to the critical role of teacher appraisals in determining whether classroom situations are manageable or stress inducing. This section of the chapter will therefore aim to expand on the research supporting Figure 16.1 by identifying (1) student misbehaviors that have the potential to cause stress, (2) recent research examining teachers' appraisals of those behaviors, and (3) the resources shown to be most effective in protecting teachers from stress. The consequences of teacher stress will then be reviewed, both for teachers' emotional well-being and for their classroom management.

Student Misbehavior as a Cause of Teacher Stress

While the role of teacher appraisals is increasingly understood as important in the stress process, research makes it clear that some types of classroom events are routinely associated with teacher stress. Clunies-Ross, Little, and Kienhuis (2008) tested 12 behaviors and identified three that contributed most to teacher stress: students talking out of turn, students hindering other students, and students being idle or slow. Students talking out of turn means that they are talking at an inappropriate time; for example, not raising their hand when a teacher has asked the class to do so before answering or interrupting a lesson by talking. Hindering other students involves distracting other students from the lesson, and idleness/slowness involves students doing work deliberately slowly on an assignment. The authors found it noteworthy that the three behaviors causing most concern for teachers were relatively minor misbehaviors, rather than major ones, such as physical aggression (Clunies-Ross, Little, and Kienhuis, 2008), suggesting that small misbehaviors occurring frequently may be primary contributors to teacher stress. Friedman (1994; 1995) found that disrespectful behaviors were most often cited as stressful for teachers. Lopez and colleagues (2008) found support for Friedman's claim that student disruptive attitude/behavior (included in the category of disrespectful behaviors) was the largest factor predicting negative emotions and a stress response in teachers.

Classroom Management Techniques That Increase Teacher Stress

It is important to be aware that demands are created not only by students: ineffective classroom management practice can also represent a classroom demand, where teachers inadvertently add to their own vulnerability to stress. Although there is a lack of research on which specific classroom management strategies increase or decrease teacher stress, it has become clear that feeling like an ineffective classroom manager, no matter what strategy a teacher uses, increases teacher stress. For example, Evers, Tomic, and Brouwers (2004) found that teachers' perceived incompetence in managing student misbehavior lead to higher levels of stress.

Additional research has shown that negative emotions can cause teachers to use negative classroom management techniques, which, in turn, can increase student misbehavior (Sutton, Mudrey-Camino, & Knight, 2009). Teachers who experience negative emotions are more likely to engage in aggressive behaviors such as yelling. Yelling at students disrupts important relationships with students that are necessary to maintaining classroom control, and when these relationships are disrupted, students tend to misbehave even more (Sutton, Mudrey-Camino, & Knight, 2009).

Lewis and associates (2011) found a positive correlation between aggressive techniques such as group punishment, yelling in anger, and humiliation, and negative attitudes and student misbehavior. Without effective strategies to cope with or ward off a stress response and the negative emotions associated with it, teacher stress can lead to teacher behaviors that inadvertently create additional demands that must be managed. For teachers who find the demands of student misbehaviors stressful, this situation can spiral out of control. Lewis and colleagues (2011) sum this up in their study as follows: "It appears that teachers who employ poor management techniques, such as aggression and punishment, contribute to their own problems by reacting with strategies that only serve to exacerbate the very problems they are intended to overcome or prevent" (p. 66).

Teacher Appraisals That Lead to Stress

Even though student misbehavior and/or ineffective classroom management are widely linked to teacher stress, the picture is incomplete without understanding the role of teacher appraisals (Chang, 2009; Hastings & Bham, 2003). Evidence for the perceptual nature of stress was reported by Kokkinos, Panayiotou, and Davazoglou (2005), who linked different teachers' appraisals of identical student misbehaviors to personality variables and levels of burnout. These authors studied how two personality traits (conscientiousness and neuroticism) and teachers' stress level correlated with teachers' appraisals of identical student behaviors. High conscientiousness is characterized by a diligent work ethic, orderliness, and thoroughness, while high neuroticism is marked by the tendency to feel negative emotions, such as anxiety and anger. Kokkinos and colleagues (2005) found that teachers who reported high levels of conscientiousness tended to rate (i.e., appraise) student misbehavior as more severe, as did teachers with high burnout levels, while neuroticism did not have the same effect. While the results of the study were correlational rather than causal, they suggest that teacher perceptions of student behavior are subjective, further emphasizing the importance of teachers' appraisals in the stress process (Kokkinos, Panayiotou, and Davazoglou, 2005).

Efficacy as a Component of the Stress Process

According to transactional models of stress, teachers are vulnerable to stress when they appraise their coping resources as insufficient for classroom demands (see Figure 16.1). It is therefore important to identify which teacher resources are most important in this determination. Research has shown that levels teacher self-efficacy, which refers to teachers' expectations that they can master the demands of the classroom (Schwerdtfeger et al., 2008) and classroom management self-efficacy, which refers to teachers' perceptions of their classroom management abilities (Brouwers & Tomic, 2000; Betoret, 2009; Friedman & Farber, 1992) are important resources that can help buffer a teacher against a stress response.

Research has shown that teachers with lower levels of general self-efficacy are more vulnerable to stress. Schwerdtfeger and associates (2008) found that teachers with low self-efficacy had greater health complaints, along with higher levels of burnout. In addition, Hong (2012) found that low self-efficacy teachers tend to experience higher levels of stress when faced with managing a classroom and handling disruptive behaviors. Lastly, Schwarzer and Hallum (2008), in a longitudinal study completed over the course of one school year, found that low general self-efficacy (measuring general coping resources not specific to teaching) and teacher self-efficacy preceded burnout symptoms.

The majority of recent research on self-efficacy, however, has focused on the construct of classroom management self-efficacy rather than global self-efficacy. In a review of research on teacher burnout, Betoret (2009) found that a positive perception of both classroom management self-efficacy and instructional self-efficacy provided a buffer against classroom stressors; having high self-efficacy "mitigated the impact that the potential stressors have on the teaching work" (p. 61), causing teachers to operate at an optimal level of functioning, whereas low self-efficacy predicted higher teacher burnout (Betoret, 2009). Researchers have elaborated on why low classroom management self-efficacy teachers might face greater levels of stress: Teachers with low classroom management self-efficacy are more likely to give up easily when faced with continuous disruptive behavior, believing that their actions have little influence (Brouwers & Tomic, 2000; Emmer & Hickman, 1991). This in turn can cause more disruptive behavior that teachers find stressful (Lewis, Roache, & Romi, 2011; Sutton, Mudrey-Camino, & Knight, 2009). As self-efficacy declines, feelings of ineffectiveness and stress increase (Brouwers & Tomic, 2000). McCormick and Barnett (2011) stated "To experience high levels of stress consistently from an inability to manage student behaviour successfully, is tantamount to failure" (p. 290). Cast in the light of transactional models of stress, such findings suggest that when teachers are faced with the demands of classroom management and have fewer resources on which to draw, they are more vulnerable to stress.

Teacher Stress and Negative Emotions

In a meta-analysis of research on teacher stress, Montgomery and Rupp (2005) found that negative emotional responses had a large impact on how teachers respond to demands, and the authors suggested future research on the relationships between negative emotions and teacher stress. Chang (2009) has described various negative emotions that emerge from appraisals of classroom events, focusing particularly on anger, frustration, anxiety, and guilt. Because these emotions are most closely linked to the stress response, this section will focus on anxiety and anger as they relate to classroom management.

According to Chang (2009), teacher anxiety may result from a number of teacher appraisals, including a perceived lack of preparedness, or ability to handle discipline issues in the classroom. Thus, teachers who are stressed because they feel ill prepared for the discipline demands of their classroom are likely to feel anxious. Anger, on the other hand, is triggered when students fail to meet teacher expectations for classroom behavior or academic performance (Chang, 2009). Student misbehavior is consistent with this category: Teachers have expectations for their students' behavior, and when these expectations are not met, their stress is manifested in anger, directed sometimes at the class as a whole or at students who are misbehaving specifically. Thus, classroom management issues can play an important role in creating stress-produced emotions. Chang makes it clear, however, that not all teachers experience negative emotions from the same student behaviors. Teachers' appraisals of both their preparedness and their students' misbehaviors play important roles in their stress responses and associated negative emotions.

Negative Effects of Teacher Stress on Classroom Management

So far, this chapter has reviewed the process whereby teachers become stressed. In this section we identify the consequences of stress for classroom management. As reviewed previously, the connection between teacher stress and classroom management is complicated by a number of variables such as the teachers' appraisals of the unique demands of their classroom and students, the sufficiency of their resources, and even their personality (Kokkinos, Panayiotou, & Davazoglou, 2005). Another reality teachers face is that when they become stressed, they cannot simply remove themselves from the classroom environment. They must still manage and teach a classroom of students, which can result in negative consequences for teachers and their students.

Poor Classroom Management

Although the literature has shown that teachers' perceptions of student misbehaviors can help explain the stress response in teachers, it has also been shown that teachers who are stressed have poorer classroom management performance in general. Brouwers and Tomic (2000) noted that low self-efficacy teachers who are stressed could actually contribute to additional student misbehaviors when compared to teachers who have higher levels of self-efficacy and lower levels of stress. These teachers tend to deal less readily with student misbehaviors, and, as a result, students tend to misbehave more (Brouwers & Tomic, 2000). The additional misbehaviors then contribute to additional stress, causing a cyclical feedback loop (Brouwers & Tomic, 2000; Lewis, Roache, & Romi, 2011). The more misbehaviors teachers face, the lower their self-efficacy in classroom management. The lower their self-efficacy in classroom management, the more disruptive student behaviors they will see, which will contribute to additional demands and an increased stress response.

Mistreatment of Students

Teacher stress is associated with teachers' negative perceptions of students in general. Teachers who are stressed because of student misbehavior are likely to experience anger, and teachers who are angry tend to react emotionally with students, engaging in behaviors such as yelling at students (Sutton, Mudrey-Camino, & Knight, 2009). Anger can also cause teachers who experience a high level of stress to blame students for their misbehavior and to be less likely to attribute student misbehavior to anything within a teacher's control (Brouwers & Tomic, 2000; Chang, 2009). Teachers then see students' misbehavior as an indication of intrapersonal characteristics, as something within the students, which can lead to labeling and marginalizing students. When teachers see students' misbehavior as an indication of intrapersonal characteristics, teachers can find it even harder to see that they can maintain order in their classrooms.

This chapter has so far examined current research and models of stress with an eye toward understanding how teachers' appraisals of classroom behaviors affect teacher stress. The information reviewed in this chapter suggests the importance of understanding teacher stress in the context of classroom management practices. Simply put, research consistently identifies classroom management as the most important factor in teacher stress. Even though this link has been established, the connection between classroom behavior and teacher stress is not linear: It is influenced by a range of factors, perhaps most importantly teachers' appraisals of classroom demands and resources (McCarthy, Lambert, O'Donnell, & Melendres, 2009).

The ultimate purpose of this line of inquiry is to find ways to reduce and prevent classroom situations that lead to teacher stress. Clearly, effective classroom practices, examined in much of the rest of this book, are central to reducing teacher stress. Therefore, our focus here will be to briefly review general factors and teaching strategies that may contribute to reducing and/or preventing teacher stress.

REDUCING AND PREVENTING CLASSROOM MANAGEMENT STRESS

Friedman (2006) asked an important question in concluding his chapter in the first edition of *The Handbook of Classroom Management*: "What can be done based on the data and information gathered and published so far?" (p. 940). This is an excellent question we will now revisit. In order to reduce and prevent stress, teachers will need to rely on coping resources, which refer to various assets in one's personal repertoire for dealing with life demands (Matheny, Curlette, Aycock, & Junker, 1993). In other words, coping resources include all of the capacities, assets, and material resources a person has to deal with life stress.

The stress literature generally recognizes two categories of coping: combative coping, which refers to coping with a stressor that has already occurred, and preventive coping, which refers to efforts at minimizing or avoiding potential stressors before they occur (for a more extensive review, see Matheny, Aycock, Pugh, Curlette, & Silva Cannella, 1986). While Figure 16.1 described the appraisal process that results in a determination that life demands are in fact stressors, Figure 16.2 depicts the combative coping process that is hypothesized to occur once a stressor has been engaged. Figure 16.2 demonstrates that, according to transactional models, after the stress response occurs, the individual taps her reservoir of combative coping resources in an attempt to find coping strategies that can lessen the intensity of the stress response and/or have the potential for altering the situation causing stress (Matheny, Aycock, Pugh, Curlette, & Silva Cannella, 1986; Pearlin & Schooler, 1978).

Coping strategies have been further distinguished in the literature as problem focused and emotion focused (Folkman & Lazarus, 1988a, 1988b). As is depicted in Figure 16.2, problem-focused coping is directed at the stressor itself, whereas emotion-focused coping is directed at the feelings generated by the stress response. As an example, teachers who are feeling stressed because of a student's behavior could attempt to use either problem-focused coping by altering their classroom management practices to attempt to stop the behavior or emotion-focused coping, such as taking a deep breath to attempt to calm their feelings of anxiety and frustration. Both problem-focused and emotion-focused coping strategies can be used together: Teachers might first need to calm themselves down (emotion-focused coping) before being able to employ classroom management techniques (problem-focused coping).

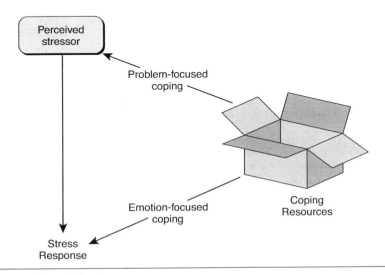

Figure 16.2 Hypothesized model of coping processes.

We next describe literature suggesting how teachers' emotion- and problem-focused coping strategies can be enhanced.

Emotion-Focused Coping

Teachers, like any other professionals, do not always experience the same emotions under the same external conditions (Lazarus, 2000). An important theory of emotion is the process model, described by Gross (2002), which states that how individuals express their emotions involves both unconscious and conscious effort. Although a complete discussion of this model is outside the scope of this chapter, in this process model of emotion, emotion-regulation strategies are described as the behavioral and cognitive ways that individuals manage their emotions. Individuals can manage several facets of their emotional responses, including expression, timing, intensity, and maintenance (Gross, 1998; 2008).

Research by Sutton and associates (2009) examined emotion regulation and classroom management and found that emotion regulation is critical to teacher effectiveness. Their research indicated that teachers who believed in displaying their positive emotions to students also showed high levels of efficacy in classroom management. As the authors describe, *up-regulating* an emotion involves an attempt to increase the intensity or duration of an emotion. For example, a teacher may intentionally recall a student's recent reading growth to enhance a feeling of joy before retrieving her students from the lunchroom. *Down-regulating* an emotion is just the opposite, involving a person intentionally reducing the intensity or duration of a negative emotional experience (Sutton, Mudrey-Camino, & Knight, 2009). Many teachers frequently down-regulate emotions (e.g., frustration with student misbehavior) in order to successfully execute a lesson plan. Down-regulating negative emotions helps teachers avoid negative and reactive behaviors, preventing students from further disruptive behaviors.

Reappraisal, an additional emotion-regulation strategy, occurs when an individual reconsiders and changes the meaning attached to a situation, thereby altering the associated emotional reaction (Gross, 2002). Research suggests that the interpretation of the meaning attached to a situation predicts both the emotion and intensity of the emotion experienced (Siemer, Mauss, & Gross, 2007), which speaks to the link between appraisal and emotion experienced in a classroom.

Despite individual differences, research suggests that there are certain socially and historically based norms for expressing emotions appropriately in the classroom. In general, during most interactions with students, teachers are expected to show positive emotions and suppress negative emotions (Aultman, Schutz, & Williams-Johnson, 2009). In a study by Sutton (2004), teachers used a variety of emotion-regulation strategies in an effort to conform to their idealized image of a teacher, believing that this would also improve their teaching effectiveness.

A recent study by Roeser, Skinner, Beers, and Jennings (2012) suggested that the emotionally demanding and unpredictable nature of the teaching profession makes the concept of mindfulness especially effective for teachers. The field of psychology has paid increasing attention to mindfulness as an emotion-focused coping strategy. Mindfulness, as defined by Kabat-Zinn (1994), involves drawing attention and awareness to the present moment in a nonreactive and nonjudgmental manner that promotes emotion regulation, stress reduction, and healthy interpersonal interactions. Mindfulness training programs for teachers include instruction on how to regulate emotions and stress more effectively. A study that taught Mindfulness Based Stress Reduction (MBSR) strategies to a small group of emotionally distressed elementary school teachers yielded promising results (Gold et al., 2010). All teachers improved on scales of anxiety, depression, and stress, and for some participants the improvements were statistically significant.

Finally, research by Frederickson and Losada (2005) suggests a difference between "flourishing" and simply "coping" with emotional episodes. These researchers suggest that a mathematical ratio of positive to negative emotions can be used to indicate the point at which a person can be considered "flourishing." When applied to the classroom, this model may also provide important insight into the question of how emotional episodes may be linked to teacher attrition. While future research is needed, these exploratory studies suggest that mindfulness may be a cost-effective and beneficial strategy for increasing the mental health and well-being of teachers.

Problem-Focused Coping

As shown in Figure 16.2, problem-focused coping is directed at managing, altering, and otherwise addressing the event is triggering the stress response. In the context of classroom management, problem-focused coping can be understood as the teacher directly addressing problematic student behaviors. McCormick and Barnett (2011) noted that "[g]reater emphasis should be placed on effective management of student behavior when assisting teachers at risk of burnout" (p. 278). Clunies-Ross and colleagues (2008) defined classroom management strategies in terms of two categories: proactive and reactive. Proactive strategies are defined as strategies designed to prevent misbehavior from arising in the first place and generally give positive responses for appropriate behavior seen in students. Reactive strategies, on the other hand, are employed only after the teacher notices student misbehavior and usually require the teacher to respond in a negative, rather than a positive, way. The authors found that reactive strategies were associated with decreased on-task behavior from students and increased teacher stress, though proactive strategies failed to demonstrate a significant relationship with increased on-task behaviors and decreased stress (Clunies-Ross, Little, and Kienhuis, 2008). The authors caution readers against making causal conclusions (i.e., that reactive strategies cause teacher stress) because of the correlational nature of the research.

Lewis and associates (2011) found support for the notion that teachers are better off using problem-focused, rather than emotion-focused, coping in dealing with classroom management situations. They examined social problem solving, relaxation, and avoidant coping as strategies for coping with student misbehavior. Social problem solving involved behaviors such as asking a mentor for help and finding a way to deal with the problem (problem-focused coping), whereas avoidant coping was defined as avoiding or worrying about the problem, and relaxation was defined as engaging in physical exercise and using humor (both emotion-focused strategies). Social problem solving was found to be the most effective strategy for dealing with student misbehavior (Lewis et al., 2009).

Increasing student engagement is another problem-focused strategy addressed in the literature. Increasing student engagement can mean positive outcomes for teachers: When students are bored and listless, engagement decreases while misbehavior increases. Covell, McNeil, and Howe (2009) conducted a study in Britain that evaluated a whole-school rights-based reform initiative called Rights, Respect, and Responsibility (RRR) over a three-year period. The results suggested the potential impact of children's rights education in increasing student engagement and reducing teacher burnout. Schools that fully implemented the reform initiative curriculum experienced an increase in student engagement and a significant decrease in teacher burnout.

Prevention: The Best Medicine

The old adage that an ounce of prevention is worth a pound of cure surely applies to the stress caused by classroom management. It is far better to help teachers prevent the classroom situations that lead to stress than to help them manage and cope with the difficulties presented by classroom misbehavior. Prevention of stress involves three key components: the events that have the potential to cause stress, the appraisals made about those events, and the resources one has to prevent demands from becoming stressors. We have already reviewed the types of demands associated with teacher stress, which include student misbehavior and ineffective classroom practices. Because these issues are already discussed in detail elsewhere in this volume, we focus here on the role of appraisal and teacher resources in preventing stress associated with classroom management.

Teacher Appraisals

A number of researchers have studied how teacher appraisals of demands play a role in teacher stress response. Evers and colleagues (2004) suggested that teachers' thinking systems be taken into account when developing and planning interventions. Lewis et al. (2010) found that teachers who appraised student misbehavior as more concerning used more punitive classroom management techniques than teachers who appraised student misbehavior as less concerning; the more punitive classroom management techniques measures were shown to be less effective and also correlated with higher stress.

Schwarzer and Hallum (2008) also suggest that teachers who have high self-efficacy tend to bounce back from setbacks more quickly than those with low self-efficacy, implying that teachers with low self-efficacy might appraise student misbehavior as a greater threat than teachers with high self-efficacy. In other words, self-efficacy can have an impact on a teacher's appraisal of student misbehavior. Lewis and colleagues (2011) concluded, "What can be said with certainty . . . is that there is a small, though statistically significant relationship between a teachers' [sic] level of concern about a student misbehavior and their classroom management techniques" (p. 65). As noted earlier in this chapter, using the CARD, Lambert and colleagues (2009) sought to better understand teacher appraisals and which are most vulnerable to stress. Measures such as the CARD could be helpful in preventing teacher stress by identifying teachers who perceive themselves as having the highest levels of classroom demands.

Increasing Teachers' Preventive Coping Resources

As discussed previously, both teacher self-efficacy and classroom management self-efficacy can be thought of as important coping resources and, as such, must be taken into account when attempting to prevent teacher stress. Recent research suggests that self-efficacy may be important to teachers not only in "withstanding" stress but in helping them avoid stress altogether; in other words, it could be an important coping resource in preventing burnout and even health issues related to burnout (Schwerdtfeger, Konermann, & Schönhofen, 2008). A preventive, wellness focus for teachers is consistent with research by Frederickson and Losada (2005) suggesting a difference between "human flourishing" and simply coping with emotional episodes. In other words, their focus is on increasing the ratio of positive to negative emotions in a teacher's life, rather than focusing only on decreasing negative emotions. These researchers even suggest that a specific ratio of positive to negative emotions could represent the point at which a person can be considered "flourishing." This research fits with Sutton and colleagues' (2009) research, described earlier, that up-regulating positive emotions and down-regulating negative emotions are both important processes.

As reviewed in the previous section, lower levels of both teacher self-efficacy and classroom management self-efficacy are correlated with higher levels of teacher burnout (Brouwers & Tomic, 2000; Betoret, 2009). Thus, increasing teacher self-efficacy can be an effective strategy in helping teachers prevent stress. Increasing classroom management self-efficacy specifically can help teachers with classroom management issues in particular, including student misbehavior. Self-efficacy measures can be used to better understand teacher self-efficacy in classroom management.

Several researchers suggest that additional training in classroom management skills could help increase self-efficacy scores, which then could reduce burnout on an organizational level by helping all teachers deal with classroom management issues more effectively (Brouwers & Tomic, 2000; Betoret, 2009). Targeting teachers who have low classroom management self-efficacy, particularly for professional development on classroom management techniques, could be even more effective. Since trainings on classroom management would address the demand of dealing with student behavior, this would be considered a problem-focused coping strategy.

CONCLUSIONS

The research reviewed in this chapter demonstrates that considerable progress has been made in recent years in better understanding the links between teacher stress, emotion, and classroom management. A number of elements in the stress process have been implicated: characteristics of student behavior, the appraisals that teachers make about these behaviors, and the resources that teachers have for combating and preventing stress. Although advances have been made in understanding teacher stress, it seems clear that we have much work to do in developing effective interventions for teachers who experience stress due to classroom management situations. We hope that this and other contributions in this volume will arm teachers with the type of information and classroom management practices that will minimize the occupational stress they experience. However, in an era of shrinking educational budgets, increasing calls for accountability, and high expectations for schools to play a role in the social and emotional lives of students, it is likely that even teachers with strong classroom management skills will experience high demand levels. It is therefore essential that researchers and all stakeholders in teacher welfare and effectiveness continue to research, promote, and support interventions for teachers experiencing stress and its consequences.

REFERENCES

Aultman, L. P., Williams-Johnson, M. R., & Schutz, P. A. (2009). Boundary dilemmas in teacher–student relationships: Struggling with "the line." *Teaching and Teacher Education, 25,* 636–646.

Bandura, A. (1982). Self-efficacy mechanism in human agency. *American Psychologist, 37*(2), 122–147. doi: 10.1037/0003-066X.37.2.122

Betoret, F. D. (2009). Self-efficacy, school resources, job stressors and burnout among Spanish primary and secondary school teachers: A structural equation approach. *Educational Psychology, 29*(1), 45–68.

Brouwers, A., & Tomic, W. (2000). A longitudinal study of teacher burnout and perceived self-efficacy in classroom management. *Teaching and Teacher Education, 16*(2), 239–253. doi: 10.1016/S0742-051X(99)00057-8

Chang, M.-L. (2009). An appraisal perspective of teacher burnout: Examining the emotional work of teachers. *Educational Psychology Review, 21*(3), 193–218. doi: 10.1007/s10648-009-9106-y

Chang, M. L., & Davis, H. A. (2009). Understanding the role of teacher appraisals in shaping the dynamics of their relationships with students: Deconstructing teachers' judgments of disruptive behavior/students. In P. A. Schutz & M. Zembylas (Eds.), *Advances in teacher emotion research: The impact on teachers' lives* (pp. 95–127). New York: Springer.

Cinamon, R. G., Rich, Y., & Westman, M. (2007). Teachers' occupation-specific work–family conflict. *Career Development Quarterly, 55*(3), 249–261.

Clunies-Ross, P., Little, E., & Kienhuis, M. (2008). Self-reported and actual use of proactive and reactive classroom management strategies and their relationship with teacher stress and student behaviour. *Educational Psychology, 28*(6), 693–710.

Covell, K., McNeil, J. K., & Howe, R. B. (2009). Reducing teacher burnout by increasing student engagement: A children's rights approach. *School Psychology International, 30*(3), 282–290.

Emmer, E. T., & Hickman, J. (1991). Teacher efficacy in classroom management and discipline. *Educational And Psychological Measurement, 51*(3), 755–765. doi: 10.1177/0013164491513027

Eskridge, D. H., & Coker, D. R. (1985). Teacher stress: symptoms, causes, and management techniques. *Clearing House, 58,* 387–390.

Evers, W. J. G., Tomic, W., & Brouwers, A. (2004). Burnout among teachers: Students' and teachers' perceptions compared. *School Psychology International, 25*(2), 131–148.

Folkman, S., & Lazarus, R. S. (1988a). Coping as a mediator of emotion. *Journal of Personality and Social Psychology, 54,* 466–475.

Folkman, S., & Lazarus, R. S. (1988b). The relationship between coping and emotion: Implications for theory and research. *Social Science Medicine, 26,* 309—317.

Frederickson, B. L., & Losada, M. F. (2005). Positive affect and the complex dynamics of human flourishing. *American Psychologist, 60,* 678–686.

Freudenberger, H. J. (1974). Staff burn-out. *Journal of Social Issues, 30,* 159–165.

Friedman, I. A. (1994). Conceptualizing and measuring teacher-perceived student behaviors: Disrespect, sociability, and attentiveness. *Educational and Psychological Measurement, 54*(4), 949–958. doi: 10.1177/0013164494054004011

Friedman, I. A. (1995). Student behavior patterns contributing to teacher burnout. *Journal of Educational Research, 88,* 281–289.

Friedman, I. A. (2006). Classroom management and teacher stress and burnout. In C. M. Evertson & C. S. Weinstein (Eds.), *Handbook of classroom management: Research, practice, and contemporary issues* (pp. 925–944). Mahwah, NJ: Erlbaum.

Friedman, I. A., & Farber, B. A. (1992). Professional self-concept as a predictor of teacher burnout. *Journal of Educational Research, 86,* 28–35. doi: 10.1080/00220671.1992.9941824

Gavish, B., & Friedman, I. A. (2010). Novice teachers' experience of teaching: a dynamic aspect of burnout. *Social Psychology of Education, 13*(2), 141–167. doi: 10.1007/s11218-009-9108-0

Gibson, S., & Dembo, M. (1984). Teacher efficacy: A construct validation. *Journal of Educational Psychology, 76,* 569–582.

Gold, E., Smith, A., Hopper, I., Herne, D., Tansey, G., & Hulland, C. (2010). Mindfulness-Based Stress Reduction (MBSR) for primary school teachers. *Journal of Child and Family Studies, 19*(2), 184–189. doi: 10.1007/s10826-009-9344-0

Gross, J. J. (1998). The emerging field of emotion regulation: An integrative review. *Review of General Psychology, 2,* 271–299. doi: 10.1037/1089-2680.2.3.271.

Gross, J. J. (2002). Emotion regulation: Affective, cognitive, and social consequences. *Psychophysiology, 39*(3), 281–291. doi: 10.1017/S0048577201393198

Gross, J. J. (2008). Emotion regulation. In M. Lewis, J. M. Haviland-Jones, & L. Feldman Barret (Eds.), *Handbook of Emotions* (3rd ed.). New York: Guilford Press.

Hastings, R. P., & Bham, M. S. (2003). The relationship between student behaviour patterns and teacher burnout. *School Psychology International, 24*(1), 115–127.

Hobfoll, S. E., Schwarzer, R., & Chon, K. K. (1998). Disentangling the stress labyrinth: Interpreting the meaning of the stress as it is studied in the health context. *Anxiety, Stress, & Coping, 11,* 181–212.

Hong, J. Y. (2012). Why do some beginning teachers leave the school, and others stay? Understanding teacher resilience through psychological lenses. *Teachers and Teaching: Theory and Practice, 18*(4), 417–440.

Ingersoll, R. (2001). Teacher turnover and teacher shortages: An organizational analysis. *American Educational Research Journal, 38*(3), 499–534.

Ingersoll, R. M., & Smith, T. M. (2003). The wrong solution to the teacher shortage. *Educational Leadership, 60*(8), 30–33.

Johnson, S., Cooper, C., Cartwright, S., Donald, I., Taylor, P., & Millet, C. (2005). The experience of work-related stress across occupations. *Journal of Managerial Psychology, 20*(2), 178–187.

Kabat-Zinn, J. (1994). *Wherever you go, there you are: Mindfulness meditation in everyday life.* New York: Hyperion.

Kaufhold, J. A., Alvarez, V. G., & Arnold, M. (2006). Lack of school supplies, materials and resources as an elementary cause of frustration and burnout in South Texas special education teachers. *Journal of Instructional Psychology, 33*(3), 159–161.

Kiziltepe, Z. (2006). Sources of teacher demotivation. In R. G. Lambert & C. J. McCarthy (Eds.), *Understanding teacher stress in an era of accountability,* Vol. 3 (pp. 145–162). Greenwich, CT: Information Age.

Klassen, R. M., & Chiu, M. (2011). The occupation commitment and intention to quit of practicing and pre-service teachers: Influence of self-efficacy, job stress, and teaching context. *Contemporary Educational Psychology, 36,* 114–129.

Kokkinos, C. M., Panayiotou, G., & Davazoglou, A. M. (2005). Correlates of teacher appraisals of student behaviors. *Psychology in the Schools, 42*(1), 79–89.

Kuzsman, F. J., & Schnall, H. (1987). Managing teachers' stress: Improving discipline. *The Canadian School Executive, 6*(3), 10.

Kyriacou, C., & Sutcliffe, J. (1977). Teacher stress: A review. *Educational Review, 29,* 299–306.

Lambert, R. G., Kusherman, J., O'Donnell, M., & McCarthy, C. J. (2006). Teacher stress and classroom structural characteristics in preschool settings. In R. G. Lambert & C. J. McCarthy (Eds.), *Understanding teacher stress in an era of accountability,* Vol. 3 (pp. 105–120). Greenwich, CT: Information Age.

Lambert, R. G., McCarthy, C. J., O'Donnell, M., & Melendres, L. (2007). Teacher stress and classroom structural characteristics in elementary settings. In G. Gates, M. Wolverton, & W. Gmelch, (Eds.), *Emerging thought and research on student, teacher, and administrator stress and coping* (pp. 109–131). Charlotte, NC: Information Age.

Lambert, R. G., McCarthy, C. J., O'Donnell, M., & Wang, C. (2009). Measuring elementary teacher stress and coping in the classroom: Validity evidence for the classroom appraisal of resources and demands. *Psychology in the Schools, 46,* 973–988.

Lazarus, R. S. (2000). Evolution of a model of stress, coping, and discrete emotions. In V. H. Rice (Ed.), *Handbook of stress, coping, and health: Implications for nursing research, theory, and practice* (pp. 195–222). Thousand Oaks, CA: Sage.

Lazarus, R. S., & Folkman, S. (1984). *Stress, appraisal, and coping.* New York: Springer.

Lewis, R., Roache, J., & Romi, S. (2011). Coping styles as mediators of teachers' classroom management techniques. *Research in Education, 85,* 53–68.

Loonstra, B., Brouwers, A., & Tomic, W. (2009). Feelings of existential fulfillment and burnout among secondary school teachers. *Teaching and Teacher Education: An International Journal of Research and Studies, 25*(5), 752–757.

López, J. M. O., Castro, C., Santiago, M. J., & Villardefrancos, E. (2010). Exploring stress, burnout, and job dissatisfaction in secondary school teachers. *International Journal of Psychology and Psychological Therapy, 10*(1), 107–123.

López, J. M. O., Santiago, M. J., Godás, A., Castro, C., Villardefrancos, E., & Ponte, D. (2008). An integrative approach to burnout in secondary school teachers: Examining the role of student disruptive behaviour and disciplinary issues. *International Journal of Psychology & Psychological Therapy, 8*(2), 259–270.

Maslach, C., Schaufeli, W. B., & Leiter, M. P. (2001). Job burnout. *Annual Review of Psychology, 52,* 397–422. doi: 10.1146/annurev.psych.52.1.397

Matheny, K. B., Aycock, D. W., Pugh, J. L., Curlette, W. L., & Silva Cannella, K. A. (1986). Stress coping: A qualitative and quantitative synthesis with implications for treatment. *The Counseling Psychologist, 14*(4), 499–549. doi: 10.1177/0011000086144001

Matheny, K. B., Aycock, D. W., Curlette, W. L., & Junker, G. N. (1993). The coping resources inventory for stress: A measure of perceived resourcefulness. *Journal of Clinical Psychology, 49,* 815–830.

McCarthy, C. J., Lambert, R. G., Crowe, E. W., & McCarthy, C. J. (2010). Coping, stress, and job satisfaction as predictors of advanced placement statistics teachers' intention to leave the field. *NASSP Bulletin, 94,* 306–326.

McCarthy, C. J., Lambert, R. G., O'Donnell, M., & Melendres, L. T. (2009). The relation of elementary teachers' experience, stress, and coping resources to burnout symptoms. *Elementary School Journal, 109*(3), 282–300.

McCarthy, C. J., Lambert, R. G., & Ullrich, A. (Eds.). (2012). *International perspectives on teacher stress.* Greenwich, CT: Information Age.

McCormick, J., & Barnett, K. (2011). Teachers' attributions for stress and their relationships with burnout. *International Journal of Educational Management, 25*(3), 278–293.

Montgomery, C., & Rupp, A. A. (2005). A meta-analysis for exploring the diverse causes and effects of stress in teachers. *Canadian Journal of Education, 28*(3), 458–486.

Moya-Albiol, L., Serrano, M. Á., & Salvador, A. (2010). Burnout as an important factor in the psychophysiological responses to a work day in teachers. *Stress and Health: Journal of the International Society for the Investigation of Stress, 26*(5), 382–393. doi: 10.1002/smi.1309

Pas, E. T., Bradshaw, C. P., & Hershfeldt, P. A. (2012). Teacher- and school-level predictors of teacher efficacy and burnout: Identifying potential areas for support. *Journal of School Psychology, 50*(1), 129–145.

Pearlin, L. I., & Schooler, C. (1978). The structure of coping. *Journal of health and social behavior, 19*(1), 2–21.

Pines, A. M. (2002). Teacher burnout: A psychodynamic existential perspective. *Teachers and Teaching: Theory and Practice, 8*(2), 121–140. doi: 10.1080/13540600220127331

Reese, R. (2004). The bottom line. *American School Board Journal, 191*(8), 26–27.

Roeser, R. W., Skinner, E., Beers, J., & Jennings, P. A. (2012). Mindfulness training and teachers' professional development: An emerging area of research and practice. *Child Development Perspectives, 6*(2), 167–173. doi: 10.1111/j.1750-8606.2012.00238.x

Schaufeli, W. B., & Enzmann, D. (1998). *The burnout component to study and practice.* London: Taylor & Francis.

Schutz, P. A., Hong, J. Y., Cross, D. I., & Osbon, J. N. (2006). Reflections on investigating emotions among educational contexts. *Educational Psychology Review, 18,* 343–360.

Schwarzer, R., & Hallum, S. (2008). Perceived teacher self-efficacy as a predictor of job stress and burnout. *Applied Psychology: An International Review, 57*(Supplement 1), 152–171. doi: 10.1111/j.1464-0597.2008.00359.x

Schwerdtfeger, A., Konermann, L., & Schönhofen, K. (2008). Self-efficacy as a health-protective resource in teachers? A biopsychological approach. *Health Psychology, 27*(3), 358–368. doi: 10.1037/0278-6133.27.3.358

Siemer, M., Mauss, I. & Gross, J. J. (2007). Same situation—different emotions: How appraisals shape our emotions. *Emotion, 7,* 592–600. doi: 10.1037/1528-3542.7.3.592

Steinhardt, M. A., Smith Jaggars, S. E., Faulk, K. E., & Gloria, C. T. (2011). Chronic work stress and depressive symptoms: Assessing the mediating role of teacher burnout. *Stress and Health: Journal of the International Society for the Investigation of Stress, 27*(5), 420–429. doi: 10.1002/smi.1394

Sutton, R. E. (2004). Emotional regulation goals and strategies of teachers. *Social Psychology of Education, 7*, 379–398.

Sutton, R. E., Mudrey-Camino, R., & Knight, C. C. (2009). Teachers' emotion regulation and classroom management. *Theory into Practice, 48*(2), 130–137.

Tschannen-Moran, M., & Woolfolk Hoy, A. (2001). Teacher efficacy: Capturing an elusive construct. *Teaching and Teacher Education, 17*(7), 783–805. doi: 10.1016/S0742-051X(01)00036-1

Tsouloupas, C. N., Carson, R. L., Matthews, R., Grawitch, M. J., & Barber, L. K. (2010). Exploring the association between teachers' perceived student misbehaviour and emotional exhaustion: The importance of teacher efficacy beliefs and emotion regulation. *Educational Psychology, 30*(2), 173–189.

von Känel, R., Bellingrath, S., & Kudielka, B. M. (2008). Association between burnout and circulating levels of pro- and anti-inflammatory cytokines in schoolteachers. *Journal of Psychosomatic Research, 65*(1), 51–59. doi: 10.1016/j.jpsychores.2008.02.007

17

TEACHER SUPPORT AND STUDENTS' SELF-REGULATED LEARNING

Co-Regulation and Classroom Management

MARY McCASLIN, VALERIE A. SOTARDI, AND RUBY I. VEGA
UNIVERSITY OF ARIZONA

We present three approaches to regulated learning that differ in recognition and resolution of the role of the self and the social in how learners come to be self-aware—"know what they know"—and act on that knowledge, or "regulate" their learning. The first, self-regulated learning (SRL), consists of an array of seven theories that share a primary focus on the individual (the "self" of the construct) and on academic achievement (the "learning" of the construct). The function of "other" typically is restricted to the conditions, persons, or situations that allow or require students learn how to or display "self-regulation" (e.g., moderately difficult tasks, distracting peers). An extensive theoretical analysis of these SRL approaches and implications for classroom management of learners who vary in SRL capabilities can be found in the first edition of this handbook (McCaslin et al., 2006). Here we summarize the array of these perspectives and refer the interested reader to the original.

Second, we expand the focus of SRL to consider the regulation of emotion, specifically, how students think about and cope with stress in the classroom. Stress is defined as those "moments of tension" (Sotardi, 2013) that are as much a part of classroom life as the curriculum and assessments that can both trigger and relieve them. Student coping behavior expands our consideration of *self*-regulated learning to more deliberately include others and situations that not only trigger and relieve the need for emotional regulation but more deliberately expand the individual's SRL capacities. SRL of emotion and activity is represented in literature chiefly on coping behavior. This literature also affords an extension of the individual into social and instructional environments that are considered part of individual regulation, similar to some aspects of social influence theories of SRL.

Third, we explicitly expand the notion of individual in our discussion of socially shared regulation of learning (SSRL), a more recent development that expands and renders even more permeable the boundaries of self. Social-regulation research and constructs systematically recognize the interpersonal context of regulation dynamics, for example, within small learning groups. This work more explicitly studies students *as a group*, compared to the more typical SRL study of students *in a group* (Bennett & Dunne, 1992), and how they share knowledge and together engage in the regulation of their own and others' learning.

Throughout, the construct of co-regulation (McCaslin, 2009; McCaslin & Good, 1996) organizes and guides interpretation of these literatures. Co-regulation is rooted in a Vygotskian-influenced sociocultural perspective. Thus, co-regulation takes as a given the social origins of higher psychological processes and hence the historical, socially situated individual whose cognition fuses the affective with the intellectual in the engagement of opportunities. A co-regulation perspective often is confused with dyadic interaction in the zone of proximal development (ZPD), perhaps the most recognizable feature of Vygotsky's work in the United States. ZPD is defined as the gap between what a learner can do alone and with assistance; thus, it is considered an appropriate learning and instructional space. For 50 years, ZPD has proved a useful vehicle for research that addressed instructional and developmental dynamics in children's thinking, or the so-called acquisition of higher psychological processes.

ZPD is an exemplar of co-regulation; however, it is not a necessary restriction of the construct to dyadic interaction or to hierarchical relationships between more and less capable persons. Co-regulation is a more inclusive construct. Co-regulation is better construed as a process of emergent interaction of regulation processes, supportive relationships, and affording opportunities of the social world that are themselves situated within the more pervasive cultural, historical time and place. Thus, while some might be tempted to arrange SRL theories on a self-dyad-group continuum, we do not conceptualize regulation dynamics in this way. Rather, we envision a dialectical progression in the theoretical conceptualizations of SRL that ultimately collapse the distinctions among self and environment, individual and social, pairs and groups. Theoretical distinctions matter if they can usefully inform teacher strategies and goals for particular students and general classroom management procedures. Toward that goal, we first define SRL and review three domains of SRL theories; behavioral, cognitive, and social influence, along with their implications for classrooms.

WHAT IS SRL?

SRL-like constructs have a long tradition in psychology and human development (e.g., Flavell, 1979; Piaget, 1983; Vygotsky, 1962); however, our focus is on modern perspectives that influence classroom practices. Most typically, SRL is a bridge construct that links student motivation, thinking, and behavior. Corno and Mandinach (1983) were among the first educational psychologists and teacher educators to define SRL in this way. They stated:

> Self-regulated learning will be shown to consist of specific cognitive activities, such as deliberate planning and monitoring, which learners carry out as they

encounter academic tasks. Learning is less self-regulated when some of the processes are overtaken by classroom teachers, other students, or features of written instruction. . . . self-regulated learning is the highest form of cognitive engagement. . . . [It] is somewhat taxing. When tasks make cognitive demands students may engage in self-regulated learning; they may also shift the mental burden by calling upon available external resources such as a willing and knowledgeable peer. (pp. 89–90)

Early work in SRL challenged the then pervasive beliefs about appropriate tasks and instructional supports for students that were rooted in automaticity and reinforcement (Rohrkemper & Corno, 1988). The development and display of SRL required challenging tasks and minimal instructional support, so that learners became more self-aware and, by necessity, strategic in the pursuit of new or uncertain learning. Indeed, SRL was believed hindered by tasks designed for ready success and by too available instructional supports, which were the normative teaching practices of the time. The early focus on the individual and academic outcomes was common across theoretical approaches; however, sociocultural perspectives (e.g., Rohrkemper [McCaslin], 1989) stressed the social and emotional realms of relationships, well-being, and identity dynamics in the "adaptive ["self"-regulated] learning" mix. These latter concerns are now more prevalent inasmuch as SRL in general has moved to a greater recognition of the role of context and social influences on individuals.

THREE BASIC THEORETICAL APPROACHES TO SRL: DIVERSE PERSPECTIVES, COMMON THEMES

Research on the sources and supports of SRL, like many domains in psychology, has been pursued within three broad theoretical orientations: behavioral, cognitive, and sociocultural. Behavioral, or "operant," approaches are at the root of each as it grapples with the role of the environment in SRL.

Behavioral

The operant approach to SRL in classrooms typically means that teacher control of students' behavior has transferred to students' control of their own behavior. Operant theorists define how this outcome might be known, basically through denial and delay ("self-control" and "commitment"), and "operationalize" the sequential ABC process. SRL in operant work is about taking control of antecedents and consequences to take control of the self. Antecedents (A) are those things that occur before a behavior's (B) consequences (C) follow the behavior. Taking control of one's self is done by taking control of A and C, just as the environment can, to deny personal impulsivity and to delay gratification. The key processes to doing so mirror the behavior modification of and by others, now applied to and by the self: self-monitoring (identifying one's behavior and linking it to consequences), self-instruction (talking one's self through it), self-evaluation (comparing one's performance with a standard), self-correction (changing behavior if performance does not meet the standard), and self-reinforcement (administering consequences) (see Mace, Belfiore, & Hutchinson, 2001).

Cognitive

Cognitive approaches in psychology typically are seen as a reaction to and the opposite of behaviorism. This is also the case in SRL work; however, cognitive approaches share many particulars with operant theory, albeit assigned to a different source. Namely, *cognitive approaches locate within the individual those processes that behaviorists assign to the environment.* Phenomenology, information processing, and volitional approaches to SRL all emphasize individual cognitive processes, yet they differ considerably in how that is done.

Phenomenology

SRL in phenomenology is personal and contemplative; self-reflection is the essential process that enables ownership of one's experience. At its core, SRL is an image of oneself as competent and in control, as an active agent in learning and regulation of advantageous learning environments. Specific SRL processes are defined similarly to social-cognitive approaches (described subsequently) that themselves borrow heavily from operant work. In the phenomenological SRL classroom, teachers provide students opportunities that require choice, completion, and time for reflection; together, these promote personal responsibility (see McCombs, 2001).

Information Processing

Information processing (IP) approaches to SRL portray the environment as an opportunity for the display of human regulation complexity (cf. Simon, 1981 [1969]) and, consistent with IP theory, adhere to cognition as goal-driven. For example, Winne (2001) asserts five basic types of deliberative (vs. automatic) processes essential to SRL: searching, monitoring, assembling, rehearsing, and translating (across multiple representations). Consistent with algorithmic learning, these processes are better remembered with the SMART mnemonic. SRL itself consists of four sequential phases, the first three required: defining the task, setting goals and plans, enacting the plans, and evaluation. Each phase is further defined by five potential information products: conditions, operations, products, evaluations, and standards (COPES).

That is a lot of detail, but two essential things to remember are the metacognitive processes of self- and environmental-awareness that make it all work: metacognitive monitoring and control. It is up to the individual to perceive environmental cues and to do the cognitive work that needs to be done. SRL is by the student, but the teacher is expected to attend to instructional conditions that can facilitate or impede that process, including such things as broken pencils, noisy neighbors, and other known assaults on the IP system. For example, opportunity for appropriate prior knowledge facilitates efficient processing in short-term memory and long-term storage: Require prerequisites. Appropriate task difficulty is a necessary condition; too difficult tasks exceed processing capabilities and too easy tasks foster automaticity rather than SRL. Mnemonics (the verbal chains of operant theorists; e.g., SMART) facilitate retrieval of information and can guide information processing.

Volition

Modern conceptions of volition are about protecting intentions and seeing tasks through to completion—getting the job done. Control is central to volitional SRL. Classrooms are workplaces rife with distractions; thus volition, or the acquisition of work habits, is necessary (although insufficient) for getting school tasks optimally done (Corno, 2011). One key volitional SRL strategy is self-monitoring to protect against intrusions, whatever the source. Another is resourcefulness, including covert and overt self and task management and control. Covert processes are about prioritizing and protecting those priorities. Overt processes are similar to the operant perspective, sharing the premise that, when we take charge of our environment, we take charge of ourselves.

Volitional strategies are learned through necessity and can develop with growing self-awareness and socialization at home and school and their fusion (e.g., homework [Corno, 1996; McCaslin & Murdock, 1991]). Volitional concerns in the classroom arise similarly to IP concerns: when tasks are too easy and support too available. Each undermines the acquisition and development of volitional SRL. Teachers support the development and enactment of volitional SRL when they provide realistic and challenging learning tasks and situations, along with the strategies to engage and complete them. "Realistic" because not all tasks are interesting and not all classmates are helpful; nonetheless, the volitional student garners strategies to persevere. It is about staying the course.

Theories of Social Influence

Social influence theories in psychology synthesize behavioral and cognitive perspectives through the mechanism of reciprocal causality (Bandura, 1977); that being said, the environment that I influence also influences me. Social influence SRL theories include social-cognitive theory in the tradition of Bandura (1997), neoconstructivism in the tradition of Piaget (1983), and sociocultural theory in the tradition of Vygotsky (1962, 1978). They differ in relative emphasis and sources of SRL.

Social-Cognitive

Social-cognitive theory, originally social learning theory (Bandura, 1977), is best known for its extension of operant (e.g., Skinner, 1976) and expectancy-reinforcement (Rotter, 1954) theories to include modeling, and thus vicarious (i.e., from others') learning, and self-efficacy (i.e., beliefs about one's ability to perform a specific behavior). More recently, Bandura (1997) has asserted "collective efficacy," that is, beliefs about the group of which one is a member to expand the affiliation emphasis to the desire for acceptance in a community. Beginning teachers, for example, observe master teachers (1) to learn management strategies (vicarious learning of specific behavior), (2) because they believe in the importance of effective classroom management for student learning potential (collective efficacy), and (3) so that they will become skilled (self-efficacy) classroom managers (and thus deserving of group membership).

SRL in social-cognitive theory focuses on internal processes, consistent with the IP perspective, and restricts consideration of behavior to a specific situation, consistent with its operant roots. SRL theorists then integrate the IP process and specific situations with self-efficacy beliefs and affiliation needs. SRL is not a trait or developmental milestone; it is a learned sequence of three phases similar to the operant antecedent, behavior, consequence (ABC) paradigm: forethought, performance control, and self-reflection (e.g., Zimmerman, 2013). The forethought phase includes goal setting and social modeling, performance control aligns with volition strategies and self-instruction that cues procedures similar to the operant approach, and self-reflection attends to internalization of external influences and the role of social supports. Each of these three phases involves learned strategies of self-observation, self-judgment, and self-reaction, each defined consistently with the operant tradition. One early difference between the social-cognitive and operant approaches, however, was the assertion that *anticipation* of consequences motivates behavior, not consequences in and of themselves. More recent work, however, attempts to reinstate the importance of actual consequences as well those imagined.

In the classroom, the social-cognitive teacher promotes SRL through modeling and guidance, along with tasks and accurate feedback that both cue and allow the practice of the three SRL phases. In addition, teachers credibly model the value of group affiliation, peer modeling, and accountability. Credibility ("this is worth doing") and accuracy ("this is how you do it") are key in social-cognitive SRL.

Neoconstructivism

Neoconstructive theories consist of Piagetian constructs that have evolved and are currently in their second iteration. Paris, Byrnes, and Paris (2001) describe a socially embedded participant who replaces earlier emphases on idiosyncratic constructions of individual learners. In addition to marked movement toward sociocultural theory consistent with the Vygotskian tradition, second-wave constructivists also shift focus to group membership (consistent with recent social-cognitive theory) and individual identity development (consistent with phenomenology). One part of identity development is the construction of coherent self-evaluative and optimistic life stories (e.g., McAdams, 1993). Like a phenomenological approach, the interpretation of experience trumps the actual. SRL in the second-wave perspective, then, is defined in terms of socially situated participation in the practices that belong to a desirable group. Group membership enhances individual self-image and optimistic beliefs about the future.

The primary source of SRL is identity confirmation; students acquire SRL strategies through invention (consistent with the original Piaget) and intervention. Teacher support of SRL is consistent with those described in the social-cognitive approach; however, a key distinction is the second-wave focus on validation. SRL is all about validated identity and finding one's place, consistent with the identity work of Erikson (1968). The teacher helps students "try on" different identities as they seek the one that fits. Thus, multidimensional classrooms (Cohen, 1994), with multiple sanctioned opportunities for exploration and learning about the self, are the stuff of neoconstructivist SRL.

Neo-Vygotskian Sociocultural Theory

A Vygotskian perspective considers SRL a "higher psychological process" and takes a developmental approach to individual mediation of cultural experience. SRL is not so much a characteristic of the self as it is an ongoing co-regulated process that is uniquely negotiated, integrated, and reconstructed through interpersonal engagement in meaningful opportunity (e.g., McCaslin, 2009), or "emergent interaction." The capacity for SRL begins in the interpersonal realm, and, through language, communication that was once by and with others becomes self-directive, or self-regulating (Vygotsky, 1962, 1978).

Neo-Vygotskian work elaborates on the role of language with the construct of "activity," defined as "tool-mediated, goal-directed action" (Wertsch, 1985). This broadens interest in SRL to include self-directive language, the types of tasks that learners engage, and the contexts in which they participate. SRL in this approach has been termed "adaptive learning." Adaptive learning involves the internalization of goals; the motivation to commit, challenge, or reform them; and the competence to enact and evaluate those commitments (Rohrkemper [McCaslin], 1989). Adaptive learning is part of emergent identity; thus, it may be expressed in the present, but it is linked to the past and informs the future.

As described previously, the best known teaching/learning space and thus opportunity for the development of SRL is the zone of proximal development (ZPD), the gap between what a learner can do alone (a proxy for SRL) and with help (an example of co-regulated learning) (Vygotsky, 1962). Co-regulation is the process by which emergent SRL, or adaptive learning, is developed, supported, and maintained in the learner's ZPD. An essential feature of the ZPD is the relationship among participants, often construed as between an expert and novice. Yowell and Smylie (1999) persuasively argue instead that each participant occupies both an expert and a novice role. For example, teachers are both experts in the cultural knowledge they (and the culture) wish to convey and novices in the contingencies of the learner's experience. Learners are experts in the contingencies of their personal experiences in their home and neighborhood and novices in the teacher's cultural knowledge. Thus, co-regulation in the ZPD is not construed as a top-down process of socialization, as in social-cognitive approaches (e.g., teacher as mastery model or expert). Rather, co-regulation is about mutual negotiation of expertise in personal, social, and cultural understandings to the betterment of both/all participants.

Co-regulation in the classroom, then, includes but is not limited to dyadic relationships in the ZPD. It is based on three concepts. First, the basic unit of analysis in school learning is the *relationship* among individuals, objects, and settings (rather than individuals or tasks). Second, students' basic task is coordination of multiple social worlds, expectations, and goals. Achievement is only one aspect of being a student; being a student is only one aspect of being a child. Third, goal coordination in the pursuit of adaptive learning is learned, and it is difficult. Teachers' basic task is to provide supportive scaffolding and to afford opportunities to promote, challenge, shape, and guide—to co-regulate—student mediation processes that enhance adaptive learning (see McCaslin, 2009; McCaslin & Good, 1996).

Student mediation processes consist of motivation, enactment, and evaluation activities that resonate with behavioral, cognitive, and other social influence theories. For example, teacher strategies for *co-regulation of motivation* are consistent with social-cognitive theory; however, in addition to goal setting, co-regulation involves goal coordination and review. This is because multiple goals are desirable despite being potentially conflicting. Thus, the larger task is to learn to coordinate among them. Goal coordination can be more or less difficult in part due to differential opportunities and their relationship with developing motive dispositions. Motive dispositions are what we value and to what and whom we make commitments. Motive dispositions inform personal identity that is rooted in prior experiences and open to validation by others, consistent with Erikson (1968); you believe and I agree that you are the person you desire to be and strive to become. One student's decision to work overtime rather than study for a final exam, another's proudly introducing a fiancé, and still another's decision to attend a local community college rather than accept a university scholarship make more "sense" to a high school teacher when they are considered in light of goal coordination, motive disposition, and identity dynamics.

Co-regulation of enactment activities is consistent with the operant, volitional, and social-cognitive approaches to covert and overt strategies for regulation. One essential difference, however, is that self-directive or "inner speech," that guides activity in pursuit of a goal in nonautomatic, "effortful" cognition is social in origin. Thus, it represents the transformation of cultural understandings in the formation of mind. Language learned through communication from (and then with) others is turned into personal thoughts that guide thinking, motivation, and regulation. In that sense, self-regulation begins in the social world. This is in marked contrast to operant and social-cognitive perspectives that consider language a "talking it through" (overtly or covertly) strategy of continuous stimulus cuing to promote rule adherence. Activities that afford inner speech, and thus "tool-mediated, goal-directed action," include novel or subjectively experienced (vs. objectively defined) moderately difficult tasks (e.g., Rohrkemper [McCaslin], 1989), whether due to wanting instruction or the task itself. Instructional supports (scaffolds) are transitional, removed when the learner has internalized their structure and are no longer needed. Co-regulation of enactment activities is not about task simplification or pursuit of response "correctness" per se so much as it is about the learner coming to understand differently. And that different understanding is as much affective as it is intellectual: Thoughts don't think themselves; people do, and meaningful learning is not a neutral event.

Co-regulation of student evaluation includes teaching students to align their self-evaluations with those of their teacher. The goal is realistic student appraisals that are more than simple accuracy. The struggle for competence in this perspective is all about the conflict of opposites—the headiness of success and the dread of failure—and understanding their place in emergent identity. Adaptive learners know their motivational and regulatory dynamics in both success and failure—knowledge that allows self-confidence, realistic self-appraisals, and the willingness to trust oneself in uncertainty. In the classroom, new work and its mastery are essential regulation and achieving opportunities; so too are reviews and tests that signal accountability (McCaslin, 2004).

Co-regulation of student mediation processes does not stop with a student who is motivated to strategically learn and who is able to prioritize intentions and realistically judge progress. The point also is to influence what students come to value and to encourage them to go beyond enlightened self-interest to contribute to the common good. In this aspect, sociocultural theory is quite different from other social-influence and constructivist perspectives that look to the social world to enhance the individual and leave it there, at individual self-interest. Personal and realistic self-evaluations, then, are one aspect of teacher co-regulation of students' SRL; another is making cultural rules and roles personally meaningful.

One goal of co-regulation as deliberate classroom management practices is the intentional construction of a bridge between school and nonschool that fosters societal acculturation of students and schools. Classroom management strategies mirror culturally sanctioned consequences for behavior; thus, they are a powerful vehicle for teaching students the rules, roles, and reasons that govern responses to help, neglect, or punish another in our culture. These understandings are fostered by management strategies that include teacher talk: stated interpretations of observed student behavior, rationales for expectations, and justifications for consequences. In this way, teacher language can scaffold student understanding of complex interpersonal behavior, especially in the younger grades (Rohrkemper, 1984). SRL is social in origin; approaches to co-regulating student cultural learning and contribution that emphasize language are more powerful than those that do not.

Concluding Comments

The array of SRL theoretical approaches affords deliberate consideration of student task engagement, broadly conceived. In practice, however, implementation of SRL perspectives primarily targets student behavior believed to promote achievement (e.g., work habits, information organizational skills). This aligns with current school reform beliefs that students are capable of and responsible for active engagement with classroom tasks and performance on mandated tests. Classrooms are about more than achievement, however, and we now extend and expand on SRL considerations for practice to include research on how elementary students regulate themselves and classmates as they cope with stressful events in the context of classroom learning and accountability demands. These events include how teachers help students manage the stressful situations they experience directly and as bystanders.

CLASSROOM MANAGEMENT FROM A STRESS AND COPING PERSPECTIVE

Classrooms are places in which students pursue the formal expectations of schooling. They are vibrant—and sometimes frenetic—social environments that change through moments of tension and relief. Whenever students and teachers encounter actual or anticipated problems in the classroom, they experience emotional shifts that motivate them to respond by using coping strategies. Coping strategies are a subset of SRL skills that are often given short shrift in theories of how students regulate their learning. Yet they are the essence of theories on stress and coping that align with SRL work. Specifically, theories of stress and coping consider individuals' appraisals of a problem, their coordination of regulatory efforts to reduce stress, and how such regulatory efforts influence the social environment (Skinner & Zimmer-Gembeck, 2007). Students view classroom events differently (e.g., Rohrkemper, 1984); thus, what may produce tension at certain times for some might signal relief for others. Research suggests that in order to reduce the negative feelings associated with stress, students cope by relying on available cognitive, emotional, and social resources (e.g., Band & Weisz, 1998).

Individual attempts to manage perceived stress influence the learning environment, and how a student copes with stress can have a personal and more generalized impact on the whole class. Thus, coping can both directly and indirectly influence classroom management. Coping begins at the point of appraisal, focusing on what is done to relieve stress. Thus, much of the environmental and personal scans of behavioral approaches to SRL (e.g., monitoring) have already occurred. So too have some of the more strategic forecasting procedures (e.g., planning) of cognitive approaches to SRL. Research on coping would do well to include these considerations. Here, coping is about regulation of emotion, thoughts, motivation, and action as well as impacting the environment in real-world time and situations. It includes immediate, reactive, and stressful emotional behavior "made sense of" and brought under control or "regulated" rather than the more dispassionate and reflective considerations more typical of cognitive approaches to SRL.

Looking at Moments of Tension in Classrooms

Classrooms are packed with emotion (Emmer & Stough, 2001). Emotions related to *academic events* such as the frustration associated with mastering a new concept, anxiety associated with taking tests, and pride associated with success influence how a student (or teacher) feels about learning. *Social events* also produce emotion in the classroom, including the fear of not being accepted by others, anxiety associated with talking in front of the class, and excitement of building and maintaining new friendships. As learning and social events come and go throughout the school day, fluctuation between moments of tension and relief can make a classroom relatively unpredictable. Research has shown that elementary school students experience threats and challenges every day ranging from comprehension obstacles to peer conflict (e.g., Humphrey, 2004). They also encounter minor, yet stressful, events at school with moderate regularity and stability (Sotardi, 2013). It is important that younger students learn to predict and avoid potentially stressful experiences and acquire a wide variety of available coping skills that can effectively manage events that are unavoidable or unexpected. Students who fail to manage stress successfully are vulnerable to learning deficits, performance declines, and conduct problems (e.g., Barrett & Heubeck, 2000). The ability to adapt to or regulate stress in the class-room is at the core of student development and personal well-being.

When people anticipate, experience, and evaluate a stressful situation, multiple processes take place. This includes how individuals try to regulate emotions, thoughts (e.g., think in a flexible and constructive way), and self- and other-directed actions to reduce perceived sources of stress (Compas, Connor-Smith, Saltzman, Thomsen, & Wadsworth, 2001). These responses are considered optimally sequential; thus, the subset of self-regulation called coping (Compas, Connor-Smith, Saltzman, Thom-sen, & Wadsworth, 2001; Eisenberg et al., 1997) aligns with most approaches to SRL. Though many different perspectives have been presented across the decades, the seminal theory on stress and coping is that by Lazarus and Folkman (1984). This transactional theory posits that people experience stress when they uniquely appraise some imbalance between threatening or challenging demands of a situation (environment) and resources they believe they currently have (person). If a person believes that he or she has sufficient coping skills to regulate, or "handle," a spe-cific problem, then the experience of stress can potentially be reduced. Importantly, the theory states that people can learn to cope with stress through different regu-latory efforts. Others have adopted similar frameworks. For instance, Skinner and colleagues view coping from a self-determination perspective (Deci & Ryan, 1985), which characterizes stress as a threat to psychological needs satisfaction, primarily needs for relatedness, autonomy, and competence. Coping, then, reflects how people regulate emotion, motivation, and action when under stress to restore those needs.

To understand how students regulate under stress and the implications for class-room management, teachers can consider stress appraisals and the types of situa-tions that students view as stress inducing. Stress appraisals are cognitive evaluations that mediate a situation and an individual's reaction to it. What is viewed as stressful depends on an array of personal variables (e.g., gender, age, and exposure to stress; e.g., Zimmer-Gembeck & Skinner, 2011) as well as environmental circumstances. Stress appraisals vary widely from one context to another; however, there are general trends in what situations children view as distressing. There have been numerous studies over recent decades investigating situations that are stressful for children (e.g., Ryan-Wenger, Sharrer & Campbell, 2005). Regrettably, there is a shortage of research on stressful school-specific situations. In part, this may be due to adult beliefs that "the kids are alright." For example, teachers and parents report/predict less stress for students across different school-related situations (e.g., discipline, performance, and peer conflict) than students actually report (Anderson & Jimerson, 2007; Bagdi & Pfister, 2006). Adults need a clearer grasp of what students view as stressful if they are to influence how students cope (i.e., regulate their emotion, thoughts, motiva-tion, and action) through supportive scaffolding and guidance that can be informed by the social influence theories of SRL.

Efforts by the teacher to predict, analyze, and evaluate moments of tension in the classroom are especially important for student development and display of SRL. From a resilience stance, not all stress is bad stress; in fact, difficult classroom events can sometimes become opportunities for growth. One important outcome of schooling is for students to develop healthy ways to cope with everyday challenges. Experiencing stress in a safe environment may strengthen students' efficacy to self-regulate problems and become adaptive thinkers and hearty kids. Classrooms with reliable social support minimize risk and maximize emotional security; here, students who feel supported may come to view school stressors as challenges rather than threats. Additionally, a teacher who consistently monitors and controls students' exposure to manageable challenges at school will serve many children. As described by Rutter (2013), this controlled exposure will promote adaptive skills in students who are not experiencing stress and will foster resilience in students who are currently facing adversity. Watching students struggle with a problem may not always be easy for teachers; however, without sufficient challenges at school, boredom can quickly ensue—an emotional state that also can be stressful. Lack of challenge also denies students the opportunity to learn how to regulate their emotions, thoughts, motivation, and coping behavior, as well as learn to recover should they fail to do so—a missed opportunity for essential learning to cope with stress (Rohrkemper & Corno, 1988; Sotardi, 2013).

Understanding Student Coping and Classroom Behavior

Literature on coping highlights a constellation of how adults, adolescents, and children cope with stress. The most comprehensive report to date is by Skinner and colleagues (Skinner, Edge, Altman, & Sherwood, 2003). The authors used factor analysis with more than 100 assessments of coping and 400 coping constructs to produce a hierarchical framework that organizes coping strategies into 13 lower-order coping strategy "families" with higher-order adaptive purposes. These coping families include problem solving (e.g., strategizing, instrumental action, and planning), escape (cognitive avoidance, behavioral avoidance, denial, and wishful thinking), support seeking (contact seeking, comfort seeking, instrumental aid, and spiritual support), accommodation (distraction, cognitive restructuring, minimization, and acceptance), and opposition (blame, projection, and aggression), among others. This is a rich, empirically based framework informed by individual factors related to coping (such as age or cultural background), as well as a range of situational stressors. Here we focus on the coping strategies of students of a particular age because development and experience influence how students are apt to respond to stress in the classroom. These age-related considerations are a welcome addition to the SRL literature, which, with few exceptions (e.g., Perry, 1998) glosses over them.

Skinner and colleagues (e.g., Zimmer-Gembeck & Skinner, 2011) identified some important age differences in children's coping capacities. For example, age trends in problem-solving strategies shift at or around 10–13 years of age. This is when children begin to employ strategies that involve more cognitive and metacognitive elaboration such as planning, instrumental support seeking, and decision making as typically described in cognitive and social influence approaches to SRL but without developmental consideration. Another example involves social support as a method of coping. Here the general age shift is at or around 8 years of age when children begin to employ strategies that rely more on seeking emotional support from friends and peers, consistent with neo-Piagetian work, and less on attachment figures. Eight-year-olds also engage in help-seeking behaviors that are more organized, flexible, and problem specific. These developmental considerations are especially important to elementary school teachers' understandings of student SRL and behavior. Teachers' expectations of and disciplinary action in response to children's conduct is more apt to successfully guide and scaffold student SRL if that action is developmentally sensitive and "within reach" of available coping resources in students' ZPD.

The basic unit of analysis in support of student coping, then, is the relationship between a specific problem at hand (the stressor) and the student's capacity to regulate it (coping). Band and Weisz (1988) conducted one of the earliest studies on stress due to a specific problem at hand and children's coping behavior. The research asked children 6, 9, and 12 years old to think about stressful episodes they might have experienced in six different situations (e.g., loss/separation, medical procedures, peer relations, school failure) and to describe how they responded when it happened. Reported coping strategies differed as a function of children's age and stressful situation. School failure experiences were more likely to involve "primary" solution strategies aimed at modifying circumstances and outcomes (e.g., study more to improve a wanting grade) as compared with stressful experiences with medical procedures like getting a vaccination. Age-related differences also revealed that younger children were more apt to cope with school failure through problem-focused avoidance, which is defined as efforts to directly avoid experiencing a stressful situation (e. g., staying away from kids who fight or tease, making efforts to avoid being taken to the doctor for a shot). Older children were more likely to directly target the achievement-related stressor (e. g., studying to improve grades, telling others to stop teasing, putting a BandAid on a cut).

This research highlights the importance of viewing coping behavior in relation to both the context and personal variables such as age and grade level. Little research examines these factors in school settings; however, Sotardi (2013) recently attempted to do so with students in grades 3–5 who attended a predominantly Latino school. Whereas stress and coping patterns were somewhat clear with respect to learning challenges, performance expectations, and teacher-related stressors, peer conflict showed the most variability and association with appraisals of personal threat (e.g., being teased or bossed around). The most frequently reported coping strategies for peer conflict were demanding change from the peer, calling for backup (e.g., seeking help from a friend, lunchroom aide, and/or teacher to attenuate the stressful situation or ask others to fix the problem altogether), and attempting to ignore the problem. Students who coped by calling for backup and demanding change also described a clear resolution to the conflict. In contrast, no clear resolution was reported when students coped by behaving aggressively, attempting to ignore the problem, or withdrawing from the situation. This research illustrates that individual coping in classroom situations appear to vary as a function of grade level and situational appraisals. Other factors, such as school climate and students' cultural background, deserve attention in these matters. Classrooms are such intensely social environments, it is also necessary to examine how an individual's coping strategies might impact selected peers and the class as a whole.

As previously discussed, social-influence SRL theories emphasize the reciprocal relationship between an individual's regulation efforts and the environment. In a specific coping episode, student action or inaction can impact the surrounding environment by introducing new stressors for others and/or by changing the coping resources that are available to others. Additionally, social-cognitive SRL reminds us that an individual's coping strategies can produce vicarious learning in others as students model one another in the classroom. Imagine Erick, a fourth-grader who is struggling to understand a new multiplication technique. He copes with the learning challenge by mentally stepping away from the task and distracting himself by doodling in a notebook. Distraction coping allows him to catch his breath before he reengages the task. Erick's seemingly adaptive coping strategy, however, can also have unintended and aversive effects on others. For instance, Jane, who sits close by, may notice that Erick gets away with not doing his work and decides to do the same. One difference: Jane's academic disengagement is the end of her regulation episode. Another student, Tom, sees students not doing work seemingly wherever he looks and tattles to the teacher. Teacher response can shape each student's self- and other-regulatory efforts. Doodling attributed to defiance or underachievement can result in teacher criticism and punishment (Brophy & McCaslin, 2009), which students agree is one consequence of student willful misbehavior (Rohrkemper, 1984). As a result, Erick may learn that distraction is not an acceptable coping strategy to regulate and temporarily relieve stress; worse yet, he may learn that feeling stress due to difficult learning is a culpable offense. Not an unusual outcome: students can confuse "good learner" with "good person" (Blumenfeld, Pintrich, Meece, & Wessels, 1982). What about Erick's peers? Jane might figure out that Erick is not the one to identify with when the going gets tough, and Tom has been reinforced for behavior certain to create future interpersonal stress with peers.

Understanding stress and coping patterns in specific classroom situations can be empowering for the teacher, student, and whole class. For teachers, gaining predictability with respect to student behavior adds to their ability to perform classroom management tasks. Looking at students' stress and coping equips teachers with questions such as, "Do students experience stress when x occurs in my class?" "What can I expect from individual students when y occurs?" "What is the likely impact on the whole class when z happens?" Moreover, a healthy balance between control and support is likely to create a classroom environment that gives way for children to cope with individual challenges in different, adaptive ways. This, in turn, transforms the teacher role. Teacher do not have to spend the school day putting out fires; they can supervise the classroom while students do the regulation on their own. For the students, sharing problems at school with a trustworthy adult/child can relieve stress. Critical analysis of one's own stress can further lead to deeper self-awareness. Moreover, seeing how others evaluate and cope with stress in the classroom can be an important educational process for student learning and social development.

Future challenges for teachers and educational researchers include understanding how stress and coping shape the learning environment in order to create a classroom that is organized yet flexible for student growth and stress management.

Concluding Comments

Integrating SRL with stress and coping literatures offers the teacher three important considerations for classroom management in general. First, it focuses on student stress from different temporal orientations to deepen teachers' knowledge of the student experience in their classroom. This includes predicting events that might trigger stress in students, analyzing stressful events as they occur, and evaluating events that students may have already experienced. Second, it takes into consideration how individual students respond to stress in the classroom and the psychological consequences that can result when effective (or ineffective) strategies are used to manage those stressors. Third, it accentuates the effects of individual stress and coping on the learning environment from a whole-class perspective. An individual student's way of handling stress can quickly produce a domino effect on others in the classroom; as such, stress and coping are at the core of what makes an entire class feel organized versus disorganized, engaged versus disengaged, and cooperative versus uncooperative. From a perspective of stress and coping, effective classroom management needs a balance of controlled stress (for order, structure, and a sense of stability) and contained chaos (for growth, engagement, and coping development to occur). Multiple perspectives of student stress and coping strategies can help the teacher to better meet students' psychological and physical needs.

SHARED REGULATION IN SMALL GROUP LEARNING FORMATS

We now examine SRL dynamics in small-group learning contexts, in which the group differs from the sum of the students in it, and ask: How might peers regulate one another in this context? The literature we review shifts from *individual* regulation and coping behavior that can be demanded by and impact others to *shared* regulation, particularly in small learning groups.

Small groups have become increasingly integral to classroom learning contexts. Over 40 years' research has examined the many ways teachers can implement small groups in their instruction and highlights the positive learning and social outcomes that can result from students working together. Although inconsistencies in findings have presented across different approaches to group learning and different populations of students, generally the documented benefits of small group learning formats include increased student achievement outcomes, increased critical thinking and deeper levels of understanding, increased metacognition and self-regulation, and increased social skills compared with whole-class lecture or independent learning formats (Cohen, 1994; Johnson & Johnson, 1995; Lotan, 2006; Vauras, Iiskala, Kajamies, Kinnunen, & Lehtinen, 2003; Whitebread, Bingham, Grau, Pasternak, & Sangster, 2007).

Although different approaches to small-group learning vary in the degree to which the teacher structures and manages group activities, essentially all approaches require students to work together in some way to achieve shared learning goals. It is generally accepted that what makes small groups powerful learning activities are the potential interactions they promote among students that center on students' mutual support of each other's learning and the co-construction of knowledge.

Theories of SRL including the ways students cope and adapt with academic and social challenges explain the *individual* learner's processes of regulation. A major focus has been on the contextual/classroom factors that promote or hinder student acquisition and use of adaptive self-regulatory skills. In contrast, the socially shared regulation (SSRL) approach describes the regulation of cognition, motivation and emotion, and behavior that occurs at the group level. SSRL refers to group members' mutually shared monitoring, planning, and evaluation of their progress toward group goals. Studies that explore SSRL focus on group-level analyses of members' collaborative efforts in engaging in regulatory behaviors during the completion of academic tasks.

Although SRL and SSRL are often presented as separate processes in the literature, these processes likely co-occur during group activities (Vauras, Iiskala, Kajamies, Kinnunen, & Lehtinen, 2003; Hadwin, Järvelä, & Miller, 2011). In small-group learning formats, the individual student's goals exist (sometimes in competition) with the group's shared goals. These tensions present unique challenges in which students must align their personal regulatory behaviors with their individual academic and social goals, as well as aligning these goals with those of the group. One result is that classroom management of small groups includes academic and social issues at the individual student and group levels. When considering classroom management issues, teachers' effective fostering and support of students' simultaneous self- and shared regulation, as well as their successful management of academic and social challenges, is of particular importance.

In small learning groups, teachers delegate primary responsibilities of managing the group and providing academic and social support to students. Studies of small groups have demonstrated that it is simply not enough to place students into groups and expect this to happen spontaneously (Cohen, 1994, Summers & Volet, 2010). Students who themselves are learning to self-regulate cannot be expected to perform this *and* collaboratively share in the process of group regulation adaptively and successfully. For students, the potential benefits of peer collaboration also come with potential costs. Peer collaboration makes significant demands of students' cognitive, motivational, and social competencies (Vauras, Iiskala, Kajamies, Kinnunen, & Lehtinen, 2003). The teacher's primary task in the management of small groups, then, is to teach and support students in adaptive regulation and coping in small groups.

So how is this done? Despite the extensive work that has investigated SRL and small groups more generally, markedly fewer studies have investigated the teacher's role in fostering and supporting group shared regulation. Though explicit empirical connections have yet to be made between teacher classroom management intervention and students' shared regulation of learning in small groups, we assert that what makes groups work successfully on a holistic level also fosters high levels of shared regulation. Hadwin, Järvelä, and Miller (2011) also suggest that "successful groups share in regulating group processes much like individuals regulate motivation, cognition and emotion" (p. 76).

Research that focuses on student interactions in successful groups note that teachers play an important role in setting the stage for productive group work. Through careful planning of tasks and preparation of students *before* activities, teachers can foster and support productive student engagement, management, and peer support. Suggestions for how teachers may achieve this include (1) careful consideration of learning objectives and appropriate assessment of these objectives; (2) careful selection of appropriately challenging, ill structured tasks that require discussion; (3) avoiding group compositions that perpetuate academic and social hierarchies and undermine collaboration and equitable distribution of responsibility; (4) providing students guidance in engaging in productive discourse, specifically how to ask for and give help.

Defining Group Learning Objectives and Assessments

Learning objectives (whether social, academic, or both) of having students work in groups should be explicit and assessed in line with these objectives. Teachers often assign group work to have students collaborate with one another and, for some, to benefit from the help of more capable peers (students as instructors consistent with the ZPD construct). However, other functions of small groups include basic skills practice and efficient instructional time management. Consequently, not all group work will result in co-construction of knowledge among "equals," or in tutorial relationships, and not all activities necessitate or elicit shared regulation to complete the task.

Different assessment and reward structures elicit different student interactions during small-group activities (Cohen, 1994; Summers & Volet, 2010). Group work assessments based on a single product (final presentation or individual test performance) rather than the process of collaboration may undermine the particular strengths of a small-group learning format. This is particularly so when individual group members' goals conflict with the group's shared goals (Webb, 2008). Ambiguous assessment structures, like those that rely on the quality of a final product, cause students stress. Individual student attempts to be self-regulating, and their coping behaviors in response to assessment challenges may undermine the teacher's intentions and the benefits of small groups. They are also detrimental to shared regulation. Summers and Volet (2010) note that if the assessment does not specifically account for collaborative engagement, students sacrifice collaborative, co-constructive interactions for the sake of efficiency. Therefore, if the teacher's intentions are to have students engage in productive collaboration, then that collaboration process (not just the learning outcome) must be a component of the assessment of the group's work. In addition to assessing group process and progress, a second management strategy to prevent student SRL dominance over SSRL goals is to stress the importance of individual as well as group accountability to students prior to starting group activities.

Choosing a Group Task

Certain instructional intentions are met with certain task structures. Studies that examine the effects of different group task structures on student interactions have found that certain task structures work in the service of shared regulation and co-construction more effectively than others. Cohen (1994) outlines two general types of task: standard (or highly structured tasks) and ill structured tasks. Standard tasks mirror individual work with structured question response formats and single correct answers. These tasks are good for practicing material and skills. However, they also promote hierarchical helping structures. These structures often result in students working on separate parts of the task together. In addition, student talk and question asking during these types of tasks primarily revolve around procedural issues and basic academic information, not higher-level or conceptual-level thinking and engagement of the material, even if the tasks intended to target "concept development" (McCaslin & Vega, 2013).

Ill structured problems are open-ended, require complex problem solving and joint attention, and consist of multiple ways for students to engage in the important content matter. For these tasks, there is no single correct answer or approach to completing the task. These types of tasks allow for or require interactions in which group members must elaborate on their knowledge to explain or clarify their understanding and that of their group members. The processes of elaborating and explaining during small group learning have been associated with deeper learning and higher levels of shared regulation and co-construction of knowledge (Vauras, Iiskala, Kajamies, Kinnunen, & Lehtinen, 2003; Lotan, 2006; Arvaja, Salovaara, Häkkinen, & Järvelä, 2007). Consistent with the IP, volitional, and co-regulation approaches to SRL discussed previously, researchers in this tradition have found that creating group tasks with an optimal level of difficulty is crucial to providing students opportunities to acquire and practice adaptive cognitive, motivation, emotion, and behavior regulatory skills.

Group Composition

Often students are grouped by ability or gender or some other characteristic. But an important component of mutual appropriation and reciprocal interdependence is creating groups in which all students' contributions are essential, important, and validated. When left to their own devices, student reports of group structure types are primarily hierarchical based on (perceived) academic competencies of individual students (Lotan, 2006). Typically, the high-achieving student is identified and becomes the student with the responsibility of managing the group activities, providing academic support for the other members, and takes on the brunt of the responsibility of getting a good grade. This type of structure results in unequal participation and contributions to the group's goals. Potential long-term negative effects of sequential interdependence are a concern for lower-achieving students (relative to group members) who can acquire or increase in passivity and helpless behavior and for those students who actively take advantage of this type of group formation who can acquire or increase in cynicism and manipulative skill. Importantly, this type of group formation does not promote shared regulation or collaboration as intended; nonetheless, it is one way in which students learn to cope with academic expectations.

Listening for Co-Construction and Shared Regulation

An important task for the teacher during small-group activities is to listen for collaboration and shared regulation and to provide immediate and specific support and feedback to students about their mutual communication and support. The teacher also plays a vital role in validating and encouraging each student's contributions to the group, particularly those of low-status (academically or socially) students (Lotan, 2006).

Vaurus and colleagues (2003) state that a feature of successful collaboration and shared regulation is "open communication" among group members. In open communication, group members nondefensively communicate their differences in understandings and approaches and are receptive to other members' contributions. They also openly discuss their misunderstandings, ask for help, and sensitively provide help to their group mates.

In addition to open communication, Arvaja and associates (2007) found that the groups of students they identified as truly collaborative reasoned and negotiated meanings by making suggestions, by clarifying their own and others' contributions, by counterarguing, and by asking high-level (as opposed to procedural) questions. Also, Volet, Summers, and Thurman (2009) reported that high-level shared regulation was often initiated when group members asked higher-level questions and provided each other with explanatory statements or summaries. High-level shared regulation was sustained by further question asking for explanations of content knowledge, for tentative explanations, for individual group members' background knowledge about the material and by shared positive emotions. These features of truly collaborative SSRL groups parallel the conditions for meaningful learning identified by information processing and volitional approaches to individual SRL.

Volet and associates (2009) do expand on the potential fusion of affective/intellectual concerns of adaptive learning (in the Vygotskian tradition) in their discussion of how student assistance might be better received among group members. They draw parallels between students' *tentativeness* and their openness and nondefensiveness. They argue that tentativeness communicates a *possible* answer that allows for negotiation, questioning, and further suggestions that are important to the process of co-construction and collaboration.

> That is, it makes room for the speaker to become a listener/learner and for the other group members to take on the role of communicating their knowledge to others. (Volet, Summers, & Thurman, 2009, p. 139)

This is consistent with the dual expert-novice roles in the ZPD advocated by Yowell and Smylie (1988). Ongoing work with elementary students suggests that "tentative" might also be about displays of modesty among peers in small groups. More assertive knowledge display or help can invite angry face-saving responses from group members (McCaslin & Vega, 2013). Finally, Volet and colleagues (2009) found that positive emotions, particularly humor, led to sustained levels of high regulation in that they sustain attention to the topic and facilitate high-level questions, elaborations, and explanations.

SSRL in the pursuit of academic learning and personal well-being requires a safe environment, one in which misunderstandings, asking for help, differing opinions, negotiation, and assistance are part of the "process" of learning. Teachers' primary tasks during group activity are to listen to student interactions and assess their questions, elaborations, and suggestions, as well as encouraging them to be kind and supportive. Teacher intervention can include modeling of and direct instruction in how to ask high-level questions, engage in attentive listening, and use tentative rather than imperative talk to pose suggestions, solutions, and elaboration. During group activities, teachers can encourage positive social interactions among students. Research on student coping behavior and temporal considerations in teacher co-regulation of these skills can inform how teachers might address both the academic and social stressors inherent in small-group learning. SSRL requires that students adaptively regulate academic and interpersonal stressors in productive ways that promote positive interactions and the meaningful learning of the intended content. There is much to be explored within the construct of SSRL, and teachers are a key component to furthering our understanding of its potential.

CONCLUDING COMMENTS

Research on the importance of the teacher–student relationship in students' academic achievement (particularly for students who attend low-income schools) continues to build even as teacher role behavior with students is increasingly mediated by external accountability pressures. The resulting tension invites our attention to how teachers and students, as individuals and as a group, confront learning objectives, tasks, and the cultural demands set for them. Each contributes to and can deliberately co-regulate—challenge, shape, and guide—students' SRL, coping behavior, SSRL, academic learning, and emotional well-being. There is much to learn.

REFERENCES

Anderson, G. A., & Jimerson, S. R. (2007). Stressful life experiences of children: The correspondence between professional judgments of teachers-in-training and children's perceptions. *Psychology in the Schools, 44,* 8, 807–821.

Arvaja, M., Salovaara, H., Häkkinen, P., & Järvelä, S. (2007). Combining individual and group-level perspectives for studying collaborative knowledge construction in context. *Learning and Instruction, 17,* 448–459.

Bagdi, A., & Pfister, I. K. (2006). Childhood stressors and coping actions: A comparison of children and parents' perspectives. *Child & Youth Care Forum, 35,* 21–40.

Band, E., & Weisz, J. (1988). How to feel better when it feels bad: Children's perspectives on coping with everyday stress. *Developmental Psychology, 24,* 247–253.

Bandura, A. (1977). Self-efficacy: Toward a unifying theory of behavioral change. *Psychological Review, 84*(2), 191–215.

Bandura, A. (1997). *Self-efficacy: The exercise of control*. San Francisco: W. H. Freeman.

Barrett, S., & Heubeck, B. G. (2000). Relationships between school hassles and uplifts and anxiety and conduct problems in grades 3 and 4. *Journal of Applied Developmental Psychology, 21*(5), 537–554.

Bennett, N., & Dunne, E. (1992). *Managing classroom groups*. London: Simon & Schuster.

Blumenfeld, P. C., Pintrich, P. R., Meece, J., & Wessels, K. (1982). The formation and role of self perceptions of ability in elementary classrooms. *The Elementary School Journal, 82* (5), 410–420.

Brophy, J., & McCaslin, M. (1992). Teachers' reports of how they perceive and cope with problem students. *Elementary School Journal, 93*, 3–68.

Cohen, E. G. (1994). Restructuring the classroom: Conditions for productive small groups. *Review of Educational Research, 64*(1), 1–35.

Compas, B. E., Connor-Smith, J. K., Saltzman, H., Thomsen, A. H., & Wadsworth, M. E. (2001). Coping with stress during childhood and adolescence: Problems, progress, and potential in theory and research. *Psychological Bulletin, 127*(1), 87–127.

Corno, L. (1996). Homework is a complicated thing. *Educational Researcher, 25*(8), 27–30.

Corno, L. (2011). Studying self-regulation habits. In B. J. Zimmerman & D. H. Schunk (Eds.), *Handbook of self-regulation of learning and performance* (pp. 361–375). New York: Routledge.

Corno, L., & Mandinach, E. (1983). The role of cognitive engagement in classroom learning and motivation. *Educational Psychologist, 18*, 88–100.

Deci, E. L., & Ryan, R. M. (1985). *Intrinsic motivation and self-determination in human behavior*. New York: Plenum.

Eisenberg, N., Guthrie, I. K., Fabes, R. A., Reiser, M., Murphy, B. C., Holmgren, R., et al. (1997). The relations of regulation of emotionality to resiliency and competent social functioning in elementary school children. *Child Development, 68*, 295–311.

Emmer, E. T., & Stough, L. M. (2001). Classroom management: A critical part of educational psychology, with implications for teacher education. *Educational Psychologist, 36*(2), 103–112.

Erikson, E. (1968). *Identity: Youth and crisis*. New York: Norton.

Flavell, J. H. (1979). Metacognition and cognitive monitoring: A new area of cognitive–developmental inquiry. *American Psychologist, 34*(10), 906–911.

Hadwin, A. F., Järvelä, S., & Miller, M. (2011). Self-regulated, co-regulated, and socially shared regulation of learning. In B. J. Zimmerman & D. H. Schunk, (Eds.), *Handbook of self-regulation of learning and performance* (pp. 65–83). New York: Routledge.

Humphrey, J. H. (2004). *Childhood stress in contemporary society*. Binghamton, NY: Haworth.

Johnson, D. W., & Johnson, R. T. (1995). Positive interdependence: Key to effective cooperation. In R. Hertz-Lazarowitz & N. Miller (Eds.), *Interaction in cooperative groups: The theoretical anatomy of group learning* (pp. 174–199). New York: Cambridge University Press.

Lazarus, R. S., & Folkman, S. (1984). *Stress, appraisal, and coping*. New York: Springer.

Lotan, R. A. (2006). Managing group work. In C. Evertson & C. Weinstein (Eds.), *Handbook of classroom management: Research, practice, and contemporary issues* (pp. 525–539). Mahwah, NJ: Erlbaum.

Mace, F. C., Belfiore, P. J., & Hutchinson, J. M. (2001). Operant theory and research on self-regulation. In B. J. Zimmerman & D. H. Schunk (Eds.), *Self-regulated learning and academic achievement* (2nd ed.) (pp. 39–65). Mahwah, NJ: Erlbaum.

McAdams, D. P. (1993). *The stories we live by: Personal myths and the making of the self*. New York: Guilford.

McCaslin, M. (2004). Co-regulation of opportunity, activity, and identity in student motivation. In D. McInerney & S. Van Etten (Eds.), *Big theories revisited*, Vol. 4 (pp. 249–274). Greenwich, CT: Information Age.

McCaslin, M. (2009). Co-regulation of student motivation and emergent identity. *Educational Psychologist, 44*(2), 137–146.

McCaslin, M., Bozack, A. R., Napoleon, L., Thomas, A., Vasquez, V., Wayman, V., & Zhang, J. (2006). Self-regulated learning and classroom management: Theory, research, and considerations for classroom practice. In C. Evertson & C. Weinstein (Eds.), *Handbook of classroom management: Research, practice and contemporary issues* (pp. 223–252). Mahwah, NJ: Erlbaum.

McCaslin, M., & Good, T. L. (1996). The informal curriculum. In D. Berliner & R. Calfee (Eds.), *Handbook of educational psychology* (pp. 622–673). New York: Macmillan.

McCaslin, M., & Murdock, T. B. (1991). The emergent interaction of home and school in the development of students' adaptive learning. In M. Maehr & P. Pintrich (Eds.), *Advances in motivation and achievement*, Vol. 7 (pp. 213–259). Greenwich, CT: JAI Press.

McCaslin, M. & Vega, R. I. (2013). Peer co-regulation of learning, emotion, and coping strategies in small-group learning. In S. Phillipson, K. Y. L. Ku, & S. N. Phillipson (Eds.), *Constructing educational achievement: A sociocultural perspective* (pp. 118–135). London/New York: Routledge.

McCombs, B. L. (2001). Self-regulated learning and academic achievement: A phenomenological view. In B. J. Zimmerman and D. H. Schunk (Eds.), *Self-regulated learning and academic achievement: Theoretical perspectives* (2nd ed.) (pp. 67–123). Mahwah, NJ: Erlbaum.

Paris, S. G., Byrnes, J. P., & Paris, A. H. (2001). Constructing theories, identities, and actions of self-regulated learners. In D. H. Schunk & B. J. Zimmerman (Eds.), *Self-regulated learning and academic achievement: Theoretical perspectives* (2nd ed.) (pp. 253–287). Mahwah, NJ: Erlbaum.

Perry, N. E. (1998). Young children's self-regulated learning and contexts that support it. *Journal of Educational Psychology, 90*, 715–729.

Piaget, J. (1983). Piaget's theory. In W. Kessen (Ed.), *Handbook of child psychology: History, theory, and methods* (pp. 103–128). New York: Wiley.

Rohrkemper, M. (1984). The influence of teacher socialization style on students' social cognition and reported interpersonal classroom behavior. *Elementary School Journal. 85*(2), 244–275.

Rohrkemper, M. (1989). Self-regulated learning and academic achievement: A Vygotskian view. In B. J. Zimmerman & D. H. Schunk (Eds.), *Self-regulated learning and academic achievement: Theory, research, and practice* (pp. 143–167). New York: Springer.

Rohrkemper, M., & Corno, L. (1988). Success and failure on classroom tasks: Adaptive learning and classroom teaching. *Elementary School Journal, 88*(3), 296–312.

Rotter, J. (1954). *Social learning and clinical psychology.* Englewood Cliffs, NJ: Prentice-Hall.

Rutter, M. (2013). Annual research review: Resilience—clinical implications. *Journal of Child Psychology and Psychiatry, 54*(4), 474–487.

Ryan-Wenger, N. M., Sharrer, V. W., & Campbell, K. K. (2005). Changes in children's stressors over the past thirty years. *Pediatric Nursing, 31*(4), 282–291.

Simon, H. (1981). *Sciences of the artificial* (2nd ed.). Cambridge, MA: MIT Press. (Original work published 1969)

Skinner, B. F. (1976). *About behaviorism.* New York: Random House.

Skinner, E. A., Edge, K., Altman, J., & Sherwood, H. (2003). Searching for the structure of coping: A review and critique of category systems for classifying ways of coping. *Psychological Bulletin, 129*(2), 216–269.

Skinner, E. A., & Zimmer-Gembeck, M. J. (2007). The development of coping. *Annual Review of Psychology, 58*, 119–144.

Sotardi, V. A. (2013). On everyday stress and coping strategies among elementary school children. Unpublished doctoral dissertation, Tucson, University of Arizona.

Summers, M., & Volet, S. (2010). Group work does not necessarily equal collaborative learning: evidence from observation and self-reports. *European Journal of Psychology of Education, 25*(4), 473–492.

Vauras, M., Iiskala, T., Kajamies, A., Kinnuen, R., & Lehtinen, E. (2003). Shared-regulation and motivation of collaborating peers: A case analysis. *Psychologia, 46*, 19–37.

Volet, S., Summers, M., & Thurman, J. (2009). High-level co-regulation in collaborative learning: How does it emerge and how is it sustained? *Learning and Instruction, 19*, 128–143.

Vygotsky, L. S. (1962). *Thought and language.* Cambridge, MA: MIT Press.

Vygotsky, L. S. (1978). *Mind in society: The development of higher psychological processes.* Cambridge, MA: Harvard University Press.

Webb, N. M. (2008). Learning in small groups. In T. L. Good (Ed.), *21st century education: A reference handbook*, Vol. 1 (pp. 203–211). Thousand Oaks, CA: Sage.

Wertsch, J. (Ed.). (1985). *Culture, communication, and cognition: Vygotskian perspectives.* New York: Cambridge.

Whitebread, D., Bingham, S., Grau, V., Pasternak, D. P., & Sangster, C. (2007). Development of metacognition and self-regulated learning in young children: Role of collaborative and peer-assisted learning. *Journal of Cognitive and Educational Psychology, 6*(3), 433–455.

Winne, P. H. (2001). Self-regulated learning viewed from models of information processing. In B. J. Zimmerman & D. H. Schunk (Eds.), *Self-regulated learning and academic achievement: Theoretical perspectives* (pp. 153–189). Mahwah, NJ: Erlbaum.

Yowell, C., & Smylie, M. (1999). Self-regulation in democratic communities. *Elementary School Journal, 99*, 469–490.

Zimmer-Gembeck, M. J., & Skinner, E. A. (2011). Review: The development of coping across childhood and adolescence: An integrative review and critique of research. *International Journal of Behavioral Development, 35*, 1–17.

Zimmerman, B. J. (2013). From cognitive modeling to self-regulation: A social cognitive career path. *Educational Psychologist, 48*(3), 135–147.

18

STUDENT PERCEPTIONS OF MISBEHAVIOR AND CLASSROOM MANAGEMENT

PAUL MONTUORO AND RAMON LEWIS
LA TROBE UNIVERSITY, VICTORIA, AUSTRALIA

INTRODUCTION

In the first edition of the *Handbook of Classroom Management*, Woolfolk Hoy and Weinstein (2006) investigated the extant literature on student and teacher perspectives of classroom management. The researchers reviewed a range of studies pertaining to two subcategories of student perceptions: perceptions of the "good teacher" and perceptions of disciplinary interventions. The former review reported students' active role in the teacher–student relationship and some fundamental expectations that students have of their teachers when it comes to being a "good teacher." For example, Woolfolk Hoy and Weinstein reported that students make considered behavioral choices that are frequently based on their liking of the teacher and in response to the teacher's own (mis)behavior. The review also reported that almost all students want teachers who care about their academic, personal, and social well-being. In fact, Woolfolk Hoy and Weinstein summarized the overwhelming body of literature in this area by simply remarking that "[g]ood teachers care" (p. 206). Furthermore, the review noted that most students perceive good teachers to be those who provide clear behavior expectations and a safe learning environment. Most students also disliked teacher meanness and threatening or aggressive behavioral directives. Finally, the review showed that students desire a fun, interactive, and participatory curriculum, as opposed to the "chalk and talk" pedagogy that is synonymous with textbooks and rote learning. These results were seen to highlight "the inseparable relationship between classroom management and instruction" (Woolfolk Hoy & Weinstein, 2006, p. 210).

The second part of Woolfolk Hoy and Weinstein's review, which examined students' "perceptions of disciplinary interventions," reported that many students have a strong moral aversion to coercive discipline, which they also claimed has no effect on their self-reported misbehavior. For example, in their review of an early study conducted by Pestello (1989), Woolfolk Hoy and Weinstein remarked that, "student perceptions of the severity, certainty, and swiftness of sanctions contributed almost nothing to the variance explained in classroom behavior" (p. 189). The review also demonstrated that many students perceive the most unacceptable interventions to be public reprimands that are shaming or personally insulting, as well as group consequences for individual misbehavior. Woolfolk Hoy and Weinstein summarized this large body of literature by remarking:

> It seems clear that teachers should avoid "public diagnosing" and "third-degree grilling," as well as other coercive, extrinsic strategies, and instead maximize the use of strategies that foster autonomy and self-regulation. In other words, teachers need to recognize that socializing students to become self-regulating is an integral part of their job. (p. 210)

Finally, Woolfolk Hoy and Weinstein reviewed a wide range of studies that reported substantial differences in student perceptions of teachers' disciplinary actions related to socioeconomic status (i.e., low- and high-income families) and racial background (i.e., African American, Asian, Latino, and white).

Our discussion of student perceptions builds on Woolfolk Hoy and Weinstein's review of the relatively new area of research examining student perceptions of classroom management, although our review also addresses student perceptions of misbehavior. Specifically, we examine studies from around the world that have been conducted since 2006, when the first edition of the *Handbook of Classroom Management* was published. Our discussion of student perceptions is organized in three parts. The first part "Research on Student Perceptions," reviews the small body of emerging literature on student perceptions of a range of schooling matters. The second part, "Student Perceptions of Misbehavior," focuses on student perceptions of what constitutes misbehavior and students' reported reasons for misbehaving. The third part, "Student Perceptions of Classroom Management," considers student perceptions of effective and ineffective classroom management techniques, as well as student perceptions of aggressive teacher responding to perceived student misbehavior.

The chapter views the literature on student perceptions through the prism of teachers' social power. The theory of social power refers to an individual's (the *influencing agent's*) *potential* to change another person's cognition, attitude, and behavior (French & Raven, 1959; Raven, 1965, 2008). The theory identifies six *bases of power*: *informational* (information- and persuasion-based influence), *reward* (positive incentive-based influence), *coercive* (negative incentive-based influence), *legitimate* (position-based influence), *expert* (knowledge-based influence), and *referent* (respect-based influence) (Raven, 2008). We will consider what the literature on student perceptions reveals about teachers as influencing agents and, further, which bases of power teachers should use to encourage social influence in the classroom.

It is important to note that this chapter repeatedly refers to the word "perception." Schunk and Meece (1992) provided a useful, rudimentary definition of student perception in their book, *Student Perceptions in the Classroom*, as "thoughts, beliefs, and feelings about persons, situations, and events" (p. xi). Therefore, in the present chapter, the word "perception" does not refer to the organization, identification, and interpretation of sensory information—the so-called foundation of cognition—(e.g., Goldstone, Medin, & Schyns, 1997) but rather to students' personal viewpoints of classroom management and misbehavior.

RESEARCH ON STUDENT PERCEPTIONS

Research examining student perceptions is a relatively new area of inquiry (Mac-Beath, 2006; Spilt, Koomen, & Mantzicopoulos, 2010; Woolfolk Hoy & Weinstein, 2006), particularly in classroom management (Riley & Docking, 2004; Sargeant, 2012). Nevertheless, research examining student perceptions continues to emerge and was recently described as an "excellent source of information about what occurs in class and why it happens" (Cothran & Kulinna, 2007, p. 222). For example, recent studies examining student perceptions have been conducted in areas such as discipline (Shirley & Cornell, 2012), bullying (Paul, Smith, & Blumberg, 2012), teacher–student relationship quality and school adjustment (Harrison, Clarke, & Ungerer, 2007), perceived safety (Cowie & Oztug, 2008), and art pedagogy (Burnard & Swann, 2010). Studies comparing teacher and student perceptions have reported little concordance between the two groups, with teachers frequently providing more positive perceptions of the classroom environment (Fraser, 2007; Rickards & Fisher, 2000). For example, Murray, Murray, and Waas (2008) reported a significant disconnection between teacher and student reports of the teacher–student relationship (i.e., teacher support, students' school liking, and students' school avoidance).

Furthermore, in an ethnographic study, Leitch and Mitchell (2007) demonstrated the discordance that exists between principals and students on matters such as student voice and how students are valued in schools. The study was conducted in five postprimary (aged 11–18 years) schools in Northern Ireland and included interviews with the five principals and 60 students from either year 9 (aged 12–13 years) or year 11 (aged 14–15 years). In one school (Vignette 1: School A), for example, the principal espoused a person-centered approach and remarked, "I don't think I could ever lead a school where child-centredness wasn't the ethos . . . [W]e try to fit the curriculum *around* the child rather than fitting the child *into* the curriculum" (p. 59). The students who were interviewed, however, saw things differently. The year 9 students saw performance and achievement as the main expectations of the school, and the year 11 students saw the school's reputation to be the top priority. One year-9 student, Marie, expressed a starkly different response from that of her principal. Marie said that the school was "like a factory" and imagined the principal presiding in "a big room of his own" (p. 60).

The student perspective reported in Leitch and Mitchell's study concurs with Francis and Mills' (2012) perspective that authoritarianism and oppressive hierarchies continue to dominate many school structures. Such variances in perception highlight the importance of research on student perceptions and research comparing teacher and student perceptions. This type of research is particularly important considering that student perceptions often concur with those of independent observers (e.g., De Jong & Westerhof, 2001; Ellis, Malloy, Meece, & Sylvester, 2007). The next section of this chapter reviews the latest research investigating student perceptions of misbehavior.

STUDENT PERCEPTIONS OF MISBEHAVIOR

A Difference of Opinion

Few recent studies have examined student perceptions of the act of misbehaving (see Hook & Rosenshine, 1979, for an exception). Nevertheless, the studies that have been conducted suggest that many students (particularly adolescents) have an inherently different perspective of misbehavior compared to their teachers (Roache & Lewis, 2011). For example, Cohen and Romi (2010) recently conducted a large questionnaire-based study that included 895 respondents in the central region of Israel. The participants included 376 teachers, 209 preservice teachers, and 310 students. The researchers examined participants' perceptions of the severity of student misbehaviors, which included relatively benign forms of misbehavior such as minor disruptions, and more serious forms of misbehavior, such as threats, vandalism, and criminal acts. The researchers reported that the students in the study perceived all forms of misbehavior as being low severity compared to the teachers' and preservice teachers' perceptions, who attributed far higher ratings of severity to all of the forms of student misbehavior.

Such apparently reckless adolescent perceptions are not unusual (e.g., Evans, Gilpin, Farkas, Shenassa, & Pierce, 1995; Quinn, Bell-Ellison, Loomis, & Tucci, 2007) and probably reflect neural changes in the brain that block the ability to think and reason logically according to the consequences (Dahl, 2004; Powell, 2006). Indeed, "adolescents appear to be prone to erratic—and . . . *emotionally influenced*—behavior, which can lead to periodic disregard for risks and consequences" (Dahl, 2004, p. 3). For example, secondary school students have been reported to perceive all forms of misbehavior, including threats, vandalism, and criminal acts, as relatively benign (Cohen & Romi, 2010).

Furthermore, adolescence has been associated with the onset of emotional and behavioral problems (Steinberg, 2005). In fact, compared to children and adults, adolescents display higher levels of troublesome behavior, including aggressive and nonaggressive conduct problems (Lahey & Waldman, 2003), and experience greater conflict with parents (Spear, 2000; Steinberg & Sheffield Morris, 2001). The link between adolescent brain development and abrupt changes in behavior was theorized as early as the 1970s (Epstein, 1974), and, in more recent times, empirical support for this theory has been reported (see Spear, 2000). For example, the adolescent brain undergoes widespread changes, including significant changes in the ratio of white-to-gray matter (Steinberg, 2005), the loss of synapses in neocortical brain regions at an approximate rate of 30,000 synapses per second over the entire cortex, and the overall remodeling of the prefrontal cortex and limbic brain regions (Spear, 2000). Indeed, "there is considerable evidence that the second decade of life is a period of great activity with respect to changes in brain structure and function, especially in regions and systems associated with response inhibition . . . and emotional regulation" (Steinberg, 2005, p. 69).

This research reveals that teachers and their students (particularly adolescent students) probably have a very different worldview. For some teachers at least, students' relatively irresponsible view of misbehavior may point to the need for *coercive power* in the classroom. On the other hand, however, the *neural divide* between teachers and their students may indicate the need for a stronger reliance on relationship-based approaches to classroom management, including *referent* and *informational power*. Indeed, student reports suggest that teacher coercion has no effect on student misbehavior (Woolfolk Hoy & Weinstein, 2006). For example, Way's (2011) research yielded "no evidence to suggest that tougher school discipline policies and practices deter student misbehavior" (p. 363).

Perceived Reasons for Misbehaving

Cothran and Kulinna (2007) conducted a large quantitative study in the United States of 2309 middle and high school students from 18 schools in the Midwestern states. The main aim of this study was to examine student perceptions of the underlying reasons for student misbehavior in physical education classes. The students reported that misbehavior primarily occurred because *the lesson was boring, the student wanted attention*, or *the student didn't believe that he or she could do the lesson and so didn't try*. More recently, Cothran, Kulinna, and Garrahy (2009) conducted a similar, albeit descriptive, study of 182 secondary school students in a variety of school districts in the United States. Once again, the participants in the study believed that *seeking attention* (both from other students and the teacher) and *boredom* were the main reasons for their classmates' misbehavior.

The results reported by Cothran and colleagues are not unusual. For example, Sargeant (2012) conducted a qualitative study of 1311 primary and secondary school students from Australia, England, and New Zealand, noting that some of the most frequently expressed reasons for student misbehavior were a *disconnect in the teacher–student relationship, a negative attitude towards school*, and *boredom*. These studies suggest that students are in search of *referent power* from their teachers—an *authentic* relationship with their older and wiser teachers. Indeed, "*Referent Power* stems from the target identifying with the agent, or seeing the agent as a model that the target would want to emulate" (Raven, 2008, p. 3).

A small handful of studies have also demonstrated the direct association between younger students' (i.e., kindergarten to the sixth grade) perceptions of the teacher–student relationship and misbehavior (Decker, Dona, & Christenson, 2007; Henricsson & Rydell, 2004). For example, Spilt and associates (2010) investigated the association between kindergarteners' perceptions of the teacher–student relationship and teacher-reported kindergartner misbehavior. The study sampled 150 young children from six regular primary schools in the Netherlands. The children provided their perceptions of the teacher–child relationship, and their teachers provided their perceptions of their young students' misbehavior. Spilt and colleagues reported that when boys experienced nonclose or distant relationships with their teachers, they displayed aggressive behavior. On the other hand, when girls experienced nonclose or distant relationships with their teachers, they became socially inhibited. These results were consistent with the gender-stereotypic behaviors of young children who had insecure attachments to their caregivers (Turner, 1991). Beyond this, however, Spilt and colleagues noted that teachers must consider misbehavior from the broader context of the teacher–kindergartner relationship. Indeed:

> It is important to recognize the possibility that children's maladaptive behaviors are manifestations of insecurity and the undermining feeling that they are not being valued . . . Teachers need to be mindful of children's need for belongingness that involves being cared about, value, and recognized as individuals. (p. 436)

In other words, Spilt and colleagues encouraged teachers to consider the relational value of *referent power* above authoritarian, surveillance-based *coercive power*. This suggestion is supported by research showing that behaviorally at-risk African American students from kindergarten to the sixth grade expressed a desire to be closer to their teachers (Decker, Dona, & Christenson, 2007). It is also supported by research reporting that warm and sensitive teachers have a positive effect on the social interactions of behaviorally at-risk preschoolers (Hamre, Pianta, Downer, & Mashburn, 2008), kindergartners (Ladd & Burgess, 2001; Rimm-Kaufman et al., 2002), students in the early years of elementary school (Hamre & Pianta, 2005; Hughes, Cavell, & Jackson, 1999; Silver, Measelle, Armstrong, & Essex, 2005), and students in the later years of elementary school (Luckner & Pianta, 2011; Stipek & Miles, 2008). These studies concur with Woolfolk Hoy and Weinstein's (2006) review, which reported that students perceived good teachers to be caring and compassionate.

Unfortunately, a recent small-scale qualitative study (Newberry & Davis, 2008) demonstrated that at-risk students are the very individuals who receive the least emotional support from their teachers. Newberry and Davis summarized why the teachers in the study distanced themselves from problematic students, remarking that "teachers appeared to operate on a very economic view of relationships—such that the amount of work they put into the relationships was dependent on the perceived likelihood of getting something in return" (p. 1983). Stated slightly differently, the students who need *referent power* the most are the students who appear to receive it the least.

The deeper reasons behind student misbehavior were also investigated by Ray, Reddy, and Rhodes (2007) in a longitudinal study that included 1451 early adolescents (middle school grades 6 through 8) from 22 Midwestern schools. The researchers reported that between the beginning and the end of middle school, student perceptions of school social climate (i.e., teacher support, peer support, student autonomy, and clarity and consistency in school rules) markedly declined. Furthermore, these declines were found to be directly associated with declines in behavioral adjustment. A similar study was also conducted by Espinoza and Juvonen (2011), focusing on the transition to middle school of a sample of 383 white and Latino students in Los Angeles. The researchers also reported that student perceptions of school social climate declined in the transition to middle school. Furthermore, the decline correlated with an increase in misbehavior only for Latino students, reinforcing previous research showing that Latino students have a heightened sensitivity to the school social climate as it relates to their self-reported misbehavior (Goodenow & Grady, 1993; Han, 2008; Slaughter-Defoe & Carlson, 1996).

Not only has student perception of school climate been identified as a causal factor in student misbehavior, but, more specifically, so has classroom discipline. Way (2011), for example, reviewed data from 10,992 students from 1132 schools in the representative National Education Longitudinal Study of 1988 (NELS:88).Way reported a positive correlation between student perceptions of restrictive school disciplinary practice and teacher reports of student misbehavior. In discussing these findings, Way remarked:

> Understanding student perception of discipline and authority is fundamental to understanding how discipline influences student behavior. In US secondary schools, the effectiveness of discipline appears to be at least partially tied to whether students view school discipline and teacher authority as fair and legitimate. By focusing on the installation of metal detectors, security guards, tougher rules, and harsher punishment, efforts to mitigate school violence may overlook the role student perceptions have for success or failure of school policy. (Way, 2011, p. 365)

These findings may be symptomatic of the large student–teacher ratios that are characteristic of mainstream education. Indeed, it has been argued that such imbalances can necessitate bureaucratized and regimented control practices, which cause students to feel dissatisfied with and resistant toward schooling (Francis & Mills, 2012; Harber, 2004). Once again, the recent literature on student perceptions of misbehavior suggests that teachers need to increase their use of *referent power* and *informational power*, particularly with students who experience emotional and behavioral difficulties: *referent power* to form closer teacher–student relationships and *informational power* to foster teacher–student communication. Such an approach would not be unlike the person-centered approach (see McCombs & Whisler, 1997; Rogers, 1969, 1983; Rogers & Freiberg, 1994), which Rogers and Freiberg described as:

> A set of values, not easy to achieve, that places emphasis on the dignity of the individual, the importance of personal choice, the significance of responsibility, the joy of creativity. It is a philosophy, built on a foundation of the democratic way, that empowers each individual. (1994, p. 123)

Rogers noted that the person-centered approach occurs when the teacher "comes into a direct personal encounter with the learner, meeting him on a person-to-person basis. It means that he is *being* himself, not denying himself" (1969, p. 106). The merits of the person-centered approach to education were recently highlighted by Cornelius-White's (2007) meta-analysis of 119 studies that examined the classical and person-centered learning models of education. Cornelius-White reported that the person-centered approach was associated with an above average association with positive student outcomes compared with other educational innovations for cognitive, affective, and behavioral outcomes. It is important to note that, in slight contrast to Rogers' person-centered approach, teachers may sometimes use punishment effectively (*coercive power*). For example, acts of student responsibility may increase when teachers use nonaggressive punishments (consequences) *within* the context of a well established teacher–student relationship (*referent power* and *informational power*), and when punishments are devised in consultation with students (Balson, 1992; Dreikurs & Cassel, 1990; Gregory & Ripski, 2008; Lewis, 2001; Roache & Lewis, 2011). Although these kinds of "consultative punishments" may only result in students *acting* responsibly as opposed to *being* responsible,[1] they ensure the safety and learning rights of others and may be reduced when students begin to develop a moral ethic of responsibility.

When Bad Is Good

Recent studies have demonstrated that students are more likely to misbehave when they perceive misbehavior to be socially acceptable (Way, 2011) or normative (Espinoza & Juvonen, 2011; Kuppens, Grietens, Onghena, Michiels, & Subramanian, 2008; Werner & Hill, 2010). However, students don't misbehave for these reasons alone. For example, students report that two of the positive consequences of misbehaving include an increase in social status (Cothran, Kulinna, & Garrahy, 2009) and better peer relationships (Fanti, Brookmeyer, Henrich, & Kuperminc, 2009). These findings are supported by recent research showing that students who misbehave dominate peer-based decision-making (Hoff, Reese-Weber, Joel Schneider, & Stagg, 2009; Woods, 2009) and are also perceived to be cool (Bellmore, Villarreal, & Ho, 2011; Hoff, Reese-Weber, Joel Schneider, & Stagg, 2009; Rodkin, Farmer, Pearl, & Acker, 2006).

For example, Becker and Luthar (2007) recruited 636 seventh-graders attending middle schools in the Northeast United States. The sample included affluent suburban and low-income urban students, who completed a questionnaire that measured their positive regard for peers, and two self-report questionnaires that measured delinquency and substance use. Regardless of their socioeconomic position, adolescents who admitted to misbehaving received ratings from their peers of high *perceived popularity* but low *sociometric popularity*. These results indicate that *popularity* does not necessarily equate to *likability*. For example, perceived popularity refers to popularity as a function of social dominance, intimidation, and self-assurance (Weisfeld, Bloch, & Ivers, 1983, 1984); students who rated highly on perceived popularity were popular inasmuch as they were socially visible, not because they were liked by their peers. On the other hand, sociometric popularity refers to popularity as a function of genuineness and kindness to others (Newcomb, Bukowski, & Pattee, 1993); students who rated highly on sociometric popularity were popular because they displayed the interpersonal skills of close friendship and because they were liked by their peers. Therefore, students who "behave bad just to get attention" or because "they wanna get popularity" (Cothran, Kulinna, & Garrahy, 2009, p. 161) are probably only developing the *interpersonally damaging* form of perceived popularity.

Furthermore, Owens & Duncan (2009) used a stimulus vignette and semi-structured focus group interviews to investigate teenage girls' (aged 14–16 years) perceptions of popularity. The small-scale study included 40 participants from diverse socioeconomic backgrounds in Adelaide, South Australia. The participants reported that, among other things, popular girls used a range of maladaptive behaviors to achieve and maintain perceived popularity, not sociometric popularity. This is exemplified in the disdainful comments made by two of the participants:

Student 1: "They think they can get away with doing anything, like, making fun of other people."

Interviewer: "What are they like in class?"

Student 2: "They think they can just yell out and make comments whenever they feel like it and then someone else who is not as popular will say something and they'll tell them to shut up." (p. 25)

Students in Owens and Duncan's study also exemplified the kind of *respect based on fear* commanded by students with perceived popularity, a kind of antithetical popularity that may be more accurately described as "negative awareness":

Interviewer: "What does popularity mean to you?"

Student 1: "Having power."

Interviewer: "What does that actually mean? Tease out having power."

Student 1: "People are scared of you. You over-rule people."

Student 4: "Their confidence. They don't care what they do—their confidence."

Student 3: "If they get into a fight with someone, everyone agrees with them."

Student 4: "And they'll go on their side."

Student 2: "It's like they're afraid to go on the other person's side."

Student 1: "There is a powerful popular and there's a nice popular. Some people are popular just because some people are scared of them." (p. 26)

These excerpts are supported by larger, quantitative studies reporting that, among elementary school students, relational aggression is associated with perceived popularity but also by peer rejection (Kuppens, Grietens, Onghena, Michiels, & Subramanian, 2008). The direction of this association, however, remains unclear. For example, Sandstrom and Cillessen (2006) conducted a longitudinal study of 466 fifth-graders in the Northeast United States. The participants completed a peer nomination survey investigating perceived popularity and sociometric popularity at the end of the fifth grade. Participant misbehaviors were then assessed through a composite peer-, teacher-, and self-report instrument at the end of the eighth grade. The researchers reported that participants who were perceivably popular in the fifth grade were more likely to show overt aggression, relational aggression, or teacher-reported disruptive behaviors in the eighth grade. Sandstrom and Cillessen surmised that perceivably popular students abuse their power by using overt aggression, relational aggression, and disruptive behaviors, or, alternatively, that these students achieve perceived popularity *through* these behaviors.

The latter hypothesis is supported in Woods' (2009) case study of three boys in the fourth and fifth grades at a primary school in West London. Woods collected sociometric, ethnographic, and interview data on the students with the aim of investigating whether status formation contributes to the association between popularity and aggression. One student in particular who was unpopular and largely rejected by his peers, Pavandeep, reported being reluctant to use aggression in response to his aggressive peers. Nevertheless, Pavandeep's nonaggressive peers described him as aggressive. Furthermore, when asked a hypothetical question about how he would respond to a disliked student interloping in a playground game, Pavandeep reported: "Miss first I say no you can't play, but when they start like bothering me, I just start, they start fighting with me, I start fighting back and then we start swearing at each other" (p. 229). Woods concluded that although Pavandeep probably did not see aggression as a legitimate basis for decision-making, he learned to use it as an effective social currency and was therefore "defined and limited by it" (p. 234). Consequently, students like Pavandeep who are socially visible because of their aggressive interactions may, in fact, be rejected and disliked by their peers. Indeed, social dominance, intimidation, and self-assuredness—the hallmarks of perceived popularity—should serve as warning flags to teachers "who may have assumed that popularity implies only positive social adjustment" (Sandstrom & Cillessen, 2006, p. 313).

For teachers, the research investigating the association between perceived popularity and student misbehavior may appear to be quite disconcerting because it suggests that student misbehavior is, at least partly, a function of the child/adolescent's social milieu, a social realm from which teachers are disconnected. On the other hand, however, these results could be interpreted as evidence that teachers need to form closer, person-centered relationships with their students (see McCombs & Whisler, 1997; Rogers, 1969, 1983; Rogers & Freiberg, 1994)—relationships that serve as models from which students can learn more prosocial strategies for navigating their peer relationships. The importance of *referent* and *informational power* is again highlighted here. The former is probably more important because, without a positive relationship, teachers may not be able to readily act as an influencing agent via the persuasive communication afforded by *informational power*. Recent research has, for example, shown strong support for the person-centered approach by demonstrating that students who feel emotionally supported by their teachers report higher levels of social and emotional wellness (Suldo, Friedrich, White, Farmer, Minch, & Michalowski, 2009).

STUDENT PERCEPTIONS OF CLASSROOM MANAGEMENT

Teacher Aggression Is Widespread and Detrimental

In the past few years, international research has demonstrated that many students are acutely aware of and generally dissatisfied with the ways in which their teachers respond to misbehavior (Bracy, 2011; Campbell, 2012; Cooper, 2006; Suldo et al., 2009).

For example, 5,521 students from the seventh to twelfth grade in Australia, Israel, and China all reported that teachers sometimes respond to student misbehavior in an aggressive manner (e.g., yelling in anger, deliberate embarrassment), which distracts them from their schoolwork and incites negativity toward the teacher (Lewis, Romi, Katz, & Qui, 2008; Romi, Lewis, Roache, & Riley, 2011). These findings are closely related to the perspectives of middle school students in the Southeast United States, who reported that coercive classroom management practices are representative of low teacher support and that these practices ultimately lead to lower levels of social and emotional wellness (Suldo et al., 2009).

Moreover, in the Netherlands, 1,208 Dutch secondary school students reported that yelling in anger at students and belittling them using sarcasm was also associated with lower teacher *proximity*[2] one week after the teacher's use of the aggressive management techniques (Mainhard, Brekelmans, & Wubbels, 2011). Mainhard and colleagues' study highlighted the lasting effects of teacher aggression on the teacher–student relationship by demonstrating that "acting coercively does not 'disappear' in the ongoing stream of teacher behavior and is not associated to mere temporal disruptions of the classroom social climate" (p. 350). They also reported that teacher coercion was not associated with greater teacher *influence*. In contrast, supportive teacher behaviors were correlated with more perceived teacher *proximity* during the lesson and the lesson one week later, although there was no effect of perceived teacher *influence*. These findings are supported by evidence suggesting that negative/corrective teacher cognitions about, and behavior toward, problematic students in the early years of elementary school partly contribute to peer disliking (McAuliffe, Hubbard, & Romano, 2009). Both of these studies, once again, hint at the limits of *coercive power* in the classroom and provide support for the use of *referent* and *informational power* and the theory that teachers should foster a moral ethic of responsibility in students, rather than using blunt external controls (i.e., *reward and coercive power*) to force students to adopt prosocial behaviors (Lewis, Montuoro, & McCann, 2013).

Students with emotional and behavioral difficulties also express general dissatisfaction with the ways in which their teachers respond to misbehavior. For example, Cefai and Cooper (2010) reviewed eight small-scale studies investigating the perceptions of secondary school students with emotional and behavioral difficulties. Many of these students said that their teachers used coercive and autocratic classroom management practices, which made them feel powerless, oppressed, and disconnected from the learning process. Nevertheless, such causality should be treated with caution. For example, it is possible that some students with emotional and behavioral difficulties feel powerless, oppressed, and disconnected from the learning process *prior to* their teachers' forceful behavioral interventions. Cefai and Cooper remarked:

> [The students] had little or no say at all, with the teachers and administration wielding the authority and making decisions without consultation. They formed part of an undemocratic system built on adult power and coercion; this left them alienated and led them to disengage from the system. (p. 189)

Many of the students included in Cefai and Cooper's meta-analysis also said that they felt humiliated and inadequate when their teachers yelled at them in anger and that such responses did not positively influence their behavior. Perhaps most notably, however, many said that they felt excluded and discriminated against by their teachers, who repeatedly failed to recognize and address the students' social and emotional needs and simply labeled them as failures and antisocial. This kind of discontent was particularly true in mainstream settings, in which the students had "unpleasant and unhappy" experiences (p. 192). These findings are not surprising. For example, earlier research reported that *didactogeny*, which refers to a faulty education that harms students, leads to deleterious educational, psychological, and somatic outcomes (Sava, 2002).

Recent studies examining student perceptions of classroom management practices reveal a continuing disconnection between teachers and students. In some countries, this disconnection appears to be perpetuated through the use of particularly aggressive classroom management techniques. For example, in South African junior secondary and high schools, student reports have revealed that teachers commonly respond to misbehavior in a reactive and punitive ways (Maphosa & Mammen, 2011). They are reported to respond to misdemeanors with a range of aggressive responses, including verbal reprimands and forcing students to kneel on the floor. More serious forms of misbehavior are met with more aggressive responses, including suspension, detention, and manual labour. "A typical example is a classroom situation when noisemakers or disruptive learners were asked to kneel on the floor. Such a disciplinary measure is not only meaningless but infringes on the rights of the learner, as it is tantamount to torture" (p. 219).

In the United States, Bracy (2011) conducted ethnographic research in two high-security public high schools in the Mid-Atlantic region to investigate student perceptions of environments that incorporate police officers, security cameras, metal detectors, and strict discipline policies. One of the high schools, Cole High School, had a predominantly white, middle-class student population, in which only 11% of students came from low-income families. The other high school, Vista High School, had a predominantly black, low-income student population. Students from both schools reported that the employment of a full-time police officer was an ineffective measure in preventing misbehavior. They also expressed widespread discontent with escalating discipline policies. Metal detectors were perceived to negatively influence the atmosphere of the schools, and the introduction of mandatory identification badges was perceived to be yet another futile disciplinary measure in an exceedingly autocratic system. Bracy remarked of one student that she expressed:

Feelings of alienation and hopelessness as a result of her school rules and the way they are in force. This account illustrates the frustration students may feel when discipline becomes too central an objective at school (i.e., discipline for discipline's sake) and students are not rewarded or acknowledged for times when they exhibit good behavior and follow rules (p. 378).

Students from both schools were also dissatisfied with the disproportionately harsh punishments that they received and the inconsistency with which rules were enforced. Furthermore, many of the students complained that they were often disciplined without being given the opportunity to explain what happened. Bracy noted that the punishment process in both schools was so oppressive that many students became disheartened and simply accepted their fate as "the way it is." One female student remarked, "I've seen students get angry, I've seen students cry, and I've seen students act like, 'oh, well.' There's not much you can do about anything in this school . . . Their mind is made up or whatever" (p. 383). Bracy's research highlights the very excesses of *coercive power* in some high-security schools. Indeed, it is apparent from Bracy's research, that, with the rise in *coercive power*, there is a systematic decline in the *referent* and *informational power*, which forms the basis of cooperative teacher–student relationships.

Good Classroom Management Is Inclusive

Some recent studies have also investigated student reactions to certain classroom management practices. For example, in Australia, Israel, and China, secondary school students have been reported to respond more responsibly to teachers who address misbehavior through discussion and who allow students to find a solution to their misbehavior on their own (Lewis, Romi, Katz, & Qui, 2008). To a lesser extent, students in all three countries were also reported to respond more responsibly to teachers who make discreet hints to them about inappropriate behavior and who involve students in the development of discipline policies. These kinds of inclusionary classroom management practices appear to do more than merely mollify students. For example, in Melbourne, Australia, Lewis, Romi, and Roache (2012) surveyed 302 secondary school students who were asked to leave their classroom due to misbehavior. The researchers reported that students were willing to take more responsibility for their behavior when the teacher's decision-making process was transparent and democratic. This included giving students warnings before asking them to leave the class, explaining the decision-making process, and conducting a conversation with the student. These student reactions are not surprising given that inclusive classroom management practices counteract the aggressive and exclusionary practices discussed earlier in this chapter.

Students with emotional and behavioral difficulties also prefer good-quality relationships with their teachers and inclusive classroom management techniques that are underpinned by clarity and fairness (Sellman, 2009). Furthermore, students with emotional and behavioral difficulties express a strong need for help and support from their teachers (Cooper, 2006). Cooper conducted an in-depth interview with a past student who was diagnosed with dyslexia and ADHD and who completed his final few years of schooling in a special school due to his emotional and behavioral difficulties. The student described the dual problem of being passive aggressively excluded by his teacher but also wanting her help:

I had one teacher—I think it was my first year of junior school. She was the worst. I used to have temper tantrums, 'cos I used to ask for help for ages and ages. Doing something. And she'd come. And she looked at me. And she looked straight at me, and she'd help someone next to me. She looked at me for ages and then just help the person beside me. (p. 19)

The relationship between teachers and at-risk students was also examined by Decker, Dona, and Christenson (2007), who conducted a number of self-report measures with 44 behaviorally at-risk African American students and 25 of their teachers. The students were from two suburban and three urban elementary schools in a Midwestern state. Many of them viewed the teacher relationship as important and reported wanting to be closer to their teachers, even though their teachers tended to view their relationships with the students as negative. Furthermore, Decker and colleagues reported that as students reported a more positive teacher–student relationship, their teachers reported that their behavior improved and that the time they spent on-task increased. Decker and colleagues summarized these findings by remarking "it is possible that when students feel that they have a positive relationship with their teacher, they may be less likely to engage in behaviors that lead to referrals and be more academically engaged in the classroom" (p. 104).

CONCLUSION

This chapter has revealed striking similarities in student perceptions of misbehavior and classroom management from around the world. For example, students tend to downplay the severity of their misbehavior and are inclined to attribute peer misbehavior to generally similar causes, including boredom, attention seeking, and work-related difficulties. Internationally, student perceptions of the school social climate appear to decline in early adolescence, and peer report studies are beginning to reveal that some students misbehave in order to develop their sense of power over others (*perceived popularity*). Students from around the world have also expressed an aversion to coercive classroom management techniques and have reported the social and emotional benefits of cooperative discipline techniques that are based on well established teacher–student relationships.

When viewed through the prism of teacher social power, this review strongly supports the increased use of *referent* and *informational power*. When a teacher manages student behavior there are two, sometimes competing, aims (Lewis, 1997). The first aim is to establish order in the classroom so that students are physically and emotionally safe and they can learn. Lewis (1997) named this aim the *managerial function of classroom management*. The second aim is to foster a moral ethic of responsibility in students. Lewis named this aim the *educational function of classroom management*. The managerial function has paramount short-term importance, and at times it warrants the use of limited forms of *coercive power*, such as "consultative consequences" (punishments) that are applied within the broader context of a well established teacher–student relationship (*referent power*), and in consultation with students (*informational power*). Nevertheless, it can be argued that the educational function of classroom management is equally important. Therefore, the ideal long-term outcome of classroom management is to foster a commitment to responsible behavior in students. This refers not to behavioral change (*acting* responsibly) but rather to attitudinal change (*being* responsible), to the development of a moral ethic of responsibility that is fostered by respectful teacher–student relationships (*referent power*) and open and honest communication (*informational power*). This review suggests that the educational function of classroom management cannot be achieved when teachers and schools use *coercive power* in isolation because it has a wide range of deleterious effects, including dislike for the teacher, feelings of social and emotional tension, feelings of oppression and powerlessness, and feelings of discrimination and unhappiness, to name a few.

This should not create the illusion that the use of *referent* and *informational power* can create problem-free teacher–student relationships. On the contrary, there appears to be a fundamental disconnection between teachers' and students' perceptions of misbehavior, and there is neural evidence to suggest that students (particularly adolescents) misbehave without the requisite regard for the consequences. But this does not automatically warrant the isolated and long-term use of *coercive power* in the classroom; student misbehavior is not *meaningless*. As discussed, students misbehave for a variety of important reasons, including boredom, attention seeking, and work-related difficulties. These reasons suggest that misbehavior is a form of "crisis communication" and not simply something that these students do for malevolent reasons. For example, unsupportive teachers and schools seem to elicit student misbehavior, whereas the opposite is true for supportive teachers. Furthermore, students with emotional and behavioral difficulties have been found to desire closer teacher–student relationships, not more distant ones. For all of these instances, the long-term use of *referent* and *informational power* promise to foster teacher–student communication and closeness, whereas the isolated use of *coercive power* threatens to alienate students and exacerbate their misbehavior.

NOTES

1. *Acting* responsibly refers to students displaying responsible behaviors in order to comply with external controls. On the other hand, *being* responsible refers to students who display responsible behaviors because they possess a moral ethic of responsibility, or internal control, that compels them to act responsibly because "it is the right thing to do" (Lewis, Montuoro, & McCann, 2013).
2. In Leary's model of the interpersonal diagnosis of personality (Leary, 1957), two dimensions of human interaction were identified: *influence* (dominance versus submission) and *proximity* (hostility versus affection) (see Wubbels, Brekelmans, Den Brok, & van Tartwijk, 2006, for a review). The *influence* dimension measures how much control an individual has in a relationship, and the *proximity* dimension measures how much affiliation is present. Mainhard, Brekelmans, & Wubbels (2011) investigated students' collective interpersonal perceptions of a teacher's *influence* and *proximity*.

REFERENCES

Balson, M. (1992). *Understanding classroom behaviour*. Melbourne: ACER (Australian Council for Educational Research).

Becker, B. E., & Luthar, S. S. (2007). Peer-perceived admiration and social preference: Contextual correlates of positive peer regard among suburban and urban adolescents. *Journal of Research on Adolescence, 17*(1), 117–144.

Bellmore, A., Villarreal, V., & Ho, A. (2011). Staying cool across the first year of middle school. *Journal of Youth and Adolescence, 40*(7), 776–785.

Bracy, N. L. (2011). Student perceptions of high-security school environments. *Youth & Society, 43*(1), 365–395.

Burnard, P., & Swann, M. (2010). Pupil perceptions of learning with artists: A new order of experience? *Thinking Skills and Creativity, 5*(2), 70–82.

Campbell, A. (2012). Administrator and student perceptions of discipline methodologies for student behavior referrals. Master of Arts in Education, Long Beach, California State University.

Cefai, C., & Cooper, P. (2010). Students without voices: The unheard accounts of secondary school students with social, emotional and behaviour difficulties. *European Journal of Special Needs Education, 25*(2), 183–198.

Cohen, E. H., & Romi, S. (2010). Classroom management and discipline: A multi-method analysis of the way teacher, students and pre-service teachers view disturbing behavior. *Educational Practice and Theory, 32*(1), 42–69.

Cooper, P. , 2006). John's story: Episode 1—Understanding SEBD from the inside: The importance of listening to young people. In Y. Hunter-Carsch, P. Tiknaz, P. Cooper, & R. Sage (Eds.), *The handbook of social, emotional and behavioural difficulties* (pp. 16–23). London: Continuum International.

Cornelius-White, C. F. , 2007). Learner-centered teacher–student relationships are effective: A meta-analysis. *Review of Educational Research, 77*(1), 113–143.

Cothran, D. J., & Kulinna, P. H. (2007). Students' reports of misbehavior in physical education. *Research Quarterly for Exercise and Sport, 78*(3), 216–224.

Cothran, D. J., Kulinna, P. H., & Garrahy, D. A. (2009). Attributions for and consequences of student misbehavior. *Physical Education and Sport Pedagogy, 14*(2), 155–167.

Cowie, H., & Oztug, O. (2008). Pupils' perceptions of safety at school. *Pastoral Care in Education, 26*(2), 59–67.

Dahl, R. E. (2004). Adolescent brain development: A period of vulnerabilities and opportunities. *Annals of the New York Academy of Sciences, 1021*, 1–22.

Decker, D. M., Dona, D. P., & Christenson, S. L. (2007). Behaviorally at-risk African American students: The importance of student-teacher relationships for student outcomes. *Journal of School Psychology, 45*(1), 83–109.

De Jong, R., & Westerhof, K. J. (2001). The quality of student ratings of teacher behaviour. *Learning Environments Research, 4*(1), 51–85.

Dreikurs, R., & Cassel, P. (1990). *Discipline without tears* (2nd ed.). New York: E. P. Dutton.

Ellis, M. W., Malloy, C. E., Meece, J. L., & Sylvester, P. R. (2007). Convergence of observer ratings and student perceptions of reform practices in sixth-grade mathematics classrooms. *Learning Environments Research, 10*(1), 1–15.

Epstein, H. T. (1974). Phrenoblysis: Special brain and mind growth period. I. Human brain and skull development. *Developmental psychobiology, 7*(3), 207–216.

Espinoza, G., & Juvonen, J. (2011). Perceptions of school social contexts across the transition to middle school: Heightened sensitivity among teenage students? *Journal of Educational Psychology, 103*(3), 749–758.

Evans, N., Gilpin, E., Farkas, A. J., Shenassa, E., & Pierce, J. P. (1995). Adolescents' perceptions of their peers' health norms. *American Journal of Public Health, 85*(8), 1064–1069.

Fanti, K. A., Brookmeyer, K. A., Henrich, C. C., & Kuperminc, G. P. (2009). Aggressive behavior and quality of friendships. *The Journal of Early Adolescence, 29*(6), 826–838.

Francis, B., & Mills, M. (2012). Schools as damaging organisations: Instigating a dialogue concerning alternative models of schooling. *Pedagogy, Culture & Society, 20*(2), 251–271.

Fraser, B. J. (2007). Classroom learning environments. In S. K. Abell & N. G. Lieberman (Eds.), *Handbook of research on science education* (pp. 103–124). Mahwah, NJ: Erlbaum.

French, J. R. P., & Raven, B. H. (1959). The bases of social power. In D. Cartwright (Ed.), *Studies in social power* (pp. 150–167). Ann Arbor, MI: Institute of Social Research.

Goldstone, R. L., Medin, D. L., & Schyns, P. G. (Eds.). (1997). *Perceptual learning.* San Diego, CA: Acadmeic Press.

Goodenow, C., & Grady, K. E. (1993). The relationship of school belonging and friends' values to academic motivation among urban adolescents students. *Journal of Experimental Education, 62*(1), 60–71.

Gregory, A., & Ripski, M. (2008). Adolescent trust in teachers: Implications for behaviour in the high school classroom. *Social Psychology Review, 37*(3), 337–353.

Hamre, B. K., & Pianta, R. C. (2005). Can instructional and emotional support in the first-grade classroom make a difference for children at risk of school failure? *Child Development, 76*(5), 949–967.

Hamre, B. K., Pianta, R. C., Downer, J. T., & Mashburn, A. J. (2008). Teachers' perceptions of conflict with young students: Looking beyond problem behaviors. *Social Development, 17*(1), 115–136.

Han, W.-J. (2008). The academic trajectories of children of immigrants and their social environments. *Developmental Psychology, 44*(6), 1572–1590.

Harber, C. (2004). *Schooling as violence: How schools harm pupils and society.* London: Routledge.

Harrison, L., Clarke, L., & Ungerer, J. (2007). Children's drawings provide a new perspective on teacher–child relationship quality and school adjustment. *Early Childhood Research Quarterly, 22*(1), 55–71.

Henricsson, L., & Rydell, A.-M. (2004). Elementary school children with behavior problems: Teacher–child relations and self-perception. A prospective study. *Merrill-Palmer Quarterly, 50*(2), 111–138.

Hoff, K. E., Reese-Weber, M., Joel Schneider, W., & Stagg, J. W. (2009). The association between high status positions and aggressive behavior in early adolescence. *Journal of School Psychology, 47*(6), 395–426.

Hook, C. L., & Rosenshine, B. V. (1979). Accuracy of teacher reports of their classroom behavior. *Review of Educational Research, 49*(1), 1–11.

Hughes, J., Cavell, T., & Jackson, T. (1999). Influence of the teacher–student relationship in childhood conduct problems: A prospective study. *Journal of Clinical Child and Adolescent Psychology, 28*(2), 173–184.

Kuppens, S., Grietens, H., Onghena, P., Michiels, D., & Subramanian, S. V. (2008). Individual and classroom variables associated with relational aggression in elementary-school aged children: A multilevel analysis. *Journal of School Psychology, 46*(6), 639–660.

Ladd, G. W., & Burgess, K. B. (2001). Do relational risks and protective factors moderate the linkages between childhood aggression and early psychological and school adjustment? *Child Development, 72*(5), 1579–1601.

Lahey, B. B., & Waldman, I. D. (2003). A developmental propensity model of the origins of conduct problems during childhood and adolescence. In B. B. Lahey, T. E. Moffitt, & A. Caspi (Eds.), *Causes of conduct disorder and juvenile delinquency* (pp. 76–117). New York: Guilford.

Leary, T. (1957). *An interpersonal diagnosis of personality.* New York: Ronald.

Leitch, R., & Mitchell, S. (2007). Caged birds and cloning machines: How student imagery "speaks" to us about cultures of schooling and student participation. *Improving Schools, 10*(1), 53–71.

Lewis, R. (1997). *The discipline dilemma* (2nd ed.). Melbourne: ACER (Australian Council for Educational Research).

Lewis, R. (2001). Classroom discipline and student responsibility: The students' view. *Teaching and Teacher Education, 17*(3), 307–319.

Lewis, R., Montuoro, P., & McCann, P. (2013). Imagining a lord of the flies-type scenario: Self-predicted classroom behaviour without external controls. *Australian Journal of Education, 57*(3), 270–291.

Lewis, R., Romi, S., Katz, Y. J., & Qui, X. (2008). Students' reaction to classroom discipline in Australia, Israel, and China. *Teaching and Teacher Education: An International Journal of Research and Studies, 24*(3), 715–724.

Lewis, R., Romi, S., & Roache, J. (2012). Excluding students from classroom: Teacher techniques that promote student responsibility. *Teaching and Teacher Education, 28*(6), 870–878.

Luckner, A. E., & Pianta, R. C. (2011). Teacher–student interactions in fifth grade classrooms: Relations with children's peer behavior. *Journal of Applied Developmental Psychology, 32*(5), 257–266.

MacBeath, J. (2006). Finding a voice, finding self. *Educational Review, 58*(2), 195–207.

Mainhard, M. T., Brekelmans, M., & Wubbels, T. (2011). Coercive and supportive teacher behaviour: Within- and across-lesson associations with the classroom social climate. *Learning and Instruction, 21*(3), 345–354.

Maphosa, C., & Mammen, K. J. (2011). Maintaining discipline: How do learners view the way teachers operate in South African schools? *Journal of Social Sciences, 29*(3), 213–222.

McAuliffe, M. D., Hubbard, J. A., & Romano, L. J. (2009). The role of teacher cognition and behavior in children's peer relations. *Journal of Abnormal Child Psychology, 37*(5), 665–677.

McCombs, B. L., & Whisler, J. S. (1997). *The learner-centred classroom and school: Strategies for increasing student motivation and achievement.* San Fransisco: Jossey-Bass.

Murray, C., Murray, K., & Waas, G. (2008). Child and teacher reports of teacher–student relationships: Concordance of perspectives and associations with school adjustment in urban kindergarten classrooms. *Journal of Applied Developmental Psychology, 29*(1), 49–61.

Newberry, M., & Davis, H. (2008). The role of elementary teachers' conceptions of closeness to students on their differential behaviour in the classroom. *Teaching and Teacher Education, 24*(8), 1965–1985.

Newcomb, A. F., Bukowski, W. M., & Pattee, L. (1993). Children's peer relations: A metanalytic review of popular, rejected, neglected, controversial, and average sociometric status. *Psychological Bulletin, 113*(1), 99–128.

Owens, L., & Duncan, N. (2009). "They might not like you but everyone knows you": Popularity among teenage girls. *Journal of Student Wellbeing, 3*(1), 14–39.

Paul, S., Smith, P. K., & Blumberg, H. H. (2012). Comparing student perceptions of coping strategies and school interventions in managing bullying and cyberbullying incidents. *Pastoral Care in Education, 30*(2), 127–146.

Pestello, F. G. (1989). Misbehavior in high school classrooms. *Youth & Society, 20*(3), 290–306.

Powell, K. (2006). How does the teenage brain work? *Nature, 442,* 865–867.

Quinn, G. P., Bell-Ellison, B. A., Loomis, W., & Tucci, M. (2007). Adolescent perceptions of violence: Formative research findings from a social marketing campaign to reduce violence among middle school youth. *Public health, 121*(5), 357–366.

Raven, B. H. (1965). Social influence and power. In I. D. Steiner & M. Fishbein (Eds.), *Current studies in social psychology* (pp. 371–382). New York: Holt, Rinehart, & Winston.

Raven, B. H. (2008). The bases of power and the power/interaction model of interpersonal influence. *Analyses of Social Issues and Public Policy, 8*(1), 1–22.

Ray, N., Reddy, R., & Rhodes, J. (2007). Students' perceptions of school climate during the middle school years: Associations with trajectories of psychological and behavioral justment. *American Journal of Community Psychology, 40*(3–4), 194–213.

Rickards, T., & Fisher, D. (2000). *Three perspectives on perceptions of teacher–student interaction: A seed for change in science teaching.* Paper presented at the Annual Meeting of the National Association for Research in Science Teaching New Orleans, Louisiana.

Riley, K., & Docking, J. (2004). Voices of disaffected pupils: Implications for policy and practice. *British Journal of Educational Studies, 52*(2), 166–179.

Rimm-Kaufman, S., Early, D. M., Cox, M. J., Saluja, G., Pianta, R. C., Bradley, R. H., & Payne, C. (2002). Early behavioral attributes and teachers' sensitivity as predictors of competent behavior in the kindergarten classroom. *Journal of Applied Developmental Psychology 23*(4), 451–470.

Roache, J., & Lewis, R. (2011). Teachers' views on the impact of classroom management on student responsibility. *Australian Journal of Education, 55*(2), 132–146.

Rodkin, P. C., Farmer, T. W., Pearl, R., & Acker, R. V. (2006). They're cool: Social status and peer group supports for aggressive boys and girls. *Social Development, 15*(2), 175–204.

Rogers, C. R. (1969). *Freedom to learn.* Columbus, OH: Charles E. Merrill.

Rogers, C. R. (1983). *Freedom to learn for the 80s.* Columbus, OH: Charles E. Merrill.

Rogers, C. R., & Freiberg, H. J. (1994). *Freedom to learn* (3rd ed.). Upper Saddle River, NJ: Prentice Hall.

Romi, S., Lewis, R., Roache, J., & Riley, P. (2011). The impact of teachers' aggressive management techniques on students' attitudes to schoolwork. *Journal of Educational Research, 104*(4), 231–240.

Sandstrom, M. J., & Cillessen, A. H. N. (2006). Likeable versus popular: Distinct implications for adolescent adjustment. *International Journal of Behavioral Development, 30*(4), 305–314.

Sargeant, J. (2012). Prioritising student voice: "Tween" children's perspectives on school success. *Education, 3–13,* 1–11.

Sava, F. A. (2002). Causes and effects of teacher conflict-inducing attitudes towards pupils: A path analysis model. *Teaching and Teacher Education, 18*(8), 1007–1021.

Schunk, D. H., & Meece, J. L. (Eds.). (1992). *Student perceptions in the classroom.* Hillsdale, NJ: Erlbaum.

Sellman, E. (2009). Lessons learned: Student voice at a school for pupils experiencing social, emotional and behavioural difficulties. *Emotional and Behavioural Difficulties, 14*(1), 33–48.

Shirley, E. L. M., & Cornell, D. G. (2012). The contribution of student perceptions of school climate to understanding the disproportionate punishment of African American students in a middle school. *School Psychology International, 33*(2), 115–134.

Silver, R., Measelle, J., Armstrong, J., & Essex, M. (2005). Trajectories of classroom externalizing behavior: Contributions of child characteristics, family characteristics, and the teacher–child relationship during the school transition. *Journal of School Psychology, 43*(1), 39–60.

Slaughter-Defoe, D. T., & Carlson, K. G. (1996). Young African-American and Latino children in high-poverty urban schools: How they perceived school climate. *Journal of Negro Education, 65*(1), 60–70.

Spear, L. P. (2000). The adolescent brain and age-related behavioral manifestations. *Neuroscience and Biobehavioral Reviews, 24,* 417–463.

Spilt, J. L., Koomen, H. M. Y., & Mantzicopoulos, P. Y. (2010). Young children's perceptions of teacher–child relationships: An evaluation of two instruments and the role of child gender in kindergarten. *Journal of Applied Developmental Psychology, 31*(6), 428–438.

Steinberg, L. (2005). Cognitive and affective development in adolescence. *Trends in Cognitive Sciences*, 9(2), 69–74.

Steinberg, L., & Sheffield Morris, A. (2001). Adolescent development. *Annual Review of Psychology*, 52, 83–110.

Stipek, D., & Miles, S. (2008). Effects of aggression on achievement: Does conflict with the teacher make it worse? *Child Development*, 79(6), 1721–1735.

Suldo, S. M., Friedrich, A. A., White, T., Farmer, J., Minch, D., & Michalowski, J. (2009). Teacher support and adolescents' subjective well-being: A mixed-methods investigation. *School Psychology Review*, 38(1), 67–85.

Turner, P. J. (1991). Relations between attachment, gender, and behavior with peers in preschool. *Child Development*, 62(6), 1475–1488.

Way, S. M. (2011). School discipline and disruptive classroom behaviour: The moderating effects of student perceptions. *The Sociological Quarterly*, 52(3), 346–375.

Weisfeld, G., Bloch, S. A., & Ivers, J. W. (1983). A factor analytic study of peer-perceived dominance in adolescent boys. *Adolescence*, 18(70), 229–243.

Weisfeld, G., Bloch, S. A., & Ivers, J. W. (1984). Possible determinants of social dominance among adolescent girls. *The Journal of Genetic Psychology*, 144(1), 115–129.

Werner, N. E., & Hill, L. G. (2010). Individual and peer group normative beliefs about relational aggression. *Child Development*, 81(3), 826–836.

Woods, R. (2009). The use of aggression in primary school boys' decisions about inclusion in and exclusion from playground football games. *British Journal of Educational Psychology*, 79(2), 223–238.

Woolfolk Hoy, A., & Weinstein, C. S. (2006). Student and teacher perspectives on classroom management. In C. A. Evertson & C. S. Weinstein (Eds.), *Handbook of classroom management: Research, practice, and contemporary issues* (pp. 181–219). New York: Routledge.

Wubbels, T., Brekelmans, M., Den Brok, P., & van Tartwijk, J. (2006). An interpersonal perspective of classroom management in secondary classrooms in the Netherlands. In C. A. Evertson & C. S. Weinstein (Eds.), *Handbook of classroom management: Research, practice, and contemporary issues* (pp. 1161–1191). Mahwah, NJ: Earnbaum.

19

TEACHER–STUDENT RELATIONSHIPS AND CLASSROOM MANAGEMENT

THEO WUBBELS AND MIEKE BREKELMANS
UTRECHT UNIVERSITY

PERRY DEN BROK
EINDHOVEN SCHOOL OF EDUCATION

LINDY WIJSMAN, TIM MAINHARD, AND JAN VAN TARTWIJK
UTRECHT UNIVERSITY

INTRODUCTION

This chapter is a follow-up of the contribution on teacher–student relationships by Pianta (2006) in the first edition of the *Handbook of Classroom Management*. Just as Pianta did, we reconceptualize classroom management in terms of the relationships between teachers and students and use a relational approach to classroom management. Evertson and Weinstein (2006) defined classroom management as "the actions teachers take to create an environment that supports and facilitates both academic and social-emotional learning" (p. 4). From a relational perspective, we both extend and confine the definition of classroom management to read all teacher actions and associated cognitions and attitudes involved in creating the social emotional aspect of the learning environment. Although this definition focuses on teacher actions, it is important to acknowledge that these actions become effective only to the degree that students interpret these. Our approach emphasizes the socio-emotional aspects of teacher actions, and this chapter is primarily interested in teacher–student relationships. Peer relationships, of course, are another important factor in the social-emotional environment but will be treated in other chapters of the handbook.

Student affective and cognitive outcomes have been shown to be related to the quality of teacher–student relationships (e.g., Cornelius-White, 2007; Roorda, Koomen, Spilt, & Oort, 2011). At the same time, teacher–student relationships are connected to teacher job satisfaction and burnout (e.g., Chang, 2009; Friedman, 2006; Spilt, Koomen, & Thijs, 2011). How exactly these outcomes are produced in interactions between teachers and students is not yet clear, but this chapter takes the strong role of teacher–student relationships as a given and reviews research on these relationships with immediate relevance for classroom management. We primarily focus on studies that have been published after the publication of the first edition of the *Handbook of Classroom Management*. A search in March 2013 in Google Scholar with the keywords "classroom management" and "teacher–student relationships" returned over 1,500 hits since 2006. However, the amount of research that explicitly goes into the connection between these two constructs is not very large and a broader search, including key terms such as "teacher–student interaction," "teacher beliefs and teacher cognitions," and "teacher–student relationships," forms the basis of this chapter.

Before reviewing the empirical research that we collected, we first describe relationships and interactions from the perspective of dynamic systems theory and introduce a conceptual model for interactions and relationships in their environment. Then we discuss two languages that can be used to describe teacher–student interactions and relationships. After describing the often neglected distinction between two types of teacher–student relationships, that is, with an individual student and with a class entailing several students, we move to an overview of research methods to collect relational data. The core of the chapter then is the review of empirical studies on teacher–student relationships guided by our conceptual framework.

INTERACTION AND RELATIONSHIPS: A DYNAMIC SYSTEMS APPROACH

Teacher–student relationships can be understood as the generalized interpersonal meaning students and teachers attach to their interactions with each other, and thus these relationships can be assumed to originate in these interactions. For example, Bronfenbrenner and Morris (1998) posit in their bioecological theory that the moment-to-moment time scale (teacher–student interaction) is the primary engine of development and therefore the basis for macro social outcomes (e.g., teacher–student relationships, teacher job satisfaction, or student emotional well-being). Dynamic systems theory can be employed to describe the development of teacher–student relationships (the macro level) from real-time interactions between teachers and their students (the micro level). According to dynamic systems theory, any human development is hierarchically nested in time, and real-time interactions are the building blocks of relationships (Granic & Hollenstein, 2003). At the same time, relationships constrain real-time processes and experiences (Hollenstein & Lewis, 2006; Mainhard, Pennings, Wubbels, & Brekelmans, 2012). For example, in a cold teacher–student relationship, interactions likely are hostile rather than friendly. Relationships become manifest in recurring patterns of real-time interactions.

A second important characteristic of dynamic systems theory is the notion that looking for causes of the development of interactions by referring to only one of the participants is usually not productive (e.g., Pianta, 2006; Wubbels, Créton, &

Holvast, 1988). The assumption of reciprocal interactions (and thus mutual influences) is basic to dynamic systems theory. Circularity in interactions is a necessary implication of this notion; that is to say, teachers and students influence each other. When a teacher, for example, is explaining subject matter very clearly, students may be more likely to listen very well. On the other hand, students may also become more docile and less inclined to ask questions. Such student behaviors, in their turn, may reinforce a strong central position of the teacher in the communication. Also, between the micro and macro levels, no cause and effect can be distinguished.

Finally, another aspect of the dynamic systems framework worth mentioning is the embedding of teacher–student relationships in wider systems such as schools, neighborhoods, and societies (Bronfenbrenner and Morris, 1998). Influences of these environments are, however, not the focus of the present chapter.

A CONCEPTUAL MODEL FOR TEACHER–STUDENT INTERACTIONS AND RELATIONSHIPS

Based on the dynamic systems approach to teacher–student interactions and relationships, we conceptualize teacher classroom management primarily as the teacher behavior at the level of interactions. Figure 19.1 visualizes the interplay between teacher–student interactions and teacher–student relationships and other variables involved in the study of teacher–student relationships and classroom management. Teacher and student characteristics, as well as characteristics of the wider social-emotional environment, are main constituents of interactions and relationships and therefore crucial variables to study in the relational approach to classroom management. Although the meaning that participants (teachers and students) attach to the interactions and relationships are of

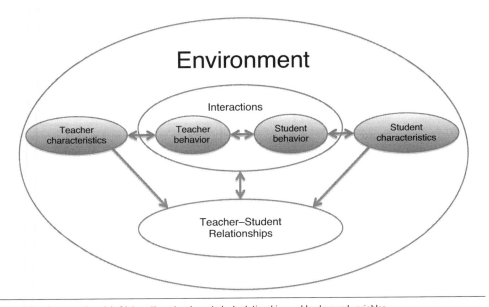

Figure 19.1 Conceptual model of interactions, teacher–student relationships and background variables.

utmost importance for the effects that interactional acts have on the participants, this chapter doesn't confine the review to studies employing student and teacher perception data but also includes research using observer data.

TWO LANGUAGES TO DESCRIBE TEACHER–STUDENT INTERACTIONS AND RELATIONSHIPS

Dynamic systems theory provides a framework for studying the interplay between teacher–student interactions and teacher–student relationships. In order to describe these relationships and interactions, a language (a specific set of concepts) is needed. As examples, we describe two frameworks providing such a language: interpersonal theory (Wubbels, Brekelmans, den Brok, & van Tartwijk, 2006) and a framework based on attachment theory (Pianta, 2001).

Interpersonal Theory

Interpersonal theory describes the (perceptions of) behavior of persons relating to and interacting in a system with other persons based on the assumption that human behavior is best understood within the context of transactional causality and reciprocal influence (Horowitz & Strack, 2011). A basic premise of interpersonal theory is that all interpersonal behavior can be described along two orthogonal dimensions, together forming the basis of a circular structure (e.g., Gurtman, 2009; Kiesler, 1983; Leary, 1957; Sadler, Ethier, & Woody, 2011; Wubbels et al., 2012). Depending on the context (e.g., psychiatry, family, education), the dimensions are designated differently with *agency* and *communion* as metalevel labels (Fournier, Moskowitz, & Zuroff, 2011; Gurtman, 2009). Agency suggests that someone is becoming individuated, dominant, has power and control, whereas communion means someone is social, shows love, union, friendliness, and affiliation (Gurtman, 2009). The two-dimensional circular structure implies that all interpersonal behavior can be ordered along the circumference of a circle. Depending on its position in the interpersonal circle, all behavior can be seen as a specific blend of agency and communion.

Teacher–student relationships are characterized by the combination of the two dimensions. To give an example of such combinations in the classroom, we describe psychological and behavioral control that have been conceptualized most clearly in the parenting literature. Behavioral control refers to the provision of regulation or structure on the child's behavioral world, whereas psychological control refers to intrusion and manipulation of the child's psychological world, such as constraining verbal interactions, and invalidating of feelings (Bean, Barber & Crane, 2006). In interpersonal theory, psychological control thus reflects a combination of a low level of teacher communion and high agency. In such a relationship, the teacher not only exerts a lot of control over the students but also puts students under pressure to think and feel in ways different from their own inclinations and utilizes coercion and restraints to reach his or her goal. Such a relationship may evoke negative feelings and anger in students and restricts students' autonomy (Frenzel, Pekrun, & Goetz, 2007; Lewis, Romi, Katz, & Qui 2008; Lewis, Romi, Qui, & Katz, 2005). Behavioral control, on the other hand, combines a high level of both teacher agency and communion. In this case, the control means that the teacher offers a structured social environment with clear expectations. Its combination with a high level of communion conveys to the students a message of empathy and mutual respect. The teacher's sense of communion helps students accept rules. Such an environment is conducive for autonomy development (Vansteenkiste, Zhou, Lens, & Soenens, 2005), student engagement, and low levels of student misbehavior (Nie & Lau, 2009).

Educational researchers have demonstrated that effective teacher–student relationships are characterized by a combination of high levels of teacher agency and communion (Ertesvåg, 2011; Walker, 2009; Wentzel, 2002; Wubbels et al., 2006) with agency being especially positively related to students' cognitive learning outcomes and communion to students' motivation (Brekelmans, 1989; Walker, 2009; Woolfolk Hoy, & Weinstein, 2006).

Attachment-Based Framework

A second language available to study teacher–student relationships, based on the attachment theory, utilizes three dimensions: closeness (openness, warmth, and security), conflict (negative, discordant, unpredictable, and unpleasant), and dependency (developmentally inappropriate degree of overreliance and possessiveness) (Koomen, Verschueren, van Schooten, Jak, & Pianta, 2012; Pianta, 2001). These three dimensions have originally been derived from concepts and assessments in parent–child relationships (Skinner, Johnson, & Snyder, 2005). In the parent-child literature these dimensions include warmth versus rejection, behavioral control versus chaos, and autonomy support versus coercion (Prinzie, Stams, Deković, Reijntjes, & Belsky, 2009). Birch and Ladd (1997) contend that attachment theorists have distinguished between the attachment construct (which has positive developmental implications) and the notion of dependency (which has negative connotations) (Bowlby, 1982). A particular teacher–student relationship may be characterized as highly close without also being highly dependent (Birch & Ladd, 1997). Koomen and colleagues (2012) argue that closeness is viewed as a positive relational factor, providing students with emotional security and support to deal with the socioemotional and academic demands they face in school. Conflict and dependence are viewed as negative relational factors, both reflecting a lack of security and consequently hampering and interfering with students' coping with demands in the school context.

The attachment and the interpersonal language may be conceived to share two dimensions. Agency and dependency can be seen as two sides of the same coin perceived from different actors. Communion and closeness are similar, and conflict might be conceived of as the negative side or absence of communion in a relationship. However, the dimensions of conflict and closeness were conceptualized to be independent, whereas when conflict is seen as the negative side of closeness, conflict and closeness should be negatively correlated. Indeed, this has been found in some studies. Koomen and associates (2012) report in two samples a correlation between closeness and conflict of −.46 and −.47. Such results suggest that conflict and closeness have a lot in common and that interpersonal theory might provide a more parsimonious model for describing teacher–student relationships.

RELATIONSHIPS WITH AN INDIVIDUAL STUDENT
AND A CLASS OF STUDENTS

In the study of relationships of teachers with their students, it is important to distinguish between relationships with individual students and their collective as a class. Although one teacher may have strong individual relationships with each of her students, she may not foster a great bond with the class as a whole because the pacing, content, or pedagogical style may not work for most of the students in the class. Another teacher may not form particularly close relationships with the individual students in his class because he keeps his interactions with students formal and restricted to classroom content; however, he may foster a strong connection with the class as a whole.

There is a distinct body of literature looking at the relationships between teachers and their individual students, primarily based on perceptions of the participants. In quantitative analyses, these perceptions are usually used to capture both individual student characteristics and teacher or class features (e.g., Buyse, Verschueren, Doumen, Van Damme, & Maes, 2008). Other approaches to the study of teacher–student relationships are based on students' or teachers' perceptions of the relationship with a class of students (e.g., Levy, den Brok, Wubbels, & Brekelmans, 2003), directly targeting the classroom or teacher level (cf. Marsh et al., 2012) and also involving multilevel analyses (den Brok, Brekelmans, & Wubbels, 2006).

The distinction between the individual and classroom levels is of direct importance when it comes to conceptualizing and operationalizing relations through student perceptions because the specific questions asked lead to different results. If students are asked whether a teacher is friendly *to the class,* the data reflect the shared view that students have of their teacher, and the concept measured comes close to a teacher characteristic (i.e., the teacher level is targeted). Asking a student whether he or she thinks a teacher is friendly *to him- or her*, the idiosyncratic view that students hold about their teacher is emphasized, and the concept measured can be conceived as a student or dyadic characteristic. Brok and colleagues (2006) showed how using such item differences affected the level of teachers' estimated interpersonal warmth and influence. On average, teachers were perceived to show more interpersonal influence and warmth in their relations with individual students than in their relationship with the class as a whole. McRobbie, Fisher, and Wong (1998) found that student perceptions that were mapped with learning environment instruments directly targeting the class or teacher level were, with a few exceptions, systematically higher than estimates based on individual forms. Unfortunately, many of the studies reviewed in this chapter do not very clearly describe at what level their data were collected.

INVESTIGATING RELATIONSHIPS AND INTERACTIONS

Teacher–student relationships and interactions can be studied in several ways. To study real-time interactions, usually observations are employed either quantitatively coded or in a more qualitative way. Videotaping improves the quality of this type of data collection because interactions can be reviewed time and time again. For mapping extended or recurring interaction patterns over time, questionnaires and interviews are widely used to gather data on students' and teachers' perceptions.

Observations

Classroom observations have a long and firm tradition. Following the development of one of the first instruments by Ned Flanders (1970), a plethora of instruments has been documented (Good & Brophy, 2007; Simon & Boyer, 1974). A recent example is the *Classroom Assessment Scoring System* (CLASS) (Pianta, La Paro, & Hamre, 2008), a standardized observation measure of global classroom quality that assesses three domains of quality—emotional supports, classroom organization, and instructional supports—and that can be used in prekindergarten classrooms through twelfth grade. Whereas this instrument and many others (e.g., Spivak & Farran, 2012) target the classroom level, others focus on moment-to-moment interactions (e.g., Roorda, Koomen, Spilt, Thijs, & Oort, 2013; Mainhard, Pennings, Wubbels, & Brekelmans, 2012). Such instruments record observer perceptions of ongoing behaviors of teacher and/or students within the classroom, for example, to analyze patterns in interactions within lessons. Scoring categories can include high inference measures such as the level of agency and communion but also lower inference measures, such as verbal elements (question type, source of initiative) and nonverbal elements (such as gesture and facial expression).

Also ethnographic (participant and nonparticipant) observations are used to investigate the relational aspect of classroom life (e.g., Milner & Tenore, 2010). Traditionally after an initial nonstructured phase of taking field notes, observations become more focused on specific topics, or a set of observation categories is developed based on open observations (e.g., Yan, Evans, & Harvey, 2011).

Questionnaires

In research on teacher–student relationships mapping, participants' perceptions comprise the second strong tradition. As compared to observational measures, this method is often easier to employ and better takes into account the sometimes longstanding acquaintance of the participants with each other. For example, Pianta's (2001) *Student–Teacher Relationship Scale* (STRS) maps teacher perceptions of the relationship with individual students. The STRS consists of 28 items rated on a five-point Likert-type scale and contains three subscales that measure conflict, closeness, and dependency. The instrument has been widely used and is available in several languages. The *Questionnaire on Teacher Interaction* (QTI) was developed specifically to map students' and teacher's perceptions of a teacher's relationship to a class of students. The QTI maps relationships on the two dimensions of agency and communion by tapping students' perceptions of eight types of teacher behavior: steering, friendly, understanding, accommodating, uncertain, dissatisfied, reprimanding, and enforcing. It has several versions with 24–77 items and is available in many languages (Wubbels et al., 2012). Similarly, Gehlbach, Brinkworth, and Harris (2012) employed the conveniently short *Teacher–Student Relationships Positivity and Negativity* scales (nine and five items) to document both teachers' and students' perceptions reliably.

Interviews

To more fully understand participants' views of teacher–student relationships, open-ended interviews are helpful because they give participants the opportunity to describe the relationships with their own words. Interviews have been used in several studies to tap underlying beliefs, attitudes, cognitions, intentions, the history of the relationship, or interpretations of differences between teachers' and students' perceptions (Gentry, Steenbergen-Hu, & Choi 2011; Suldo et al., 2009).

REVIEW OF EMPIRICAL WORK

We now present the results of our search for empirical work on classroom management and teacher–student relationships carried out since the publication of the previous *Handbook on Classroom Management*. We review only studies on teacher–student relationship with direct importance for classroom management, and therefore several topics, such as the role of learning in the relationships, change in relationships over the course of the school year, and developmental differences that all are critical to these relationships, are not covered. The review starts with studies on student and teacher characteristics relevant for interactions and teacher–student relationships. Then we discuss research on teacher–student interactions with an emphasis on circularity in interactions (see inner circle in Figure 19.1). After a section on the interplay between interactions and relationships, we discuss what evidence research has produced regarding efforts to promote classroom management–related effective interactions and relationships in teacher education and professional development.

Student Characteristics

Students bring a variety of goals, feelings, needs, and behavioral tendencies into the classroom, which will ultimately affect the quality of the relationships they form with teachers (Pianta, 2006). The individual characteristics of students and the make-up of a classroom group as a whole represent a central determinant of the teaching context (Nurmi, 2012). In this section we discuss recent research that has focused on student characteristics, both directly visible for teachers in the classroom (e.g., student behavior or gender) and more latent (like student motivation), that elicit teacher behavior in classroom interactions or are associated with the quality of teacher–student relationships.

Studies on the effect of student *gender* have shown that low levels of conflict and high levels of closeness characterize girls' relationships with their teachers more than those of boys (e.g., Hamre & Pianta, 2001). Gender differences, however, are entangled with behavioral differences. Boys more often show behavior teachers perceive as *disrupting* classroom processes (e.g., verbal disrespect, violence) (Koles, O'Connor, & Collins, 2013). Several authors explain how disruptive student behavior affects teachers (Alvarez, 2007; O'Conner, 2010). Alvarez (2007) describes how disruptive student behavior heightens teachers' stress level and negatively affects their interactions with students. According to Alvarez, teachers tend to use harsher discipline strategies and spend less time in engaging in a positive way with disruptive students than with other students. Students and teachers thus may get caught in a negative vicious cycle of deteriorating teacher–student interactions and escalating student problem behavior (e.g., Brackett, Reyes, Rivers, Elbertson, & Salovey, 2011; Doumen et al., 2008).

Not only *aggressive* but also *shy* students tend to develop less close and more dependent relationships with their teachers (e.g., Arbeau, Coplan, & Weeks, 2010; Rudasill & Rimm-Kaufman, 2009; Rudasill, Rimm-Kaufman, Justice, & Pence, 2006). Notably, according to Koles and colleagues (2013), higher levels of shyness seem to be less harmful for girls than for boys. Shy boys may develop more conflictual relationships with their teachers than shy girls due to potential gender-based coping mechanisms. Because girls are stereotypically expected to be more shy, shy girls may not as readily seize the teacher's attention, and thus the teacher may not initiate more (negative) interactions with shy girls (Koles, O'Connor, & Collins, 2013). While student gender differences seem to be predictive of teacher perceptions and teacher–student interactions, Mitchell and Bradshaw (2013) and O'Conner (2010) reported that boys and girls did not differ in their perceptions of general teacher fairness or order and discipline in the classroom.

Some studies approached the effect of student behavior on teacher–student interactions and relationships, differentiating between *externalizing* (i.e., aggressive and hyperactive) and *internalizing* (anxious, shy) student behavior (Nurmi, 2012; Vick Whittacker & Jones Harden, 2010a). From his meta-analysis, Nurmi (2012) concludes that higher levels of both internalizing and externalizing student behaviors are linked to more conflict and less closeness in teacher–student relationships. Nurmi (2012) notes that while externalizing and internalizing student behavior may differ in their effects on classroom interactions, perceptions of the relationship as such may be quite similar.

Another student characteristic that has received some attention recently is *ethnicity* (Mitchell & Bradshaw, 2013; O'Connor, 2010). Garza (2009), for example, found that in the United States, Latino and white high school students valued the same themes in caring teacher behaviors in classrooms. However, the priority of these behaviors differed somewhat with Latinos valuing most teachers' scaffolding behaviors and white students emphasizing teachers' generic positive dispositions toward students. den Brok, van Tartwijk, Wubbels, and Veldman (2010) showed that, in the Dutch context, minority students from Turkish, Moroccan, and Surinamese backgrounds perceived higher levels of influence and proximity in the teacher–student relationship. This implies that their perceived relationship with the teacher was better than that of indigenous Dutch students. O'Conner (2010), based on teacher perception data, showed that African American students have lower-quality relationships with their teachers, especially when teachers had lower levels of self-efficacy and in classrooms with less positive social climates. The effect of ethnicity on teacher–student interactions and relationships is likely to be dependent on the school context. In a predominantly European American or nonethnic context, ethnicity may have a different effect on individual relationships than in highly multicultural schools (cf. Lüdtke, Robitzsch, Trautwein, & Kunter, 2009).

Myers and Pianta (2008) emphasize the importance of students' *reactivity* (i.e., the frequency and intensity of emotional reaction) and *teachability* (i.e., high attention, task orientation, and adaptability) as predictors of teacher–student interactions. Students scoring higher on these dimensions elicit, according to Keogh (2003), more open and positive interactions, whereas students perceived lower on these dimensions are more likely to be involved in purely instructional exchanges. Myers and Pianta (2008) related this to a goodness-of-fit between the student and what the teacher in the school context expects of the students.

Regarding student *achievement*, Nurmi (2012) concluded that teachers who interacted with highly motivated and engaged students and with students with a high level of academic performance reported to experience higher-quality teacher–student relationships.

Teacher Characteristics

During the last decade, a host of studies have investigated associations between a variety of teacher characteristics and teacher behavior, teacher–student relationships, and student behavior. In this section, we first discuss recent research that has focused on teacher characteristics (e.g., experience, self-efficacy, practical knowledge) that are associated with particular teacher behaviors or with the quality of teacher–student relationships. Then we focus on the student behavior and outcomes elicited in these relationships.

Teacher Characteristics, Teacher Behavior, and Relationships

Consistent and positive associations have been found between teacher *experience* and students' perceptions of the quality of the teacher–student relationship, with more experienced teachers being perceived as higher in terms of agency and communion (i.e., control and affiliation) (Brekelmans, Wubbels, & van Tartwijk, 2005; Vick Wittaker & Jones Harden, 2010a; Wubbels et al., 2006). Interestingly, the relationship between teacher experience and teachers' self-perceptions of the quality of the teacher–student relationship displays a less consistent pattern across studies. Some studies show similar patterns for teacher and student data (e.g. Brekelmans, Wubbels, & van Tartwijk, 2005; Riley, 2009; Wubbels et al., 2006), while others showed mixed (Pianta, 2006) or reversed patterns, with younger and less experienced teachers reporting more positive relationships than more experienced teachers (Mashburn, Hamre, Downer, & Pianta, 2006; Yeo, Ang, Chong, Huan, & Quek, 2008).

Strong and positive associations have been found between teachers' *self-efficacy* and students' and teachers' perceptions of the quality of teacher–student relationships (Hamre, Pianta, Downer, & Mashburn, 2008; Mashburn, Hamre, Downer, & Pianta, 2006; Myers & Pianta, 2008; O'Connor, 2010; Pianta, 2006).

Teachers' *emotional states*, as well as their *personality characteristics*, have been found to be associated with the quality of teacher–student relationships. Jennings and Greenberg (2009) concluded in their review that teachers' negative feelings and emotions were associated with less caring for students and less involved student behaviors. Similarly, Hosotani and Imai-Matsumura (2011) found that more positive teacher emotions were associated with more caring teacher behavior. Higher teacher emotional intelligence has been linked to more teacher closeness in the classroom (Nizielski, Hallum, Lopes, & Schutz, 2012). Pianta (2006), in the previous *Handbook of Research on Classroom Management*, also reported that better teacher mental health was associated with higher quality of teacher–student relationships. Koles and colleagues (2013) indeed found that teacher neuroticism and depression resulted in more teacher–student conflicts, which consistently appeared in different countries involved in this study.

Teacher *(practical) knowledge* has also been linked to teacher behavior and the quality of teacher–student relationships in the classroom. Studies have reported that more knowledge of teacher–student and between-student relationships in class and the factors that shape these relationships are beneficial for the creation of positive and high-quality teacher–student relationships. Milner and Tenore (2010) argued that, in the context of multicultural classes, relationship quality improves if teachers can better distinguish between equity and equality, if they have more knowledge of power structures in the classroom, if they have better self-understanding, and if they are more willing to immerse themselves in the lives of their students. Empirical evidence for such assertions also were reported in a study in multicultural classes by Van Tartwijk, den Brok, Veldman and Wubbels (2009). Interestingly, in both studies in the multicultural classroom context, knowledge of relationships and social processes in the classroom appeared to be more important for the teachers than the actual knowledge of their students' ethnic and cultural backgrounds.

Finally, mixed results have been found regarding the association of teacher *attitudes, emotions and beliefs* and the quality of teacher–student relationships. Beliefs may vary from more custodial orientations toward classroom management (Van Tartwijk, den Brok, Veldman, & Wubbels, 2009) to more caring and student-oriented beliefs (Hosotani & Imai-Matsumura, 2011; Riley, Lewis, & Wang, 2012). A study by Myers and Pianta (2008) suggested that teachers who view themselves as instructors may negatively respond to underachieving and disruptive students, whereas teachers who view themselves as socializers may respond negatively to aggressive or disconnected students (see also Riley, Lewis, & Wang, 2012). In sum, although different orientations of teachers toward teacher–student relationships may lead to diverse responses to subpopulations of students in the classroom, no clear patterns have been reported.

Teacher Characteristics, Student Behavior, and Student Outcomes

Many studies have investigated the connection of teacher–student communion or (emotional) proximity and student behaviors. Several of these studies have shown positive associations between the degree of teacher closeness, warmth, respect for students, or empathy and *desired* student behaviors in the classroom, such as positive student conduct (Brackett, Reyes, Rivers, Elbertson, & Salovey, 2011), positive student work habits (Myers & Pianta, 2008), prosocial student behavior (Jennings & Greenberg, 2009; Spivak & Farran, 2012), high student well-being and engagement in the classroom

(Cooper, 2011), high student behavioral self-control (Merritt, Wanless, Rimm-Kaufman, Cameron, & Peugh, 2012), teacher liking by students (Gest & Rodkin, 2011), and friendships and connections between students in class (Gest & Rodkin, 2011). Findings were inconsistent, however, regarding associations of teacher warmth and closeness on the one hand and student prosocial behavior on the other. Some studies, using observations and teacher perception data, did not find associations between these variables (Ocak, 2010; Spivak & Farran, 2012).

Specific behaviors associated with teacher warmth and closeness, such as eye contact, open body positioning, and teacher self-talk, have been found to be associated with positive student behaviors such as on-task student behavior (Hall & Smotrova, 2013; Mazer, Murphy & Simonds, 2007). Other teacher behaviors that have been found to be associated with more student attentiveness and engagement are teacher praise and error correction, clarity, care, monitoring behavior, and behavioral control (Conroy, Sutherland, Haydon, Stormont, & Harmon, 2009; Nie & Lau, 2009). Cooper (2011) found that seating arrangements created by teachers with more physical proximity to the teacher led to higher student engagement. In a similar fashion, student perceptions of teacher care, opportunity to ask questions, taking time to help, or giving structure is related to higher degrees of student well-being in class (Suldo et al., 2009) and student resilience (Johnson, 2008). On a more general level, high teacher autonomy support is also associated with increased student engagement and better teacher–student relationships (Reeve, 2006). Similarly, a consistent finding across studies is that higher degrees of warmth, empathy, and closeness are associated with lower amounts of *undesired* student behaviors, such as disruptions (Hall & Smotrova, 2013; Myers & Pianta, 2008), conflicts between students (Hamre, Pianta, Downer, & Mashburn, 2008; Myers & Pianta, 2008), student discipline problems or misconduct (Holt, Hargrove, & Harris, 2011; Nizielski, Hallum, Lopes, & Schutz, 2012), in-class text messaging via mobile phones (Johnson, 2013), student distraction (Lewis, Romi, Katz, & Qui, 2008), student aggression in the classroom (Merritt, Wanless, Rimm-Kaufman, Cameron, & Peugh, 2012; Myers & Pianta, 2008), or more moderate behaviors such as resistance or reactance (Zhang & Sapp, 2013).

The Conroy and associates (2009) study also reported that lower amounts of teacher clarity and inconsistent responses to students led to more *distraction and student aggression*. Nie and Lau (2009) reported that more behavioral control was related to lower levels of classroom misbehavior. Good classroom rules and procedures have also been found to be associated with less discipline problems (Holt, Hargrove, & Harris, 2011). Teacher recognition of students, hinting students, involving them in classroom interactions, and rewarding them are associated with less student distraction (Lewis, Romi, Katz, & Qui, 2008). Higher degrees of teacher–student conflict behaviors, teacher misbehaviors, teacher aggression, teacher negative remarks to students, and teacher disapproval of students and student behaviors are associated with more *externalizing* and *internalizing* student behavior (Buyse, Verschueren, Doumen, Van Damme, & Maes, 2008; Vick Whittaker & Jones Harden, 2010b), more antisocial student behavior (Claus, Booth-Butterfield & Chory, 2012), increased student distraction (Lewis, Romi, Katz, & Qui, 2008; Romi, Lewis, Roache, & Riley, 2011), student noncompliance (Vick Whittaker & Jones Harden, 2010b), more student aggression and conflict (Gest & Rodkin, 2011; Hamre, Pianta, Downer, & Mashburn, 2008; Jennings & Greenberg, 2009; Ocak, 2010), increased student behavioral problems (Myers & Pianta, 2008), less cooperative behavior between students in the classroom (Jennings & Greenberg, 2009), and lower ratings of peers by students (Jennings & Greenberg, 2009; Romi, Lewis, Roache, & Riley, 2011). In a related fashion, lower amounts of negative or oppositional teacher behaviors are associated with more student on-task behavior and less student talking-out behavior (Leflot, van Lier, Ongenha, & Colpin, 2010).

Interestingly, some teacher oppositional behaviors also have been found to relate positively to desired student behaviors. For example, Gest and Rodkin (2011) found that physically separating students by teachers led to more liking of the teacher by students and to stronger between-student friendships and contact in class. Lewis, Romi, and Roache (2012) found that excluding students from class led to improved student behavior. However, their study also showed that this was the case only if several conditions were met, such as giving prior warnings to students before exclusion, explaining to students the reason(s) for exclusion, and having follow-up meetings with the student(s) concerned after exclusion.

Circularity in Interactions

Several studies show that generally in the course of a school year teacher–student relationships change and more often tend to become less positive than more positive (Doumen et al., 2008; Gehlbach, Brinkworth, & Harris, 2012; Mainhard, Brekelmans, den Brok, & Wubbels, 2011). Reciprocity in aggressive circular interactions may be the origin of these deteriorating relationships, and the Doumen and associates (2008) study hinted at such mutual influences of teacher and student behaviors. For example, at the micro level, aggressive student behavior may lead to increased teacher hostile behaviors, which in turn can foster increased levels of aggressive student behavior. Thus such processes at the micro level may over time have caused a vicious cycle of deteriorating teacher–student interactions, leading at the macro level to worsening relationships from the onset to the end of the year.

Interpersonal theory through the notions of circularity and complementarity helps to understand the origin of recurring patterns in interactions. Complementarity describes what reaction most probably is invited by interactional behaviors. Complementarity differs for the two interpersonal dimensions agency and communion, with behavior on the agency dimension inviting contrasting and behavior on the communion dimension inviting similar responses (Dryer & Horowitz, 1997; Tracey, 2004). Thus for teacher–student interactions, interpersonal theory predicts that teacher behavior high on agency probably invites a submissive reaction from the students and that submissive behavior of the students invites active or dominant behavior of the teacher, thus reinforcing the original teacher behavior (De Jong, Van Tartwijk, Veldman, Verloop, & Wubbels, 2012). Thus an interaction pattern comes to life in which the teacher is in control and active and students become passive followers. On the communion dimension, similar behavior is invited: a teacher conveying high levels of communion most probably invites an equally warm reaction from students, and a teacher low on communion invites similar aggressive or hostile behavior of the students. Thus, in the former case, a friendly and caring classroom atmosphere may be the result, and in the latter a climate characterized by unliking and aggressive feelings and behavior on the part of teacher and students.

Few studies explicitly investigated to what degree teacher–student interactions were complementary, and the results do not straightforwardly confirm or reject the complementarity principle. One example is a study by Roorda, Koomen, Spilt, Thijs, and Oort (2013) on kindergarten teacher and student behavior. Both teachers and students reacted complementarily on the control but not on the affiliation dimension. For kindergarten teachers, Thijs, Koomen, Roorda, and ten Hagen (2011) also reported complementarity for teacher control. For students, they reported complementarity for affiliation and for control only if they were shy or shared positive relationships with their teachers. In case studies in secondary education in classrooms with a positive and a less positive climate, teacher behaviors were found in both classes to be rather complementary on both dimensions (Mainhard, Pennings, Wubbels, & Brekelmans, 2012). De Jong and colleagues (2012) investigated teachers' expectations of student responses to teacher behavior. They found that teachers' expectations of student behavior were complementary except for hostile teacher behaviors. For these behaviors, teachers expected more submissive student responses than would be expected according to the complementarity principle.

The mixed results regarding the complementarity principle may be due to the hierarchical nature of teacher–student relationships. For example, in the de Jong and associates (2012) study a noncomplementary submissive student response may be the result of the generally expected student obedience when teachers correct student behavior. Hence the student response to teacher hostile behavior is not the aggression postulated by the complementarity principle, but submission. Thus, although complementarity is theorized to be the most probabilistic pattern of behavior, other responses may occur. This is fortunate because it may help teachers to prevent the development of escalated aggression, which represents a situation of rigid complementarity (Wubbels, Créton, & Holvast, 1988).

Interactions and Relationships

The heart of our conceptual model in Figure 19.1 is the interplay between real-time moment-to-moment interactions (the micro level) and relationships (the macro level). Suldo and associates (2009) found that students perceive the relationship with their teacher positively when the interactions with the teacher are interpreted as attempts to connect with students on an emotional level. Thijs, Koomen, and van der Leij (2008) found that teachers reported more socioemotional support behaviors and more behavior regulation for students with whom they had unfavorable (dependent, conflicted, or distant) relationships. Buyse and colleagues (2008), however, found that teacher-reported management behavior did not predict relationship quality. Van Tartwijk and associates (2009) showed that teachers who were successful in creating positive teacher–student relationships in multicultural classrooms were generally aware of the importance of providing clear rules and correcting student behavior whenever necessary and also of the potential negative consequences of corrections for the relationship with their students. These teachers were said to use deliberate strategies to reduce the potential negative consequences. In all these studies, however, interactions and behaviors were investigated with teacher or student interviews or questionnaires, which were not mapping real-time interactions but over time generalized perceptions of these interactions. Thus, in essence, these results reflect associations of two macro-level variables instead of relating the micro to the macro levels.

The number of studies explicitly addressing the interplay between the micro and the macro levels is small. Research by Mainhard and colleagues (2012), Mainhard, Brekelmans, and Wubbels (2011), and Vick Whittaker and Jones Harden (2010b) comes most closely to investigating this interplay. The Mainhard and associates (2011) study showed that teacher supportive behaviors in one lesson were positively correlated to the teacher–student relationship in terms of affiliation during that same lesson and also in the lesson a week later. These supportive behaviors were not, however, correlated with the relationship in terms of teacher interpersonal influence. Coercive teacher behaviors in one lesson were negatively correlated with the relationship in terms of affiliation during that lesson and the lesson a week later but almost did not correlate with the level of a teacher's influence in the classroom. Thus when a teacher showed coercive behavior in order to improve the teacher–student relationship, this had a counterproductive effect. Mainhard and colleagues (2012) compared interactions in one classroom with a positive and one with a negative teacher–student relationship. Most of the time, interaction in both classrooms was characterized by teacher behaviors on control somewhat higher than student behaviors and by complementary medium to high teacher and student affiliation behaviors. This might reflect the commonly assumed social hierarchy in classrooms, which combines legitimate teacher power with a basically nonoppositional attitude of both teacher and students (cf. Thijs, Koomen, Roorda, & ten Hagen, 2011). One difference between the interactions in the two classrooms was found: for the more positive teacher–student relationship, interactions including high teacher affiliation behavior were frequently observed, whereas reciprocated hostile interaction behaviors occurred only with the less positive teacher–student relationship. Mainhard and colleagues (2012) also suggested that variability in interaction might explain differences between positive and negative teacher–student relationships. Interactions varied far more within the less favorable than in the more favorable relationship. Finally, Vick Whittaker and Jones Harden (2010b) reported only weak associations between teacher–student relationships and observed interactions. The strongest (negative) association was found between conflict in the relationship and positive interactions.

Teacher Education and Professional Development

A number of publications are available on interventions that aim to help teachers and student teachers to build productive relationships with students, in particular students with severe behavioral problems. Many of these publications, however, are not based on thorough effect studies.

Conroy and associates (2009) describe an ecological, classroom-based approach that aims at serving the behavioral needs of young students that demonstrate chronic behavior problems. The starting point for this approach is the notion that the behavior of teacher and students in interactions mutually influence each other. Thus changes in a student's behavior impact the teacher's behavior and the teacher's changed expectations and behavior, in turn, affect the behavior of the student (Conroy 2009, p. 4).

They suggest that a system of positive behavior support should take various levels of challenging behavior into account and include instructional practices such as increased rates of praise, clear classroom rules, and precorrection (identifying contexts in which a student is likely to engage in problem behavior and provide precorrective prompts to teach the student how to respond appropriately in that situation). An example of such an approach is the Child Teacher Relationship Therapy, in which a teacher is trained as a therapeutic agent to assist in the change process of the child's life. Studies investigating the effect of this therapy indicated that students whose teachers were trained in this approach made statistically significant improvements in behavior compared with control groups (Morrison Bennett & Bratton, 2011; Pretz Helker & Ray, 2009).

In the context of kindergarten, Roorda, Koomen, Thijs, and Oort (2013) investigated the effects of short-term training for teachers (twice, 45 minutes each time) based on interpersonal theory and the complementarity principle and targeting negative interaction cycles between teachers and socially inhibited (shy) students. The training elicited decreased teacher control and increased teacher affiliation, especially in interactions with shy students. Hemmeter, Snyder, Kinder, and Artman (2011) developed an intervention targeting the improvement of preschool teachers' descriptive praise. This intervention consisted of a brief training session on the use of descriptive praise, e-mail contact entailing performance feedback by coaches who observed teachers at work during a large-group activity, and hyperlinks to descriptive praise video exemplars. A small-scale pilot revealed positive effects on teachers' use of descriptive praise and, as a consequence, diminishing students' challenging behavior. In a study on the development of the behavior of young primary school students with high levels of oppositional behavior and hyperactivity, Leflot and colleagues (2010) showed that training aimed at reducing the use of negative remarks and increasing the use of teacher praise resulted in a long-term reduction of student problem behavior.

In several school settings, Pianta and Hamre (2009) developed a program to conceptualize, measure, and ultimately improve the quality of teacher–student interactions. This program focused initially on the preschool and early elementary period but was later extended to secondary education. This work resulted in an approach to enhance the quality of teacher–student interactions (MyTeachingPartner) based on the Classroom Assessment Scoring System (CLASS) observational system. MyTeachingPartner is an ongoing, systematic professional development program for teachers, with four "levers" to produce developmental change for teacher–student interactions: (1) teachers' knowledge and cognitions related to their interactions with students, (2) ongoing relational supports for teachers themselves, (3) teachers' regular exposure to individualized feedback about their actual interactions with students, and (4) a standard and valid target around which to focus efforts to change interactions. The MyTeachingPartner program builds on a supportive consultation relationship using web-based interactions in which teachers have the opportunity to view annotated videos of their own and others' interactions with students. Positive effects have been reported for the quality of teacher–student interactions.

Brown, Jones La Russo, and Aber (2010) investigated the effects of the 4R program on classroom quality in urban elementary schools. The 4Rs Program is a school-based intervention in literacy development, conflict resolution, and intergroup understanding that trains and supports teachers in how to integrate the teaching of social and emotional skills into the language arts curriculum. Teachers take an introductory training of five days just prior to the beginning of the school year and/or within the first two weeks after school begins. After this training, they receive ongoing coaching by program staff developers. Also in this study, classroom quality was measured using the CLASS observational instrument. Teachers' self-reported emotional ability and burnout were included in the analyses. The 4R program had significant positive effects on classroom quality.

In the context of a teacher education program, the positive effects of a focus on the teacher–student relationship was supported by a study investigating the influence of teacher preparation on responses to the aggression of students with behavioral problems in the classroom (Alvarez, 2007). In this study it was assumed that the students' aggression negatively affects student teachers' stress levels, such that they use harsher discipline and spend less time engaging students in a positive manner, thereby eliciting negative relationships. Teacher training focusing on teaching students with emotional problems or emotional disabilities moderated the relation between attributions of intentionality and negative affective reactions to student aggression.

Kaya, Lundeen, and Wolfgang (2010) found that student teaching significantly increased preservice elementary teachers' preferences toward a more assertive discipline model (Rules and Consequences) and decreased their preferences for the humanistic discipline model (Relationship–Listening). A study by Van Tartwijk, Veldman, and Verloop (2011) investigated the effects of a transition in a secondary teacher education program from teaching classroom management in a separate course with a strong focus on training behavioral techniques to teaching classroom management in a curriculum that aimed at linking practice and theory by stimulating students to reflect on their experience and using a relationship perspective on classroom management. Their study showed a significant increase in how well student teachers felt prepared for classroom management.

In sum, these studies show that the improvement of teachers' classroom management competencies through professional development programs and specific activities in teacher education on teacher–student relationships is a fruitful avenue to pursue.

CONCLUDING REMARKS

When reflecting on the results presented in this chapter from the perspective of the dynamic systems theory, it is striking how few studies have explicitly looked at relationships from two tenets of this theory: (1) reciprocity instead of one-directional causality as a fundamental feature of interactions and relationships and (2) the hierarchical nesting of interactions and relationships.

Reciprocity and Causality

Reciprocity is a fundamental feature of interactions, and it is important to note that most studies reviewed do not allow for causal inferences. Most studies on the association between student or teacher characteristics and teacher–student interactions or relationships test unidirectional models providing evidence, for example, either for the statistical effect of student characteristics on teacher–student relationships (e.g., Ladd & Burgess, 1999; Murray & Murray, 2004) or, vice versa, for the statistical effect of teacher–student relationships on student characteristics (e.g., nonstatic behavior) (Pianta & Stuhlman, 2004). Most studies mentioned that associations between variables were correlational and that no causality could be assumed—for example, that more behavioral control was related to lower levels of classroom misbehavior (Nie & Lau, 2009)—or that good classroom rules and procedures were associated with less discipline problems (Holt, Hargrove, & Harris, 2011). On the other hand, some of the studies reviewed on teacher professional development give indications that changing teacher behavior may help change student behavior.

One of the few studies that took a bidirectional perspective on the association of student characteristics and teacher–students relationships (Doumen et al., 2008) provided evidence for reciprocal influences between teacher–student conflict and aggressive student behavior over time. Aggressive behavior at the onset of kindergarten led to increased levels of teacher–student conflict by the middle of the school year, which in turn led to increased levels of aggressive behavior by the end of the year.

Given the low number of studies with a bidirectional approach or allowing for causal inferences, we advocate that future research should focus on reciprocal influences (cf. Luckner & Pianta, 2011) and causal effects, for example, by employing longitudinal (e.g., O'Connor, 2010) or experimental designs. In a longitudinal design, in particular, cross-lagged panel analyses (Jöreskog, 1970) are useful for disentangling causal effects.

Nesting of Interactions and Relationships

According to dynamic systems theory, the moment-to-moment time scale (teacher–student interaction) is the primary engine of development for macro-level outcomes (e.g., teacher–student relationships, teacher job satisfaction, students' emotional well-being). It is striking that most studies in school settings on interactions in the field of classroom management and teacher–student relationships did not gather data on the real-time scale of the micro level, let alone look at the interplay between the micro and the macro levels. In various other social contexts, studies on relationships have been carried out using a dynamic systems approach and focusing on the micro level. Examples are studies on parent–child relationships (Granic & Hollenstein, 2003), family relationships (Chuang, 2005), homogeneous interaction partners (Markey, Lowmaster, & Eichler 2010), and mixed-sex relationships (Sadler & Woody, 2003).

In order to understand what teachers can do in their classroom management behaviors to improve teacher–student relationships, further research on the interplay between the level of real-time moment-to-moment interactions and generalized perceptions of teacher–student relationships is dearly needed.

REFERENCES

Alvarez, H. K. (2007). The impact of teacher preparation on responses to student aggression in the classroom. *Teaching and Teacher Education, 23*, 1113–1126.

Arbeau, K. A., Coplan, R. J., & Weeks, M. (2010). Shyness, teacher–child relationships, and socio-emotional adjustment in grade 1. *International Journal of Behavioral Development, 34*, 259–269.

Bean, R. A., Barber, B. K., & Crane, D. R. (2006). Parental support, behavioral control, and psychological control among African American youth: The relationships to academic grades, delinquency, and depression. *Journal of Family Issues, 27*, 1335–1355.

Birch S. H., & Ladd, G. W. (1997). The teacher–child relationship and children's early school adjustment. *Journal of School Psychology, 35*, 61–79.

Bowlby, J. (1982). *Attachment and loss*: Vol. 1. *Attachment* (2nd ed.). New York: Basic Books.

Brackett, M. A., Reyes, M. R., Rivers, S. E., Elbertson, N. A., & Salovey, P. (2011). Classroom emotional climate, teacher affiliation, and student conduct. *Journal of Classroom Interaction, 46*(1), 27–36.

Brekelmans, M. (1989). *Interpersonal teacher behavior in the classroom*. Utrecht, The Netherlands: W.C.C. [in Dutch].

Brekelmans, M., Wubbels, T., & van Tartwijk, J. (2005). Teacher–student relationships across the teaching career. *International Journal of Educational Research, 43* (1–2), 55–71.

Brok, P. den, Brekelmans, M., & Wubbels, T. (2006). Multilevel issues in studies using students' perceptions of learning environments: The case of the Questionnaire on Teacher Interaction. *Learning Environments Research, 9* (3), 199–213.

Brok, P. den, Tartwijk, J. van, Wubbels, Th., & Veldman, I. (2010). The differential effect of the teacher–student interpersonal relationship on student outcomes for students with different ethnic backgrounds. *British Journal of Educational Psychology, 80*, 199–221.

Bronfenbrenner, U., & Morris, P. A. (1998). The ecology of developmental processes. In W. Damon (Series Ed.) & R. M. Lerner (Vol. Ed.), *Handbook of child psychology*, Vol. 1. *Theoretical models of human development* (5th ed.) (pp. 993–1028). New York: Wiley.

Brown, J. L., Jones, S. M., LaRusso, M. D., & Aber, J. L. (2010). Improving classroom quality: Teacher influences and experimental impacts of the 4Rs program. *Journal of Educational Psychology, 102*(1), 153–167.

Buyse, E., Verschueren, K., Doumen, S., Van Damme, J., & Maes, F. (2008). Classroom problem behavior and teacher–child relationships in kindergarten: The moderating role of classroom climate. *Journal of School Psychology, 46*, 367–391.

Chang, M. (2009). An appraisal perspective of teacher burnout: Examining the emotional work of teachers. *Educational Psychology Review, 21*, 193–218.

Chuang, Y. (2005). Effects of interaction pattern on family harmony and well-being: Test of interpersonal theory, Relational-Models theory, and Confucian ethics. *Asian Journal of Social Psychology, 8*(3), 272–291.

Claus, C. J., Booth-Butterfield, M., & Chory, R. M. (2012). The relationship between instructor misbehaviors and student antisocial behavioral alteration techniques: The roles of instructor attractiveness, humor, and relational closeness. *Communication Education, 61*, 161–183.

Conroy, M., Sutherland, K., Haydon, T., Stormont, M., & Harmon, J. (2009). Preventing and ameliorating young children's chronic problem behaviors: An ecological classroom-based approach. *Psychology in the Schools, 46*(1), 3–17.

Cooper, P. (2011). Teacher strategies for effective intervention with students presenting social, emotional and behavioural difficulties: an international review. *European Journal of Special Needs Education, 26,* 71–86.

Cornelius-White, J. (2007). Learner-centered teacher student relationships are effective: A meta-analysis. *Review of Educational Research, 77*(1), 113–143.

de Jong, R. J., Van Tartwijk, J., Verloop, N., Veldman, I., & Wubbels, T. (2012). Teachers' expectations of teacher–student interaction: Complementarity and distinctive expectancy patterns. *Teaching and Teacher Education, 28,* 948–956.

Doumen, S., Verschueren, K., Buyse, E., Germeijs, V., Luyckx, K., & Soenens, B. (2008). Reciprocal relations between teacher–child conflict and aggressive behavior in kindergarten: A three-wave longitudinal study. *Journal of Clinical Child & Adolescent Psychology, 37,* 588–599.

Dryer, D. C., & Horowitz, L. M. (1997). When do opposites attract? Interpersonal complementarity versus similarity. *Journal of Personality and Social Psychology, 72,* 592–603.

Ertesvåg, S. K. (2011). Measuring authoritative teaching. *Teaching and Teacher Education, 27,* 51–61.

Evertson, C. M., & Weinstein, C. S. (2006). Classroom management as a field of inquiry. In C. M. Evertston & C. S. Weinstein (Eds.), *Handbook of classroom management: Research, practice, and contemporary issues* (pp. 3–15). Mahwah, NJ: Erlbaum.

Flanders, N. A. (1970). *Analyzing teacher behavior.* Oxford: Addison-Wesley.

Fournier, M. A., Moskowitz, D. S., & Zuroff, D. C. (2011). Origins and applications of the interpersonal circumplex. In L. M. Horowitz, & S. Strack (Eds.), *Handbook of interpersonal psychology* (pp. 37–56). New York: Wiley.

Frenzel, A. C., Pekrun, R., & Goetz, T. (2007). Perceived learning environment and students' emotional experiences: A multilevel analysis of mathematics classrooms. *Learning and Instruction, 17*(5), 478–493.

Friedman, I. A. (2006). Classroom management and teacher stress and burnout. In C. Evertson & C. Weinstein (Eds.), *Handbook of classroom management: Research, practice, and contemporary issues* (pp. 925–944). Mahwah, NJ: Erlbaum.

Garza, R. (2009). Latino and white high school students' perceptions of caring behaviors: Are we culturally responsive to our students? *Urban Education, 44,* 297–321.

Gehlbach, H., Brinkworth, M. E., & Harris, A. D. (2012). Changes in teacher–student relationships. *British Journal of Educational Psychology, 82,* 690–704.

Gentry, M., Steenbergen-Hu, S., & Choi, B. (2011). Student-identified exemplary teachers: Insights from talented teachers. *Gifted Child Quarterly, 55*(2), 111–125.

Gest, S. D., & Rodkin, P. C. (2011). Teaching practices and elementary classroom peer ecologies. *Journal of Applied Developmental Psychology, 32,* 288–296.

Good, T. L., & Brophy, J. (2007). *Looking in classrooms* (10th ed.). Boston: Allyn & Bacon.

Granic, I., & Hollenstein, T. (2003). Dynamic systems methods for models of developmental psychopathology. *Development and Psychopathology, 15*(3), 641–669.

Gurtman, M. B. (2009). Exploring personality with the interpersonal circumplex. *Social Psychology Compass, 3,* 1–19.

Hall, J. K., & Smotrova, T. (2013). Teacher self-talk: Interactional resource for managing instruction and eliciting empathy. *Journal of Pragmatics, 47,* 75–92.

Hamre, B. K., & Pianta, R. C. (2001). Early teacher–child relationships and the trajectory of children's school outcomes through eighth grade. *Child Development, 72,* 625–638.

Hamre, B. K., Pianta, R. C., Downer, J. T., & Mashburn, A. J. (2008). Teachers' perceptions of conflict with young children: Looking beyond problem behaviors. *Social Development, 17,* 115–136.

Hemmeter, M. L., Snyder, P., Kinder, K., & Artman, K. (2011). Impact of performance feedback delivered via electronic mail on preschool teachers' use of descriptive praise. *Early Childhood Research Quarterly, 26,* 96–109.

Hollenstein, T., & Lewis, M. D. (2006). A state space analysis of emotion and flexibility in parent–child interactions. *Emotion, 6*(4), 663–669.

Holt, C., Hargrove, P., & Harris, S. (2011). An investigation into the life experiences and beliefs of teachers exhibiting highly effective classroom management behaviors. *Teacher Education and Practice, 24,* 96–113.

Horowitz, M. L., & Strack, S. (2011). *Handbook of interpersonal psychology.* New York: Wiley.

Hosotani, R., & Imai-Matsumura, K. (2011). Emotional experience, expression, and regulation of high-quality Japanese elementary school teachers. *Teaching and Teacher Education, 27,* 1039–1048.

Jennings, P. A., & Greenberg, M. T. (2009). The prosocial classroom: Teacher social and emotional competence in relation to student and classroom outcomes. *Review of Educational Research, 79*, 491–525.

Johnson, B. (2008). Teacher–student relationships which promote resilience at school: A micro-level analysis of students' views. *British Journal of Guidance & Counselling, 36*, 385–398.

Johnson, D. I. (2013). Student in-class texting behavior: Associations with instructor clarity and classroom relationships. *Communication Research Reports, 30*, 57–62.

Jöreskog, K. G. (1970). A general method for analysis of covariance structures. *Biometrika, 57*, 239–251.

Kaya, S., Lundeen, C., & Wolfgang, C. H. (2010). Discipline orientations of pre-service teachers before and after student teaching. *Teaching Education, 21*(2), 157–169.

Keogh, B. K. (2003). *Temperament in the classroom: Understanding individual differences.* Baltimore, MD: Paul H. Brookes.

Kiesler, D. J. (1983). The interpersonal transaction circle: A taxonomy for complementarity in human processes. *Psychological Bulletin, 77*, 421–430.

Koles, B., O'Connor, E. E., & Collins, B. A. (2013). Associations between child and teacher characteristics and quality of teacher–child relationships: The case of Hungary. *European Early Childhood Education Research Journal, 21*, 53–76.

Koomen, H. M. Y, Verschueren, K., van Schooten, E., Jak, S., & Pianta, R. C., et al. (2012). Validating the student–teacher relationship scale: Testing factor structure and measurement invariance across child gender and age in a Dutch sample. *Journal of School Psychology, 50*(2), 215–234.

Ladd, G. W., & Burgess, K. B. (1999). Charting the relationship trajectories of aggressive, withdrawn, and aggressive/withdrawn children during early grade school. *Child Development, 70*, 910–929.

Leary, T. (1957). *An interpersonal diagnosis of personality.* New York: Ronald.

Leflot, G., van Lier, P. A. C., Onghena, P., & Colpin, H. (2010). The role of teacher behavior management in the development of disruptive behaviors: An intervention study with the good behavior game. *Journal of Abnormal Child Psychology, 38*, 869–882.

Levy, J., den Brok, P., Wubbels, T., & Brekelmans, M. (2003). Students' perceptions of interpersonal aspects of the learning environment. *Learning Environments Research, 6*, 5–36.

Lewis, R., Romi, S., Katz, Y. J., & Qui, X. (2008). Students' reaction to classroom discipline in Australia, Israel, and China. *Teaching and Teacher Education, 24*, 715–724.

Lewis, R., Romi, S., Qui, X., & Katz, Y. J. (2005). Teachers' classroom discipline and student misbehavior in Australia, China and Israel. *Teaching and Teacher Education, 21*(6), 729–741.

Lewis, R., Romi, S., & Roache, J. (2012). Excluding students from classroom: Teacher techniques that promote student responsibility. *Teaching and Teacher Education, 28*, 870–878.

Luckner, A. E., & Pianta, R. C. (2011). Teacher–student interactions in fifth grade classrooms: Relations with children's peer behavior. *Journal of Applied Developmental Psychology, 32*, 257–266.

Lüdtke, O., Robitzsch, A., Trautwein, U., & Kunter, M. (2009). Assessing the impact of learning environments: How to use student ratings of classroom or school characteristics in multilevel modeling. *Contemporary Educational Psychology, 34*(2), 120–131.

Mainhard, M. T., Brekelmans, M., den Brok, P., & Wubbels, T. (2011). The development of the classroom social climate during the first months of the school year. *Contemporary Educational Psychology, 36*, 190–200.

Mainhard, T., Brekelmans, M., & Wubbels, Th. (2011) Coercive and supportive teacher behaviour: Within- and across-lessons associations with the classroom social climate. *Learning and Instruction, 21*, 345–354.

Mainhard, M. T., Pennings, H. J. M., Wubbels, T., & Brekelmans, M. (2012). Mapping control and affiliation in teacher–student interaction with state space grids. *Teaching and Teacher Education, 28*, 1027–1037.

Markey, P. M., Lowmaster, S. E., & Eichler, W. C. (2010). A real-time assessment of interpersonal complementarity. *Personal Relationships, 17*, 13–25.

Marsh, H. W., Lüdtke, O., Nagengast, B., Trautwein, U. Morin, A. J. S., & Köller, O. (2012). Classroom climate and contextual effects: Conceptual and methodological issues in the evaluation of group-level effects. *Educational Psychologist, 47*, 106–124.

Mashburn, A. J., Hamre, B. K., Downer, J. T., & Pianta, R. C. (2006). Teacher and classroom characteristics associated with teachers' ratings of prekindergartners' relationships and behaviors. *Journal of Psychoeducational Assessment, 24*, 367–380.

Mazer, J. P., Murphy, R. E., & Simonds, C. J. (2007). I'll see you on "Facebook": The effects of computer-mediated teacher self-disclosure on student motivation, affective learning, and classroom climate. *Communication Education, 56*, 1–17.

McRobbie, C. J., Fisher, D. L., & Wong, A. F. L. (1998). Personal and class forms of classroom environment instruments In B. J. Fraser & K. G. Tobin (Eds.), *International handbook of science education* (pp. 581–594). Dordrecht: Kluwer Academic.

Merritt, E. G., Wanless, S. B., Rimm-Kaufman, S. E., Cameron, C., & Peugh, J. L. (2012). The contribution of teachers' emotional support to children's social behaviors and self-regulatory skills in first grade. *School Psychology Review, 41*, 141–159.

Milner IV, H. R., & Tenore, F. B. (2010). Classroom management in diverse classrooms. *Urban Education, 45*, 560–603.

Mitchell, M. M., & Bradshaw, C. P. (2013). Examining classroom influences on student perceptions of school climate: The role of classroom management and exclusionary discipline strategies. *Journal of School Psychology, 51*(5), 599–610.

Morrison Bennett, M. O., & Bratton, S. C. (2011). The effects of child teacher relationship training on the children of focus: A pilot study. *International Journal of Play Therapy, 20*(4), 193–207.

Murray, C., & Murray, K. M. (2004). Correlates of teacher–student relationships: An examination of child demographic characteristics, academic orientations and behavioral orientations. *Psychology in the Schools, 41*, 751–762.

Myers, S. S., & Pianta, R. C. (2008). Developmental commentary: Individual and contextual influences on student–teacher relationships and children's early problem behaviors. *Journal of Clinical Child and Adolescent Psychology, 37*, 600–608.

Nie, Y., & Lau, S. (2009). Complementary roles of care and behavioral control in classroom management: The self-determination theory perspective. *Contemporary Educational Psychology, 34*, 185–194.

Nizielski, S., Hallum, S., Lopes, P. N., & Schütz, A. (2012). Attention to student needs mediates the relationship between teacher emotional intelligence and student misconduct in the classroom. *Journal of Psychoeducational Assessment, 30*, 320–329.

Nurmi, J. (2012). Students' characteristics and teacher–child relationships in instruction: A meta-analysis. *Educational Research Review, 7*, 177–197.

Ocak, S. (2010). The effects of child-teacher relationships on interpersonal problem-solving skills of children. *Infants & Young Children, 23*, 312–322.

O'Connor, E. (2010). Teacher–child relationships as dynamic systems. *Journal of School Psychology, 48*, 187–218.

Pianta, R. C. (2001). *Student-Teacher Relationship Scale. Professional manual.* Lutz, FL: Psychological Assessment Resources.

Pianta, R. C. (2006). Classroom management and relationships between children and teachers: Implications for research and practice. In C. M. Evertston & C. S. Weinstein (Eds.), *Handbook of classroom management: Research, practice, and contemporary issues* (pp. 685–710). Mahwah, NJ: Erlbaum.

Pianta, R. C., & Hamre, B. K. (2009). Classroom processes and positive youth development: Conceptualizing, measuring, and improving the capacity of interactions between teachers and students. *New Directions For Youth Development, 121* (Spring 2009), 33–46.

Pianta, R. C., La Paro, K. M., & Hamre, B. K. (2008). *Classroom Assessment Scoring System [CLASS]: Manual, Pre-K.* Baltimore, MD: Paul H. Brookes.

Pianta, R. C., & Stuhlman, M. W. (2004). Teacher–child relationships and children's success in the first years of school. *School Psychology Review, 33*, 444–458.

Pretz Helker, W., & Ray, D. C. (2009). Impact of child teacher relationship training on teachers' and aides' use of relationship-building skills and the effects on student classroom behavior. *International Journal of Play Therapy, 18*(2), 70–83.

Prinzie, P., Stams, G. J. J., Deković, M., Reijntjes, A. H., & Belsky, J. (2009). The relations between parents' Big Five personality factors and parenting: A meta-analytic review. *Journal of Personality and Social Psychology, 97*, 351–362.

Reeve, J. (2006). Teachers as facilitators: What autonomy-supportive teachers do and why their students benefit. *The Elementary School Journal, 106*, 225–236.

Riley, P. (2009). An adult attachment perspective on the student–teacher relationship & classroom management difficulties. *Teaching and Teacher Education, 25*, 626–635.

Riley, P., Lewis, R., & Wang, B. (2012). Investigating teachers' explanations for aggressive classroom discipline strategies in China and Australia. *Educational Psychology, 32*, 389–403.

Roorda, D. L., Koomen, H. M. Y., Spilt, J. L., & Oort, F. J. (2011). The influence of affective teacher–student relationships on students' school engagement and achievement. *Review of Educational Research, 81*(4), 493–529.

Roorda. D, L., Koomen, H. M., Spilt, J. L., Thijs, J. T., & Oort, F. J. (2013). Interpersonal behaviors and complementarity in interactions between teachers and kindergartners with a variety of externalizing and internalizing behaviors. *Journal of School Psychology*, 51(1), 143–158.

Roorda, D. L., Koomen, H. M. Y., Thijs, J. T., & Oort , F. J. (2013). Changing interactions between teachers and socially inhibited kindergarten children: An interpersonal approach. *Journal of Applied Developmental Psychology*, 34(4), 173–184.

Romi, S., Lewis, R., Roache, J., & Riley, P. (2011). The impact of teachers' aggressive management techniques on students' attitudes to schoolwork. *Journal of Educational Research*, 104, 231–240.

Rudasill, K. M., & Rimm-Kaufman, S. E. (2009). Teacher–child relationship quality: The roles of child temperament and teacher–child interactions. *Early Childhood Research Quarterly*, 24, 107–120.

Rudasill, K. M., Rimm-Kaufman, S. E., Justice, L. M., & Pence, K. (2006). Temperament and language skills as predictors of teacher–child relationship quality in preschool. *Early Education and Development*, 17, 271–291.

Sadler, P., Ethier, N., & Woody, E. (2011). Interpersonal complementarity. In L. M. Horowitz, & S. Strack (Eds.), *Handbook of interpersonal psychology* (pp. 123–142). New York: Wiley.

Sadler, P., & Woody, E. (2003). Is who you are who you're talking to? Interpersonal style and complementarity in mixed-sex interactions. *Journal of Personality and Social Psychology*, 84, 80–95.

Simon, A., & Boyer, E. G. (1974). *Mirrors for behaviour III: An anthology of observation instruments*. Wyncote, PA: Communication Materials Center.

Skinner, E., Johnson, S., & Snyder, T. (2005). Six dimensions of parenting: A motivational model. *Parenting: Science and Practice*, 5, 175–235.

Spilt, J. M., Koomen, M. Y., & Thijs, J. T. (2011). Teacher wellbeing: The importance of teacher–student relationships. *Educational Psychology Review*, 23, 457–477.

Spivak, A. L., & Farran, D. C. (2012). First-grade teacher behaviors and children's prosocial actions in classrooms. *Early Education and Development*, 23, 623–639.

Suldo, S. M., Friedrich, A. A., White, T., Farmer, J., Minch, D., & Michalowski, J. (2009). Teacher support and adolescents' subjective well-being: A mixed-methods investigation. *School Psychology Review*, 38, 67–85.

Thijs, J., Koomen, H., Roorda, D., & ten Hagen, J. T. (2011). Explaining teacher–student interactions in early childhood: An interpersonal theoretical approach. *Journal of Applied Developmental Psychology*, 32, 34–43.

Thijs, J. T., Koomen, H. M. Y., & van der Leij, A. (2008). Teacher–child relationships and pedagogical practices: Considering the teacher's perspective. *School Psychology Review*, 37, 244–260.

Tracey, T. J. G. (2004). Levels of interpersonal complementarity: A simplex representation. *Personality and Social Psychology Bulletin*, 30, 1211–1225.

Vansteenkiste, M., Zhou, M., Lens, W., & Soenens, B. (2005). Experiences of autonomy and control among Chinese learners: Vitalizing or immobilizing? *Journal of Educational Psychology*, 97, 468–483.

Van Tartwijk, J., den Brok, P., Veldman, I., & Wubbels, Th. (2009). Teachers' practical knowledge about classroom management in multicultural classrooms. *Teaching and Teacher Education*, 25, 453–460.

Van Tartwijk, J., Veldman, I., & Verloop, N. (2011). Classroom management in a Dutch teacher education program: A realistic approach. *Teaching Education*, 22(2), 169–184.

Vick Whittaker, J. E., Jones Harden, B. (2010a). Beyond ABCs and 123s: Enhancing teacher–child relationship quality to promote children's behavioral development. *NHSA Dialog*, 13, 185–191.

Vick Whittaker, J. E., & Jones Harden, B. (2010b). Teacher–child relationships and children's externalizing behaviors in Head Start. *NHSA Dialog*, 13, 141–167.

Walker, J.M.T. (2009). Authoritative classroom management: How control and nurturance work together. *Theory into Practice*, 48, 122–129.

Wentzel, K. R. (2002). Are effective teachers like good parents? Teaching styles and student adjustment in early adolescence. *Child Development*, 73, 287–301.

Woolfolk-Hoy, A., & Weinstein, C. S. (2006). Student and teacher perspectives on classroom management. In C. Evertson & C. S. Weinstein (Eds.), *Handbook of classroom management: Research, practice, and contemporary issues* (pp. 181–219). Mahwah, NJ: Erlbaum.

Wubbels, Th., Brekelmans, M., den Brok, P., Levy, J., Mainhard, T., & Tartwijk, J. (2012). Let's make things better: developments in research on interpersonal relationships in education. In Th. Wubbels et al. (Eds.), *Interpersonal Relationships in Education: An Overview of Contemporary Research* (pp. 225–250). Rotterdam/Boston/Taipei: Sense Publishers.

Wubbels, T., Brekelmans, M., den Brok, P., & van Tartwijk, J. (2006). An interpersonal perspective on classroom management in secondary classrooms in the Netherlands. In C.M. Evertston & C.S. Weinstein (Eds.), *Handbook of classroom management: Research, practice, and contemporary issues* (pp. 1161–1191). Mahwah, NJ: Erlbaum.

Wubbels, T., Créton, H., & Holvast, A.J.C.D. (1988). Undesirable classroom situations. *Interchange*, 19, 25–40.

Yan, E. M., Evans, I. M., & Harvey, S. T. (2011). Observing emotional interactions between teachers and students in elementary school classrooms, *Journal of Research in Childhood Education*, 25(1), 82–97.

Yeo, L. S., Ang, P. A., Chong, W. H., Huan, V. S., & Quek, C. L. (2008). Teacher efficacy in the context of teaching low achieving students. *Current Psychology*, 27, 192–204.

Zhang, Q., & Sapp, D. A. (2013). Psychological reactance and resistance intention in the classroom: Effects of perceived request politeness and legitimacy, relationship distance, and teacher credibility. *Communication Education*, 62, 1–25.

20

COMMUNICATION AND INTERPERSONAL SKILLS IN CLASSROOM MANAGEMENT

How to Provide the Educational Experiences Students Need and Deserve

KATHERINE A. RACZYNSKI AND ARTHUR M. HORNE
UNIVERSITY OF GEORGIA

Teaching is an art and a science that demands exceptionally skilled practitioners. Teachers are expected to know their subject matter very well, and that is just the beginning. Teachers also must understand managing classroom activities, the learning modes and processes of students, the developmental characteristics for the age level they teach, and the dynamics of student relationships. They must understand the structure of schools, how to relate to colleagues and administrators, and how to tailor their teaching to meet the needs of their individual students, especially given students' diverse backgrounds and family circumstances. Most teachers entering the field know their subject matter and are able to pass certification standards required for their discipline. Once they become teachers, however, a large exodus of well educated early career teachers occurs over the first few years (Ingersoll, 2003; Ingersoll & Merrill, 2010; Ingersoll & Smith, 2003; Kopkowski, 2008; Riggs, 2013).

Very few teachers leave the field because they don't know the material they are supposed to teach; rather they are more likely to leave the field because of the other demands, such as classroom management and discipline issues, overly restrictive curricula and testing programs, and lack of administrative support (Kopkowski, 2008; Ravitch, 2013). It doesn't have to be this way. In fact, in some districts the exodus of early career educators is minimal because teachers report being well prepared academically, having the skills to manage their classrooms, receiving strong administrative and family support for their efforts, and enjoying positive relationships with their students (Zaloom & Klinenberg, 2012). The good news is that the skills needed for effective approaches to teaching—skills that lead to students who are nurtured academically, socially, and emotionally—are learnable.

In the first edition of this handbook, classroom management was presented as

the actions teachers take to create an environment that supports and facilitates both academic and social learning. In other words, classroom management has two distinct purposes: It not only seeks to establish and sustain an orderly environment so students can engage in meaningful academic learning, it also aims to enhance students' social and moral growth. From this perspective, how a teacher achieves order is as important as whether a teacher achieves order.

In the service of these two purposes, teachers carry out a number of specific tasks. They must (1) develop caring, supportive relationships with and among students; (2) organize and implement instruction in ways that optimize students' access to learning; (3) use group management methods that encourage students' engagement in academic tasks; (4) promote the development of students' social skills and self-regulation; and (5) use appropriate interventions to assist students with behavior problems. Clearly, classroom management is a multifaceted endeavor that is far more complex than establishing rules, rewards, and penalties to control students' behavior. (Evertson & Weinstein, 2006, p. 5).

In this chapter we describe how positive communication and successful interpersonal skills serve as the foundation for effective classroom management and positive teacher–student and student–student relationships.

BACKGROUND AND FOUNDATIONS

During a classroom observation, the following situation occurred, as described by our colleague Hein (2004). One student called another student a negative ethnic term. The teacher could have scolded the offending student, lost her cool, doled out a punishment, or given a lecture about the importance of respect. Instead, immediately after the incident, the teacher stopped the lesson and gathered the whole class in a circle. As a group, they discussed what happened, how it was a violation of their values, and why it needed to be addressed immediately. The offending student apologized to the offended student and to the classmates. They discussed briefly the importance of treating all people respectfully and ways of providing "put-ups" (i.e., compliments) rather than put-downs. Then students immediately returned to their work. What could have been a potentially fraught disciplinary issue was resolved in a straightforward manner to the satisfaction of everyone involved. The entire process took less than five minutes. In that time, the classroom values were reviewed, expectations were reiterated, and remediation occurred; the incident turned into a positive learning experience for the entire classroom.

Clearly, this is an example of a capable teacher skillfully resolving a dicey situation. What differentiates this teacher from others who might not have managed the problem as capably? Is it simply that talented teachers know how to apply a process (such as holding a classroom meeting) when things go wrong in the classroom? On one hand, classroom meetings have been described frequently over many years in education (Dreikurs, Grunwald, & Pepper, 1982; Orpinas & Horne, 2006) and serve as a valuable asset for teachers. On the other hand, perhaps something else was needed in addition to knowledge of a particular technique. The teacher in the example set about creating a classroom of respect, dignity, and affirmation from the very first day of school. The students "knew the drill" and could move quickly to addressing issues of concern as a classroom issue. This foundation created the environment whereby a particular process (i.e., classroom meeting) could be implemented swiftly and effectively.

The Helping Relationship

If you were to ask a group of teachers, "What is your job, essentially?" we would hope that very few would respond with answers such as "to get through the textbook" or "to raise test scores." Instead, we hope that teachers would articulate their role in terms of *helping* students—helping them learn, grow, and become equipped as responsible citizens. That is, teaching is fundamentally a helping and facilitating profession that contributes to an informed and capable citizenry.

To best help students, adults must provide a combination of support and structure. Support and structure can both be conceptualized as falling along a continuum. In terms of support, the continuum extends from warmth to coldness, with "warm" adults providing interest, care, and love to students and "cold" adults exhibiting little emotional connection to students or concern for their well-being. In terms of structure, the continuum ranges from strict to lenient. Students thrive in environments of high support and high structure, where adults value and care for each child and consistently enforce clear expectations for appropriate behavior (Gregory et al., 2010).

Gazda and colleagues (2005) described eight core conditions (in the following list) of a helping relationship within the context of the classroom. Carl Rogers (1951) defined the essential characteristics of the therapeutic relationship (i.e., therapist–client) in his writings about counseling. Others in the fields of counseling and education then translated these conditions to the teacher–student relationship. (Aspy, 1972; Combs & Gonzalez, 1993; Danish & Hauer, 1973; Gazda, et al., 2005; Gordon, 1974). To build positive relationships with students characterized by high support and high structure, teachers should strive to establish the following conditions:

1. *Empathy:* Teachers need to understand students' emotional experiences, that is, where students are coming from. Later in this chapter, we provide a framework to help teachers get a better sense of the factors that impact students emotionally and that influence student behavior.
2. *Respect:* Teachers show respect to students by learning about their individual characteristics and capabilities. In respecting students, we show them that we believe in them and have faith in their abilities.
3. *Warmth:* Teachers need to care about students and demonstrate a positive regard for them. Some students are easier to like than others, but teachers must develop a working relationship with *all* students, even those who actively try to push away.

4. *Concreteness:* Teachers need to be capable of being concrete and specific with students. For instance, a teacher can help students become more successful by modeling specific techniques, such as a conflict resolution process. In this chapter, we provide several examples of specific skills that can be taught to students.
5. *Genuineness:* Teachers must be genuine and real with students. Often, students can easily detect falseness in teachers. For instance, if a teacher is demonstrating a problem-solving strategy but does not believe in or understand the strategy, the lesson will likely be a wasted effort.
6. *Self-disclosure:* When appropriate and relevant, a teacher can strengthen relationships with students by sharing personal stories, such as a time when the teacher struggled with a similar decision or problem or by disclosing personal feelings, such as "I know this work is hard, but I'm confident we can master it if we continue to work together."
7. *Confrontation:* Confrontation, when practiced together with other factors such as warmth, respect, and empathy, can help strengthen a relationship. After all, setting and enforcing appropriate limits is a way to demonstrate care. Consider again the example at the beginning of this section. In that situation, the teacher demonstrated care for all the students in the classroom by swiftly confronting hurtful behavior in an empathic, respectful, warm, and concrete manner.
8. *Immediacy:* Immediacy refers to the ability to be present in the moment and to address issues as they occur, when appropriate. For instance, a teacher may exhibit immediacy by saying something like, "Rebecca, I appreciate your enthusiasm, but right now your interruptions are distracting me and other students. If you'd like, we can discuss this topic one on one at a different time." Also, in our earlier example, the teacher demonstrated immediacy by responding in the moment to a student being disrespectful.

These eight conditions of the helping relationship form the core of a positive and helping relationship between teachers and students. In the next section, we describe how teachers can use specific skills for effective communication within the helping relationship.

THE BASICS: SKILLS FOR COMMUNICATION AND INTERPERSONAL INTERACTION

Nearly all of the teachers we speak to want to have warm and inviting relationships with their students. They don't want to resort to yelling and threats to get students to follow directions. They don't want to brush off the student who discloses a personal concern, but they may be at a loss for other options. Most teachers enter the profession with the best of intentions—they desire to help children. But without specific skills for how to handle difficult situations, teachers can easily wind up feeling overwhelmed, underprepared, and may resort to undesirable strategies in an effort to force compliance and make their students "act right." In this section, we present specific skills to assist teachers in their communication with students. These skills include ways of listening, speaking, and helping to solve problems.

Listening Skills

Of all the skills teachers may bring to create an effective classroom environment, the most important is listening—not just listening but listening with respect, dignity, empathy, and caring. With all the competing demands and nonstop motion of a teacher's life, it can seem almost impossible to take the time to have a quiet, uninterrupted conversation. And yet many times a focused conversation with a student or coworker is the only way to make progress on solving a problem or dilemma. Further, making that connection with another person feels good. It is enormously satisfying to understand another person and feel understood. It makes working together in the future easier, and it strengthens the bonds we share as members of a community.

To effectively communicate with another person, we must accurately hear, interpret, and understand what the other person is saying. It is all too common for people to spend one half of a conversation speaking and the other half planning what to say next. This can be an acceptable strategy when we are making small talk or when the topic is of no great import. Plenty of conversations don't require being fully engaged. When students ask for a bathroom pass or want to know how to find the computer lab, it's possible to respond to these requests while completing other tasks, such as monitoring a class change. But when a conversation is significant—when you want to understand what is going on with someone or solve a problem—we must step out of this casual mode and work harder.

A first consideration is assessing whether a serious conversation is possible within the current context. At the very beginning of the class period, you may not be able to discuss a troubling incident that happened in the hallway with a student until you get the class up and running. Late on Friday afternoon might not be the best time to bring up a dilemma with a coworker.

When you find time to talk, a good way to show that you value your conversation partner is by setting aside other work and distractions and being fully present for the discussion. Our body language speaks volumes (Corey, 2012; Danish & Hauer, 1973; Egan, 2013; Hill, 2009; Ivey, Ivey, & Zalaquett, 2014; Skovholt, 2012). Think of how hard it is to speak with a person whose body language seems stiff, uncomfortable, or rejecting. Warm, inviting body language—facing the student, leaning in slightly, and using empathic facial expressions—can put students at ease. A smile at the end of the conversation reinforces a caring attitude and a willingness to talk in the future.

To help students open up about a topic, it can be helpful to use statements or questions that encourage students to keep talking through the problem without the listener expressing judgment. This can be accomplished by (1) using encouraging verbalizations such as "mmmmm" and "uh-huh," (2) repeating back what was said (i.e., "You wanted to play on the swing, but Sarah said you couldn't use it?"), and (3) reflecting back the feelings associated with what was said ("You feel hurt and left out because Sarah scared you away from the swings."). Listening intently communicates to students that their experiences and feelings are important. Everyone wants to feel understood. Sometimes just being listened to is enough to smooth over a situation. This is why social support is so important to people of all ages. There have probably been many times in your life when a supportive friend has helped you get through a difficult situation, just by being there and listening to you.

The field of counseling has a rich literature on developing effecting communications skills, especially the process of empathic understanding and engaged discussions. Readers are encouraged to explore the contributions of the many counseling texts available on this topic (see, for example, Corey, 2012; Egan, 2013; Gazda, et al., 2005; Hill, 2009; Ivey, Ivey, & Zalaquett, 2014; Skovholt, 2012).

Talking with Students to Develop Understanding

Teachers spend a good amount of time every day talking with students: giving directions, delivering lessons, providing one-on-one assistance, chatting informally during class changes and at lunch. It is not the goal of this section to discuss all of the various ways that teachers talk with students, such as being a clear communicator during academic lessons. Rather, we focus on the interpersonal skills that help teachers connect and understand where students are coming from, even during difficult situations. Gordon (1974) differentiates between teacher-owned problems and student-owned problems. Teacher-owned problems are those that tangibly and directly affect the teacher, such as a student disrupting class, messing with another student's belongings, or defacing classroom property. Student-owned problems are those that teachers might not know about unless students share them. These include experiences such as a student feeling frustrated, lonely, or rejected because of something that happened at home, with friends, or in the classroom. In this section, we consider teacher responses to student-owned problems.

Gazda and colleagues (2005) provide an overview of several types of ineffective communication styles. How many of these sound familiar to you? As you read through the list, imagine if you wanted to talk to a friend or coworker about a problem. How would you respond to each type of response? Would you want to continue the conversation, or would you likely clam up or get angry?

- *The Detective:* The detective immediately responds with a barrage of questions in an attempt to get to the bottom of what happened. The detective is more interested in finding out the who, what, when, and where than in attending to the feelings of the person having the problem.
- *The Magician:* The magician wants to make the problem disappear. The magician will try to smooth over whatever trouble there is by saying that the problem is not a big deal or worth getting upset about.
- *The Drill Sergeant:* The drill sergeant responds to the student by issuing commands about exactly what the person needs to do to fix the problem.
- *The Guru:* The guru dispenses wisdom in the form of unhelpful clichés or proverbs.
- *The Florist:* The florist avoids talking about problems by prettying up anything uncomfortable, for example, by saying that it is all a misunderstanding.

In each of these cases, the student may feel misunderstood, lose confidence in the teacher or helper, and be less forthright (intentionally or unintentionally) about the situation. A positive resolution is not likely to be found. We are probably all guilty of using these ineffective response styles at one time or another. How can we avoid them? Let us return to the characteristics of the helping relationship presented earlier in the chapter. Helpful responses are those that combine warmth, empathy, respect, and genuineness. The goal is to better understand students' experiences. The more information students are willing to share, the more helpful our responses can be. That means we should take the time to listen without expressing judgment by using listening skills (such as those described earlier) to encourage the student to continue to talk through any concerns or issues.

We can also help students gain a better understanding of their own motivations and responses by reflecting back the emotions that they may be experiencing. Teachers demonstrate empathy and understanding by perceiving emotions and helping students work through them. This can be accomplished in the form of a guess, ("Could it be that you are angry that Sam won the spelling bee and not you?"), a question ("Are you feeling lonely because Mika moved away?), or a statement ("You seem to be worried that people may laugh at you if you audition for the play."). The most skillful teachers are able to identify surface feelings—those that are most obviously related to the situation at hand, like anger, loneliness, and worry—and underlying feelings—those that go deeper, such as feelings of inferiority or vulnerability (Aspy, 1972; Combs & Gonzalez, 1993; Ivey, Ivey, & Zalaquett, 2014).

Skills for Solving Problems

Listening and developing an understanding of where students are coming from are important components of being an interpersonally skilled teacher. Teachers are also called on to help solve problems. In some cases, students are able to work out their own solutions in the process of talking with the teacher. But when this doesn't occur, teachers can apply skills to help students solve problems. These problem-solving skills can be applied both to teacher-owned and to student-owned problems.

Solution-focused problem solving (Franklin, Trepper, McCollum, & Gingerich, 2012; Metcalf, 2008; O'Connell, 2005) is one approach to resolving problems. Often in life, people spend considerable time with an emphasis on the problem: what is the background, what caused it, why did it happen, who is to blame? (Think of The Detective described earlier.) The solution-focused approach shifts to a different emphasis: This happened, and so what can we do about it? The solution-focused approach emphasizes what works now or what has worked in the past instead of what is the problem? A solution-focused approach is more optimistic ("What can we do?") rather than punitive ("Look at the mess you made!"). It also elicits a sense of hope and a sense of control ("Let's see if we can figure out how to do this differently.") rather than despair ("You never do it right!"). A problem-focused emphasis often tries to find a guilty party ("Who did this?"), whereas a solution-focused approach is more interested in changing the outcome ("What do we need to do to change this? How can we make sure this doesn't happen again? Let's practice doing it in a better way.").

Table 20.1 Problem-focused and solution-focused questions.

Problem-Focused Approach	Solution-Focused Approach
Why is this student aggressive?	What can I do to help this student?
Why doesn't this student have the skills needed? What's wrong with this child? It must be the parents!	What steps can I take to help this student learn the skills necessary to manage these issues?
What did you do? Why? When? Where? What made you do such a thing?	How can we find a solution to this dilemma? How can we prevent this from happening again?

One way to look at the solution-focused versus problem-focused approach is for the teacher to examine how a solution-focused approach might differ from a problem-focused model. We will present four examples from our Bully Busters program (Horne, Bartolomucci & Newman-Carlson, 2003; Newman, Horne & Bartolomucci 2000), which, of course, have been adapted from other sources over the years, to illustrate the solution-focused approach. The first activity consists of identifying questions teachers might ask using the problem-focused versus the solution-focused approach. Examples of two types of questions are provided in Table 20.1.

A second activity, the Act NICE plan (Newman, Horne, & Bartolomucci, 2000), is another way of conceptualizing a solution-focused approach:

N = Notice what, where, when, with whom, and under what conditions the child isn't having the problem. When are things going well?
I = Increase what already works.
C = Create opportunities for success based on what's worked in the past.
E = Encourage success, even in small steps toward a goal.

The solution-focused approach does not come naturally to many people, and yet it is a learnable skill. This is a positive, encouraging, and affirming approach to solving problems and one that leads to less conflict for teachers while educating students in better self-control and effective problem solving.

A third activity from the Bully Busters program (Horne, Bartolomucci, & Newman-Carlson, 2003) are the Big Questions, which was adapted from Glaser's work on reality therapy (1975). This is a process that teachers can use to walk students through problems. In working in classrooms, we have found many educators who are quite successful in helping their students deal with problems and conflicts. Rather than addressing conflict or problems with anger or with coercive interactions, these teachers model respectful and successful ways of managing adversity, as with this approach.

1. What is your goal?
2. What are you doing?
3. Is what you are doing helping you achieve your goal?
4. If not, what can you do differently?

These questions are a basic problem-solving model that helps people clarify what their goals are, whether what they are currently doing is working, and whether other actions might be more beneficial. We encourage you to ask yourself these questions and apply them in your life, particularly when you are feeling emotional about a situation—for example, when you find yourself getting frustrated with a student.

The STOPP procedure (Orpinas & Horne, 2006) is another problem-solving strategy that can be used in place of or in addition to the Big Questions.

S = *Stop:* Stop, settle down, and be calm.
T = *Think:* Think about the problem and your goals.
O = *Options:* Think about the options or solutions to the problem.
P = *Plan:* Examine the consequences of different options, choose the best, and do it.
P = *Plan working?* If it is, congratulations. This is a signal to continue. If it isn't, consider what you could do differently to cause the plan to work better or select another plan to carry out.

Both the STOPP procedure and the Big Questions can be taught to students, posted in the classroom, practiced as a group, and modeled when problems occur.

THE ADDED INGREDIENTS: AN EMPATHIC ORIENTATION

To this point, we have highlighted some specific skills that teachers can use to become better communicators. In this section, we describe two "added ingredients" that serve to enhance relationships and interpersonal interactions between teachers and students. These areas form a backdrop for creating a climate of positive communication and respectful relationships. First, we assert that skilled teachers strive to understand their students, and we provide a framework to assist this process. That is, they get to know their students and develop an awareness of the specific characteristics of each child, such as family and community influences. This awareness and understanding can help educators foster a more empathic orientation and enhance their ability to "join and connect" with students. Further, we describe the concept of positive school climate. School climate refers to the personality of a school (Orpinas & Horne, 2006), that is, how people feel about being in the school community. We posit that positive school climate influences the quality of relationships and interpersonal interactions among teachers and students.

Understanding Students Using the Ecological Model

Imagine the student who falls asleep every day in class. Or the one who refuses to open the book or turn in homework. Or the student who talks incessantly through the class. Or one who won't speak at all. These are the students who can try our patience as teachers. Standing at the front of the room, it can be easy to start to feel self-doubt, wondering what the problem is: Is this classroom activity not engaging enough? Have I been talking too long? Although the instinct may be to question what's wrong with you as the teacher, it is often the case that the problem is better explained by what is going on in the life of the student.

To facilitate teachers' understanding of the factors that can influence student behavior and learning in the classroom, we emphasize an ecological model that helps explain what makes a student more or less likely to be an engaged learner in class. That is, what is going on in the life of the child that contributes to engagement in the classroom versus disruptive or withdrawn behavior? The ecological model developed by Bronfenbrenner (1979) suggests that there are risk factors (those that contribute to the development of problems related to learning and engagement) and protective factors (those that contribute to effective learning and engagement). These risk and protective factors exist across multiple levels of influence, including the individual, family, peer group, school, community, and society.

For example, consider the student who falls asleep in class every day. This behavior could be a result of several overlapping risk factors. This student may have some physiological characteristics that make it challenging to get a restful night's sleep (individual level). She may also have a somewhat chaotic family life that makes getting to sleep at a reasonable hour difficult (family level), and this may be exacerbated by friends who send text messages late at night (peer level), living on a noisy street (community level), and belonging to an academic environment that places excessive emphasis on testing, thus creating anxiety and fear (school or society level). Once the teacher has a better understanding of the factors contributing to the undesirable behavior, it will be a lot easier to treat this student with empathy rather than exasperation and to develop possible solutions to the problem. That is, having an awareness of students' risk and protective factors can lead to a more empathic response to students and their troubles, and in turn, better communication patterns between students and teachers.

One example of the ecological model applied to classroom disruptive behavior, bullying, violence, and aggression is presented in Figure 20.1, which is based on the work of Orpinas and Horne (2006), Newman, Horne, and Bartolomucci (2000), and Horne, Bartolomucci, and Newman-Carlson (2003). While no child has all of either risk or protective factors, problems arise when there are many risk factors and insufficient offsetting protective factors. Within the realm of schools, educators need to be aware of the risk factors for each stage of development for students and be able to create experiences to increase protective factors in students' lives while reducing the risks. It is beyond the scope of this chapter to provide a comprehensive discussion of all the influencing units (child, family, school, community, society). However, teachers can refer to the framework of the ecological model to help identify possible risk and protective factors of behavior of the students they teach. That is, what might be going on with the student's family, peers, or community that is influencing what happens (good or bad) in the classroom.

It is also critical that teachers understand their sphere of influence on shaping the cognitive, behavioral, and emotional development of students. It is just not possible for one individual to change risk and protective factors across all of the levels of the ecological model. In the case of the sleepy student, there is likely nothing that the teacher can do about the fact that the student lives on a noisy street. The teacher could suggest to the parents that they enforce a consistent bedtime and to the student that she turn off her cell phone at night to sleep more soundly. But this influence is

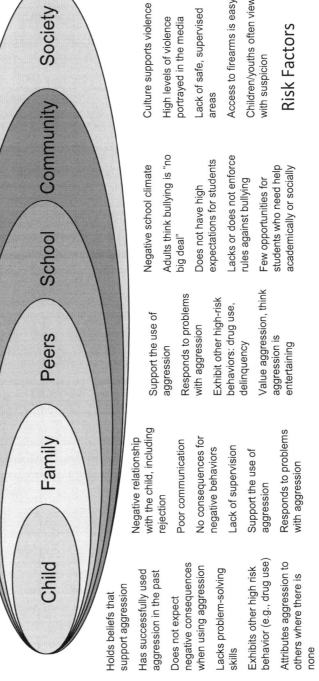

Protective Factors

Child
Socially competent

Has a sense of purpose in life

Displays positive values: honesty, friendship, peace & respect

Connected to school & friends

Values learning

Family
Loving and caring

Positive communication

Clear rules and consequences

Appropriate supervision

Model respect and peaceful conflict resolution

Involved and interested in child's life

Peers
Supportive and caring

Connected to school and academics

Hold positive values: honesty, friendship, peace, respect

Model peaceful solutions to problems

Don't accept aggression in others

School
Positive relationships between teachers and students

Clear policies against bullying

High expectations for all students

Appropriate supervision

Fosters excellence in teaching

Offers opportunities for meaningful participation in school

Society
Opportunities for youths to meaningfully participate in community activities (sports, educational programs, volunteer opportunities)

Safe, supervised areas available for all children

Attitudes toward children are caring and supportive

Risk Factors

Child
Holds beliefs that support aggression

Has successfully used aggression in the past

Does not expect negative consequences when using aggression

Lacks problem-solving skills

Exhibits other high risk behavior (e.g., drug use)

Attributes aggression to others where there is none

Family
Negative relationship with the child, including rejection

Poor communication

No consequences for negative behaviors

Lack of supervision

Support the use of aggression

Responds to problems with aggression

Peers
Support the use of aggression

Responds to problems with aggression

Exhibit other high-risk behaviors: drug use, delinquency

Value aggression, think aggression is entertaining

School
Negative school climate

Adults think bullying is "no big deal"

Does not have high expectations for students

Lacks or does not enforce rules against bullying

Few opportunities for students who need help academically or socially

Society
Culture supports violence

High levels of violence portrayed in the media

Lack of safe, supervised areas

Access to firearms is easy

Children/youths often viewed with suspicion

Figure 20.1 The ecological model for bullying and aggression (adapted from Orpinas & Horne, 2006).

limited; the teacher can't force these changes to happen. What the teacher can control is what happens in the classroom. The teacher can provide friendly and understanding support, while making it clear that sleeping in class is not an acceptable behavior. When teachers have a better sense of where their students are coming from, it is a first step in building connections. These connections are a vital component of positive relationships and effective communication.

Positive School Climate

Imagine a place where you feel welcome and at ease—a place you would choose to return to time and time again. It could be your childhood home or your current abode. It might be your favorite booth in your favorite restaurant or the memory of a special place from a treasured vacation. No matter the details, what makes this place appealing is likely a combination of the physical characteristics (comfortable, pleasing) and the people who are there—people who are happy to see you. Now contrast this with a place that makes you feel unsettled or uncomfortable. Perhaps, if you enjoy peace and quiet, it could be a busy, unfamiliar airport. The sights and sounds can be intrusive and jarring. It can be overcrowded, difficult to navigate, and challenging in terms of meeting basic needs (e.g., finding decent food and a comfortable place to sit). It is easy to feel small, unimportant, irritated, and in the way.

We believe that schools and classrooms should strive to be more like areas of refuge than places that add stress to the lives of students and teachers. That is, schools and classrooms should be places where students and teachers feel safe and welcome and, in fact, places where they *want* to be. It is the responsibility of the teacher to establish this welcoming climate, including demonstrating the characteristics of the helper described earlier in this chapter. That is, teachers who are empathic, warm, concrete, respectful, and genuine in their communications with students foster a climate of inclusion and welcome—a safe and comfortable place to be. In this section, we describe aspects of a positive school climate, and we emphasize that a teacher's communications process helps determine the quality of the classroom and school environment. We contend that without the foundation of a positive school climate at a system level, it will be much more challenging for individual teachers and students to interact effectively with each other. On the other hand, when a positive school climate exists, it occurs in part because of talented teachers with effective communications skills and an empathic orientation toward students.

A positive school climate can be defined in a variety of ways. We have identified eight characteristics of a positive school environment (Orpinas & Horne, 2006), as displayed in Figure 20.2: excellence in teaching, school values, policies and accountability, awareness of strengths and weaknesses, positive expectations, caring and respect, support for teachers, and physical environment.

Excellence in Teaching

Successful and inviting schools value and support excellence in teaching. Administrators strive to hire and retain the best teachers, and these teachers are expected to

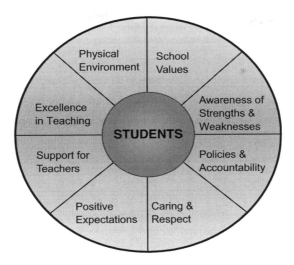

Figure 20.2 Components of positive school climate (adapted from Orpinas & Horne, 2006).

foster student growth in academic, social, and emotional learning. Excellent teachers are well trained in content area knowledge, pedagogy, classroom management, childhood development, and social skills, among other areas. They also must be skilled at classroom management and effective communications to develop positive interpersonal relationships with students. The importance of teaching excellence was highlighted in Hattie's (2009) evaluation of more than 800 meta-analyses. He found that excellence in teaching, teacher clarity, and the student–teacher relationship had the greatest relationship with academic achievement from dozens of variables studied, including teacher knowledge and principal support.

Several programs emphasize incorporating academic subjects with the behavioral, emotional, and cognitive skills necessary to become socially and emotionally mature and adept; these skills are often called the "21st Century Skills" (Marzano & Heflebower, 2012) or social-emotional learning (SEL) (Zins, Weissberg, Wang, & Walberg, 2004). An excellent description of SEL is available on the website for the Collaborative for Academic, Social, and Emotional Learning (CASEL) (http://www .casel.org/social-and-emotional-learning/) and in Chapter 6 of this volume. This effort—to focus education on both academic subject matter and developing social and emotional skills—is not new. In fact, decades ago, John Dewey emphasized a model of pragmatism in teaching emphasizing that when students find meaning in their learning, they would become engaged and participative rather than disruptive (Dewey, 1938). Today an extension of this model exists in programs that emphasize prosocial skills (e.g., cooperation, assistance, empathy) and cooperative learning, which requires students to learn and master effective communication skills.

Innovative teaching often requires greater effort and planning than didactic or rote learning models; it emphasizes individuality and creativity, as well as the ability to think in diverse and innovative ways on the part of both the students and teachers.

And yet the payoff is greater student engagement, increased social skills development, enhanced problem-solving ability, and stronger decision-making capabilities.

School Values

All schools have values. In some schools, the values are explicitly stated and universally understood and endorsed, while in other schools, the values are less clearly defined. Yet the values of the school influence the learning environment and most definitely the behavioral issues of students. Curwin and Mendler (1997) developed four steps to facilitate the process of defining values: (1) identify the school's core values, (2) create rules and consequences based on these values, (3) model these values, and (4) eliminate interventions that are incongruent with these values. We add to this that schools should effectively communicate these values throughout the school community.

In the best of circumstances, the whole school community engages in the decision-making process for the school's values. That is, teachers, parents, students, administrators, and other staff are involved in helping to define school values and rules/consequences, so that there can be ownership and buy-in. This requires valuing the members of the school and trusting their judgment. It also involves communications among all the constituent groups of a school: students, teachers, administrators, parents, community leaders, and others. A good values clarification exercise is to examine two of the most valuable assets schools have: their calendars and their checkbooks. How do teachers and administrators spend their time and their money? Is the emphasis on engagement, learning, and enjoyable discussions? Or is it on rote memorization? Is the time spent on learning effective management and prevention skills, or is time spent instead on punishment, reparation, and coercive exchanges? If the school values an environment of respect and dignity for all people, there is no tolerance of abusive language, name-calling, put-downs, and other forms of negative or disruptive communication. The values become clear when examining a school's functioning.

We hold three values as essential, and we always invite teachers and administrators to consider endorsing them as well. They always do because the values are highly consistent with a positive educational environment. Unfortunately, endorsing the three values does not always translate into action. The values are as follows:

1. *All children can learn.* Of course, educators endorse this value, but then we often see violations of the value because best intentions sometimes fail to translate to the classroom. This happens when teachers begin labeling children (e.g., "he's a 'special needs' child and can't learn like the others," "her family is very dysfunctional, so you can't expect her to do well in school," and so on). Many children bring poor learning habits with them; that doesn't mean they are incapable of learning. Rather, it means it is critical that educators figure out positive and respectful teaching methods to engage them.

2. *All people in the school environment are to be treated with respect and dignity.* Children who have had previous negative experiences in school or who

have been harassed and belittled often believe they don't have a right to be treated respectfully; it is critical to challenge this belief. Also, children—and teachers—often respond to a negative experience with aggression. An old expression sums it up: "Nastiness begets nastiness." Turning around negative responses to respectful but assertive positions is critical. It is particularly critical that teachers model management of self-control, respect, and connectedness and to communicate the importance of these values to all students.

3. *Violence, aggression, bullying, and disruptive and disrespectful behavior are not acceptable in our schools.* We have little authority over other places. We cannot make reality show actors and pop musicians behave respectfully. We cannot force legislators to engage their colleagues respectfully. But we can model classrooms where the expectation is an environment of safety, respect, and dignity, in which all students feel ownership of the experiences in their classrooms and teachers communicate this with both words and action.

Policies and Accountability

Policies and accountability tie in closely with school values. Schools in which responsible engagement and connectedness are prioritized identify the values of the school and then develop policies that reflect those values. A school that emphasizes all members being treated with respect and dignity will engage the school community in developing and communicating the policies that will guide them. Administrators will involve teachers in policy development, and teachers will engage students and their family members. When all members have buy-in with policies, they are more likely to understand and support them. But there also must be accountability when policies are violated.

Curwin and Mendler (1997, 1999) have examined different approaches to classroom management and indicate that when accountability focuses on punitive and coercive approaches to maintaining school policies, students will have a clear message of the values: punishment for not adhering to rules. In an obedience model, the goal is for students to obey the teacher, obey school rules, and maintain appropriate decorum, or receive punishment for the misbehavior. On the other hand, a responsibility model emphasizes that students are responsible and accountable for what they do. Students will make poor judgments—it is inevitable—and with the responsibility approach teachers focus on helping students identify what happened, take responsibility for correcting the problem, and identify what they have learned from the experience. The punitive model teaches students to avoid being caught doing something wrong because they will be punished for it; the accountability model teaches students that errors happen and that when they do, being responsible and addressing the problem are positive steps to take. With the responsibility model, we frequently engage in role-playing, modeling, skills practice, and behavior rehearsal activities to help students acquire the skills they need both as students in today's classes and as adults in tomorrow's world.

The responsibility approach may take more time and effort on the part of teachers because it becomes an emphasis for the classroom discussions, as in the example of the teacher stopping a lesson to have the classroom discuss one student calling another student an ethnic epithet. However, the time is well spent; it is a process of teaching responsibility taking, problem solving, and active engagement in developing more appropriate ways of being. A drawback is that the approach requires administrative support, additional teacher time, and some individualization of the work.

Awareness of Strengths and Weaknesses

Effective teachers are aware of what is working and what isn't in their classrooms. At the same time, it is critical to seek input, engagement, and discussion with students, other educators, and family members to be certain that there is an environment of understanding and appreciation for the learning experience.

Surveying students and family members is an effective way of becoming aware of concerns and issues in the classroom. We use an activity called the Prouds and Sorries. Whether a teacher is working with a classroom, an administrator is working with teachers, or school members are working with parents and community leaders, the process is the same. A teacher may ask students to divide a sheet of paper into two columns and in one column write about what they are proud of related to school. What is working, what is fun, what is engaging, what do they really enjoy? Then on the other side they write their sorries, or the issues in school that they wish were altered, were done differently, or are not sufficiently engaging and connected. When done effectively, this little exercise can be used as a class project to help both the teacher and the students identify ways to strengthen the classroom climate so that there can be ownership of how the class is doing. A second part to the process is helps and hindrances. After identifying prouds and sorries, we then ask the participants to identify (1) what helps them move toward the prouds (helps) and (2) what impedes them and leads to sorries (hindrances). The goal is to identify and increase the helps and reduce the hindrances. When these topics are discussed openly in the classroom and steps are taken to address problems while celebrating successes, a strong connection develops among the group members and opens lines of communications about what is working and what isn't.

Positive Expectations

Under the topic of school values, we indicated our first value is that *all students can learn*. This value sounds great on paper. What teacher would disagree? But at times it may not be put into practice. This is not to say that teachers are purposefully discriminatory toward students, but based on several decades of social science research (see, for example, Rosenthal, 1994), we do know that teachers form expectations or biases. Some of the expectations may be based on gender ("Boys can't sit still in class." "Girls can't learn sports."). Others are based on social class ("His family lives in *that* side of town." "We know she will do well; her family is always successful in everything they do.") or on demographics ("We can't expect much from kids who go to this school; after all, it is the dumping ground of the city.") or even on past experiences ("Boy, have you got your job waiting for you. I had both that kid's siblings and they were nightmares."). Even though there can be many reasons to form bias toward students, it is imperative that they be examined and set aside to see the actual performance of the student. If we truly believe all children can learn and should be treated respectfully, it behooves us to think in terms of how to work with the bias to prove it wrong rather than letting it become a self-fulfilling prophecy.

This is not a call for gratuitous praise unfounded on skills and abilities; if a child hasn't been able to accomplish a task, it should be acknowledged. Of the following examples, which approach is more likely to be motivating?

> *Teacher:* "You haven't been able to do this, but that doesn't matter because all of our students are exceptional and bright. We'll just move you on to the next level, and you'll probably understand it later."

A statement such as this ignores the student's failure to accomplish a task, thus placing her at a disadvantage moving forward; a student who doesn't understand basics isn't likely to master more advanced work. It appears to be a statement about teacher needs ("I need to move on; I don't have time for this") rather than the student's needs.

> *Teacher:* "You haven't been able to do this. I'm wondering, do we need extra time on this project, or do we need to approach it differently? It is important that you understand this task before moving on, so let's see if we can find a better way to approach it."

This teacher comment demonstrates an awareness of the progression of the student and communicates an empathic and caring commitment to the student.

Caring and Respect

Earlier in this chapter, we described the importance of caring and respectful behaviors of teachers. It is clear from the discussion to this point that caring and respectful behavior is a core component of a positive school environment. Students who feel connected to their school, affirmed by their teachers, and accepted by their peers are more likely to be successful as students and then more successful as adults (Phillips, Linney, & Pack, 2008; Pianta, 2000). In a school climate characterized by caring and respect, students have the opportunity to learn the social and "soft" skills that are so valuable later in life. Considering people that we have known with employment or family problems, it is often the case that these problems are not caused by a lack of knowledge about a particular subject (such as world history). Instead, often job losses or the breakup of families are a result of poor problem-solving skills, a lack of ability to engage in conflict resolution, or poor anger management abilities. A safe and respectful school environment characterized by caring relationships provides an important incubator for learning skills that help people thrive across the life span.

Support for Teachers

Teachers juggle many competing demands—most of them complex and tremendously important. Schools characterized by a positive school climate provide teachers with the support and encouragement they deserve. This support can come in a variety of ways, both formal and informal. Instead of summarizing all such possibilities, we focus here on one particular model: teacher support groups (Orpinas & Horne, 2006). In our work, we have used teacher support groups as the basis for the elementary and middle school Bully Busters curricula (Horne, Bartolomucci, & Newman-Carlson, 2003; Newman, Horne, & Bartolomucci, 2000). The goal of this approach is to support teachers in understanding and preventing bullying in their classrooms and schools. Within the support group, teachers serve as resources for each other. About once a week, teachers meet in small groups of about four to eight to discuss their day-to-day experiences and discuss disruptive classroom behavior. Most often, the groups are led by an experienced mentor teacher, school counselor, or administrator. In our experience, teachers quickly master the operation of the group and can facilitate the group experience as peers rather than needing an ongoing leader. The group meetings serve as an opportunity for teachers to learn from their peers, practice new skills, and develop a deeper understanding of their students and the problems they are facing. Although some teachers resist professional development, we find that they are grateful to have time to discuss problems and brainstorm solutions with their colleagues. Groups can be very supportive if they are used to help build strengths, share concerns (think prouds and sorries, helps and hindrances), and offer recommendations. Whatever the format, teachers need to feel supported at school in order to excel.

Physical Environment

In the rush to make our schools safer, in some cases schools have instead been made to seem more like lockdown units in a correctional setting. Correctional settings should be austere; they should be places people don't want to be—we want the incarcerated to want to be somewhere else. But we shouldn't model our schools after settings where we want people to do everything they can to avoid being there. Schools should be inviting.

Schools don't have to be new to accomplish this. In our projects working with many schools across the nation (e.g., Orpinas, Horne, and Multisite Violence Prevention Project, 2004), we found that some of the most inviting buildings were older institutions, places whose prime has passed. And yet, in big and little ways, the physical environment of some of the schools speaks to the warm and inviting atmosphere that can be created for all students and teachers, regardless of the age of the physical building. The hallways are clean and orderly. Student accomplishments—academic, athletic, in the arts, and otherwise—are celebrated. Signs are friendly. ("We are so glad you are here. Please sign in so we can help you." vs. "No visitor may enter the school without first signing in.") There is a tangible sense of, "This is our school, and we enjoy being here." This is a school where teachers and students want to be and can thrive.

OTHER RESOURCES AND PUTTING IT TOGETHER

Interpersonal and communication skills are a vital component of masterful teaching. In fact, it is nearly impossible to imagine an effective classroom teacher who isn't skilled at both. At the college level, sometimes brilliant but socially maladroit "nutty professor" types exist whose academic genius outweighs their interpersonal awkwardness. But in a K–12 setting, this simply isn't possible. The role of educators at the elementary and secondary level is to help students develop academically, socially, and emotionally. This requires relating to students in caring and empathic ways and modeling appropriate communication and interpersonal skills. It takes practice, but as educators hone these skills, their daily experiences and interactions with students will become increasingly satisfying and rewarding.

The skills and empathic orientation we have described up to this point may seem simple, but the implementation and engagement process may require considerable practice and certainly much more information than could be provided in this chapter. A number of excellent programs focus on assisting teachers and administrators to develop the positive interpersonal and communications skills that are so critical for our students. A few of them include:

- *CASEL* (http://www.casel.org/about/) is an organization that champions the development of social-emotional competence in students through research, practice, and advocacy. The CASEL website offers a wealth of information for educators, including issue briefs, a resource library, and a guide to selecting evidence-based SEL programs for use in the classroom.
- Community Matters (http://community-matters.org/programs-and-services/safe-school-ambassadors) has been involved with more than 1,300 schools in the United States. Their emphasis is on changing the whole school climate by assessing the current level of operation and identifying means of improving the school framework so that a positive environment evolves. One of their programs is the Safe School Ambassadors (Phillips, Linney, & Pack, 2008), which provides training for students to become facilitators of safe and welcoming schools. Community Matters programs emphasize relational competence in respectful circumstances.
- The *Partnership for 21st Century Skills* (http://www.p21.org/) prepares students for the current century by providing tools and resources to enhance academic success but also places equal emphasis on creativity and innovation, effective communications skills, and training in problem solving and critical thinking. The partnership addresses the whole school climate and addresses ways for educators to develop the school environment that educates students to be well prepared for life in today's complex world.
- *Safe and Welcoming Schools* (http://www.coe.uga.edu/sws/) is a project from the University of Georgia's College of Education. Safe and Welcoming Schools conducts research and outreach on issues of school safety and school climate, including annual conferences, regular trainings, and consultation services. The emphasis of the program is the subject of this chapter: how to prepare teachers, administrators,

and others to create a school environment that is truly inviting and safe, in which a strong level of commitment to learning in the broadest sense can occur.

- The *Search Institute* in Minneapolis was founded more than 50 years ago to provide social science approaches to understanding schools and the processes of effective child development. Through the development of their program of studying developmental assets—those personal/emotional/affective characteristics of children—they have identified personal, family, school, and community assets that can be taught in schools, community agencies, and service facilities. Their broad research program examining characteristics of successful vs. troubled youth have been very influential for helping schools identify specific programs that can be incorporated into the school curriculum.
- Housed at the University of Virginia, Youth-Nex (http://curry.virginia.edu/research/centers/youth-nex) advocates the promotion of healthy youth development and educational experiences by creating respectful and inviting school environments. While emphasizing high-quality learning outcomes, the program also stresses the importance of relationships and personal physical and mental health as essential components of effective citizenship.

CONCLUSION

In this chapter, we have described communication and interpersonal skills for teachers. These skills are not just a grab bag of techniques, although there clearly are processes and procedures (i.e., classroom meetings, Prouds and Sorries, The Big Questions, STOPP) that can be used to improve relationships and solve problems in the classroom. Instead, the most important aspect is the overall orientation of the teacher—appreciative of students and their diverse experiences and willing to work to provide them with both support and structure.

As we move forward in examining what works and what doesn't in education, it is critical to frame the discussion in relationship to the values of education. Do schools exist solely to train students to be future employees in the workplace? If so, creating inviting and engaging classrooms may not be seen as a top priority. Or is the purpose of education to develop well prepared citizens for the various roles and responsibilities in our democracy? If so, classrooms should emphasize healthy communication, warm and welcoming relationships, and an environment of trust, respect, and dignity. Students should learn to engage in effective problem solving, decision making, and conflict resolution. Teaching these skills requires acuity in communication and interpersonal interactions. Future research on this topic needs to focus on evaluating how to best prepare teachers to model and teach these vital skills.

REFERENCES

Aspy, D. (1972). *Toward a technology for humanizing education.* Champaign, IL: Research Press.
Bronfenbrenner, U. (1979). *The ecology of human development: Experiments by nature and design.* Cambridge, MA: Harvard University Press.
Combs, A., & Gonzalez, D. (1993). *Helping relationships: Basic concepts for the helping profession.* Upper Saddle River, NJ: Pearson.

Corey, G. (2012). *Theory and practice of counseling and psychotherapy*. Pacific Grove, CA: Brooks-Cole.

Curwin, R. L., & Mendler, A. N. (1997). *As tough as necessary: Countering violence, aggression, and hostility in our schools*. Alexandria, VA: Association for Supervision and Curriculum Development (ASCD).

Curwin, R. L., & Mendler, A. N. (1999). *Discipline with dignity*. Alexandria, VA: Association for Supervision and Curriculum (ASCD).

Danish, S. J., & Hauer, A. L. (1973). *Helping skills: A basic training program*. New York: Behavioral Publications.

Dewey, J. (1938). *Experience and Education*. Indianapolis, IN: Kappa Delta Pi.

Dreikurs, R., Grunwald, B., & Pepper, F. (1982). *Maintaining sanity in the classroom: Classroom management techniques*. New York: Harper & Row.

Egan, G. (2013). *The skilled helper: A problem-management and opportunity development approach to helping*. Pacific Grove, CA: Brooks/Cole.

Evertson, C. M., & Weinstein, C. S. (2006). Classroom management as a field of inquiry. In C. M. Evertson & C. S. Weinstein (Eds.), *Handbook of classroom management: Research, practice, and contemporary issues*. Mahwah, NJ: Erlbaum.

Franklin, C., Trepper, T. S., McCollum, E. E., & Gingerich, W. (2012). *Solution-Focused Brief Therapy: A Handbook of Evidence-Based Practice*. New York: Oxford University Press.

Gazda, G. M., Balzer, F. J., Childers, W. C., Nealy, A. U., Phelps, R. E., & Walters, R. P. (2005). *Human relations development: A manual for educators*. New York: Pearson.

Glaser, W. (1975). *Reality therapy*. New York: Harper and Row.

Gordon T., (1974). *Teacher effectiveness training*. New York: Three Rivers Press.

Gregory, A., Cornell, D., Fan, X., Sheras, P., Shih, T.-H., & Huang, F. (2010). Authoritative school discipline: High school practices associated with lower bullying and victimization. *Journal of Educational Psychology, 102*, 483–496. doi: 10.1037/a0018562

Hattie, J. (2009). *Visible learning: A synthesis of over 800 meta-analyses relating to achievement*. New York: Routledge.

Hein, K. (2004). Preventing aggression in the classroom: A case study of extraordinary teachers. Doctoral dissertation, Athens, University of Georgia.

Hill, C. (2009). *Helping skills: Facilitating exploration, insight, and action*. Washington, DC: American Psychological Association.

Horne, A. M., Bartolomucci, C. L., & Newman-Carlson, D. (2003). *Bully Busters: A teacher's manual for helping bullies, victims, and bystanders (Grades K–5)*. Champaign, IL: Research Press.

Ingersoll, R. (2003). *Is there really a teacher shortage?* (Report R-03-4) Seattle: University of Washington, Center for the Study of Teaching and Policy and The Consortium for Policy Research in Education.

Ingersoll, R., & Merrill, L. (2010). Who's teaching our children? *Educational leadership, 67*, 14–20.

Ingersoll, R. & Smith, T. (2003). The wrong solution to the teacher shortage. *Educational leadership, 60*, 30–33.

Ivey, A., Ivey, M. B., & Zalaquett, C. (2014). *Intentional interviewing and counseling: Facilitating client development in a multicultural society* (8th ed.). Pacific Grove, CA: Brooks/Cole.

Kopkowski, C. (2008, April). Why they leave. *NEA Today Magazine*. Retrieved from http://www.nea.org/home/12630.htm.

Marzano, R. J., & Heflebower, T. (2012). *Teaching and assessing 21st century skills: The classroom strategies series*. Bloomington, IN: Marzano Research Laboratory.

Metcalf, L. (2008). Counseling toward solutions: A practical solution-focused program for working with students, teachers and parents. San Francisco: Jossey Bass.

Newman, D. A., Horne, A.M., & Bartolomucci, C. L. (2000). *Bully Busters: A teacher's manual for helping bullies, victims, and bystanders (Grades 6–8)*. Champaign, IL: Research Press.

O'Connell, B. (2005). *Solution-focused therapy*. London: Sage.

Orpinas, P., & Horne, A. M. (2006). *Bullying prevention: Creating a positive school climate and developing social competence*. Washington, DC: American Psychological Association.

Orpinas, P., Horne, A. M., & Multisite Violence Prevention Project. (2004). A teacher-focused approach to prevent and reduce students' aggressive behaviors: The GREAT Teacher Program. *American Journal of Preventive Medicine, 26*, 1S, 29–38.

Phillips, R., Linney, J., & Pack, C. (2008). *Safe school ambassadors: Harnessing student power to stop bullying and violence*. San Francisco: Jossey-Bass.

Pianta, R. (2000). *Enhancing relationships between children and teachers*. Washington, DC: American Psychological Association.

Ravitch, D. (2013). *Reign of error: The hoax of the privatization movement and the danger to America's public schools*. New York: Random House.

Riggs, Elizabeth (2013, October). Why do teachers quit? *The Atlantic*. Retrieved from http://www.theatlantic.com/education/archive/2013/10/why-do-teachers-quit/280699/.

Rogers, C. (1951). *Client-centered therapy: Its current practice, implications, and theory*. Boston: Houghton Mifflin.

Rosenthal, R. (1994). Interpersonal expectancy effects—A 30-year perspective. *Current Directions in Psychological Science, 3,* 176–179.

Skovholt, T. (2012). *Becoming a therapist*. Hoboken, NJ: Wiley.

Zaloom, C., & Klinenberg, E. (2012). *A life of consequence, a profession of status enhancing respect, recognition, and retention of talented teachers*. Princeton, NJ: Woodrow Wilson Foundation.

Zins, J. E., Weissberg, R. P., Wang, M. C., & Walberg, J. J. (2004). *Building academic success on social and emotional learning: What does the research say?* New York: Teachers College Press.

V

Influential Forces and Factors

21

CULTURALLY RESPONSIVE CLASSROOM MANAGEMENT

GWENDOLYN CARTLEDGE
THE OHIO STATE UNIVERSITY

YA-YU LO
UNIVERSITY OF NORTH CAROLINA AT CHARLOTTE

CLAUDIA G. VINCENT
UNIVERSITY OF OREGON

PORSHA ROBINSON-ERVIN
NORTHERN KENTUCKY UNIVERSITY

The overall goal of classroom management is to minimize disruption so that teachers can teach and students can learn; a well managed classroom is traditionally defined as an orderly environment that facilitates student engagement (Emmer & Stough, 2001; Marzano, Marzano, & Pickering, 2003). Establishing an "orderly environment" can pose challenges in multicultural classrooms, since the term seems to imply that all individuals populating the environment share a common understanding of what constitutes order and how it is maintained through individual action. Similarly, "student engagement" assumes positive and trusting peer as well as student–teacher relationships and a common understanding of what it means to be on-task and academically engaged. An emerging body of literature focuses on addressing these challenges by merging the principles of classroom management with the principles of cultural responsiveness.

Fundamental to creating culturally responsive preventative classroom management is the need to acknowledge that conventional classroom management strategies intended to create orderly environments are not culturally neutral but are often an expression of predominantly white, middle-class sensibilities (Cartledge & Johnson, 2004; Weinstein, Tomlinson-Clarke, & Curran, 2004). Teachers' awareness of their own actions as an expression of their cultural identity is thus a prerequisite to culturally responsive classroom management. Understanding of one's own cultural identity often facilitates greater awareness of the cultural identities of others and the larger sociocultural contexts that shape them (Bondy, Ross, Gallingane, & Hambacher, 2007; McCready & Soloway, 2010). The more teachers know about their students' cultural and linguistic backgrounds, the better they can create classrooms where all of their students can succeed socially and academically, regardless of their cultural and linguistic differences. Teacher awareness of differences in communication styles, concepts of authority, and individualistic vs. collectivistic orientations is necessary for culturally responsive classroom management (Cartledge, Singh, & Gibson, 2008; Ladson-Billings, 1995). Most importantly, however, the literature recommends that teachers use specific culturally responsive classroom management practices to ensure that all students share a common understanding of what is expected of them and that all students feel valued and encouraged to contribute to their own learning and that of their peers (Cartledge & Kourea, 2008; Klingner et al., 2005). Seen through the lens of cultural responsiveness, the primary goal of classroom management appears not singularly focused on establishing order but rather emphasizes mutual understanding and respect among students and teachers, which—when achieved—sets the stage for an orderly environment and student compliance. Although classroom management is often considered first and foremost the teacher's responsibility, culturally responsive classroom management might be conceived as a responsibility shared by a learning community, including all school personnel, students, parents, and members of the immediate and larger environment.

CULTURAL RESPONSIVENESS

Cultural Responsiveness Defined

Culture has been variously defined but we typically think of it as the ways of doing things. The culture of a group is determined by its shared traditions, beliefs, values, and norms. It also includes language or communication systems as well as distinguishing artifacts such as fashion or music (Cartledge, Gardner, & Ford, 2009; Sugai, O'Keeffe, & Fallon, 2012). Cultural norms, for example, may be thought of as

> the collective expectations of what constitutes "*proper*" or "*improper*" behavior in a given situation and guide the scripts to be followed (e.g., how we greet someone; how we introduce ourselves; how we eat; how we show gratitude; how we discipline children; how we treat the elderly, etc.). (Cartledge, Gardner, & Ford, 2009, p. 13)

Cultural responsiveness has been studied extensively in recent years, focused on the most effective pedagogy for culturally and linguistically diverse (CLD) learners. Culturally responsive instruction involves a variety of components, but essentially it means that educators are nonjudgmental (Brown-Jeffy & Cooper, 2012) and make an effort to understand, embrace, respect, and meet the needs of students who are from cultural backgrounds that are different from their own (Ford & Kea, 2009). Some of the key components include cultural understanding, caring, fairness, culturally appropriate management strategies, and commitment (Cartledge, Gardner, & Ford, 2009). Culturally aware teachers not only learn about the culture of their students but also are aware of their own ethnocentrism and bias, recognizing that their worldview is not universal and their cultural norms are not absolute (Chamberlain, 2005; Weinstein, Tomlinson-Clarke, & Curran, 2004). Caring is considered to be critical to culturally responsive management where teachers display concern for the students' overall development through developing good positive relationships while setting and maintaining high academic and behavioral standards (Brown, 2003; Howard, 2001). Students from diverse backgrounds also must perceive that the classroom management practices are fair, that the disciplinary actions are appropriate for the infraction, and that the severity of the actions does not discriminate according to subgroup (Weinstein, Tomlinson-Clarke, & Curran, 2004). Culturally appropriate management strategies need to be considered so that students socialized under one set of disciplinary actions will not encounter drastically different and confusing behaviors at school. For example, American Indian students, who often experience discipline through teachings at home, can be shocked with the harsh punishments meted out at school (Dykeman, Nelson, & Appleton, 1995). Committed teachers embrace the previously noted culturally responsive traits, and they are flexible, resourceful, persistent, and dedicated to the success of their CLD students (Cartledge, Gardner, & Ford, 2009).

Culture and Behavior

Culture dictates our ways of doing things and, to a large extent, specific social actions. The dominant U.S. culture emphasizes the individual and competition (Cartledge & Milburn, 1995). Under these conditions, our schools are structured to be competitive, and the most valued students are those who are at the top of the class in academics, athletics, performing arts, visual arts, and so forth. Children socialized within collectivistic-oriented societies, where the emphasis is on the group rather than on the individual, may find themselves at odds with the culture pervasive within U.S. schools. American Indian youth, reared in collectivistic traditions, for example, have been found to prefer small-group rather than individualistic structures (Ledlow, 1992). These youth might view high achievers as models to emulate rather than as competitors and are reluctant to be placed in competitive situations (Cartledge & Milburn, 1996).

One of the most distinctive cultural differences for ethnic and racial subgroups pertains to communication styles and language. Although the dominant U.S. culture espouses assertive communication styles (i.e., stating a position with mutual respect for oneself and the listener), many CLD subgroups are characterized with nonassertive language, ranging from extremely passive to loud and expressive exuberance (Chamberlain, 2005; Cartledge, Gardner, & Ford, 2009). Various researchers have noted the different interpretations of eye contact, with teachers from dominant culture often viewing a child's looking away as a sign of disrespect while at home the child has been taught just the opposite (Gay, 2000; Ledlow, 1992). Delpit (1995) discusses the communication differences for African American children who may have been socialized in direct language as opposed to the veiled, indirect language typical of the European American middle-class school culture. A direct command would be, "Take out your book, and let's begin reading," as opposed to, "Don't you think we should get started?" or "What do you think you should be doing right now?" The latter two questions might be confusing and viewed as optional to a youngster who is used to more straightforward commands, which, in turn, leads the teacher to perceive the student as uncooperative or defiant.

Another important aspect of communication is listening. Brown (2003) writes about the importance of teachers listening to their students as a means of being effective in developing communication systems and teaching CLD students. The verbal and nonverbal communication styles of subgroups vary so that children from some groups may be extremely quiet out of deference for the teacher's authority (e.g., Asian Americans), whereas other youth may be quite vociferous, such as in a call–response style (e.g., African Americans). In both cases, students may be attempting to affirm the speaker, and the teacher must have cultural knowledge and understanding in order to refrain from reacting negatively to the student behavior (Brown, 2003).

Although culture plays a major role in human behavior, it is important to realize that no group is a monolith and that we are cautioned not to stereotype the behavior of youth in any group or subgroup. Sugai and colleagues (2012) advise that, even though individuals may share similar learning histories, each individual is unique, and we should avoid overly generalizing from the group to the individual, recognizing that individual differences and cultural groups change over time. Within the same racial/ethnic group, individuals will have different levels of participation, shaping the degree of racial/ethnic identity, as well as a set of experiences that can combine to prompt relatively unique responses from individuals of the same cultural background. These differences in experiences may help to explain why two youth from the same cultural background and learning histories may similarly perceive an event as being unfair but respond differently according to direct instructional opportunities and reinforcing consequences.

DISCIPLINE DISPROPORTIONALITY FOR CLD LEARNERS

Disproportionality in behavior discipline for CLD learners has been a long-standing, pervasive, and difficult issue since the 1990s and became especially evident with the widespread adoption of zero tolerance policies and exclusionary practices in schools as a means to eliminate student problem behaviors (Skiba & Peterson, 2000). In particular, the research literature consistently documents discipline overrepresentation for African American students (e.g., Krezmien, Leone, & Achilles, 2006; Noltemeyer & Mcloughlin, 2010; Skiba, Michael, Nardo, & Peterson, 2002), with a few studies reporting overrepresentation for Native American and Latino students (Skiba et al., 2011; Wallace, Goodkind, Wallace, & Bachman, 2008). For example, Wallace and associates examined racial and ethnic differences in school discipline of a nationally representative sample of high schools within the 48 contiguous U.S. states from 1991 to 2005. They found that Native American, African American, and Latino students were one to two times more likely to be sent to the office or detained and two to five times more likely to be suspended or expelled when compared to their White and Asian American peers. African American students presented the highest level of overrepresentation. Skiba and colleagues (2011), for example, examined office referral data from a national sample involving 272 elementary schools and 92 middle schools and found that African American students were twice as likely at the elementary level and four times as likely at the middle school level to receive office referrals, compared to their white counterparts. Latino students were overrepresented in office referrals at the middle school level but underrepresented at the elementary level. Additionally, data from the Skiba and associates study showed that both African American and Latino students were likely to receive more serious consequences than their white peers for the same behavioral infractions, suggesting racial disparities at the administrative level. These discipline patterns for some CLD students are alarming and require close attention from policy makers, administrators, and educators.

Causes for Discipline Disproportionality

There are a number of hypothesized causes for discipline disproportionality of CLD learners, including poverty, different student rates of inappropriate behaviors, adoption of questionable disciplinary practices, cultural mismatch or misinterpretation of culturally based student behavior, and poor instructional and behavioral practices (Skiba et al., 2011; Townsend, 2000). Poverty and economic disadvantage is one widely suggested explanation for racial disparity in discipline disproportionality due to the close link between socioeconomic status and race (Skiba et al., 2008). This explanation is based on the notion that risk factors associated with poverty such as limited resources and educational opportunities are likely to result in poor academic outcomes and more behavioral challenges. Despite the associated risk factors, research has shown poverty to be a weak and inconsistent predictor of discipline disproportionality and that racial disparities remained after controlling for socioeconomic status (Skiba, Michael, Nardo, & Peterson, 2002; Wallace, Goodkind, Wallace, & Bachman, 2008). Similarly, the hypothesis that students of color have higher rates of inappropriate behavior is not empirically confirmed (Kelly, 2010). For example, Bradshaw, Mitchell, O'Brennan, and Leaf (2010) examined factors contributing to disciplinary disproportionality in 21 elementary schools and found that African American students were significantly more likely to receive disciplinary referrals than white students even after controlling for teachers' perceptions of students' misbehaviors and teacher ethnicity. African American students have consistently received more severe punishments at disproportionately higher rates than white students for lesser or more subjective misbehaviors (Shaw & Braden, 1990). These findings indicate that factors other than the inherent higher rates of inappropriate student behavior are contributing to discipline disproportionality.

Cultural mismatch or discontinuity between teachers and CLD students is viewed as an important contributing factor (Monroe, 2005; Townsend, 2000). Monroe (2005), for example, reported that many teachers may perceive African American males as troublesome or threatening and therefore are implicitly guided by stereo-typical perceptions that greater control and more punitive disciplinary measures are needed. In their five-year ethnographic study examining sociocultural factors affect-ing two teachers' decisions to suspend students in an urban high school, Vavrus and Cole (2002) found that suspensions often occurred during moments of teacher–student tension, likely in the absence of clearly defined physical or verbal violence, and that suspended students were most likely those of color (e.g., African American and Latino). These findings represent cultural incongruity, that is, the subjective nature of teachers' disciplinary practices with CLD students. Further, a related underlying concern is the inadequacy of the instructional and behavioral practices in the class-rooms due to misperceptions of students' behaviors and the lack of culturally respon-sive behavioral management skills (Harris-Murri, King, & Rostenberg, 2006).

Effects of Discipline Disproportionality

Particularly disconcerting in disciplinary overrepresentation are the higher rates of exclusionary practices, which include detention, suspension, expulsion, or other actions resulting in removal of the student from instructional settings. Losen and Gillespie (2012) analyzed national data collected by the Office for Civil Rights address-ing the out-of-school suspension reports from 85% of all K–12 public schools in the United States during the 2009–2010 school year. These authors found that African Americans (1 in every 6 students, 17%), Native American (1 in 13, 8%), and Latino students (1 in 14, 7%) were suspended at least one time substantially more often than white students (1 in 20, 5%) or Asian students (1 in 50, 2%). Additionally, students with disabilities were suspended at alarming rates of 13% across racial groups, com-pared to only 7% of students without disabilities, with one out of every four African American students with disabilities (25%) being suspended at least once in 2009–2010. Students with disabilities, especially African American students, were also at a much higher risk for being suspended multiple times throughout the year than those without disabilities or white students. Although exclusionary practices are intended to serve as punishment to reduce problem behavior occurrences or encourage appro-priate behaviors, they often result in counterproductive and detrimental outcomes (Losen, 2011; Skiba & Peterson, 1999). Specifically, exclusionary practices have been associated with higher rates of grade retention, dropping out of school, accessing the criminal justice system, and academic underachievement (e.g., Fabelo et al., 2011; Heitzeg, 2009; Rausch & Skiba, 2006). Further, it has been reported that exclusion-ary practices had little effect on improving the safety of schools (Skiba & Peterson, 1999); such practices, inadvertently, may have increased student misbehavior, emo-tional harm, and alienation (Hyman & Perone, 1998). There is also research evidence that students who reported unfair treatment from a teacher were likely to receive disciplinary referrals from that teacher (Gregory & Ripski, 2008), further supporting the connection between poor student–teacher relationships and exclusionary prac-tices. Finally and most importantly, exclusionary practices deprive students of the opportunities to learn, further placing them at risk for school failure and academic underachievement. Discipline disproportionality suggests that traditional classroom management strategies, intended to minimize disruption through student compliance with established classroom rules, might not be sufficiently sensitive to cultural differences existing in classrooms with CLD students. If non-white students find it difficult to comply with behavioral expectations as the research suggests, either the behavioral expectations, as defined and taught, might seem alien to them, or their teachers might interpret students' culturally conditioned behaviors as noncompliance.

The risk of discipline disproportionality is great for CLD students and therefore must be addressed with a sense of urgency through prevention and culturally responsive practices before resorting to exclusionary practices (Skiba et al., 2011).

CULTURALLY RESPONSIVE PREVENTION METHODS

To improve the educational outcomes of CLD students, prevention is the preferred and arguably best option. There seems to be widespread consensus on the overall need of a positive, respectful, and consistent classroom management to prevent disciplinary incidents from disrupting instruction (Sailor, Dunlap, Sugai, & Horner, 2009). In a well managed classroom, CLD students can benefit specifically from (1) effective academic instruction and (2) parental involvement as culturally responsive prevention approaches. Skiba and colleagues (2008) defined culturally responsive practices as ones that "are not only intended to improve academic and behavioral outcomes in general, but are also specifically designed and evaluated in terms of their capability to reduce measured inequity" (p. 282). The implementation of culturally responsive practices holds great promise for CLD students.

Effective Academic Instruction

The importance of effective instruction on managed behavior cannot be overstated, especially for low-income CLD students who disproportionately experience disruptive classroom environments (Kellam, Rebok, Ialongo, & Mayer, 1994). A thoroughly researched feature of effective instruction pertains to high rates of academic responding, with empirical evidence that lower rates are found more often in urban settings compared to more affluent classrooms (Greenwood, Hart, Walker, & Risley, 1994; Stichter et al., 2009) and higher rates are associated with improved academic and social behavior (Lambert, Cartledge, Heward, & Lo, 2006; Haydon, et al., 2009). In a study of academic responding, Stichter and associates (2009) found a significant inverse correlation between instructional talk and negative student verbalizations. In other words, as the classroom instructional levels increased, the amount of pupil problem behavior decreased. Another finding was that higher instructional levels and lower pupil negativity were found more often in the more affluent schools than the low-income settings. This study supports the relationship between academic responding and behavior and also points to the greater need for more effective instruction within classrooms with low-income CLD students.

Academic responding may take a variety of forms such as choral responding, response cards, written responses or guided notes, and collaborative learning groups (Heward, 1994). A basic principle in active student responding is that all students consistently have the opportunity to respond to classroom instruction compared to single-student responding where one student has the opportunity to respond and other students may or may not attend. Typically, the more capable students attend and respond while less skilled students are likely to become disengaged or disruptive. Haydon et al. (2009) used choral responding to increase the academic responses of an elementary student with behavior problems. As academic responses increased, there were corresponding increases in correct academic responding and decreases in disruptive behavior. Lambert, Cartledge, Heward, & Lo (2006) used write-on response cards to increase correct math responses and reduce disruptive behavior in fourth-grade urban students. During the intervention phases, all students in the class received wipe-off boards to respond to the teacher's questions, which occurred after modeling how to calculate the math problem. Data were collected on nine students who exhibited the highest rates of disruptive behavior. The results of the study showed pronounced reductions in disruptive behavior during the response cards condition, with means of academic responses increasing from 0.12 per minute during single-student responding to 0.82 during response cards. This school, like many other urban, low-income schools, had very high office disciplinary referral rates, with the most common reason given for referral being classroom disruption. Students who are academically engaged are much less likely to become disruptive, and academically engaged students will benefit from classroom instruction. Peer tutoring is another viable strategy found to contribute to both academic performance and classroom management. Lo and Cartledge (2004) provide one example with African American urban learners by pairing an entire class of fourth-grade students to teach each other the social studies lessons. The researchers also used a group contingency in different phases of the study to determine the effects of added incentives on performance scores. Results showed improved social study scores and greater on-task behavior during the intervention. The group contingency did not appear to have an additive effect for these students. A particular advantage for peer tutoring for some CLD groups such as African Americans is that it allows for communal or peer learning. Students who have a collectivistic orientation are inclined to highly value peer interactions, and under these circumstances, when well structured, group learning can be quite beneficial. These studies support that teachers need to employ an array of strategies by promoting active student responding in order to create well managed, highly productive learning environments for CLD students.

Parental Involvement

The importance of parental involvement for improving the educational outcomes of CLD students has been widely discussed (Al-Hassan & Gardner, 2002; Musti-Rao & Cartledge, 2004). Research suggests that there is a strong correlation between the level of parental involvement and improved social competence of CLD students (Day-Vines & Terriquez, 2008; Waterman & Harry, 2008). For example, creating open and reciprocal communication between home and school (Adams, Womack, Shatzer, & Caldarella, 2010; Delgado-Gaitan, 2004) and involving parents in home-based learning (Fantuzzo & McWayne, 2002; Middleton & Cartledge, 1995) have been found to support the social development of African American students and Latino English language learners. In her single-subject design study, Brophy (2011) conducted a small-group culturally responsive social skill instruction program with parental involvement to improve the social behaviors of three African American high school students with mild intellectual disability. In this study, parents received scripted activities in a workbook to review and practice with their child the targeted skills of responding to teasing, self-control, and standing up for their own rights three times a week. The parents were instructed to review the skill steps, discuss situations when the skill would be used, and participate in role-play activities with their child. The results of the study showed that all three students increased their appropriate use of targeted social skills during role-play situations with their peers at school and family members at home. Anecdotal data also suggested that the students were able to use the targeted social skills in naturally occurring aggression-inducing situations.

An important outcome of parental involvement is family empowerment that is likely to promote positive child and family outcomes. Hall and colleagues (2007) trained six family members of preschoolers with ethnically diverse and low-income backgrounds (i.e., Latino, African American, European American) across 28 intervention hours. The training workshops addressed parent–child relationships, culturally appropriate family goals, family strengths, positive behavior support strategies (e.g., reinforcement, ignoring, redirection, environmental changes, establishing routines, offering choices, and teaching skills), and functional behavioral assessments for challenging behaviors. These authors reported that the families (1) felt more capable of using the taught strategies to effectively reduce their child's challenging behavior, (2) reported reduced stress about their child's challenging behavior, and (3) believed that the training addressed their needs.

Educators who make a strong commitment in extending school-based agendas of parental involvement and family engagement to community-based agendas can further empower families of CLD learners. As Auerbach (2009) demonstrated in her qualitative study, educational leaders who proactively promoted community-oriented activities—such as organizing annual colloquiums or conferences for teachers and Latino families, making home visits, and supporting Latino parents as "authors" to engage them in writing and "voicing" their experiences—had greater and more positive effects on their outreach to support CLD families and build family–school collaboration.

CULTURALLY RESPONSIVE INTERVENTIONS

In addition to the prevention effort, classroom teachers also need an instructional repertoire that enables them to determine the individual behavioral needs of their students and to intervene accordingly. Two effective strategies are (1) using culturally responsive procedures to conduct functional behavioral assessments of student behaviors to determine behavior strengths and (2) implementing culturally responsive social skill instruction to promote desired social behaviors.

Culturally Responsive Functional Assessment

Functional assessments are intended to help identify the cause or function of problem behaviors and to identify interventions useful in providing desired replacement behaviors. Considering that middle-class Caucasians are the standard for most existing behavioral measures (Haack & Gerdes, 2011), functional assessments that are based mainly on direct observations within the problem setting may be especially appropriate for CLD learners. Functional assessments have been used increasingly in recent years (Alter, Conroy, Mancil, & Haydon, 2008), since being mandated in the Individual with Disabilities Education Act Amendments (1997). Stoiber and Gettinger (2011), for example, trained 35 teachers of kindergarten and first-grade children who presented challenging behavior in the combined strategies of functional assessments and positive behavior supports. Following the intervention, the teachers evidenced greater competence and reported more self-confidence in these skills compared to the 35 control teachers. The children of the experimental teachers also displayed fewer challenging behaviors compared to the children of the control teachers.

Lo and Cartledge (2006) used functional assessments and behavior intervention plans to reduce the problem behaviors of four African American elementary-aged males. Functional assessments, consisting of direct observations, classroom analyses, and pupil and teacher interviews, revealed that adult attention was the primary function for the off-task behaviors for all four students. The students tended to use inappropriate teacher attention-seeking behavior, mainly in the form of talking out, which resulted in negative teacher attention. According to Cartledge and colleagues (2008), this study adhered to the guidelines for culturally responsive functional behavior assessments. First, a professional team devised the assessments and interventions rather than its being left to untrained classroom teachers. The team included someone who was familiar with the learner's cultural background and was able to distinguish between problem- and culture-specific behaviors (Salend & Taylor, 2002). The team determined how the teachers were inadvertently reinforcing the problem behavior. Student strengths as well as problem behaviors were assessed, and the team determined how to use this information to promote more positive interactions between the students and the teachers. Specifically, in this study the students were taught how to monitor their own behavior and how to use a specific strategy to recruit appropriately the teacher's attention. Part of this strategy was to request the teacher's approval and to thank her for her attention. As noted elsewhere in this chapter, positive teacher–student interactions are a cornerstone of culturally responsive teaching. In this study, teaching students to recruit appropriately and express gratitude for teacher attention was intended to foster positive and possibly caring teacher attitudes/behaviors. Finally, the intervention plan did improve the students' behaviors, which minimized disciplinary actions, in addition to eliminating considerations for more restrictive educational placements. Functional assessments allow for assessments of the cultural as well as the social environment for the most appropriate behavioral and cultural interventions.

Culturally Responsive Social Skill Instruction

According to Cartledge and Loe (2001), the social competence of CLD students is mediated by school culture and teacher perception, as well as by students' skills in traversing different social environments with socially appropriate behaviors in specific settings. Cultural biases or misconceptions can often lead to inappropriate disciplinary consequences for CLD students. For instance, African American students who walked with a "stroll" were often perceived by teachers as being aggressive or needing more academic support (Neal, McCray, Webb-Johnson, & Bridgest, 2003), whereas Latino students from economically poor backgrounds were likely rated by teachers as having lower social competence than their white counterparts (Galindo & Fuller, 2010). Culturally responsive social skill instruction provides a means for educators to be aware of cultural biases and to provide direct and explicit teaching of important social skills that reflect the lifestyle, values, and experiences of CLD students (Cartledge & Kourea, 2008; Cartledge, Singh, & Gibson, 2008; Ford & Kea, 2009). To be effective, social skill instruction should consist of several important components, including clear skill identification, presentation of rationale for performing the skill, modeling, opportunities for role plays or independent behavioral rehearsal, provision of reinforcement and performance feedback, and strategies to promote maintenance and skill generalization across settings (Cartledge & Milburn, 1995). Robinson-Ervin, Cartledge, and Keyes (2011) further delineated five features for implementing culturally responsive social skill instruction, including (1) teaching skills most important to the target CLD student population, (2) using culturally relevant materials, (3) including culturally competent peer models, (4) embedding CLD students' personal experiences, and (5) creating opportunities to allow students to apply learned skills in natural and specific environments. Culturally responsive social skill instruction with these five features is likely to affirm and empower CLD students within both their subculture and the larger society.

Lo, Mustian, Brophy, and White (2011) developed a culturally responsive social skill program and trained seven African American elementary students to serve as tutors or tutees in the peer-mediated, computer-assisted social skill instruction to learn classroom-based skills (e.g., finishing school work on time, following teachers' directions) and aggression-resolution skills (e.g., ignoring or leaving bad situations, negotiating conflict). The social skill curriculum targeted critical social skills for the participants considering their cultural experiences and challenges, embedded student's prior experiences in role-play situations, and included student dyads in the instruction based on the peer-oriented strengths of African American students. These authors found that all participants improved their response accuracy on social skill knowledge and decreased their inappropriate classroom behavior during the culturally responsive social skill instruction implementation. Robinson-Ervin (2012) also used computer software to deliver a culturally responsive social skill instructional curriculum to six African American urban youth with emotional behavior disorders. The researcher employed the previously noted template for culturally responsive social skill instruction (Robinson-Ervin et al., 2011). Direct observations and interviews of authority figures and the students were conducted to determine which behaviors were most important to the participants. Problem situations taken from students' lives or literature reflecting their lives were used to make a case for teaching and learning the skills. For example, in a lesson on dealing with situations that are perceived to be unfair, Robinson-Ervin used a true narrative of an African American youth complaining about the unfairness associated with the shooting death of a teenage relative. The youth complained about the unfairness of the situation and pondered alternatives ranging from avenging with violence to sharing his anger and despair in a letter. Unfortunately, the youth in this class could easily relate to this scenario and needed to explore alternatives to aggression when dealing with unfair situations. Results showed the culturally responsive social skill instruction to be effective in improving the target behaviors for all six participants.

As noted by Robinson-Ervin and colleagues (2011), competent same-race peer models are important in culturally responsive social skill instruction. Authorities in this area note the importance of the learner being able to identify with the model (Bandura, 1977; Glick & Goldstein, 1987; Yung & Hammond, 1995) and that peers could potentially have an even greater effect on social learning than adult trainers (Blake, Wang, Cartledge, & Gardner, 2000). Additionally, practice activities or role-plays should reflect the students' daily experiences, and the applications or consequences should be authentic. For example, in structuring rewarding consequences, Robinson-Ervin (2012) simulated the corner store that the students frequented with highly coveted items. These items ranged from posters and small electronic devices to edible reinforcers, such as snacks and fruit. Interestingly, fruit was chosen as a very popular reward item, possibly due to the lack of fresh fruit and vegetables in the students' neighborhood. Another culturally specific item used in this study was a "black card," made popular by the students' favorite rap stars but used in this study as a means to collect points for appropriate social behaviors and used to purchase from the class "store."

Lo, Correa, and Anderson (2013) tackled the issue that Latino students tended to build their friendship networks exclusive to Spanish-speaking peers due to their strong family unity and ties within the same cultural friendship group. The researchers trained eight Latino elementary male students to participate in peer-mediated, computer-assisted culturally responsive social skill instruction to learn friendship-building skills (e.g., skills related to importance of friendship, starting a conversation, continuing a conversation, and joining in an activity). Specifically, four Latino students served as peer tutors to deliver 12 PowerPoint® social skill lessons with video peer models on friendship-building skills to their same-age Latino peers. Prior to the instruction, all participants engaged in social interactions during recess, primarily with Latino peers with limited interactions with non-Latino peers; however, all students clearly increased the number of positive verbal social interactions with their non-Latino peers during recess after the culturally responsive social skill instruction was implemented.

A common feature of these three studies showed the benefits of peer-mediated instruction with CLD learners. Including peers as the behavioral support agents in social skill instruction allows CLD students to exercise cooperation and appropriate peer interactions during monitored situations, which has been found to enhance student engagement (Spencer, 2006) and skill generalization outside of the training sessions (Prater, Serna, & Nakamura, 1999; Wu, Lo, Feng, & Lo, 2010).

EVALUATING MANAGEMENT AND INTERVENTION EFFECTS

Evaluation of culturally responsive classroom management comprises evaluations of implementation fidelity as well as evaluations of student outcomes. Administrators can periodically assess the extent to which teachers implement recommended practices and provide teachers with necessary assistance and support based on the obtained fidelity outcomes. Similarly, administrators and teachers can assess the extent to which students are successful and use data to modify classroom management practices to promote greater equity across students from different cultural and linguistic backgrounds.

Evaluation of Implementation Fidelity

Many instruments designed to evaluate implementation fidelity of practices in school and classroom environments (such as *Effective Behavior Support Self-Assessment Survey* [Sugai, Horner, & Todd, 2000] or *School-wide Benchmarks of Quality* [Kincaid, Childs, & George, 2010]) allow teachers and school teams to rate the extent to which core classroom management practices are currently in place; however, these rating scales often do not specifically evaluate whether classroom management practices are culturally responsive. The *Cultural Responsiveness Assessment* (Indiana University Equity Project, 2011b) and its companion measure, the *5×5 Walkthrough* (Indiana University Equity Project, 2011a), are exceptions. The CRA is a self-assessment instrument that allows teachers and team members to rate current status and improvement priority of key components of culturally responsive classroom management. The CRA consists of five subscales: (1) Curriculum, Instruction and Classroom Management, (2) Assessment and Accountability, (3) Family and Community Engagement, (4) Professional Development, and (5) Environment. Specifically, these scales include items on culturally appropriate acknowledgment of students for expected behaviors in the classroom; on consideration of cultural influences in discipline outcomes; on efforts to include parents from traditionally underrepresented backgrounds; on professional development opportunities for teachers to learn about their own cultural identity; on opportunities to engage in ongoing discussions about race, culture, and equity; and on teacher collaboration to implement culturally responsive classroom practices. The 5×5 is a direct observation instrument that measures the same domains as the CRA but is completed by an outside observer based on review of permanent products, classroom observations, and interviews of school personnel and students. These instruments can provide school teams with valuable information about the extent to which teachers use culturally responsive classroom management practices. Based on the outcomes of the evaluation, resources and support should be made available (1) to assist teachers in building the necessary skills to manage their classrooms and provide instruction in a culturally responsive manner, (2) to make issues related to cultural differences and equity visible in the school community and openly discuss them, and (3) to encourage teachers to help each other with implementing classroom management practices that facilitate equitable outcomes for students regardless of their cultural and linguistic backgrounds.

Evaluation of Intervention Effects

Generally, the effectiveness of classroom management practices is assessed through student discipline outcomes. Student discipline outcomes, as well as disciplinary inequity for CLD students, are often measured in office discipline referrals. In the majority of schools, discipline referral data are routinely collected and used as punitive and reactive approaches to inappropriate behavior. Overall reductions in the number of office discipline referrals are commonly interpreted as improved student behavioral compliance (Horner, Sugai, Todd, & Lewis-Palmer, 2005), and distributions of referrals across racial/ethnic student groups compared to the enrollment of those groups tend to be interpreted as a measure of disciplinary equity (Kaufman et al., 2010; Vincent, Swain-Bradway, Tobin, & May, 2011). Given our focus on prevention of inappropriate behavior that might disrupt instruction through culturally responsive classroom management, it may be useful to consider alternative measures of student outcomes focusing on documenting positive behaviors.

A number of measures exist that allow teachers to rate their students' engagement in appropriate behaviors, including the *BASC-2 Behavioral and Emotional Screening Systems* (Kamphaus & Reynolds, 2007), the *Social Skills Improvement System* (Elliott & Gresham, 2007), and the *Strengths and Difficulties Questionnaire* (Goodman, 1997). Lane, Oakes, and Menzies (2010) provide a summary of the strengths and weaknesses, as well as completion times for these and similar tools. Many behavioral screening measures tend to be time intensive, and many make aggregations across the entire classroom difficult. A recently developed web-based tool, the *Elementary Social Behavior Assessment* (ESBA) delivered via the *iris*Progress Monitoring Tool (*iris*PMT™) (Marquez, Yeaton, & Vincent, 2013), was specifically designed to allow teachers to efficiently assess the extent to which all students in their classrooms engage in a number of behaviors that have been associated with academic success (Walker & Rankin, 1980). Based on comparisons with the other students, teachers can rate each student on 12 key behaviors (e.g., "listens to and respects the teacher," "follows rules," and "gets along with peers"). A three-point rating scale consisting of 1 being "cause for concern," 2 being "needs improvement," and 3 being "mastery" maps onto the support tiers commonly used within a multitiered prevention framework. Completing the ESBA for a classroom of about 25 students takes about 15–30 minutes (Sprague et al., 2012).

After rating all students in their classroom on all behaviors using the ESBA, teachers have instant access to a number of reports that allow them to see (1) how many students received low ratings across the majority of behaviors, (2) which desirable behaviors appear problematic for the majority of students, and (3) which individual students received low ratings on the majority of behaviors. These three reports provide valuable information about the effectiveness of classroom management practices. If the majority of students receive low ratings in the majority of behaviors, the teacher likely needs assistance with overall classroom management. If the majority of students who receive low ratings share a specific cultural and linguistic background, the teacher likely needs assistance with culturally responsive classroom management. If many students receive low ratings on one or two behaviors, these behaviors might have to be retaught. If many of these students share a specific cultural and linguistic background, these behaviors need to be retaught in a culturally responsive manner. Finally, if a few students receive low ratings across many behaviors, these students might need more intensive behavioral support.

Data on students' performance of desirable behaviors keep teachers' attention focused on the overall effectiveness and cultural responsiveness of their classroom management practices and the need to teach students how to behave appropriately. It might also help teachers in making specific adjustment to their classroom management strategies based on the patterns emerging from the data. Knowing which students do not perform well on specific appropriate behaviors also provides useful information about how to shape additional support for these students. A student who receives low ratings on "gets along with peers," for example, can receive additional support designed to improve peer interactions.

To assess the effectiveness of culturally responsive classroom management practices, it is imperative that teachers and administrators regularly disaggregate and review student outcome data by student race/ethnicity (Cartledge & Kourea, 2008; Gregory & Ripski, 2008; Losen & Skiba, 2010). Only if data are disaggregated by student race/ethnicity can potential patterns of inequitable student outcomes be observed. Once patterns emerge, hypotheses about their causes can be constructed and action plans developed to address these causes. Continuous review of disaggregated data will allow school personnel to evaluate the effectiveness of their action plans and make further adjustment as necessary.

CONCLUSIONS

The first step in culturally responsive behavior management is to assess the climate of the school in terms of student demographics and administrative actions. Culturally responsive management means that school personnel regularly and deliberately study discipline referral data, noting patterns of referral for individuals and groups, disciplinary actions taken, and the corresponding effects. Disproportionate patterns for subgroups or individuals indicate the need to take action to reduced disproportionality and to increase the school success for all students. Culturally responsive schools will realize that they are not meeting student needs and will take action in the interest of the student, making sure that school environments are wholesome, humane, and fair for everyone, that disciplinary practices are proactive with emphasis on prevention, that interventions are effective in teaching and maintaining school expectations, that they involve families and the extended community, and that CLD students feel valued and successful.

Culturally responsive schools focus on prevention where school expectations are made explicit and all students, including CLD students, are engaged in identifying expectations, policies, and practices that help the school and classrooms to be orderly, caring, and fair. Students have a sense of ownership, they feel wanted, they have a sense of academic and behavioral efficacy, and they believe that school personnel will help them meet the desired goals. For CLD students, teachers need to teach the behaviors the student needs to learn and provide supportive and reinforcing contingencies that will establish the behavior and mild reductive consequences for competing undesired actions. Except for the rare occasions when students are a threat to themselves or others, exclusionary practices should be avoided.

Effective academic instruction is extremely important to classroom management and is undoubtedly most important in settings characterized by academic underachievement. Classrooms where students are actively engaged and where there is commensurate academic progress are critical to CLD learners. Again, students need to believe in themselves as learners, that they belong in the classroom and that they can achieve academically as well as socially.

We all know that children cannot learn in a poorly managed, chaotic classroom and that such environments will have lasting and possibly damaging effects on students, especially those with poor behavior controls (Kellam, Rebok, Ialongo, & Mayer, 1994). Too much emphasis is placed on exclusionary practices, which help neither the children being excluded nor their classmates. Culturally responsive schools are focused on keeping all students in the classroom and actively learning while in class; they emphasize academic productivity and positive social development for all students, and they give top priority to creating positive environments where students feel valued and learn to respect and value others.

REFERENCES

Adams, M., Womack, S., Shatzer, R., & Caldarella, P. (2010). Parent involvement in school-wide social skills instruction: Perceptions of a home note program. *Education, 130*(3), 513–528.

Al-Hassan, S., & Gardner, R. (2002). Involving immigrant parents of students with disabilities in the educational process. *TEACHING Exceptional Children, 34*(5), 52–58.

Alter, P. J., Conroy, M. A., Mancil, G. R., & Haydon, T. (2008). A comparison of functional behavior assessment methodologies with young children: Descriptive methods and functional analysis. *Journal of Behavioral Education, 17*, 200–219.

Auerbach, S. (2009). Walking the walk: Portraits in leadership for family engagement in urban schools. *The School Community Journal, 19*(1), 9–32.

Bandura, A. (1977). *Social learning theory*. Englewood Cliffs, NJ: Prentice Hall.

Blake, C., Wang, W., Cartledge, G., & Gardner, R. (2000). Middle school students with serious emotional disturbances serve as social skill trainers and reinforcers for peers with SED. *Behavioral Disorders, 25*, 280–298.

Bondy, E., Ross, R., Gallingane, C., & Hambacher, E. (2007). Creating environments of success and resilience: Culturally responsive classroom management and more. *Urban Education, 42*, 326–348.

Bradshaw, C. P., Mitchell, M. M., O'Brennan, L. M., & Leaf, P. J. (2010). Multilevel exploration of factors contributing to the overrepresentation of Black students in office disciplinary referrals. *Journal of Educational Psychology, 102*, 508–520.

Brophy, A. A. (2011). Effects of a social skill instruction program on the social skill acquisition of African American high school students with mild intellectual disabilities and challenging behaviors. Doctoral dissertation. Available from ProQuest Dissertations and Theses database (UMI No. 3491400).

Brown, D. F. (2003). Urban teachers' use of culturally responsive management strategies. *Theory into Practice*, *42*, 277–282.

Brown-Jeffy, S., & Cooper, J. E. (2012). Toward a conceptual framework of culturally relevant pedagogy: An overview of the conceptual and theoretical literature. *Teacher Education Quarterly*, *38*(1), 65–84.

Cartledge, G., Gardner, R., & Ford, D. (2009). *Diverse learners with exceptionalities: Culturally responsive teaching in the inclusive classroom*. Upper Saddle River, NJ: Merrill.

Cartledge, G., & Johnson, C. T. (2004). School violence and cultural sensitivity. In J. C. Conoley & A. P. Goldstein (Eds.), *School violence intervention: A practical handbook* (2nd ed.) (pp. 441–482). New York: Guilford Press.

Cartledge, G., & Kourea, L. (2008). Culturally responsive classrooms for culturally diverse students with and at risk for disabilities. *Exceptional Children*, *74*, 351–371.

Cartledge, G., & Loe, S. A. (2001). Cultural diversity and social skill instruction. *Exceptionality*, *9*(1&2), 33–46.

Cartledge, G., & Milburn, J. F. (1995). *Teaching social skills to children and youth: Innovative approaches* (3rd ed.). Boston, MA: Allyn & Bacon.

Cartledge, G., & Milburn, J. F. (1996). *Cultural diversity and social skill instruction: Understanding ethnic and gender differences*. Champaign, IL: Research Press.

Cartledge, G., Singh, A., & Gibson, L. (2008). Practical behavior management techniques to close the accessibility gap for students who are culturally and linguistically diverse. *Preventing School Failure*, *52*(3), 29–38.

Chamberlain, S. (2005). Recognizing and responding to cultural differences in the education of culturally and linguistically diverse learners. *Intervention in School and Clinic*, *40*, 195–211.

Day-Vines, N. L., & Terriquez, V. (2008). A strengths-based approach to promoting prosocial behavior among African American and Latino students. *Professional School Counseling*, *12*, 170–175.

Delgado-Gaitan, C. (2004). *Involving Latino families in schools: Raising student achievement through home-school partnerships*. Thousand Oaks, CA: Corwin Press/SAGE.

Delpit, L. (1995). *Other people's children: Cultural conflict in the classroom*. New York: New Press.

Dykeman, C., Nelson, J. R., & Appleton, V. (1995). Building strong working alliances with American Indian families. *Social Work in Education*, *17*, 148–158.

Elliott, S. N., & Gresham, F. M. (2007). *Social Skills Improvement System: Performance Screening Guides*. Bloomington, MN: Pearson Assessments.

Emmer, E. T., & Stough, L. M. (2001). Classroom management: A critical part of educational psychology and teacher education. *Educational Psychologist*, *36*, 103–112.

Fabelo, T., Thompson, M. D., Plotkin, M., Carmichael, D., Marchbanks, M. P., & Booth, E. A. (2011). *Breaking schools' rules: A statewide study of how school discipline relates to students' success and juvenile justice involvement*. New York: Council of State Governments Justice Center. Retrieved from http://justicecenter.csg.org/resources/juveniles/report.

Fantuzzo, J., & McWayne, C. (2002). The relationship between peer-play interactions in the family context and dimensions of school readiness for low-income preschool children. Journal of Educational Psychology, 94, 79–87.

Ford, D. Y., & Kea, C. D. (2009). Creating culturally responsive instruction: For students' sake and teachers' sake. *Focus on Exceptional Children*, *41*, 1–18.

Galindo, C., & Fuller, B. (2010). The social competence of Latino kindergartners and growth in mathematical understanding. *Developmental Psychology*, *46*, 579–592.

Gay, G. (2000). *Culturally responsive teaching: Theory, research, & practice*. New York: Teachers College Press.

Glick, B., & Goldstein, A. P. (1987). Aggression replacement training. *Journal of Counseling and Development*, *65*, 356–362.

Goodman, R. (1997). The Strengths and Difficulties Questionnaire: A research note. *Journal of Child Psychology and Psychiatry*, *38*, 581–586.

Greenwood, C. R., Hart, B., Walker, D., & Risley, T. R. (1994). The opportunity to respond revisited: A behavioral theory of developmental retardation and its prevention. In R. Gardner, D. M. Sainato, J. O. Cooper, T. E. Heron, W. L. Heward, J. W. Eshleman, & T. A. Grossi (Eds.), *Behavior analysis in education: Focus on measurably superior instruction* (pp. 213–223). Pacific Grove, CA: Brooks/Cole.

Gregory, A., & Ripski, M. B. (2008). Adolescent trust in teachers: Implications for behavior in high school classrooms. *School Psychology Review*, *37*, 337–353.

Haack, L. M., & Gerdes, A. C. (2011). Functional impairment in Latino children with ADHD: Implications for culturally appropriate conceptualization and measurement. *Clinical Child and Family Psychology Review*, *14*, 318–328. doi: 10.1007/s10567-011-0098-z

Hall, T. P., Turnbull, A. P., Mccart, A., Griggs, P., Choi, J.-H., Markey, U., . . . Sailor, W. (2007). The effects of positive behavior support parent-training programs on parent-child relationships in culturally and linguistically diverse families. *Multiple Voices, 10*(1 & 2), 191–210.

Harris-Murri, N., King, K., & Rostenberg, D. (2006). Reducing disproportionate minority representation in special education programs for students with emotional disturbances: Toward a culturally responsive response to intervention model. *Education & Treatment of Children, 29*, 779–799.

Haydon, T., Conroy, M. A., Scott, T. M., Sindelar, P. T., Barber, B. R., & Orlando, A. (2009). A comparison of three types of opportunities to respond on student academic and social behaviors. *Journal of Emotional and Behavioral Disorders, 18*, 27–40. doi: 10.1177/1063426609333448

Heitzeg, N. A. (2009). Education or incarceration: Zero tolerance policies and the school to prison pipeline. *Forum on Public Policy Online, 2009*(2), 1–21. Retrieved from http://forumonpublicpolicy.com/papers.htm.

Heward, W. L. (1994). Three "low-tech" strategies for increasing the frequency of active student response during group instruction. In R. Gardner III, D. M. Sainato, J. O. Cooper, T. E. Heron, W. L. Heward, J. Eshleman, & T. A. Grossi (Eds.), *Behavior analysis in education: Focus on measurably superior instruction* (pp. 283–320). Pacific Grove, CA: Brooks/Cole.

Horner, R. H., Sugai, G., Todd, A. W., & Lewis-Palmer, T. (2005). School-wide positive behavior support. In L. Bambara & L. Kern (Eds.) *Individualized supports for students with problem behaviors: Designing positive behavior plans* (pp. 359–390). New York: Guilford Press.

Howard, T. C. (2001). Telling their side of the story: African-American students' perceptions of culturally relevant teaching. *The Urban Review, 33*, 131–149.

Hyman, I. A., & Perone, D. C. (1998). The other side of school violence: Educator policies and practices that may contribute to student misbehavior. *Journal of School Psychology, 36*, 7–27.

Indiana University Equity Project (2011a). *5x5 Walkthrough*. Bloomington, IN: Center on Education & Lifelong Learning/Equity Project, Indiana University.

Indiana University Equity Project (2011b). *Cultural Responsiveness Assessment*. Bloomington, IN: Center on Education & Lifelong Learning/Equity Project, Indiana University.

Individual with Disabilities Education Act Amendments of 1997, 20 U.S.C. Section 1400 et seq. (1997).

Kamphaus, R. W., & Reynolds, C. R. (2007). *BASC-2, Behavioral and Emotional Screening System*. San Antonio, TX: Pearson.

Kaufman, J. S., Jaser, S. S., Vaughan, E. L., Reynolds, J. S., Di Donato, J., Bernard, S. N., & Hernandez Brereton, M. (2010). Patterns in office discipline referral data by grade, race/ethnicity, and gender. *Journal of Positive Behavior Interventions, 12*, 44–54.

Kellam, S. G., Rebok, G., Ialongo, N., & Mayer, L. (1994). The course and malleability of aggressive behavior from early first grade into middle school: Results of a developmental epidemiologically-based prevention trial. *Journal of Child Psychology and Psychiatry, 35*, 259–281.

Kelly, S. (2010). A crisis of authority in predominantly black schools? *Teachers College Record, 112*, 1247–1274.

Kincaid, D., Childs, K., & George, H. (2010). School-wide benchmarks of quality (rev. ed.). Unpublished instrument, Tampa, University of South Florida.

Klingner, J. K., Artilles, A. J., Kozleski, E., Harry, B., Zion, S., Tate, W., . . . Riley, D. (2005). Addressing the disproportionate representation of culturally and linguistically diverse students in special education through culturally responsive educational systems. *Education Policy Analysis Archives, 13*(38), 1–42. Retrieved from http://epaa.asu.edu/epaa/v13n38/.

Krezmien, M. P., Leone, P. E., & Achilles, G. M. (2006). Suspension, race, and disability: Analysis of statewide practices and reporting. *Journal of Emotional and Behavioral Disorders, 14*, 217–226.

Ladson-Billings, G. (1995). Toward a theory of culturally relevant pedagogy. *American Educational Research Journal, 32*, 465–491.

Lambert, M. C., Cartledge, G., Heward, W. L., & Lo, Y.-y. (2006). Effects of response cards on disruptive behavior and academic responding during math lessons by fourth-grade students in an urban school. *Journal of Positive Behavior Interventions, 8*, 88–99.

Lane, K., Oakes, W., & Menzies, H. (2010). Systematic screenings to prevent the development of learning and behavior problems: Considerations for practitioners, researchers, and policy makers. *Journal of Disability Policy Studies, 21*, 160–172.

Ledlow, S. (1992). Is cultural discontinuity an adequate explanation for dropping out? *Journal of American Indian Education, 31*(3), 21–36.

Lo, Y.-y., & Cartledge, G. (2004). Total class peer tutoring and interdependent group-oriented contingency: Improving the academic and task-related behaviors of fourth-grade urban students. *Education & Treatment of Children, 27*, 235–262.

Lo, Y.-y., & Cartledge, G. (2006). FBA and BIP: Increasing the behavior adjustment of African American boys in schools. *Behavioral Disorders, 31*, 147–161.

Lo, Y.-y., Correa, V. I., & Anderson, A. L. (2013). *Culturally responsive social skill instruction for Latino male students.* Manuscript submitted for publication.

Lo, Y.,-y., Mustian, A. L., Brophy, A., & White, R. B. (2011). Peer-mediated social skill instruction for African American males with or at risk for mild disabilities. *Exceptionality, 19*, 191–209. doi: 10.1080/0936283 5.2011.579851

Losen, D. J. (2011). *Discipline policies, successful schools, and racial justice.* Boulder, CO: National Education Policy Center. Retrieved from http://nepc.colorado.edu/publication/discipline-policies.

Losen, D. J., & Gillespie, J. (2012). *Opportunities suspended: The disparate impact of disciplinary exclusion from school.* Los Angeles, CA: The Civil Rights Project, Center for Civil Rights Remedies. Retrieved from http://civilrightsproject.ucla.edu/resources/projects/center-for-civil-rights-remedies/school-to-prison-folder/federal-reports/upcoming-ccrr-research.

Losen, D. J., & Skiba, R. J. (2010). *Suspended education: Urban middle schools in crisis.* Bloomington: Indiana University, Center for Evaluation and Education Policy.

Marquez, B., Yeaton, P., & Vincent, C. (2013). *Delivering quick, efficient, and accurate behavioral universal screening and progress monitoring assessments using web-based, electronic technology.* In H. M. Walker & F. Gresham (Eds.), *Handbook of research in emotional and behavioral disorders.* New York: Guilford.

Marzano, R., Marzano, J., & Pickering, D. (2003). *Classroom management that works: Research-based strategies for every teacher.* Alexandria, VA: Association for Supervision and Curriculum Development.

McCready, L. T., & Soloway, G. B. (2010). Teachers' perceptions of challenging student behaviours in model inner city schools. *Emotional and Behavioural Difficulties, 15*, 111–123.

Middleton, M., & Cartledge, G. (1995). The effects of social skills instruction and parental involvement on the aggressive behaviors of African American males. *Behavior Modification, 19*, 192–210.

Monroe, C. R. (2005). Why are "bad boys" always Black? Causes for disproportionality in school discipline and recommendations for change. *The Clearing House, 79*, 45–50.

Musti-Rao, S., & Cartledge, G. (2004). Making home an advantage in the prevention of reading failure: Strategies for collaborating with parents in urban schools. *Preventing School Failure, 48*(4), 15–21.

Neal, L. I., McCray, A. D., Webb-Johnson, G., & Bridgest, S. T. (2003). The effects of African American movement styles on teachers' perceptions and reactions. *The Journal of Special Education, 37*, 49–57.

Noltemeyer, A., & Mcloughlin, C. S. (2010). Patterns of exclusionary discipline by school typology, ethnicity, and their interaction. *Perspectives on Urban Education, 7*(11), 27–40.

Prater, M. A., Serna, L., & Nakamura, K. K. (1999). Impact of peer teaching on the acquisition of social skills by adolescents with learning disabilities. *Education & Treatment of Children, 22*, 19–35.

Rausch, M. K., & Skiba, R. J. (2006). *The academic cost of discipline: The relationship between suspension/expulsion and school achievement.* Cambridge, MA: The Achievement Gap Initiative, Harvard University. Retrieved from http://agi.harvard.edu/.

Robinson-Ervin, P. (2012). The effects of culturally responsive computer-based social skills instruction on the social skill acquisition and generalization of urban 6th-grade students with emotional and behavioral disorders. Unpublished doctoral dissertation, Columbus, The Ohio State University.

Robinson-Ervin, P., Cartledge, G., & Keyes, S. (2011). Culturally responsive social skills instruction for adolescent black males, *Multicultural Learning and Teaching, 6*(1), Article 7. doi: 10.2202/2161-2412.1075

Sailor, W., Dunlap, G., Sugai, G., Horner, R. (Eds.). (2009). Handbook of positive behavior supports. In M. Roberts (Series Ed.), *Handbook of Clinical Child Psychology.* New York: Springer.

Salend, S. J., & Taylor, L. S. (2002). Cultural perspectives: Missing pieces in the functional assessment process. *Intervention in School and Clinic, 38*, 104–112.

Shaw, S. R., & Braden, J. P. (1990). Race and gender bias in the administration of corporal punishment. *School Psychology Review, 19*, 378–383.

Skiba, R. J., Horner, R. H., Chung, C.-G., Rausch, M. K., May, S. L., & Tobin, T. (2011). Race is not neutral: A national investigation of African American and Latino disproportionality in school discipline. *School Psychology Review, 40*, 85–107.

Skiba, R. J., Michael, R. S., Nardo, A. C., & Peterson, R. (2002). The color of discipline: Sources of racial and gender disproportionality in school punishment. *Urban Review, 34*, 317–342.

Skiba, R. J., & Peterson, R. (1999). The dark side of zero tolerance: Can punishment led to safe schools? *Phi Delta Kappan, 80*, 372–376, 381–382.

Skiba, R. J., & Peterson, R. L. (2000). School discipline at a crossroads: From zero tolerance to early response. *Exceptional Children, 66*, 335–346.

Skiba, R. J., Simmons, A. B., Ritter, S., Gibb, A. C., Rausch, M. K., Cuadrado, J., & Chung, C.-G. (2008). Achieving equity in special education: History, status, and current challenges. *Exceptional Children, 74,* 264–288.

Spencer, V. (2006). Peer tutoring and students with emotional behavioral disorders: A review of the literature. *Behavioral Disorders, 31,* 204–222.

Sprague, J. R., Marquez, B., Yeaton, P., Marquez, J., Pennefather, J., & Vincent, C. G. (2012). Elementary Social Behavior Assessment: Integrating universal screening and progress monitoring to measure behavioral response to intervention. Paper session presented at the meeting of the Annual Washington PBIS Conference, Bellevue, Washington, November.

Stichter, J. P., Lewis, T. J., Whittaker, T. A., Richter, M., Johnson, N. W., & Trussell, R. P. (2009). Assessing teacher use of opportunities to respond and effective classroom management strategies: Comparisons among high- and low-risk elementary schools. *Journal of Positive Behavior Interventions, 11,* 68–81. doi: 101177/1098300708326597

Stoiber, K. C., & Gettinger, M. (2011). Functional assessment and positive support strategies for promoting resilience: Effects on teachers and high-risk children. *Psychology in the Schools, 48,* 686–705.

Sugai, G., Horner, R. H., & Todd, A. (2000) *Effective Behavior Support Self-Assessment Survey (EBS–SAS).* Eugene: University of Oregon, Educational and Community Supports.

Sugai, G., O'Keeffe, B. V., & Fallon, L. M. (2012). A contextual consideration of culture and schoolwide positive behavior support. *Journal of Positive Behavior Interventions, 14,* 209–219. doi: 10.1177/1098300711426334

Townsend, B. L. (2000). The disproportionate discipline of African-American learners: Reducing school suspensions and expulsions. *Exceptional Children, 66,* 381–391.

Vavrus, F., & Cole, K. (2002). "I didn't do nothin'": The discursive construction of school suspension. *The Urban Review, 34,* 87–111.

Vincent, C. G., Swain-Bradway, J., Tobin, T. J., & May, S. (2011). Disciplinary referrals for culturally and linguistically diverse students with and without disabilities: Patterns resulting from school-wide positive behavior support. *Exceptionality, 19,* 175–190.

Walker, H. M., & Rankin, R. (1980). *The Social Behavior Skills Inventory of teacher social behavior standards and expectations.* Eugene: University of Oregon Press.

Wallace, J. M., Goodkind, S., Wallace, C. M., & Bachman, J. G. (2008). Racial, ethnic, and gender differences in school discipline among U.S. high school students: 1991–2005. *The Negro Educational Review, 59*(1–2), 47–62.

Waterman, R., & Harry, B. (2008). *Building collaboration between schools and parents of English language learners: Transcending barriers, creating opportunities.* Tempe, AZ: National Center for Culturally Responsive Educational Systems.

Weinstein, C. S., Tomlinson-Clarke, S., & Curran, M. (2004). Toward a conception of culturally responsive classroom management. *Journal of Teacher Education, 55,* 25–38.

Wu, C., Lo, Y.-y., Feng, H., & Lo, Y. (2010). Social skills training for Taiwanese students at risk for emotional and behavioral disorders. *Journal of Emotional and Behavioral Disorders, 18,* 162–177.

Yung, B. R., & Hammond, R. W. (1995). *PACT positive adolescent choices training: A Model for violence prevention groups with African-American youth.* Champaign, IL: Research Press.

22

CLASSROOM MANAGEMENT AND THE LAW

MITCHELL L. YELL
UNIVERSITY OF SOUTH CAROLINA

MICHAEL ROZALSKI
BINGHAMTON UNIVERSITY

JASON MILLER
ANNE ARUNDEL COUNTY, MD PUBLIC SCHOOLS

CLASSROOM MANAGEMENT AND THE LAW

Classroom management has been an issue of concern to teachers and administrators since the early days of public education in the United States. In fact, the first textbook providing advice to educators on managing their classrooms was published in 1907 (Bagley, 1907). A management-related issue that has caused apprehension among school personnel is how the law affects teachers' ability to manage their classrooms and administrators' ability to manage student behavior on a school-wide basis.

In the majority opinion of a seminal education case heard by the U.S. Supreme Court, Justice Byron White wrote, "Discipline and order is [sic] essential if the educational function is to be performed" (*Goss v. Lopez*, 1975, p. 584). In this case, it was recognized that for teaching and learning to occur in schools and classrooms, teachers must be able to manage student behavior. At the same time, the Supreme Court has also recognized that students have rights that need to be balanced with this need to maintain order in the classroom. Such rights include a reasonable expectation of privacy, expression, and due process.

The purpose of this chapter is to examine teachers' rights and responsibilities when they develop programs to prevent and control student misbehavior in the classroom. First, we examine general issues regarding the law and education, including the basis of a teacher's authority over students' behavior in the classroom and the rights of students in public schools when they are subjected to disciplinary sanctions because of misbehavior. Next, we discuss the legal responsibilities of teachers when employed by public school districts. Lastly, we consider the implications of law for administrators when developing school-wide management procedures and teachers when developing classroom management techniques.

SOURCES OF LAW

The three sources of law in the United States are Constitutional law, statutory law, and case law. These sources exist on both the federal and state levels.

Constitutional Law

The U.S. Constitution is the basic source of law in our legal system. The Constitution defines the fundamental rules by which the American system functions and sets the parameters for governmental action. All 50 states have their own constitutions, each of which plays a role similar to the federal constitution at the state level. State constitutions tend to be more detailed than the federal Constitution. Often they address the day-to-day operations of the state government, in addition to ensuring the rights of the state's citizens (McCarty, Cambron-McCabe, & Eckes, 2014).

Statutory Law

The U.S. Constitution gives Congress the authority to make laws. The laws passed or enacted by Congress are referred to as *statutes*. In Congress, the formal process begins with the introduction of a bill by a senator or representative. The bill is assigned a designation as originating in either the House (H.R.) or Senate (S.) and a number that reflects the order of introduction. The bill is then referred to the appropriate House or Senate committee. If a bill passes both the House and the Senate but in different forms, a conference committee comprised of representatives and senators is appointed to develop a compromise bill. The compromise bill is then voted on again, and the final version of the bill is sent to the president, who either signs or vetoes it. State statutes or laws are created and enacted in a manner similar to federal statutes. For the most part, bills are introduced and passed by state legislative bodies and signed into law by the governor of the state. Most statutes concerning matters of education are state rather than federal laws.

Case Law

Case law refers to the published opinions of judges in court cases. As is the case with Constitutional and statutory law, there is one federal court system and a court system in each of the 50 states. The opinions that arise from either federal or state court cases are used to interpret federal or state statutes. Our system relies heavily on these decisions because they establish legal precedents that other courts often follow. The importance of case law arises from the English tradition known as "common law." English common law was developed as a set of customs, rules, and traditions that were handed down through generations and reflected in the reports of decisions of the courts. Once a legal principle or precedent was established, it would be applied to cases with similar facts by subsequent courts.

IN LOCO PARENTIS

A common law principle that forms the basis of much of the legislation and litigation on classroom management is the doctrine of *in loco parentis*. The courts have long recognized the importance of giving school administrators and teachers the authority to manage student behavior. Thus, the principal and teachers have the authority not only to organize their schools and to teach but also to guide, correct, and discipline students. Clearly, such control is necessary to accomplish the mission of schools. Much of this authority originates from the English common law doctrine of *in loco parentis*, which translates to "in the place of the parent." When the term is applied to schools, it essentially means that school personnel have authority over students while they are at school or traveling to and from school. *In loco parentis* does not mean, however, that school personnel have the same degree of authority as parents have over their children. The *in loco parentis* doctrine implies that teachers have a duty to see that school order is maintained by requiring students to obey reasonable rules and commands, respect the rights of others, and behave in an orderly and safe manner when at school. This means that students should clearly know which behaviors are acceptable and which are prohibited. If students violate reasonable school rules by behaving in ways that are prohibited, they should be held accountable. Although *in loco parentis* does not have the legal force it once had because courts and legislatures have limited it, it is nonetheless still an active concept used by courts (Schimmel, Stellman, & Fischer, 2011).

FEDERALISM

We live in a federal system, which means that the government of the United States of America is a union of states joined under a federal government. The federal government protects the people's rights and liberties and acts to achieve certain ends for the common good while simultaneously sharing authority and power with the states (Yell, 2012). This relationship is set forth in the U.S. Constitution, the basic source of law in our legal system, and specifically in the 10th Amendment to the Constitution. The 10th Amendment limits excessive concentration of power in the national government while simultaneously limiting full dispersal of power to the states. It accomplishes this by giving the federal government only those powers that are specifically granted in the Constitution. All powers not specifically granted to the federal government are the province of the states. Because the Constitution contains no mention of education, the power to regulate education is a state prerogative. The laws in each of the states, therefore, govern education. In fact, in the case *San Antonio Independent School District v. Rodriquez* (1973), the U.S. Supreme Court ruled that education is not a fundamental Constitutional right. This is important in understanding the role of the law in classroom management because the federal government does not exert direct control over education. Although the federal government can influence how the states educate children (e.g., consider how the federal Individual with Disabilities Education Act influences the provision of special education services in all U.S. schools), it does so by requiring states to establish minimum requirements to access federal funds. States therefore exert more direct control over education.

Although the Constitution does not mention education and contains no explicit federal provisions for it, the basic rights that the Constitution guarantees to citizens do affect and influence education. Three amendments in particular, the 1st, 4th, and 14th, have an influence on educational practice.

The U.S. Supreme Court has repeatedly emphasized the authority of school district officials and educators to prescribe and control student conduct in schools (see *Bethel School District v. Fraser*, 1986; *New Jersey v. T.L.O.*, 1965; *Tinker v. Des Moines Community School District*, 1969). An especially important Supreme Court education case was *Goss v. Lopez* (1975), in which the Court noted that the 14th Amendment to the U.S. Constitution forbids states from depriving any person of life, liberty, or property without due process of law. Moreover, when a state provides a free public education to its citizens, it essentially is a right that a state or local education agency may not deprive a citizen of without also providing due process protections to ensure fundamental fairness. We next address the due process rights of students. It is in this area that the law may directly influence school-wide discipline policies and classroom management practices.

DUE PROCESS PROTECTIONS AND CLASSROOM MANAGEMENT

Students have two categories of due process rights: procedural and substantive. In terms of discipline, *procedural due process* involves the fairness of methods and procedures used by the schools; *substantive due process* refers to the protection of student rights from violation by school officials and involves the reasonableness of the disciplinary processes (Valente & Valente, 2005). Educators are vested with broad authority for establishing rules and procedures to maintain order and discipline; however, the due process rights of students must be considered in the development of establishing such rules and procedures.

Procedural Due Process: The Right to Fair Procedures

The importance of education to a student's future certainly requires that disciplinary actions that result in the student being deprived of an education (e.g., suspension, expulsion) be subjected to the standards of due process. The purpose of due process procedures is to ensure that disciplinary actions are made in a fair manner. Due process procedures in school settings do not require the full range of protections that a person would get in a formal court trial (e.g., representation by counsel, cross-examination of witnesses). Due process procedures in school settings do, however, include the basic protections such as notice and hearing.

The U.S. Supreme Court in *Goss v. Lopez* (1975) outlined the due process protections that must be extended to all students. This case involved nine high school students who had been suspended from school without a hearing. The students filed a lawsuit claiming that they had been denied due process of law under the 14th Amendment. The Supreme Court agreed, ruling that the students had the right to at least minimal due process protections in cases of suspension. The high court stated: "Having chosen to extend the right to an education . . . [the state] may not withdraw the right on grounds of misconduct absent fundamentally fair procedures to determine whether the misconduct had occurred" (p. 574).

The Court noted that schools have broad authority to prescribe and enforce standards of behavior. However, in their decision, the Supreme Court held that students are entitled to public education as a property interest, which is protected by the 14th Amendment. Because education is protected, it may not be taken away without adhering to the due process procedures required by the Constitution. The school's lawyers had argued that a 10-day suspension was only a minor and temporary interference with the student's education; the high court disagreed, stating that a 10-day suspension was a serious event in the life of the suspended child. When school officials impose 10-day suspensions, therefore, they must grant the suspended student the fundamental requisite of due process of law, the opportunity to be heard.

The opportunity to be heard, when applied to the school setting, involves the right to notice and hearing. The right to notice and hearing requires that students are presented with the charges against them and have an opportunity to state their case (Schimmel, Stellman, & Fischer, 2011). These protections will not shield students from properly imposed suspensions. The protections will, however, protect them from an unfair or mistaken suspension. The court in *Goss v. Lopez* (1975) recognized the necessity of order and discipline and the need for immediate and effective action, stating that suspension is a "necessary tool to maintain order [and] a valuable educational device" (p. 572). The prospect of imposing lengthy and cumbersome hearing requirements on every suspension case was a concern to the Court. However, the majority believed that school officials should not have the power to act unilaterally, free of notice and hearing requirements. The Court held that when students are suspended for a period of 10 days or less, the school must give them oral or written notice of the charges, an explanation of the reasons for the suspension, and an opportunity to present their side of the story.

The notice and hearing requirement does not mean that a formal notice to a student and a meeting must always precede suspension. It is permissible to a have reasonable delay between the time the notice is given and the student's hearing. For example, if the behavior poses a threat to other students or the academic process, a student can be immediately removed from school. The notice and hearing should then follow within 24 to 72 hours. A teacher or an administrator who is disciplining the student could also informally discuss the misconduct with the student immediately after the behavior occurred. This would give the student notice and an opportunity to explain his or her version of the facts before the teacher or administrator carried out the disciplinary sanction. In this case, the notice and hearing would precede the discipline.

It is important to remember that the basic due process protections outlined by the Supreme Court in *Goss v Lopez* (1975) apply only to short suspensions of under

10 school days. According to the Court, longer suspensions, or expulsions, require more extensive and formal notices and hearings. Although many common disciplinary procedures such as time-out, detention, response cost, and overcorrection do not require that due process procedures be extended to students, it is a reasonable assumption that notice and hearing procedures should be followed when using in-school suspension.

Substantive Due Process: The Right to Reasonableness

The courts have tended to give great authority to teachers and school officials to write rules that govern student behavior in school. Courts have also granted school officials the authority to develop and impose consequences on students who break their rules. There is a limit to this power, however. These rules and consequences must not violate students' constitutional protections discussed earlier (e.g., due process). Generally, rules and consequences will not violate students' constitutional rights when they are reasonable. Reasonable rules and consequences have a carefully considered rationale and a school-related purpose. Schools may not prohibit or punish behavior that has no adverse effect on the school environment. Furthermore, schools cannot use disciplinary penalties or restraints that are unnecessary or excessive to achieve safety and order in school. School and classroom rules and consequences must be rational, fair, and related to legitimate educational purposes (i.e., maintaining order and ensuring safety).

Rules must be sufficiently clear and specific to allow students to distinguish permissible from prohibited behavior. School rules that are too vague or general may result in the violation of students' rights because students will not have a clear understanding of them. Appropriate school rules are specific and definitive. They provide students with information regarding behavioral expectations.

A federal district court in Indiana addressed the issue of the reasonableness of a school's use of discipline in *Cole v. Greenfield-Central Community Schools* (1986). The plaintiff, Christopher Bruce Cole, was diagnosed as emotionally disturbed under Indiana state law. The student exhibited behavior management and adjustment problems. The school had attempted and documented numerous positive behavioral procedures that it had used to improve Christopher's behavior. When these procedures failed, school officials decided to use behavior reduction strategies such as time-out, response cost, and corporal punishment. The plaintiff sued the school, contending that in using these procedures the school had violated his civil rights.

The court recognized that Christopher, although he had a disability covered by the Individuals with Disabilities Education Act (IDEA), was not immune from the school's disciplinary procedures. The court held that the validity of the plaintiff's claim, therefore, rested on the "reasonableness" of the disciplinary procedures used by the school in attempting to manage Christopher's behavior. The court analyzed four elements to determine whether the rules and consequences were reasonable, which included: (1) Did the teacher have the authority under state and local laws to discipline the student? (2) Was the rule violated within the scope of the educational function? (3) Was the rule violator the one who was disciplined? and (4) Was the discipline in proportion to the gravity of the offense? Finding that all four elements of reasonableness were satisfied, the court held for the school district. The ruling provided further guidance to school districts developing and implementing discipline procedures.

FEDERAL LAW AND CLASSROOM MANAGEMENT

Whereas education is a state prerogative, federal involvement has played an important role in the growth of education in the United States. The federal government's role provided under the authority given Congress by the Constitution's General Welfare Clause is indirect (Yell, 2012). The primary way in which the federal government influences education in the states is through categorical grants. The purposes of the categorical grants have been to provide supplementary assistance to the state systems of education and to influence educational policy in the states. States have the option of accepting or rejecting the categorical grants offered by the federal government. If a state accepts a categorical grant from the federal government, the state must abide by the federal guidelines for the use of any funds they receive through the grants. Examples of categorical grants include the Elementary and Secondary Education Act of 1965 and IDEA. The federal government may also influence education in the states by either requiring agencies that are supported by federal dollars to take certain actions or prohibiting these agencies from taking certain actions. Two examples of this type of federal law is Section 504 of the Rehabilitation Act of 1973, which prohibits discrimination against persons with disabilities based solely on their disability in all agencies receiving federal funding, and the Children's Health Act of 2000, which prohibits hospital and other health care agencies supported by federal dollars from using seclusion and restraint except in emergencies.

Federal laws may also address classroom management issues. For example, IDEA required that the individualized education programs (IEPs) of students with disabilities "consider the use of positive behavioral interventions and supports for any student whose behavior impedes his or her learning or the learning of others (IDEA, 20 U.S.C. § 1414[d][3][B])[i]). Another example of such a federal law addressing a management/discipline issue is the proposed Keeping All Students Safe Act (2013), which if passed would "prevent and reduce the use of physical restraint and seclusion in schools" (H.R. 1893 § 3[1], [2013]). The bill allows restraint and seclusion to be used in school only when the student's behavior poses an imminent danger of physical injury to the student, school personnel, or others and less restrictive interventions would be ineffective in stopping such imminent danger of physical injury.

STATE LAW AND CLASSROOM MANAGEMENT

Because the U.S. Constitution does not grant the federal government the power to regulate education, the states have this responsibility. State constitutions create a right to an education for its citizens. Thus, most laws that affect education and therefore classroom management are state laws. States clearly have the right to require school districts to establish and enforce reasonable codes of student conduct to protect the rights and safety of students and to ensure that school environments are conducive to learning (McCarty, Cambron-McCabe, & Eckes, 2014). A complete review of all state laws is beyond the scope of this chapter, however. Interested readers can access their state laws regarding education and classroom management in states where such laws exist, on state websites. All states now publish the unofficial versions of their laws on the Internet in some format. State legislative websites generally allow interested persons to search by keyword (e.g., "classroom management," "discipline") and to browse by title of the law. For access to legislative websites for all states, readers can consult the website for the National Conference of State Legislatures (www.plol.org/Pages/Search.aspx) and other state resource websites maintained by entities such as FindLaw (www.findlaw.com/11stategov/index.html), Cornell's Legal Information Institute (www.law.cornell.edu/states/listing.html), and the Public Library of Law (www.plol.org/Pages/Search.aspx).

Generally, state education laws do not specifically address classroom management. In fact, according to Rapp (2013), state laws impose few limits on school district actions in establishing rules to regulate student conduct. When they do, state laws often prohibit certain disciplinary sanctions. Although these state laws vary widely, the types of discipline that are commonly prohibited or restricted by states are seclusion, restraint, and corporal punishment. Although the Supreme Court ruled that the U.S. Constitution does not prohibit the use of corporal punishment in schools (*Ingraham v. Wright*, 1977), currently corporal punishment is illegal in 31 states and the District of Columbia (for a list of the states and their corresponding laws on corporal punishment, go to The Center for Effective Discipline website at www.stophitting.com/index.php?page = statesbanning). Courts have upheld terminations of teachers who have used corporal punishment in states in which its use is prohibited (McCarthy, Cambron-McCabe, & Eckes, 2014). Similarly, seclusion and restraint are also prohibited in some states. Seclusion is the involuntary isolation of a single student in a room from which staff member(s) physically prevent the student from leaving by locking or blocking the door (Peterson, Ryan, & Rozalski, 2013). Physical restraint is defined by federal regulation as "the application of physical force without the use of any device, for the purposes of restraining the free movement of a resident's body. The term personal restraint does not include briefly holding without undue force a resident in order to calm or comfort him or her, or holding a resident's hand to safely escort a resident from one area to another" (42 CFR IV § G[483][352]).

According to the Committee on Education and the Workforce (Butler, 2013), 19 states have some sort of meaningful protections regarding the use of seclusion and restraint, 20 states prohibit restraints that restrict breathing, 13 states limit the use of restraints to emergencies involving immediate risk of harm, 15 states ban the use of mechanical restricts, and 30 states have a requirement that parents be notified if their child was secluded or restrained at school. Usually, if a state's laws address teachers' use of disciplinary procedures, these laws will be reflected in the disciplinary policies in that state's school districts.

Many states also have policies requiring schools to implement stringent security measures and zero tolerance policies (McCarty, Cambron-McCabe, & Eckes, 2014).

While implementing such measures to create safe schools has been quite controversial and subject to little research, when states require school districts to implement such policies, school officials must adhere to and implement them.

CASE LAW AND CLASSROOM MANAGEMENT

Case law has clearly established the right of a state and its local education agencies to establish and enforce reasonable standards of student conduct to ensure a safe, secure, and orderly learning environment that is conducive to student leaning (Rapp, 2013; Schimmel, Stellman, Fischer, 2014). In fact, courts have seldom addressed individual teacher's classroom management systems. Moreover, courts have traditionally been reluctant to interfere with student conduct codes, and students have seldom been successful in challenging school-wide discipline policies and procedures (Yell, 2012). As the U.S. Supreme Court noted in *Wood v. Strickland* (1975), "It is not the role of the federal courts to set aside decisions of school administrators" (p. 308). Similarly, courts must "refrain from second-guessing the disciplinary decisions made by school administrators" (*Gabrielle M. v. Park Forest-Chicago Heights Illinois School District 163*, p. 825). This is because courts see school district rights to impose disciplinary policies and procedures as a right that is bestowed by the states (McCarty, Cambron-McCabe, & Eckes, 2014). For example, the U.S. Circuit Court of Appeals for the Seventh Circuit in *Boucher v. School Board* (1998) noted that the U.S. Supreme Court had repeatedly affirmed the comprehensive authority of the states and of school officials, consistent with fundamental constitutional safeguards, to prescribe and control conduct in the schools. That is, reasonable school discipline policies and procedures have been consistently upheld as long as they serve a legitimate educational purpose, do not conflict with federal or state law, do not abridge a student's Constitutional rights, and are not discriminatory.

All rules and disciplinary sanctions should also be reviewed to determine whether they may violate a student's Constitutional rights or are discriminatory. According to the U.S. Supreme Court in *Bethel v. Fraser* (1965), "students do not shed their Constitutional rights at the schoolhouse gate" (p. 681). Students are "persons" under the Constitution and have fundamental rights that a state must respect. Constitutional issues that should be respected are those that involve freedom of speech, freedom from search and seizure, and procedural due process (Rapp, 2013). Nonetheless Constitutional considerations must be applied in light of the special characteristics of the school environment (*Long v. Board of Education*, 2000). Rules and disciplinary sanctions should therefore be reviewed to ensure that they are consistent with Constitutional standards.

Additionally, rules should be consistent with statutory law. Federal and state laws prohibit discrimination on the basis of race, color, national orientation, sex, and disability (Rapp, 2013). Seldom are rules or sanctions discriminatory on their face. It is usually in the application of nondiscriminatory rules or sanctions that discrimination may occur. Thus, the use of rules and sanctions should be monitored to ensure there is no discriminatory impact.

Another problem that may derail school conduct policies is a lack of specificity. School-wide discipline policies have been overturned if they are so vague that the policies have not specified what constitutes prohibited student behavior (*Killion v. Franklin School District*, 2001). In the case of *Woodis v. Westark Community College* (1998), the U.S. Court of Appeals for the 8th Circuit noted that the wording of a discipline policy should be exact enough to alert students specifically what behavior is unacceptable. According to Rapp (2013), school district officials should prepare a comprehensive document covering school-wide rules and consequences. McCarty, Cambron-McCabe, and Eckes (2014) suggested that school district officials should ensure that students and parents are knowledgeable about rules of conduct by having students and parents read and sign a form indicating that they understand the school rules. When behavioral issues arise that are not covered in such documents, educators have flexibility to address these situations (Rapp, 2013). In such situations when disciplinary sanctions are applied, a warning should usually precede the sanction.

SCHOOL DISTRICT POLICIES ON CLASSROOM MANAGEMENT

Many, if not most, school districts have established policies on the use of discipline with students. It is important that school district officials provide training to their administrators, teachers, and staff on school-wide policies. School districts have also established policies that call for zero tolerance of weapons, drugs, and violent acts that are committed on school grounds. Some schools, especially middle and high schools, have implemented security measures such as metal detectors. Moreover, many school districts throughout the United States have implemented procedures to prevent disciplinary problems and to teach proactive social skills. An example of such a procedure is school-wide positive behavior intervention and support (PBIS) (see Chapter 3 in this text). When such policies and procedures exist, it is incumbent on employees of the district to understand and adhere to these policies. In fact, failure of an administrator, teacher, or staff members to follow school district policies could be grounds for terminating employment.

LEGAL RESPONSIBILITIES OF TEACHERS

Statutes and case law impart special responsibilities upon teachers. These responsibilities, especially with respect to maintaining a safe and orderly school and classroom environment, can be gleaned from an examination of tort laws in the 50 states. Tort laws offer remedies to individuals harmed by the unreasonable actions of others. Tort claims usually involve state law and are based on the legal premise that individuals are liable for the consequences of their conduct if it results in injury to others (Schimmel, Stellman, & Fischer, 2011). Tort laws involve civil suits, which are actions brought to protect an individual's private rights. Such civil actions may be brought against individual teachers, but they are most likely brought against a school district. This is because of the doctrine of *respondent superior*, which infers that the master is responsible for the servant or let the master answer. Under this doctrine, in many situations the employer is responsible for the actions performed by his or her employees during the course of employment.

Two major types of tort violations are most likely to involve teachers: intentional and negligence torts. Intentional torts are usually offenses committed by a person who attempts or intends to do harm. For intent to exist, the individual committing the offense must be aware that injury will be the result of the act. Courts have typically given teachers great leeway in cases involving intentional torts because such cases often arise from a teacher's attempt to discipline a student or stop a student from injuring another, and courts traditionally have been reluctant to interfere with a teacher's authority to discipline students (Valente & Valente, 2005). When teachers are found to have injured a student and to be liable under tort laws, it has often involved a teacher administering a consequence for a disciplinary infraction that was cruel, excessive, and administered with malice, anger, or intent to injure.

Negligence torts are the most common type of tort case involving teachers. In negligence, unlike unintentional tort claims, acts that lead to injury are unexpected and unintended. Typically, persons who bring negligence claims against teachers or a school district must prove that school personnel could have foreseen and prevented an injury by exercising proper care. Accidents that could not have been prevented by reasonable care do not constitute negligence (Schimmel, Stellman, & Fischer, 2011).

Four elements must be present for negligence to be proven: (1) The teacher must have a duty to protect students from unreasonable risks; (2) the teacher must have failed in that duty by not exercising a reasonable standard of care; (3) there must be a causal connection between the breach of the duty to care and the resulting injury; and (4) there must be an actual physical or mental injury resulting from the negligence. In a court, all four elements must be proven before damages will be awarded for negligence.

These four elements—duty, failure to exercise a reasonable standard of care, connection between a teacher's negligence and injury, and actual injury—essentially outline a teacher's responsibility to his or her students. Thus, teachers have a duty to supervise students, maintain a safe environment, provide instruction, and be conscientious in fulfilling their duties. According to Morrison (2011), the standards for avoiding negligence provide the following two lessons to teachers: (1) Always keep the best interests of students in the forefront of their planning, and (2) always act in a manner that can pass the reasonable, prudent person test (i.e., in similar circumstances would a reasonable person have acted in this manner?). With respect to classroom management, teachers need to (1) maintain a safe and orderly classroom; (2) teach students the behaviors that are expected of them; (3) be aware of, and plan for, potentially dangerous situations; and (4) supervise students at all times.

THE LAW AND CLASSROOM MANAGEMENT

Maintaining a safe and orderly education environment is one of the most important and difficult duties that teachers face. If schools and classrooms are to be orderly environments where teachers can teach and students can learn, teachers should develop and implement classroom management strategies and adopt rules to indicate what behaviors are unacceptable. When teachers have to use disciplinary procedures, it is important that they understand their rights and responsibilities as well as those of their students. It is also important that school officials fashion school district policies and procedures that comport with the law. Following are suggested guidelines that will help to ensure that administrators and teachers meet federal, state, and court requirements when using discipline with public school students.

Implications for Administrators

The law is clear regarding the responsibilities of administrators for events that occur in their schools. A school's principal is responsible for actions taken in his or her school, and a school district's superintendent is responsible for actions that occur in his or her school district. We believe that district and school administrators should take the following actions with respect to school-wide discipline policies and teacher's classroom management programs.

Develop School District Disciplinary Policies and Procedures

School district administrators should develop written policies and procedures for teaching appropriate behavior and disciplining students when they violate school rules. These policies and procedures should be developed to ensure that schools are safe and orderly environments in which students are provided with an appropriate public education. That is, the rules must have a legitimate education purpose. The policies should include rules of student conduct, prohibited student behaviors, and disciplinary sanctions when those rules are broken. Developing the policies with the participation of administrators, teachers, parents, and students will help to ensure that they are reasonable and related to a legitimate educational function. Moreover, school district policies must be in line with state laws and regulations and must not be discriminatory or violate students' Constitutional rights.

After school-wide policies and procedures are developed school district officials should ensure that teachers, administrators, staff, and parents have access to and understand these policies and procedures. Methods that district officials can use to ensure parental access include mailing discipline policy brochures to parents and having teachers explain the procedures in parent–teacher conferences. It is important that policies and procedures apply equally to all students and that they are administered fairly and consistently.

Provide Professional Development Activities

Administrators should ensure that all staff and teachers receive professional development in the district's school-wide discipline policies and procedures and on how to construct their own classroom management plans. In addition to familiarizing teachers with the school district policies, such training should include the use of positive behavioral programming (e.g., developing rules and consequences, reinforcing appropriate behavior), acknowledging and encouraging appropriate student behavior, and using consequences when students violate rules. It is especially important that teachers understand their legal responsibilities to their students. Professional development activities should stress the importance of thorough documentation in situations in which students are disciplined. Documentation should include the problem behaviors, warnings given to the student, the actions taken to correct the behavior, the disciplinary procedures administered, and the results.

Ensure that Disciplined Students Are Afforded Due Process Protections

Minor disciplinary sanctions, such as removing points, assigning detention, and brief periods of time-out, only require minor procedural protections, such as an explanation of the behavior that led to the sanction. More significant sanctions, such as in-school or out-of-school suspension, require a more formal notification of a student and his or her parents and an opportunity to tell their side of the story. Additionally, students with disabilities are afforded additional procedural protections under Section 504 of the Rehabilitation Act and the IDEA (1973). Administrators and staff should know how to provide these procedural protections with students who are disciplined.

Implications for Teachers

Teachers should develop classroom management plans that consist of rules for student conduct and consequences for violating the code of conduct. Moreover, these plans must be fair, reasonable, and implemented with consistency. Classroom management plans may include reasonable sanctions that are used when students violate classroom rules. Teachers should ensure that the following conditions are met in the classroom policies and procedures.

Align Classroom Management Procedures with School-Wide Behavior Systems

When there is a school- or district-wide behavior or discipline system, teachers should develop their individual classroom management systems to align with the larger system. Of course, the management system must also comport to any state laws or regulations. Teachers should not develop classroom management systems that include procedures that are prohibited by the school district in which a teacher works.

Ensure That Students and Parents Understand the Classroom Management System

It is imperative that students and their parents understand the classroom management policies and procedures that are in place. The management policy should be specific enough that students know specifically what behaviors are unacceptable and the consequences for engaging in such behaviors. Classroom management systems that are too vague or general may result in the violation of students' rights because students will not have a clear understanding of them. Thus, appropriate management systems should be specific and definitive and should provide students with information regarding behavioral expectations. Teachers can take steps to ensure that students and their parents understand the classroom rules of conduct by having them read and sign a form indicating that they have reviewed and understand the school rules.

Classroom Management Systems Must Be Reasonable, Serve a Legitimate Educational Purpose, and Be Applied Fairly and Consistently

The most effective classroom management systems have a minimum number of rules on student conduct, the purpose of which is to ensure that a classroom environment is conducive to learning (Smith & Yell, 2013). The rules that a teacher develops should serve an important educational purpose. When rules are arbitrary and unrelated to the teaching function, they are more likely to be problematic from an educational and legal standpoint. Reasonable rules and consequences in a classroom management system should have a carefully considered rationale and a school-related purpose. Moreover, rules and consequences should be applied fairly and consistently. Teachers may not prohibit or punish behavior that has no adverse effect on the school environment. Classroom management systems designed to achieve safety and order in school should not include disciplinary penalties or restraints that are unnecessary or excessive.

Document Disciplinary Actions

When using disciplinary procedures with students, teachers should keep thorough written records of all disciplinary actions taken. An examination of court rulings in disciplinary matters indicates that in many instances, decisions turned on the quality of the school's records (Yell, 2012). That is, when a school district is sued over a particular disciplinary incident, a court may examine the records of the incident. Keeping records on emergency disciplinary actions is also important. Such records should contain an adequate description of the incident, warnings (if any) that were given to allow a student to stop the misbehavior, and avoid the disciplinary sanction, disciplinary action taken, results of the disciplinary actions, and the signatures of witnesses present. Documenting a disciplinary action is advisable when serious disciplinary sanctions are used (e.g., seclusion timeout, in- or out-of school-suspension) but would not be necessary in situations involving minor disciplinary sanctions (e.g., removing points, after school detention).

SUMMARY

An important issue with teachers and administrators is how the law affects teachers' ability to manage their classrooms and administrators' ability to manage student behavior on a school-wide basis. State law and court cases have allowed school officials and teachers great latitude when developing and implementing school-wide and classroom management systems. In developing such systems, it is important that teachers not deprive students of the right to an education, which is guaranteed to students by the constitutions of all 50 states. Neither should school-wide and classroom management systems deprive students of the due process protections guaranteed by the U.S. Constitution. School district administrators and teachers must adhere to state laws in implementing classroom management policies and procedures. Teachers can ensure that their classroom management system is educationally beneficial to students and legally sound if the system is reasonable, is related to a legitimate educational purpose, and is applied in a fair and consistent manner.

REFERENCES

Bagley, W. C. (1907). *Classroom Management.* Norwood, MA: MacMillan.

Bethel v. Fraser, 478 U.S. 675 (1986).

Boucher v. School Board, 134 F.3d 821 (7th Cir. 1998).

Butler, J. (2013). *An analysis of state seclusion and restrain laws and policies.* Retrieved on March 18, 2013 from www.autcom.org/pdf/HowSafeSchoolhouse.pdf.

Children's Health Act of 2000. Retrieved on June 2, 2013 from govtrack.us (www.govtrack.us/congress/bills/106/hr4365).

Cole v. Greenfield-Central Community Schools, 657 F. Supp. 56 (S.D. Ind. 1986).

Elementary and Secondary Education Act (ESEA) of 1965, 20 U.S.C. §16301 *et seq.*

Gabrielle M. v. Park Forest-Chicago Heights Illinois School District 163, 315 F.3d 817, (7th Cir. 2003).

Goss v. Lopez, 419 U.S. 565 (1975)

H.R. 1893, 113th Congress, 1st Session, (2013, May 8). "Keeping All Students Safe Act." Downloaded from www.govtrack.us/congress/bills/113/hr1893/text.

Individuals with Disabilities Education Act (IDEA), 20 U.S.C. § 1400 *et seq.*

Ingraham vs. Wright, 430 U.S. 651 (1977).

Keeping All Students Safe Act of 2013, Retrieved on June 2, 2013 from Congress.Gov (http://beta.congress .gov/congressional-record/2013/05/09/house-section/article/H2538–5).

Killion v. Franklin School District, 136 F. Supp. 2d 459 (W.D. PA, 2001).

Long v. Board of Education, 121 F. Supp. 2d 621 (E.D. KY 2000).

McCarty, M. M., Cambron-McCabe, N. H., & Eckes, S. E. (2014). *Public school law: Teachers' and students' rights* (7th ed.). Upper Saddle River, NJ: Pearson/Merrill Education.

Morrison, G. S. (2008). *Teaching in America* (5th ed.). Upper Saddle River, NJ: Pearson/Merrill Education.

New Jersey v. T.L.O., 469 U.S. 325 (1985).

Rapp, James A. (2013). *Education law,* Vol. 3. San Francisco, CA. LexisNexis.

Peterson, R. L., Ryan, J. B., & Rozalski, M. (2013). *Physical Restraint and Seclusion in School.* Alexandria, VA: Council for Exceptional Children.

San Antonio School District v. Rodriquez, 411 U.S. 1 (1973).

Schimmel, D., Stellman, L. R., & Fischer, L. (2011). *Teachers and the law* (8th ed.). Upper Saddle River, NJ: Pearson/Merrill Education.

Section 504 of the Rehabilitation Act of 1973 Regulations, 34 C.F.R. § 104 *et seq.*

Smith, S. W., & Yell, M. L. (2013). *Teacher's guide to preventing behavior problems in the elementary classroom.* Upper Saddle River, NJ: Pearson/Merrill Education.

Tinker v. Des Moines Independent Community School District, 393 U.S. 503 (1969).

Valente, W. D. & Valente, C. M. (2005). *Law in the schools* (6th ed.). Upper Saddle River, NJ: Pearson/Merrill Education.

Wood v. Strickland, 420 U.S. 308 (1975).

Woodis v. Westark Community College, 160 F.3d 435 (8th Cir. 1998).

Yell, M. L. (2012). *The law and special education* (3rd ed.). Upper Saddle River, NJ: Pearson/Merrill Education.

23

HOW TEACHERS LEARN TO BE CLASSROOM MANAGERS

LAURA M. STOUGH AND MARCIA L. MONTAGUE
TEXAS A&M UNIVERSITY

Seven decades of research have documented the central importance of classroom management in providing quality instruction (see Brophy, 2006; Brophy & Evertson, 1978; Emmer, Evertson, & Anderson, 1980; Fuller, 1969; Gilberts & Lignugaris-Kraft, 1997; Kounin & Gump, 1958). Teacher educators (e.g., Doyle & Carter, 1996; Emmer & Stough, 2001; Evertson & Weinstein, 2006) have repeatedly argued that classroom management is a critical pedagogical skill that teachers must master in order to maximize classroom instruction. Studies have also demonstrated that when teachers are effective classroom managers, their students achieve at a higher level (Freiberg, Stein, & Huang, 1995; Omoteso & Semudara, 2011; Stronge, Ward, & Grant, 2011; Stronge, Ward, Tucker, & Hindman, 2008) and display more interest in the subject matter of the class (Kunter, Baumert, & Köller, 2007). Plainly, teachers must learn to competently manage instruction and behavior if they are to become effective instructors.

Several chapters in the earlier edition of this book (Brophy, 2006; Jones, 2006; Stough, 2006) provided in-depth reviews of research on the necessity of training in classroom management. In this current chapter, we provide an update on that research, noting where more recent findings intersect with those established previously. First, we discuss recent research on the different ways in which classroom management is integrated into preservice training. Second, we discuss research on in-service professional development and present several effective models of classroom management that have been used in school settings. In our last section, we summarize the current status of research on training teachers to be classroom managers.

PRESERVICE PROGRAMS AND CLASSROOM MANAGEMENT

Teacher educators have repeatedly identified the importance of classroom management, while simultaneously lamenting that teachers receive limited classroom training during their preservice education (see Brophy, 2006; Brownell, Ross, Colón, &

McCallum, 2005; Jones, 2006). In the previous edition of this handbook, the first author suggested that the root of this divide is that state certification and professional accreditation standards seldom identify classroom management as a required competency (Stough, 2006). Given the national emphasis on content area preparation for teaching, coursework in general pedagogy, such as classroom management, has been deemphasized over the last several decades (Imig & Imig, 2008). This change in focus has not, however, changed the view of most academics that classroom management is an essential element of teacher preparation.

Traditional Routes to Preservice Training

In the early part of the 20th century, preservice teachers were commonly prepared at normal schools or teacher's colleges, rather than at universities, and coursework was focused on preparing the student for the educational profession (Labaree, 2008). During the last half of the century, most teachers' colleges were incorporated into public universities, and the first several years of teacher preparation became equivalent to that required of all undergraduates (Labaree, 2008). Currently, 79 percent of those seeking certification receive their training through higher education–based preparation programs (U.S. Department of Education [DOE], 2011). Preservice teachers typically enter undergraduate degree programs soon after graduating from high school. These traditionally prepared teachers then spend four to five years completing their coursework conjointly with their teacher certification requirements.

Along with general coursework, teachers prepared through the traditional undergraduate route complete subject-specific coursework. For example, aspiring math teachers take additional coursework in mathematics, along with related pedagogical coursework, such as math for elementary school teachers. Education support courses, such as in child development or inclusive education, are also part of the typical teacher preparation curriculum. Pedagogical coursework that focuses on instructional design and delivery or classroom management then rounds out the coursework requirements. Reforms since the passing of No Child Left Behind have tended to shift the balance in this coursework and increased the amount of content matter required, while the amount of general pedagogy coursework has decreased (Brownell, Ross, Colón, & McCallum, 2005; Stough, 2006). In addition to coursework, supervised field practica are typically embedded within or accompany the coursework (Brownell, Ross, Colón, & McCallum, 2005). The curriculum is usually concluded with a student teaching experience during the final year of teacher preparation. The Department of Education (2011) reports that traditionally trained teachers receive an average of 177 hours of supervised classroom practica offered alongside their coursework, followed by an additional average of 514 hours in the classroom as part of the student teaching experience.

The goals of classroom management are to create positive teacher–student relationships, manage student groups to sustain on-task behavior, and use psychological strategies to aid students who present persistent psychosocial problems (Emmer

& Stough, 2001). Classroom management content, however, does not fit neatly into the curriculum because its focus is primarily pedagogic, and it does not correspond to a specific content area (Stough, 2006). Studies affirm that classroom management content is minimal within most teacher training programs. Only a minority of teacher preparation programs in the United States includes classroom management as a stand-alone course (Brophy, 2006; Stough, 2006), and Wesley and Vocke (1992) found that only 39% of teacher preparation programs included classroom management as a stand-alone course. More recent studies show that this trajectory has continued. In a study of preparation programs in the top 50 U.S. schools of education, Stough, Williams, & Montague (2004) found only 44 percent of the top 50 colleges of education in the United States listed a stand-alone course in classroom management. In an examination of 26 special education programs in Florida, Oliver and Reschly (2010) similarly found that only 27% had a course devoted to classroom management. An Australian study of 35 teacher preparation programs (O'Neill and Stephenson, 2011) also found only 30% of teacher preparation programs included stand-alone classroom management content. However, O'Neill and Stephenson (2011) did find, after additional analysis, at least some management content embedded within 30 of the 35 programs they reviewed. In these embedded units, however, the mean number of hours spent on the topic of classroom management hours was 2.3 compared to 25.5 mean hours covering the content in the stand-alone coursework. In the United States, classroom management content is often embedded in introductory courses in educational psychology; however, given the range of topics in this subject, its inclusion in these courses is probably limited to several lectures at best (Jones, 2006).

Preservice programs differ not only in the *extent* to which classroom management content is taught but also in the *type* of classroom management content taught (Stough, Williams-Diehm, & Montague, 2004). This difference is highlighted when the content of special education programs is compared to the content of general education programs. Preservice training for general education teachers typically focuses on content and group instruction, whereas training for special education preservice teachers tends to focus on modifications and individual instruction (Brownell, Ross, Colon, & McCallem, 2005; Gilberts & Lignugaris-Kraft, 1997). While early in their college careers, general and special education preservice teachers typically take most of the same courses, their training paths diverge about the third year of training (Stough, Williams, & Montague, 2004). In examining course syllabi (Stough, Montague, Williams-Diehm, & Landmark, 2006), we have found that classroom management is taught with two primary emphases: either a whole-class/generalist approach or an individual/behaviorist approach. The first of these two approaches has its roots in the seminal work of the educational psychologist Kounin (1970), while the second aligns with the theoretical work of B. F. Skinner. As a result, when classroom management appears as part of a general education program, the pedagogical emphasis tends to be on management and procedures for the whole class, while special education coursework emphasizes individual interventions for students, rather than whole-group instruction (Stough, Williams, & Montague, 2004).

Fieldwork and Student Teaching during Preservice Training

Much less is known about classroom management knowledge acquired during student teaching or other fieldwork experiences. Although teachers report that they learn the most about classroom management through experience in the field (Stough, Montague, Williams-Diehm, & Landmark, 2006) it cannot be assumed, and indeed there is no evidence, that new teachers acquire classroom management skills simply with time and experience (Oliver & Reschly, 2007). With respect to learning management skills as part of practica, Jones (2006) suggests that related field experiences should be of high quality and sufficient duration. Further, he advocates (as would most teacher educators) that there should be congruence between the university coursework content and the field experiences. Oliver and Reschly (2007) point out that teachers need ample opportunity and feedback in order to learn how to implement behavior management strategies. Brownell and colleagues (2005), in a review of 64 preservice special education programs, found that effective field experiences were those that were carefully supervised and tied to practices acquired in coursework.

Research has shown that collaboration with cooperating or mentor teachers has successful outcomes for novice, beginning, and preservice teachers (Brownell, Ross, Colón, & McCallum, 2005; Krull, Oras, and Sisask, 2007). Jones (2006) recommends that cooperating teachers be selected who appropriately demonstrate classroom management strategies that are taught in university coursework. In addition, Jones recommends that teachers-in-training have numerous visits from university supervisors who can provide frequent and ongoing feedback on how to create learning environments that promote positive student behavior. Brownell and colleagues (2005) state that preservice field experiences that accompany classroom management coursework should include diverse students and collaboration between preservice and in-service teachers.

Oliver and Reschly (2007) point out that most preservice teachers begin their field experiences after the commencement of the school year and are placed in classrooms that already have established management routines and procedures. However, new teachers will need to know how to establish routines and procedures once they are in charge of their own classrooms. Oliver and Reschly (2007) suggest that professional development school models are an ideal environment in which preservice teachers might practice and receive supportive feedback on their classroom management skills. Professional development schools established in partnership with teacher education programs and providing teacher candidates with intensive preservice classroom experiences have demonstrated their potential to increase new teachers' classroom and behavior management skills (Emmer & Stough, 2001; Siebert, 2005). In addition, instructional components such as journal writing, reflective activities, and portfolios enhance field-based management competencies by providing additional opportunities for reflection on classroom practice. There is also evidence that video of classroom situations may provide a useful medium for analysis and discussion of appropriate classroom management strategy use in fieldwork settings (Stough, 2001). Also recommended are experiences in multiple classroom contexts as a strategy to strengthen classroom management skills (Emmer & Stough, 2001; Soodak, 2003).

It is important to note that most of the published work on fieldwork and classroom management gives recommendations rather than providing empirical results on the effect that fieldwork has on developing classroom management skills. Much more work is needed to test the veracity of many of these claims, commonsensical as they may appear.

Alternative Routes to Preservice Training

An increasing number of teachers in the United States complete their teacher certification requirements through alternative certification programs (Schonfeld and Feinman, 2012; U.S. Department of Education, 2011). Alternative certification programs serve teacher candidates who are acting as teacher of record in a classroom while simultaneously participating in training (U.S. Department of Education, 2011). Alternative preparation programs may be based either within, or independently from, a college or university. Of the over 230,000 teachers who complete their teaching requirements each year, approximately 9 percent do so through an alternative certification program associated with an institution of higher education, while 11 percent complete nonassociated alternative routes to certification (U.S. Department of Education, 2011).

Alternative routes to certification are reported to vary widely with respect to the time required to complete the program and the content of these programs. Some research has indicated that teachers who complete alternative preparation programs are less skilled in classroom management than those who complete traditionally trained programs (e.g., Darling-Hammond, 2001; Good et al., 2006; Schonfeld & Feinman, 2012). Other studies suggest that alternative certified teachers have different attitudes toward classroom management in their first years of teaching (e.g. Ritter & Hancock, 2007; Schonfeld & Feinman, 2012; Sokal, Smith, & Mowat, 2003). Given the variability in alternative programs, however, it is difficult to make general assumptions about the classroom management skills of teachers prepared through alternative programs. Given the shorter length of time of preservice training usually required in alternative preparation programs (U.S. Department of Education, 2011), a more appropriate analysis may be of the number of instructional hours devoted to learning classroom management skills in alternative programs vs. those hours spent in traditional programs.

Several studies have examined classroom management as an element within alternative teacher training. Tricario & Yendol-Hoppey (2012) found that 15 teachers-in-training in a university-affiliated alternative training program exhibited significant challenges in monitoring student learning and providing differential instruction due to their struggles with classroom management. Schonfeld and Feinman (2012) studied 252 beginning teachers in New York public schools. They found those teachers who were alternatively certified were significantly more likely to experience classroom management problems than were their colleagues. These studies suggest that the amount of time spent in preservice training is an important variable in developing skill in the area of classroom management. Because teachers usually spend less time receiving preservice training in alternative certification programs (U.S. Department of Education, 2011), it is logical to assume that the number of hours that they spend receiving classroom management training is also reduced.

PROFESSIONAL DEVELOPMENT AND CLASSROOM MANAGEMENT

Professional development (previously termed in-service training) refers to the additional education that teachers receive after receiving certification and while they are employed. Professional development can benefit teachers in a number of ways: filling gaps of knowledge, keeping teachers up-to-date with changing theories and legal mandates, and allowing teachers to reflect on their educational practices and beliefs (Charland, 2006). For teachers in the field, professional development training can serve as a critical bridge from learning about research on evidence-based practices to implementing such practices in their classrooms (Kretlow, Cooke, & Wood, 2011).

Research has identified a number of components that, when implemented within a professional development program, have positive impacts on teacher strategy use and confidence. Effective professional development programs are typically provided by experts in the field, conducted in a way that allows for application, aligned to school goals, and practical in meeting current classroom needs (Hough, 2011a). The majority of teachers report a preference for in-district workshops in which teams of teachers participate (Coalition for Psychology in Schools and Education, 2006).

Recent studies emphasize the need for professional development that is provided in a continuous manner (Oliver & Reschly, 2007), rather than provided piecemeal through workshops. A program evaluation of a professional development training program found that training must be sustained for at least two years and implemented in the classroom for at least 1.5 years by 75% of the participating teachers in order for positive teaching and student outcomes to result (Hough, 2011a, 2011b). Similarly, a national survey of over 1000 in-service teachers revealed that length of time and number of hours of professional development had a substantial positive influence on active learning by teachers. Researchers reported that professional development is more effective and of higher quality if it is sustained over time and engages teachers for a substantial number of hours (Garet, Porter, Desimone, Birman, &Yoon, 2001).

Numerous studies have emphasized teachers' ongoing need for classroom management as part of their professional development (e.g. Baker, 2005; Coalition for Psychology in Schools and Education, 2006; Nahal, 2010; Stough, Montague, Williams-Diehm, & Landmark, 2006), and even highly effective classroom managers benefit from professional development on classroom management (Montague, 2009). A national sample of over 2,000 teachers identified the most frequent need was to "ensure that students' negative behaviors are not an ongoing distraction to you (the teacher) and your classroom" (Coalition for Psychology in Schools and Education, 2006, p. 93). Further areas of need identified by teachers in the study included physical safety, time management, and active student participation.

Effective classroom management professional development emphasizes the use of positive, preventive, and proactive strategies to both prevent student behavior problems (Boulden, 2010; Carlson, Tiret, Bender, & Benson, 2011; Sugai & Horner, 2002) and to decrease teacher stress (Clunies-Ross, Little, and Kienhuis, 2008). Also, training in classroom management has been found to increase teacher use of positive strategies and lessen teacher negative emotional effects (Alvarez, 2007). Conversely, reactive management approaches tend to increase student off-task behaviors (Clunies-Ross, Little, and Kienhuis, 2008). The use of proactive or preventive classroom management as a more effective practice has been frequently supported in the literature (e.g. Emmer & Stough, 2001; Oliver & Reschly, 2007) and is considered best practice when used as part of professional development. In addition, Hough (2011a) found that sustained professional development resulted in teachers implementing a number of effective classroom management practices at high levels of proficiency.

Teachers receive professional training in classroom management skills through a variety of methods. In the United States, professional development workshops are often used as a medium through which to improve the classroom management skills of in-service teachers. Teachers participate in training sessions either within their school districts or through universities, conferences, or regional workshops (Coalition for Psychology in Schools and Education, 2006). Examples of professional development training programs teachers report receiving frequently include Applied Behavior Analysis, Boys Town, Capturing Kids' Hearts, and Love and Logic (Stough, Montague, Williams-Diehm, & Landmark, 2006). Professional development programs such as the Good Behavior Game (GBG), The First Days of School, Classroom Organization and Management Program (COMP), Assertive Discipline, Teacher Effectiveness Training, and Conflict Resolution Education in Teacher Education (CRETE) are referenced widely in the literature (see Jones, 2006; van Lier, Muthén, van der Sar, & Crijnen, 2004; Webster-Stratton, 2000). Jones (2006), in the first edition of this *Handbook*, provides additional detail about the COMP and Consistency Management and Cooperative Discipline programs. Two additional programs that have professional development components and that have become increasingly popular over the last several decades are detailed in the following sections.

Positive Behavior Support

An increasingly popular program is Positive Behavior Support (PBS). PBS is a school-wide approach in which systematic educational and systems change methods are used to redesign the school environment (Carr et al., 2002; Sugai & Horner, 2002). Preventive strategies rather than punishment are used to enhance quality of life and minimize problem behavior. As such, school-wide PBS provides a "framework for prevention and the foundation for effective classroom organization and management" (Oliver & Reschly, 2007) and has been shown to effectively reduce disruptive student behaviors (Horner & Sugai, 2000; Sugai & Horner, 2002). Although Positive Behavior Support (PBS) is not a stand-alone professional development program, part of the PBS systems change includes in-service teacher training. PBS also provides the same type of training to both special educators and general educators.

The National Technical Assistance Center on Positive Behavioral Interventions and Supports provides a "blueprint" for states, regional centers, districts, and/or campus-level teams to utilize in building professional development training in PBS (Lewis, Barrett, Sugai, & Horner, 2010). Teams are provided with strategies to implement PBS through each of the blueprint phases, including exploration, installation, initial implementation, full implementation, and sustainability. Teams are provided with information on Tier I, II, and III interventions and given campus evaluation questions that are needed to begin and continue the process of school-wide PBS implementation (Lewis, Barrett, Sugai, & Horner, 2010).

Although school-wide PBS does not specifically target individual teacher classroom management strategies, it does provide a school-wide behavioral plan that transcends classrooms, as well as a tertiary model of behavioral support. Within the classroom, the PBS model relies on teachers to directly teach routines and expectations, actively supervise students, prompt desired behaviors, and organize the classroom in effective ways (Sugai & Horner, 2002). However, Jones (2006) pointed out that most of the data from the PBS approach have been either based on individual student cases or aggregated by school rather than examining the management practice of individual teachers.

The Incredible Years Teacher Classroom Management Program

The Incredible Years Teacher Classroom Management Program for children is an evidence-based model that includes professional development in the area of classroom management. Developed by Webster-Stratton, the Incredible Years Training Series contains a number of research-validated components, including parent training, teacher training, and child training (see Carlson, Tiret, Bender, & Benson, 2011; Shernoff & Kratochwill, 2007; Webster-Stratton & Reid, 1999a, 1999b). As is the case with PBS, it is not designed solely as a teacher development program, but teachers often receive Incredible Years training as part of their professional development. The teacher professional development program emphasizes decreasing problem behavior and preventing behavior problems through proactive teaching strategies, providing effective praise, motivating students and building positive relationships with students, and outreach to families. A key component of the training is the use of video modeling, whereby teachers model effective management of challenging classroom behaviors. Video narration, teacher manuals, and readings accompany the video modeling (Shernoff & Kratochwill, 2007). Research validating the effectiveness of the teacher training component was first published in the literature in 1999. Results show that students in classes with teachers trained in the program demonstrate higher levels of social competence, higher levels of engagement in the class, and lower rates of noncompliance and aggression (Webster-Stratton & Reid, 1999a, 1999b, Webster-Stratton, Reid, & Hammond, 2004). Further, studies have shown that teachers trained in the program utilize higher rates of praise and lower rates of criticism than do control groups of teachers (Webster-Stratton & Reid, 1999a, 1999b; Webster-Stratton, Reid, & Hammond, 2001, 2004). Researchers have also assessed the effectiveness of specific components of the Incredible Years Teacher Training

Program. Shernoff and Kratochwill (2007) compared teachers trained using video modeling and those using video modeling with added consultation and found students in both groups showed decreased problem behaviors. The additional use of consultation following the teachers' self-directed video modeling produced even greater positive effects on teacher confidence. It should be noted that a large number of the studies that have found the Incredible Years program effective have been conducted by the developer or her colleagues.

Mentoring as a Form of Professional Development Training

Mentoring is another well researched method for training teachers in effective classroom management strategies (e.g. Evertson & Smithey, 2000). Mentoring provides in-service teachers with the opportunity to provide collegial support, examine their own methods, and support their peers (Jones, 2006). Mentors provide support by assisting the teacher to consider new educational practices (Knight, 2004). Numerous studies support the efficacy of coaching novice teachers in classroom management skill development (Certo, 2005a, 2005b; Edwards, 2011; Hough, 2011a). Baker (2005) found that teachers typically report high self-efficacy and willingness to ask and consult with colleagues for advice and assistance. Consultation with colleagues can provide guidance and external validation for the mentee teachers and lead to increased confidence and competence. Research has also shown that collaboration with mentor teachers has successful outcomes for novice teachers (Certo, 2005a, 2005b; Krull, Oras, and Sisask, 2007).

Mentoring is implemented in a number of ways. Mentoring is often provided as a component of teacher induction where new teachers are welcomed, trained, and valued. Mentoring is also a way to build relationships and provide needed support. Coaching, which is a form of mentoring, is also a frequently cited method for assisting novice teachers (Edwards, 2011; Shernoff et al., 2011). Coaching usually is directed at supporting the teacher in carrying out specific classroom functions. Hough (2011a) found that classroom-based coaching, as part of a classroom management professional development program with more than 2,300 teachers across 25 states, resulted in enhanced professional development training and improved student outcomes in terms of behavior, attendance, and achievement. Coaching, paired with pre- and post-conferences, as well as teacher support groups, has been demonstrated as an effective approach for professional development in classroom management (Edwards, 2011; Shernoff et al., 2011).

A Model of Effective Mentoring and Coaching

A recently developed promising practice for professional development in classroom management is the Teachers Supporting Teachers in Urban Schools (TST) model. Within this model, teachers who are socially connected and influential on the campus are labeled Key Opinion Leaders (KOLs) (Atkins et al., 2008). These KOLs serve as mentors and are matched with novice teachers (Shernoff et al., 2011). KOL mentors receive training and promote effective classroom management strategies (Neal et al., 2008). A second group of teachers, KOL Coaches, then provide evidence-based classroom management and motivation support through preconferences, classroom visits, and postconferences.

KOLs mentors lead group seminars twice a month for novice teachers where classroom management and motivational strategies are shared. Coaches are invited to attend these group seminars. Further, KOL mentors lead Professional Learning Communities (PLCs) monthly for all teachers in which reflection, shared responsibility, and collaboration are central components (Shernoff et al., 2011). Together, the mentors and coaches serve in complementary roles that center on addressing persistent problems and promoting teacher effectiveness. The mentor model of using learning communities has been highlighted in other research as well (Edwards, 2011).

FUTURE DIRECTIONS IN CLASSROOM MANAGEMENT

In reflecting on the studies reviewed in this chapter, we confirm the critical need for classroom management training while simultaneously agreeing with the National Research Council's (2010) statement: "There is currently little definitive evidence that particular approaches to teacher preparation yield teachers whose students are more successful than others." Reports from novice and experienced teachers alike strongly point to the need for more training in the area of classroom management, but the number of efficacy studies continue to be few and have limited generalizability. While several models, such as PBS and the Incredible Years, have established effectiveness, classroom management training is only part of larger intervention and takes place during professional development. In the first edition of this *Handbook*, Stough (2006) asserted that classroom management should be integrated as a fundamental part of all preservice teacher training programs. Several models for how to integrate classroom management into preservice training exist, and research suggests that more intensive instruction in this area is more effective. Research, too, is abundant on the use of mentoring to help teachers develop effective classroom management practices. However, as was the case in the first edition of the *Handbook*, we actually know little about how these different types of teacher training ultimately affect classroom management practice, student achievement, and student behavior (see Jones, 2006). Most recently, the National Research Council (2010) ranked classroom management training as one of the three highest-priority research areas in teacher preparation. For the most part, however, contemporary educational researchers have yet to take up this charge.

REFERENCES

Alvarez, H. K. (2007). The impact of teacher preparation on responses to student aggression in the classroom. *Teaching and Teacher Education, 23*, 1113–1126.

Atkins, M. S., Frazier, S. L., Leathers, S. J., Graczyk, P. A., Talbott, E., Jakobson, L., Adil, J. A., Marinez-Lora, A., Demirtas, H., Gibbons, R. B., & Bell, C. C. (2008). Teacher key opinion leaders and mental health consultation in urban low-income schools. *Journal of Consulting and Clinical Psychology, 76*, 905–908.

Baker, P. H. (2005). Managing student behavior: How ready are teachers to meet the challenge? *American Secondary Education, 33*(3), 51–64.

Boulden, W. T. (2010). The behavior intervention support team (BIST) program: Underlying theories. *Reclaiming Children and Youth, 19*(1), 17–21.

Brophy, J. (2006). History of research on classroom management. In C. M. Evertson & C. S. Weinstein (Eds.), *Handbook of classroom management: Research, practice, and contemporary issues* (pp. 17–43). Mahwah, NJ: Erlbaum.

Brophy, J., & Evertson, C. (1978). Context variables in teaching. *Educational Psychologist, 12,* 310–316.

Brownell, M. T., Ross, D. D., Colón, E. P., & McCallum, C. L. (2005). Critical features of special education teacher preparation: A comparison with general teacher education. *The Journal of Special Education, 38*(4), 242–252.

Carlson, J. S., Tiret, H. B., Bender, S. L., & Benson, L. (2011). The influence of group training in the Incredible Years Teacher Classroom Management Program on preschool teachers' classroom management strategies. *Journal of Applied School Psychology, 27*(2), 134–154.

Carr, E. G., Dunlap, G., Horner, R. H., Koegel, R. L., Turbull, A. P., Sailor, W., Anderson, J., Albin, R. W., Koegel, L. K., & Fox, L. (2002). Positive behavior support: Evolution of an applied science. *Journal of Positive Behavior Interventions, 4*(1), 4–16.

Certo, J. (2005a). Support and challenge in mentoring: A case study of beginning elementary teachers and their mentors. *Journal of Early Childhood Teacher Education, 26*(4), 395–421.

Certo, J. (2005b). Support, challenge, and the two-way street: Perceptions of a beginning second grade teacher and her quality mentor. *Journal of Early Childhood Teacher Education, 26*(1), 3–21.

Charland, W. (2006). The art association/higher education partnership: Implementing residential professional development. *Arts Education Policy Review, 107*(6), 31–39.

Clunies-Ross, P., Little, E., & Kienhuis, M. (2008). Self-reported and actual use of proactive and reactive classroom management strategies and their relationship with teacher stress and student behaviour. *Educational Psychology, 28*(6), 693–710.

Coalition for Psychology in Schools and Education. (2006). *Report on the Teacher Needs Survey.* Washington, DC: American Psychological Association, Center for Psychology in Schools and Education.

Darling-Hammond L. (2001). The challenge of staffing our schools. *Educational Leadership, 58*(8), 12–17.

Doyle, W., & Carter, K. (1996). Educational psychology and the education of teachers: A reaction. *Educational Psychologist, 31*(1), 23–28.

Edwards, S. (2011). Managing a standards-based classroom. *Mathematics Teaching in the Middle School, 17*(5), 282–286.

Emmer, E., Evertson, C., & Anderson, L. (1980). Effective classroom management at the beginning of the school year. *Elementary School Journal, 80,* 219–231.

Emmer, E., & Stough, L. (2001). Classroom management: A critical part of educational psychology, with implications for teacher education. *Educational Psychologist, 36,* 103–112. doi: 10.1207/S15326985EP3602_5.

Evertson, C., & Smithey, M. (2000). Mentoring effects on proteges' classroom practice: An experimental field study. *The Journal of Educational Research, 93*(5), 294–304.

Evertson, C. M. & Weinstein, C. S. (2006). Classroom management as a field of inquiry. In C. M. Evertson & C. S. Weinstein (Eds.), *Handbook of classroom management: Research, practice, and contemporary issues* (pp. 3–15). Mahwah, NJ: Erlbaum.

Freiberg, H. J., Stein, T. & Huang, S. (1995). Effects of a classroom management intervention on a student achievement in inner-city elementary schools. *Educational Research and Evaluation: An International Journal on Theory and Practice, 1,* 36–66.

Fuller, F. (1969). Concerns of teachers: A developmental conceptualization. *American Educational Research Journal, 6*(2), 207–226. doi: 10.3102/00028312006002207

Garet, M. S., Porter, A. C., Desimone, L., Birman, B. F., & Yoon, K. S. (2001). What makes professional development effective? Results from a national sample of teachers. *American Educational Research Journal, 38*(4), 915–945.

Gilberts, G. H., & Lignugaris-Kraft, B. (1997). Classroom management and instruction competencies for preparing elementary and special education teachers. *Teaching and Teacher Education, 13*(16), 597–610.

Good, T. L., McCaslin, M., Tsang, H. Y., Zhang, J., Wiley, C. R. H., Bozack, A. R., & Hester, W. (2006). How well do 1st-year teachers teach: Does type of preparation make a difference? *Journal of Teacher Education, 57*(4), 410–430.

Horner, R. H., & Sugai, G. (2000). School-wide behavior support: An emerging initiative (special issue). *Journal of Positive Behavioral Interventions, 2,* 231–232.

Hough, D. L. (2011a). Characteristics of effective professional development: An examination of the developmental designs character education classroom management approach in middle grades schools. *Middle Grades Research Journal, 6*(3), 129–143.

Hough, D. L. (2011b). An evaluation of the developmental designs approach and professional development model on classroom management in 22 middle schools in a large, midwestern school district. *Middle Grades Research Journal, 6*(3), 177–192.

Imig, D. G., & Imig, S. R. (2008). From traditional certification to competitive certification: A twenty-five year retrospective. In M. Cochran-Smith, S. Feiman-Nemser, & D. McIntyre (Eds.), *Handbook of research on teacher education: Enduring questions in changing context* (3rd ed.) (pp. 886–907). New York: Erlbaum/ Taylor & Francis.

Jones, V. (2006). How do teachers learn to be effective classroom managers? In C. M. Evertson & C. S. Weinstein (Eds.), *Handbook of classroom management: Research, practice, and contemporary issues* (pp. 887–907). Mahwah, NJ: Erlbaum.

Knight, J. (2004). Instructional coaches make progress through partnership: Intensive support can improve teaching. *National Staff Development Council, 25*(2), 32–37.

Kounin, J. S. (1970). *Discipline and group management in classrooms.* NY: Holt, Rinehart, and Winston.

Kounin, J., & Gump, P. (1958). The ripple effect in discipline. *Elementary School Journal, 35*, 158–162.

Kretlow, A. G., Cooke, N. L., & Wood, C. L. (2011). Using in-service and coaching to increase teachers' accurate use of research-based strategies. *Remedial and Special Education, 33*(6), 348–361.

Krull, E., Oras, K., & Sisask, S. (2007). Differences in teachers' comments on classroom events as indicators of their professional development. *Teaching and Teacher Education, 23*, 1038–1050.

Kunter, M., Baumert, J., & Koller, O.(2007). Effective classroom management and the development of subject-related interest. *Learning and Instruction, 17*(5), 494–509.

Labaree, D. F. (2008). An uneasy relationship: The history of teacher education in the university. In M. Cochran-Smith, S. Feiman-Nemser, & D. McIntyre (Eds.), *Handbook of research on teacher education: Enduring questions in changing context* (3rd ed.) (pp. 290–306). New York: Erlbaum/Taylor & Francis.

Lewis, T. J., Barrett, S., Sugai, G., & Horner, R. H. (2010). *Blueprint for schoolwide positive behavior support training and professional development.* Eugene, OR: National Technical Assistance Center on Positive Behavior Interventions and Support. Retrieved from www.pbis.org.

Montague, M. L. (2009). Expert secondary inclusive classroom management. Doctoral dissertation, College Station, Texas A&M University. Available electronically at https://repository.tamu.edu/handle/1969.1/ ETD-TAMU-2009-12-7343

Nahal, S. P. (2010). Voices from the field: Perspectives of first-year teachers on the disconnect between teacher preparation programs and the realities of the classroom. *Research in Higher Education, 8*, 1–19.

National Research Council. (2010). Preparing teachers: Building evidence for sound policy. Committee on the Study of Teacher Preparation Programs in the United States, Center for Education, Division of Behavioral and Social Sciences and Education. Washington, DC: National Academies Press.

Neal, J., Shernoff, E. S., Frazier, S. L., Stachowicz, E., Frangos, R., & Atkins, M. (2008). Change from within: Engaging teacher key opinion leaders in the diffusion of interventions in urban schools. *The Community Psychologist, 41*, 53–57.

Oliver, R. M., & Reschly, D. J. (2007). Effective classroom management: Teacher preparation and professional development. Washington, DC: The National Comprehensive Center for Teacher Quality.

Oliver, R. M., & Reschly, D. J. (2010). Special education teacher preparation in classroom management: Implications for students with emotional and behavioral disorders. *Behavioral Disorders, 35*(3), 188–199.

Omoteso, B., & Semudara, A. (2011). The relationship between teachers' effectiveness and management of classroom misbehaviours in secondary schools. *Psychology, 2*, 902–908. doi: 10.4236/psych .2011.29136

O'Neill, S., & Stephenson, J. (2011). Classroom behaviour management preparation in undergraduate primary teacher education in Australia: A web-based investigation. *Australian Journal of Teacher Education, 36*(10), article 3. Available at http://ro.ecu.edu.au/ajte/vol36/iss10/3.

Ritter J. T., Hancock D. R. (2007). Exploring the relationship between certification sources, experience levels, and classroom management orientations of classroom teachers. *Teaching and Teacher Education, 23*(7), 1206–1216.

Schonfeld, I. S., & Feinman, S. J. (2012). Difficulties of alternatively certified teachers. *Education and Urban Society, 44*(3), 215–246.

Shernoff, E. S., & Kratochwill, T. R. (2007). Transporting an evidence-based classroom management program for preschoolers with disruptive behavior problems to a school: An analysis of implementation, outcomes, and contextual variables. *School Psychology Quarterly, 22*(3), 449–472.

Shernoff, E. S., Marinez-Lora, A. M., Frazier, S. L., Jakobson, L. J., Atkins, M. S., & Bonner, D. (2011). Teachers supporting teachers in urban schools: What iterative research designs can teach us. *School Psychology Review, 40*(4), 465–485.

Siebert, C. J. (2005). Promoting preservice teachers' success in classroom management by leveraging a local union's resources: A professional development school initiative. *Education, 125*(3), 385–392.

Sokal, L., Smith, D. G., & Mowat, H. (2003). Alternative certification teachers' attitudes toward classroom management. *The High School Journal, 86*(3), 8–16.

Soodak L. C. (2003). Classroom management in inclusive settings. *Theory into Practice, 42*(4), 327–333.

Stough, L. M. (2001). Using stimulated recall in classroom observation and professional development. Paper presented at the annual meeting of the American Educational Research Association, Seattle, Washington, April. (ERIC Document No. ED457214)

Stough, L. M. (2006). The place of classroom management and standards in teacher education. In C. Evertson & C. Weinstein (Eds.), *Handbook of Classroom Management. Research, Practice, and Contemporary Issues* (pp. 909–923). Mahwah, NJ: Erlbaum.

Stough, L., Montague, M., Williams-Diehm, K., & Landmark, L. (2006). *The effectiveness of different models of classroom management instruction.* Paper presented at the annual meeting of the American Educational Research Association, San Francisco, April.

Stough, L., Williams, K., & Montague, M. (2004). Classroom management content in teacher preparation programs. Paper presented at the annual meeting of the Teacher Education Division of the Council for Exceptional Children, Albuquerque, New Mexico, November.

Stronge, J. H., Ward, T. J., & Grant, L. W. (2011). What makes good teachers good? A cross-case analysis of the connection between teacher effectiveness and student achievement. *Journal of Teacher Education, 62*(4), 339–355.

Stronge, J. H., Ward, T. J., Tucker, P. D., & Hindman, J. L. (2008). What is the relationship between teacher quality and student achievement? An exploratory study. *Journal of Personnel Evaluation in Education. 20*(3–4), 165–184.

Sugai, G. & Horner, R. (2002). The evolution of discipline practices: School-wide positive behavior supports. *Child & Family Behavior Therapy, 24*(1/2), 23–50.

Tricario, K., & Yendol-Hoppey, D. (2012). Teacher learning through self-regulation: An exploratory study of alternatively prepared teachers' ability to plan differentiated instruction in an urban elementary school. *Teacher Education Quarterly, 39*(1), 139–158.

U.S. Department of Education, Office of Postsecondary Education. (2011). *Preparing and Credentialing the Nation's Teachers: The Secretary's Eighth Report on Teacher Quality; Based on Data Provided for 2008, 2009, and 2010.* Washington, DC: Author.

van Lier, P. A. C., Muthén, B. O., van der Sar, R. M., & Crijnen, A. A. M. (2004). Preventing disruptive behavior in elementary schoolchildren: Impact of a universal classroom-based intervention. *Journal of Consulting and Clinical Psychology, 72*(3), 467–478.

Webster-Stratton, C. (2000). The Incredible Years Training Series. *Juvenile Justice Bulletin,* (June), 1–24.

Webster-Stratton, C., & Reid, J. (1999a). Treating children with early-onset conduct problems: The importance of teacher training. Paper presented at the American Association of Behavior Therapy, Toronto, Ontario, November.

Webster-Stratton, C., & Reid, J. (1999b). Effects of teacher training in Head Start classrooms: Results of a randomized controlled evaluation. Paper presented at the Society for Prevention Research, New Orleans, June.

Webster-Stratton, C., Reid, M. J., & Hammond, M. (2001). Preventing conduct problems, promoting social competence: A parent and teacher training partnership in Head Start. *Journal of Clinical Child Psychology, 30*(3), 283–302.

Webster-Stratton, C., Reid, M. J., & Hammond, M. (2004). Treating children with early-onset conduct problems: Intervention outcomes for parent, child, and teacher training. *Journal of Clinical Child and Adolescent Psychology, 33*(1), 105–124.

Wesley, D. A., & Vocke, D. E. (1992). *Classroom discipline and teacher education.* Paper presented at the annual meeting of the Association of Teacher Educators, Orlando, Florida. (ERIC Document Reproduction Services No. ED 341 690)

24

PARENTAL ENGAGEMENT AND CLASSROOM MANAGEMENT

Unlocking the Potential of Family–School Interactions and Relationships

JOAN M. T. WALKER
PACE UNIVERSITY

KATHLEEN V. HOOVER-DEMPSEY
VANDERBILT UNIVERSITY

Our central thesis in this chapter is that parents' active engagement in their students' school learning is important because it can make teachers' classroom management and instruction more effective. Parent engagement has been positively related to achievement across grade levels and ethnic groups (e.g., Wilder, 2014), and research demonstrates that when teachers and parents work together, student learning and engagement are enhanced (Christenson & Reschly, 2010; Henderson, Mapp, Johnson & Davies, 2007; Hill & Chao, 2009; Hughes & Kwok, 2007). Exactly *how* parents and teachers contribute to student learning outcomes remains unclear. This leads to our second purpose in writing this chapter—identifying the mechanisms or "active ingredients" of parents' and teachers' interactions with students and with one another. Understanding how and why these dyadic relationships function is essential to promoting effective teaching and parenting practice and school improvement.

We assert that one fruitful place to look for explanations is research on parenting and families as developmental contexts. Over recent decades, developmental research has more fully defined family influence on child and adolescent outcomes as a complex *process*. Drawing in part from Bronfenbrenner's (1986) ecology of human development, several investigators have focused on understanding how, why, and under what circumstances specific elements of family, school, and family–school relationships support students' school success across the preschool through secondary years (Bryk & Schneider, 2002; Christianson & Reschly, 2010; Crosnoe, 2009; Fan &

Williams, 2010; Grolnick, Kurowski, & Gurland, 1999; Lavenda, 2011; Pomerantz, Moorman, & Litwack, 2007).

One prominent example of these efforts is the Hoover-Dempsey and Sandler (1995, 1997, 2005) *process model* of parental involvement. The model begins by explaining *why* parents become involved and continues in identifying *what* parents do when they are involved with their children's learning (their varied forms of engagement such as home- and school-based activities, as well as their use of several psychological learning mechanisms within the course of those activities including encouragement, modeling, reinforcement, and teaching). In its culminating levels, the model articulates *how* parents' involvement translates into student outcomes. Central to this last link, the model suggests that the relationship between families' engagement practices and students' learning and engagement is mediated by students' perceptions of their parents' behaviors and expectations related to their learning. In this process framework, students are active architects of their own development; they are not simply bystanders who passively receive resources from socializing agents.

Taken as a whole, Hoover-Dempsey and Sandler's process approach deepened earlier work that examined links between how frequently parents engaged in a range of specific involvement behaviors on the one hand and the distal outcome of student achievement on the other. Essentially, the model has attempted to fill in the "black box" between family engagement and student outcomes.

Trends in family engagement research and theory are paralleled in research on teachers' classroom management practices. For example, seminal research on classroom management examined the relationship between observable teacher behaviors and objective measures of student learning, such as the relation between teachers' use of time and student achievement tests (e.g., Emmer, Evertson, & Anderson, 1980). Later, researchers began to articulate psychological aspects of teachers' classroom management practices, such as the structure of teachers' classroom goals and authority and how these dimensions are related to subjective student outcomes, including motivation, ability beliefs, and use of self-regulated learning strategies (Urdan & Midgley, 2003; Urdan, Midgley & Anderman, 1998). In recent years, research on classroom management has grown still more diverse, examining an array of factors believed to influence student learning and engagement, including students' backgrounds and characteristics, their perceptions of the classroom environment and teacher–student relationship (TSR) quality, the influence of school structure on classroom processes, how teachers learn about classroom management, and tests of varied classroom management interventions (Evertson & Weinstein, 2006).

These varied endeavors to understand classrooms as developmental contexts can be organized according to the process-oriented questions posed in Hoover-Dempsey and Sandler's (1995, 1997, 2005) parent engagement model: *Why* do teachers adopt the specific classroom management practices they use? *What* is the range—and what are the active ingredients, or mechanisms—of teachers' successful classroom management practices? What student outcomes do these management strategies and mechanisms influence? *How* do teachers' management practices influence students' social development and school learning?

As in the earlier version of this chapter (Walker & Hoover-Dempsey, 2006), we draw on ecological systems theory to organize the chapter. In the first two sections, we examine the microsystems of home and school by reviewing research on (1) parents' contributions to student learning outcomes within the family context and (2) teachers' contributions to student learning within the classroom context. Grounded in developmental and educational theories that bridge the contexts of home and school, we focus on three specific characteristics of parents' and teachers' engagement with students that support student learning and school success. These characteristics are (1) behavioral control/demandingness, (2) responsiveness, and (3) developmentally appropriate autonomy support. Drawing parallels between the literatures on families and classrooms as developmental contexts is important to achieving full understanding of students' social and cognitive development because, as Grolnick, Deci, and Ryan (1997) have noted, "parents and teachers face the important challenge of how . . . to promote socially sanctioned behav[ior] without killing the spirit of the child" (p. 135).

The third section of the chapter considers research on *interactions* between home and school (the mesosystem level of Bronfenbrenner's ecological systems theory). Here we examine whether and how the relational quality of one dyad influences the quality of other dyadic interactions. For example, does the quality of the parent–child relationship influence the quality of the teacher–student relationship? Does the quality of the teacher–student relationship influence the quality of parent–teacher interactions? To learn more about the unique and additive nature of parent and teacher contributions to student learning and school-related outcomes, we also summarize what researchers have learned when family engagement and teacher practices are considered together in models predicting student outcomes. The chapter concludes with recommendations for how schools and families can create and use their partnerships to enhance student success beyond levels generally attained when the two developmental systems function in relative isolation.

We note that the major issues addressed in the chapter are pertinent to all schools and the families they serve. However, some issues related to developing positive and productive family–school relationships may require more school knowledge and outreach when families the school serves (1) are very poor or have very limited education, (2) are first- or second-generation immigrants or refugees from countries and cultures outside the United States, and (3) had limited or nonexistent models in their own schooling of how schools and families can work together to support successful student learning.

CULTURE, PARENTING, AND FAMILIES AS DEVELOPMENTAL CONTEXT

Macro-Level Systems: The Influence of Culture on Families and Parenting

A sample of research over recent decades from anthropological, developmental, and educational perspectives (Hill, 2010; LeVine, 1988; Maccoby, 1992; Okagaki & Bingham, 2010; Rodriguez, 2009; White & Carew, 1973; Whiting & Whiting, 1975) has suggested strongly that families' cultural beliefs, values, and goals play a major role in shaping the practices that parents engage in as they raise their children. This research also suggests that the specific culture in which a child is born, grows, and develops is likely to manifest similarities and differences when compared with other cultures in which families live and raise their children. Further, even within countries where citizens share many cultural values and practices, families across the country may live in quite varied environments (e.g., rural, urban, suburban) and may hold perspectives, values, beliefs and goals that differ in some respects from those of other families within the same country. Finally, this research base also suggests that when families immigrate into a new "cultural home" and country, they—and the schools serving the communities in which they live—often benefit considerably from engaging in collaborative work that supports the development of *mutual* understanding of the values and goals that family and school bring to the task of ensuring students' effective education and learning.

Against this background, LeVine's (1988) work has suggested strongly that *families across cultures hold in common* a hierarchy of three values and goals fundamental to their thinking and behavior as they raise their children. Primary in this hierarchy is the goal that the family's children *survive*; that is, if a child's life is in danger (from illness, community violence, war, etc.), parents across cultures and circumstances will focus on doing whatever is necessary and possible to ensure that the child survives. Second in the hierarchy of common goals across cultures is parents' belief that their *children must acquire knowledge and skills essential to an economically productive adult life.* As the Whitings' (1975) classic study of six culturally different families in communities around the world suggested, specific manifestations of this goal may vary widely across cultures. For example, in one culture they studied, successful families emphasized teaching their young children to engage in useful home-based activities, such as caring for younger siblings, tending crops in the family garden, and preparing simple food. In another culture, parents focused on helping their children acquire cognitive, social, and emotional skills that they believed would be essential for the child's school success and future economic survival. The third universal goal that parents hold focuses on ensuring that their *children develop an understanding of, appreciation for, and commitment to the basic values, goals, and practices of the family's culture.* For example, some families may emphasize young children's learning to respect all elders' needs and demands, while families in another culture might emphasize with equal strength the early development of the child's cognitive and school-readiness skills.

Because schools and school systems serve as a deeply important micro system in the educational success of students in the United States, LeVine's research thus suggests strongly that schools and school personnel work to understand the values and goals driving parents' behaviors with their children and with their children's schools. Such understanding, as well as families' understanding of schools' goals in the culture that they share, is often essential to the creation and support of family–school collaboration that offers critical support for students' school success from early childhood through adolescence.

Micro-Level System: Family and the Influence of Parenting on Student Outcomes

Within this set of universal goals for child rearing just described are a multiplicity of specific parenting values, goals, intentions, and practices within and across many cultures. Within the United States, research on parenting practices and their implications for varied child outcomes received notable impetus in the late 1950s as Baumrind (1966, 1971, 1989) began a program of research focused on (1) patterns of parenting practices within and among families and (2) links between these patterns of parenting behaviors and patterns of developmental outcomes (cognitive, social, emotional) manifested by children in these families from preschool through the secondary years (see also Darling & Steinberg, 1993; Maccoby & Martin, 1983). Baumrind's early work identified three distinct patterns or styles of parenting (authoritative, authoritarian, permissive), which varied in levels of parental *responsiveness* (i.e., emotional and affective support and encouragement for the child) and *demandingness* (i.e., the assertion of principles, rules, and requirements for the child's behavior, work, and engagement with others). She found authoritative parenting, with its strong focus on parental responsiveness *and* demandingness, to be consistently linked with the most positive patterns of child outcomes—that is, strong cognitive, social, and emotional development. The other two styles—authoritarian (strongly focused on demandingness, generally low in responsiveness) and permissive (strongly focused on responsiveness, very low in demandingness)—were often markedly less effective than authoritative parenting in promoting strong overall competence in the child. Over subsequent decades, this body of work was influential in shaping other investigators' examination of parenting style as developmental context (Darling & Steinberg, 1993; Steinberg, Elmen, & Mounts, 1989; Steinberg, Lamborn, Dornbusch, & Darling, 1992).

Across time, varied investigators noted that the broad pattern of authoritative parenting style and related patterns of children's developmental outcomes emerged primarily in samples of predominantly white, middle- and upper-middle class families. As studies in this area incorporated more diverse samples of families, there were reports that poor and ethnic minority parents often practiced *authoritarian* parenting (strong focus on demandingness, low use of responsiveness) and that the school outcomes for students growing up in authoritarian families were poorer than those generally reported for children growing up with parents using authoritative parenting practices (Dornbusch, Ritter, Leiderman, Roberts, & Fraleigh, 1987). Other studies reported, however, that when families within low-income communities engaged in *some* authoritative parenting practices, especially responsiveness, student outcomes tended to be more positive than in families with *non*authoritative parenting styles (Brody & Flor, 1998; Murry et al., 2005; see also Chao, 1994, 2001).

This research is important because it demonstrated that in some family and community contexts, the potentially negative influence of parents' firm behavioral control and limited support for student autonomy could be mitigated by adequate levels of parental responsiveness (Le, Ceballo, Chao, Hill, Murry, & Pinderhughes, 2008). In sum, current thinking about parenting's contributions to student academic and social outcomes is grounded not so much in a strict interpretation of parenting *style* but rather in identifying and recognizing parents' use of specific practices that reflect the larger constructs of responsiveness (e.g., expressions of positive regard for the child, his/her work, effort, interests, accomplishments) in *combination* with practices that reflect demandingness and control (e.g., monitoring) across varied community settings and contextual influences.

CLASSROOMS AS DEVELOPMENTAL CONTEXTS

Macro-Level Systems: Public Policy and School Culture as Influences on Teacher Practices

For Bronfenbrenner, public policy and school culture constitute macro-level systems that exert a distal but distinct influence on children's school outcomes through their impact on the more local, or micro-level, developmental spheres of home and school. As is true of most families' basic goals for their children's survival and development, education policy and school governance are driven by the goals of enhancing the skills and productivity of its citizens and perpetuating the national culture. Since 2006, U.S. education policy has reflected increasing attention to the overlap between the contexts of home and school and the role each plays in the larger societal aims of schooling. For example, policy focused on family engagement has included increasing calls to offer families the right to choose educational avenues for their children that diverge from the traditional options of private and public schooling (e.g., charter schools, home schooling). In terms of policy relevant to schools and classrooms, there has been intense scrutiny of teacher practice and the adoption of performance benchmarks that focus on holding teachers and schools accountable for student achievement.

Although these policy trends are often controversial, from a developmental perspective, they represent efforts to distribute responsibility for children's education across schools and families. They also demonstrate increased awareness that effective teaching pertains to both skillful classroom management *and* to teachers' family engagement skills. These two areas of professional competence are embodied in Danielson's (2007) Framework for Teaching, which contains four domains of teacher performance: Planning and Preparation, Classroom Environment, Instruction, and Professional Responsibilities. The Classroom Environment domain (Domain 2) articulates abiding challenges in classroom management, including management of instructional groups, transitions and materials, and monitoring and responding to student misbehavior. It also recognizes the importance of the psychological dimensions of classroom management such as teacher expectations, student pride, and the value of academic learning. The Professional Responsibilities domain (Domain 4) includes classroom-related activities such as providing families with information about instructional programs and their individual student. Perhaps most importantly, this domain also emphasizes teachers' efforts to *engage* families in the school's instructional programs or goals. Within each domain, teacher performance is compared to four levels of effectiveness (ranging from highly effective, effective, developing and ineffective). Grounded in this framework, many school districts across the

United States now use a formal approach to teacher evaluation that views classroom management and family engagement as interdependent professional obligations.

Against the national backdrop of school choice and accountability, however, there is wide variation in how local school communities support families and teachers. For example, the No Child Left Behind Act requires that all Title I schools and school districts (including charter schools) have a written plan that makes parents partners in their children's education; unfortunately, most school districts have an uneven record of translating written policy into systematic and equitable opportunities for family engagement (Weiss, Lopez, & Rosenberg, 2010). Moreover, as evidenced in a status report on teacher professional development, teachers across the United States have few high-quality opportunities to learn about classroom management and family engagement (Darling-Hammond, Wei, Andree, Richardson, & Orphanos, 2009). This latter issue is particularly troublesome given that most teacher preparation programs also fail to offer substantial training in these areas (Epstein & Sanders, 2006; Stough, 2006). The question remains: How will teachers meet new and increasingly rigorous standards for classroom management and family engagement without support?

In sum, just as culture, family, and community exert pressures on parents' behaviors and in turn on children's development and learning, the affordances and restrictions of public policy and local school context shape how teachers engage with families and connect with students.

Micro-Level/Classroom Systems: Teaching Style

As true of research examining parental engagement and its contributions to student outcomes, classroom management research has firmly established that the prevalence and quality of specific teacher practices can support a range of student social and academic outcomes (Evertson & Weinstein, 2006). Evidence of these effects has been aggregated over time and through a breadth of methodologies including teacher and student self-report, objective observation, and, more recently, biological science. For example, children who experienced a supportive classroom learning environment produced levels of salivary cortisol consistent with effective stress regulation (Blair, 2010). Now the field seeks to understand the specific psychological mechanisms behind these effects and to articulate what they look like across the span of K–12 education.

To understand classrooms as developmental contexts and teachers as socializing agents, several investigators have drawn explicitly from the parenting literature to argue that effective teachers are like good parents in that they use responsiveness, autonomy support, and firm behavioral control to support student learning and engagement (Walker, 2009; Wentzel, 2002). In this section, we summarize recent research on teachers' use of these three authoritative practices and each one's relation to varied student outcomes. To explain *how* the three teacher behaviors influence student learning and development, we integrate parenting style theory with self-determination theory. Self-determination theory (Ryan & Deci, 2000) is a robust framework arguing that all humans have an intrinsic need for relatedness, autonomy, and competence. When these intrinsic needs are met, healthy social development and learning ensues; when they are not met, less healthy outcomes ensue.

How do parenting style theory and self-determination fit together? Recall Darling and Steinberg's (1993) assertion that parenting style alters the effectiveness of a given parenting practice by influencing student openness to parental influence. From this standpoint, constellations of parent and teacher practices that reflect responsiveness *and* demandingness influence student social and cognitive development only to the extent that students are willing to "tune in" to parents' and teachers' socialization efforts. Essentially, style theory affirms that student socialization is a co-constructed process in which parents/teachers and students play active roles. Self-determination theory complements style theory by offering an explanation for *how* parents and teachers can engage students in the socialization process. From a self-determination perspective, students are more likely to attend to and internalize parent and teacher expectations when their intrinsic needs have been met. Thus, to foster positive student social and academic outcomes, teachers and parents must express support and warmth to meet students' need for relatedness and use behavioral control, adjusted to students' developing capacity for self-sufficiency, to meet students' needs for competence and autonomy.

Responsiveness

Teacher responsiveness can be defined as emotional support (e.g., providing comfort, warmth) and as meeting students' needs as individual learners (e.g., connecting academic content to student interests). In a notable meta-analytic study, learner-centered or responsive teacher–student relationships (TSRs) were linked to a range of K–12 student outcomes including increased participation, critical thinking, satisfaction, achievement, motivation, social connection, and reduced disruptive behavior (see Cornelius-White, 2007). From a self-determination perspective, responsive TSRs affect learning through their impact on students' feelings of psychological safety, which lead, in turn, to increased student engagement and academic self-efficacy. Given this, it is logical to assume that negative TSRs can accelerate problematic behaviors and hinder students' success; however, few studies have examined this trajectory (cf. Clotfelter, Ladd, & Vigdor, 2007).

Positive TSRs at entry to school have been found to predict positive social and academic outcomes in middle school (Hamre & Pianta, 2001), and they hold particular benefits for at-risk students and those with learning difficulties (e.g., Baker, 2006; Hamre & Pianta, 2005). In general, African American and Latino students benefit more from positive TSRs than their white peers (Hamre & Pianta, 2005); however, African American students tend to have less supportive TSRs than their Latino and White counterparts (Hughes & Kwok, 2007). Sadly, levels of teacher responsiveness are generally low but variable across elementary school classrooms (Pianta, Belsky, Houts, Morrison & the NICHD ECCRN, 2007). Moreover, the average quality of TSRs declines across the elementary school years (O'Connor & McCartney, 2007). This is troubling given that the transition to secondary school is often the beginning of a downward motivational and academic spiral for many adolescents (Barber &

Olson, 2004). At a developmental period when they might benefit most from positive TSRs, adolescents are least likely to experience them. Helping secondary teachers learn the critical role of positive TSRs in adolescent learning and how to forge positive relationships with adolescents holds promise as a tool for increasing teacher effectiveness and enhancing adolescent school outcomes.

Autonomy Support

Teacher support for student autonomy can be defined as teacher speech and behaviors that rely on students' inner motivational resources, such as personal interest, rather than on extrinsic reasons for learning, such as grades or consequences. Teacher support for student autonomy has been linked to a range of important student outcomes including engagement, content understanding, grades, and well-being (Reeve, 2009). Consistent with the idea that autonomy support is an instructional "signal" that leads students to choose to tune in rather than tune out (Walker, 2009), adolescents' perceptions of autonomy support fosters their engagement in learning, and its perceived absence can lead to deliberate student disengagement (Collins & Laursen, 2004). Autonomous environments promote learning and engagement by increasing cognitive involvement and effort and by decreasing boredom (Ryan & Deci, 2000). So, like good parenting, effective teaching involves provision of choice, the avoidance of intrusion, and connecting student choice to personal interests and goals. Again, however, Reeve's (2009) research indicates that teachers, especially at the secondary level, tend to be more controlling than autonomy supportive during instruction.

The benefits of students' perceived autonomy support can accrue to teachers over time. For example, Hafen and colleagues (2012) found that if high school students perceived that their classroom encouraged autonomy in the first few weeks of the year, their engagement increased throughout the course. By contrast, students in classrooms with less perceived autonomy typically declined in engagement. These findings echo classroom management research indicating that the opening weeks of school are a developmentally sensitive period and that classroom norms and culture established early on by teachers can result in very different student outcomes later in the year (Bohn, Roehrig, & Pressley, 2004; Emmer, Evertson, & Anderson, 1980; Walker, 2008). Although autonomy support might seem more developmentally appropriate during adolescence, as early as third grade students can distinguish among different forms of teacher autonomy support (i.e., providing choice versus explaining relevance) and, like adolescents, are negatively influenced by forms of autonomy suppression (e.g., intrusiveness; Assor, Kaplan, & Roth, 2002).

Firm Control/Structure

The term "classroom management" is synonymous with structure. Structure involves setting expectations, giving clear directions, and generally establishing order (Doyle, 1986), and it has been positively associated with student learning and engagement (Emmer & Stough, 2010; Evertson & Weinstein, 2006). Teachers who provide structure help students understand what is required and offer guidance on how to achieve an expected outcome; these teacher characteristics, in turn, support learning because they foster students' sense of competence (Jang, Reeve, & Deci, 2010). Structure is often confused with control or the lack of student choice; however, in effectively managed classrooms, teacher structure and autonomy support are positively correlated. Moreover, both variables promote student engagement but in different ways. For example, Jang, Reeve, and Deci (2010) found that high school teachers who gave clear directives were actually *more* likely to support student interest and initiative than less structured teachers. Further, these authors found that structure supported students' behavioral engagement, whereas autonomy support was associated with cognitive engagement. Put simply, effective classroom managers tell students what they expect, make academic work personally relevant to students, and then get out of the way.

DRAWING PARALLELS ACROSS THE CONTEXTS OF HOME AND SCHOOL

Although families and teachers each make significant contributions to student school success, few studies have directly examined how home–school interactions contribute to student outcomes. In this section, we review research set within the overlap between the spheres of home and school (i.e., the mesosystem level of the ecology). We organize this section along two questions. First, does the quality of dyadic relationships among parents, teachers, and students influence other dyadic interactions: Does the parent–child relationship quality predict teacher–child relationship quality? Does the quality of parent–teacher interactions predict teacher–student interactions? Second, what is the nature of parent and teacher contributions to student learning and related student outcomes when both socializing agents are considered in predictive models? Are the contributions of each interactive, additive, or compensatory?

Does the Quality of the Parent–Student Relationship Influence Teacher–Student Interactions?

The answer to this question is yes, especially during entry to school and the early childhood years. Grounded in attachment theory, which views the mother–child bond as a foundational interpersonal relationship whose quality serves as a template for all subsequent social interactions, young children's attachment or feelings of emotional security with their mothers extends to their relationships with other caregivers (Booth, Kelly, Spieker, & Zuckerman, 2003). For example, preschool children with secure attachments to parents had secure attachment to teachers (Ahnert, Pinquart, & Lamb, 2006); insecurely attached children had lower-quality relationships with teachers (O'Connor & McCartney, 2007). Observational work across the transition to kindergarten suggests that the negative effects of less secure maternal attachment can be moderated by teacher responsiveness (Buyse, Verschueren, & Doumen, 2011).

Attachment is important to students' school outcomes because it is fundamentally related to the quality of the TSR, which predicts student engagement. If parent–child attachment serves as a relational template for children's connections with teachers, then it is also possible that students' early TSRs serve as a model for connecting to future teachers. Indeed, despite the fact that students experience different teachers each year, once formed, the quality of teacher–student attachment appears stable across the preschool, kindergarten, and first-grade years (O'Connor & McCartney, 2006). Unfortunately, very few studies have examined links between parent–child relationship quality and student social and academic functioning beyond early childhood and into adolescence. In one of the few examples of research in this area, Barber and Olsen (2004) reported, consistent with findings for earlier developmental stages, that positive parent–student interactions supported adolescents' relational functioning in the classroom.

Do Parent–Teacher Interactions Influence the Teacher–Student Relationship?

In general, higher levels of family involvement are associated with more positive TSRs, whereas lower levels of family involvement are associated with teacher–student conflict. For example, Mantzicopoulos (2005) found that when kindergarten teachers reported less positive home–school relationships within the school, their students were more likely to report higher levels of conflict with their teacher. In longitudinal work following over 300 low-income students from kindergarten through fifth grade, mothers' reported that involvement in school was directly and positively related to students' reported relationships with teachers and indirectly related to students' positive feelings about school, as well as their perceptions of competency in literacy and math (Dearing, Kreider, Simpkins, & Weiss, 2006).

The connection between family involvement and TSR quality has been found to differ along lines of class and gender. Wyrick and Rudasill (2009), for example, examined the extent to which teachers' perceptions of TSR quality in third grade varied as a function of parents' self-reported school involvement and child characteristics. Controlling for child gender and family income, regression analyses revealed that higher levels of parents' school involvement predicted positive TSRs, while less parent school involvement predicted teacher–student conflict. However, parent involvement and family income worked together to explain teacher–student conflict; specifically, higher parent school involvement predicted less teacher–student conflict for low-income students.

These and related findings (e.g., Hughes & Kwok, 2007) demonstrating that higher levels and quality of teacher–parent interactions produce social and academic benefits for students suggest that if the tenor of dyadic interactions between parents and teachers can be improved, the teacher–student relationship will also improve. In fact, students' perceptions of their relationship to their teacher have been shown to fully mediate the link between parent involvement and teacher ratings of the child's classroom academic performance (Topor, Keane, Shelton, & Calkins, 2010). In sum, research suggests that positive parent–teacher interactions enhance student outcomes in part by shaping teachers' attention to and perceptions of students.

What Is the Nature of Parent and Teacher Contributions to Student Learning and Related Outcomes When Both are Considered in Predictive Models?

In general, research addressing this question has found that, during secondary school, some aspects of the TSR predict student academic and social variables over and above similar aspects of parent–child relationships. For example, middle school students' perceptions of teacher emotional support have been positively related to students' perceived self-competence and interest in academics, over and above the influence of perceived parental support (Marchant, Paulson, & Rothlisberg, 2001). Similarly, Wentzel (1998) found that perceived support from parents was related to students' motivational orientations, whereas perceived teacher support was uniquely related to student interest in class and social goals (i.e., compliance with classroom norms). It should be noted, however, that the student outcomes examined in this work often pertain exclusively to the classroom context. In such cases, it is logical that teacher variables would be more strongly related to student classroom-specific outcomes than to parent variables.

Although TSRs can perform a compensatory function in the preschool and elementary school years (e.g., Buyse, Verschueren, & Doumen, 2011), the effects of these relationships during adolescence appear to be unique and additive. Gregory and Weinstein (2004), for example, examined adolescents' perceptions of (1) connection with and (2) regulation received from both parents and teachers. Parent and teacher regulation uniquely predicted students' academic growth in math from eighth to twelfth grade, strongly suggesting additive effects of home and school. The combination of teacher connection and regulation (i.e., an authoritative teaching style) predicted greater academic growth in math for adolescents from low socioeconomic backgrounds. Similarly, in a study comparing the relative impact of students', parents', and teachers' positive expectations, each party's expectations uniquely contributed to tenth-graders' postsecondary status four years later (Gregory & Huang, 2013). Teacher and parent expectations for how far the student would go in his or her education were stronger predictors of student postsecondary status than were student characteristics (e.g., achievement, race, and gender). Related to the question of mechanisms, although parental expectations are one of the most robust predictors of student outcomes across socioeconomic groups (e.g., Jeynes, 2007), we know little about how this psychological construct is translated into parental behaviors and, in turn, students' inner resources for school success.

RECOMMENDATIONS FOR PRACTICE

Educational and developmental theory and research, as well as federal policy focused on improving the learning outcomes of *all* students across all communities, offer an increasingly rich base of questions and evidence pertinent to the successful education of children from early childhood through adolescence in the United States. The evidence incorporates an increasingly wide range of communities, from relative homogeneity to notable heterogeneity across variables often found to influence students' learning success, including family socioeconomic status, ethnicity, immigrant or refugee status, and cultural background. Schools' abilities to meet all students' learning needs as well as varied policy standards depends more than ever on schools staffed by highly competent teachers, administrators, and support personnel, who focus on developing and using the potential inherent in the major goals that families across community circumstances hold for their children: health and survival, the development of skills essential to economic well-being across childhood and adulthood, and the capacity and knowledge to engage positively in their culture and community.

As implicit in our chapter's title, we suggest strongly that families' and schools' abilities to effectively educate the students they share—consistent with societal goals for children's full, positive, and successful development across childhood and into adulthood—require the development of fully functional and effective family–school *relationships*. The relationship is critical because it is only when both home and school are fully engaged and committed to sharing perspectives, knowledge, and information that each party's goals for children's learning are achieved.

We focus on major recommendations for schools because schools and teachers hold the major share of knowledge and power essential to the effective education of students across childhood and adolescence. Because of this, the development of effective family–school relationships most often requires that the school—collectively, incorporating teachers, administrators, and staff—*invite* and support processes essential to creating productive family engagement in mutual support of students' motivation for and success in learning.

Our first recommendation is that schools must invite—consistently, effectively, and creatively—students' families into their students' educational processes at multiple levels. While normal beginning points (e.g., back-to-school night, parent–teacher conferences, student events) are important, even more important are meetings where teachers, administrators, and support staff affirm the school's valuing of parents and the power of parents and teachers *sharing* their knowledge about students. The goal of this information exchange is to support *families'* ability to offer effective learning support and to support *teachers' and schools'* ability to develop classroom management approaches and practices that engage, motivate, and support students' learning. In many circumstances, this requires that school personnel understand the conditions of family life in the community, as well as families' goals for their students. It is also often equally important that parents understand teachers' educational goals for their students and the specific practices their children's teachers enact in the classroom in support of effective student learning. (For more on how parents' perceptions of invitations from teachers and schools promote their engagement, see Green, Walker, Hoover-Dempsey, & Sandler, 2007; Hoover-Dempsey, Whitaker, & Ice, 2010; Walker, Ice, Hoover-Dempsey, & Sandler, 2011).

Our second recommendation is that schools support teachers' and parents' sharing of information regarding effective ways of supporting individual students' learning and engagement in learning. Conversations about this may incorporate suggestions from each party regarding elements and experiences of effective teaching and parenting, as well as suggestions for teacher and parent support of more effective student learning at home and at school. One-on-one (as well as group) conversations can be notably helpful in supporting teachers' *and* parents' understanding of specific practices that offer significant support for individual student (or many students') learning.

In an example of a formal effort to enact this recommendation, Auerbach and Collier (2012) reported on parents' involvement in a school-based program focused on improving young students' performance on statewide tests of reading skills. Parents and participating school personnel (teachers, administrators, support staff) reported that the most important learning experienced by each group was the information and knowledge shared by the other. Elements of this shared knowledge that were new for parents included an expanded understanding of their children's learning processes and understanding of teaching processes and practices used at school to support their students' learning. School personnel identified their new learning from interacting with parents as including (1) new awareness of how school program activities support parents' confidence about their own abilities to help their children learn, (2) new information about some of the specific ways parents worked with their children to support learning, (3) more substantive understanding of participating families' culture and stronger awareness of parents' hopes for their children's success, as well as their wish to be effective in supporting that learning, and (4) increased personal motivation to continue direct work with parents and families as valued participants in supporting student learning (for more specific recommendations for practice, see Clarke, Sheridan & Woods, 2010; Hoover-Dempsey, Walker, Sandler, Whetsel, Green, Wilkins, & Closson, 2005; Walker, Hoover-Dempsey, Whetsel, & Green, 2004).

Our third recommendation is that schools and parents work with others in their communities to develop system- and community-wide opportunities for parent and family learning pertinent to the ongoing development of family skills important to effective support of students' school learning from early childhood through adolescence (see, for example, Lawson & Alameda-Lawson, 2012; Warren, Hong, Rubin, & Uy, 2009; Warren & Mapp, 2011).

Two programs currently in action offer snapshots of success, or models that other schools, districts, and states might emulate to enact these recommendations. The first program, developed at Arizona State University, is the Realizing the American Dream (RAD) parent education program. Since 2006, more than 21,000 Arizona parents in over 190 public schools have completed the program at their child's school. The 10-week RAD program is grounded in Hoover-Dempsey and Sandler's (1995, 1997, 2005) theoretical model of the parent involvement process and emphasizes the role that parents play in their children's education, strategies for creating a positive learning environment at home, basic elements of schooling in the United States (e.g., standardized testing, parent–teacher conferences), and how to work with teachers to prepare for students' postsecondary education. The program is offered in both Spanish and English; Latino families, many of whom are immigrants to the United States, are the majority of program completers. Recent tests of the program's impact on over 2,000 participating parents showed significant self-reported change in knowledge of how schools work, as well as increased involvement behaviors related to children's school learning (Walker, 2013). Parents' post-RAD engagement behaviors were predicted primarily by their post-RAD knowledge, their postprogram beliefs about the role they and home-based learning activities play in their children's education, and finally, their pre-RAD beliefs and knowledge. Consistent with large-scale survey studies testing the program's guiding theoretical model (e.g., Green, Walker, Hoover-Dempsey, & Sandler, 2007), family demographics (including level of education and income) played only a small role in predicting participating parents' involvement behaviors.

The second program, Academic Parent–Teacher Teams (APTT), is notable for its reframing of a traditional home-school communication practice: the parent–teacher conference (Paredes, 2010). Teachers who elect to participate in APTT agree to hold 75-minute team meetings with parents from each class three times a year and briefer individual parent–teacher meetings once a year. During team meetings, teachers provide data on students' aggregate classroom performance. Each parent also receives a folder containing his or her child's academic data in relation to the rest of the class on standards for reading and math. The teacher then helps parents set 60-day goals for children based on their academic scores. After goals are set, the teacher models different ways parents can support their children's learning at home. Parents then practice these activities with other parents. Results for this approach include higher attendance rates at parent–teacher conferences, increased father involvement, and more teacher-reported efficiency and time use (Paredes, 2010). This program's success in engaging families and teachers in a dialogue about student learning is likely due to its grounding in evidence that families need and want instruction and modeling in order to support their children's academic learning in the home (e.g., Dearing et al., 2006).

Finally, schools may consider and develop school-wide opportunities for more formal teacher education pertinent to developing their own capacity and skills for engaging families. Such efforts might involve in-house teacher-led efforts such as reading and discussion of teacher-friendly literature describing the challenges and rewards of family engagement practices (e.g., Walker & Hoover-Dempsey, 2008) and how those promises and pitfalls apply to teachers' current work life and school community. They might also involve more formal professional learning opportunities focused on developing teachers' beliefs about their abilities and their perceptions of families, reflecting on teachers' current family engagement practices and their impact, as well as on using teachers' current practices and family engagement systems as a platform for introducing and adopting evidence-based forms of home–school collaboration that fit the local school community's goals and capacities (e.g., Hoover-Dempsey, Walker, Jones, & Reed, 2002).

CONCLUSION

This chapter has drawn from the literatures on parent engagement and classroom management with an eye toward understanding and underscoring the potential that families—and productive family–school relationships—hold for increasing teachers' and parents' effectiveness in supporting student learning and school success. We have articulated parallel traditions of research across the two fields and have identified a set of specific parent and teacher practices or mechanisms of development that have been found to support student learning and related positive outcomes. Finally, we have drawn from a small but growing body of research demonstrating that both parties—parents and teachers—perform essential socialization activities that uniquely support varied aspects of students' school success, from early childhood through secondary school. Grounded in this summary of research, we have offered a set of recommendations for how to transform our knowledge into action across schools and communities. If our society is to achieve its aim of a good education for every child, then parents and teachers *both* must be informed about—and empowered to fulfill—the critical part each plays in the collaborative enterprise of students' successful schooling.

REFERENCES

Ahnert, L., Pinquart, M., & Lamb, M. E. (2006). Security of children's relationships with nonparental care providers: A meta-analysis. *Child Development, 77*(3), 664–679.

Assor, A., Kaplan, H., & Roth, G. (2002). Choice is good, but relevance is excellent: Autonomy-enhancing and suppressing teacher behaviours predicting students' engagement in schoolwork. *British Journal of Educational Psychology, 72*(2), 261–278.

Auerbach, S. & Collier, S. (2012). Bringing high stakes from the classroom to the Parent Center: Lessons from an Intervention program for immigrant families. *Teachers College Record, 114*(3), 1–40.

Baker, J. A. (2006). Contributions of teacher–child relationships to positive school adjustment during elementary school. *Journal of School Psychology, 44*(3), 211–229.

Barber, B. K., & Olsen, J. A. (2004). Assessing the transitions to middle and high school. *Journal of Adolescent Research, 19*(1), 3–30.

Baumrind, D. (1966). Effects of authoritative parental control on child behavior. *Child Development, 37*, 887–907.

Baumrind, D. (1971). Current patterns of parental authority. *Developmental Psychology, 4*(1, pt. 2), 1–103.

Baumrind, D. (1989). Rearing competent children. In W. Damon (Ed.), *Child development today and tomorrow* (pp. 349–378). San Francisco: Jossey-Bass.

Blair, C. (2010). Stress and the development of self-regulation in context. *Child Development Perspectives, 4*(3), 181–188.

Bohn, C. M., Roehrig, A. D., & Pressley, M. (2004). The first days of school in the classrooms of two more effective and four less effective primary-grades teachers. *The Elementary School Journal, 104*, 269–287.

Booth, C. L., Kelly, J. F., Spieker, S. J., & Zuckerman, T. G. (2003). Toddlers' attachment security to child-care providers: The Safe and Secure Scale. *Early Education and Development, 14*(1), 83–100.

Brody, G. H., & Flor, D. L. (1998). Maternal resources, parenting practices, and child competence in rural, single-parent African American families. *Child Development, 69*(3), 803–816.

Bronfenbrenner, U. (1986). Ecology of the family as a context for human development: Research perspectives. *Developmental Psychology, 22*(6), 723–742.

Bryk, A. S., & Schneider, B. L. (2002). *Trust in schools: A core resource for improvement.* New York: Russell Sage Foundation.

Buyse, E., Verschueren, K., & Doumen, S. (2011). Preschoolers' attachment to mother and risk for adjustment problems in kindergarten: Can teachers make a difference? *Social Development, 20*(1), 33–50.

Chao, R. K. (1994). Beyond parental control and authoritarian parenting style: Understanding Chinese parenting through the cultural notion of training. *Child Development, 65*(4), 1111–1119.

Chao, R. (2001). Integrating culture and attachment. *The American Psychologist, 56*(10), 822–823.

Christenson, S. L., & Reschly, A. L. (Eds.). (2010). *Handbook of school-family partnerships.* New York: Routledge/Taylor & Francis.

Clarke, B. L., Sheridan, S. M., & Woods, K. E. (2010). Elements of healthy family–school relationships. In S. L. Christenson & A. L. Reschly (Eds.), *Handbook of school–family partnerships* (pp. 61–79). New York: Routledge/Taylor & Francis Group.

Clotfelter, C. T., Ladd, H. F., & Vigdor, J. L. (2007). Teacher credentials and student achievement: Longitudinal analysis with student fixed effects. *Economics of Education Review, 26*(6), 673–682.

Collins, W. A., & Laursen, B. (2004). Changing relationships, changing youth interpersonal contexts of adolescent development. *The Journal of Early Adolescence, 24*(1), 55–62.

Cornelius-White, J. (2007). Learner-centered teacher-student relationships are effective: A meta-analysis. *Review of Educational Research, 77*(1), 113–143.

Crosnoe, R. (2009). Family-school connections and the transitions of low-income youth and English language learners from middle school into high school. *Developmental Psychology, 45*(4), 1061–1076.

Danielson, C. (2007). *Enhancing professional practice: A framework for teaching.* Alexandria, VA: Association for Supervision and Curriculum Development.

Darling, N., & Steinberg, L. (1993). Parenting style as context: An integrative model. *Psychological Bulletin, 113*, 487–487.

Darling-Hammond, L., Wei, R. C., Andree, A., Richardson, N., & Orphanos, S. (2009). *Professional learning in the learning profession.* Washington, DC: National Staff Development Council.

Dearing, E., Kreider, H., Simpkins, S., & Weiss, H. B. (2006). Family involvement in school and low-income children's literacy: Longitudinal associations between and within families. *Journal of Educational Psychology, 98*(4), 653–664.

Dornbusch, S. M., Ritter, P. L., Leiderman, P. H., Roberts, D. F., & Fraleigh, M. J. (1987). The relation of parenting style to adolescent school performance. *Child Development, 58*, 1244–1257.

Doyle, W. (1986). Classroom organization and management. In M. Wittrock (Ed.) *Handbook of Research on Teaching* (3rd ed., pp. 392–431). New York: MacMillan Publishing.

Emmer, E. T., Evertson, C. M., & Anderson, L. M. (1980). Effective classroom management at the beginning of the school year. *The Elementary School Journal, 80*(5), 219–231.

Emmer, E. T., & Stough, L. M. (2001). Classroom management: A critical part of educational psychology, with implications for teacher education. *Educational Psychologist, 36*(2), 103–112.

Epstein, J. L., & Sanders, M. G. (2006). Connecting home, school, and community. In *Handbook of the sociology of education* (pp. 285–306). Philadelphia: Springer US.

Evertson, C. M, & Weinstein, C. S. (2006). *Handbook of classroom management: Research, practice, and contemporary issues.* Mahwah, NJ: Erlbaum.

Fan, W., & Williams, C. M. (2010). The effects of parental involvement on students' academic self-efficacy, engagement and intrinsic motivation. *Educational Psychology, 30*(1), 53–74.

Green, C. L., Walker, J. M. T., Hoover-Dempsey, K. V., & Sandler, H. M. (2007). Parents' motivations for involvement in children's education: An empirical test of a theoretical model of parental involvement. *Journal of Educational Psychology, 99*, 532–544.

Gregory, A., & Huang, F. (2013). It takes a village: The effects of 10th grade college-going expectations of students, parents, and teachers four years later. *American Journal of Community Psychology* (April 6). Online publication.

Gregory, A., & Weinstein, R. S. (2004). Connection and regulation at home and in school predicting growth in achievement for adolescents. *Journal of Adolescent Research, 19*(4), 405–427.

Grolnick, W. S., Deci, E. L., & Ryan, R. M. (1997). Internalization within the family: The self-determination theory perspective. *Parenting and children's internalization of values: A handbook of contemporary theory* (pp. 135–161). New York: Wiley.

Grolnick W. S., Kurowski, C. O., & Gurland, S. T. (1999). Family processes and the development of children's self-regulation. *Educational Psychologist, 34*, 3–14.

Hafen, C. A., Allen, J. P., Mikami, A. Y., Gregory, A., Hamre, B., & Pianta, R. C. (2012). The pivotal role of adolescent autonomy in secondary school classrooms. *Journal of Youth and Adolescence, 41*(3), 245–255.

Hamre, B. K., & Pianta, R. C. (2001). Early teacher–child relationships and the trajectory of children's school outcomes through eighth grade. *Child Development, 72*(2), 625–638.

Hamre, B. K., & Pianta, R. C. (2005). Can instructional and emotional support in the first-grade classroom make a difference for children at risk of school failure? *Child Development, 76*(5), 949–967.

Henderson, A. T., Mapp K. L., Johnson, V. R., & Davies, D. (2007). *Beyond the bake sale: The essential guide to family–school partnerships.* New York: The New Press.

Hill, N. E. (2010). Culturally-based worldviews, family processes, and family-school interactions. In S. L. Christenson & A. L. Reschly (Eds.), *Handbook of school–family partnership* (pp. 101–127). New York: Routledge/Taylor & Francis Group.

Hill, N. E., & Chao, R. K. (Eds.). (2009). *Families, schools, and the adolescent: Connecting research, policy, and practice.* New York: Teachers College Press.

Hoover-Dempsey, K. V., & Sandler, H. M. (1995). Parental involvement in children's education: Why does it make a difference? *Teachers College Record, 95,* 310–342.

Hoover-Dempsey, K. V., & Sandler, H. M. (1997). Why do parents become involved in their children's education? *Review of Educational Research, 67*(1), 3–42.

Hoover-Dempsey, K. V., & Sandler, H. M. (2005). Final performance report for OERI grant # R305T010673: The social context of parental involvement: A path to enhanced achievement. Paper presented to Project Monitor, Institute of Education Sciences, U.S. Department of Education, March 22.

Hoover-Dempsey, K. V., Walker, J. M. T., Jones, K. P., & Reed, R. P. (2002). Teachers Involving Parents (TIP): An in-service teacher education program for enhancing parental involvement. *Teaching and Teacher Education, 18,* 843–867.

Hoover-Dempsey, K. V., Walker, J. M. T., Sandler, H. M., Whetsel, D., Green, C. L., Wilkins, A. S., & Closson, K. (2005). Why do parents become involved? Research findings and implications. *The Elementary School Journal, 106*(2), 105–130.

Hoover-Dempsey, K. V., Whitaker, M. C., & Ice, C. L. (2010). Motivation and commitment to family-school partnerships. In S. L. Christenson & A. R. Reschley (Eds.), *Handbook of family–school partnerships* (pp. 30–60). New York: Routledge.

Hughes, J., & Kwok, O. M. (2007). Influence of student–teacher and parent–teacher relationships on lower achieving readers' engagement and achievement in the primary grades. *Journal of educational psychology, 99*(1), 39–51.

Jang, H., Reeve, J., & Deci, E. L. (2010). Engaging students in learning activities: It is not autonomy support or structure but autonomy support and structure. *Journal of Educational Psychology, 102*(3), 588.

Jeynes, W. H. (2007). Urban secondary school student academic achievement. *Urban Education, 42*(1), 82–110.

Lavenda, O. (2011). Parental involvement in school: A test of Hoover-Dempsey and Sandler's model among Jewish and Arab parents in Israel. *Children and Youth Services Review, 33*(6), 927–935.

Lawson, M. A., & Alameda-Lawson, T. (2012). A case study of school-linked, collective parent engagement. *American Educational Research Journal, 49*(4), 651–684.

Le, H. N., Ceballo, R., Chao, R., Hill, N. E., Murry, V. M., & Pinderhughes, E. E. (2008). Excavating culture: Disentangling ethnic differences from contextual influences in parenting. *Applied Developmental Science, 12*(4), 163–175.

LeVine, R. A. (1988). Human parental care: Universal goals, cultural strategies, individual behavior. *New Directions for Child Development, 40,* 3–12.

Maccoby, E. E. (1992). The role of parents in the socialization of children: An historical overview. *Developmental Psychology, 28*(6) (November), 1006–1017.

Maccoby, E. & Martin, J. (1983). Socialization in the context of the family: Parent–child interaction. In E. M. Heatherington (Ed.), *Handbook of child psychology,* Vol. 4: *Socialization, personality and social development* (pp. 1–101). New York: Wiley.

Mantzicopoulos, P. (2005). Conflictual relationships between kindergarten children and their teachers: Associations with child and classroom context variables. *Journal of School Psychology, 43*(5), 425–442.

Marchant, G. J., Paulson, S. E., & Rothlisberg, B. A. (2001). Relations of middle school students' perceptions of family and school contexts with academic achievement. *Psychology in the Schools, 38*(6), 505–519.

Murry, V. M., Brody, G. H., McNair, L. D., Luo, Z., Gibbons, F. X., Gerrard, M., & Wills, T. A. (2005). Parental involvement promotes rural African American youths' self-pride and sexual self-concepts. *Journal of Marriage and the Family, 67,* 627–642.

O'Connor, E., & McCartney, K. (2006). Testing associations between young children's relationships with mothers and teachers. *Journal of Educational Psychology, 98*(1), 87–98.

O'Connor, E., & McCartney, K. (2007). Examining teacher–child relationships and achievement as part of an ecological model of development. *American Educational Research Journal, 44*(2), 340–369.

Okagaki, L., & Bingham, G. E. (2010). Diversity in families: Parental socialization and children's development and learning. In S. L. Christenson & A. R. Reschly (Eds.), *Handbook of family–school partnerships* (pp. 80–100). New York: Routledge.

Paredes, M. (2010). Academic parent–teacher teams: Reorganizing parent–teacher conferences around data. (FINE) Newsletter, 2(3) (June). Retrieved from www.hfrp.org/family-involvement/publications-resources/effective-home-school-communication.

Pianta, R.C., Belsky, J., Houts, R., Morrison, F., NICHD Early Child Care Research Network (2007). Opportunities to learn in America's elementary classrooms. *Science*, 315(5820): 1795–1796.

Pomerantz, E. M., Moorman, E. A., & Litwack, S. D. (2007). The how, whom, and why of parents' involvement in children's academic lives: More is not always better. *Review of Educational Research*, 77(3), 373–410.

Reeve, J. (2009). Why teachers adopt a controlling motivating style toward students and how they can become more autonomy supportive. *Educational Psychologist*, 44(3), 159–175.

Rodriguez, J. L. (2009). Considering the context of culture: Perspectives in the schooling of Latino adolescents from the classroom, home, and beyond. In N. H. Hill & R. K. Chao (Eds.), *Families, schools and the adolescent: Connecting research, policy and practice* (pp.37–52).New York: Teachers College Press.

Ryan, R. M., & Deci, E. L. (2000). Intrinsic and extrinsic motivations: Classic definitions and new directions. *Contemporary Educational Psychology*, 25(1), 54–67.

Steinberg, L., Elmen, J. D., & Mounts, N. S. (1989). Authoritative parenting, psychosocial maturity, and academic success among adolescents. *Child Development*, 60, 1424–1436.

Steinberg, L., Lamborn, S. D., Dornbusch, S. M., & Darling, N. (1992). Impact of parenting practices on adolescent achievement: Authoritative parenting, school involvement, and encouragement to succeed. *Child Development*, 63(5), 1266–1281.

Stough, L. (2006). The place of classroom management in the standards in teacher education. In C. M. Evertson & C. S. Weinstein (Eds.), *Handbook of classroom management. Research, practice, and contemporary issues* (pp. 909—924). Mahwah, NJ: Erlbaum.

Topor, D. R., Keane, S. P., Shelton, T. L., & Calkins, S. D. (2010). Parent involvement and student academic performance: A multiple mediational analysis. *Journal of Prevention & Intervention in the Community*, 38(3), 183–197.

Urdan, T., & Midgley, C. (2003). Changes in the perceived classroom goal structure and pattern of adaptive learning during early adolescence. *Contemporary Educational Psychology*, 28(4), 524–551.

Urdan, T., Midgley, C., & Anderman, E. M. (1998). The role of classroom goal structure in students' use of self-handicapping strategies. *American Educational Research Journal*, 35(1), 101–122.

Walker, J. M. T. (2008). Looking at teacher practices through the lens of parenting style: Three case studies at entry to middle school. *Journal of Experimental Education*, 76, 218–240.

Walker, J. M. T. (2009). Authoritative classroom management: How control and nurturance work together. *Theory into Practice*, 48(2), 122–129.

Walker, J. M. T. (2013). Realizing the American Dream: A parent education program designed to engage Latino families' involvement. Paper presented at the annual meeting of the American Educational Research Association, San Francisco.

Walker, J. M. T., & Hoover-Dempsey, K. V. (2006). Why research on parental involvement is important to classroom management. In C. M. Evertson & C. S. Weinstein (Eds.), *Handbook of classroom management: Research, practice, and contemporary issues* (pp. 665–684). Mahwah, NJ: Erlbaum.

Walker, J. M. T., & Hoover-Dempsey, K. V. (2008). Parent involvement: Barriers and resources pre-service teachers should know about. In C. Ames, D. Berliner, J. Brophy, L. Corno, T. Good, & M. McCaslin (Eds.), *21st Century education: A reference handbook*, Vol. 2 (pp. 382–391). Thousand Oaks, CA: Sage.

Walker, J. M. T., Hoover-Dempsey, K. V., Whetsel, D. R., & Green, C. L. (2004). Parental involvement in homework: A review of current research and its implications for teachers, after school program staff, and parent leaders. Cambridge, MA: *Harvard Family Research Project*. Retrieved from www.hfrp.org/publications-resources/browse-our-publications/parental-involvement-in-homework-a-review-of-current-research-and-its-implications-for-teachers-after-school-program-staff-and-parent-leaders.

Walker, J. M. T., Ice, C. L., Hoover-Dempsey, K. V., & Sandler, H. M. (2011). Latino parents' motivations for involvement in their children's schooling: An exploratory study. *The Elementary School Journal*, 111(3), 409–429.

Warren, M., Hong, S., Rubin, C., & Uy, P. (2009). Beyond the bake sale: A community-based relational approach to parent engagement in schools. *The Teachers College Record*, 111(9), 2209–2254.

Warren, M. R., & Mapp, K. L. (2011). *A match on dry grass: Community organizing as a catalyst for school reform*. New York: Oxford University Press.

Weiss, H. B., Lopez, M. E., & Rosenberg, H. (2010). Beyond random acts: Family, school, and community engagement as an integral part of education reform. Washington, DC: National Policy Forum for Family, School, & Community Engagement, Harvard Family Research Project.

Wentzel, K. R. (1998). Social relationships and motivation in middle school: The role of parents, teachers, and peers. *Journal of Educational Psychology*, 90, 202–209.

Wentzel, K. R. (2002). Are effective teachers like good parents? Teaching styles and student adjustment in early adolescence. *Child development*, *73*(1), 287–301.

White, B. L., & Carew, J. C. (1973). *Experience and environment: Major influences on the development of the young child*. Englewood Cliffs, NJ: Prentice Hall.

Whiting, B. B., & Whiting, J. W. M. (1975). *Children of six cultures: A psycho-cultural analysis*. Cambridge, MA: Harvard University Press.

Wilder, S. (2013). Effects of parental involvement on academic achievement: A meta-synthesis. *Educational Review* (ahead of print), 1–21.

Wyrick, A. J., & Rudasill, K. M. (2009). Parent involvement as a predictor of teacher–child relationship quality in third grade. *Early Education and Development*, *20*(5), 845–864.

25

CLASSROOM MANAGEMENT AND TECHNOLOGY

CHERYL MASON BOLICK
UNIVERSITY OF NORTH CAROLINA AT CHAPEL HILL

JONATHAN T. BARTELS
UNIVERSITY OF ALASKA ANCHORAGE

Computer technologies are a set of dynamic tools that continue to evolve and transform classroom teaching and learning. As new technologies emerge and develop over time, they are often at the forefront of educational innovation and play an increasingly significant role in society. The majority of students have access to an Internet-connected computer in their classrooms today, and almost all students have access to one in their schools. Access to computers, mobile devices, and the Internet is making a significant impact on teaching and learning. A recent Pew Research Center report (2013) states that 92% of surveyed teachers report the Internet has a "major impact" on access to curriculum resources, 69% report the Internet has a "major impact" on collaborating with colleagues, and 67% report the Internet has a "major impact" on parent communication. The impact of technology on our society and our schools is so radical that Darnton (2008) claims the transitional moment we are living in has come to be known as one of only four other times in our history in which learning, communication, and business have changed so dramatically. He argues that our current information age is as transformative as the invention of writing around 4000 BCE, the development of movable type in 10th-century China and 15th-century Europe, the invention of the printing press during the end of the 18th century. It is overwhelming to consider that the changes we are experiencing now with technology are as monumental as such historical moments as the invention of the printing press.

Although widely promoted and now generally accepted, the integration of technology into the classroom is by no means an effortless process. There is a clear disconnect between the optimism of those advocating technology in the classroom and the realities of teaching and learning in 21st-century classrooms (Cuban,

2001; Pew Research Center, 2013). Teaching and learning with computers presents a series of new challenges and demands related to education professionals. These challenges include, but are not limited to, teacher training, digital equity, funding, maintenance, and classroom management. In addition to these challenges, it is important that teachers keep in mind issues resulting from the digital divide that reveal inequalities in access to technology between schools and homes in rural, suburban, and urban areas often related to socioeconomic differences (Schrum & Levin, 2009). Some schools are addressing these issues by implementing one-to-one laptop initiatives, providing computer access to every student and/or making use of free, open-source software instead of high-priced commercial software (Solomon & Schrum, 2007). Recent studies have shown that the recent increase in mobile technologies has lessened the extent of the digital divide, though it is still present (Pew Research Center, 2013).

Although adding technology to a classroom equips teachers with a new range of classroom management tools, such as tablets and social media tools to manage school and classroom records and information, technology also presents a series of new classroom management issues, such as monitoring students working in a Bring Your Own Device classroom or managing a class of students when they are out in the field collecting data and uploading it to a shared network space.

As an example, the following scenario describes one teacher's attempt to integrate technology into the classroom while maintaining an effective classroom learning environment. The students in Mr. Williams' seventh-grade social studies class are studying the different branches of government. The students are clustered into small groups of five or six students scattered throughout the room, while a buzz of talking and typing pervades the room. One cluster of students is gathered around a single computer, engaged in a video conference call with their local congresswoman. Prior to sitting down at the computer, these students generated a list of questions to ask their representative and now are engaging in an interactive video conference call with her. When the congresswoman wants to highlight an example for the students, she is able to share video clips from her computer for the students to watch as she discusses them. As the students listen and talk with her, they are all furiously scripting notes on their handheld tablets.

Another group of students is gathered in the back corner, all sitting at individual computer stations. The students are wearing headphones and completing a web-based research assignment that Mr. Williams developed. The research assignment requires students to access specific websites to answer a carefully sequenced set of questions. Many of the sites include podcasts for the students to listen to and videos for the students to watch. The predetermined websites have been bookmarked to help the students follow the activity with relative ease. If the students have questions, they send an instant message to the other students working on the same assignment. They are often able to help each other before turning to the teacher for assistance. Mr. Williams monitors the instant messages from his tablet as he circulates the classroom.

The third group of students gathered around the interactive whiteboard in the front of the room. They are working together to create a multimedia presentation about the roles and responsibilities of the different branches of government. The students, who outlined the presentation as a group, each developed an individual section to share with the group. Now they are sharing their sections with one another on the whiteboard. Each component is a myriad of text, images, video, and audio. The assignment list that Mr. Williams prepared for them requires them next to review each others' entries and collectively develop a summary of each student's contributions.

The fourth group of students has pulled a group of desks together and is working on the classroom laptops to edit a series of digital video clips they recorded. The students interviewed members of the community about the branches of government and are now editing the videos to create a documentary video to share with the class. All of the students in the group have an assigned role, such as scriptwriter, editor, or interviewer, that helps to ensure equal participation.

Even though this scenario may be the dream of many high-tech teachers, it may be a nightmare for many teachers who are uncomfortable with managing the technology-infused classroom. Integrating technology tools into the classroom introduces variables that may make some teachers uncomfortable. There is an unpredictable nature of using technology in the classroom. Hardware issues such as the network being down or a computer freezing during a lesson often cause unpredictability in employing technology. In each of these cases, planned instruction is interrupted, possibly leading to classroom management issues. This chapter will address the managerial issues that teachers encounter as they attempt to use technology in teaching.

RESEARCH ON TECHNOLOGY AND CLASSROOM MANAGEMENT

The field of research on computer technology use in classrooms has exploded over the past decade. Despite the expansion of publications in this area, little research exists to document how the introduction of technology affects classroom management. There certainly is no scientifically based research using random assignments to treatment and control groups to investigate how technology impacts classroom management issues and practices. Instead, there are a number of small investigations, typically using qualitative methods such as surveys, interviews, and observation techniques to examine the interactions between technology use and classroom management.

A number of these reports and studies describe how technology can be used to manage school and classroom records and information (Brindley, Walti, & Blaschke, 2009; Kahn, 1998; McNally & Etchison, 2000; Niles, 2013). Tools that can facilitate this type of classroom management have moved from being solely software programs such as word processors and spreadsheets to include social networking tools and mobile devices. These technologies can be used to gather and analyze grades, track attendance, store and share curriculum resources, provide classroom seating charts, communicate with parents, and increase student interaction. Used in this way, classroom management refers to the use of technology to improve record keeping, to reduce paperwork, and to free up teachers' time to focus more on instructional activities and planning. The use of these tools will be addressed later in the chapter.

However, a less studied and written about aspect of classroom management and technology concerns how the introduction of technology into classrooms changes and/or affects the dynamics of the classroom. Only a few studies examine such issues as designing and maintaining the physical classroom environment, establishing and maintaining classroom rules and routines, interactions among students, interactions between teacher and students, academic engaged time, managing transitions among activities, and many other aspects of classroom management that are affected by the presence and use of instructional technologies (Brindley, Walti, & Blaschke, 2009; Dwyer, 1994; Gross, 2002; Sandholtz, Ringstaff, & Dwyer, 1990; Wetzel & Marshall, 2012; Xu, 2002). There are also reports of teacher concerns about classroom management when using technology, including fears that unruly students may damage expensive equipment and concerns about children using mobile devices as they move about the classroom or other learning environments (Irving, 2003; Pew Research Center, 2013).

Reports of effective technology use in classrooms often describe how students actively engage with the technology in inquiry-based, knowledge-construction strategies. Because many traditional classrooms are teacher centered and favor direct instruction methods, using technology effectively may require a paradigm shift to promote constructivist behavior—student problem solving, exploring the learning environment, conducting learning activities, and monitoring their own learning. This shift may threaten some teachers who fear a loss of control. Currently, when technology is used in classrooms, it is most often assigned as homework or to practice discrete skills and seen largely as a motivational device, as opposed to being used to increase cognitive, social, or psycholinguistic skills (Dredger, Woods, Beach, & Sagstetter, 2010). However, teachers are beginning to use more digital media in their classrooms. A majority of teachers (78%) strongly agree that digital media are best used when they are soundly integrated into instruction as opposed to serving as an add-on piece to a lesson (PBS, 2009). Using technology effectively for instructional use requires considerable planning on the part of the teacher, with the ever present potential malfunction of the technology looming in the background. Teachers need to perform the activity and test the equipment for possible problems before students become involved (Saurino, Bouma, & Gunnoe, 1999). Planning and managing the technology adds additional tasks to a teacher's already full plate. Teachers with poor or average classroom management skills may shy away from using instructional technology for fear of losing control of the classroom (Margerum-Leys & Marx, 2000; Pew Research Center, 2013). It is difficult for teachers to integrate technology into their instruction if they have poor classroom management skills because computers add another layer of complexity to classroom management and to monitoring student work.

SUMMARY

Research concerning classroom management and the use of technology is scant, but what does exist provides some insight into the intersection of these two topics. As the classroom context changes, so do the classroom management issues. When technology is first introduced into classrooms, management issues are likely to arise.

When classrooms have only one or two computers, students are likely to vie for access to this equipment, and teachers have to develop rules regarding their use. In technology-rich classrooms, teachers must deal with issues related to the physical arrangement of the classroom to accommodate computers, printers, and other paraphernalia. As teachers become comfortable with the technology and develop more skill in its use, technology seems to save teachers time rather than requiring additional time. Getting to this point, however, may take a couple of years.

Creative use of technology for instructional purposes also seems to lead to a different teaching style, one that is less teacher centered and more student centered. Many teachers are uncomfortable with this new role as guide or facilitator and resist integrating technology into instruction in a meaningful way. Teachers who struggle with classroom management issues are unlikely to embrace technology because it introduces more variables into an already complicated situation. Even teachers who are skilled in classroom management will have to deal with issues such as managing access to the equipment, monitoring student time on task, and being alert to new forms of possible cheating.

TEACHER USE OF TECHNOLOGY FOR NONINSTRUCTIONAL ACTIVITIES

It has been documented that 4 hours and 1 minute (or 45.4%) of a teacher's school day is dedicated to classroom instruction (Bruno, Ashby, & Mazo, 2012). This leaves that over half of a teacher's school day is spent on noninstructional activities. Noninstructional activities include communicating with parents, providing student feedback on assignments, and engaging in professional development activities. Noninstructional activities are essential for creating an effective classroom learning environment; however, they detract from the amount of time teachers are able to spend directly interacting with students. Teachers find that spreadsheets, social media, and file synchronization systems are effective technology tools that aid in streamlining noninstructional activities, facilitating communication and access to resources. A recent study published by the Pew Internet and American Life Project (Pew Research Center, 2013) found that 92% of teachers identify that the Internet is a significant resource they use to locate content, resources, and material.

Software such as spreadsheet and database programs may be used to manage school and classroom records and information. A spreadsheet is a piece of software that allows users to arrange text or numbers in rows and columns. It allows users to enter data, much like data would be entered onto a ledger form. The data entered can be analyzed using formulas, charts, and graphs. Teachers report that they find a spreadsheet to be a helpful classroom management tool by using it specifically to track student progress. For example, by entering student grades into a spreadsheet program, teachers can sort the grades to track one student's progress throughout a grading cycle or to compare all student grades on one particular assignment. Teachers can chose to track the scores either by listing the raw number or by creating different charts or graphs. Recording and organizing data in this manner not only enables teachers to streamline their paperwork but also is a helpful way to share student progress with parents and students. Spreadsheets also may be used to streamline teachers' noninstructional tasks, such as creating and maintaining a class budget, creating class lists, scheduling student projects, and keeping student attendance.

Word processing software is another technology tool used by teachers to stream-line their noninstructional activities. Word processing software enables users to edit, store, and print documents. It is an efficient way to make revisions and to save and file documents. Teachers' most frequent use of this software is to create lesson plans and instructional materials (Berson et al., 2002). Examples of instructional materials that teachers can create include worksheets, tests, lab reports, outlines, book report forms, and unit guides. In addition to creating instructional materials, word process-ing software can be used to prepare documents such as letters home to parents or class newsletters.

Multiuser file synchronization systems are another essential classroom manage-ment tool for teachers. Teachers may store data in a cloud, school network, a soft-ware program such as Dropbox. For example, teachers may upload lesson plans or student information to share with colleagues. Today, some schools solely use Google to share documents and calendars. This not only is an effective way to share pro-fessional information, but it is an efficient way to track student achievement and behavior. By storing student grades and behavior on a shared space, teachers can trace student grades or behavior issues over time and across classes. For example, a high school teacher having classroom behavior issues with a student can easily pull up the student's behavior chart to see if the behavior issues occur across all subject areas or just one class.

Communication and Web 2.0 tools also assist teachers with classroom manage-ment. Teachers report that communicating with parents via e-mail, Twitter, or a class blog provides them a flexible and efficient way to share classroom news with parents. The increased parental involvement and awareness with the school that results from frequent e-mail communication between teacher and parent has been shown to have a positive impact on student classroom behavior (Sumner, 2000). Approximately 67% of teachers identify the Internet as having a "major impact" on their ability to communicate with parents and 57% with students (Pew Research Center, 2013).

The Web 2.0 paradigm is hung on a business model referred to as the "architecture of participation," which simply states that it is the responsibility of the users, not the programmers, to create and maintain content (O'Reilly, 2004). Web 2.0 capitalizes on participatory culture by co-opting collaboration and creation (Jenkins, 2006). Even though it is characterized by technical markers such as rich site summary (RSS) and script that allows user-generated modifications, Web 2.0 is also centered on a differ-ent way of thinking—a collective intelligence (O'Reilly, 2004). The functions of Web 2.0 technologies have created a philosophy that is embodied in web-based applica-tions whereby multiple parties are able to collaborate on content to be consumed and modified by other users, without the need for coding knowledge or access to server space (Gordon-Murnane, 2006; Salz, 2005). Instead of providing content or a con-sumable product, the business provides the consumer an interface. This generation of web-based applications often involves prefabricated templates for users to upload and download content of various forms (Macnamara, 2010). Web 2.0 technologies are a naturally collaborative, simple means of sharing multimedia content in an interchangeable and personal way (Cormode & Krishnamurthy, 2008). This conceptual shift created a new type of media that can be defined in many ways, but most definitions include similar characteristics: multimodal, networked, digitally interactive, and dialogic (Logan, 2010). These tools have altered the ways we communicate and have diminished the time it takes to share information; however, the wealth of possibility found in these tools for education is not yet entirely clear (West, 2012).

In education, this new generation of web-based tools provides a wealth of potential for both instructional and noninstructional application by making tools more widely available by lowering the barriers to entry. For instance, creating a website or robust digital news feed no longer requires technical knowledge of Internet systems. The ease of use of Web 2.0 technologies makes a wide variety of tools available for teachers to use with the educational content they need to more efficiently manage their teaching. While some tools are general in their design, others are specifically designed for education. Some of the more popular tools designed for classroom teachers are Edmodo, a classroom-based social network; CourseSites, a learning management system; and ClassDojo, a tool for tracking student behavior. All of these tools, as well as the others like them, are supported by a great deal of anecdotal evidence.

Although individual Web 2.0 tools provide great resources, it is argued by many that the collaborative approach promoted in Web 2.0 technologies is more significant than any individual tool and is how we should conceptualize our future approaches to education (e.g. Houle & Cobb, 2011; Lankshear & Knobel, 2011; West, 2012). Among the most popular Web 2.0 tools in classrooms are blogs, wikis, collaborative websites, and social media.

Potential noninstructional uses of blogs. Blogs, short for web logs, are a type of journaling application that organizes posts in reverse chronological order. The uses of blogs range from personal online diaries to professional news reporting. A great benefit of blogs is the ease with which anyone can publish his or her thoughts or ideas on the web, as well as the fact that topical blogs can also function as a platform for people to share topic-related information (Collins & Halverson, 2009). When used for noninstructional activities, blogs are typically used as communication tools to share information with parents about classroom or school happenings (Schachter, 2011).

Blogs have many possible functions for use as a noninstructional tool. Teachers can use blogs to share information about classroom happenings or to highlight exemplary student work for parents to browse. Blogs can function as a place where students can find lesson objectives and assignments posted by their teacher. Finally, many teachers have their own blogs about education and their experiences in the classroom; this type of blog use can be a great reflection tool for examining professional practices.

Potential noninstructional uses of wikis. A wiki is a collection of web pages at which anyone with appropriate access can add, remove, or modify content. Collaborative websites, such as Google sites, function in the same way. These types of tools "allow individuals from varying backgrounds and viewpoints to work together to accumulate knowledge and offer opinions" on any topic (West, 2012, p. 37). Wikis are designed to allow for collaborative authoring in organized ways around topics (Parker & Chao, 2007). These tools can easily be used to create a teacher or classroom website to share general information with students and parents. Or, because these types of tools can be organized by topics, they can be used to archive lesson plans for an individual teacher or a group of teachers.

Potential noninstructional uses of social media. Social media, also referred to as social networking sites, emphasize the creation and exchange of all types of user-generated media within a digitally mediated community (Kaplan & Haenlein, 2010). Social media platforms often engage mobile technologies in addition to web-based interfaces. This portability is a contributing factor to the massive influence social media has had on the way our society communicates (Kietzmann & Hermkens, 2011). The practices enacted by the users of these technologies are often regarded as participatory culture. Jenkins (2006) defines participatory culture as one:

1. with relatively low barriers to artistic expression and civic engagement.
2. with strong support for creating and sharing one's creations.
3. with some type of informal mentorship whereby what is known by the most experienced is passed along to novices.
4. where members believe their contributions matter.
5. where members feel some degree of social connection with one another (p. 7).

Some predominant social media tools include Facebook, Twitter, and YouTube. In educational settings, social media is often greeted with a great deal of hesitation because of the lack of content control (Schachter, 2011). There are, however, social media platforms that are specifically designed for education—Edmodo, TeacherTube, engrade, etc. These types of Web 2.0 tools are only now beginning to find their way into educational practice.

The primary emphasis with social media tools is that they are intended for communication. Teachers can use tools such as Twitter or Facebook to post homework assignments or field questions from students and parents. Currently, many educational organizations use various forms of social media to disseminate information. Additionally, many teachers use social media platforms, such as Google+ and Twitter, to connect with other educators around the world.

TEACHER AND STUDENT USE OF TECHNOLOGY FOR INSTRUCTIONAL ACTIVITIES

Managing the learning environment when using technology also varies according to the configuration of the technologies. A teacher-centered lesson using a single computer with a display station calls for different classroom management than a student-centered classroom in which all students are equipped with mobile devices and pursuing individual assignments. Issues that emerge from integrating a variety of technologies and their impact on classroom management will be explored, along with the implications of how instructional technologies are organized for managing the learning environment.

Of a different nature, as more courses and programs are offered online, instructors must manage multiuser learning environments to provide for individual expression while also building a safe community. Among the issues arising from these virtual contexts are ways of establishing appropriate norms for student computer responses, monitoring appropriate language and potentially offensive language in online discussions, and responding to bullying or teasing of other online students.

One-Computer Classroom

The function of a computer in a one-computer classroom may simply be teacher use for noninstructional activities such as those discussed in the previous section. However, there are varied and powerful opportunities to use the one computer for effective instructional purposes. Student use of the one-computer classroom has been likened to students lining up to drink water from a hallway drinking fountain (Anderson, 2004). The bottleneck created by this line of eager students is ripe for classroom behavior problems. Although many classrooms today have more than one computer, teachers often lead instruction in a way that reverts to the one-computer-in-a-classroom model.

Classroom management strategies are essential for creating a successful learning environment in the one-computer classroom. Issues that must be considered are as basic as ensuring that the location of the one computer is appropriate for its intended use. Ashmus (2004) reminds teachers to check to be certain that the placement of the hardware ensures convenient access. Convenient access may be defined as a central location for classroom display for all students or as a center that is to the side of the classroom. Because students often will be working on the one computer on their own or in small groups, it is vital for teachers to be appropriately prepared. Being prepared requires teachers to precheck the computer for all required software and to ensure that students have detailed directions to lead them through the assignment.

Beyond being prepared, teachers should consider specific instructional strategies that have proven effective for teaching in the one-computer classroom (Ashmus, 2004). Among these strategies are creating "trained experts" from the students in the class, asking the volunteers or parents to assist, implementing cooperative learning methods, rotating student computer time, creating standardized methods for saving student work, and providing students with a template or checklist to guide them through the assignment.

Multicomputer Classroom

Teachers who have access to multiple computers in the classroom typically design classroom instruction so that students either cluster around the computers in groups to complete the same assignment or set up a station model in which students rotate to different computers, completing a different task at each station. Burns' (2002) research of technology-enhanced instruction revealed a variety of classroom management patterns being practiced in the multicomputer classroom. She named and defined the four more prominent models as:

1. *Learning stations model (13 students to 2 computers).* Teams of four to five students are rotated through three different "learning stations" to gather data and information for their project. In one particular application of this structure, one station used a digital camera to gather images, another station used a simple electronic spreadsheet to analyze data, and a third station used printed materials about the community. Each of the stations had roles for every team member, as well as instructions for completing the tasks at that station.
2. *Navigator model (4 students to 1 computer).* Using a road trip analogy, teams of four to five were assembled and given role cards. The "driver" controlled the mouse and keyboard, while the "navigator" helped the driver operate the computer. "Backseat driver 1" managed the group's progress, and "backseat driver 2" served as the timekeeper. The navigator attended a 10- to 20-minute training session in which the facilitator provided an overview of the basics of particular software. Once trained, the navigators returned to their teams and instructed team members in use of the software. The navigator could only give instructions but could not touch the mouse or keyboard. The rest of the team rotated "driving" the computer so that everyone had a chance to use the software.
3. *Facilitator model (6 students to 1 computer).* This model was useful for carrying out more complex projects that required different skill sets and levels of expertise. The designated facilitator had some experience with the software in use and showed the most novice users (students) how to use the software application to create a layout for a final product. Like the navigator in the third model, the facilitator worked with the layout group, and the content group worked without a computer to create content for the newsletter or report. All group members, with the exception of the facilitator, rotated through the layout and content groups to ensure that each member gained experience with the software and the content.
4. *Collaborative groups model (7 students to 1 computer).* In the collaborative groups model, each small group was responsible for creating some component of the whole group's final product. For example, one part of the group wrote a report, another created a map, and a third used the computer to gather census data and display it in graphs (Burns, 2002, p. 38–39).

Classroom Lab

In the classroom computer lab, the ratio of student to computer is one to one. Given the influx of money that has been dedicated to student use of computers, one would expect teachers to be using lab-based computers more often for instruction. Currently, approximately 91% of teachers have access to computers in their classrooms (PBS, 2012). However, only 67% of teachers report that they use the computer during class time (Technology Counts, 2003). Teachers report that the number is not higher because they find it difficult to schedule time to take their classes to the school computer lab, they are fearful of losing control of their students in the lab, and they cite the inordinate amount of preparation time required for taking students to the lab (Burns, 2002). Although these obstacles may be valid concerns for teacher avoidance of the computer lab, a number of guides and reports for teachers list suggested strategies for effective classroom management in the computer lab. These guides often provide helpful classroom management tips for the classroom teacher.

Starr (2004) surveyed a team of education technology specialists to arrive at suggested classroom lab management tips. Consistent across the specialists was to begin by setting the classroom up for success. They suggest that, before students' ever engage with the technology, teachers should establish clear expectations of etiquette for using the technology and clear guidelines for the tasks to be completed. Most schools have an acceptable-use policy that students and parents sign. The policy spells out the code of conduct of accessing materials on the Internet. Classroom teachers should go beyond just accessing online materials to include proper care of technology equipment. Suggestions for caring for equipment include how to carry a laptop, properly store equipment, power devices on and off, and save files. To remind students of the protocol, it is suggested that teachers type directions for frequently used computer operations—opening programs, inserting clip art, printing documents, and so on—onto laminated index cards. These reminders can be stored next to each computer station. Other procedural strategies include:

- Placing different colored sticker dots on the left and the right bottom corners of each monitor. Use these to indicate which side of the screen you are talking about.
- Appointing classroom technology managers. Consider an Attendance Manager, who takes attendance and serves as a substitute teacher helper when necessary; a Materials Manager, who passes out materials and runs errands; a Technical Manager, who helps resolve printer and computer issues; and an End-of-Class Manager, who makes sure work areas are neat—keyboards pushed in, mice straight, and programs closed—before students are dismissed.

It is recommended that teachers invest extra time to ensure that students understand the procedural expectations of using technology in the classroom. Taking the extra time will reduce the classroom management distractions that could arise from students misusing technology tools.

Web 2.0

A major facet of computers in the classroom is having access to the Internet. Web 2.0 technologies, such as blogs, wikis, and social media, provide many possibilities for instructional use.

Potential instructional uses of blogs. In classrooms, blogs are often used in place of journaling activities. Utecht (2007) argues that blogs should be seen more as conversations, through the commenting features, than just classroom journals. He goes on to point out that this can carry educational discussions outside the classroom and beyond an individual lesson. When used for instruction, blogs are often used to promote reflection and critical thinking, as well as to enhance writing skills and collaboration. In the classroom, this may take the form of students writing blogs about materials they are reading as a review or reflection activity, students writing blogs reflecting on classroom activities and/or topics, students using blogs to document their learning process as the academic year progresses, or students using blogs to house and reflect back on learned information about a topic.

Potential instructional uses of wikis. In the classroom setting, most instructional uses of wikis can be categorized in one of four ways: a knowledge repository—or portfolio—for a single user, a knowledge repository for a group, a space for collaborative note taking, or a collaborative writing space (Tonkin, 2005). In the classroom, wikis can allow groups of students to compile and organize information for various sources. Students can collaboratively take notes on classroom activities in a wiki; this could be in the form of a collaborative lab notebook, reading notes, or any other activity that may require students to take notes. Students can create writing or reading portfolios in which they can compile and share their writing or reading commentary with their peers. Instead of writing a traditional research paper, students can create a multimodal website that shares their research findings via a wiki.

Potential instructional uses of social media. Although the use of social media spaces in education are dominated by noninstructional applications, instructional use of these tools can provide a valuable, though underresearched addition to a classroom. For instructional use, social media platforms can extend classroom space by expanding discussions around digital resource collections. Social media spaces can also provide an environment for students to engage one another on personal levels in order to develop and promote classroom community.

Virtual Learning Environments

Virtual learning environments such as online learning, telecollaboration activities, and multiuser virtual learning environments present innovative learning opportunities for students, yet also present a new series of classroom management challenges for teachers. Online learning can take many forms in the classroom. The most prevalent model of online learning is based on the virtual high school model. That is, individual or small groups of students from a traditional school enroll in a course sponsored by an organization outside the student's school building. The course activities are primarily asynchronous, meaning that students and teachers do not engage in online discussion at the same time.

The typical student enrolled in a virtual class chooses to enroll to have access to course content unavailable in the local community. Beyond access to locally unavailable courses, students seek out online learning opportunities because of the flexibility of being able to take classes anytime, anywhere, and to have the opportunity to engage in learning experiences with learners from around the globe. It becomes the responsibility of the student and the student's school to identify an appropriate time and place for online learning. Some schools have designated specific labs or individual computers in computer labs for use by students enrolled in online courses. It is important for teachers and students in the school to mutually agree on when and where online students should work on their online course assignments. Agreeing on the time and location will minimize classroom management issues.

Telecollaborative activities are another category of virtual learning environments that allow students to learn in ways not possible before the advent of the Internet. Harris (1999) defines telecollaboration as "an educational endeavor that involves people in different locations using Internet tools and resources to work together." Students engaged in telecollaborative activities may use e-mail to correspond with an expert, such as an archaeologist on an international expedition or with other students across the globe about the effects of global warming on their local community. Web-based discussion boards provide students the opportunity to engage in asynchronous chats with an author of the novel that they just completed reading. Synchronous chats through programs such as instant messenger allow students to collect and share local weather data with classrooms in other locations. Students can participate in real-time communication that allows audio and video through videoconferencing. An example is the Model United Nations project, in which students throughout the globe video-conference with one another to discuss and debate global issues. Multi-user virtual environment experiential simulators (MUVEES) are another category of technology that empowers students to communicate with others in geographically disparate locations. MUVEES engage students in virtual spaces that have been created for learning, such as virtual museums or historical situations (Dede & Ketelhault, 2003).

Because Instant Messenger and MUVEES link students with others in geographically disparate locations, they are two powerful technologies that allow students to learn in a way that was not possible when students were limited to resources and learning experiences within their schools and local communities. Yes, these two technologies can cause classroom management problems. For instance, it is very easy for students to get off-task and engage in online conversations that do not relate to the assignment. This happens when students strike up conversations with students or experts that do not relate to the assigned task or topic. Students may also use the tools to engage in conversation with friends who are not a part of the assignment. For example, a ninth-grade student who is assigned to have an instant messenger conversation about a collection of poetry with a ninth-grade student in another state may choose to contact his friend who is home sick from school for the day rather than the student in the other state. Teachers should address classroom management issues such as these before students ever turn on the computers. There should be a clear set of classroom expectations and consequences related to online communication. Students should understand that off-task communication is not permitted, why it is not permitted, and what the consequences will be. Teachers should monitor students' online communication by ensuring that student computers are positioned so that a teacher can easily circulate around the room and view what is on each computer screen. Teachers may also require students to print out transcriptions of their online discussions. Printed transcripts allow teachers to ensure students stay on task and also help teachers stay in touch with what students are learning from the activity.

Telecollaborative activities provide students with powerful learning opportunities. Yet they present teachers with a new set of classroom management issues. These issues reveal the dark side of technology, such as cyber bullying, child pornography, child molestation, and kidnapping (Berson, Berson, & Ferron, 2002). It is essential that teachers discuss Internet safety issues with students before permitting them to engage in telecollaborative activities. Given the increase in cyber crimes against students, it is essential to prepare students for telecollaborative activities as much for classroom management issues as for their own safety. Most schools have acceptable-use policies (AUP) that oversee student use of the Internet. AUPs serve three primary functions: to educate students, parents, and teachers about the Internet, to define boundaries of online behavior, and to specify the consequences of online misconduct (CoVis, 2004).

CONCLUSION AND RECOMMENDATIONS

The literature reviewed in this chapter may be organized into two categories: descriptive and research based. The majority of the literature that has been published about classroom management and technology is descriptive and exploratory. A large number of publications and web sites are dedicated to this topic. We attribute this to the fact that classroom teachers are grappling with how to create effective learning environments with the emergence of new technologies in their classrooms. Relatively few published studies are related to the nexus of classroom management and technology. The lack of research studies is most likely attributed to the fact that research on computer technology use in schools is a relatively evolving niche and scholars in the field are just beginning to recognize the need for such studies. In order for the field of educational technology to advance, more empirical, as opposed to anecdotal, research on the use and impact of technology tools as pertaining to classroom management is needed. Additionally, it is imperative that researchers begin to move beyond focusing on individual technology tools in order to more holistically address issues surrounding the usage of genres of tools. For example, instead of focusing research on the use of Apple's iMovie in a classroom, focus on the use of digital movie editing software in a classroom; this shift will allow the field to move beyond the glorification of individual tools and will create more technology research that is not as quickly outdated by the rapid pace of changing technologies.

Based on this review, it is our recommendation that traditional textbooks on classroom management should begin to address the issue of technology and how its introduction affects classroom management dynamics. Additionally, teacher education programs should incorporate technology and classroom management issues into preservice education experiences. It is also our recommendation that as school systems develop technology-based professional development activities for in-service teachers, they should incorporate classroom management strategies for teachers into the staff development. By this we mean that when teachers are introduced to a new piece of hardware or software, they not only learn how to use it, but they also learn related classroom management strategies.

The research would also indicate that teachers need time to go through "stages" of using technology before they become comfortable with it and can actually start saving time through its use. Also, students have certain needs, according to Glasser (1990)—survival, love and belonging, power, freedom, and fun—and teachers should recognize and take advantage of these needs vis-à-vis computer use. Glasser maintains that inappropriate behaviors by students are often misguided efforts to achieve power. Teachers need to address this need for power by combining the needs of students with classroom assignments or activities. By understanding and incorporating basic human needs into the classroom structure, the more students will be convinced that their schoolwork satisfies their needs, the harder they will try, and the better work they will produce. Related to this is teacher understanding of student motivation. Research (Jang, 2008) indicates that when teachers present clear rationales for why tasks are to be completed, students have a heightened sense of motivation to engage with the tasks. Practically speaking, this means that when teachers articulate the value of completing an assignment, the students are more often focused and engaged, resulting in few classroom management issues. Organizing computer technology assignments to allow and encourage learning teams and to give students opportunities to fulfill needs for power or self-importance will help to establish an effective classroom management system and reduce undesirable attention-getting behaviors.

REFERENCES

Anderson, W. (2004). *That's not a drinking fountain or how to survive in a one computer classroom.* Retrieved from www.ncrtec.org/tl/digi/onecomp/.

Ashmus, D. (2004). *But I don't have a computer lab! Using one computer in the classroom.* Retrieved from www.serve.org/seir-tec/present/onecomptr.html.

Berson, I. R., Berson, M. J., & Ferron, J. M. (2002). *Emerging risks of violence in the digital age: Lessons for educators from an on-line study of adolescent girls in the US.* Retrieved from www.ncsu.edu/meridian/sum2002/cyberviolence/index.html.

Brindley, J., Walti, C., & Blaschke, L. M. (2009). Creating effective collaborative learning groups in an online environment. *International Review of Research in Open and Distance Learning, 19*(3). Retrieved from www.irodl.org.

Bruno, R., Ashby, S., & Mazo, F. (2012). *Beyond the classroom: An analysis of Chicago public teacher's actual workday.* Retrieved from www.illinoislabored.org/.

Burns, M. (2002). From black and white to color: Technology, professional development and changing practice. *THE Journal, 29*(11), 36–42.

Collins, A., & Halverson, R. (2009). *Rethinking education in the age of technology: The Digital revolution and schooling in America.* New York: Teachers College Press.

Cormode, G., & Krishnamurthy, B. (2008). Key differences between Web 1.0 and Web 2.0. *First Monday, 13*(6), Retrieved from http://firstmonday.org/htbin/cgiwrap/bin/ojs/index.php/fm/article/view/2125/1972.

CoVis (2004). *What you need to know about Acceptable Use Policies.* Retrieved from www.covis.nwu.edu/info/network-use-policy.html.

Cuban, L. (2001). *Oversold and underused: Computers in the classroom.* Cambridge, MA: Harvard University Press.

Darnton, R. (2008). *The library in the digital age. New York review of books.* Retrieved from www.nybooks.com/articles/archives/2008/jun/12/the-library-in-the-new-age.

Dede, C., & Ketelhut, D. (2003). *Designing for motivation and usability in a museum-based multi-user virtual environment.* Retrieved from http://muve.gse.harvard.edu/muvees2003/documents/DedeKetelMUVE aera03final.pdf.

Dredger, K., Woods, D., Beach, C., & Sagstetter, V. (2010). Engage me: Using new literacies to create third space classrooms that engage student writers. *Journal of Media Literacy Education, 2*(2), 85–101.

Dwyer, D. (1994). Apple classrooms of tomorrow: What we've learned. *Educational Leadership, 51*(7), 4–10.

Glasser, W. (1990). *The quality school.* New York: Harper and Row.

Gordon-Murnane, L. (2006). Social bookmarking, folksonomies, and web 2.0 tools. *Searcher, 14*(6), 26–38.

Gross, D. (2002). *An analysis of perceptions of factors that influence microcomputer use in three urban public schools.* Unpublished doctoral dissertation, Detroit, Michigan, Wayne State University.

Harris, J. (1999). First steps in telecollaboration. *Learning and Leading with Technology, 27*(3), 54–57.

Houle, D., & Cobb, J. (2011). *Shift ed: A call to action for transforming K–12 education.* Thousand Oaks, CA: Corwin.

Irving, K. E. (2003). *Preservice science teachers' use of educational technology during student teaching.* Unpublished doctoral dissertation, Charlottesville, University of Virginia.

Jang, H. (2008). Supporting students' motivation, engagement, and learning during an uninteresting activity. *Journal of Educational Psychology, 100*(4), 798.

Jenkins, H. (2006). *Confronting the Challenges of Participatory Culture: Media Education for the 21st Century* [white paper]. Chicago: The MacArthur Foundation.

Jenkins, H. (2010). Afterword: Communities of readers, clusters of practices. In M. Knobel & C. Lankshear (Eds.), *DIY media: creating, sharing and learning with new technologies* (pp. 231–253). New York: Peter Lang.

Kahn, J. (1998). *Ideas and strategies for the one-computer classroom.* Eugene, OR: International Society for Technology in Education.

Kaplan, A. M., & Haenlein, M. (2010). Users of the world, unite! The challenges and opportunities of Social Media. *Business Horizons, 53*(1), 59–68.

Kietzmann, J. H., & Hermkens, K. (2011). Social media? Get serious! Understanding the functional building blocks of social media. *Business Horizons, 54*(3), 241–251.

Lankshear, C., & Knobel, M. (2011). *New literacies: Everyday practices and social learning* (3rd ed.). Maidenhead, UK: Open University Press.

Logan, R. K. (2010). *Understanding new media: Extending Marshall McLuhan.* New York: Peter Lang.

Macnamara, J. (2010). *The 21st century media (r)evolution: Emergent communication practices.* New York: Peter Lang.

Margerum-Leys, J., & Marx, R.W. (2000). *Teacher knowledge of educational technology: A study of student teacher/mentor teacher pairs.* Paper presented at the annual meeting of the American Educational Research Association, New Orleans, April. Retrieved from ERIC Database. (ED442763).

McNally, L., & Etchison, C. (2000). Strategies of successful technology integration, Part 1. *Learning and Leading with Technology, 28*(2), 6–12.

Niles, T. (2013). *DROPBOX brings course management back to teachers. Teaching English with Technology, 13*(1), 20–28.

O'Reilly, T. (2004). *The Architecture of participation.* Retrieved from www.oreillynet.com/pub/a/oreilly/tim/articles/architecture_of_participation.html.

Parker, K. R., & Chao, J. T. (2007). Wiki as a teaching tool. *Interdisciplinary Journal of Knowledge and Learning Objects, 3*(1), 57–72.

PBS (2009). *Digitally inclined: Teachers increasingly value media and technology.* Arlington, VA: Author.

PBS (2012). National PBS survey finds teachers want more access to classroom tech: Cost is biggest barrier, pointing to need for free digital classroom resources. Retrieved from: http://www.pbs.org/about/news/archive/2012/teacher-survey-fetc/.

Pew Research Center (2013). *How teachers are using technology at home and in their classrooms.* Retrieved from: http://pewinternet.org/Reports/2013/Teachers-and-technology.

Salz, P. (2005). People powered: Content and collaboration combine forces. *EContent, 28*(11), 24–29.

Sandholtz, J. H., Ringstaff, C., & Dwyer, D.C. (1990). *Teaching in high-tech environments: Classroom management revisited.* Paper presented at the annual meeting of the American Educational Research Association, Boston, April. Retrieved from ERIC Database. (ED327172).

Saurino, D. R., Bouma, A., & Gunnoe, B. (1999). *Science classroom management techniques using graphing calculator technology: A collaborative team action research approach.* Paper presented at the annual meeting of the National Association of Research in Science Teaching, Boston, March. Retrieved from ERIC Database. (ED429828).

Schachter, R. (2011). The social media dilemma. *District Administration* (July), 27–33.

Schrum, L., & Levin, B. B. (2009). *Leading 21st century schools: Harnessing technology for engagement and achievement.* Thousand Oaks, CA: Corwin.

Solomon, G., & Schrum, L. (2007). *Web 2.0: New tools, new schools.* Washington, DC: International Society for Technology in Education.

Starr, L. (2004). *Managing technology: Tips from the experts.* Retrieved from www.education-world.com/a_tech/tech/tech116.shtml.

Sumner, S. (2000). *Parent communication? Try a classroom web page.* Retrieved from www.4teachers.org/testimony/sumner/index.shtml.

Technology Counts. (2003). E-defining education. *Education Week, XXI(35).* Retrieved from www.edweek.org/media/ew/tc/archives/TC02full.pdf.

Tonkin, E. (2005). Making the case for a wiki. *Ariadne, 42.* Retrieved from www.ariadne.ac.uk/issue42/tonkin/.

Utecht, J. (2007). Blogs aren't the enemy: How blogs enhance learning. *Technology & Learning, 27*(9), 32.

West, D. M. (2012). *Digital schools: How technology can transform education.* Washington, DC: Brookings Institute Press.

Wetzel, K., & Marshall, S. (2012). TPACK goes to sixth grade: Lessons from a middle school teacher in a high-technology-access classroom. *Journal of Digital Learning in Teacher Education, 28*(2), 73–81.

Xu, C. (2002). *Teaching mathematics; Implementation of a learning information system in a middle school special education program.* Unpublished doctoral dissertation, Lincoln, University of Nebraska.

26

REWARDS[1]

JOHNMARSHALL REEVE
KOREA UNIVERSITY (SEOUL)

A reward is any environmental offering one person gives to another in exchange for some service or achievement. A service is typically a requested action (e.g., read the chapter), whereas an achievement is typically performing to a standard (e.g., make the highest score). In the classroom, such teacher offerings set in motion several important downstream effects, including subsequent changes in students' motivation, behavior, and development.

Teachers offer rewards because they believe that these environmental offerings can do for students what very few other classroom events can—namely, rather suddenly transform a classroom event from "something not worth doing" into "something worth doing." For instance, a student may view "sitting still" as something not worth doing until the teacher offers "extra recess time" for doing so. Such an attractive offer can almost magically transform the requested behavior into something worth doing.

REWARDS, MOTIVATION, AND BEHAVIOR

Rewards work—they change motivation and they change behavior (Cangelosi, 2008; Emmer & Evertson, 2012; Evertson & Emmer, 2012). But just as readers do not need an ornithologist to tell them that birds fly, readers similarly do not need an educational psychologist to tell them that rewards work. It is obvious. A student offered an attractive enough reward will willingly engage in almost any teacher-requested behavior. There is, however, a great deal to be learned in asking questions such as the following:

- Why do rewards work?
- When (i.e., under what conditions) do rewards work?
- Do rewards produce any troubling side effects?
- Is offering rewards the best way for teachers to motivate students?

The Brain's Reward Center

To understand why rewards work, it is helpful—even necessary—to look to neuroscience. This is so because the energetic, enthusiastic reaction that educators see from students who have just been promised an attractive reward arises from subcortical brain events. The experience of reward begins as the student perceives that the environmental offering has rewarding and beneficial properties (e.g., it tastes sweet, it brings social acceptance). This stimulus evaluation occurs largely in the amygdala (Baxter & Murray, 2002). What the amygdala detects, responds to, and learns about is the presence vs. absence of reward, the value or quality of the available reward, the predictability of the reward, and the costs associated with trying to obtain the potential reward (Berridge & Kringelbach, 2008; Whalen, 2007). If there is an attractive, rewarding, and personally beneficial stimulus in the environment, the amygdala will detect it, evaluate it, and respond to it.

Once the person encounters an environmental object that has rewarding properties (e.g., it is attractive, it is personally beneficial), the amygdala cues the ventral tegmental area to release dopamine, and that dopamine release activates the ventral striatum in general and the nucleus accumbens in particular (Berridge & Kringelbach, 2008; Jennings et al., 2013). As illustrated in Figure 26.1, the amygdala, nucleus

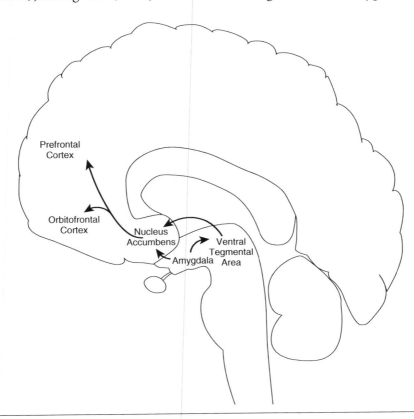

Figure 26.1 The dopamine-based reward center.

accumbens, and the ventral tegmental area are closely interconnected, and they collectively serve as the neural basis of the dopamine-based reward center. As shown in Figure 26.1, the amygdala–to–ventral tegmental area–to–nucleus accumbens reward circuit also projects fibers upstream into the cortical brain. In the prefrontal cortex, the person has a conscious experience of pleasure (e.g., "I like it."), and the orbitofrontal cortex stores the learned reward value of environmental objects so that the person will know (will remember) that a particular object has produced rewarding consequences in the past.

Students learn the reward value of environmental objects and events mostly through the extent of dopamine release those objects and events are able to produce (Hampton & O'Doherty, 2007; McClure, Laibson, Loewenstein, & Cohen, 2004; O'Doherty, 2004). Through the reward-related information that is dopamine release, students learn what to like, what to prefer, and what to value (Smith, Tindell, Aldridge, & Berridge, 2009).

The brain's reward center has an interesting anatomical relationship with other brain areas. These subcortical structures send projections to almost every part of the brain, whereas a smaller number of projections return information back to the ventral striatum (Cardinal, Parkinson, Hall, & Everitt, 2002). This anatomical and communication-pathway imbalance helps explain why emotion and reward tend to overpower cognition and self-control more than cognition self-regulates emotion and reward. In addition, the prefrontal cortex (cortical brain) of children and adolescents matures more slowly than does the early maturing subcortical brain (Gladwin, Figner, Crone, & Wiers, 2011). This lesser capacity for executive self-control may explain some of the reason why reward-based motivational and behavioral programs are often found in classrooms of children and students with special needs.

Why Rewards Work

Why do students get so excited about the prospect of receiving an attractive extrinsic reward? Why do these rewards enliven positive emotion and approach behavior? What all behavior-energizing rewards do is signal the opportunity for personal gain, and this environmental signal that personal gain is imminent is what triggers dopamine release[2] (D'Ardenne, McClure, Nystrom, & Cohen, 2008). Routine and expected classroom events leave the subcortical brain unexcited, and dopamine release does not occur. However, dopamine release and behavioral approach occur when events take an unexpected turn for the better, as one encounters a pleasant image (looking at a beautiful face), a pleasant taste (sipping sweet juice), or a learned cue (teacher dims the lights before showing an interesting video)—trigger dopamine release (Sabatinelli, Bradley, Lang, Costa, & Versace, 2007; Wise, 2002). As rewards become predictable (the teacher gives the same praise or bonus points day after day), they lose their capacity to trigger dopamine release and hence their capacity to energize reward-directed behavior (D'Ardenne, McClure, Nystrom, & Cohen, 2008).

Some level of dopamine is always present in the brain. When classroom events offer rewards in ways that are better than expected (more frequent, higher quality), the ventral tegmental area releases greater dopamine, and the increased dopamine serves as information that the event is producing more reward than it was anticipated to deliver. Dopamine release is therefore greatest when rewarding events occur in ways that are unpredicted ("Wow, I didn't know that would be so good!") or underpredicted ("Wow, that was better than I thought it would be!") (Mirenowicz & Schultz, 1994). In contrast, when classroom events offer rewards in ways that are worse than expected (less frequent, lower quality), a lesser dopamine release serves as information that a particular course of action is producing less reward than it was anticipated to deliver (Montague, Dayan, & Sejnowski, 1996). In addition, it is not the receipt of reward that triggers dopamine release but rather the *anticipation* of reward. That is, dopamine release occurs when the student first learns that he or she is about to receive praise, a special privilege, or a good grade (reward anticipation), not when the student actually receives the praise, privilege, or good grade (reward receipt). Thus, extent of dopamine release is the essence of reward-related information, and it occurs (1) when the environment signals that personal gain is imminent, (2) when the reward is better than expected, and (3) during reward anticipation rather than during reward receipt.

Rewards Work—But Only in a Qualified Way

Rewards work: They increase motivation, and they increase behavior. But rewards increase a particular kind of motivation and a particular kind of behavior. Rewards increase extrinsic motivation, and rewards increase extrinsically motivated behavior. Extrinsic motivation is an environmentally created (i.e., reward-created) reason to initiate a specific behavior. It arises from a do-this-in-order-to-get-that behavioral contract between teacher and student, where "this" is the teacher-requested behavior, and "that" is the teacher-offered reward. From the student's point of view, extrinsic motivation exists as a what's-in-it-for-me? type of motivation.

For the person who is externally regulated (i.e., reward regulated), the presence vs. absence of a reward and the high versus low quality of the reward regulate the rise and fall of (extrinsic) motivation. A student who is externally regulated does not have a difficult time beginning a task if there is an attractive high-quality reward at stake, but that same student will have a difficult time beginning the task if there is no attractive reward or only a low-quality reward at stake. The problem with externally regulated behavior is that, compared to other types of motivation and other ways of regulating behavior, it produces relatively poor classroom functioning and outcomes (Kohn, 1993; Ryan & Connell, 1989; Ryan & Deci, 2000).

Relying on a classroom management strategy that yields a relatively poor-quality motivation and classroom functioning seems like a low-grade compromise for teachers to make. Rewards do gain teachers classroom compliance from students, but there are better and more effective classroom management strategies to employ. These alternatives will be discussed later in the chapter, but first it is just as important to point out the problems with rewards as it is to point out their benefits.

Problems with Rewards

Research on a qualitatively different type of motivation—intrinsic motivation—began with this question: "If a person is involved in an intrinsically interesting activity and begins to receive an extrinsic reward for doing it, what happens to his or her intrinsic motivation for that activity?" (Deci & Ryan, 1985, p. 43). For example, what happens to the motivation of the student who reads for the fun of it but then begins to receive a $2 prize for each book read during a school-sponsored program (e.g., Book it!)? One might suppose that rewarding reading behavior with a monetary prize would add to the student's motivation—that the intrinsic (enjoyment) and extrinsic (money) motivations might sum to produce supermotivation. And if you ask preservice teachers to make predictions about what happens to a student's motivation under these conditions, increased supermotivation is most predicted (Hom, 1994).

Supermotivation does not occur. Rather, the imposition of an extrinsic reward to engage in an intrinsically interesting activity typically undermines (has a negative effect on) future intrinsic motivation (Deci, 1971; Deci, Koestner, & Ryan, 1999; Lepper, Greene, & Nisbett, 1973; Wiechman & Gurland, 2009).

To understand the undermining effect, consider a neuroscience-based test of the undermining effect (Murayama, Matsumoto, Izuma, & Matsumoto, 2010). Participants played an interesting game for two consecutive sessions. During session 1, half of the participants were promised a monetary reward for playing the game, while the other half of the participants simply played the game. Then, during session 2, all participants played the game without rewards involved. Throughout both sessions, researchers recorded participants' neural activations in the brain's reward center (ventral striatum, ventral tegmental area). Participants who played the game without reward experienced activations in the brain's reward center during both sessions 1 and 2 because the game itself was intrinsically motivating. Participants who played the game for reward in session 1 but not in session 2 showed strong activations when playing for reward in session 1 (super-motivation), but those activations literally disappeared when playing for no reward in session 2 (undermining effect). What this study shows is that attractive rewards motivate when offered but actually demotivate when removed.

The reward's adverse effect on intrinsic motivation is termed a "hidden cost of reward" (Lepper & Greene, 1978) because society typically regards rewards as positive contributors to motivation (Boggiano, Barrett, Weiher, McClelland, & Lusk, 1987). Like everyone else, teachers use rewards expecting to gain the benefits of increased motivation and behavior, but, in pursuing these objectives, they often incur the unintentional side effect of undermining intrinsic motivation (Deci, Koestner, & Ryan, 1999; Greene & Lepper, 1974; Lepper & Greene, 1975, 1978; Lepper, Greene, & Nisbett, 1973; Ryan & Deci, 2000; Wiechman & Gurland, 2009). However, rewards do not always undermine intrinsic motivation (Cameron & Pierce, 2002; Deci, Koestner, & Ryan, 1999). Expected, tangible, and contingent rewards ("After you turn in your homework, then you will get a candy bar.") typically undermine intrinsic motivation, but unexpected, verbal, and non-contingent rewards generally do not (Anderson, Manoogian, & Reznick, 1976;

Deci, Koestner, & Ryan, 1999; Henderlong & Lepper, 2002; Lepper, Greene, & Nisbett, 1973; Pallak, Costomiris, Sroka, & Pittman, 1982; Ryan, Mims, & Koestner, 1983; Tang & Hall, 1995).

Expected, tangible, and contingent rewards produce two additional problematic side-effects. They generally interfere with both the *process* and the *quality* of learning. When offered in an expected, tangible, and contingent way, extrinsic rewards tend to shift the student's goal away from optimal challenge, attaining mastery, and focusing on what is to be learned in favor of easy success, attaining reward, and focusing on what is to be gained extrinsically (Harter, 1978; Pittman, Boggiano, & Ruble, 1983; Shapira, 1976). These types of rewards also tend to orient learners toward convergent thinking, trying to get the right answer quickly, and a search for factual knowledge, but away from creativity, divergent thinking, the search for an optimal solution, and the desire to conceptually understand the lesson (Amabile, 1985; Benware & Deci, 1984; Grolnick & Ryan, 1987; Harter, 1978; Vansteenkiste, Simons, Lens, Sheldon, & Deci, 2004; Vansteenkiste, Simons, Lens, Soenens, & Matos, 2005).

Expected, tangible, and contingent rewards further interfere with students' developmental capacity for autonomous self-regulation (Cannella, 1986; Kohn, 1993; Lepper, 1983; Ryan, 1993). After a history of always being rewarded for doing something, reward recipients understandably begin to have difficulty regulating their behavior when not offered the reward. The student wonders, "Why should I do it?" This reward dependency occurs because the presence vs. absence of rewards—rather than one's own autonomous self-regulation—comes to regulate the initiation and persistence of one's behavior. When these types of rewards are not at stake, students generally engage in academic activities in ways that reflect the rise and fall of their inner motivations, such as curiosity, intrinsic motivation, and personal goals (Joussemet, Koestner, Lekes, & Houlfort, 2004). In contrast, the offering of an attractive extrinsic contingency essentially asks students to neglect and desensitize themselves to their own inner motivations and autonomous self-regulation and instead have their behavior come under environmental (reward) regulation.

COGNITIVE EVALUATION THEORY

When teachers offer students extrinsic rewards, they generally do so because they want to motivate students to engage in a particular, desired behavior. Much of the spirit behind the use of an extrinsic reward is therefore to influence, determine, or outright control a student's behavior. But there is a second purpose behind the offering of rewards. Rewards also provide feedback that informs students about their competence at the task. Rewards not only function to increase behavior (i.e., control behavior) but also to communicate a message of a job well done (i.e., inform competence). This insight on the dual function of rewards raises the practical question of *why* a teacher offers students a reward: Is it to control their behavior, or is it to inform their competence?

Rewards serve two purposes: to elicit a desired behavior (control behavior) and to affirm a job well done (inform competence). According to cognitive evaluation theory, this first purpose is referred to as the "controlling aspect" of a reward, whereas the second purpose is referred to as its "informational aspect" (Deci & Ryan, 1985). The theory goes farther, however, to state that *all* extrinsic rewards have *both* a controlling aspect and an informational aspect. That is, all rewards both control behavior and inform competence, so the important distinction is whether the teacher's purpose in administering the reward is mostly to control behavior or mostly to inform competence.

Figure 26.2 illustrates cognitive evaluation theory (based on Deci & Ryan, 1980, 1985; Ryan & Deci, 2002). As shown on the left-hand side of the figure, any reward serves the twin purposes of controlling behavior and informing competence. As shown in the upper half of the figure, the more the reward is used to control behavior, the more it will increase extrinsic regulation, frustrate student autonomy, and undermine intrinsic motivation. In general, rewards offered in an expected, tangible, and contingent way ("If you do X, you'll get Y.") are used to control students' behavior and produce these undermining effects. If the reward is not used in a controlling

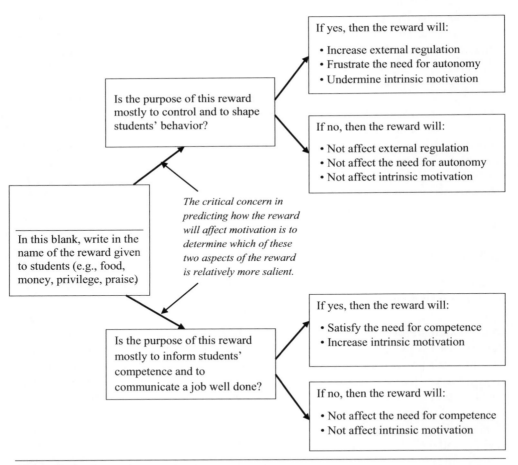

Figure 26.2 Graphical representation of cognitive evaluation theory.

Table 26.1 Three different ways teachers may offer rewards to students.

Type of Offering	Definition and Example
Expected (vs. Unexpected)	Reward given on a prearranged and contingent basis, such as, "If you turn in your homework, then you can expect two bonus points." An unexpected reward is given without a preannounced, prearranged contingency or contract.
Tangible (vs. Verbal)	Reward that the student can touch, smell, see, or taste, such as food or a prize. A verbal reward is one of symbolic value, such as praise or positive feedback.
Contingent (vs. Noncontingent)	Reward given in exchange for carrying out a requested behavior or task. For instance, teacher gives students a reward because he or she completed a worksheet assignment. A noncontingent reward is given irrespective of whether the student actually engages in the behavior or task. The reward is given with no strings (no contingency) attached.

way (if it is offered in an unexpected, verbal, and noncontingent way, such as, "I noticed that you did X well. Congratulations!"), it tends to leave these same student outcomes unaffected. As shown in the lower half of the figure, the more a reward is used to inform competence, the more it will satisfy competence and enhance intrinsic motivation. If the reward is not used in an informational way, however, it tends to leave students' competence and intrinsic motivation unaffected. Tests of cognitive evaluation theory have consistently supported the theory (Deci, Koestner, & Ryan, 1999; Rummel & Feinberg, 1988; Tang & Hall, 1995; Wiersma, 1992).

Offering Rewards

Because rewards can be presented to students in relatively controlling or in relatively informational ways, skill is needed when administering rewards. Table 26.1 summarizes the three different ways that teachers can offer a reward and provides a definition and example for each way.

Expected rewards are typically experienced as highly controlling because they are given on a contractual do-this-get-that basis (Lepper, Greene, & Nisbett, 1973; Pallak, Costomiris, Sroka, & Pittman, 1982). Unexpected rewards, however, are typically experienced as noncontrolling, which allows their competence-affirming informational aspect to become salient. An important practical point, however, is that if the same unexpected reward is repeated over time, then it too becomes an expected reward.

Tangible rewards are rewards that students can see, touch, feel, and taste, such as money, awards, and food. Tangible rewards are typically experienced as controlling because they tend to attract so much of the student's attention that his or her focus shifts from the task to the reward. Verbal rewards, such as praise, positive feedback, awards, and scholarships, however, have symbolic value and are therefore more likely to be experienced as informational events (Anderson, Manoogian, & Reznick, 1976; Dollinger & Thelen, 1978; Kast & Connor, 1988; Swann & Pittman, 1977).

Contingent rewards are those given only in exchange for some service or achievement (the reward depends, or is contingent, on a prespecified service or achievement). Contingent rewards are typically experienced as highly controlling because they are given simply in exchange for doing what is asked. The more the student perceives that there is a "string attached" (a contingency attached) to the reward, the more he or she will experience it as a controlling event.

Implications

These discussions on (1) the problems with rewards, (2) cognitive evaluation theory, and (3) the skill needed in offering rewards yield two key implications. The first implication is that it is the experience of reward—and not the environmentally offered object itself—that increases motivation and behavior. The experience of reward is a neural event that takes place inside the student (i.e., dopamine release), and this brain activity occurs or fails to occur following the student's perceptions of the quality of the reward, the person/reward fit, the student's need for that reward, the student's perceived value of that reward, how unexpected the reward is, how competence affirming the reward is, and how noncontingent the reward is. Thus, teacher-offered rewards sometimes do but other times do not produce in students an experience of reward because it is dopamine release that energizes and directs behavior, not environmental objects themselves such as a sticker, praise, privilege, or money.

The second implication is that why and how the teacher offers the reward is more important than what reward is offered. Unexpected, competence-enriching, and noncontingent rewards increase students' motivation and behavior, and they do so without engendering the problematic hidden costs of rewards. According to cognitive evaluation theory, this means that rewards need to be offered in a noncontrolling, informational way. This implication fundamentally challenges the historical purpose or function of classroom rewards. Rewards have traditionally been recommended ways for teachers to get students to engage in specific, desired, targeted, and teacher-prescribed ways (e.g., "If you clean your desk in the way I showed you and if you clean it before the end of class, then you will gain 5 bonus points."). But the more teachers use extrinsic rewards to control students' behavior, the more motivational, educational, and developmental damage these offerings produce (i.e., undermine intrinsic motivation, interfere with learning, and undermine autonomous self-regulation).

All this notwithstanding, reward-induced external regulation is not always bad or counterproductive (Covington & Mueller, 2001). Recognizing this, researchers and practitioners alike have tried to use rewards in ways that minimize their hidden costs. One way to do this, as discussed, is to use rewards that are unexpected and verbal (e.g., praise) and refrain from using those that are expected and tangible (e.g., bribes). This actually turns out to be harder to do than first meets the eye. The experienced teacher needs simply to reflect on how and why each of the following rewards is typically offered in the classroom setting: grades, gold stars, bonus points, check marks, awards, trophies, certificates, honor roll lists, prizes, scholarships, privileges, public recognition, food, parties, celebrations, money, and incentive plans of all kinds (i.e., expected, tangible, and contingent offers to get students to do what the teacher requests).

A second means to limit the hidden costs of rewards is to use them only on those tasks and behaviors that have low intrinsic interest but high social importance. A key practical question is whether rewards will have detrimental effects on *un*interesting tasks. In other words, if, with respect to a given task, a student has little or no intrinsic motivation to undermine, then intrinsic motivation is not likely to be put at risk by offering a reward. Indeed, research shows that the negative impact of rewards on intrinsic motivation is limited to interesting activities (Deci et al., 1999). Under conditions of low interest but high social importance, teachers offer rewards because their experience tells them that, without a reward at stake, students will not sit quietly, participate in class, and start their homework. Given this dilemma, some educators come to the practical conclusion that it is fine and well to use expected, tangible, and contingent extrinsic rewards when students' intrinsic motivation is low (Witzel & Mercer, 2003). This is a mistake, however, because even if they increase students' compliance, expected, tangible, and contingent rewards still undermine the quality of performance, interfere with the process and quality of learning, and undermine autonomous self-regulation. Their use under these conditions also distracts teachers' attention away from asking the hard question of why they are asking students to do uninteresting tasks, and it fails to acknowledge that there are better ways than bribery to encourage students' classroom engagement (Kohn, 1993).

FROM TARGETING BEHAVIOR TO SUPPORTING ENGAGEMENT

Within a behavioral framework, controlling classroom management strategies makes sense. A controlling approach represents an ideal way to manage students' behavior—that is, to produce students' on-task, teacher-prescribed behavior. Offering rewards (and offering positive reinforcers in particular) certainly has its place with such an approach to classroom management. It is helpful, however, to step back and ask whether there might be merit in expanding one's approach to classroom management beyond the relatively narrow goal of targeting behavior (via rewards) to the more general classroom aspiration of supporting students' classroom engagement. To speak to this larger goal, the chapter introduces the two classroom management strategies of providing structure and providing autonomy support.

Teacher-Provided Structure

Classroom behavior does not need to be controlled, targeted, or prescribed. It may alternatively be guided, mentored, and supported. With teacher control, the teacher tries to transition the students from "not doing X" to "doing X" (from "not cooperating with peers" to "cooperating with peers"). With guidance, mentoring, and support, the teacher tries to help the student advance his or her way of behaving from a relatively immature, poor functioning, and maladaptive pattern of activity toward one that is more mature, better functioning, and adaptive. To help students advance toward such a constructive way of behaving, teachers can provide rewards, but they can further offer clear expectations of what student are to do, endorse high standards for behavior and achievement, provide step-by-step how-to directions, set goals, make plans, offer suggestions, provide help and assistance, make available role models to emulate, and administer feedback (Brophy, 1986; Skinner, 1995). That is, teachers might advance from offering rewards to providing structure.

Structure refers to the amount and clarity of information that teachers provide to students regarding what to do, how to do it, and the best ways to develop the desired skills and achieve valued outcomes (Farkas & Grolnick, 2010; Grolnick & Pomerantz, 2009; Skinner, Zimmer-Gembeck, & Connell, 1998). At the opposite end of structure are chaos and confusion. Confused students do not know what to do (e.g., "What should I do?"). Generally speaking, the more teachers provide students with a highly structured classroom environment, the more they prepare students for effective class-room behavior and grow a sense of competence that helps them develop the skills and attain the outcomes they seek (Skinner, Zimmer-Gembeck, & Connell, 1998). In practice, teacher-provided structure is typically a three-step process of (1) communicating clear expectations and high standards, (2) helping students to adjust their behavior in ways that will allow them to meet those expectations and standards, and (3) providing a future pathway to more effective functioning. Rewards can and do play an important role in the delivery of a highly structured classroom, but the use of rewards is only a subset of the larger classroom management concept of structure.

Figure 26.3 provides a three-part framework to illustrate not only a highly structured classroom environment but also the role of rewards within that structured

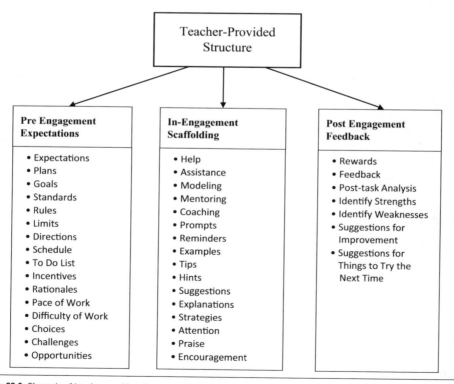

Figure 26.3 Elements of teacher-provided classroom structure.

environment. Before asking students to engage themselves in a learning activity (solve a math problem) or in a stream of behavior (show social skill during group interaction), the teacher prepares students by communicating his or her expectations, standards, and a script for what students will be asked to do. What all these aspects of structure shown on the left-hand side of Figure 26.3 have in common is that they help students formulate intentions to act. If rewards are used at this point in the lesson, they are usually offered as incentives in exchange for students' service. As students engage themselves in the learning activity or in the stream of behavior, the teacher helps students develop competence and skill by providing modeling, coaching, scaffolding, hints, suggestions, and encouragement. What all these aspects of structure shown in the middle of Figure 26.3 have in common is that they help students develop greater competence and skill. If rewards are used at this point in the lesson, they are usually employed as behavioral supports to maintain students' positive emotion and on-task behavior. As students complete the learning activity or stream of activity, the teacher provides feedback, analysis, and a reflective commentary to ready students for future learning and behavioral opportunities. What all these aspects of structure on the right-hand side of Figure 26.3 have in common is that they help students adjust and revise their goals, intentions, strategies, and sense of what needs to be done differently during future encounters with the same learning activity or stream of behavior. If rewards are used at this point in the lesson, they are given either spontaneously or in exchange for students' achievement.

Student Engagement

Engagement refers to how actively involved a student is in a learning activity (Christenson, Reschly, & Wylie, 2012). As shown in Figure 26.4, engagement is a multidimensional construct that consists of the four distinct, yet intercorrelated and mutually supportive aspects of behavior, emotion, cognition, and agency (Christenson, Reschly, & Wylie, 2012; Fredricks, Blumenfeld, & Paris, 2004; Reeve, 2013; Reeve & Tseng, 2011; Skinner, Kindermann, Connell, & Wellborn, 2009). Behavioral engagement refers to how involved the student is during a learning activity in terms of on-task attention, exertion of effort, and persistence. This aspect of student engagement is widely emphasized in discussions of classroom management strategies. Emotional engagement refers to the presence of positive emotions during task involvement such as curiosity and interest and to the absence of negative emotions such as anxiety and anger. Cognitive engagement refers to how strategically the student attempts to process information and to learn in terms of employing sophisticated rather than superficial learning strategies (e.g., elaboration rather than memorization). Agentic engagement refers to how proactive the student is in contributing constructively to the flow of the instruction he or she receives in terms of asking questions, expressing preferences, and letting the teacher know what he or she wants and needs.

Engagement is important because it functions as a student-initiated pathway to highly valued educational outcomes, such as academic progress and achievement (Jang, Kim, & Reeve, 2012; Ladd & Dinella, 2009; Skinner, Kindermann, Connell, & Wellborn, 2009; Skinner, Zimmer-Gembeck, & Connell, 1998). Engagement is what

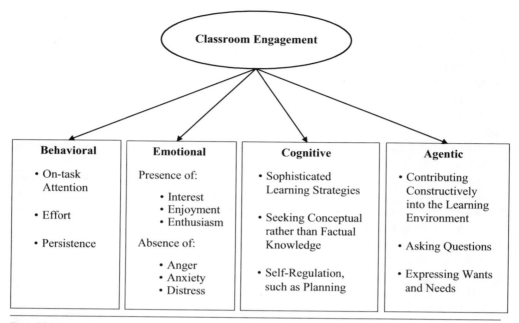

Figure 26.4 Four interrelated and mutually supportive aspects of students' classroom engagement.

students do to make academic progress; it is what students do to know, understand, and achieve. To make progress in learning a foreign language, for instance, students can pay close attention to sources of information, invest effort, and persist in the face of setbacks, which is behavioral engagement. Or they can enhance their curiosity and minimize their anxiety and frustration, which is emotional engagement. Or students can apply sophisticated learning strategies and carry out mental simulations to diagnose and solve problems, which is cognitive engagement. Or, proactively, students can contribute to the flow of instruction they receive, both to personalize that instruction and to negotiate for the interpersonal support they need to energize their motivation and learning.

Inner Motivational Resources

Environmentally offered rewards can be used to promote students' behavioral engagement, but the motivational source of the fuller four-dimensional conceptualization of engagement typically lies outside of reward. Classroom engagement arises out of and overtly expresses the underlying status of students' inner motivational resources. An inner motivational resource is an inherent energizing, directing, and sustaining force that all students possess, irrespective of their age, gender, nationality, or academic ability that, when supported, vitalizes engagement and enhances well-being. In a motivational analysis, inner motivational resources such as curiosity, interest/intrinsic motivation, and psychological needs provide the ultimate source of students' classroom engagement in learning activities (Reeve,

Deci, & Ryan, 2004). When classroom environments involve, nurture, and support students' inner motivational resources during instruction, students show strong classroom engagement (just as students show disengagement when the classroom environment neglects or frustrates their inner motivational resources) (Jang, Kim, & Reeve, 2012; Reeve, 2013).

Teacher-Provided Autonomy Support

Autonomy support is what teachers say and do during instruction to support students' inner motivational resources. When autonomy supportive, teachers strive to identify, nurture, and vitalize the inner motivational resources listed in the previous section (Reeve, 2009). The opposite of autonomy support is teacher control. When controlling, teachers pressure students to think, feel, and behave in a teacher-prescribed way. Generally speaking, the more teachers support student autonomy, the more students experience a personal endorsement of their own thinking (goals), feeling (emotions), and behaving (actions). "Personal endorsement of one's behavior" is a conceptual synonym for autonomy (Ryan & Deci, 2000), and the more autonomous students are during classroom learning activities and streams of behavior, the more behavioral, emotional, cognitive, and agentic engagement they show (Reeve, 2013). In practice, teacher-provided autonomy support can be understood within the same three-step framework provided earlier in the discussion of structure. When autonomy supportive, teachers first work to take the students' perspective and then, secondly, vitalize students' inner motivational resources so that their autonomous motivation (rather than a teacher's environmental incentives and rewards) energizes and directs classroom activity; lastly, teachers return to the effort to take the students' perspective so that future instruction can be redesigned to better incorporate students' inner motivational resources into tomorrow's instruction (Deci & Ryan, 1985; Reeve, 2009).

Figure 26.5 provides a three-part framework to illustrate a highly autonomy-supportive classroom environment. Before asking students to engage in a learning activity or in a stream of behavior, the teacher adopts the students' perspective and frame of reference on the forthcoming lesson (e.g., Is it interesting? Is it relevant to student's personal goals? What would students want to change about this lesson?). To help inform the teacher's design of instruction, he or she invites and welcomes students' suggestions about the lesson and incorporates their thoughts, feelings, and behaviors into the lesson plan and learning objective. What the aspects of autonomy support on the left-hand side of Figure 26.5 have in common is that the teacher extends his or her own goals, priorities, and agenda (i.e., perspective) for the upcoming lesson to incorporate students' goals, priorities, and agenda. As students engage themselves in the learning activity or in the stream of behavior, the teacher introduces elements of instruction that can vitalize students' inner motivational resources, provides explanatory rationales for requests, uses informational language, displays patience, and acknowledges and accepts students' complaints and expressions of negative affect. What all these aspects of autonomy support, shown in the middle of Figure 26.5, have in common is that they allow student activity to flow

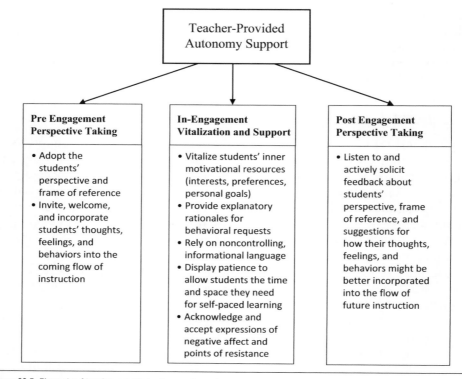

Figure 26.5 Elements of teacher-provided autonomy support.

out of an internal locus of causality, a sense of volitional freedom, and a perception of choice (i.e., autonomy) (Reeve, Nix, & Hamm, 2003). As students complete the learning activity, the teacher listens carefully and actively solicits students' inputs and suggestions for how to incorporate students' need for autonomy into tomorrow's instruction and classroom activity. What the aspects of autonomy support, shown on the right side of Figure 26.5, have in common is that the teacher seeks ways to develop students' capacity for greater autonomous self-regulation.

Several classroom-based studies confirm that teacher-provided autonomy support—operationally defined objectively by trained raters' assessments and subjectively by students' perceptions (Reeve & Jang, 2006; Su & Reeve, 2011)—predicts high levels of students' inner motivational resources (e.g., psychological need satisfaction, intrinsic motivation) (Cheon & Reeve, 2013; Cheon, Reeve, & Moon, 2012), classroom engagement (Reeve, Jang, Carrell, Jeon, & Barch, 2004), and positive educational outcomes (e.g., conceptual learning, skill development, and achievement) (Cheon, Reeve, & Moon, 2012; Reeve, 2009).

Other studies show that teachers do not need to make a decision between "offer structure" or "support autonomy" because structure and autonomy support work in complementary and synergistic ways to promote student motivation and positive classroom functioning (Jang, Reeve, & Deci, 2010; Sierens, Vansteenkiste, Goossens,

Soenens, & Dochy, 2009). As one case in point, it is a constructive mental exercise to take literally any individual element of structure listed in Figure 26.3 and ask the question, "How can I, as a classroom teacher, provide that aspect of structure to students in a highly autonomy supportive way?" As a point of reference, one group of researchers showed how classroom teachers can provide elementary-grade students with rules and limits in an autonomy supportive way and what the motivational, behavioral, and developmental fruits of doing so were (Koestner, Ryan, Bernieri, & Holt, 1984).

EPILOGUE

Given the preceding discussion, a final question that needs to be addressed is why teachers are still so often controlling in the classroom and why teachers continue to use rewards in expected, tangible, and contingent ways (Reeve, 2009). For the past decade, I have hosted many in-service events to help experienced teachers become more autonomy supportive toward their students (Cheon & Reeve, 2013; Cheon, Reeve, & Moon, 2012; Reeve, Jang, Carrell, Jeon, & Barch, 2004). A key part of all these visits is to explain the benefits of autonomy support and the costs of teacher control. This is always a controversial discussion. This is so because many teachers believe in the effectiveness and necessity of teacher control. They ask, "Well, how do you get the motivated engagement in the first place?" I recommend that teachers continue to offer all the external events and elements of structure that they have offered in the past, extrinsic rewards included, but to experiment with presenting these classroom objects and events in an autonomy-supportive way (for examples, see Reeve, 2009). A script, schedule, goal, or expectation often provides an initial engagement spark, but for that engagement to persist and include cognitive and agentic aspects of engagement (in addition to behavioral aspects), the chosen element of structure needs to be provided in an autonomy-supportive way (Jang, Reeve, & Deci, 2010). While I espouse a motivation-based "support engagement" paradigm, my viewpoint is not accepted by all, particularly scholars with strong behavioral beliefs and perspectives on classroom management for difficult-to-teach students (e.g., Alberto & Troutman, 2013; Kerr & Nelson, 2010; Scheuermann & Hall, 2012; Witzel & Mercer, 2003).

In addition, I recommend teachers consider new instructional strategies to vitalize students' otherwise dormant inner motivational resources, such as asking a curiosity-inducing question, offering an optimal challenge to involve the psychological need for competence, or framing the learning activity as an opportunity for personal growth to involve an intrinsic goal. As they enact these alternative motivation- and engagement-fostering instructional strategies, I ask teachers to keep an eye out for an immediate and rather pronounced spike in students' classroom engagement. Sometimes I get asked back to the school and therefore have the chance to follow up on teachers' classroom experiences. They always smile because classroom life is much improved, and it tends to improve not only for the students (in terms of motivation, engagement, and learning) (Cheon, Reeve, & Moon, 2012) but for the teachers as well.

The positive response from teachers was so consistent that Sung Hyeon Cheon and I conducted an experimentally designed, longitudinal study to assess the *teacher* benefits of offering greater autonomy support. Compared to a control group of teachers who used their existing motivating style throughout the semester, teachers who participated in an intervention program designed to help them incorporate autonomy-supportive instructional behaviors showed greater teaching efficacy, greater passion for teaching, greater psychological need satisfaction of their own, greater vitality (energy) while teaching, higher job satisfaction, and lesser postclass emotional exhaustion (Cheon & Reeve, in press). What teacher could ask for more?

NOTES

1. This writing of this chapter was supported by the WCU (World Class University) Program, funded by the Korean Ministry of Education, Science and Technology, consigned to the Korea Science and Engineering Foundation (Grant no. R32–2008–000–20023–0).
2. The neuroscientific analysis on reward can be considered a modern update on E. L. Thorndike's (1932) well-known law of effect. According to the law of effect, behaviors that have good effects tend to become more frequent, whereas behaviors that have bad effects tend to become less frequent. "Good effects" in a neuroscientific analysis are defined by dopamine release in the subcortical brain's reward center.

REFERENCES

Alberto, P. A., & Troutman, A. C. (2013). *Applied behavior analysis for teachers* (9th ed.). Upper Saddle River, NJ: Pearson.

Amabile, T. M. (1985). Motivation and creativity: Effect of motivational orientation on creative writers. *Journal of Personality and Social Psychology, 48*, 393–399.

Anderson, R., Manoogian, S. T., & Reznick, J. S. (1976). The undermining and enhancing of intrinsic motivation in preschool children. *Journal of Personality and Social Psychology, 34*, 915–922.

Baxter, M. G., & Murray, E. A. (2002). The amygdala and reward. *Nature Reviews: Neuroscience, 3*, 863–873.

Benware, C., & Deci, E. L. (1984). Quality of learning with an active versus passive motivational set. *American Educational Research Journal, 21*, 755–765.

Berridge, K. C., & Kringelbach, M. (2008). Affective neuroscience and pleasure: Reward in humans and animals. *Psychopharmacology, 191*, 391–431.

Boggiano, A. K., Barrett, M., Weiher, A. W., McClelland, G. H., & Lusk, C. M. (1987). Use of the maximal-operant principle to motivate children's intrinsic interest. *Journal of Personality and Social Psychology, 53*, 866–879.

Brophy, J. (1986). Teacher influences of student achievement. *American Psychologist, 41*, 1069–1077.

Cameron, J., & Pierce, W. D. (2002). *Rewards and intrinsic motivation: Resolving the controversy.* Westport, CT: Greenwood.

Cangelosi, J. S. (2008). *Classroom management strategies: Gaining and maintaining students' cooperation.* Hoboken, NJ: Wiley.

Cannella, G. S. (1986). Praise and concrete rewards: Concerns for childhood education. *Childhood Education, 62*, 297–301.

Cardinal, R. N., Parkinson, J. A., Hall, J., & Everitt, B. J. (2002). Emotion and motivation: The roles of the amygdala, ventral striatum, and prefrontal cortex. *Neuroscience and Biobehavioral Reviews, 26*, 321–352.

Cheon, S. H., & Reeve, J. (2013). Do the benefits from autonomy-supportive training program endure? A one-year follow-up investigation. *Psychology of Sport & Exercise, 14*, 508–518.

Cheon, S. H., & Reeve, J. (in press). Teacher benefits from giving students autonomy support during physical education instruction. *Journal of Sport and Exercise Psychology.*

Cheon, S. H., Reeve, J., & Moon, I. K. (2012). Experimentally based, longitudinally designed, teacher-focused intervention to help physical education teachers be more autonomy supportive toward their students. *Journal of Sport & Exercise Psychology, 34*, 365–396.

Christenson, S. L., Reschly, A. L., & Wylie, C. (Eds.). (2012). *The handbook of research on student engagement.* New York: Springer Science.

Covington, M. V., & Mueller, K. J. (2001). Intrinsic versus extrinsic motivation: An approach/avoidance reformulation. *Educational Psychology Review, 13*(2), 157–176.

D'Ardenne, K., McClure, S. M., Nystrom, L. E., & Cohen, J. D. (2008). BOLD responses reflecting dopaminergic signals in the human ventral tegmental area. *Science, 319,* 1264–1267.

Deci, E. L. (1971). Effects of externally mediated rewards on intrinsic motivation. *Journal of Personality and Social Psychology, 18,* 105–115.

Deci, E. L., Koestner, R., & Ryan, R. M. (1999). A meta-analytic review of experiments examining the effects of extrinsic rewards on intrinsic motivation. *Psychological Bulletin, 125,* 627–668.

Deci, E. L., & Ryan, R. M. (1980). The empirical exploration of intrinsic motivational processes. In L. Berkowitz (Ed.), *Advances in experimental social psychology,* Vol. 13 (pp. 39–80). New York: Academic Press.

Deci, E. L., & Ryan, R. M. (1985). *Intrinsic motivation and self-determination in human behavior.* New York: Plenum.

Dollinger, S. J., & Thelen, M. H. (1978). Over-justification and children's intrinsic motivation: Comparative effects of four rewards. *Journal of Personality and Social Psychology, 36,* 1259–1269.

Emmer, E. T., & Evertson, C. M. (2012). *Classroom management for middle and high school teachers* (9th ed.). Boston: Pearson.

Evertson, C. M., & Emmer, E. T. (2012). *Classroom management for elementary teachers* (9th ed.).Boston: Pearson.

Farkas, M. S., & Grolnick, W. S. (2010). Examining the components and concomitants of parental structure in the academic domain. *Motivation and Emotion, 34,* 266–279.

Fredricks, J. A., Blumenfeld, P. C., & Paris, A. H. (2004). School engagement: Potential of the concept, state of the evidence. *Review of Educational Research, 74,* 59–109.

Gladwin, T. E., Figner, B., Crone, E. A., & Wiers, R. W. (2011). Addiction, adolescence, and the integration of control and motivation. *Developmental Cognitive Neuroscience, 1,* 364–376.

Greene, D., & Lepper, M. R. (1974). Effects of extrinsic rewards on children's subsequent intrinsic interest. *Child Development, 45,* 1141–1145.

Grolnick, W. S., & Pomerantz, E. M. (2009). Issues and challenges in studying parental control: Toward a new conceptualization. *Child Development Perspectives, 3,* 165–170.

Grolnick, W. S., & Ryan, R. M. (1987). Autonomy in children's learning: An experimental and individual differences investigation. *Journal of Personality and Social Psychology, 52,* 890–898.

Hampton, A. N., & O'Doherty, J. P. (2007). Decoding the neural substrates of reward-related decision making with fMRI. *PNAS, 104,* 1377–82.

Harter, S. (1978). Pleasure derived from optimal challenge and the effects of extrinsic rewards on children's difficulty level choices. *Child Development, 49,* 788–799.

Henderlong, J., & Lepper, M. R. (2002). The effects of praise on children's intrinsic motivation: A review and synthesis. *Psychological Bulletin, 128,* 774–795.

Hom, H. L., Jr. (1994). Can you predict the overjustification effect? *Teaching of Psychology, 21,* 36–37.

Jang, H., Kim, E.-J., & Reeve, J. (2012). Longitudinal test of self-determination theory's motivation mediation model in a naturally-occurring classroom context. *Journal of Educational Psychology, 104,* 1175–1188.

Jang, H., Reeve, J., & Deci, E. L. (2010). Engaging students in learning activities: It is not autonomy support or structure but autonomy support and structure. *Journal of Educational Psychology, 102,* 588–600.

Jennings, S. H., Sparta, D. R., Stamatakis, A. M., Ung, R. L., Pleil, K. E., Kash, T. L., & Stuber, G. D. (2013). Distinct extended amygdala circuits for divergent motivational states. *Nature, 496,* 224–228.

Joussemet, M., Koestner, R., Lekes, N., & Houlfort, N. (2004). Introducing uninteresting tasks to children: A comparison of the effects of rewards and autonomy support. *Journal of Personality, 72,* 139–166.

Kast, A., & Connor, K. (1988). Sex and age differences in response to informational and controlling feedback. *Personality and Social Psychology Bulletin, 14,* 514–523.

Kerr, M., & Nelson, M. (2010). *Strategies for addressing behavior problems in the classroom.* Upper Saddle River, NJ: Pearson.

Koestner, R., Ryan, R. M., Bernieri, F., & Holt, K. (1984). Setting limits on children's behavior: The differential effects of controlling versus informational styles on intrinsic motivation and creativity. *Journal of Personality, 52,* 233–248.

Kohn, A. (1993). *Punished by rewards: The trouble with gold stars, incentive plans, A's, praise, and other bribes.* Boston: Houghton Mifflin.

Ladd, G. W., & Dinella, L. M. (2009). Continuity and change in early school engagement: Predictive of children's achievement trajectories from first to eighth grade? *Journal of Educational Psychology, 101,* 190–206.

Lepper, M. R. (1983). Social-control processes and the internalization of social values: An attributional perspective. In E. T. Higgins, D. N. Ruble, & W. W. Hartup (Eds.), *Social cognition and social development* (pp. 294–330). New York: Cambridge University Press.

Lepper, M. R., & Greene, D. (1975). Turning play into work: Effects of adult surveillance and extrinsic rewards on children's intrinsic motivation. *Journal of Personality and Social Psychology, 31,* 479–486.

Lepper, M. R., & Greene, D. (Eds.). (1978). *The hidden costs of rewards.* Mahwah, NJ: Erlbaum.

Lepper, M. R., Greene, D., & Nisbett, R. E. (1973). Undermining children's intrinsic interest with extrinsic rewards: A test of the overjustification hypothesis. *Journal of Personality and Social Psychology, 28,* 129–137.

McClure, S. M., Laibson, D. I., Loewenstein, G., & Cohen, J. D. (2004). Separate neural system value immediate and delayed monetary rewards. *Science, 506,* 503–507.

Mirenowicz, J., & Schultz, W. (1994). Importance of unpredictability for reward responses in primate dopamine neurons. *Journal of Neurophysiology, 72,* 1024–1027.

Montague, P. R., Dayan, P., & Sejnowski, T. J. (1996). A framework for mesencephalic dopamine systems based on predictive Hebbian learning. *Journal of Neuroscience, 16,* 1936–1947.

Murayama, K., Matsumoto, M., Izuma, K., & Matsumoto, K. (2010). Neural basis of the undermining effect of monetary reward on intrinsic motivation. *PNAS Early Edition,* 1–6.

O'Doherty, J. (2004). Reward representations and reward-related learning in the human brain: Insights from human neuroimaging. *Current Opinion in Neurobiology, 14,* 769–776.

Pallak, S. R., Costomiris, S., Sroka, S., & Pittman, T. S. (1982). School experience, reward characteristics, and intrinsic motivation. *Child Development, 53,* 1382–1391.

Pittman, T. S., Boggiano, A. K., & Ruble, D. N. (1983). Intrinsic and extrinsic motivational orientations: Limiting conditions on the undermining and enhancing effects of reward on intrinsic motivation. In J. Levine & M. Wang (Eds.), *Teacher and student perceptions: Implications for learning* (pp. 319–340). Mahwah, NJ: Erlbaum.

Reeve, J. (2009). Why teachers adopt a controlling motivating style toward students and how they can become more autonomy supportive. *Educational Psychologist, 44*(3), 159–175.

Reeve, J. (2013). How students create motivationally supportive learning environments for themselves: The concept of agentic engagement. *Journal of Educational Psychology, 105,* 579–595.

Reeve, J., Deci, E. L., & Ryan, R. M. (2004). Self-determination theory: A dialectical framework for understanding the sociocultural influences on student motivation. In D. McInerney & S. Van Etten (Eds.), *Research on sociocultural influences on motivation and learning: Big theories revisited,* Vol. 4 (pp. 31–59). Greenwich, CT: Information Age Press.

Reeve, J., & Jang, H. (2006). What teachers say and do to support students' autonomy during learning activities. *Journal of Educational Psychology, 98,* 209–218.

Reeve, J., Jang, H., Carrell, D., Jeon, S., & Barch, J. (2004). Enhancing students' engagement by increasing teachers' autonomy support. *Motivation and Emotion, 28,* 147–169.

Reeve, J., Nix, G., & Hamm, D. (2003). Testing models of the experience of self-determination in intrinsic motivation and the conundrum of choice. *Journal of Educational Psychology, 95,* 375–392.

Reeve, J., & Tseng, M. (2011). Agency as a fourth aspect of student engagement during learning activities. *Contemporary Educational Psychology, 36,* 257–267.

Rummel, A., & Feinberg, R. (1988). Cognitive evaluation theory: A meta-analytic review of the literature. *Social Behavior and Personality, 16,* 147–164.

Ryan, R. M. (1993). Agency and organization: Intrinsic motivation, autonomy and the self in psychological development. In J. Jacobs (Ed.), *Nebraska symposium on motivation: Developmental perspectives on motivation,* Vol. 40 (pp. 1–56). Lincoln,: University of Nebraska Press.

Ryan, R. M., & Connell, J. P. (1989). Perceived locus of causality and internalization: Examining reasons for acting in two domains. *Journal of Personality and Social Psychology, 57,* 749–761.

Ryan, R. M., & Deci, E. L. (2000). Self-determination theory and the facilitation of intrinsic motivation, social development, and well-being. *American Psychologist, 55,* 68–78.

Ryan, R. M., & Deci, E. L. (2002). An overview of self-determination theory: An organismic-dialectical perspective. In E. L. Deci & R. M. Ryan's (Eds.), *Handbook of self-determination research* (pp. 3–33). Rochester, NY: University of Rochester Press.

Ryan, R. M., Mims, V., & Koestner, R. (1983). Relation of reward contingency and interpersonal context to intrinsic motivation: A review and test using cognitive evaluation theory. *Journal of Personality and Social Psychology, 45,* 736–750.

Sabatinelli, D., Bradley, M. M., Lang, P. J., Costa, V. D., & Versace, F. (2007). Pleasure rather than salience activates human nucleus accumbens and medial prefrontal cortex. *Journal of Neurophysiology, 98,* 1374–1379.

Scheuermann, B. K., & Hall, J. A. (2012). *Positive behavioral supports for the classroom* (2nd ed.). Upper Saddle River, NJ: Pearson.

Shapira, Z. (1976). Expectancy determinants of intrinsically motivated behavior. *Journal of Personality and Social Psychology, 34,* 1235–1244.

Sierens, E., Vansteenkiste, M., Goossens, L., Soenens, B., & Dochy, R. (2009). The synergistic relationship of perceived autonomy support and structure in the prediction of self-regulated learning. *British Journal of Educational Psychology, 79,* 57–68.

Skinner, E. A. (1995). *Perceived control, motivation, and coping.* Newbury Park, CA: Sage.

Skinner, E. A., Kindermann, T. A., Connell, J. P., & Wellborn, J. G. (2009). Engagement and disaffection as organizational constructs in the dynamics of motivational development. In K. Wentzel & A. Wigfield (Eds.), *Handbook of motivation in school* (pp. 223–245). Mahwah, NJ: Erlbaum.

Skinner, E. A., Zimmer-Gembeck, M. J., & Connell, J. P. (1998). Individual differences and the development of perceived control. *Monographs of the Society for Research in Child Development, 63,* Serial number 254.

Smith, K. S., Tindell, A. J., Aldridge, J. W., & Berridge, K. C. (2009). Ventral pallidum roles in reward and motivation. *Brain Research, 196*(2), 155–167.

Su, Y.-L., & Reeve, J. (2011). A meta-analysis of the effectiveness of intervention programs designed to support autonomy. *Educational Psychology Review, 23,* 159–188.

Swann, W. B., Jr., & Pittman, T. S. (1977). Initiating play activity in children: The moderating influence of verbal cues on intrinsic motivation. *Child Development, 48,* 1125–1132.

Tang, S.-H., & Hall, V. C. (1995). The overjustification effect: A meta-analysis. *Applied Cognitive Psychology, 9,* 365–404.

Thorndike, E. L. (1932). *The fundamentals of learning.* New York: Teachers College Press.

Vansteenkiste, M., Simons, J., Lens, W., Sheldon, K. M., & Deci, E. L. (2004). Motivated learning, performance, and persistence: The synergistic role of intrinsic goals and autonomy-support. *Journal of Personality and Social Psychology, 87,* 246–260.

Vansteenkiste, M., Simons, J., Lens, W., Soenens, B., & Matos, L. (2005). Examining the motivational impact of intrinsic versus extrinsic goal framing and autonomy-supportive versus internally controlling communication style on early adolescents' academic achievement. *Child Development, 2,* 483–501.

Whalen, P. J. (2007). The uncertainty of it all. *Trends in Cognitive Science, 11,* 499–500.

Wiechman, B. M., & Gurland, S. T. (2009). What happens during the free-choice period? Evidence of a polarizing effect of extrinsic rewards on intrinsic motivation. *Journal of Research in Personality, 43,* 716–719.

Wiersma, U. J. (1992). The effects of extrinsic rewards in intrinsic motivation: A meta-analysis. *Journal of Occupational and Organizational Psychology, 65,* 101–114.

Wise, R. A. (2002). Brain reward circuitry: Insights from unsensed incentives. *Neuron, 36,* 229–240.

Witzel, B. S., & Mercer, C. D. (2003). Using rewards to teach students with disabilities: Implications for motivation. *Remedial and Special Education, 24,* 88–96.

VI
Research Methodology

27

STATISTICAL MODELING METHODS FOR CLASSROOM MANAGEMENT RESEARCH

S. NATASHA BERETVAS, TIFFANY A. WHITTAKER, AND ROSE E. STAFFORD
THE UNIVERSITY OF TEXAS AT AUSTIN

In recent years, increasing use has been made of structural equation modeling (SEM) and multilevel modeling to examine the relationships among variables in large-scale data sets. These approaches make it possible to represent, compare, and test models that preserve more realistically the complex nature of intercorrelation and causality that exists in real-world phenomena. The purpose of this chapter is to provide readers with descriptions of these modeling approaches so that when they are encountered in the literature, they will be more accessible. We also hope to encourage researchers in the field of classroom management to consider using these analytic approaches when their data sets are appropriate. Classroom management researchers may also find it helpful to apply these models to answer questions in databases like the National Educational Longitudinal Study (NELS), data compiled by the National Center for Education Statistics (NCES), and other longitudinal data sets. Each section of this chapter will describe models that could be of interest to classroom management researchers or that may be encountered when reading widely in the literature related to classroom management. This chapter will focus on understanding the contexts in which the models might be used and on giving examples of how the models might answer certain types of research questions, rather than technical details of the statistical procedures. References will be provided for further study.

The chapter contains two primary sections. The first section will focus on the conventional multilevel modeling framework. The second section will focus on the conventional SEM framework. Note that both of these frameworks can be subsumed under a single modeling framework; however, it is easier for most applied researchers to think of these models separately when being introduced to their use. Methodological research is constantly enhancing modeling techniques and estimation procedures, and there is room here only to introduce the most basic forms of these kinds of models.

Once these basics have been mastered, then the more complicated extensions can be considered. Lastly, the models and techniques described in this chapter are designed for applied classroom management researchers who have reasonably large data sets. The definition of "large" depends on many factors, including model complexity and the number and even the true value of the parameters being estimated. Researchers intending to estimate the models introduced here are encouraged to reference texts like Kline's (2011) SEM text and the multilevel modeling texts by Hox (2010) and Raudenbush and Bryk (2002) to find out recommendations for the relevant minimum sample sizes as a function of model type and complexity and other factors.

MULTILEVEL MODELING

A fundamental assumption made when using analysis of variance (ANOVA) or multiple regression analyses is that the cases are independent of each other. Unfortunately, in many scenarios in classroom- and school-based research, this assumption is violated. For example, an educational researcher might have access to student-level variables from several classrooms with multiple students per classroom. Academic outcomes for students within the same classroom cannot be assumed to be independent of one another. Alternatively, a researcher might have longitudinal data for students, and the repeated measures of each student cannot be assumed independent. It is also possible to have doubly nested data sets such as data that include repeated measures on students with multiple students sampled per classroom, or multiple students per classroom and multiple classrooms per school sampled in a data set. In any of these and related scenarios, it is possible that the assumption of independence of observations has been violated and will compromise the validity of inferences associated with use of ordinary least squares (OLS) regression or of ANOVA. If the dependence found in clustered data is ignored, then the resulting standard errors may be underestimated, and the test statistics' type I error rates may be inflated. It is also likely that some test statistics' type II error rates will be affected (e.g., see Snijders & Bosker, 1999). One option for handling data that violate the assumption of independence is the use of multilevel modeling.

The multilevel model has several different names across various social science disciplines, including the hierarchical linear model, random or mixed effects model, and random coefficients model, among others. Use of the multilevel model permits appropriate handling of hierarchically clustered data by partitioning variability into the components associated with the different clustering levels and also providing corrected error rates. As will be demonstrated, the multilevel model also provides a flexible framework for modeling relationships among variables across levels of the data's hierarchy.

Two-Level Models

It is possible to have many levels of clustering; however, this discussion will start with the simplest scenario in which there is only one level of clustering in the data set. For example, a data set might consist of student mathematics achievement scores (*Math_Ach*) for multiple students sampled from each of multiple classrooms.

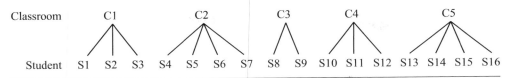

Figure 27.1 Network graph of a two-level data set with students clustered within classrooms.

The researcher might be interested in assessing the relationship between students' engagement scores (*Engage*) and *Math_Ach*. In the data set, students are clustered within classrooms, and thus classroom constitutes the clustering variable. Using Raudenbush and Bryk's (2002) nomenclature, this data set is a two-level data set, with classrooms representing the level-two clustering unit and students measured at level-one. Figure 27.1 contains a network graph depicting a subset of a two-level data set with students clustered within classrooms.

In Figure 27.1, it is clear that this subset of the data set consists of variables describing multiple classrooms and multiple students per classroom. Note that, as can be seen in Figure 27.1, although there are multiple level-one units (here, students) per level-two unit (classroom), each level-one unit is associated with only a single level-two unit comprising a "pure" hierarchy. (There are scenarios that will be described later in which data are nested although the nesting is not purely hierarchical).

The student variables (here, *Engage* and *Math_Ach*) for students in the same classroom will vary less than if they were measured for students who had been sampled from different classes. Thus, if a simple (or multiple) regression model is estimated that ignores the nesting of students while assessing the association between *Engage* and *Math_Ach*, then the resulting test statistics will be biased. For example, the type I error rates associated with testing predictors' effects might be inflated, or spurious relationships between variables might be found (Hox, 2010). Another researcher might be interested in assessing the effect of a classroom management program intended to reduce the relationship between a preintervention math achievement measure (*pre_Math*) and postintervention score, *Math_Ach*. Again, if a researcher simply tested this moderating relationship using multiple regression and ignored the dependencies inherent in clustered data sets (here, of students within classrooms), then the resulting statistical inferences might be misleading.

Instead of disaggregating the data and ignoring the clustering, the researcher could use multilevel modeling to handle the dependency among measures of students in the same classroom. Use of multilevel modeling allows partitioning of the total variability in the outcome (here, for example, *Math_Ach*) into the component attributable to students' individual differences as separate from the variability that has to do with classrooms differences. The higher the proportion of the total variability in the outcome that has to do with differences among classrooms, the more classroom-based dependence there is in the data, and the more important it is that it is handled appropriately. This proportion (i.e., the ratio of the cluster-level variance in the outcome out of the total variance in the outcome) is termed the intraclass correlation (ICC). And, as just noted, the larger the ICC, the greater the likelihood of errors in the resulting statistical inferences if the dependence is ignored.

When using multilevel modeling to handle two-level data, it is possible to add multiple predictors at each of the two levels in the model. Thus, student-level variables (like *Engage* and *pre_Math*) can be explored as predictors of the outcome (e.g., of *Math_Ach*). Classroom-level variables (like a classroom-based intervention variable) can also be investigated as predictors of the outcome. In addition, classroom-level variables can be assessed as moderators of relationships between student-level variables (or vice versa). In the current example, this means that a researcher could examine whether a classroom management intervention (classroom-level variable *CM_Tx*) randomly assigned to classrooms (i.e., a cluster-level variable), as compared to business-as-usual classrooms, could reduce the relationship between *pre_Math* and *Math_Ach* (level-one predictor and outcome). A researcher might not have an observed classroom variable that is hypothesized to explain variability in the relationship between a level-one predictor (student *Engage* values) and the outcome (*Math_Ach*) scores. Instead, the researcher might wish to model that the relationship between *Engage* and *Math_Ach* varies as a function of some unobserved clustering variable. The multilevel model could model this variability in the relationship between the predictor and outcome across clusters.

Three-Level Models

Real-world data sets typically entail more than one level of clustering. For example, a large-scale educational data set might consist of measures of multiple students (level one) sampled from several classrooms (level two) within multiple elementary schools (level three). Figure 27.2 depicts a (small) subset of such a data set with clusters of students nested within classrooms and clusters of classrooms nested within each elementary school. As has been emphasized in the section on two-level models, the validity of statistical inferences made about relationships between pairs of variables is compromised if dependencies inherent in clustered data are ignored. Use of the three-level model allows appropriate partitioning of variability in the outcome into the three levels (the part having to do with each of the following: the individual student, the classroom, and the school). For example, a researcher might be interested in the prediction of students' *Math_Ach* scores using student-, classroom-, and/or school-level variables (like *Engage*, *CM_Tx*, and a school climate measure, *Sch_Cli*, respectively). The relationships between the predictors and the student-level

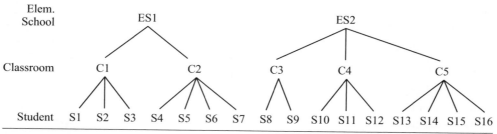

Figure 27.2 Network graph of a three-level data set with clusters of students nested within classrooms and clusters of classrooms nested within each elementary school.

outcome (*Math_Ach*) can be explored using a three-level model. In addition, within- and across-level interactions between predictors and their effects on the outcome of interest can be explored using the multilevel model. For example, an applied researcher might hypothesize that the effect of a classroom management intervention on individual student *Math_Ach* scores might depend on the global (school-wide) perception of how safe a school feels to enrolled students. The researcher could estimate a three-level model including *Math_Ach* as the outcome and the following predictors: main effects of the level-two *CM_Tx* and level-three *Sch_Cli* predictors and a term capturing the interaction of the two variables. As with a two-level model, additional predictor and covariate variables can also be included in the model, and the resulting slopes (coefficients representing relationships between predictors and the outcome) can be modeled as fixed or randomly varying across higher-level clustering factors (classrooms and/or schools).

Longitudinal Models

The two- and three-level model examples have focused on contexts (like classrooms or schools) as clustering variables. However, it is also possible to conceive of individuals as clustering variables. For example, a longitudinal data set might consist of multiple measures of individual students across time. As depicted in Figure 27.3 for a subset of longitudinal data, the repeated measures (level one) of an individual student can be considered clustered within the student at (level two). The scores for a student measured on occasions cannot be assumed to be independent. Instead, the three scores are related largely as a function of characteristics of the student. It is important to handle the within-person dependency inherent in longitudinal data. It is possible to investigate the degree to which individual students differ in their math scores at the first time point of the measurement period (a random intercept model), as well as differing in their linear growth in mathematics achievement over elementary school (a random slopes model). It is also possible to assess whether within-student and across-student characteristics influence growth trajectory parameters. Note that many of these simple two-level (measurement occasion within students) longitudinal models have exactly equivalent parameterizations when using the SEM framework (as described in the next section).

One of the benefits of using the multilevel modeling framework for modeling growth trajectories is that the individuals being measured might themselves be sampled within clusters (such as classrooms, intervention groups or schools). For example, a subset of a longitudinal data set in which measurement occasions (level one) are clustered within students (level two) with multiple students sampled from each

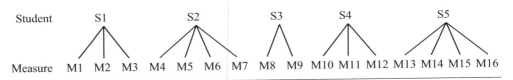

Figure 27.3 Network graph of repeated measures that are clustered within each student.

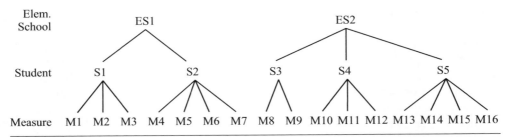

Figure 27.4 Network graph of repeated measures that are clustered within students who are sampled from multiple elementary schools.

of multiple elementary schools (level three) is depicted in Figure 27.4. A three-level model can be used to explore hypotheses about growth in an outcome for individuals nested within contexts or clusters. This model can also be used to investigate predictors of growth trajectory parameters. For example, a researcher might hypothesize that there are gender differences (level-two predictor) in linear growth in student *Engage* scores but that in schools in which a school-wide antibullying program has been implemented, this difference might not occur.

Multilevel Modeling Notes

Although not described here, it is, of course, possible to estimate a multilevel model with an outcome that cannot be assumed to be normally distributed. For example, a researcher might be interested in whether a school-based intervention to reduce bullying ultimately impacts whether students graduate or not (i.e., a dichotomous outcome). It is also possible under the multilevel modeling framework to handle models with multiple related outcomes (i.e., a multivariate multilevel model). Readers interested in learning more about multilevel models are encouraged to refer to excellent textbooks on the topic (including, e.g., Goldstein, 2010; Hox, 2010; Raudenbush & Bryk, 2002; Snijders & Bosker, 1999). Several statistical software programs, including HLM, MLwiN, Mplus, among others, facilitate estimation of multilevel models. More general-purpose statistical software programs, including R, SAS, SPSS and STATA, also include multiple procedures that can be used to estimate multilevel models.

In addition, use of the conventional multilevel modeling framework involves the assumption that variables (outcomes and predictors) are measured without error. Given the types of outcomes typically encountered in educational and social science research in general, it is more appropriate and more powerful (statistically speaking) to be able to incorporate the modeling of measurement error. Use of the structural equation modeling (SEM) framework facilitates modeling of more complex systems of variables in which there might be quasi endogenous variables. SEM is also designed to partition observed variables into the components resulting from measurement error as separate from the latent variable component underlying the score values. The next section focuses on the use of structural equation models to handle (1) complex systems of variables, (2) measurement error, and (3) both together.

STRUCTURAL EQUATION MODELING (SEM)

Structural equation modeling subsumes several techniques that can be used to model the relationships only among observed variables or among a combination of observed and unobserved, or latent, variables. A description of selected techniques in SEM that are relevant to classroom management research will be subsequently presented. Prior to presenting examples of selected SEM techniques, however, it is first important to briefly introduce some SEM notation and discuss issues related to causal inferences in SEM.

Causal Inference in SEM

In SEM illustrations, observed variables are symbolized using squares or rectangles, whereas unobserved or latent variables are symbolized using circles. The relationships among observed and unobserved variables are demonstrated by way of single- and double-headed arrows. Single-headed arrows connecting two variables ($X \rightarrow Y$) in SEM imply that the variable from which the arrow is originating (X) has a direct or causal effect on the variable receiving the causal contribution (Y). Double-headed arrows connecting two variables ($X \leftrightarrow Y$) imply that the two variables are simply related to one another without a directional hypothesis. It is essential that the connections between variables in SEM be based on justifiable theory and logic.

Although the relationships among all variables connected with single- or double-headed arrows may be theoretically important in a model, the single-headed arrows, which imply causal direction, are of substantive interest in SEM and require more consideration here. For instance, including $X \rightarrow Y$ in a model does not suggest that X is the singular cause of Y. Instead, it implies that X is a hypothesized cause of Y, which may be among other hypothesized causes that may also be included in the model.

In general, some select conditions must hold for researchers to be more assured of cause–and–effect relationships in SEM, including temporal precedence, association, and isolation (Davis, 1985; Mulaik, 2009; Pearl, 2000; Sobel, 1995). Temporal precedence stipulates that the hypothesized cause (X) must precede the hypothesized effect (Y) in time. Association signifies that the cause (X) and effect (Y) covary or correlate with one another. Isolation specifies that the cause (X) and effect (Y) should still be associated once they are isolated from all other influential variables. Temporal precedence may be satisfied with methods such as those implemented in experimental or quasi experimental designs by way of manipulation or by collecting data concerning the causal variables prior to the effect variables. Isolation tends to be the most difficult condition to satisfy entirely, but it is more likely to be fulfilled by collecting data on extraneous variables and statistically controlling for them in a model.

Path Analysis

In SEM, a path analysis model offers an extension of a multiple regression model in which the relationships among observed variables are modeled. The observed (directly measured) variables are represented as squares. For example, Figure 27.5 illustrates a path model in which *Classroom Climate, Years of Teaching Experience,*

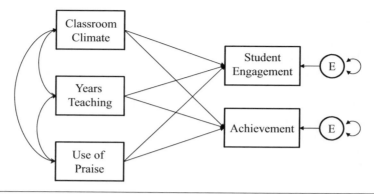

Figure 27.5 Observed variable path model predicting *Student Engagement* and *Achievement* with three correlated predictors (including *Classroom Climate, Years Teaching,* and *Use of Praise*).

and *Teacher Use of Praise* are exogenous, or independent, variables that are theorized to directly affect two endogenous, or dependent, variables, including *Student Engagement* and *Achievement*. As depicted in Figure 27.5, the direct effects are represented in the path model with the single-headed arrows from the three exogenous variables to the two endogenous variables. The double-headed arrows connecting the three exogenous variables symbolize that they are simply related or correlate, but there are no directional hypotheses concerning the relationships among the exogenous variables in the figure.

Similar to multiple regression analysis, direct effects correspond to unstandardized or standardized partial regression coefficients, and the two-headed arrows correspond to covariances or correlations when interpreting unstandardized or standardized output, respectively. Also similar to multiple regression analysis, an R^2 value can be calculated for each endogenous variable in the model and is interpreted as the proportion of variance in the endogenous variable explained by the causal relationships. Unless perfectly predicted, errors will be associated with endogenous variables, which also have direct effects on their respective endogenous variables. Because errors or residuals (also sometimes referred to in the SEM framework as "uniquenesses") cannot be directly measured, they are represented in path models as E's enclosed in circles in order to indicate that the errors are latent or unobserved. The unexplained variance of an endogenous variable is generally symbolized as a double-headed arrow loop, which is associated with the error for the endogenous variable (see Figure 27.5).

Mediation Models

Researchers often hypothesize that certain variables intervene or mediate the relationship between two other variables. Estimation of mediation models is popular using the SEM framework because of the ability to simultaneously estimate several direct and indirect effects within a single model. Mediated, or indirect, effects are comprised of two or more single-headed arrows pointing in the same direction with

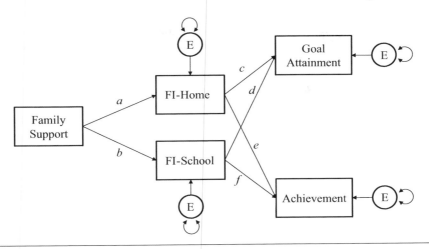

Figure 27.6 Observed variable path model in which the prediction of *Goal Attainment* and *Achievement* by *Family Support* is mediated by *Family Involvement (FI)* at *Home* and *School.*

one arrow pointing at the mediator and the other arrow emanating from the mediator. For instance, a researcher may hypothesize that family support programs have an indirect effect on student outcomes via two types of family involvement (the mediators). Figure 27.6 is an example of this hypothesis in which the perception of *Family Support* availability at school has a direct impact on *Family Involvement at Home* (FI-Home) and *Family Involvement in the School* (FI-School) each of which also has a direct impact on *Student Goal Attainment* and *Achievement* at school. In this model, the perception of family support availability is modeled to have a direct effect on family involvement at home and on family involvement in the school, which correspond to paths *a* and *b*, respectively. In turn, family involvement at home has a direct effect on student goal attainment and on student achievement (corresponding to paths *c* and *d*, respectively). Family involvement at school also is modeled as having a direct effect on student goal attainment and on achievement (corresponding to paths *e* and *f*, respectively).

Although the direct effects are theoretically important, the indirect effects in this model would be of considerable interest to researchers given the hypothesis of mediation. The indirect effects of perception of family support availability on student goal attainment and on achievement via family involvement at home correspond to the products of the path coefficients, namely *ac* and *ae*, respectively. The indirect effects of perception of family support availability on student goal attainment and achievement via family involvement at school correspond to the products *bd* and *bf*, respectively (see Figure 27.6). Typically, researchers present the results from a mediation model in so-called effects decomposition tables in which the direct, indirect, and total effects within a model are summarized.

Several procedures can be used to estimate the statistical significance of these indirect effects, including the Sobel test and bootstrapping estimation techniques. Available SEM software programs (e.g., Mplus and Amos) do have the capability of performing bootstrapping to provide bootstrapped confidence interval estimates of indirect effects. MacKinnon, Fritz, Williams, and Lockwood created easy-to-use free software (named PRODCLIN) that also provides a better statistical test of indirect effects (2007). For more information concerning mediation analysis and the testing of indirect effects, see MacKinnon (2008) and Preacher and Hayes (2008), respectively.

Latent Variable SEM

The causal relationships described for path analysis models may be extended to include unobserved or latent variables. Latent variable SEM involves a combination of both observed and unobserved variables. In path analysis, observed variables may be comprised of a single score (e.g., time-on-task score) or an aggregate of items from a scale (e.g., average or summed score) and are used to measure some construct of interest (e.g., student engagement). In a path analysis, it is assumed that each observed exogenous variable and aggregated variable (either exogenous or endogenous) are measured with perfect reliability and hence have no measurement error. If this assumption is incorrect, which will most likely be the case with social science and educational measures, the results in a path model may be inaccurate (Bollen, 1989). Because researchers are ultimately interested in the relationships among the constructs of interest, latent variable SEM allows for the incorporation of latent or unobserved factors underlying the measured variables. Latent variable SEM counters the negative effects of measurement error found in path models by modeling the error associated with the measured variables.

Confirmatory Factor Analysis (CFA)

Confirmatory factor analysis (CFA) models are often referred to as measurement models and allow researchers to test the factorial validity of a construct of interest. CFA models are *a priori* models in that researchers must specify the number of factors in the model, which items load onto which factors, and whether or not the factors covary. Figure 27.7 illustrates a simple one-factor CFA model in which the latent factor, *Job Satisfaction*, underlies four indicator, or measured, variables. These four indicators may represent Likert scores (ranging from 1 = *Never* to 7 = *All of the Time*) on items included on a short job satisfaction scale in which teachers respond to how often they believe their thoughts and ideas are heard (*Heard*), how often they feel respected by their peers (*Respect*), how often they feel valued at work (*Valued*), and how often they feel a sense of autonomy at work (*Auton*). In this model, the *Job Satisfaction* factor is an exogenous or independent variable and has direct effects on each of the measured variables. The direct paths from the factor to the measured or indicator variables, also known as the "factor loadings" (paths *a* through *d*), may be interpreted as partial regression coefficients and compared using the standardized loading values. The value of the factor loading quantifies how closely a single indicator of the factor (e.g., *Heard*) is related to the other factor indicators (here, *Respect*, *Valued*, and *Auton*). The sign (positive or negative) of the

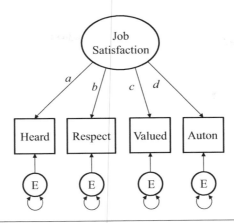

Figure 27.7 One-factor confirmatory factor analysis (CFA) model in which a *Job Satisfaction* factor underlies the following four indicator variables: *Heard, Respect, Value,* and *Autonomy (Auton)*.

factor loading indicates whether the relationship is positive or negative similar to the sign for a correlation coefficient. For example, if the *Respect* item was actually a measure with a higher score representing the teacher-felt *Disrespect*, then its factor loading would likely be negative.

The indicator or measured variables are endogenous variables in CFA models. As in path models with observed variables, the endogenous variables will each have an R^2 value indicating the proportion of variance explained by, in this case, the single factor. Measurement error associated with each measured item is modeled and is denoted with circles in which E is encompassed. Thus, there will be unexplained or error variance, represented by the double-headed arrow loop associated with each indicator's error term (see Figure 27.7). It is important to note that at least three indicator variables must be used for single-factor models in order for parameters to be estimated and the model to be identified. See Brown (2006) for more discussion concerning CFA models.

Latent Variable Path Models

Latent variable path models (also called "structural equation models") are simply extensions of a path analysis model to a path model that includes latent variables. For example, Figure 27.8 illustrates a latent variable path model in which perceived *Teacher Support* and *Principal Leadership* factors are modeled as correlated and have a direct effect on the *Teacher Self-Efficacy* and *Job Satisfaction* factors. In turn, the *Teacher Self-Efficacy* and *Job Satisfaction* factors are modeled to have a direct effect on the teacher use of *Positive Feedback* in the classroom factor. Although not illustrated in the model, each factor separately represents a measurement model in which the factor has underlying measured or indicator variables. For instance, the *Job Satisfaction* factor, as illustrated in Figure 27.7, has four indicator variables as previously described in the CFA subsection.

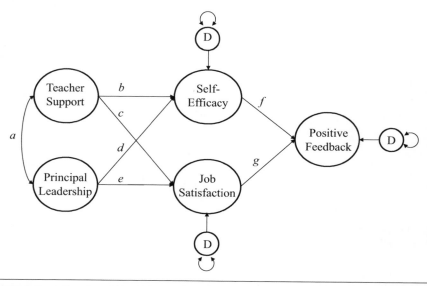

Figure 27.8 Latent variable path model in which the prediction of *Positive Feedback* by *Teacher Support* and *Principal Leadership* is mediated by *Self-Efficacy* and *Job Satisfaction* factors.

One may notice the similarities between this model and a path analysis model with observed variables. More specifically, the single-headed arrows represent direct effects (*b*, *c*, *d*, *e*, *f*, and *g*) that correspond to partial regression coefficients, and the two-headed arrow (*a*) represents covariation between two factors. An R^2 value will be calculated for each endogenous factor in the model indicating the proportion of variance in the endogenous factor explained by the model. Likewise, error will be associated with endogenous factors that directly influence their respective endogenous factor. In latent variable path models, however, these errors are more often called "disturbances," simply representing the error associated with a factor as opposed to that of an observed variable. These disturbances are symbolized as circles in which a D is encompassed (see Figure 27.8).

One may also notice in Figure 27.8 that indirect effects are modeled. Specifically, the *Teacher Support* and *Principal Leadership* factors are modeled as indirectly affecting the classroom environment factor via *Teacher Self-Efficacy* and *Job Satisfaction* (corresponding to the products *bf*, *cg*, and *df*, *eg*, respectively). As in mediational analyses with observed variables, indirect effects among latent variables may also be tested for statistical significance.

Multiple-Group SEM

Thus far, the previously mentioned SEM techniques have been discussed with respect to a single group of participants. Nonetheless, SEM is a popular framework in which models for multiple groups may be compared. All of the techniques previously described, including path analysis, CFA, and latent variable path analysis, may be incorporated into a multiple-group context. In brief, multiple-group SEM allows researchers to test whether certain parameter estimates of interest (e.g., direct paths, covariances, factor loadings) are equivalent or nonequivalent across groups.

Measurement Invariance

Multiple-group SEM is commonly introduced as a way to test measurement invariance (equivalence). When testing measurement invariance, SEM models with increasingly restrictive equality constraints that are imposed on parameters across groups are compared to evaluate the parameters' equivalence across groups. As a simple example, a researcher might like to assess whether the factor *Job Satisfaction* (see Figure 27.7) can be assumed to be measured equivalently across males and females. This means that the researcher might be interested in testing whether the factor loadings for the four measures of the *Job Satisfaction* factor (see paths *a* through *d* in Figure 27.7) can be assumed equivalent across the two gender groups. If support were found for the equivalence of these factor loadings, then this would help justify general use of the *Job Satisfaction* factor for both males and females. Equivalence of other parameters and across more than two groups can also be tested. Measurement invariance is an extensive topic, and a thorough treatment of invariance is beyond the scope of this chapter (see Vandenberg & Lance, 2000, for more information concerning measurement invariance and multiple-group SEM). Succinctly, measurement invariance concerns the extent to which the relationships among latent factors and the measured, or indicator, variables that they underlie are comparable across groups.

Support for measurement invariance is typically provided by statistical difference tests (i.e., chi-square difference tests; Lagrange multiplier tests, which are also called "modification indices") or by change in model fit indices. Statistically nonsignificant difference tests and unsubstantial changes in fit indices would indicate that invariance (equivalence) is supported because inclusion of the equality constraints does not significantly or substantially decrease model fit. In contrast, statistically significant difference tests and considerable changes in fit indices would indicate that invariance is not supported because inclusion of the equality constraints significantly or substantially decreased model fit. Identification of unequal parameter values across groups would support that the parameter is noninvariant or unequal across groups.

More general parameter invariance can be tested for parameters in both observed and latent variable path models. For instance, paths *a–f* in Figure 27.6 may be constrained to be equal across groups to test which of the paths in the mediation models might be assumed equivalent across groups (e.g., genders, ethnicities, middle versus elementary schools, etc.). Further, the covariance (parameter *a*) and direct paths (*b–g*) in Figure 27.8 may also be tested for equality across groups.

Moderation Models

When noninvariance is detected using a multiple-group SEM approach, it is indicative of an interaction between variables because the parameter values differ for the different groups (Schumacker & Lomax, 2004). For example, suppose that invariance testing indicated that path *b* in Figure 27.8 differed significantly for teachers from small schools as compared to teachers from large schools. This would indicate that the relationship between teacher support and self-efficacy differs depending on the type of school. The inference might be that there is a stronger relationship between the two constructs in one group (e.g., large schools) than in the second group (e.g., small schools). Continuous latent variable interactions may also be modeled in SEM; however, a presentation of these models is beyond the scope of this chapter (see Marsh, Wen, & Hau, 2006, for more information concerning latent variable interactions).

Latent Growth Models in SEM

As mentioned in an earlier subsection of the multilevel modeling section, researchers are often interested in assessing the stability or the growth in an outcome across time. Latent growth modeling (LGM) in SEM allows for the modeling of individual growth in outcomes measured during several measurement occasions. The SEM parameterization of the basic LGM is exactly equivalent to that based in the multilevel modeling framework. For completeness sake, however, Figure 27.9 is presented to provide the SEM representation of a basic latent growth model in which children's aggressive behavior is measured at four different measurement occasions (for example, yearly in grades 2–5 of elementary school). A latent growth model is an extension of a CFA model in which each indicator variable is the outcome score measured at each time point. Oftentimes,

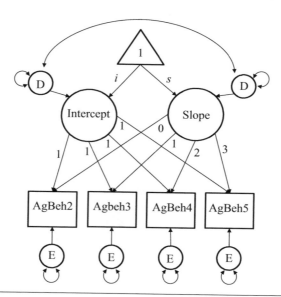

Figure 27.9 Latent growth model of *Aggressive Behavior (AgBeh)* scores measured on four occasions.

two factors are used to represent the different dimensions of change across time. Specifically, an *Intercept* factor signifies the standing of the students on the outcome variable (e.g., aggressive behavior) at a selected temporal reference point, and the *Slope* factor captures the children's linear growth trajectory on the outcome variable across measurement occasions. The most commonly used temporal reference point is the initial measurement occasion. Means of the *Intercept* and *Slope* factors are estimated by regressing each factor on a constant or unit predictor equal to one (represented in SEM diagrams using the 1 in a triangle as in Figure 27.9). The paths from the constant to the *Intercept* and *Slope* factors in this illustration, then, would denote the average on the outcome variable (e.g., aggressive behavior) at the initial measurement time and the average linear growth rate across time (paths *i* and s, respectively, in Figure 27.9). The variability of the disturbances associated with the *Intercept* and *Slope* factors in this illustration would indicate whether significant variability existed among the children with respect to the outcome at the initial time point and whether significant variability existed among the children with respect to their linear rate of change, respectively. The covariance between the disturbances associated with the *Intercept* and *Slope* factors signals whether there is a relationship between children's outcome scores at the initial measurement occasion and their linear growth trajectory.

It is important to note that, in addition to other more technical details, at least three measurement occasions are required to model growth in a latent growth model for model identification purposes. LGM is an extremely flexible modeling technique allowing for the modeling of various temporal reference points and growth trajectories (see Hancock & Lawrence, 2006, and Lawrence & Hancock, 1998, for more information concerning time-coding and nonlinear growth trajectories in latent growth SEM models). Observed and/or latent predictor variables may be included to help explain the variability in the intercept and slope factors, and these predictor variables may be time variant or time invariant. The flexibility of LGM will also allow for the modeling of equally or unequally spaced measurement occasions. Further, the basic latent growth model may be extended to a multivariate latent growth model in which multiple outcome variables are measured during each measurement wave (see McArdle, 1988, and Sayer & Cumsille, 2001, for more information concerning multivariate latent growth models). Many of the benefits of using the SEM framework for testing LGMs apply also to use of the multilevel modeling framework for modeling growth across time.

Model Fit

An appealing quality of SEM is that model fit may be assessed via a large variety of different criteria. A chi-square (χ^2) test statistic is available and is commonly used as a test of overall model fit. Although numerous fit indices exist, some of the more commonly used ones are the Non-Normed Fit Index (NNFI), which is also called the Tucker-Lewis Index (TLI) (Tucker & Lewis, 1973); the Comparative Fit Index

(CFI) (Bentler, 1990); the Adjusted Goodness-of-Fit Index (AGFI) (Jöreskog & Sörbom, 1984); the Root Mean-Square Error of Approximation (RMSEA) (Steiger & Lind, 1980); and the Standardized Root Mean-Square Residual (SRMR) (Bentler, 1995). In general, a chi-square (χ^2) test statistic that is *not* statistically significant supports overall model fit. Values for the NNFI, TLI, CFI, and AGFI fit indices should be equal to or greater than .90 to support adequate model fit. The RMSEA and the SRMR values typically need to be equal to or less than .05 to denote acceptable model fit.

ADDITIONAL MODELS

Although not detailed here, additional modeling techniques might prove useful to classroom management researchers for handling data structure complexities. For example, all of the clustered data examples described in the "Multilevel Modeling" section involved pure hierarchies in which, for example, lower-level units (e.g., students) were associated with only a single higher-level unit (e.g., school). It is far more likely that there are some lower-level units associated with more than one higher-level clustering unit. For example, mobile students attend more than one school. Clustered data in which multiple lower-level units are associated with each higher-level unit *and* some lower-level units are associated with more than one higher-level unit can be conceptualized as cross-classified data structures. Extensions to the conventional multilevel model—such as the cross-classified or multiple-membership random effects models—can be used to handle these additional data structure complications (see, e.g., Beretvas, 2010; Goldstein, 2010; Hox, 2010; Rasbash & Browne, 2001). Another form of dependency that might be encountered in classroom management data sets results from measuring dyads such as teacher–student, peer, parent–child pairs. Both the multilevel model and SEM models can be adapted to appropriately handle the resulting dependencies (see, e.g., Newsom, 2002).

Mixture Modeling

Mixture modeling is increasingly being utilized by applied researchers. In contrast to multiple-group modeling in which groups are distinguished *a priori* based (most likely) on observable characteristics (e.g., sex, SES), mixture modeling allows researchers to estimate model parameters in different populations that are not distinguishable by directly observed characteristics. These mixture models may consist of path models, CFA models, latent variable models, and latent growth models (see Gagné, 2006, for an accessible introduction to mixture modeling). Mixture modeling has many similarities to exploratory factor analysis (EFA). In EFA, the researcher has a set of correlated variables and hypothesizes that one or more latent factors might explain the correlations among the variables. The researcher then specifies the number of factors to extract that might explain the correlations. After estimating the EFA model, the researcher uses the results and data to interpret (even name) the latent factor(s). With mixture modeling, a researcher might hypothesize that differences (heterogeneity) in a model's parameters are a function of some unobserved (latent) grouping variable. For example, a researcher might hypothesize that some measures of aggressive behavior are more reliable for some groups of children than for others. However, the researcher might not have an explicit measure that corresponds with the grouping (e.g., high vs. low identification with school) and might first wish to use the data to inform whether there might be heterogeneity. As with EFA, the researcher then has to specify the number of latent classes (unobserved groups) that are hypothesized to lie at the root of the differences and then uses the mixture model's parameter estimates and the data to make sense of the results. In our current example, the researcher might find support for a two-latent-class-factor model for measures of aggressive behavior. After investigating the results and further information about the child respondents in the data set, the researcher might be able to understand what characterizes membership in each of the two latent classes.

Multilevel SEM

All of the previously described structural equation models, including mixture models, can be analyzed with the appropriate statistical adjustments incorporated when clustering or nesting is evident in the data. Stapleton (2006) provides a readable chapter describing how to estimate and interpret multilevel SEM models.

Other Model Extensions

The models described in this chapter can be estimated using specialized statistical software, including programs like Mplus, HLM, AMOS, and MLwiN. Given sufficient programming expertise, researchers can write their own code using software such as R and Mathematica or WinBUGS and OpenBUGS for using Bayesian estimation to estimate these same models or complex extensions thereof that do not necessarily require the same parametric assumptions as are typically made.

As improved technology continues to facilitate the gathering of and access to large data sets, researchers in the area of classroom management may need to understand how to handle the methodological complexities that are typically encountered by using some of the models described here. Figure 27.10 contains a flowchart that can help applied researchers with one- or two-level data (i.e., with only up to a single level of clustering in their data) choose the model or modeling technique that might best fit the data. This flowchart offers only a few of the basic models briefly reviewed in this chapter. Some real data sets might incorporate additional challenges and complexities that could not be addressed here. This chapter has provided a brief description of some modeling options, and readers are encouraged to refer to primary statistics sources (see asterisked references) to build their repertoire of statistical tools to maintain and even improve the caliber of applied classroom management research involving larger data sets.

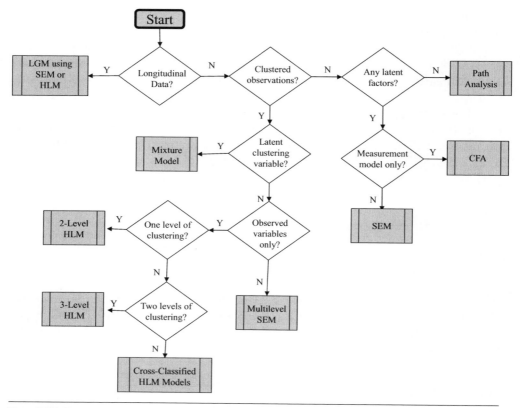

Figure 27.10 Flowchart providing overview of decisions leading to choice of general model or modeling technique for one- or two-level data.

REFERENCES

Seminal Textbook References have been Asterisked

Bentler, P. M. (1990). Comparative fit indexes in structural models. *Psychological Bulletin, 107,* 238–246.

Bentler, P. M. (1995). *EQS structural equations program manual.* Los Angeles: BMDP Statistical Software.

Beretvas, S. N. (2010). Cross-classified and multiple membership random effects models. In J. Hox & J. K. Roberts (Eds.), *The handbook of advanced multilevel analysis* (pp. 313–334). New York: Routledge.

*Bollen, K. A. (1989). *Structural equations with latent variables.* New York: Wiley.

*Brown, T. A. (2006). *Confirmatory factor analysis for applied research.* New York: Guilford.

Davis, J. A. (1985). *The logic of causal order.* Beverly Hills, CA: Sage.

Gagné, P. (2006). Mean and covariance structure mixture models. In G. R. Hancock & R. O. Mueller (Eds.), *Structural equation modeling: A second course* (pp. 197–224). Greenwich, CT: Information Age.

*Goldstein, H. (2010). *Multilevel statistical models* (4th ed.). New York: Hodder Arnold.

*Hancock, G. R., & Lawrence, F. R. (2006). Using latent growth models to evaluate longitudinal change. In G. R. Hancock & R. O. Mueller (Eds.), *Structural equation modeling: A second course* (pp. 171–196). Greenwich, CT: Information Age.

*Hox, J. (2010). *Multilevel analysis: Techniques and Applications* (2nd ed.). New York: Routledge.

Jöreskog, K. G., & Sörbom, D. (1984). *LISREL VI user's guide* (3rd ed.). Mooresville, IN: Scientific Software.

*Kline, R. (2011). *Principles and practice of structural equation modeling* (3rd ed.). New York: Guilford.

Lawrence, F. R., & Hancock, G. R. (1998). Assessing the change over time using latent growth modeling. *Measurement and Evaluation in Counseling and Development, 30*(4), 211–224.

*MacKinnon, D. P. (2008). *Introduction to Statistical Mediation Analysis*. New York: Lawrence Erlbaum Associates.

MacKinnon, D. P., Fritz, M. S., Williams, J., & Lockwood, C. M. (2007). Distribution of the product confidence limits for the indirect effect: Program PRODCLIN. *Behavior Research Methods, 39*, 384–389.

Marsh, H. W., Wen, Z., & Hau, K-T. (2006). Structural equation models of latent interaction and quadratic effects. In G. R. Hancock & R. O. Mueller (Eds.), *Structural equation modeling: A second course* (pp. 225–265). Greenwich, CT: Information Age.

McArdle, J. J. (1988). Dynamic but structural equation modeling of repeated measures data. In J. R. Nesselroade & R. B. Cattell (Eds.), *Handbook of multivariate experimental psychology*, Vol. 2 (pp. 561–614). New York: Plenum Press.

Mulaik, S. A. (2009). *Linear causal modeling with structural equations*. Boca Raton, FL: Chapman & Hall/CRC.

Newsom, J. T. (2002). A multilevel structural equation model for dyadic data. *Structural Equation Modeling, 9*, 431–477.

Pearl, J. (2000). *Causality: models, reasoning, and inference*. New York: Cambridge University Press.

Preacher, K. J., & Hayes, A. F. (2008). Asymptotic and resampling strategies for assessing and comparing indirect effects in multiple mediator models. *Behavior Research Methods, 40*, 879–891.

Rasbash, J. L., & Browne, W. J. (2001). Modeling non-hierarchical structures. In A. H. Leyland and H. Goldstein (Eds.), *Multilevel modeling of health statistics* (pp. 93–105). Chichester, UK: Wiley.

*Raudenbush, S. W., & Bryk, A. S. (2002). *Hierarchical linear models: Applications and data analysis methods*. Thousand Oaks, CA: Sage.

Sayer, A. G., & Cumsille, P. E. (2001). Second-order latent growth models. In L. M. Collins & A. G. Sayer (Eds.), *New methods for the analysis of change* (pp. 179–200). Washington, DC: American Psychological Association.

Schumacker, R. E. & Lomax, R. G. (2004). *A beginner's guide to structural equation modeling*, (2nd ed.). Mahwah, NJ: Erlbaum.

Snijders, T. A. B., & Bosker, R. J. (1999). *Multilevel analysis: An introduction to basic and advanced multilevel modeling*. London: Sage.

Sobel, M. E. (1995). Causal inference in the social and behavioral sciences. In G. Arminger, C. Clogg, & M. E. Sobel (Eds.), *Handbook of Statistical Modeling for the Social and Behavioral Sciences* (pp. 1–35). New York/London: Plenum.

Stapleton, L. M. (2006). Using multilevel structural equation modeling techniques with complex sample data. In G. R. Hancock & R. O. Mueller (Eds.), *Structural equation modeling: A second course* (pp. 345–383). Greenwich, CT: Information Age.

Steiger, J. H., & Lind, J. C. (1980, May). Statistically based tests for the number of common factors. Paper presented at the annual meeting of the Psychometric Society, Iowa City, IA.

Tucker, L. R., & Lewis, C. (1973). A reliability coefficient for maximum likelihood factor analysis. *Psychometrika, 38*, 1–10.

Vandenberg, R. J., & Lance, C. E. (2000). A review and synthesis of the measurement invariance literature: Suggestions, practices, and recommendations for organizational research. *Organizational Research Methods, 3*(1), 4–70.

28

SINGLE-CASE EXPERIMENTAL DESIGNS

Contributions to Classroom Management Research

THOMAS R. KRATOCHWILL, MARGARET R. ALTSCHAEFL,
BRITTANY J. BICE-URBACH, AND JACQUELINE M. KAWA
UNIVERSITY OF WISCONSIN–MADISON

INTRODUCTION

Single-case research designs are increasingly used in intervention research in psychology and education and have special application in experimental research on classroom management procedures and techniques. This methodology allows the researcher to structure an experiment in which replication and/or randomization can be used to document intervention outcomes while ruling out various threats to internal validity. Although methodologies in research on classroom management are diverse (Brophy, 2006), a rather large body of research in classroom management is based on investigations in which the researcher used single-case research design, and, for the most part, this research base emanates from the field of applied behavior analysis (Landrum & Kauffman, 2006). In fact, the *Journal of Applied Behavior Analysis* publishes the highest number of research articles in which single-case design methodology is used, followed by *Behavior Modification* and *Research in Autism Spectrum Disorders* (Shadish & Sullivan, 2011). These journals typically feature intervention research investigations.

In recent years, there has also been strong interest in conducting literature reviews to summarize the research base in various intervention domains including classroom management, and these have often focused on meta-analysis. Moreover, with the increasing reliance on meta-analysis, there have been calls for improving this methodology (see Ahn, Ames, & Meyers, 2012), as well as suggestions for how reviews of prior reviews (dubbed variously "overviews of reviews," "meta-reviews," etc.) can be improved (see Cooper & Koenka, 2012). Although meta-analysis is less frequent in the literature involving single-case research design (in part due to controversy over the best methods to reflect effect size estimates; see Shadish, Rindskopf, & Hedges, 2008), advances in this area are also increasing. Nevertheless, literature reviews, whether based on narrative presentation or formal meta-analysis, require an appraisal of the investigations that enter into the data base.

In the process of conducting literature reviews involving single-case design, various appraisal guidelines have been developed that structure the conceptual and methodological process of synthesis reports. It is beyond the scope of this chapter to review the various single-case design appraisal guidelines (see Smith, 2012, and Wendt & Miller, 2012, for an overview of several guidelines). Among the appraisal guidelines that have been developed and applied recently to some literature reviews in classroom management, the What Works Clearinghouse (WWC) Pilot Single-Case Design *Standards* (see Kratochwill et al., 2010; Kratochwill et al., 2013) have appeared prominent. A special issue of *Remedial and Special Education* was devoted to issues and advances in synthesizing single-case research with a focus on the WWC *Standards* as part of the series (see Maggin & Chafouleas, 2013, and Wolery, 2013, for a critical analysis of the *Standards*).

In this chapter, we review two elements of the WWC *Standards*, the design standards and evidence criteria. Specifically, we review how single-case research designs contribute to the evidence-based classroom management/intervention literature within the context of the WWC *Standards* for single-case intervention research. The primary goals of the chapter are to provide the reader with (1) the conceptual logic of single-case research designs, (2) an overview of traditional design options (including ABAB, multiple-baseline, and alternating treatment designs), and (3) and an overview of some data analysis strategies. Examples of single-case design research from the classroom management literature are also presented to illustrate application of the WWC *Standards*.

THE WWC SINGLE-CASE DESIGN PILOT *STANDARDS*

A large number of authors have presented the foundations of single-case design methodology in texts devoted to the topic (see, for example, some recent texts: Gast, 2010; Kazdin, 2011; Kennedy, 2005; Kratochwill & Levin, 2014). To add to the standards for randomized controlled trial and regression discontinuity designs, the Institute for Education Sciences WWC developed pilot *Standards* for single-case designs. The *Standards* were developed by a panel to provide criteria and appraisal guidelines for reviewing intervention studies in education-related investigations (Kratochwill et al., 2010; Kratochwill et al., 2013). The *Standards* can also be used to design research on classroom management. An important aspect of the WWC *Standards* is that they are divided into two separate elements: *design standards* and *evidence criteria* (see Figure 28.1). This design and evidence distinction is important because a research report may have met a credible design element (design standard), but, following the fair test of the intervention, there may be no evidence for an effect (evidence criteria). We now elaborate on each of these elements of the WWC *Standards*.

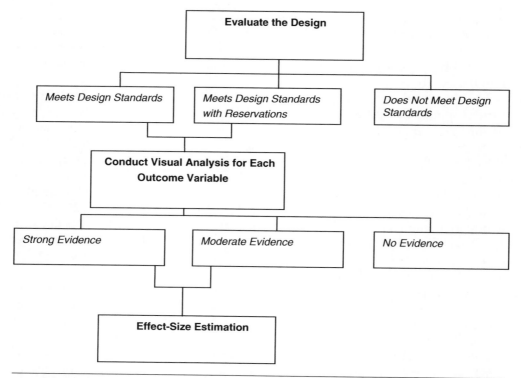

Figure 28.1 Procedure for applying SCD Standards: First evaluate the design, and then evaluate the evidence. (Source: Institute of Education Sciences, 2010.)

Design Criteria

The design criteria, when applied to a single-case design investigation, will result in one of three outcomes: *Meets Design Standards, Meets Design Standards with Reservations*, or *Does Not Meet Design Standards*. Each of these categories and its definition as applied to the three major classes of single-case designs (ABAB designs, multiple-baseline designs, and alternating treatment designs, all to be discussed in this chapter), are illustrated in Table 28.1.

Supplemental criteria have also been developed for multiple-probe designs, variations of alternating treatment designs, and nonconcurrent multiple baseline designs, but these will not be illustrated in this chapter.

Evidence Criteria

Evidence criteria refer to an evaluation of the evidence for an intervention effect and are applied subsequent to application of the design standards; these criteria are illustrated in Table 28.2. An evaluation of the evidence in a single-case design involves determining whether there is a functional relation between the independent variable and dependent variable (as outlined in Table 28.2). In the WWC *Standards*, the

Table 28.1 What Works Clearinghouse Single-Case Design Standards.

In order to *Meet Design Standards*, the following design criteria must be present:

1. The independent variable (i.e., the intervention) must be systematically manipulated (i.e., implemented and/or withdrawn), with the researchers determining when and how changes in independent variable conditions brings about changes in the outcome variable. If this standard is not met, the study *Does Not Meet Design Standards*.

2. Each outcome variable must be measured systematically over time by more than one assessor. Interobserver agreement (for the dependent variable) must be documented on the basis of an accepted psychometric measure of agreement. Although there are more than 20 psychometric measures to represent interassessor agreement (see Berk, 1979; Suen & Ary, 1989), commonly used techniques include percentage agreement (or proportional agreement) and Cohen's kappa coefficient (Hartmann, Barrios, & Wood, 2004). According to Hartmann and colleagues (2004), minimum acceptable values of interassessor agreement range from 0.80 to 0.90 (on average) if measured by percentage agreement and at least 0.60 if measured by Cohen's kappa. Regardless of the statistic, interassessor agreement must be assessed for each case on each outcome variable. A study must report interassessor agreement in all phases. It must also report interassessor agreement for at least 20% of all sessions (total across phases) within a given condition (e.g., baseline, intervention.). If this standard is not met, the study *Does Not Meet Design Standards*. Some additional criteria have been advanced for permanent product dependent variables or those that rely on existing data sources (e.g., multiple choice responses, words spelled correctly).

3. The study must include at least three attempts to demonstrate an intervention effect at three different points in time or with three different phase repetitions (i.e., tiers within MBDs). If this procedure is not followed, the study *Does Not Meet Design Standards*. Examples of designs meeting this standard include ABAB designs; multiple-baseline designs with at least three baseline conditions; alternating and simultaneous treatment designs with at least three data points per condition; changing criterion designs with at least three different criteria; and more complex variants of these designs. Examples of designs not meeting this standard are AB, ABA, and BAB designs.

4. For a phase to qualify as an attempt to demonstrate an effect, the phase must have a minimum of three data points:
   - To *Meet Standards*, a reversal/withdrawal design (i.e., ABAB) must include a minimum of four phases per case with at least 5 data points per phase. To *Meet Standards with Reservations*, a reversal/withdrawal design must include a minimum of four phases per case with 3–4 data points per phase. Any phases based on fewer than 3 data points cannot be used to demonstrate existence of or lack of an effect.
   - To *Meet Standards*, a multiple-baseline design must include a minimum of six phases (i.e., at least three A and three B phases) with at least 5 data points per phase. To *Meet Standards with Reservations*, a multiple-baseline design must include a minimum of six phases within 3–4 data points per phase. Any phases based on fewer than 3 data points cannot be used to demonstrate existence of or lack of an effect. As of this writing, additional criteria have recently been advanced for variants of the multiple-baseline design, including the nonconcurrent multiple-baseline design and the multiple-probe design.
   - An alternating treatment design requires at least five repetitions of the alternating sequence to *Meet Standards*. Designs such as ABABBABAABBA, BCBCBCBCBC, and AABBAABBAABB would qualify, even though randomization or brief functional assessment may lead to only one or two data points in a phase. A design with four repetitions would *Meet Standards with Reservations* and a design with fewer than four repetitions *Does Not Meet Standards*. In the case of the alternating treatment design each treatment comparison is rated separately (e.g., A vs. B, A vs. C, and C vs. B in a three condition design).

Source: Kratochwill et al., 2010. Single-Case Design Technical Documentation retrieved from What Works Clearinghouse website: http://ies.ed.gov/ncee/wwc/pdf/wwc_scd.pdf.

researcher must first verify that there are three demonstrations of an intervention effect (i.e., all three design types require a functional relation in the data). Visual analysis of graphic data is then used to determine if study results meet WWC evidence criteria.

A number of supplementary visual analysis aids can be used to make a judgment of an intervention effect. The interested reader should consult some resources that

Table 28.2 The What Works Clearinghouse Evidence Criteria for Single-Case Design.

For studies that meet standards (with and without reservations), the following rules are used to determine whether the study provides *Strong Evidence, Moderate Evidence,* or *No Evidence* of a causal relation:

- Documenting the consistency of level, trend, and variability within each phase.
- Documenting the immediacy of the effect, the proportion of data overlap between phases, the consistency of the data across phases in order to demonstrate an intervention effect, and comparing the projected and observed patterns of the outcome variable.
- Examining external factors and anomalies (e.g., a sudden change of level within a phase).

Note: If a SCD does not provide at least three demonstrations of an effect, then the study is rated as providing *No Evidence.* If a study provides three demonstrations of an effect and also includes at least one demonstration of a noneffect (this is possible in, for example, a multiple-baseline design with four baselines), the study is rated as providing *Moderate Evidence.* The following characteristics must be considered when identifying a noneffect:

- Data within the baseline phase do not demonstrate a stable enough pattern that can be compared with data patterns obtained in subsequent phases.
- Failure to establish a consistent pattern within a phase (e.g., high variability of outcomes within a phase).
- Difficulty in determining whether the intervention is responsible for a claimed effect as a result of either (1) long latency between introduction of the independent variable and change in the outcome variable or (2) overlap between observed and projected patterns of the outcome variable between baseline and intervention phases.
- Inconsistent patterns across similar phases (e.g., an ABAB design in which the outcome variable data points are high during the first B phase but low during the second B phase).
- Major discrepancies between the projected and observed between-phase patterns of the outcome variable.

Note: When examining the outcomes of a multiple-baseline design, reviewers must also consider the extent to which the time in which a basic effect is initially demonstrated with one series (e.g., first five days following introduction of the intervention for Case 1) is associated with change in the data pattern over the same time frame in the other series of the design (e.g., same five days for Cases 2, 3, and 4). If a basic effect is demonstrated within one series and there is a change in the data patterns in other series, the highest possible design rating is *Moderate Evidence.* If a study has either *Strong Evidence or Moderate Evidence,* then effect size estimation follows.

Source: Kratochwill et al., 2010. Single-Case Design Technical Documentation retrieved from What Works Clearinghouse website: http://ies.ed.gov/ncee/wwc/pdf/wwc_scd.pdf.

provide an overview of visual analysis strategies (see Gast, 2010; Horner & Spaulding, 2010; Kratochwill, Levin, Horner, & Swoboda, in press; Parsonson & Baer, 1978). Figure 28.2 (from Horner & Spaulding, 2010) provides a list of salient steps and variables that are part of the visual analysis process. In the context of using visual analysis, a limitation of the *Standards,* and field of single-case research as a whole is that a standard set of protocols for training and application do not exist. (Kratochwill, Levin, Horner, & Swoboda, 2014). It is for this reason that statistical analysis of single-case data can often provide an important supplement to visual analysis (Kratochwill & Levin, 2014).

APPLICATIONS OF SINGLE-CASE RESEARCH DESIGNS IN CLASSROOM MANAGEMENT RESEARCH

Single-case designs share some important methodological features that appear in intervention research. First, data in single-case designs are collected repeatedly across time and phases of the design. Thus, dependent variables that allow repeated and frequent assessment must be used in these designs (e.g., direct measures of

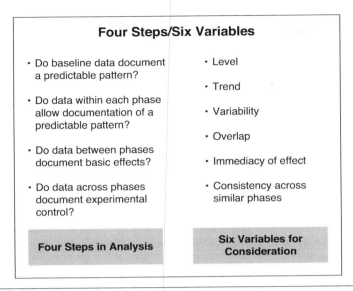

Figure 28.2 The four steps and six variables considered in visual analysis of single-case data. (Source: Horner & Spaulding, 2010. Reproduced with permission.)

student behavior, academic measures). Second, the designs are structured so that the intervention effect is replicated in the design structure. The type of replication varies as a function of the design (e.g., replication can occur across time in within-series ABAB designs or across participants in combined series designs, such as the multiple-baseline design). The number of replications required to establish functional relationships has no formal empirical basis, but the WWC *Standards* require at least three replications across each of the design types.

In this section of the chapter, we discuss three major classes of single-case research design: ABAB, multiple-baseline, and alternating treatment designs. We will also illustrate the basic features of these designs previously noted and apply the WWC *Standards* to some selected examples from the classroom management literature.

Overview of ABAB Designs

The ABAB design involves the repeated implementation and withdrawal of an intervention over phases of the experiment. Thus, a case or unit is exposed to changing conditions in the following sequence: a first baseline phase (A_1), a first intervention phase (B_1), a second baseline phase (A_2), and a second intervention phase (B_2). (Note: Traditionally, baseline phases are represented by an "A" and intervention phases are represented by a "B" and are extended when additional interventions are added to the design such as "C" or "D.") The ABAB design is also called a "withdrawal design" because the intervention is withdrawn from the experimental sequence in the second baseline phase, and it is predicted that data collected on the outcome variable will return to the levels and/or trend documented in the first baseline phase. An experimenter manipulates the introduction and removal of the intervention to provide at least three replications of the intervention effect at each transition between a base-line and intervention phase (as per the current WWC *Standards*). The goal of this design is to document a stable baseline trend in the first baseline phase, an expected change in the outcome variable in the first intervention phase, a return to baseline performance in the second baseline phase, and another expected change in the out-come variable in the second intervention phase. In a successful ABAB design, the initial absence or removal of the intervention would predict a stable data pattern if nothing is added to the environment and the introduction of an intervention would result in a desired change in the outcome variable. Additional phases can be added to this design to increase the complexity, number, and type of phases. For example, an ABAB design could be extended by increasing the number of times the intervention is introduced and removed, leading to an ABABABAB design. The ABAB design can also be used to evaluate the effects of different components of an intervention pack-age, wherein the "C" in a ABABA(B+C)A(B+C) design is used to denote a new phase and added intervention component (Horner et al., 2005; Kazdin, 2011).

ABAB Design Example

Our first classroom management design example comes from Banda and Sokolosky (2012) who used an ABAB design to examine the effect of noncontingent attention (NCA) on the frequency of disruptive talking-out behavior with a seven-year-old student (see Figure 28.3). The intervention took place in a general education class-room of 19 students. The goal was to decrease the number of talk-outs (e.g., calling out to the teacher from the student's desk, asking questions aloud) during whole-group instruction. Using a functional analysis procedure, the function of the student's

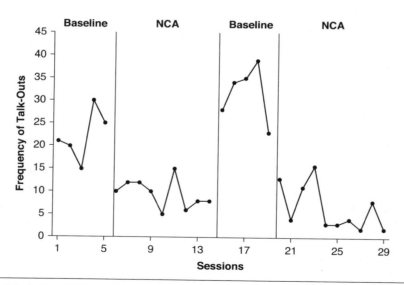

Figure 28.3 Example of an ABAB design that meets *Standards* for WWC design criteria with *Strong Evidence* for a causal relation. (Source: Banda & Sokolosky, 2012.)

behavior was determined to be obtaining teacher attention. The conditions occurred within the language arts class and were 5 minutes in duration. In the baseline, or A phases, the teacher verbally redirected the student in response to the talk-out behavior and provided the student with verbal (e.g., "good work") and tangible (i.e., stickers) reinforcement when a task was completed. In the intervention, or B phases, the teacher implemented an NCA intervention. More specifically, the teacher provided the student with attention (e.g., smile, "Let's keep working.") for the first 20 seconds of the session and for 5 seconds every 20 seconds thereafter for the entire session. The number of talk-outs was recorded throughout the 5-minute sessions.

According to the WWC design criteria, this study *Meets Design Standards*. Banda and Sokolosky (2012) systematically introduced and removed the intervention throughout the investigation (point 1 in Table 28.1). The mean interobserver agreement (IOA) for talk-outs was 96% with a range of 95–97%. The IOA data were collected for 37% of sessions (point 2). There were three opportunities to demonstrate an effect, with the transition in phases from the first baseline phase to the first intervention phase (introduction of the NCA intervention), first intervention phase to the second baseline phase (withdrawal of the NCA intervention), and second baseline phase to the second intervention phase (reintroduction of the intervention) (point 3). Lastly, there were at least five data points in each of the phases (point 4).

For the *WWC evidence criteria,* Banda and Sokolosky (2012) present graphic data (see Figure 28.3) that indicate *Strong Evidence* of an effect (see Table 28.2). Additionally, noneffects do not appear to be present in the data collected in this study. There is consistency in level, trend, and variability in the baseline phases, as well as in the intervention phases. However, the level of the frequency of talk-outs is slightly higher in the second baseline phase than in the first baseline phase. There is a discrepancy between the projected outcomes and observed outcomes in frequency of talk-outs from the first baseline to the first intervention phase, first intervention phase to the second baseline phase, and second baseline phase to the second intervention phase. Nevertheless, there is evidence of sufficient nonoverlapping data among the baseline and intervention phases. The data also show an immediate effect of the NCA intervention on the frequency of talk-outs wherein the behavior decreases in the first session of the first intervention phases, increases in the first session of the second baseline phase, and finally increases in the first session of the second intervention phase. Overall, there is sufficient evidence to suggest a functional relationship between the NCA intervention and decreases in the frequency of talking-out behavior by the target student.

ABAB Design Considerations

The repeated introduction and removal of the intervention in an ABAB design offers three opportunities to demonstrate an effect of the intervention. Yet there are a number of conceptual and methodological factors to consider when evaluating the usability of the design for a particular intervention research protocol. First, the ABAB design is not helpful for documenting functional relationships for interventions whose goal is to change a behavior that is unlikely to be reversed when the intervention is removed. This situation may occur when an intervention targets specific academic or social skills, and it is unrealistic to expect a student to not use a recently acquired problem-solving strategy or skill. Additionally, the experimental control of the design becomes limited when there is not a return to baseline levels and trend in the second baseline phase. Researchers would need to examine the possible reasons for a continued data pattern observed in the first intervention phase, such as unintended continued implementation of all or some components of the intervention and maturation effects. Finally, it is necessary to examine the acceptability and/or ethical implications of removing a potentially successful intervention from the classroom environment. Care must be taken to acknowledge that stakeholders may be uncomfortable temporarily removing the positive outcomes experienced in the first intervention phase. This is especially the case when an intervention target involves the safety of an individual participant or the safety of other individuals in the surrounding environment.

Overview of Multiple-Baseline Designs

The multiple-baseline design (MBD), another type of single-case design that can establish functional relationships, uses multiple AB design series but with a staggered order of intervention implementation across participants, behaviors, or settings. Thus, this research design is useful for investigating changes in performance between baseline and intervention phases across multiple units (Kazdin, 2011). The MBD involves the introduction of an intervention to different baselines series at different points in time. Once a stable baseline has been established across all units, intervention start times are systematically staggered. If intervention effects are observed only after the introduction of the intervention phase, causal inferences can be attributed to the intervention and not to extraneous variables (Kratochwill & Levin, 2010). Intervention effectiveness can then be determined by differences observed between baseline and treatment conditions. For example, if a researcher examines the impact of an intervention on the reduction of a particular problem behavior across five students in a classroom, baseline data collection would begin for all five students, followed by the staggered introduction of the intervention for each student. Data collection would continue for all five students until the last student had completed treatment. The MBD could also be used to evaluate an intervention's effect across multiple classrooms. For instance, if six teachers examine the effectiveness of a bullying intervention in each of their classrooms, all teachers would begin baseline data collection, documenting the number of observed occurrences of bullying over the course of a predetermined time period (e.g., class period/day/week/ etc.). Once a stable baseline had been established, the first teacher would begin intervention implementation. The other participating teachers would continue baseline data collection until it is demonstrated that the intervention had a clear effect on the dependent variable and the baseline for the other participants had remained stable. This process is sometimes called a vertical analysis and is critical to the internal validity of the MBD. Once this condition of the study is established, the next teacher would begin intervention implementation. This sequence would continue until all teachers were implementing the intervention. If changes between baseline and treatment phases were observed in most or all of the classrooms, treatment effects would likely be attributed to the bullying intervention program.

As indicated by the WWC *Standards* design criteria to *Meet Standards*, the MBD must include at least six phases (at least three baseline and three intervention phases), with a minimum of five data points per phase. To *Meet Standards with Reservations*, the MBD must include at least six phases with a minimum of three to four data points per phase (see Table 28.1) (Kratochwill, Hitchcock, Horner, Levin, Odom, Rindskopf, & Shadish, 2010). Consequently, by providing at least three opportunities for replications of observable treatment effects, the researcher allows for the preservation of internal validity. In addition, multiple replications further support the external validity of the study outcomes.

The MBD also provides unique advantages for the classroom management researcher: as noted, there are a number of possible variations across series (i.e., at least across the participants, behaviors, or settings to which the intervention was extended) that can be used to examine intervention effectiveness. In addition, the MBD is useful when treatment withdrawal or a return to baseline is not appropriate or preferable (Kazdin, 2011). Nevertheless, for cases in which prolonged or delayed intervention start times may not be ethical or desired, the MBD may not be a suitable option. Lastly, due to the flexibility of the design, the MBD can provide a more efficient way to collect data in practical settings such as schools and classrooms where time, resources, and rigorous data collection may not be feasible.

Multiple Baseline Design Research Example

Hoff and Ervin (2013) conducted an MBD study in which they examined the effectiveness of a self-management program across three second-grade students exhibiting disruptive behaviors (i.e., violation of rules, defiance, classroom disruption, yelling, aggressive interactions, passive off-task behavior). Throughout baseline and intervention phases, the percentage of intervals that disruptive behaviors occurred (both class-wide and target student data) was recorded. The MBD consisted of a (1) baseline phase (BP); (2) a teacher-directed phase (TD) in which teachers instructed their students on classroom rules, a self-monitoring rating scale, and provided feedback on their performance as a class; and (3) a self-management phase (SM) in which students monitored their own behaviors and class-wide behaviors and then voted on a number in the attempts to match their teacher's classroom rating. For Classroom 3, in an attempt to establish a more stable BP, a return to baseline after the SM was implemented, followed by an additional SM Phase. Figure 28.4 reflects the percentage of intervals in which disruptive behaviors were observed for target students and class-wide.

In considering WWC design standards, this study *Meets Standards* for the MBD because of the systematic manipulation of the independent variable (self-management intervention) (point 1 in Table 28.1) and the systematic measurement of the outcome variable (15-second partial-interval recording system) (point 2 in Table 28.1). IOA data were collected on 21% of all sessions observed, with a mean percentage of

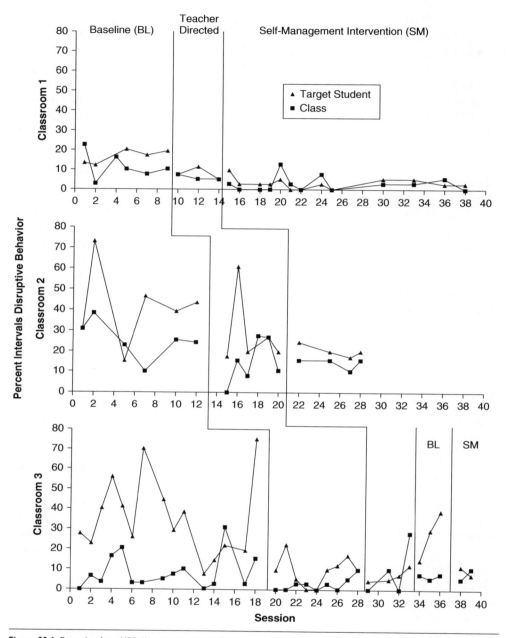

Figure 28.4 Example of an MBD that meets *Standards* for WWC design criteria with *Moderate Evidence* (target students) to *No Evidence* (class students) for a causal relation. (Source: Hoff & Ervin, 2013.)

92.5% in overall agreement. In addition, the study design reflects three phase repetitions for both the target students and classroom observations with all BP and intervention phases (point 3 in Table 28.1), including at least five data points in each of the phases (point 4 in Table 28.1).

When using WWC *Standards* evidence criteria to evaluate the causal relation between the self-management intervention and class-wide self-management program (see Table 28.2), target student data reflect some change in level and trend and a decrease in the variability of disruptive behavior. As reported by the researchers, students' mean occurrences of disruptive behaviors decreased across classrooms, became similar to that of their peers, and were more stable during the intervention phases. Class-wide data appear to reflect slightly less variability in baseline and treatment phases but from our perspective lack marked changes in level or trend across all three classrooms. Data point overlap between BP and intervention phases occurs, and, in our judgment, the target students' outcomes provide only *Moderate Evidence* for an intervention effect and the class-wide outcomes provide *No Evidence* for an intervention effect.

In this study, the researchers also included a return to baseline phase in Classroom 3, thereby adding a within-series design in this condition. This procedure can strengthen the validity of the design if it meets the conditions of a withdrawal design discussed in the previous section. Nevertheless, the within-series design used in this study does not meet design standards because it would involve only a B/A/B design format with fewer than three replications. It is also noteworthy to indicate that their overall MBD involves an order effect in that the SM intervention is always followed by the TD condition.

Multiple-Baseline Design Considerations

The MBD poses a number of potential challenges that should be taken into consideration prior to selecting this design (Kazdin, 2011). For example, it is important to consider the interdependence of baselines. Changes in one baseline, behavior, or individual may inadvertently produce a carryover effect, thereby influencing subsequent baselines and threatening the study's internal validity. Close monitoring of baseline level, trend, and consistency of the data can help identify any unintended or residual effects of an intervention and prevent inaccurate interpretations of intervention effects or noneffects.

MBDs with prolonged baselines can also pose a problem (Kazdin, 2011). Some MBD applications may require the withholding of an intervention for an extended period of time, thereby raising several practical, ethical, and methodological concerns. If an intervention has been shown to work for a particular problem, it may not be ethical or practical to continue collecting baseline data while favorable intervention effects are being observed for other individuals or behaviors. In a practical setting such as a school or classroom, time constraints and a paucity of resources may make prolonged baseline data collection unrealistic. Lastly, methodological issues could include the generalization of baselines as a result of carryover effects or unpredictable changes occurring in performance over time.

Overview of Alternating Treatment Designs

The alternating treatment design (ATD), the final design discussed in this chapter, is valuable for comparing the effectiveness of multiple interventions. ATDs are structured with a rapid alternation of at least two conditions during the intervention phase. The design is intended to demonstrate the level of student performance during contrasting conditions and to determine the most effective intervention for continued use. The ATD is advantageous for treatment comparisons over a short period of time in that it does not require a stable baseline to begin the intervention phase, and it does not require a reversal condition where students would be receiving no intervention (Kazdin, 2011).

A critical component of the ATD is the rapid alternation of conditions (usually two distinct interventions) during the intervention phases. All intervention conditions typically occur during the same day over multiple time periods. The intervention conditions must be counterbalanced or randomized equally across all stimulus conditions (e.g., time of day, setting, teacher) to ensure that changes in student performance are due exclusively to the intervention condition (Kazdin, 2011). This structure allows for the control of confounding variables. Due to the need for counterbalancing across intervention conditions, it is recommended that no more than three conditions or interventions be examined within an ATD. With each addition of an intervention, the number of sessions required to counterbalance (or randomize) the design increases. Thus, the design can become too complex and time-consuming when trying to counterbalance across four or more intervention conditions.

Alternating Treatment Design Example

Faul, Stepensky, and Simonsen (2012) used an ATD to examine the off-task behavior of two middle school students within the general education classroom. The targeted off-task behaviors included getting out of the seat, talking out, disruptive noises, and talking to peers. The school within the study engaged in positive behavior supports (PBS) and wanted to determine whether the students' off-task behaviors would change when prompted about the expectations within the classroom (i.e., Be Respectful, Be Responsible, and Have Pride). Student off-task behavior was observed during two class periods each day, during which students were either prompted about the expectations at the beginning of class or were not prompted about the expectations. During both intervention conditions, the teacher ignored the student's behavior, and no additional prompts were provided.

The baseline phase was conducted over five days. Each day, researchers observed 15 minutes at the beginning of one class period to determine the percent of partial intervals each student was off-task. A coin was flipped to determine which of the two classes the researchers would observe. During the baseline phase, teachers were expected to teach their classes according to their usual routines. After baseline, the treatment phase occurred for eight days. Each day, the researchers observed student behavior in both classes for the first 15 minutes. A coin was flipped daily to determine which class would act as the no-prompt condition and which class would act as the prompt condition. The researchers found that the prompt condition reduced off-task behavior for both students. The data for one of the students is presented in Figure 28.5.

Under the WWC design standards, this study *Meets Evidence Standards*. The baseline phase and both conditions within the intervention phase contain at least five data points (in Table 28.1). The design also allows for no more than two consecutive data points within the same condition prior to alternation to the second condition. Researchers also conducted ample IOA data; more specifically, IOA was examined for 40% of the baseline observations with 99% agreement. Additionally, IOA was conducted on 31% of observations during the intervention phase with 98% agreement.

For the WWC *Standards* evidence criteria, the student data presented in Figure 28.5 demonstrate *Moderate Evidence* for a causal relationship between receiving a prompt and a reduction in off-task behavior. Although there is a slight downward slope for off-task behavior during baseline, this student would appear to remain off-task approximately 55% of the time with no intervention. Once in the intervention phase, the no-prompt condition rather consistently shows an increasing slope of off-task behavior, whereas the prompt condition displays a decreasing slope of off-task behavior. In both conditions during the intervention phase, only one data point does not follow the trend. There is a change in off-task behavior immediately after baseline, with the no-prompt condition increasing the behavior and the prompt condition decreasing the behavior. Finally, one outlier data point overlaps between the baseline, the prompt condition, and the no-prompt condition, demonstrating one noneffect. Overall, the prompt condition is displaying a greater reduction in off-task behavior for this student based on visual analysis of the data.

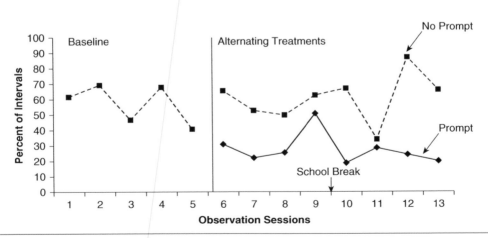

Figure 28.5 Example of an ATD that meets *Standards* for WWC design criteria, with strong evidence for a causal relation. (Source: Faul, Stepensky,& Simonsen, 2012.)

Alternating Treatment Design Considerations

When using an ATD, there are a number of factors to consider. The first consideration is to determine whether the behavior being observed is sensitive enough to demonstrate change over a short period of time. Some behaviors require long periods of time to display meaningful change (e.g., acquiring a complex skill). The ATD would typically not be appropriate for interventions that will not show behavioral changes in the short term (Kazdin, 2011).

A second consideration relates to whether the behavior occurs at a rate that would allow the researcher to demonstrate observable differences between intervention conditions. It may not be possible to examine low-frequency and high-frequency behaviors using an ATD (Kazdin, 2011). A low-frequency behavior may not be displayed at a rate that allows an observable difference between the two interventions. For example, if a student engages in a behavior only once a week, there would not be enough reliable data to know whether a change in behavior was due to one of the interventions examined. Similarly, and in contrast, if a behavior occurs at a very high frequency, it may be difficult to observe a meaningful difference between the two intervention conditions.

A third consideration relates to whether the interventions used within the design are different enough for the participant to discriminate between or among them. With the rapid shift between interventions, usually within the same day, a researcher needs to determine whether the participant will be able to differentiate between or respond differently to the intervention conditions provided (Kazdin, 2011). If the conditions are too similar, the participant may perform or respond in the same manner under both conditions, thereby not allowing the researcher to determine which intervention is the most effective option.

A final consideration is whether one intervention condition will create spillover or carryover effects during the other intervention conditions. With the rapid alternation of conditions, the impact of the first condition may lead to added behavioral changes during subsequent intervention conditions (Kazdin, 2011). If this factor occurs, the researcher would not be able to identify whether a single intervention was effective or it was the combination of multiple interventions on the same day. In a similar light, one intervention could lead to a reduction in the effectiveness of a different intervention. Due to the potential positive or negative carryover effects, it is important to consider whether the interventions used within an ATD will be able to be tested independently.

REVIEW APPLICATIONS OF SINGLE-CASE RESEARCH DESIGNS IN CLASSROOM MANAGEMENT RESEARCH

As noted previously, the WWC *Standards* were developed to assist with reviews of the intervention research literature involving single-case designs. Although there have been reviews of the classroom management literature on various topics (see numerous examples in the *Handbook of Classroom Management*, Evertson & Weinstein, 2006), due to the recent availability of the WWC *Standards*, only a few formal reviews have been conducted with the *Standards* criteria applied to the literature base that involves single-case designs.

The WWC Single-Case Design Panel proposed a 5-3-20 criterion for a literature review that results in an "intervention report." Ultimately, in this context, the goal would be to designate a particular classroom intervention or management program as an evidence-based practice (see also Horner & Spaulding, 2010). The following three criteria were presented in the *Standards*:

1. A minimum of five (5) Single-Case Design studies examine the intervention with a design that either *meets evidence standards* or *meets evidence standard with reservations.*
2. The studies are conducted by at least three (3) research teams with no overlapping authorship at three different institutions.
3. The combined number of cases (i.e., participants, classrooms, etc.) totals at least 20.

Next we feature two example reviews of classroom management research in which the WWC *Standards* were used in appraisal of single-case design intervention research.

Token Economy Classroom Management Research

Token economies have been applied in classroom management quite frequently with research literature dating back many years. Maggin, Chafouleas, Goddard, and Johnson (2011) reviewed the literature on token economies as a classroom management "tool" while adopting the WWC *Standards* as a framework for evaluation of this literature. Out of a total of 834 studies, they found 67 where the student was the unit of analysis and 23 in which the classroom was the unit of analysis. After applying the WWC design standards and evidence criteria, they concluded that token economies *cannot* be regarded as an evidence-based practice. They reported that methodological quality is the major limitation of the literature base, including problems with treatment integrity, interobserver agreement measures, quality of research designs (not meeting replication standards), and limitations in the social validity of the reported findings.

Self-Management Research

Maggin, Briesch, and Chafouleas (2013) applied the WWC *Standards* to single-case design intervention studies that were part of a previous review of the self-management literature between 1988 and 2008 (Briesch & Chafouleas, 2009). Their results, when applying the design standards, suggested that approximately two-thirds of the studies met standards with or without reservations ($n = 68$; 64%); the primary reason for not meeting design standards was the failure of the investigator to schedule three replications of the intervention in the design. With regard to the evidence criteria, Maggin and his colleagues reported that the majority of researchers met evidence criteria ($n = 55$; 81%) based on a visual analysis protocol that they developed for the review. The authors also reported effect sizes based on the percentage of nonoverlapping data and generalized least squares regression; based on the 5-3-20 criterion, they designated self-management interventions as an evidence-based practice for classroom management.

FINAL CONSIDERATIONS

In this chapter, we provided an overview of single-case intervention research designs, including ABAB, MBD, and ATDs. We also featured the WWC *Standards* as a framework for appraisal guidelines of single-case design intervention studies conducted in the area of classroom management research. The *Standards* require that the investigator assess design standards and evidence criteria (see Tables 28.1 and 28.2). The use of randomization in the design structure is an option in single-case intervention research (see Kratochwill & Levin, 2010) and presents a number of options for application of randomization tests to add to evidence criteria.

Two illustrative reviews were featured in the area of classroom management interventions in which the design standards and evidence criteria were applied to an existing literature base (Maggin, Chafouleas, Goddard, & Johnson, 2011; Maggin, Briesch, & Chafouleas, 2013). Based on the application of the *Standards* in these two reviews of classroom management research, a few considerations can be extended to the classroom management literature and future research. First of all, in contrast to research reviews based on group randomized controlled trials, there is no agreement on effect size estimates for single-case designs (see Shadish, Rindskopf, & Hedges, 2008; Kratochwill et al., 2013 for further information on this issue). Thus, the effect size metrics reported by Maggin and associates in both reviews must be interpreted with caution. The future will likely see growing consensus on what effect sizes are acceptable and how effect sizes in single-case design can be combined with those from randomized controlled trial group design research. This is an important consideration because the goal would be to designate a particular procedure or practice as evidence-based by the 5-3-20 criterion and combine single-case and group research.

Second, although effect size estimates can allow researchers to describe the effect of an intervention (and compare effects across studies), it does not address the social validity of the outcomes. For example, a researcher may meet design standards and evidence criteria in a particular study, but the determination of the clinical significance of the outcomes are usually determined by care providers in the applied setting (e.g., teachers, parents). The WWC *Standards* do not address a metric for the importance or clinical significance of the outcomes of research.

Third, as noted by Maggin and colleagues (2013) in their discussion of the WWC *Standards*, there is no formal agreed-upon protocol for conducting a visual analysis. To address this issue, Maggin and his associates presented a protocol that could be used or adapted in future research in which the investigator is interested in applying the *Standards* for the appraisal process. Nevertheless, the reviews conducted by the WWC are done with a protocol for their own use but eventually could be made available for researchers using the *Standards*.

Finally, we wish to note that some of the applications of the WWC *Standards* might be made in cases where the classroom is the unit of analysis (as was the case in some of the studies we featured as examples and those in the two literature reviews). In such cases, there are additional internal validity considerations over and above those when a single participant is the unit of analysis in the design (e.g., attrition, differential response to the intervention among members of the group). These issues are currently not addressed in the *Standards*.

Classroom management research includes a mix of descriptive, correlational, and experimental research that investigators have used to support practices in applied educational and clinical settings. Among the options for developing the scientific basis for practice, experimental research is generally the best option (Levin & Kratochwill, 2013). Nevertheless, many classroom practices continue without an evidence base to support their application. The reasons for this circumstance are many, but two are emphasized here. First, classroom management research has traditionally focused on documenting what works in terms of a management practice. Traditional group and single-case experimental research paradigms have been effective for investigators to document experimentally an effective practice or procedure, and the number of such programs is growing. But investigators have increasingly realized that research must also document key elements of the *implementation* of a practice. This development includes a focus on implementation science and is critical to advancing effective practices in schools because it includes analysis of such variables as barriers to implementation, fidelity and core components of a practice, and consideration of diverse students and settings (Forman et al., 2013). Implementation science holds great promise to actually get evidence-based practices in place where they are most needed: in schools and classrooms.

Second, although implementation science can be helpful to understand (and perhaps overcome) the barriers to adoption and implementation of evidence-based classroom management practices, there will always be factors that must be addressed on a local level that influence use of the evidence base. As an example, interpretation of what research actually consists of despite what might be consensus in the scientific community will influence what is acceptable at the local level (Asen, Gurke, Solomon, Conners, & Gumm, 2011). Asen and his colleagues compared the definition of research in the No Child Left Behind Act (NCLB) with those definitions of three school districts/school boards in Wisconsin. They found that the narrow and specific definition of research in NCLB was given "an expansive meaning" in which school professionals combined scientific research with other types of evidence, some of which was based on the local community needs and values. Often, this hybrid of information was not anywhere near the scientific evidence base. The future of classroom management research depends on careful study of these local and contextual factors that may influence selection, adoption, and implementation of evidence-base practices.

REFERENCES

Ahn, S., Ames, A. J., & Myers, N. D. (2012). A review of meta-analyses in education: Methodological strengths and weaknesses. *Review of Educational Research, 82*, 436–476.

Asen, R., Gurke, D., Solomon, R., Connors, P. and Gumm, E. (2011). "The research says": Definitions and uses of a key policy term in federal law and local school board deliberations. *Argumentation and Advocacy, 47*, 195–213.

Banda, D. R., & Sokolosky, S. (2012). Effectiveness of noncontingent attention to decrease attention-maintained disruptive behaviors in the general education classroom. *Child & Family Behavior Therapy, 34*, 130–140.

Berk, R. A. (1979). Generalizability of behavioral observations: A clarification of interobserver agreement and interobserver reliability. *American Journal of Mental Deficiency, 83*, 460–472.

Briesch, A. M., & Chafouleas, S. M. (2009). Review and analysis of literature on self-management interventions to promote appropriate classroom behavior. *School Psychology Review, 24*, 106–118.

Brophy, J. (2006). History of research on classroom management. In C. M. Everson & C. S. Weinstein (Eds.), *Handbook of classroom management: Research, practice, and contemporary issues* (pp. 17–43). Mahwah, NJ: Erlbaum.

Cooper, H., & Koenka, A. C. (2012). The overview of reviews: Unique challenges and opportunities when research syntheses are the principal elements of new integrative scholarship. *American Psychologist, 67*, 446–462.

Evertson, C. M., & Weinstein, C. S. (2006) (Eds.). *Handbook of classroom management: Research, practice, and contemporary issues.* Mahwah, NJ: Erlbaum.

Faul, A., Stepensky, K., & Simonsen, B. (2012). The effects of prompting appropriate behavior on the off-task behavior of two middle school students. *Journal of Positive Behavior Interventions, 14*, 47–55.

Forman, S. G., Codding, R. S., Reddy, L. A., Sanetti, L. M. H., Shapiro, E. S., Gonzales, J. E., Rosenfield, S. A., & Stobier, K. C. (2013). Implementation science and school psychology. *School Psychology Quarterly, 28*, 77–100.

Gast, D. L. (2010). *Single subject research methodology in behavioral sciences.* New York: Routledge.

Hartmann, D. P., Barrios, B. A., & Wood, D. D. (2004). Principles of behavioral observation. In S. N. Haynes and E. M. Hieby (Eds.), *Comprehensive handbook of psychological assessment. Vol. 3: Behavioral assessment* (pp. 108–127). New York: John Wiley & Sons.

Hoff, K. E., & Ervin, R. A. (2013). Extending self-management strategies: The use of a classwide approach. *Psychology in the Schools, 30*, 151–164.

Horner, R. H., Carr, E. G., Halle, J., McGee, G., Odom, S., & Wolery, M. (2005). The use of single subject research to identify evidence-based practice in special education. *Exceptional Children, 71*, 165–179.

Horner, R., & Spaulding, S. (2010). Single-case research designs. In N. J. Salkind (Ed.), *Encyclopedia of Research Design* (pp. 1386–1394). Thousand Oaks, CA: Sage.

Institute of Education Sciences. (2010). What Works Clearinghouse Single-Case Design Technical Documentation. Retrieved http://ies.ed.gov/ncee/wwc/pdf/wwc_scd.pdf.

Kazdin, A. (2011). *Single-case research designs: Methods for clinical and applied settings* (2nd ed.). Oxford/New York: Oxford University Press.

Kennedy, C. H. (2005). *Single-case designs for educational research.* Boston: Allyn and Bacon.

Kratochwill, T. R., Hitchcock, J., Horner, R. H., Levin, J. R., Odom, S. L., Rindskopf, D. M & Shadish, W. R. (2010). Single-case designs technical documentation. Retrieved from What Works Clearinghouse website: http://ies.ed.gov/ncee/wwc/pdf/wwc_scd.pdf.

Kratochwill, T. R., Hitchcock, J., Horner, R. H., Levin J. R., Odom, S. L., Rindskopf, D. M., Shadish, W. R. (2013). Single-case intervention design standards. *Remedial and Special Education, 34*, 26–38.

Kratochwill, T. R., & Levin, J. R. (2010). Enhancing the scientific credibility of single-case intervention research: Randomization to the rescue. *Psychological Methods, 15*, 124–144.

Kratochwill, T. R., & Levin, J. R. (2014). *Single-case intervention research: Methodological and data-analysis advances.* Washington, DC: American Psychological Association.

Kratochwill, T. R., Levin, J. R., Horner, R. H., & Swoboda, C. M. (2014). Visual analysis of single-case intervention research: Conceptual and methodological considerations. In T. R. Kratochwill & J. R. Levin (Eds.), *Single-case intervention research: Methodological and data-analysis advances.* Washington, DC: American Psychological Association.

Landrum, T. J., & Kauffman, J. M. (2006). Behavioral approaches to classroom management. In C. M. Everson and C. S. Weinstein (Eds.), *Handbook of classroom management: Research, practice, and contemporary issues* (pp. 47–71). Mahwah, NJ: Erlbaum.

Levin, J. R., & Kratochwill, T. R. (2013). Educational/psychological intervention research circa 2012. In I. B. Weiner (Series Ed.) & W. M. Reynolds & G. E. Miller (Vol. Eds.), *Handbook of psychology,* Vol. 7 (2nd ed.). Educational psychology (pp. 465–492). New York: Wiley.

Maggin, D. M., Briesch, A. M., & Chafouleas, S. M. (2013). An application of the What Works Clearinghouse *Standards* for evaluating single-subject research: Synthesis of the self-management literature base. *Remedial and Special Education, 34*, 44–58.

Maggin, D. M., & Chafouleas, S. M. (2013). Introduction to the special series: Issues and advances of synthesizing single-case research. *Remedial and Special Education, 34*, 3–8.

Maggin, D. M., Chafouleas, S. M., Goddard, K. M., & Johnson, A. H. (2011). A systematic evaluation of token economies as a classroom management tool for students with challenging behavior. *Journal of School Psychology, 49*, 529–554.

Parsonson, B., & Baer, D. (1978). The analysis and presentation of graphic data. In T. Kratochwill (Ed.), *Single subject research* (pp. 101–166). New York: Academic Press.

Shadish, W. R., Rindskopf, D. M., & Hedges, L. V. (2008). The state of the science in the meta analysis of single-case experimental designs. *Evidence-Based Communication Assessment and Intervention, 3*, 188–196.

Shadish, W. R. & Sullivan, K. J. (2011). Characteristics of single-case designs used to assess intervention effects in 2008. *Behavior Research Methods, 43*(4), 971–980. doi: 10.3758/s13428-011-0111.

Smith, J. D. (2012). Single-Case Experimental Designs: A Systematic Review of Published, Research and Recommendations for Researchers and Reviewers. *Psychological Methods, 17*, 510–550.

Suen, H. K. & Ary, D. (1989). *Analyzing quantitative behavioral observation*. Hillsdale, NJ: Erlbaum.

Wendt, O., & Miller, B. (2012). Quality appraisal of single-subject experimental designs: An overview and comparison of different appraisal tools. *Education and Treatment of Children, 35*, 235–268.

Wolery, M. (2013). A commentary: Single-case design technical document of the What Works Clearinghouse. *Remedial and Special Education, 43*, 39–43.

LIST OF CONTRIBUTORS

Margaret R. Altschaefl (maltschaefl@gmail.com) is a graduate student in the School Psychology Program at the University of Wisconsin–Madison. Her research interests include problem-solving consultation, home–school partnerships, multitiered service delivery, and intervention implementation and treatment integrity. In addition, she is interested in the applications of single-case design methodology in school settings.

Jonathan T. Bartels (jbartels2@uaa.alaska.edu) is an assistant professor in the College of Education at The University of Alaska, Anchorage, where he teaches courses in secondary education, 21st-century literacies, and research methods. His areas of scholarly interests include English education, new literacies, and classroom technologies.

George G. Bear (gbear@udel.edu) is professor of school psychology at the University of Delaware. His research focuses on school climate, school discipline, and children's social, emotional, and development. Among his many publications is the book entitled *School Discipline and Self-Discipline: A Practical Guide to Promoting Prosocial Behavior* (2010).

S. Natasha Beretvas (tasha.beretvas@austin.utexas.edu) is a professor in the Quantitative Methods Program, Educational Psychology Department, The University of Texas at Austin. Her research interests include evaluation and innovative application of statistical models used in educational and social science research with a focus on extensions to the conventional multilevel model for handling student mobility and other data structure complexities.

Brittany J. Bice-Urbach (bjbice@wisc.edu) is a graduate student in the School Psychology Program at the University of Wisconsin–Madison. Her research interests include incorporating technology into consultation services and evidence-based interventions for social-emotional and behavioral concerns.

Cheryl Mason Bolick (cbolick@unc.edu) is an associate professor in the School of Education at The University of North Carolina at Chapel Hill. Her pedagogical interests include elementary-level social studies methods and social studies and technology, and her areas of scholarly concentration comprise social studies teacher education and the integration of technology into the social studies curriculum.

Mieke Brekelmans (m.brekelmans@uu.nl) is professor of education in the Faculty of Social and Behavioral Sciences, Department of Education, Utrecht University. She is director of the Research Centre Learning in Interaction and the Undergraduate Program in Educational Sciences. Her main research interest is the study of classroom social climate.

Perry den Brok (p.j.d.brok@tue.nl) is professor and research director of the Eindhoven School of Education at Eindhoven University of Technology. His research deals with the link between teacher professional learning and teacher performance, teacher education, classroom learning environments, and teacher–student interpersonal relationships, especially within the context of science education.

Robert V. Bullough Jr. (bob_bullough@byu.edu) is emeritus professor of educational studies, University of Utah. He is also professor of teacher education and associate director of the Center for the Improvement of Teacher Education and Schooling (CITES) in the McKay School of Education and a fellow in the Humanities Center, Brigham Young University. He has published widely in education and teacher education, including a series of studies of Head Start and Head Start teacher well-being. His most recent book is *Adam's Fall*.

James L. Byo (jbyo@lsu.edu) is the Carl Prince Matthies Professor of Music Education and a University Distinguished Teaching Professor at Louisiana State University. He has published and presented research extensively in music teacher effectiveness and aural perception in music. He is currently serving on the executive committee of the Society for Research in Music Education.

Gwendolyn Cartledge (cartledge.1@osu.edu) is professor emeritus at The Ohio State University, College of Education and Human Ecology. Her professional research and writing have centered on the social and academic skills of individuals with and without disabilities. Currently she is the principal investigator on an IES grant to develop a reading fluency intervention.

Donetta Cothran (dcothran@indiana.edu) is a professor in the School of Public Health at Indiana University. Her research focuses on participant perspectives of the educational experience, particularly curricular reform. She is a fellow of the National Academy of Kinesiology and the Research Consortium of the American Alliance for Health, Physical Education, and Recreation.

Maurice J. Elias (rutgersmje@aol.com) is professor, Psychology Department, Rutgers University. His interests include students' emotional intelligence, school success, and social-emotional and character development. A recipient of the Sanford McDonnell Award for Lifetime Achievement in Character Education, among

Dr. Elias' numerous books is *Talking Treasure: Stories to Help Build Emotional Intelligence and Resilience in Young Children.*

Edmund T. Emmer (emmer@austin.utexas.edu) is a professor of educational psychology at the University of Texas at Austin. His research has examined the identification of effective teaching and classroom management practices, the role of emotion in teaching, and programs for management and discipline. He has also studied cooperative learning approaches, teacher efficacy and its relationship with classroom management factors, and research methodology.

Dorothy L. Espelage (espelage@illinois.edu) is Edward William Gutgsell & Jane Marr Gutgsell Endowed Professor and Hardie Scholar of Education, in the Department of Educational Psychology at the University of Illinois, Urbana–Champaign. She has conducted research on bullying, homophobic teasing, sexual harassment, and dating violence for the last 20 years and is author of 100 peer-reviewed journal articles and 25 chapters.

Collette Fischer (cfischer4@wisc.edu) is a doctoral student in the University of Wisconsin–Madison's School Psychology Program. She works as a teaching assistant in a professional master's degree program for teachers. Her main area of interest is interdisciplinary early childhood prevention and intervention.

Maribeth Gettinger (mgetting@wisc.edu) is a professor in the Department of Educational Psychology, University of Wisconsin–Madison. Her research focuses on the development and evaluation of class-wide interventions to promote social-emotional and early literacy skills among high-risk preschoolers. She consults with early childhood programs throughout Wisconsin to implement Positive Behavior Support approaches and evidence-based literacy programs.

Robyn M. Gillies (r.gillies@uq.edu.au) is professor of education at The University of Queensland, Brisbane, Australia. She has worked extensively in primary and secondary schools to help teachers to embed student-centered pedagogical practices into their curricula. Her research interests include cooperative learning, small-group interactions, inquiry-based learning, classroom discourses, and classroom processes related to learning outcomes.

Kathleen V. Hoover-Dempsey (kathy.hoover-dempsey@vanderbilt.edu) is Professor Emerita, Vanderbilt University. Her research has focused on parents' engagement in schooling and the influence of their involvement on students' learning success. Her model has been examined and adapted by local programs concerned with increasing family–school relationships in support of students' success.

Arthur M. Horne (ahorne@uga.edu) is Dean Emeritus and Distinguished Research Professor of the University of Georgia. His career has focused on developing safe and effective families, schools, and community services, and he has worked extensively on violence prevention programs at the local, state, and national level.

Jacqueline M. Kawa (jmflint@wisc.edu) is a PhD student in school psychology at the University of Wisconsin–Madison. Her research interests include evidence-based interventions and cultural considerations, culturally responsive mental health care within school settings, treatment of anxiety disorders such as post-traumatic stress disorder, and single-case research.

Thomas R. Kratochwill (tomkat@education.wisc.edu) is Sears-Bascom Professor at the University of Wisconsin–Madison. His research interests include problem-solving consultation, transportability of evidence-based interventions to practice, children's anxiety disorders, and single-case research design and data analysis.

Pamela Kulinna (p.kulinna@asu.edu) is a professor in the Mary Lou Fulton Teachers College at Arizona State University. She studies teaching, learning, and curricula in physical education, along with comprehensive school health programming. She is a fellow of the National Academy of Kinesiology and the Research Consortium of the American Alliance for Health, Physical Education, and Recreation.

Kathleen Lynne Lane (Kathleen.Lane@ku.edu) is a professor in the Department of Special Education at the University of Kansas. Her research interests focus on school-based interventions (academic and behavioral) with students at risk for emotional and behavioral disorders. She has designed, implemented, and evaluated comprehensive, integrated, three-tiered models of prevention in elementary, middle, and high school settings to prevent the development of learning and behavior challenges and to respond to existing behavioral challenges.

Ramon Lewis (rlewis@latrobe.edu.au) is a professor in the Faculty of Education at Latrobe University. He has published extensively in the field of classroom management and explores the relationship between theory and practice by conducting and evaluating the effect of professional development programs for teachers in schools.

Timothy J. Lewis (LewisTJ@missouri.edu) is professor and chair in the Department of Special Education at the University of Missouri. He is also codirector of the Office of Special Education Program Center for Positive Behavioral Interventions and Support, codirector of the Institute for Education Sciences, Center for Adolescent Research in Schools, and director of the University of Missouri Center for School-Wide Positive Behavior Support. His research focuses on school-wide positive behavior supports, social skill instruction, and functional behavioral assessment.

Sally Lineback (sallylineback@gmail.com) is a doctoral student in counseling psychology at the University of Texas at Austin. Before attending graduate school, she taught kindergarten in a rural public school and worked for an educational non-profit. She is continuing her work on the mental health issues of teachers.

Ya-yu Lo (ylo1@uncc.edu) is an Associate professor in the Department of Special Education and Child Development at the University of North Carolina at Charlotte.

Her research interests include social skill instruction, effective academic and behavioral interventions, urban students with culturally and linguistically diverse backgrounds, functional behavioral assessments, and positive behavior support.

Tim Mainhard (M.T.Mainhard@uu.nl) is an assistant professor of education in the Department of Education at Utrecht University. His research interests include social relations in educational settings and how affective and cognitive regulation affects learning.

Christopher J. McCarthy (cjmccarthy@austin.utexas.edu) is a professor in the Department of Educational Psychology at the University of Texas Austin. His area of specialization is counseling psychology. Dr. McCarthy's research interests include examining ways to promote health and coping among K–12 teachers, group counseling, and career development.

Mary McCaslin (mccaslin@email.arizona.edu) is professor of educational psychology and codirector of the Center for Research on Classrooms at the University of Arizona. Her scholarship focuses on the relationships among cultural, social, and personal sources of influence that co-regulate student adaptive learning, motivational dynamics, and emergent identity.

Holly Mariah Menzies (hmenzie@exchange.calstatela.edu) is an associate professor in the Charter College of Education at California State University, Los Angeles, and the program coordinator in mild-moderate disabilities in the Division of Special Education and Counseling. She worked as both a general educator and special educator for over 10 years and has provided staff development in the areas of assessment, language arts, and SWPBS. Her research interests are inclusive education and school-based interventions.

Jason Miller (miller.j33@gmail.com) is a doctoral candidate in special education at the University of Maryland and a special education teacher in Anne Arundel County Public Schools. His research interests include identifying supports for teaching mathematics to students with learning disabilities and teaching social skills to students with behavior problems.

H. Richard Milner IV (rmilner@pitt.edu) is Helen Faison Professor of Urban Education, Professor of Education and Director of the Center for Urban Education at the University of Pittsburgh. His interests are urban education, teacher education, African American literature, and the sociology of education. His most recent books are *Start Where You Are But Don't Stay There: Understanding Diversity, Opportunity Gaps, and Teaching in Today's Classrooms* and *Handbook of Urban Education* (coedited with Kofi Lomotey). Currently, he is editor-in-chief of *Urban Education.*

Barbara S. Mitchell (MitchellBS@missouri.edu) is an adjunct assistant professor in the Department of Special Education and Tier II/III consultant in the University of

Missouri Center for School-Wide Positive Behavior Support. Her research interests include Tier II supports within SWPBS and supports for students with mental health concerns.

Marcia L. Montague (mmontague@tamu.edu) is an adjunct assistant professor in the Special Education Program within the Educational Psychology Department at Texas A&M University. She has taught undergraduate and graduate-level teacher preparation coursework, which includes a focus on classroom management and teacher effectiveness.

Paul Montuoro (paul.montuoro@hotmail.com) is a doctoral student at La Trobe University in Melbourne. His thesis focuses on identifying the combined causes of aggressive teacher responding to perceived acts of student misbehavior. His research interests also include the role of attachment theory in the teacher–student relationship and the application of phenomenological research in education.

Lori Newcomer (NewcomerL@missouri.edu) is associate research professor in the Department of Educational, Counseling and School Psychology, University of Missouri. Her research interests include prevention, SWPBS, and instructional supports.

Malinda Leigh Pennington (mlpennin@ncsu.edu) is a PhD candidate in the Department of Curriculum, Instruction and Counselor Education, North Carolina State University. Her areas of interest include supports for students with autism in general education and teacher preparation to meet the needs of students with autism spectrum disorders in all educational environments.

Katherine A. Raczynski (krac@uga.edu) is the director of the Safe and Welcoming Schools project at the University of Georgia. Much of her research has been in the area of bullying and peer victimization, with a particular emphasis on early prevention and student-led efforts.

M. Karega Rausch (marausch@indiana.edu) is a research associate with the Equity Project at the Center for Evaluation and Education Policy and PhD candidate, both at Indiana University. Rausch founded the Indianapolis affiliate of an education advocacy nonprofit, and his research interests center on the creation of more effective and equitable schools, particularly for marginalized students.

Johnmarshall Reeve (reeve@korea.ac.kr) is a professor in the Department of Education at Korea University in Seoul, South Korea. His research interests include all aspects of human motivation and emotion, with a particular emphasis on teachers' motivating styles and students' motivation and engagement during learning activities. He is widely published in these areas and is editor of the journal *Motivation and Emotion*.

Jenson Reiser (jenson.reiser@gmail.com) is a doctoral student in counseling psychology at the University of Texas at Austin. Before attending graduate school, she taught first grade in an urban public school and worked for an educational non-profit. She also trains incoming teachers on classroom management, curriculum, and instruction.

Michael Richardson (michael_richardson@byu.edu) is an assistant professor of teacher education at Brigham Young University. He teaches adolescent development and classroom management. His research and scholarly interests include understanding and improving social and emotional well-being for adolescent students and, more broadly, moral development and education.

Porsha Robinson-Ervin (robinsonep1@nku.edu) is an assistant professor in the College of Education at Northern Kentucky University. Her research interests include teaching social skills and the education of students with emotional and behavior disorders.

Michael Rozalski (rozalski@binghampton.edu) is an associate professor in the Graduate School of Education at Binghamton University. His research interests include classroom and school-wide supports, including alternatives to aversive procedures like seclusion and timeout, and legal issues related to students with disabilities.

Edward J. Sabornie (edward_sabornie@ncsu.edu) is professor of special education in the Department of Curriculum, Instruction, and Counselor Education at NC State University. His areas of interest and scholarship include applied behavior analysis and classroom management, social status of students with disabilities in inclusive classrooms, and secondary-level instruction and behavioral interventions for students with high-incidence disabilities.

Yoni Schwab (dr.yschwab@gmail.com) is the founding assistant head of school of the Shefa School (a Jewish day school for children with language-based learning disabilities) and an adjunct clinical supervisor at Ferkauf Graduate School of Yeshiva University. He publishes and lectures on social-emotional learning, behavior management, and effective interventions for children with learning disabilities.

Brandi Simonsen (brandi.simonsen@uconn.edu) is associate professor in special education in the Neag School of Education at the University of Connecticut. Her interests are school-wide positive behavior support, applied behavior analysis, behavior and classroom management, school discipline, and education of students with behavior disorders in alternative settings.

Wendy L. Sims (simsw@missouri.edu) is professor, Director of Music Education, and Director of Teacher Education at the University of Missouri. She has published and presented research extensively on aspects of children's musical development and effective instruction in early childhood and elementary music. She is currently serving as the editor of the *Journal of Research in Music Education*.

Russell J. Skiba (skiba@indiana.edu) is a professor in the school psychology program at Indiana University. His research is in the areas of disproportionality, school discipline, and school violence. He directs the Equity Project, a consortium of federal, state, and foundation-funded grants, providing evidence to practitioners and policy makers in the areas of school violence, zero tolerance, and equity in education.

Valerie A. Sotardi (vsotardi@email.arizona.edu) is a recent graduate of the doctoral program in educational psychology at the University of Arizona in Tucson. Her interests include the study of everyday stress and coping development, and motivation/learning outcomes of children in public schools and lower-income communities.

Rose E. Stafford (rose.stafford@austin.utexas.edu) is a doctoral student in the Quantitative Methods program, Educational Psychology Department, The University of Texas at Austin. Her research interests include multilevel modeling, structural equation modeling, and growth curve modeling and their application in education, social, and developmental studies.

Laura M. Stough (lstough@tamu.edu) is associate professor of educational psychology and the coordinator of the Learning Sciences Program at Texas A&M University. She conducts research on effective classroom practices of special educators and within the interdisciplinary area of disability studies.

George Sugai (george.sugai@ucann.edu) is professor and Carole J. Neag Endowed Chair in Special Education in the Neag School of Education at the University of Connecticut with specializations in school-wide positive behavior support, applied behavior analysis, behavior and classroom management, school discipline, and education of students with behavior disorders.

Jan van Tartwijk (j.vantartwijk@uu.nl) is professor of education at the Faculty of Social and Behavioral Sciences, Department of Education, Utrecht University. His research is concerned with the interpersonal significance of teacher behavior, communication processes between students and teachers, and teachers' cognitions about classroom communication processes and how these cognitions affect teacher behavior.

Robert Trussell (RPTrussell@utep.edu) is associate professor of special education and associate dean in the College of Education at the University of Texas, El Paso. His areas of specialization include SW-PBS, behavioral supports for students with autism, and supports for immigrant children.

Ruby I. Vega (rvega@email.arizona.edu) is a doctoral candidate and graduate associate of research and teaching in the Department of Educational Psychology at the University of Arizona. She is interested in the regulation of student adaptive learning, emotion, and motivation.

Claudia G. Vincent (clavin@uoregon.edu) is a research assistant at the Institute on Violence and Destructive Behavior at the University of Oregon. Her research focuses on the cultural dimensions of positive behavior support, social skills measurement, and evaluation.

Joan M. T. Walker (jwalker@pace.edu) is associate professor at Pace University. Her research examines teacher preparation and professional development for classroom management and family–school partnerships. She has used innovative technologies, including simulations and online platforms, as tools for developing teachers' knowledge, skills and dispositions for their numerous professional obligations.

Tiffany A. Whittaker (tiffany.whittaker@austin.utexas.edu) is associate professor in the Quantitative Methods program, Educational Psychology Department, The University of Texas at Austin. Her research interests include procedures used to model the relationships among variables, such as structural equation modeling (SEM), multilevel modeling (MLM), and item response theory (IRT) with a particular focus on model specification.

Lindy Wijsman (l.a.wijsman@fsw.leidenuniv.nl) is a PhD student at Leiden University. Her research interests are related to underachievement in secondary education and evaluation of cognitive, metacognitive, and socio-emotional student effects, and student differentiation and talent development in school.

Theo Wubbels (t.wubbels@uu.nl) is professor of education and associate dean of the Faculty of Social and Behavioural Sciences at Utrecht University. His main research interests developed from the pedagogy of physics education and have evolved to include problems and supervision of beginning teachers, teaching and learning in higher education, and studies of learning environments, especially interpersonal relationships in education.

Mitchell L. Yell (myell@sc.edu) is the Fred and Francis Lester Palmetto Chair of Teacher Education and a professor of special education at the University of South Carolina. His scholarly interests are IEP development, legal issues in special education, classroom management, progress monitoring, and evidence-based practices in special education. He is a due process hearing officer in South Carolina.

AUTHOR INDEX

Aber, J.L. 379
Aber, M.S. 120, 127, 128
Abrami, P. 261, 274
Abril, C.R. 232
Abu-Teneh, A. M. 284, 293
Achilles, G.M. 118, 414
Acker, R.V. 351
Adams, M. 418
Adderly, C. 232
Adkins-Coleman, T.A. 180
Ahn, H. 82
Ahn, S. 538
Ahnert, L. 468
Akin-Little, A. 32
Alameda-Lawson, T. 472
Alber, S.R. 215
Alberto, P.A. 116, 120, 511
Albiero, P. 83
Albin, R.W. 69, 190, 196
Alder, N. 213
Aldridge, J.W. 498
Algozzine, B. 49
Al-Hassan, S. 418
Alleman, J.R. 131
Allensworth, E. 123
Alley, J.M. 225
Aloe, A.M. 202
Alter, P.J. 145, 285, 420
Altman, J. 333
Altoè, G. 83
Altschaefl, Margaret R. 11
Alvarez, H.K. 285, 291, 370, 371, 379
Alvarez, V.G. 302, 305
Amabile, T.M. 501
Ames, A.J. 538
Ames, C. 225, 227
Amo, L.C. 202
Anderman, E.M. 460
Anderson, A.L. 422
Anderson, A.R. 27, 51, 78
Anderson, C.A. 49

Anderson, C.M. 50, 61
Anderson, G.A. 332
Anderson, K.L. 200
Anderson, L. 446
Anderson, L.M. 16, 460, 467
Anderson, R. 500, 503
Anderson, W. 487
Andree, A. 465
Ang, P.A. 372
Angold, A. 76
Anthony, L.J. 161
Anthony, S. 117, 118
Appleton, V. 413
Aragon, S.R. 78, 79
Arbeau, K.A. 371
Arbogast, G. 241, 242
Arbuckle, C. 289, 292
Arcia, E. 118, 121, 122, 128, 131
Arguelles, M. 273
Armendariz, F. 212
Armstrong, J. 349
Arnold, D.H. 147
Arnold, E.H. 147
Arnold, M. 302, 305
Arseneault, L. 81
Artman, K. 150, 378
Arum, R. 20
Arvaja, M. 339, 340
Asen, R. 555
Ashby, S. 483
Ashmus, D. 487
Asmus, E.P. 226, 227
Aspy, D. 389, 393
Assor, A. 467
Astor, R.A. 22
Atjonen, P. 289
Atkins, M.S. 31, 454
Au, W. 296
Auerbach, S. 419, 472
Auld, R.G. 177
Aultman, L.P. 314

Johnson, S. 301, 367, 374
Johnson, V.R. 459
Jolivette, K. 50, 119, 144, 149
Jones, C. 129
Jones, K.P. 473
Jones, M. 189, 190, 197
Jones, S.E.L. 47
Jones, S.M. 26, 146, 152, 154, 289, 379
Jones, V. 446, 447, 448, 449, 452, 453, 454, 455
Jones Harden, B. 371, 374, 377
Jordan, W.J. 120, 121
Jöreskog, K.G. 380, 534
Joseph, G.E. 144, 146, 150, 161
Joubert, M. 117, 118, 121, 131
Joussemet, M. 501
Joyner, E.T. 28
Jung, L.A. 149
Junker, G.N. 305, 312
Justice, L.M. 149, 371
Juvonen, J. 76, 79, 80, 81, 83, 349, 351

Kabat-Zinn, J. 315
Kaderavek, J.N. 149
Kaff, M.S. 199
Kahn, J. 481
Kaibel, C. 51
Kaiser, A.P. 142
Kaiser, B. 144
Kajamies, A. 336, 337, 339
Kalberg, J.R. 206, 216
Kam, C.M. 157
Kame'enui, E.J. 45, 61
Kamphaus, R.W. 424
Kamps, D. 176
Kaplan, A.M. 486
Kaplan, H. 467
Karns, K. 273, 275
Karp, D.R. 130
Karvonen, M. 49
Kast, A. 503
Katon, W. 76, 79
Katsiyannis, A. 158
Katz, Y.J. 354, 356, 366, 374
Kauffman, J.M. 4, 31, 54, 187, 206, 538
Kaufhold, J.A. 302, 305
Kaufman, D. 291, 292, 294
Kavanagh, K. 157
Kawa, Jacqueline M. 11
Kaya, S. 379
Kazdin, A. 539, 544, 546, 547, 549, 550, 552
Kea, C.D. 413, 421
Keane, S.P. 469
Keating, X.D. 244
Kelk, M.J. 49
Kellam, S.G. 28, 30, 118, 126, 129, 417, 426
Kelly, J.F. 468

Kelly, S. 415
Kennedy, B.L. 180, 183
Kennedy, C.H. 539
Kennedy, E.F. 251
Kennedy, M. 232
Kenter, B. 263
Keogh, B.K. 372
Kerivan, A.S. 146
Kern, L. 22, 31, 207, 211
Kerr, I.G. 252
Kerr, M. 511
Kesner, C. 172
Ketelhut, D. 491
KewalRamani, A. 118
Keyes, S. 421
Khalaileh, H. A. 284, 293
Khan, A. 261, 264, 270
Khasawneh, S.A. 284, 293
Khoury-Kassabri, M. 287
Kidder-Ashley, P. 145
Kienhuis, M. 308, 315, 452
Kiesler, D.J. 366
Kietzmann, J.H. 486
Killian, J.N. 223
Kim, C.Y. 122
Kim, E.-J. 507, 509
Kim, S. 289
Kim, S.E. 223
Kim, T.E. 76, 77, 80
Kincaid, D. 423
Kinchin, G. 254
Kindall-Smith, M. 231, 232
Kinder, K. 150, 378
Kindermann, T.A. 507
King, Alison 265, 267, 268, 269
King, K. 416
Kingsbury, W.L. 77
Kinney, D.W. 222, 232
Kinnunen, R. 336, 337, 339
Kirk, D. 254
Kirkpatrick, C.L. 285, 288, 297
Kiziltepe, Z. 301
Klassen, R.M. 287, 289, 301
Klinenberg, E. 387
Klinger, J. 273
Klingner, J.K. 267, 272, 412
Kloeppel, T. 253
Knight, C.C. 174, 177, 290, 302, 307, 309, 310, 312, 314
Knight, J. 454
Knitzer, J. 142, 152
Knobel, M. 485
Knoff, H.M. 33, 118, 121
Knoster, T. 49
Kochenderfer-Ladd, B. 82
Koenig, B.W. 78, 79
Koenka, A.C. 538

McCarthy, Christopher J. 10, 301, 302, 303, 304, 305, 307, 308, 312
McCarthy, J.D. 125, 171
McCartney, K. 466, 468, 469
McCarty, M.M. 432, 438, 439, 440
McCaslin, Mary 10, 30, 95, 107, 322, 323, 324, 326, 328, 329, 330, 333, 334, 341
McCaughtry, N. 253
McClellan, B.E. 16
McClelland, G.H. 500
McClure, S.M. 498
Maccoby, E.E. 461, 463
McCollum, E.E. 393
McCombs, B.L. 112, 325, 350, 353
McCormack, A. 244, 248, 251, 252
McCormick, J. 229, 230, 310, 315
McCormick, K.M. 149
McCoy, C.L. 231
McCray, A.D. 421
McCready, L.T. 412
McCurdy, B.L. 50, 176
Mace, F.C. 325
McElroy, H.K. 25
McEvoy, M. 154
McFadden, A.C. 123
McFadden, L. 153
McGavock, K. 276
McGee, E. 175
McGinnis, J.C. 149
Machalicek, W. 200
MacIntosh, K. 129
McIntosh, K. 49, 50, 51
MacKenzie, M. 261
McKinney, R. 130, 132
MacKinnon, D.P. 528
McLaughlin, A. 205
MacLeod, K.S. 50
MacLeod, S. 50
McLeskey, J. 206
Mcloughlin, C.S. 118, 124, 127, 128, 414
McMahon, P.M. 80, 85
McNally, L. 481
Macnamara, J. 484
McNeely, C.A. 117, 120
McNeil, J.K. 316
McNeill, K. 265
MacPhail, A. 254
McPherson, G.E. 228, 229, 230
McRobbie, C.J. 368
McTighe, J. 209, 210
McWayne, C. 419
McWilliam, R.A. 148
McWilliams, L. 147
Madden, N.A. 119
Madsen, C.K. 223, 224, 225, 234
Madsen, K. 234

Maes, F. 368, 374
Maggin, D.M. 201, 539, 553, 554
Mainhard, M.T. 354, 364, 369, 375, 376, 377
Malloy, C.E. 347
Mammen, K.J. 355
Mancil, G.R. 213, 420
Mandinach, E. 323
Mann, E.L. 121
Manning, M.A. 25, 32
Mannon, S.E. 119
Manoogian, S.T. 500, 503
Mansfield, W. 118
Mantegna, M.E. 207
Mantzicopoulos, P.Y. 346, 469
Manz, P. 211
Maphosa, C. 355
Mapp, K.L. 459, 472
Marachi, R. 22
March, G.E. 123
Marchand-Martella, N.E. 141
Marchant, G.J. 470
Marchant, M.R. 50
Margerum-Leys, J. 482
Markey, P.M. 381
Markson, S. 120
Marquez, B. 424
Marsh, H.W. 368, 532
Marsh, S. 46, 207, 213
Marshall, M. 106, 107
Marshall, S. 482
Martella, R.C. 49, 141
Martens, B.K. 187
Martin, A.J. 230
Martin, E. 241
Martin, J.J. 253, 463
Martin, M. 119
Martin, N.K. 6, 7, 284, 285
Martinez, T.E. 116, 117, 118
Martinez-Pons, M. 228
Marx, R.W. 482
Marzano, J.S. 61, 94, 411
Marzano, R.J. 94, 399, 411
Mashburn, A. J. 27, 349, 372, 374, 375
Mashek, D.J. 25
Maslach, C. 301, 304
Maslow, A.H. 106
Mason, B.A. 28
Mason, W.A. 187
Mason Bolick, Cheryl 11
Mastergeorge, A. 264
Masyn, K.E. 118
Matheny, K.B. 303, 305, 312, 313
Matos, L. 501
Matsumoto, K. 500
Matsumoto, M. 500
Matthews, R. 302

SUBJECT INDEX